1,000,000 Books

are available to read at

Forgotten Books

www.ForgottenBooks.com

Read online
Download PDF
Purchase in print

ISBN 978-0-260-97432-7
PIBN 11110386

This book is a reproduction of an important historical work. Forgotten Books uses state-of-the-art technology to digitally reconstruct the work, preserving the original format whilst repairing imperfections present in the aged copy. In rare cases, an imperfection in the original, such as a blemish or missing page, may be replicated in our edition. We do, however, repair the vast majority of imperfections successfully; any imperfections that remain are intentionally left to preserve the state of such historical works.

Forgotten Books is a registered trademark of FB &c Ltd.
Copyright © 2018 FB &c Ltd.
FB &c Ltd, Dalton House, 60 Windsor Avenue, London, SW19 2RR.
Company number 08720141. Registered in England and Wales.

For support please visit www.forgottenbooks.com

1 MONTH OF FREE READING

at

www.ForgottenBooks.com

By purchasing this book you are eligible for one month membership to ForgottenBooks.com, giving you unlimited access to our entire collection of over 1,000,000 titles via our web site and mobile apps.

To claim your free month visit: www.forgottenbooks.com/free1110386

* Offer is valid for 45 days from date of purchase. Terms and conditions apply.

English
Français
Deutsche
Italiano
Español
Português

www.forgottenbooks.com

Mythology Photography **Fiction**
Fishing Christianity **Art** Cooking
Essays Buddhism Freemasonry
Medicine **Biology** Music **Ancient Egypt** Evolution Carpentry Physics
Dance Geology **Mathematics** Fitness
Shakespeare **Folklore** Yoga Marketing
Confidence Immortality Biographies
Poetry **Psychology** Witchcraft
Electronics Chemistry History **Law**
Accounting **Philosophy** Anthropology
Alchemy Drama Quantum Mechanics
Atheism Sexual Health **Ancient History**
Entrepreneurship Languages Sport
Paleontology Needlework Islam
Metaphysics Investment Archaeology
Parenting Statistics Criminology
Motivational

REPORTS

OF

CASES ARGUED AND DETERMINED

IN THE

SUPREME COURT OF TENNESSEE

DURING THE YEARS

1858-9.

BY JOHN W. HEAD,
STATE REPORTER.

VOLUME II.

NASHVILLE:
J. O. GRIFFITH & CO., PRINTERS—UNION AND AMERICAN OFFICE.
1860.

Rec Nov 28. 1860

CASES REPORTED IN THIS VOLUME.

Adams v. Mayor and Aldermen of Somerville 863
Adams, Nored v 449
Allen v. Bain 100
Allen, Parks v 528
Allison, Anderson & Co., Anderson v 122
Allison, Starnes & Wife v 221
Allison v. Stephens 251
Alston v. Davis 266
Ament, Perkins v 110
Ammon, Baker v 898
Anderson v. Allison, Anderson & Co 122

Bain, Allen v 100
Baker v. Ammon 898
Baker v. Compton 471
Bandy, Scott, Baker & Co. v 197
Bank of the Union, Golladay, Cheatham & Co. v 57
Bates v. Whitson 155
Beadle, Wilson v 510
Beasley v. Jenkins 191
Belote v. White 703
Bigelow v. Mississippi Central and Tennessee R. R. Co 624
Birdsong v. Birdsong 289
Birdsong v. Birdsong 608
Bivens, Croone v 889
Bond v. Clay 879
Bonner, State v 185
Bowers v. Douglass 876
Bradford v. Caldwell 496
Brazelton v. Brooks 194
Brooks, Brazelton v 194
Brown v. State 180
Brown, Ryland v 270
Bullock v. Tipton 408
Burrough, Woods v 202
Burroughs v. Goodall 29
Burton, Mitchell v 618
Bushart v. Swails 561

Caldwell, Bradford v 496
Cardwell v. Cheatham 14
Carter & Pulliam v. Turner 52
Catham v. The State 553
Chapman v. The State 86
Cheatham, Cardwell v 14
Cheek, Park v 451
Clark v. Clark 336
Clay, Bond v 879
Cleveland v. Martin 128
Cochrane, Egnew v 820
Cockrell, McWhirter v 9
Coleough v. Nashville and Northwestern R. R. Co 171
Coleman v. Satterfield 259

CASES REPORTED IN THIS VOLUME.

Coleman, Fletcher v. 384
Collins, Kellogg & Kirby, Thompson v. 441
Compton, Baker v. 471
Compton, Henry v. 549
Connell v. County Judge of Davidson 189
Conner v. Crunk. 246
Cooley v. Steele. 605
Cope & Co. v. McFarland. 543
Cornelius & Davis v. Merritt. 97
County Judge of Davidson, Connell v. 189
Cozart, Smith v. 526
Crawford, McNeill & Co., State v. 460
Criner v. Pike. 398
Crittenden v. Terrill. 588
Cromwell v. Winchester. 389
Croone v. Bivens 339
Crunk, Conner v. 246
Cruse v. McKee. 1
Cunningham v. Edgefield and Kentucky R. R. Co 23
Ourd & White, Venable & Co. v. 582

Darnall, Tomlinson v. 588
Davis, Alston v. 266
Davis, Gray v. 360
Dean v. Vaccaro & Co. 488
Dement v. Scott. 367
Dement v. The State. 505
Donell, Williams v. 695
Douglass, Bowers v. 376
Douglass, Planters' Bank v. 699
Drewry v. Vaden. 312

Edgefield & Kentucky R. R. Co., Cunningham v. 23
Egnew v. Cochrane. 320
Elrod v Myers. 38
Elrod v. Lancaster. 571
Epperson, Gage, Dater & Massey v. 669

Faulker, Louisville & Nashville R. R. v. 65
Felts v Mayor and Aldermen of Memphis 650
Fisher, Hopper v. 253
Fisher v. Pollard. 814
Fleming v. Martin. 48
Fletcher v. Coleman. 384
Fogg v. Williams. 474
Ford v. Grieshaber. 435
Ford, Frazer v. 464
Forsey v. Luton. 183
Frazer v. Ford. 464

Gambill, Smiley v. 164
Gates, Haynes v. 598
Gage, Dater & Massey v Epperson 669
Gaugh and Wife v. Henderson. 628
Gee v. Graves 239
Gibbs v. Ross. 437
Golladay, Cheatham & Co. v. Bank of the Union 57
Goodall, Burroughs v. 29
Goss v. Singleton. 67
Graves, Gee v 239
Gray v. Davis. 360

CASES REPORTED IN THIS VOLUME.

Green, State v.	856
Grieshaber, Ford v.	435
Griffin & Co., Wells v.	568
Hall, Parker v.	641
Hassell v. Southern Bank of Kentucky.	381
Haynes v. Jones.	872
Haynes v. Gates.	598
Henry & Shackleford, Philips v.	138
Henry v. Compton	549
Henderson, Gaugh and Wife v.	628
Hess, Sandeford v.	680
Hill v. Hinton	124
Hinton, Hill v.	124
Hopper v. Fisher.	253
Hunter, Lownes, Orgill & Co. v.	343
Isaac (a slave) v. The State	458
Jenkins, Beasley v.	191
Jones, Haynes v.	872
Jones, Memphis and Charleston R. R. Co. v.	517
Jones, Taylor v.	565
Joyner, Leslie v.	514
Lancaster, Elrod v.	571
Larry, O'Sullivan v.	54
Lashley v. Wilkinson.	482
Leetch v. The State.	140
Leslie v. Joyner.	514
Levick, Brother & Co., Venable & Co. v.	851
Lillard v. Porter.	177
Lincoln v. Purcell.	148
Louisville and Nashville R. R. Co. v. Faulkner	65
Love v. Williams.	80
Lownes, Orgill & Co. v. Hunter	843
Luton, Forsey v.	183
Maley v. Tipton.	403
Marr v. Marr.	303
Martin, Fleming v.	43
Martin, Cleveland v.	128
Matthewson v. Spencer.	424
Mayer & Co. v. Pulliam.	346
Mayor and Aldermen of Somerville, Adams v.	303
Mayor and Aldermen of Memphis, Felts v.	650
McKee, Cruse v.	1
McLellan v. McLean.	684
McMannus v. The State.	218
McWhirter v. Cockrell.	9
McFarland, Cope & Co. v.	543
McComb, Relfe & Co. v.	558
McLean, McLellan v.	684
Memphis & Charleston R. R. Co. v. Jones.	517
Memphis and Little Rock R. R. Co v. Walker	467
Merritt, Cornelius & Davis v.	97
Mississippi Central and Tennessee R. R. Co., Bigelow v.	624
Mitchell v. Burton.	613
Moore v. Simmons.	545
Morgan v. Reed.	276
Morris, Tanner & Co., Neely v.	595

Mt. Olivet Cemetery Co. v. Shubert	116
Murphy, Weisinger v.	674
Myers, Elrod v.	83
Nashville and Chattanooga R. R. Co., Woodruff v.	87
Nashville and Northwestern R. R. Co., Colcough v.	171
Neely v. Morris, Tanner & Co.	595
Nelson & Co., Patrick v.	507
Nolen v. The State	520
Nored v. Adams	449
O'Sullivan v. Larry	54
Overton v. Phelan	445
Owens v. The State	455
Park v. Cheek	451
Parker v. Hall	641
Parks v. Allen	528
Patrick v. Nelson & Co.	507
Perkins v. Ament	110
Phelan, Overton v.	445
Philips v. Henry & Shackleford	133
Philips v. Sampson	429
Pike, Criner v.	398
Pilcher & Cataulis v. Smith	208
Planters' Bank v. Douglass	699
Pollard, Fisher v.	314
Porter, Lillard v.	177
Price & Bell, Scott v.	532
Pugh v. The State	227
Pulliam, Mayer & Co. v.	346
Purcell, Lincoln v.	143
Reed, Morgan v.	276
Reeves v. Steele	647
Relfe & Co. v. McComb	558
Rippy v. The State	217
Roberts v. The State	501
Rogers v. Rogers	660
Ross, Gibbs v.	437
Rowley, Ashburner & Co., Stockley v.	493
Rucker v. Wynne	617
Ryland v. Brown	270
Sampson, Philips v.	429
Sandeford v. Hess	680
Sanders, Tipton v.	690
Saterfield, Coleman v.	259
Saunders v. Wilder	577
Scott, Baker & Co. v. Bandy	197
Scott, Dement v.	367
Scott v. Price & Bell	532
Seay v. Young	417
Shubert, Mt. Olivet Cemetery v.	116
Simmons, Moore v.	545
Singleton, Goss v.	67
Smiley v. Gambill	164
Smith and Wife, Pilcher & Cataulis v.	208
Smith v. Cozart	526
Southern Bank of Kentucky, Hassell v.	381
Spencer, Matthewson v.	424
Starnes and Wife v. Allison	221
State, Chapman v.	36
State v. Bonner	185

State, Leetch v.	140
State, Brown v.	180
State, McMannus v.	218
State, Rippy v.	217
State, Pugh v.	227
State v. Green	856
State, Owens v.	455
State, Isaac v.	458
State v. Crawford, McNeill & Co.	460
State, Roberts v.	501
State, Dement v.	505
State, Nolen v.	520
State, Catham v.	553
State, Tucker & Oaks v.	555
State, Trice v.	591
Steele, Cooley v.	605
Steele, Reeves v.	647
Stephens, Allison v.	251
Stipe v. Stipe	169
Stockley v. Rowley, Ashburner & Co.	498
Street & Co., Ware v.	609
Swails v. Bushart	561
Taylor v. Jones	565
Terrill, Crittenden v.	588
Thomas, Wood v.	160
Thompson v. Thompson	405
Thompson v. Collins, Kellogg & Kirby	441
Tomlinson v. Darnall	588
Threadgill v. Timberlake	895
Timberlake, Threadgill v.	895
Tipton, Maley v.	403
Tipton v. Sanders	690
Tipton, Bullock v.	408
Trice v. The State	591
Tucker & Oaks v. The State	555
Turner, Carter & Pulliam v.	52
Vaccaro & Co., Dean v.	492
Vaden v. Drewry	312
Venable & Co. v. Levick, Brother & Co.	851
Venable & Co. v. Curd & White	582
Walker, Memphis and Little Rock R. R. Co. v.	467
Ware v. Street & Co.	609
Weisinger v. Murphy	674
Wells v. Griffin & Co.	568
Whitson, Bates v.	155
White, Belote v.	708
Wilder, Saunders v.	577
Wilkinson, Lashley v.	482
Williams v. Love	80
Williams, Fogg v.	474
Williams v. Donell	695
Wilson v. Beadle	510
Winchester, Cromwell v.	889
Wood v. Thomas	160
Woodruff v. Nashville and Chattanooga Railroad Company	87
Woods v. Burrough	202
Wynne, Rucker v.	617
Young, Seay v.	417

JUDGES OF THE SUPREME COURT
OF TENNESSEE.

Hon. ROBERT J. McKINNEY, - - - - Knoxville.
 " ROBERT L. CARUTHERS, - - - Lebanon.
 " ARCHIBALD WRIGHT, - - - - - Memphis.

ATTORNEY GENERAL OF TENNESSEE,
JOHN W. HEAD,
Gallatin.

TO THE

HON. JOHN J. WHITE,

GALLATIN, TENN.,

This Volume

IS RESPECTFULLY DEDICATED,

As a Testimonial

OF MY HIGH APPRECIATION OF HIS PROFOUND LEGAL LEARNING,
RIPE SCHOLARSHIP, PURE MORALS, EXALTED PATRIOTISM,

AND COURTEOUS BEARING AS A

GENTLEMAN AND LAWYER.

REPORTER.

CASES ARGUED AND DETERMINED

IN THE

SUPREME COURT OF TENNESSEE,

FOR THE

MIDDLE DIVISION.

NASHVILLE: DECEMBER TERM, 1858.

M. Cruse, Adm'r, *v.* A. McKee *et al.*

1. WILL. *Construction of. Power of appointment.* The will of David Baggerly contained the following clauses: "To my beloved wife, Rebecca, I give and bequeath all the lands owned by me, lying on the south side of the Yadkin river, in Iredell county, during her life time; and also, all my household goods and effects of every description, and also my negro women, Fanny and Rina, and a negro boy named James." * * * "It is further my will and desire, that my negroes, Fanny, Rina and James, be disposed of by my wife Rebecca, with their increase, *to the whole, or any one or more of my children she may think proper, at her decease.*" Upon these clauses, it is held:

1. That the wife took an estate for life, with power to dispose of the property to one or more of the *children,* as she chose; but, in the event she failed to exercise the power, or made an invalid appointment, it would go, equally, to the children and grandchildren of the testator.

2. That the power of appointment to children does not embrace grandchildren, and the exercise of it in their favor, is void.

3. That the appointments of the wife, so far as they are in conformity with the power, are not void, because others, invalid, are included in her will. Those in accordance with the power will be sustained, and those not, rejected.

4. That the property not diposed of in conformity with the power will be equally divided among the children and grandchildren, *per*

stirpes, under the will of the testator, without regard to the property held under the valid appointments of the wife. It is not, as in a case of intestacy, a case for collation of advancements.

2. SAME. Same. Same. *A power must be executed in good faith.* A person clothed with a power of appointment, must exercise it in good faith for the end and purposes designed; and, in all cases when a discretion is given in the selection of the objects amongst a class, good faith must be observed, and if discriminations are made to secure advantage to the trustee, or a stranger, his act will be held vicious and corrupt, and the appointment declared void.

3. POWER. *Fraud in its exercise. Question reserved* If fraud intervenes in the exercise of a power of appointment, does it vitiate the entire acts of the trustee, or only such appointments as are fraudulent?

FROM LINCOLN.

This cause was heard before Chancellor RIDLEY, at the August Term, 1858. The facts are stated in the opinion of the Court.

JOHN M. BRIGHT, for the respondents who contest the appointment, argued:

1. The bequest in David Baggerly's will, to Rebecca during life, with power of disposition to the whole, or any one or more of his children, was a power coupled with a trust, which she was required to execute in good faith. Hill on Trustees, 85, 86, top pages.

2. In default of the exercise of the power, the objects of the trust would all take, in equal parts, under the will of David Baggerly. Hill on Trustees, 87 and note; also, 88, 89, 90 and 91; also, 721, 722 and 723.

3. If the power of distribution or appointment be *improperly* exercised, the objects of the power will take, equally, as in default of any appointment. Hill on Trustees, 723; *Kemp* v. *Kemp*, 5 Ves., 849; *Aleyn* v. *Belcher*, 1 Leading Cases in Eq. by Hare & Wallace, 322-326 and notes.

4. Again, we insist that the execution of the trust is void, because the widow, by will, did not pretend to dispose of the slaves by virtue of her authority as trustee, but disposed of them in her own name as her absolute property. If she held the property in trust she could, alone, communicate the title in trust. If, being a trustee, she conveyed by deed or will in her own name, it would communicate no title to the donee or legatee, and would leave the property, as in default of any execution at all. A trustee can exercise a power, alone, as trustee. See Story's Eq. Jur.

KERCHEVAL, for the other respondents, cited and commented upon the following authorities: Sugd. Pow. 86; *Jarnagin* v. *Conway*, 2 Hum., 51; Sug. Pow., 42, 58 and 54; also, pages 377 and 380: *Bostick* v. *Winton*, 1 Sneed, 588.

CARUTHERS, J., delivered the opinion of the Court.

This bill is filed as administrator with the will annexed of Rebecca Baggerly, deceased, for the construction of her will, upon the interpleading of the parties whose interests conflict. The difficulty arises upon the exercise of a power by the widow, given to her, in relation to the disposition of certain slaves in the will of her husband.

David Baggerly, a citizen of North Carolina, made his will in 1816, and the same was admitted to probate by the County Court of Iredell, in 1819. It contains these two clauses, upon which the difficulty arises.

"To my beloved wife Rebecca, I give and bequeath all the lands owned by me, lying on the south side of the Yadkin river, in Iredell county, during her lifetime, and also all my household goods and effects of every description, and also my negro women, Fanny and Rina, and a negro boy named James."

In a subsequent clause, he says: "It is further my will and desire, that my negroes, Fanny, Rina, and James, be disposed of by my wife Rebecca, with their increase, *to the whole, or any one, or more of my children she may think proper, at her decease.*"

In March, 1856, she made her will, and died in Lincoln county, Tennessee, to which she had removed many years ago. These slaves, or their increase were disposed of in her will, unequally, among such of her children as were then living, and to some of the grandchildren. Some were to be sold, and the proceeds to go, partly, to grandchildren.

She had a power of appointment under restrictions; it was to be, to any one or more of her children. Her power was coupled with an interest, as well as a trust.

A power of appointment to children does not embrace grandchildren, and the exercise of it in their favor is without authority, and void. *Jarnagin* v. *Conway*, 2 Hump., 50, and authorities there cited. This is not disputable. But the more difficult question here is, whether that avoids the appointments of her will to children, so as to leave the whole property undisposed of by her, or, is it good *pro tanto;* and if so, how shall the balance go? This does not fall under the head of *illusory* appointments. That only applies to a case where one invested with a power to apportion property amongst a class, with full discretion as to the amount to be given to each, gives to one a merely *nominal* share. That will be set aside as *illusory*, as a fraud upon the donor of the power, as he certainly intended by making all the objects of his bounty, or of the power, that each should have a *substantial* share. 1 Hare & Wallace, L. C. Eq., 832. But in this case she had full and express power to give all to one, or two, or more, with an unrestricted discretion. It was not to his children as a class, without distinction, but she might exclude one or more if she chose, entirely. Not so in cases to which illusory appointment applies; though in these cases discriminations may be made, yet not to the entire exclusion of any one, or a *nominal* share to one.

In this case the widow's estate is for life only, by implication with power to control the remainder to a limited extent, and in a certain mode. The limitation was to his children. They, as a class, had a vested joint remainder under the will; but power was given to her to defeat this interest of any one or more, by the exercise of the power given, but in case she failed to appoint, or made an invalid appointment, then the property would go to all, *equally*, under his will, at her death.

There is no doubt but that a person having a power,

must execute it in good faith for the end and purposes designed, or it will be void. In the leading case of *Aleyn* v. *Belcher*, 1 White and Tudor, 290, this principle is illustrated, and in the notes, the cases are collected. In that case, the power of appointing was given, but it was exercised in favor of the wife, upon *an agreement* on her part that she should receive only a part as an annuity, and that the residue should be applied to the payment of the husband's debts. This was held to be a fraud upon the power, and set aside, *except so far as related to the annuity*. A Court of Equity will guard the exercise of these powers, so as to prevent any fraud upon the donor of the power. In all cases where a discretion is given in the selection of the objects amongst a class, good faith must be observed, and if discriminations are made to secure advantage to the trustee himself, or a stranger, his act will be held vicious and corrupt. If there be a secret understanding that the appointee shall assign a part of the fund to a stranger, or pay the debts of the appointor, or loan him the fund, the appointment would, thereby, be vitiated and declared void. Notes to the same case, 295, citing 8 Iredell's Eq. R., 55, 59; 1 Sim. 343, and other authorities; also, *Bostick* v. *Winton*, 1 Sneed, 538. Any exercise of such a power in fraud of the original intention with which the power was created, would, in equity, render the appointment void.

A question sometimes arises, as to the extent the Courts will go in setting aside fraudulent appointments; whether to the extent of the fraud, or entirely. But that question does not come up in this case, as there is no pretence that any advantage was received, in this case, by the appointor to herself or any one else, to induce the appointment. The objection is, that she undertook by mistake, or misconstruction of her authority, to give a part of the property to grandchildren. There was no fraud contemplated by her, nor can it be so considered. The rules in relation to fraudulent appointments do not, then, apply to the case, but it is, simply, a question of the validity of its exercise, so far as it is in favor of grandchildren.

The result is, that her appointment, so far as it is exercised in favor of her children, is valid, and the appointment to her grandchildren is void.

The slave Tillman, given at valuation in the third clause, to her daughter, Mrs. McKee, is not properly disposed of, as the amount of the value is distributed in a manner not authorized by her power. The dispositions in clauses 4, 5 and 7, being to children of the donor, are good; so are the bequests of the eighth clause, as that relates to property not embraced in the trust, that being limited to the slaves.

A valid appointment, though in the same deed or will with others not valid, will be maintained. 2 Sug. on Pow. 87.

The other slaves, not disposed of by the widow under the trust, must be distributed, equally. among all the objects of the power, under the will of David Baggorly. We have felt strongly inclined to produce equality, by compelling those to account who have received slaves by the valid exercise of the discretionary power confided to the widow, but have been unable to find any principles to authorize it. She had the express power to give the whole to "any one or more," and exclude the others.

She could have given all to one. All would have been equal on failure to exert the power, or in case of an invalid or void exercise of it. The unrestricted power of selection and discrimination entrusted to her, enabled her, legally, to produce any inequality she desired. So far then as she has appointed, that must stand, with its advantages to the objects selected. As to that portion of the property she has left untouched by her power, it must pass under the will of the testator, as a vested remainder, exempt from the contingent power of appointment given to her over it, to all his children, and their representatives, where any are dead. It is not a case for collation of advancements, as in cases of intestacy; but the right is derived from the will. All the children then are embraced, without regard to what any may have received under the exercise of the power, that is, from a different source. Sug. on Pow., 508.

Where a discretionary power is not exercised, the whole of the objects who are within it, will take in equal shares. Hill on Trustees, 70-492. So it must be, where it is not exercised as to part, in the disposition of that.

The decree of the Chancellor will be reversed, and decree here in accordance with this opinion.

GEORGE F. MCWHIRTER *et al. v.* M. R. COCKRELL.

1. ROADS. *Practice. Contest to be decided by the Court, and not submitted to a jury.* In contests about roads, the jurisdiction, in the first instance, is given, exclusively, to the County Court; and, upon appeal to the Circuit Court, to the Judge. It is the duty of the Circuit Judge to hear and determine the controversy, and not shift the labor and responsibility from himself to a jury.

2. SAME. *When to be established. Rights of the community and of individuals.* Whenever the necessity for a road is imperative, it is the duty of the Court to establish it, although injurious to individuals, upon making compensation for the injury, as provided by law. This is to be done with as little injury to private property as practicable, and only when the advantage to the public is sufficiently great to outweigh the private injury. The Court should look, carefully, to the interest of all citizens, and never exercise the right of eminent domain, unless it is clearly and imperatively demanded for the public good.

FROM DAVIDSON.

This cause was tried upon appeal from the County Court, at the September Term, 1858, of the Circuit Court, BAXTER, J., presiding. The decision of the County Court was reversed, and the petitioners appealed to this Court.

N. S. BROWN, DEMOSS, and M. M. BRIEN, for the petitioners.

R. J. MEIGS and ANDREW EWING, for the defendant.

George F. McWhirter *et al.* *v.* M. R. Cockrell.

CARUTHERS, J. delivered the opinion of the Court.

This is a contested road case. The plaintiffs are petitioners for a county road, to pass over the lands of the defendant, in Robertson's Bend, on Cumberland river, about six miles from Nashville. The petitioners live in White's Bend, on the opposite side of the river from Robertson's Bend, and propose to establish a ferry, by which to pass over to the bank of defendant, and then over his land in the direction of Nashville, about the distance of ——.

The defendant has the whole bend enclosed and arranged for stock-raising at considerable expense, and resists the application to run a public road through it, because it would inflict irreparable injury upon him, without any corresponding advantage to the public. Much proof was introduced to support the positions assumed on both sides—the public demand for the road on the one part, and the private injury on the other.

The County Court decided in favor of the petitioners, and ordered the laying out and establishment of the road; but upon an appeal to the Circuit Court that judgment was reversed and the petition dismissed, and an appeal to this Court. It is now for us to decide upon the evidence presented in the bill of exceptions, which tribunal gave the proper judgment.

It is assigned for error here, first, that the Circuit Judge refused to refer the question to a jury, instead of passing upon the evidence himself. We think he did not err in this. Such a practice has never been adopted, and it is not contemplated by any act of Assembly on the subject of roads. It is not a proper

George F. McWhirter *et al.* *v.* M. R. Cockrell.

matter for a jury. The jurisdiction is given, exclusively, to the County Court in the first instance, and then, upon appeal to the Circuit Court, to the judge. These contests are often of the most exciting character. They generally array many against one, and arouse whole communities against a single individual. It would be unsafe, in such cases, to leave them to a jury of the vicinage. At all events it would be more safe and appropriate to intrust them to an impartial, unexcited Court. But it is enough that the Legislature has confided all such questions to the Courts, without any provisions for a jury. It would be an evasion of duty for a Judge to shift this labor and responsibility from himself to a jury, and, probably, it would be held erroneous to do so.

The public is entitled to all *necessary* roads and thoroughfares, and it is the duty of the Courts to grant them, wherever they are needed, although they may be injurious to individuals, upon making compensation for the injury, as provided by law. This is to be done, however, with as little injury to private property as practicable. It does not follow that a road is to be granted because a portion of the people may desire it; not even in every case where it is manifest that it would be of some convenience or advantage to them. The advantage to the public must be sufficiently great to overbalance the private injury. That is, in a case where the necessity is not imperative, very serious harm will not be done to individuals by the establishment of a public road. In the exercise of this very delicate and important jurisdiction, by which private property is taken for public use, the Courts should look, carefully, to the

George F. McWhirter *et al. v.* M R. Cockrell.

interests of all the citizens, and never exercise the right of eminent domain unless it is clearly and urgently demanded for the public good. That a few miles in distance would be saved, or a road some degrees better provided for a portion of the community, is not a sufficient reason, in all cases, to justify the running a road over private property. The Courts should wisely and fairly judge of each case upon the facts presented. On the one hand the public prosperity and convenience should not be retarded because individual interests might be in the way; and, on the other, private rights ought not to be infringed without manifest necessity. This would not only be unjust to those who would be immediately affected by it, but to the whole community, who would have to be taxed to pay the damages that might be assessed for the appropriation of private property to public use. This must necessarily be done, because the constitution, as well as the acts of Assembly, require it. So a good many considerations are involved in the question.

Both parties have used every exertion to present all the facts in this case calculated to assist the Courts in arriving at a correct conclusion. We have a map of the two bends, the river, adjacent turnpikes, and other public roads and ferries. The situation of all the families in "White's Bend," together with the opinions of men as to the necessity of the proposed road for each inhabitant. From all which it appears that a few of the families would be benefitted by shortening the distance to Nashville, provided they succeeded in getting a good ferry kept up. But taking all the circumstances into view, as they are presented in the proof, we are

George F. McWhirter *et al. v.* M. R. Cockrell.

satisfied that a majority of the people in this bend would not only receive no advantage by opening the road, but that it would not be used by them if opened on the opposite side of the river. The proximity of two good turnpike roads—the one leading from Charlotte to Nashville, and the other to Hyde's, Ferry without much increase of distance, would prevent very much use of the contemplated road, even if it were opened and a ferry kept up. The character of the ground near the river in Robertson's Bend would make it a bad road in the winter and spring seasons, and some of the witnesses say almost impassable—entirely so, without throwing up an embankment for three or four hundred yards from the river, to an elevation of three or four feet, and building a bridge over a slough or ravine.

Some of the witnesses are of opinion that the road would be of vital importance to the families in White's Bend "—at least for some of them—and others think it would be of very little or no benefit to them. Some say that the ferry to be established upon the new road, at the head of Robertson's Island, would be safe and convenient, and others, that it would be exceedingly dangerous, and, in high water, almost impassable. So we are left, as in most cases of this kind, to judge between them upon the reasons they assign and the facts they state. The proof shows that there are from twenty to forty families in the bend—some of them renters; that most of them, by proper roads leading to the turnpikes on either side, could reach Nashville more easily and safely than by the proposed road, though the distance might be somewhat greater to a majority of them. It is clear that the general public have no interest in the question, but that it would be confined to the small community in the bend. We are not satisfied from the proof that the benefit to them would be sufficient to authorize the injury to private property that would result. The County Court, in 1850, discontinued a county road through Robertson's Bend, upon the report of a jury of view, and we can see no sufficient reason for opening it again at present.

We concur with the Circuit Judge in his conclusion upon the facts, and affirm his judgment disallowing the petition.

MARTHA A. P. CARDWELL *v.* F. R. CHEATHAM *et al.*

1. TRUST AND TRUSTEE. *Husband and wife. Sale of real estate settled upon the wife. Privy examination of the wife.* If real estate is conveyed by the husband to a trustee, for the sole and separate use of the wife, with power to the trustee, at her request in writing, to sell and convey the same, and reinvest the proceeds as she may direct, a simple request in writing is sufficient. A formal power to the trustee, accompanied with the *privy examination* of the wife, is not required.

2. SAME. *Same. Same. Breach of Trust. Fraud.* It is the duty of both the trustee and purchaser, in the event the property is sold, to see that the fund is paid over to the trustee, and reinvested for the benefit of the wife, as directed by the terms of the trust. And if, in violation of the provisions of the deed, the purchaser contract with the husband, pays him the purchase money, and, upon the written authority of the wife, the trustee conveys title to him, such sale and conveyance is a breach of trust—a fraud upon the power, and will, upon the application of the wife, be set aside.

3. SAME. *Same. Same. Innocent purchaser* If the purchase is made *bona fide,* without notice of the breach of a trust reposed in the

trustee, the purchaser is not bound to see that the purchase money is reinvested in other property for the use of the wife.

4. SAME. *Same. Same. Same. How this defence to be made.* If a party rely upon the defence that he is an innocent purchaser without notice, he must set it out, specifically, by plea or answer; and establish the facts relied on by proof.

FROM DAVIDSON.

At the May Term, 1858, Chancellor FRIERSON dismissed complainant's bill. She appealed. The lot was sold by Davis to Johnson, but no deed appears to have been made to him by Davis.

BRIEN & COX, for the complainant, argued:

1st. The sale by Cheatham to Davis is void, complainant at the time being a *feme covert*, and not having been *privily examined. Coppedge v. Threadgill*, 8 Sneed, 577.

2d. Suppose complainant had the power under the deed to sell the lot, still she had no power over the fund, and Cheatham could not appropriate it in any way except as directed by the deed. He had no power to pay the funds to complainant's husband. The deed expressly states that if the land is sold, Cheatham is to re-invest the proceeds, and of course he had no power, only as given by the deed. 3 Johnson, ch. Rep. 78, 1 W. & T. Cases in Equity, 66, 67, 76, 77, 869, 870, 873, 875, 876.

3d. Cheatham was and is the Clerk of the County Court, and therefore had no power to acknowledge his own deed. As to the liability of Johnson, see Meigs Dig. 244, 245.

Ewing & Cooper, for the defendants:

1st. The allegations of fraud being fully met by the answers, and not sustained by proof, the only questions that can arise in the case are questions of law.

2d. The trustee is authorized to "sell and convey" the lot "at her (Mrs. C's) request in writing." A simple request in writing, without witnesses, or privy examination, would meet the requirements of this provision. The attestation of two witnesses to the act, was unnecessary except to perpetuate the evidence of its occurrence. The fact that these witnesses have not been examined by the complainant, demonstrates that the allegations of fraud and coercion are utterly without foundation, even if such demonstrations were required.

3d. The deed of trust was, manifestly, drawn up for the express purpose of meeting the very contingency which has happened; a sale and receipt of the purchase money by husband and wife, without the intervention of the trustee. The sale, as we have seen, is authorized at the wife's "*request in writing.*" The reinvestment of the proceeds is also to be "*as she may direct in writing,*" and the deed expressly provides that the trustee is to be responsible "*for fraud or gross neglect of duty only, and not for any mismanagement* of said Martha A. P. Cardwell." Complainant has suffered loss, if at all, by her own act.

4th. It is now the well settled rule in England and in this country, that a purchaser is not bound to see to the application of the purchase money, when the conveyance is made in conformity with the trust, and without any fraud or collusion. 1 W. & T. Lead. Cases in Eq. 58–76, and cases cited.

WRIGHT, J., delivered the opinion of the Court.

On the 1st of March, 1852, James W. Cardwell, the husband of complainant, made a conveyance by deed in fee simple, to the defendant, Felix R. Cheatham, of a lot in the city of Nashville.

The deed, upon its face, was in trust, that said Cheatham should hold the legal title of the lot for the sole and separate use and benefit of complainant; the same not to be liable to the control, or for any debt, or responsibilities to be contracted or incurred by the said James W. Cardwell, and that the said Cheatham should permit her to use, occupy, rent out, or improve the lot as she might think proper; and at her request in writing, to sell and convey the same, and to re-invest the proceeds as she, in writing, might direct; and that the property acquired by the re-investment should be held by the trustee, in like manner as the original estate; and that said trustee should be responsible only for fraud or gross neglect of duty, and not for any mismanagement of complainant, in the premises.

On the 17th day of November, in the same year, the said Cheatham, in his character of trustee, signed and executed a deed of conveyance, in fee simple, of said lot to the defendant, A. L. Davis, for the consideration of $300, as stated in the deed, which is therein admitted to have been received by said Cheatham. At the foot of the deed to Davis, and upon the same paper, the complainant executed the following writing: "It is at my desire and request that F. R. Cheatham, trustee, has made and executed the above deed, and I hereby ratify and confirm it in every respect; and I hereby warrant and defend the title to said lot specified in the above deed, against the right, title, interest or claim of all and every person or persons whatsoever. In witness whereof, I have hereunto set my hand and seal, this the 17th of November, 1852.

MARTHA A. CARDWELL, [L. S.]

Test: JOHN COLTART, H. G. BENNETT.

Complainant's husband has since departed this life, and she now brings this bill against defendants, Cheatham, Davis and Johnson, to recover this lot.

Among other things, she charges that her husband, in violation of the express terms of the conditions of said deed of trust, and in fraud of her rights, sold said lot to the defendant, Davis, for $300, and received the pay, and that said Davis and Cheatham fraudulently combined with said James W. Cardwell to deprive her of the benefit of said deed, and that said Cheatham executed a deed to said lot to defendant Davis, he, at the time, well knowing the condition of her title, and permitted said James W. to use and consume the proceeds thereof, and failed to re-invest the same as directed in said deed.

She also alleges, that she was forced to sign the writing at the foot of the deed, and did so in ignorance of her rights.

Martha A. P. Cardwell v. F. R. Cheatham *et al.*

The defendants, Davis and Cheatham, in their answers, deny the charges of fraud and coercion, in detail; and Davis avers that the title was made in accordance with the terms of the trust deed, and that the complainant's rights were fully protected by her trustee. He admits, however, that the trade for the lot was made with complainant's husband.

The defendant, Cheatham, states in his answer, that his name was used as trustee in the deed without his knowledge or assent; that he has no recollection of ever seeing it, until he saw it as an exhibit in complainant's bill. He, however, admits his signature to the deed, to Davis, but has no recollection of ever executing it, and is certain he never saw complainant to know her, and never received one dollar of the consideration recited in the deed.

He supposes that complainant's husband, for his own purposes, used his name in the first deed without consulting him, and that he afterwards brought the deed, to Davis, with his wife's authority appended, and requested him to execute it, stating, doubtless, that it was all right, and that it was a mere matter of form—the legal title having been conveyed to him, and that he signed his name accordingly. That "his whole and sole agency in the business was the execution of the deed to Davis when it was brought to him, with complainant's written authority appended."

He states further, that he has no doubt complainant's husband resorted to the plan of conveying the lot in trust for his wife, to protect it from his creditors, and with such provisions as enabled him, readily, to dispose of it whenever a fit opportunity presented itself.

Martha A. P. Cardwell *v.* F. R. Cheatham *et al.*

Cheatham was the Clerk of the County Court, and the deed of trust was duly acknowledged by James W. Cardwell, before his deputy, upon the day of its date, and duly registered the next day.

No proof was taken in the cause. The Chancellor, in his decree, denied complainant any relief, and dismissed her bill.

In this, we think, he erred. We do not place our objections to the decree upon any want of formality in the execution of the power. It may be conceded that the wife's request was sufficient, and that it was given simultaneously with the deed, and as a part of it; and that if it were not for other difficulties in the way, a valid title would have passed.

It may also be true, that if Davis, in this transaction, had occupied the position of a *bona fide* purchaser, without notice of a breach of the trust reposed in Cheatham, he would not have been bound to see to the application of the purchase money, by its re-investment in other property, for the use of complainant. 1 W. & T. Leading Cases in Eq., and notes to *Elliott* v. *Merryman*, 66, 67, 76, 77; *Wormley* v. *Wormley*, 8 Wheat. 421.

We may concede too, as we do, that Cheatham is free of all intentional wrong. We are obliged to take it that he accepted this trust, and that he and Davis had full knowledge of the terms of the deed. Indeed, Davis' title depends upon his acceptance. Then what is the nature of this transaction? It was the duty of the defendant, Cheatham, as the trustee of the complainant, upon her written request, personally, himself, to sell this lot, and to receive the proceeds, and re-invest it in other property, under her written directions. A sale by the husband was totally unauthorized by the trust. The trustee could not, legally, pay the purchase money to him, or permit Davis to do so, without a plain violation of the terms of the deed. To do so would be a gross neglect of duty, and if allowed, would, in effect, annul the trust altogether.

We have no evidence, nor is it alleged, that the husband received this fund with the complainant's consent. But this could make no difference; for by the very terms of the deed, he was to have no control over it. Neither was she to have the fund produced by the sale of the lot. It was to be re-invested by the trustee in *other property*. She was to *use, occupy, rent out, or improve* the original or substituted property as she might think proper; and for any mismanagement on her part, as to these things, the trustee was not to be liable. But the body of the estate, the fund itself, was not to be consumed or destroyed, but the same was secured, in the hands of the trustee, against the power of the husband, and weakness of the wife. *Methodis Episcopal Church* v. *Jaques:* 3 Johns. Ch. R. 78; Notes to *Hulme* v. *Tenant*, 1 W. & T. Leading Cases in Eq., 369, 370, 373, 375, 376.

Now what has been done in this case? and what part did Cheatham and Davis take in it? Why, simply, the husband, himself, sold the lot to Davis, and received and used the money, and Cheatham, simply, signed the deed to carry out the husband's sale. There has been no re-investment; nor was the sale made for any such purpose, but exclusively for the husband's use. And, both Davis and Cheatham knew it at the time, and became directly parties to it, the one by making the purchase and paying the money, and the other by signing the deed to carry it out. This is the plain meaning of the answers. If so, there was a palpable breach of trust, in fraud of the power, and Davis cannot, in equity, be allowed to hold property thus acquired.

The principles laid down in the cases of *Wormley* v. *Wormley*, 8 Wheat. 421, and *Champlin* v. *Hoight*, 10 Paige 274, are, it seems to us, decisive against this purchase.

To be sure, in the notes to *Elliott* v. *Merryman*, 1 W. & T. Leading Cases in Eq. 77, the case in Paige is stated to have been reversed, on another point, upon appeal. (7 Hill 245.)

The defendant, Johnson, can be in no better condition. There is nothing in this record to show that he is an innocent purchaser. There is no plea or answer as to him, and no proof. No deed is shown as to him, or that he paid anything. Neither he nor any of his co-defendants have given him the attitude of an innocent purchaser. 1 Meigs Dig. 244, 245.

Decree reversed.

ENOCH CUNNINGHAM v. EDGEFIELD AND KENTUCKY RAILROAD COMPANY.

1. RAILROAD COMPANY. *Conditional subscription of stock. Notice.* If a party, who has subscribed stock to a railroad company, can renounce and abandon his subscription, it can be only done by notice to the agent, or to the company, in proper time.

2. SAME. *Same. Fraud vitiates subscription, if notice is given in a reasonable time.* If a subscription is fraudulently obtained from a person, and he is injured thereby, the contract of subscription would be void, although the name of the subscriber was accepted and entered upon the stock-book of the company, unless, by his failure to notify them in a reasonable time after the fraud was discovered, the company would be injured by its release.

3. SAME. *Same. Effect of parol condition.* A parol condition to the subscription of stock to a railroad company will not, if violated, invalidate the subscription, because it forms no part of the written contract of the parties.

4. SAME. *Same. Effect of an innocent mistake. Contract.* If a party is induced to take stock in a railroad company by false representations which are not fraudulent, and which form no part of the contract of subscription, he is not entitled to be relieved from the payment of the amount of his subscription. But if he acts upon such representations to his injury, he is entitled to relief, although they may have been innocently made.

FROM DAVIDSON.

Tried at the February Term, 1858, before Judge BAXTER. Defendant appealed.

A. L. DEMOSS, for the plaintiff in error.

REID, for the plaintiff in error.

1. We contend that the subscription of Cartwright was *a condition precedent* to the taking of stock by

Enoch Cunningham v. Edgefield and Kentucky Railroad Company.

Cunningham. That is clear. Cunningham avers in his plea that he would not take stock unless Cartwright did first, and then he would take the same number of shares.

Now it is clear that if the subscription of Cunningham was a verbal contract, not reduced to writing, he would not be bound. I understand the law to be, that "where the condition is precedent, it must be strictly performed in every particular, in order to entitle the party, whose duty it is to perform it, to enforce the contract against the other party." *Story on Contracts*, § 32. "Nor does it matter that such condition is difficult or foolish; for, if it be so, it is the fault of the party who engages to perform it, and he should suffer the consequences." *Ibid.*

But I wish to say, that the condition imposed by Cunningham may not have been foolish or unreasonable. He and Cartwright were possessed of about the same wealth, and were pretty much the same character of men, and he might very well have said that I can bear as much as he, and I would prefer to risk his judgment, as to the propriety or profit of taking the stock, than to trust my own. Or he may have been so situated (and such was the fact) that, because of their propinquity, if the road was a peculiar benefit to the one, it would be to the other. He might have been very unwilling to have trusted the judgment or will of Enoch P. Connell. Mr. Connell might be, in his opinion, inconsiderate in his acts, or he might have possessed large real estate about Goodlettsville, and have been very willing and very able to take one thousand shares instead of twenty.

2. But the subscription was in writing. Does that

Enoch Cunningham v. Edgefield and Kentucky Railroad Company.

preclude us from proving the condition upon which it was made? We think not.

If Mr. Cunningham was induced by fraud to subscribe, it is clear that the fraud could be shown by parol, and the contract would be null.

Mr. Story, in his work on contracts, goes further. In section 675, he lays down the law as follows: "Parol evidence will also be admitted to show that an instrument is void, *and never had any legal existence or binding force.*" In the conclusion of the same section he says: "Whatever would vitiate the contract *ab initio*, may be given in evidence to invalidate a written contract."

Now, if the allegations of the plea, or the facts proved on the trial, be true, the road will have perpetrated a most wicked fraud on Mr. Cunningham, if he be held responsible on this subscription. It was well known he would not subscribe unless Cartwright did. The road, by its agent, pretends that it is authorized to subscribe Cartwnight's name, and does do it. Cunningham, in the act of signing, asks if he may feel assured that his name is there in good faith. He is told, yes. Cunningham signs his name, and the trap is let down upon him, and he is told you are ours. If this is not fraud, what is? Redfield on Railways, page 70, and note 2.

In conclusion, we doubt, if the subscription under any circumstances had been binding, whether it was not revoked before it was accepted. The persons who got his signature were mere volunteers, and did not hand in the names, or, if they did, they were not accepted until long after Mr. Cunningham had said he would not be bound by his subscription.

Enoch Cunningham v. Edgefield and Kentucky Railroad Company.

EWING & COOPER, for the defendant in error.

The rejection of evidence as to the organization of the railroad company was certainly proper in the absence of a special plea, because this company was already organized when defendant subscribed. His subscription recognizes their proper organization, and is an estoppel on him. Redfield on Railways, 9, and 85; 5 Vermont.

The action Connell, as to Cartwright, was unguarded, but not fraudulent, and the jury found that it operated no injury to Cunningham. False representations, if not fraudulent and forming no part of the contract itself, are immaterial, (Chitty on Contracts, 682,) more especially as to written agreements. Chitty, 683; 10 M. & W., 147.

The jury are the judges as to materiality. Chitty, 684. Fraud and misrepresentation alone are not sufficient to invalidate a contract. There must also be injury resulting to the person complaining. 1 Meigs' Digest, 189; 2 Parsons on Contracts, 268.

It was necessary for Mr. Cunningham to give notice to the company, when he discovered the fraud, that he would avoid the contract. It was a conditional contract, and the company, in locating their route, were governed by these conditional subscriptions. They were, certainly, innocent and ignorant of any fraud on Cunningham. If he intended to avoid his obligation, he ought, certainly, to have notified the railroad company soon after he discovered the fraud, and his failure to do so was a waiver of his right. 2 Parsons, 278.

The failure to make payment in money of fifty cents on the share, at the time of the subscription, does not

Enoch Cunningham *v.* Edgefield and Kentucky Railroad Company.

give defendant the power to avoid it. Redfield on Railways, § 37, note 3, § 51.

CARUTHERS, J., delivered the opinion of the Court.

This is an action of assumpsit for calls on stock subscribed by Cunningham in the Edgefield and Kentucky Railroad Company.

The main defence is, that at the time the stock was subscribed, there was fraud and deception practiced upon him by one Enoch P. Connell, who was acting as agent of the road in obtaining stock, in this: He refused to take stock unless one Cartwright, a son-in-law of Connell, would do so before him; and Connell, without authority from Cartwright, entered his name for twenty shares under a pretended power from him, but, in fact, without authority, and the same was never sanctioned, but positively repudiated by Cartwright. The book of stock was returned by Connell to, and accepted by the company. No notice to the company, or to Connell, that the subscription was repudiated, was given; but proof was offered to show, that, as soon as Cunningham ascertained that the subscription for Cartwright was without authority, he repudiated, and announced that he would not pay his. This evidence was rejected by the Court, and that was certainly right, because, if the power existed at all to renounce and abandon his subscription, it clearly could only be done by notice to the agent, or to the company, in proper time.

If that defence could be made available at all, which

Enoch Cunningham *v.* Edgefield and Kentucky Railroad Company.

we need not decide in this case, the facts here presented are not such as to raise the question.

But, still, if the subscription was *fraudulently* obtained, and any injury resulted to him therefrom, he would have a good defence, though his name was accepted and entered upon the stock book of the company, unless by his failure to notify them in a reasonable time after he discovered it, they would sustain an injury by its release. If he was deceived and defrauded, it would have been his duty to have notified the company, or its agent, of it, and his intention not to pay, before they incurred liabilities on account of it in the construction of the road. 2 Par. on Con., 278. Delay is evidence of a waiver.

It does not appear that there was any intentional wrong on the part of Connell, but that he had reasonable grounds to believe that his son-in-law, Cartwright, had made up his mind to take stock against his first determination. But, as it turned out, this was not so, and his name was entered without and against his consent, and he refused to ratify the act. But Connell made it good himself, and there was no injury on the score of the money, to the extent of those twenty shares. Yet Cunningham was deceived as to that fact, and so was Connell; and the latter sustained the injury by taking the stock upon himself. Still, it is true, that the condition upon which Cunningham subscribed failed. But, as a condition, it would not invalidate his subscription, because it was not part of the writing signed by him. *East Tennessee and Virginia Railroad* v. *Gammon*, 5 Sneed, 567.

If it were an innocent mistake, on the part of Connell, upon which he acted, he would be entitled to relief; but only in case he were injured by it, and took advantage of it in proper time. This he did not do, and the misrepresentation has done him no harm. It could not be material to his interest, as a stockholder, whether the amount was paid by Cartwright or another.

False representations in general, if not fraudulent, and form no part of the contract itself, will not vacate it. Chitty on Contracts, 682. But even if innocent, if the party acts upon them to his injury, relief will be afforded. 2 Parsons, 268. But there can be no relief against fraud which is not operative, and in its effects produces no injury or loss to the party seeking redress on account of it. 1 Meigs' Digest, § 337; 2 Parsons on Contracts, 268.

The law and the facts are against the plaintiff in error, and he was, properly, subjected to the payment of his stock by the verdict and judgment below.

We affirm it.

JOSEPH M. BURROUGHS *v.* W. W. GOODALL, *et al.*

1. SUMMARY PROCEEDING. *Motion against Sheriff and securities. Revivor by motion. Act of* 1858, *ch.* 89. Prior to the act of 1858, the remedy by motion did not extend to the personal representative of a deceased officer, or of his security, and could not be maintained against either. By that act, if the officer, or either of his securities, shall die during the pendency of a suit by motion, against them, it may be revived against the personal representative of such officer, or security,

Joseph M. Burroughs v. W. W. Goodall *et al.*

in the same way that suits are revived against personal representatives in other cases.*

2. SAME. *Same. Same. Act of* 1858 *does not have a retrospective operation.* If the Legislature could have given the act of 1858 a retrospective operation, it is manifest that it was not done; and is, therefore, to be construed as applicable, only, to cases arising after its passage.

3. SAME. *Same. Same. Death of the principal abates the motion as to the securities.* It is only through their principal, and jointly with him, that the securities can be reached by motion. And the abatement of the motion as to the principal, of necessity, works an abatement as to the securities. Even under the act of 1858, no step can be taken against the securities until the motion is revived against the personal representative of the principal.

FROM JACKSON.

This cause was heard at the November Term, 1858, GOODALL, J., presiding. The plaintiff appealed. The facts are stated by the Court.

H. DENTON and M. M. BRIEN, for the plaintiff.

J. P. MURRAY, for the defendants.

McKINNEY, J., delivered the opinion of the Court.

On the 21st of July, 1856, the plaintiff obtained judgment, by motion, against Goodall, the Sheriff of Jackson county, and his sureties, before a Justice of said county, for $135,54, for the failure of his deputy to make return of a justice's execution, issued upon a judgment in favor of the plaintiff against one Settle. From this

---

* The provisions of the act of 1858 are carried into the Code, section 3597.

Joseph M. Burroughs v. W. W. Goodall et al.

judgment the defendants appealed to the Circuit Court. At the November Term of said Court, 1856, the death of Goodall, the Sheriff, was suggested and admitted. No other step appears to have been taken in the case until the July Term, 1858, when the defendant moved the Court to dismiss the motion. This motion was refused. And, thereupon, on motion of the plaintiff, a *scire facias* was awarded against the administrator of said Goodall, to shew cause why said motion should not be revived against him.

The administrator appeared and demurred to the *scire facias;* and, on argument, the Court sustained the demurrer, and gave judgment that the motion be abated as to all the parties—the sureties as well as the principal.

On the foregoing facts two questions arise. First: Did the Court err in holding that the motion could not be revived against the personal representative of the Sheriff? and, secondly, in holding that the motion stood abated as to the sureties.

We are of opinion that the judgment is right upon both points. 1st. It is well settled that, by the law as it stood prior to the act of 1858, ch. 89, this remedy by motion, did not extend to the personal representative of a deceased officer, or of his surety; and could not be maintained against either. *Park* v. *Walker*, 2 Sneed 503, and cases there referred to. But the law upon this subject has been changed by the act of 1858, which provides, in substance, that in cases of motions against sheriffs, coroners, or constables, and their sureties, where the officer or either of his securities shall die during the pendency of the motion, it may be re-

Joseph M. Burroughs v. W. W. Goodall *et al.*

vived against the personal representative of such officer, or security, in the same manner that suits are revived against personal representatives in other cases.

This act is supposed by the plaintiff's counsel, to be applicable to the present case; and in holding otherwise it is insisted that the Circuit Judge erred. It is not thought proper to discuss the question, whether it would have been competent for the Legislature to have given the law a retrospective operation, as we feel very clear that the act upon its face evidences no such intention, and is, therefore, upon a well established general principle, to be construed as applicable, only, to cases arising after its passage. And such, indeed, is the true import of the second section of the act.

2d. We think it equally clear, that the abatement of the motion as to the principal, of necessity worked an abatement as to the sureties also. We are aware of no decision of this Court upon this identical question; but the principle declared in the case of *Balew* v. *Clark*, 4 Hum. 505, by analogy fully maintains our conclusion. But if there were no authority to be found, in reason, it must be so. It is only through their principal, and jointly with him, that the securities can be reached at all. They cannot be proceeded against separately from him in this summary method. And any cause, founded either on matter of law, or fact, which precludes the party injured from proceeding, *by motion*, against the principal, personally, constitutes an insuperable barrier to such proceeding, against his securities.

It matters not that the motion was properly instituted against the sheriff and his securities, in the lifetime of the former; his death, pending the motion, arrests all further proceedings, and is an end of the case, under the law as it stood until the passage of the act of 1858. And, even under that act, no step can be taken against the securities until the motion shall have been revived against the personal representative of the principal.

Judgment affirmed.

EPHRAIM ELROD, GUARDIAN, &c. *v.* W. & C. E. MYERS.

GUARDIAN AND WARD. *When an infant may bind himself, or guardian, or parent, for necessaries.* If an infant is under the care of a parent, or guardian, who has the means and is willing to furnish him what is actually necessary, he can make no contract for any article whatever, that will bind himself, his parent, or guardian, without the consent of his legal protector and adviser. But an infant is liable for necessaries suitable to his rank and condition, when he has no other means of obtaining them except by the pledge of his own personal estate.

FROM JACKSON.

Verdict and judgment for the plaintiff, at the July Term, 1857; GOODALL, J., presiding. The defendant appealed.

JAMES W. MCHENRY, for the plaintiff in error, cited and commented upon, 2 Kent's Com., side page, 239; 9 John. R. 141; 2 Paige's Ch. R. 419.

Ephraim Elrod, Guardian, &c., v. W. & C. E. Myers.

J. P. MURRAY, for the defendants in error, referred to 2 Kent's Com. 192–218; 2 Greenl. on Ev. §§ 365, 366.

McKINNEY, J., delivered the opinion of the Court.

The plaintiff in error, as guardian of Susan Clarke, a minor, was sued before a justice, upon a store account, for about $17,00, for goods furnished to his ward, by the defendant in error. And, on appeal to the Circuit Court, judgment was rendered against said guardian for the amount of said account.

From the proof, it appears that the goods,—which were certain articles of dress—were sold and delivered to the minor herself, without the knowledge of, or any authority from, her guardian. Whether or not the goods sold to the minor were necessaries suitable to her condition, and what was her fortune or condition in life, are matters as to which there is no proof in the record. The proof shows that she was furnished with some goods by her guardian; and there is no evidence that he refused to provide reasonable necessaries for her. It also appears that the minor, without the knowledge or consent of her guardian, had contracted several other store accounts.

Upon this proof the Judge instructed the jury, that the defendant, as guardian, was liable for *necessaries* furnished his ward, provided the amount did not exceed the interest of the fund in his hands belonging to the ward; and that he would be liable although he had not requested or authorized the plaintiff to furnish the goods to his ward, if they were *necessaries*.

Ephraim Elrod, Guardian, &c., v. W. & C. E. Myers.

This instruction is entirely erroneous. All the authorities concur, that, if an infant lives with his parent, or guardian, and their care and protection are duly exercised, he cannot bind himself even for necessaries. 2 Kent's Com. 239.

An infant is liable for necessaries suitable to his rank and condition, when he has no other means of obtaining them except by the pledge of his own personal credit.

But if he is under the care of a parent or guardian, who has the means and is willing to furnish him what is actually necessary, the infant can make no binding contract for any article whatever, without the consent of his legal protector and adviser. 2 Paige's Ch. Rep. 419.

And where it is claimed that the goods furnished were *necessaries*, the evidence may be rebutted by proof that the infant lived under the parental roof, and was furnished with such real necessaries of life as, in the judgment of his parent, seemed proper. Addison on Con. 83. It may also be shown that he was furnished in like manner by his guardian, or that a competent allowance was made to him for his support; or that he was supplied with necessaries from other sources. 2 Greenleaf's Ev., sec. 366, and authorities referred to in note.

From these principles it is clear that the contract, in the present case, was not binding on the infant—upon the facts in this record—neither did it impose any obligation whatever upon the guardian.

The judgment will be reversed.

Sarah Chapman *v.* The State.

SARAH CHAPMAN *v.* THE STATE.

1. CODE. *When it went into effect. Act of* 1847, *ch.* 89. There is no positive enactment as to the time when the Code should go into effect. The general rule is, that all statutes are in force from the date of their enactment, unless some other time is prescribed therein; but the act of 1847, ch. 89, enlarged this rule to forty days after the passage of any general law. The Code adopts the act of 1847. ch. 89, computing, however, the forty days from the adjournment of the Legislature, *sine die.* The Legislature that enacted the Code adjourned on the 22d day of March, 1858, and the Code went into operation on the first day of May, thereafter.

2. CRIMINAL LAW. *False pretence. Act of* 1842, *ch.* 48. *Release of the penalty.* The power to release the penalty imposed by the act of 1842, for obtaining goods under false pretences, on the recommendation of the jury, where the goods do not exceed ten dollars, is vested, *alone,* in the Circuit Judge. If he decline to do so, the power cannot be exercised by the Supreme Court.

3. SAME. *Same. Same. False pretence to be taken in its legal sense.* It is not every falsehood or pretence that will constitute the offence created by the act of 1842. False pretence is to be taken in its legal, and not in its literal sense. The obtaining a quart of whiskey by falsely pretending to be sent for it by another is not sufficient to constitute the offence.

FROM OVERTON.

The prisoner was convicted at the June Term, 1858, GARDENHIRE, J., presiding. Motions in arrest and for a new trial having been overruled, an appeal in error was taken to the Supreme Court.

JONES, for the prisoner, argued that there was no time fixed for the Code to go into effect, and, therefore, it took effect forty days after the adjournment of the

Legislature. This would be about the first day of May, 1858. The time of holding the Circuit Court for Overton county was changed by the Code; consequently there was no law authorizing the holding of said Court at the time the plaintiff in error was tried. This being so, the judgment should have been arrested.

Again, the prisoner was recommended to the mercy of the Court. Under the act of 1842, ch. 89, § 8, the Court has the power to release the penalty. His honor, the Circuit Judge, refused to do so. Under all the circumstances of this case, the penalty, certainly, should have been released; and this Court can now do what it was the duty of the Court below to have done.

I further insist that the case made out does not fall within the provisions of the act of 1842. If parties are to be convicted for every falsehood perpetrated to get whiskey, the walls of the penitentiary will have to be enlarged. Many cases analogous to this are to be found in which it was held the offence was not made out. 8 Arch. C. P., 468; Roscoe's Crim. Ev., 465, *et seq.* Roscoe refers to several cases analogous to the one now before the Court.

SNEED,. Attorney General, for the State.

CARUTHERS, J., delivered the opinion of the Court.

This is an indictment, in the Circuit Court of Overton, for obtaining one quart of whiskey from Joseph Morton by "false and fraudulent pretences." She is charged to have falsely "represented and pretended that she was sent by one James Brown to get the spirits

Sarah Chapman v. The State.

for him." This is under the act of 1842, ch. 48, and was found 23d June, 1858. A conviction was had at the same term, and sentenced to three years confinement in the penitentiary. The jury recommended the defendant to the mercy of the Court, but the Court declined to "release the penalty imposed by the act," as he was authorized to do on the recommendation of the jury, by the third section, where the goods obtained do not exceed the value of ten dollars.

We are now urged to grant the release. We doubt our power to do so, as it was probably intended to confine this discretionary power to the judge trying the case, who would have all the facts before him, and on that account be better able to form a correct opinion upon the merits of the case. He failed to notice the recommendation in any way, and thereby tacitly rejected it. We held, at Knoxville, that the power given to the Circuit Judge to commute the punishment in the penitentiary to confinement in the common jail, in cases of petit larceny, was given, alone, to the judge below, and could not be exercised by this Court. That is analogous to this case.

This small case brings up an important question upon one of the reasons in arrest, which is, to settle the time when the Code went into effect. The question arises in this way: The Code changes the times of holding Overton Circuit Court from the third Mondays of February, June, and October, to the fourth Mondays of January, May, and September. So if the act constituting the Code was in force before the third Monday in June, it is insisted that there was no authority for the proceedings and judgment in this case, as the Court was sitting at

Sarah Chapman v. The State.

the wrong time, being different from that fixed by the latest act. This question might be avoided by disposing of the present case upon other grounds; but we prefer to meet it at once, as there seems to be some diversity of opinion on the question; and it is certainly very important, for many weighty reasons, that the question should be put to rest by judicial determination.

It would seem a little remarkable that this point had not been settled by positive enactment in the Code itself. But this can well be accounted for by the impatience and hurry which generally attend an adjournment, after a long and tedious session, of any legislative body. Although the great body of the Code consists of the statutes before enforced, with some changes of phraseology, yet there are many new and important provisions and changes which it would seem reasonable should not go into effect until after knowledge of their nature on the part of the people, which could only be given by publication of the work. It would be proper, therefore, if it could be done upon any provision, or correct principle, to hold that it only takes effect from the time it was published. But can this be done?

The Code purports to embody all the general acts of the State in one act, divided into *parts, titles, chapters, articles,* and *sections.* The chapter on the limitation of actions, by section 47, is not to apply to any causes of action accruing before the 6th of October, 1858. An argument is made that this has the effect to postpone the whole Code to that day. But in this we are not able to concur. If such was the intention, why single out that chapter, when it would have been as easy and more natural to embrace the whole, expressly.

This would rather tend to show, that as the mind of the Legislature was upon the subject at the time when the Code should take effect, and they confined the provision to one single subject, that it was not intended to extend any further.

It is a general rule that all statutes take effect from the time they are passed, unless some other time is prescribed in the act. But, for the purpose of avoiding the injustice and hardship, if not absurdity, of holding the people bound by laws before they had any opportunity of knowing what they were even by their publication in the newspapers, or the return of their members, a general law was passed in 1847, ch. 39, providing that "no general law" should "go into operation, or have any binding effect, until after the expiration of forty days *after its passage*, unless otherwise provided in the act."

This is adopted in the Code, section 162, with the single alteration that the forty days are to be counted from "*the adjournment without day*" of the Legislature. The whole Code is but one general act of the Legislature, and the only provision in it in relation to the point under consideration, with the exception before stated, in relation to the limitation chapter, is in conformity to the act of 1847. Then is it possible to avoid the conclusion that it went into operation and effect at the expiration of forty days from the adjournment? We think not, and so decide. There is no question but that was long before the session of the Court at which these proceedings occurred, for that was late in June, 1858. The Legislature adjourned on the 22d day of March, and the Code went into operation on the first day of May, 1858.

But still it does not follow that the judgments of the Court were unauthorized and illegal. The Code provides in section 41, that "in case of any *conflict* between the acts of this session and this Code, the latter shall be controlling." The concluding paragraph of the act of last session, chapter 98, which fixes the terms of all the Courts precisely as does the Code—the one must have been copied from the other—excludes the change therein made from affecting the first terms to be held within "forty days" from the end of the session. Now this provision is not in conflict with the Code. The latter has no provision on that subject, but only adopts and continues the time fixed by the act as a permanent regulation. Both may stand without inconsistency. We will not say that there are not other grounds upon which the judgments of this Court might be maintained, independent of the one stated; but that is sufficient for the purpose, and we need not go in search of additional arguments. The judgments of Courts and the acts of officers, judicial or ministerial, will always be sustained, if it can be done upon any correct principle.

Another ground in arrest is, that the indictment does not charge a case of felony under the act of 1842.

The first section creates this new class of felonies in general terms. It consists in feloniously obtaining or getting into possession the personal goods or choses in action of another "by means of any false or fraudulent pretence." The third section defines the words used. Among other things, it provides that the phrase, "shall include all cases where a person feloniously gets the money or goods or choses in action of another into possession by any (1) false token, (2) or counterfeit letter, or (3) by falsely personating another, or (4) by falsely pretending to be the owner of such goods," &c., " or *by any other false and fraudulent pretence,* with the intention at the time of feloniously stealing them." The four specified cases in the above extract are plain enough and of easy application; but under the general clause it is difficult to find any settled rule which pervades all the cases. The construction placed upon the English statutes on that subject, and those of the several States of the Union on their respective statutes, (for almost every State, with slight variations, has an act of the kind,) present such a conflicting variety of decisions that it is difficult to extract any settled principle from them. In 3 Arch. Crim. Prac., 468, there is a case cited from 2 East. P. C., 672, very analogous to this, which was held not to fall under the statute. So at page 471 of the same book, in 43 Eng. Com. Law Rep., 92, where a case very much like this was held not to constitute the felony. There are other cases cited by the same author and other books on the subject, that it would be difficult to distinguish from this, where similar acts were held to constitute the felony. We are not disposed to open the door so wide in the construction of this severe and penal act as to convert every case of falsehood and dishonesty by which one may get the advantage of another in the most insignificant matter into a felony. It surely was not intended that barely telling a *lie,* for the purpose of getting twenty-five cents worth of something to eat or drink, should constitute a felony punishable by, at least, three years confinement in the penitentiary. " False pretence" is to be taken in its legal, not literal sense. It is not every falsehood or pretence that will constitute the offence. But we will not now go into the distinctions. The defendant must be a very degraded creature, but she seems to have been a customer of the prosecutor. The *lie* was not calculated in itself, under the circumstances, to impose upon the prosecutor, and there is some reason to doubt whether it really did so.

The judgment will be arrested, upon this ground, and the defendant discharged.

ELI G. FLEMING *et al. v.* MATT MARTIN *et al.*

1. CHANCERY. *Sale of land. Rescission of contract. Registration. Attachment.* If a contract for the sale of a tract of land is entered into, and a title bond executed; and, thereafter, said contract is rescinded by the parties, either in writing or by parol, a specific performance can not be enforced by the vendee. The creditors of the vendee stand upon no higher ground than he occupies, and can not claim a specific performance of such contract, so as to subject the land to the payment of their debts, although the contract of rescission is not registered before the levy of their attachments upon the same.

2. SAME. *Same. Same. Same. Fraud.* If the rescission of the contract was prompted by a motive to benefit the vendee, or injure his creditors, it would be a *fraud* upon the creditors; and would not affect them. Otherwise, if it was made to save the vendor. The registration laws do not apply to such a contract.

3. SAME. *Same. Sale of equitable interest. Question reserved.* If, instead of a rescission of the contract of sale, the vendee sells his equitable interest to a third person, and the contract of sale is not registered before the land is attached, a different question would arise. It would, then, be a contest between a purchaser and the creditors of the vendee, and the question, as to the effect of a non-registration of the sale of such equitable interest, as against the creditors, is reserved.

Eli G. Fleming *et al. v.* Matt Martin *et al.*

4. SAME. *Lien of vendor for other debts. Question reserved.* Would the vendor, if the contract is executory, have the right to retain a lien upon the land by virtue of his having the legal title, until all his debts against his vendee, both for the land and otherwise, as well as liabilities for him, are paid or secured, in preference to attaching creditors?

FROM BEDFORD.

Upon the hearing, at the November Term, 1858, Chancellor RIDLEY, dismissed complainants' bills. They appealed.

E. COOPER, for the complainants.

W. H. WISENER, for the defendants.

CARUTHERS, J., delivered the opinion of the Court.

The complainants are creditors of Wm. G. Loughry, and seek to reach his equitable interest in the tract of land described, for the satisfaction of their debts.

Loughry purchased of Matt Martin on the 31st, December, 1851, his large and valuable tract of land in Bedford county. The consideration was $47,000, of which $20,000 were to be paid upon judgments then existing against Martin, in favor of the Bank of Tennessee and others, which were a lien upon the land, and the remaining $27,000 in three equal annual payments of $9,000 each; the first to be due on the 1st of January, 1854. A bond for title was then executed, in a penalty of $100,000. Possession was given immediately, and Loughry used and occupied the place as his own, until early in April, 1854, when he became desperate in his circumstances, and absconded and left the country. He did not return for two years.

His creditors, which were numerous and large, not being able to find anything else out of which to make their debts, filed these attachment bills, to reach the equitable interest of their debtor in this land. The first bills were filed, and attachments issued, on the 7th of April, 1854, and the others in quick succession. They allege that Loughry had paid a large amount of the consideration, and to that extent has an interest in the land; and that after the payment of Martin, whatever may be due him of the *purchase money*, they are entitled, as creditors, to the balance, and to ascertain that, they have a right to a decree for the sale of the land, and an account.

Martin resists the prayer of the bills upon two grounds:

1. That the contract of sale was "annulled and rescinded," by an agreement in writing between him and Loughry, on the 31st of March, 1854, and that upon a settlement of accounts between them on that day, and set forth in said writing, the amount which Loughry had paid him on the land trade, was to be applied to his other demands against, and liabilities incurred for, said Loughry. So that whatever interest the latter had in said land, was released and extinguished. Also, that by another written agreement, more formally drawn up, but to the same effect, dated on the 6th of April, 1854, the said Loughry denuded himself, of any and all interest he may have had in said land.

Eli G. Fleming *et al.* *v.* Matt Martin *et al.*

2. That he has a right to retain the legal title with which he has never parted, not only for the unpaid purchase money, but for all other debts due to him by his vendee, or liabilities incurred for him, before the attachments; and that these debts and liabilities will exceed the amount he has received of the consideration, leaving no interest in Loughry, even if the sale had not been rescinded.

Upon the decision of these questions, the rights of the parties must depend:

The writing of 31st of March, 1854, is severely contested, and boldly charged to be a forgery. Much proof is taken on this point; and among others, Loughry himself is examined as a witness. We pass by the question of competency, which may be doubtful. He swears most positively, that he never executed or saw such a paper, but admits the signature is genuine. He says, about that time, and before, he was in the habit of giving Martin his name in blank, for the purpose of raising money, &c., but does not remember that particular case, but knows he never executed, or even knew of the existence of the paper in question. His credit is then impeached and sustained, upon his general character. Thirty-odd witnesses are examined, a majority of whom would give him credit, but many would not. Martin, on the other hand, in his answers, relies upon this instrument, and in response to an amended bill for a discovery in relation to it, under a charge that it is fabricated and forged, positively denies it, and states the circumstances under which it was executed with minute detail. He states that he became alarmed at Loughry's condition; met him at Murfreesboro' by appointment, where he had gone for the purpose of making a deed of trust upon his property to secure his creditors; that they slept in the same room at the hotel, and agreed upon the terms of settlement, and he drew it up and signed it, and. read it over to Loughry, who said it was right, and would sign it next morning; and that on the next morning, in the bar-room, he presented it to him, and after some explanation he signed it, as he thinks, at a desk or table in the public room. This is, he says, his best recollection, or it may be that Loughry did not sign until they got to Shelbyville, which was the next morning after it is dated, 1st of April. In corroboration of this, James Mullins proves that he was with the parties at Murfreesboro' at that time, and saw them just before, or after breakfast, in the public room at the hotel, standing together near "a long writing desk, or something of that sort. Martin had an instrument of writing, and was reading or showing it to Loughry; it was laid down on the desk, and I saw Mr. Loughry have a pen in his hand, and my impression is, that he signed the instrument of writing." Mr. Wisener, a witness, states, that on the return of Loughry, after an absence of two years, he came to his office to learn something about the state of his business, and among other things, he told him what Col. Martin said about his article of rescission, and how it was executed, as set out in Martin's answer; and he understood him to say, that "it was all right, and that he and Col. Martin would have no difficulty on that subject."

We think that the instrument is established by the weight of proof, and that Loughry cannot be credited

Eli G. Fleming *et al. v.* Matt Martin *et al.*

on that point. There is nothing to overthrow the answer, which is responsive, but the swearing of a single witness, and he of a doubtful and slender character. But the answer has to sustain it, the very strong circumstances stated by Mullins and by Wisener.

The Chancellor came to the same conclusion, but held, that not being registered before the bills were filed, it could not stand in the way of the attaching creditors. But he held that Martin had a right to satisfaction of all other claims and liabilities against Loughry, before he could be compelled to part with the legal title. He ordered the necessary accounts on that basis, and upon the taking of the same, it appeared that there was nothing left for the complainants upon the principles adopted, and the bills were dismissed. To the account and report producing this result, many exceptions were filed on both sides, but the Chancellor, in his action upon them, came to the conclusion just stated.

The first sentence in the writing thus established, is this: "We, the undersigned, William G. Loughry, and Matt Martin, both of the county of Bedford, and State of Tennessee, have this day mutually agreed to *rescind and annul* the trade made and entered into by the above named parties, on or about the 1st day of January, 1852, of a tract of land lying in the county of Bedford, District No. 1, on the Garrison Fork of Duck river."

Loughry then agrees to re-convey the land to Martin as soon as the boundaries can be ascertained from the title bond, which was not then present. The writing then proceeds to adjust the accounts between the

Eli G. Fleming *et al.* *v.* Matt Martin *et al.*

parties, by which it is agreed, that what may have been paid by Loughry upon the contract of sale, shall stand against the various amounts paid, and to be paid for him by Martin, and the use of the place for three years, and the overplus, which may be due from Loughry upon settlement, is to be secured by his note at one day after date. By an account taken under the decree of the Chancellor, it turns out that there was a balance due to Martin upon the basis of this agreement. It seems that the paper executed by Loughry on the 6th of April, was intended, more effectually, to carry out the stipulations of that of the 31st of March.

The question arises upon this state of facts, whether, on the 7th of April, the time of the filing of the first of these bills, there was any interest, legal or equitable, in Loughry, which could be attached. Certainly he had no interest remaining of which *he* could avail himself. A bill filed by him for a specific performance, it will not be contended, could have been maintained. Even a parol rescission would have been sufficient to resist him. 2 Hum., 119; 8 Hum., 584.

But it is contended that his creditors stand upon higher ground, and as against them the rescission could have no effect until proved and registered. We think differently. The registration laws do not apply to such a case. There was no fraud here on the part of Martin. His object was to extricate himself, by prompt and decisive action, from the embarrassing difficulties with which he found he was surrounded and the ruin which threatened him by his unwarranted confidence in Loughry. His action was not prompted by any motive to benefit Loughry or to injure his creditors, but to save himself.

Eli G. Fleming *et al.* *v.* Matt Martin *et al.*

It was a race of diligence between creditors. As Martin's involvment with the common debtor arose out of his connection with him in this land, it was surely proper to make himself secure if he could, by regaining the equitable title to it. That he has succeeded in doing so, and thereby defeated the prospect of complainants to make their debts by his loss, is no just ground of complaint on their part. They are struggling to cast the loss upon him, and each are entitled to any legal advantages they can obtain.

If Loughry, in the absence of fraud, could not ask a specific performance against Martin, how can his creditors? It is only upon that ground that they can claim anything. They ask that the land be sold, and after paying the unpaid purchase money to Martin, the balance shall be appropriated to their debts, and the title divested out of him. The answer is, that the contract of which you demand the performance, has been annulled by the contracting parties, and your debtor, therefore, has no interest under it, and your right must depend upon his; you can only claim through him. The case would of course be otherwise if the rescission were fraudulent—made to defeat creditors, for in that case they would have a right to regard it as a nullity, and do what the party himself could not, because of his complicity in the fraud. But, otherwise, the creditors would occupy no higher ground than the debtor, in this respect.

We cannot see what the registration law has to do with the question. The complainants seek an equity of their debtor in the land; it turns out that he has none, that the contract in which it originated has been rescinded in a legal mode, and the equity has again been

Eli G. Fleming *et al. v.* Matt Martin *et al.*

united with the legal estate before they attach it. It is but an illusion—a thing that once was, but now has no existence.

If Loughry had sold his equitable interest to a third person, and the sale had not been registered, a different question would arise. That would raise a contest between a purchaser, and creditors of the vendor. But this was a rescission, and not a sale; the release and abandonment of a past contract, not the making of a new one.

We are aware of no authority that would invalidate this instrument, even as to creditors, for want of registration. This is decisive of the case, and renders it unnecessary to examine the second ground assumed in relation to the right of Martin to retain the legal title until all his debts against Loughry, both for the lands and otherwise, as well as liabilities for him, are paid or secured, in preference to attaching creditors. That question may present some difficulty, and need not be decided until it becomes necessary. *

We come to the conclusion of the Chancellor, though by a different process, and upon other grounds, and without the necessity of taking any accounts.

His decree, dismissing the bills, is affirmed.

---

*As to this question, see the case of *Williams* v. *Love*, reported in this volume, p. 80.

CARTER & PULLIAM v. B. F. TURNER.

PRACTICE AND PLEADING. *Suit prematurely instituted. Abatement. Demurrer.* The fact that a suit has been prematurely brought is, properly, matter for what is termed a plea in abatement to the action of the writ, unless the objection is apparent upon the face of the record; and then it is ground of demurrer, or may be taken advantage of on the trial. But, if not so apparent, it must be pleaded in abatement. And if this be not done, the defendant loses the benefit of the defence.

FROM RUTHERFORD.

This cause was tried before Judge DAVIDSON, at the July Term, 1858. Verdict and judgment for the defendant. Plaintiffs appealed.

KEEBLE & PALMER, for the plaintiff.

AVENT, for the defendant.

McKINNEY, J., delivered the opinion of the Court.

This was an action on the case to recover damages for the wrongful suing out of an attachment, without probable cause.

The attachment was sued out, not as an original process, but under the act of 1843, ch. 29, as auxiliary to a suit at law then pending.

It seems that Turner had sued the plaintiff, in assumpsit, to recover the value of certain services, and labor performed for him. In aid of this suit, the attachment was procured to issue. The ground of the attachment need not now be noticed, as the case turns upon a question altogether aside from the merits of the case.

The facts of the case are, in some respects, very imperfectly and obscurely presented in the record. It would seem, however, that the main ground of defence relied upon on the trial, was, that the present suit, for the wrongful issuance of the attachment, was commenced before the attachment itself, or the suit to which it was auxiliary, had been disposed of.

The Court held that the suit having been prematurely brought, the plaintiff must fail; and verdict and judgment were rendered for defendant.

From anything in the record, it does not appear that this ground of defence was taken by plea, or that the objection was made until the trial. The bill of exceptions states—that it was shown from the record, that the present suit was commenced on the 13th of July, and the attachment was disposed of on the 16th of July, 1857. And on this proof, made on the trial, the case went off. We will not decide whether this defence, if made in the proper form and at the proper time, ought to have prevailed; but will restrict our inquiry to the simple question, whether it was admissible for the defendant to avail himself of it, by proving the facts on the trial.

The fact that a suit has been *prematurely brought*, is properly matter for what is termed a plea in abatement to the action of the writ, unless the objection is apparent upon the face of the record, and then it is ground of demurrer, or may be taken advantage of on the trial. But, if not so apparent, it must be pleaded in abatement; and if this be not done, the defendant loses the benefit of the defence. 1 Chitty on Pl. 453.

Upon this ground alone the judgment must be reversed, and the case remanded for a trial on the merits.

Timothy O'Sullivan *v.* Patrick Larry *et al.*

1. CERTIORARI AND SUPERSEDEAS. *What the petition must show. Code,* § 3130. By § 3180 of the Code, when the certiorari extends only to a part of the judgment, or the cause is brought up by one of several parties, a certified copy of the proceedings complained of shall be made out by the proper officer and filed in lieu of the original papers and the suit, as to parties who do not join in the application, shall not be affected. And if the whole judgment is not complained of the petition must show in what the error consists, and the amount of the same. A general statement that the judgment is for a much larger amount than the plaintiff is entitled to, is not sufficient.

2. SAME. *Petition must show merits. Abatement.* When a party has lost his right of appeal, and is driven to the extraordinary remedy furnished by the writ of certiorari, he must show merits. A trial in the wrong civil district is a matter in abatement, and cannot be taken advantage of by certiorari. It does not involve the merits of the case.

3. SAME. *Justice of the peace. Civil district. Code,* §§ 4114 *and* 4118. If it were conceded that objection to a trial out of the proper district could be made available by certiorari, the petition for the writ must state such facts as will enable the Court to see that the case was tried

Timothy O'Sullivan *v.* Patrick Larry *et al.*[1]

in the wrong district, as regulated by §§ 4114 a..d 4118 of the Code. A statement that the trial was had without the civil district of, both, the plaintiff and defendant, is not sufficient.

FROM SUMNER.

The petition of the defendant below for writs of certiorari and supersedeas, was dismissed upon motion at the June Term, 1858. TURNER, J., presiding. The petitioner appealed.

BAXTER SMITH, for the plaintiff in error.

HEAD & TURNER, for the defendants in error.

WRIGHT, J., delivered the opinion of the Court.

The Circuit Judge did not err in dismissing the petition for writs of certiorari and supersedeas in these cases.

Section 3129 of the Code of Tennessee, provides that where the error complained of is in the amount of the judgment, the petition shall show the amount of the mistake, and the supersedeas shall not issue for more than such amount; and the plaintiff in the judgment shall be entitled to execution for the balance not complained of, as if no such writ had been obtained.

And section 3130 provides that when the certiorari extends only to a part of the judgment, or it is brought up by one or more of several parties only, a certified copy of the proceedings complained of shall be made

Timothy O'Sullivan *v.* Patrick Larry *et al.*

out by the proper officer, and filed in lieu of the original papers and proceedings as to parties who do not join in the application, shall not be affected.

Now it is palpable the petitioner did not complain of the whole amount of these judgments; yet he failed to state wherein the error consisted, or its amount. The language of the petition is, that "petitioner will be able to show upon a new trial, that the judgments were for a much greater amount than the plaintiffs were entitled to."

This language implies that a large portion, if not the greater part of these judgments is correct.

The objection that these trials and judgments were not had in the proper civil district, if true, at this stage of the cause, has nothing in it, because it does not involve the merits of the case; and when the party has lost his appeal, and is driven to the extraordinary remedy furnished by the writ of certiorari, he must show merits.

But when we examine the petition it does not appear from anything stated therein, that the trials and judgments were had in the wrong district. The petitioner's objection is that he was tried out of his own district and that of the plaintiff. The form of the actions were in debt, and by the 4114th section of the Code, he was not entitled to be tried in his own district because he disputed the plaintiff's claim. And in that case—unless the magistrate was incompetent, or absent, or there was no magistrate of the plaintiff's district—the trial should have been in that district. But in case of incompetency, absence, or want of a magistrate in the proper district, the trial may be had in any adjoining district. Code, section 4118. Now, if we concede that the defendant had a right to call in question the want of a trial in the plaintiff's district—a requirement evidently for the plaintiff's benefit—yet he nowhere in his petition states anything from which it may be seen that these cases were tried in the wrong district.

But, as before stated, this is matter in abatement, and does not go to the merits.

Judgment affirmed.

GOLLADAY, CHEATHAM & CO. *v.* THE BANK OF THE UNION.

1. BILLS AND NOTES. *Demand and notice. What sufficient evidence of notice.* Act of 1820, ch. 25, § 4. Code §§ 1800 and 1801. A Notary Public is a public officer, and when he certifies that he has done an official act, it is presumed that he has performed that duty according to law, until the contrary is shown. Hence, if he certify *in* or *on* his protest, that he notified the drawers and endorsers, it is, *prima facie,* good; and it is not necessary that he should state the time when the notice was given, the post office to which it was sent, &c. The act of 1825, carried into the Code, Secs. 1800 and 1801, does not expressly, require it.

2. SAME. *Same. Effects in the hands of the drawee.* If the drawer of a bill has no effects in the hands of the drawee to meet it, or some good reason to believe it will be accepted, he is bound to the payee, or holder, without demand or notice. It is, however, presumed that the drawee has such effects, until the contrary appears; and this presumption is not changed by a waiver, or want of acceptance of the bill.

3. SAME. *Same. Waiver of notice.* If the drawer of a bill, with a

knowledge that he is discharged from its payment for want of notice, acknowledge the debt and promise to pay it, he, thereby, waives demand and notice, and is liable for the same.

FROM DAVIDSON.

At the September Term, 1858, BAXTER, J., presiding, there were verdict and judgment for the plaintiff. The defendants appealed.

THOS. WASHINGTON and A. L. DEMOSS, for the plaintiffs in error.

F. B. FOGG and J. H. MCDONALD, for the defendant in error.

CARUTHERS, J., delivered the opinion of the Court.

The Bank of the Union recovered a judgment against Golladay, Cheatham & Co., as the drawers, in Tennessee, of a bill of exchange for $1200, upon Traber & Aubery, of Cincinnati, Ohio, in the Circuit Court of Davidson. "Acceptance waived," was written upon the face of the bill.

The errors assigned, are upon the charge of the Court.

The defence was upon the ground of failure of notice of the demand and refusal to pay. The official protest of the notary is in evidence, which shows that the protest was on the proper day, 23d of October, 1857; the bill having been drawn on the 22d of July preceding, at ninety days. The only proof of notice is this sentence in the body of the protest: "I then notified the drawers and endorsers." The act of 1820, ch. 25, sec. 4, is, that

Golladay, Cheatham & Co. v. The Bank of the Union.

when "the notary shall have certified *either in*, or *on* his protest, that he has given notice of demand of payment, and refusal, or the dishonor of such bill," &c., "to the endorsers, makers, or others concerned, such protest shall be *prima facie* evidence of the fact of notice."

The Code, in sections 1800 and 1801, continues, in substance, the same provision. This was done to save the parties from the expense of taking depositions, and the loss of rights by the accident of death.

The fact is to be stated by the notary, either *in* or *on* his protest. But it is said that he must state the time when the notice was given, the post office to which it was sent, and all the particulars necessary to make out a good legal notice, under the law merchant. The act does not expressly require this. The notary is a public officer and when he certifies that he has done an official act it must be presumed that he has done it correctly, unless some statute or rule of law prescribes a particular mode, until the contrary appears. It is only made *prima facie* evidence. It is no hardship on a defendant who is relying upon strict law and, generally, without merit to get clear of a debt, to require him to rebut this presumption. It would be easy to prove the facts by the notary if he had not done enough to fix the liability. We are not prepared to agree with his honor, that this proof unrebutted, was not sufficient on the question of notice. We think it was *prima facie*, under the statute, and cast the burthen of proving the contrary upon the defendants. But the plaintiff recovered upon other grounds, with this error against him.

The defendants complain of two positions in the charge against them:

Golladay, Cheatham & Co. v. The Bank of the Union.

1. The Court stated to the jury, "that if the defendants had no effects in the hands of the drawee, with which to meet the bill, they would not be entitled to notice of the dishonor; and that in the absence of an acceptance by the drawee, or a waiver of an acceptance upon the bill, the law would not raise a presumption of effects in the hands of the drawee, and the burthen of proof of effects would lie upon the defendants."

2. "That the letter marked exhibit 'C,' although it specified no particular debt as being due from the defendants to the plaintiff, might, in the absence of proof of the existence of any other debt, be presumed to apply to this debt; and that if they believed it to apply to this debt, it would be a waiver of notice, and a promise to pay the debt, notwithstanding there had been no notice. And that the said letter was admissible under the present state of the pleadings, to prove a waiver of notice, and subsequent promise to pay, where the declaration contained but one count, with an averment that there had been due and legal notice, and without any excuse for the want of notice, or any count founded on a subsequent promise."

The letter marked exhibit "C," was written by Archer Cheatham, one of the firm, and is as follows:

At Home, December 30th, 1857.

"DAN'L F. CARTER, Esq.,

"*Dear Sir:*—Golladay, Cheatham & Co., have stopped their furnace, and will wind up their business just as rapidly as possible. We have about 1000 tons pig iron, with negroes and mules, all which we are going to sell as soon as possible, in order to pay off all the indebtedness of said firm. We are owing money, and among

Golladay, Cheatham & Co. v. The Bank of the Union.

the rest, are indebted to your Bank. It has been our wish to pay off all our debts promptly, but no one, six months ago, looked for the times we have had for the past four months. Like many others, we have found it impossible to pay our debts at maturity. But we have stopped our furnace, and will sell everything belonging to the firm, and go ahead and pay what we owe, without the mortification of suit. If you think, however, upon consultation with those engaged with you, that a suit is the safest and quickest way to collect your debt, I have not one word of complaint to utter. We are abundantly able to pay all we owe, and will devote ourselves to this purpose until we get through."

Dan'l Carter, to whom this letter was addressed, was proved to be the President of the Bank of the Union, and it was also proved, that this letter was in the hand writing of the said Archer Cheatham, of the firm of defendants. There is but little other proof in the case, except as to the residences of the defendants, their post offices, and place of doing business, and that they were in the habit of doing business by consigning their iron to the drawees of this bill. But whether they had any effects in their hands to meet this bill, or had given any assurances that it would be met, does not appear. There is no proof that we can notice upon either side on that point.

In reference to this state of facts, are the legal positions assumed in the charge erroneous?

1. There can be no doubt but that the *drawer* of a bill is bound to the payor or holder, without demand or notice, where he has *no effects* in the hands of the drawee to meet it, or some good reason to believe it

Golladay, Cheatham & Co. v. The Bank of the Union.

will be accepted. Story on Prom., notes, secs. 311, 268; Story on Bills, 311, 369. But this is an exception to the general rule; Chitty on Bills, 436, and note 2. But it is always *presumed* that the drawee has such effects, until the contrary appears. Chitty on Bills, 327, 436. The holder must prove this to excuse notice, note 2; and 2, Marsh. 152; Byles on Bills, 234, note 1. So the only question upon this part of the charge, is, whether the waiver of acceptance upon the bill, or the absence of acceptance, changes the presumption of law in favor of effects being in the hands of the drawee, and throws the burthen of proving that fact upon the drawer, before he can defend himself upon the ground of want of notice of dishonor at maturity, upon the demand of payment.

There are some exceptions to the rule that want of effects dispenses with notice; Chit. on Bills, 329, 436, and note; but they need not be referred to, as the facts of this case did not require that they should be brought to the attention of the jury. Upon this precise question we have been referred to no authority, and are unable to find any. The position of the charge is that where there is no acceptance, and this may be for want of presentation, or refusal to accept upon presentation, the presumption of law that the drawee has effects of the drawer in his hands is overthrown. In other words, there is no such presumption unless the bill is accepted, or that it does not arise until actual acceptance. It goes further, and holds that the presumption is against effects to meet the bill, and the drawer must show he had them there before he can insist upon his right to notice of demand and refusal to

Golladay, Cheatham & Co. *v.* The Bank of the Union.

pay. This was certainly conclusive of the case upon that point, as it was not pretended that the bill had been presented for acceptance, or that it was intended by the parties that this should be done. The duty of doing this was waived on the face of the paper. And this last fact, also, the Judge charges, would have the same effect to change the burthen of proof.

In the absence of authority, we are not prepared to adopt this principle, which seems to us to be an innovation upon the established practice. We are not able to see how the fact of want of acceptance, or waiver of acceptance, could change the legal presumption in relation to the existence of effects to meet the bill in the hands of the drawee. We can perceive no good reason why it should have the effect to change the burthen of proof on that subject. The law does not require the presentation of a bill at all before maturity in order to hold the drawer or endorsers liable. The holder may do this, or not, at his option, and he loses nothing by the failure, but the obligation of the drawee, in case he would accept. Can the waiver of acceptance have any other effect? The drawee in this does not waive the presentation for payment, and if not, it would seem clear that his right to notice of refusal to pay, would remain unaffected, and that any excuse for the failure to give him notice of that, would have to be made out by the holder, by proving, against the existing presumption of effects, that there was no provision made to meet the bill. The charge on this point introduces, as it seems to us, a new rule and distinction in this branch of the law, which is already sufficiently complicated.

This practice of waiving acceptance is, perhaps, a

Golladay, Cheatham & Co. *v.* The Bank of the Union.

modern invention to avoid the charges generally made by business men, of a certain per cent. for the act of accepting. It is difficult to see what legal effect it would have upon the rights of the parties to a bill, or how it can in any way change the law merchant on the questions of notice, or the established presumptions of law, or burthen of proving matters to exonerate holders from the performance of acts required to fix drawers with liability. So, we think, there is error in this point of the charge.

2d. On the second point, we think his Honor was right throughout, with the exception of the important qualification, that an acknowledgment of the debt, and promise to pay it, in order to amount to a waiver of demand or notice, must be made *with a knowledge of his discharge* at the time. Ad. on Con., 998; 3 Kent 113. Our own adjudication in the case of *Spurlock* v. *The Union Bank*, 4 Hum., 336, makes the full knowledge of his discharge indispensable to the binding effect of such a subsequent provision. As to the identity of the debt referred to in the letter, and the admissibility of the evidence under the count averring demand and notice, the charge was right upon the authorities. But this position as to a promise to pay, amounting to a waiver of notice, is erroneous without the qualification that they knew at the time that they were discharged for want of notice.

It may be that the same verdict would have been proper, notwithstanding these errors of the grounds of waiver of the want of notice, if the Court had let in the protest as proof of notice; and, therefore, a new trial should not be given, as the merits have been reached. Yet we cannot tell but the defendants were prepared to disprove the *prima facie* evidence afforded by the statement of notice in the protest, if it had been admitted against them.

The result is that the judgment must be reversed.

LOUISVILLE AND NASHVILLE R. R. Co. *v.* JAMES F. FAULKNER.

RAILROAD COMPANY. *Liability to tenant for trespass.* If a railroad company, in violation of a contract with the landlord, enter upon land held by a tenant, and commit a trespass upon the tenant's possession, by destroying his vegetables, &c., said company is liable, in an action on the case, to the tenant for the damages sustained by him. Otherwise, if there is no contract with the company, by which the tenant is protected in his possession of the premises.

FROM DAVIDSON.

This cause was heard at the January Term, 1858, BAXTER, J., presiding. Verdict and judgment for the plaintiff. The defendant appealed.

A. L. DEMOSS, for the plaintiff in error.

J. C. THOMPSON, for the defendant in error.

CARUTHERS, J., delivered the opinion of the Court.

Faulkner sued the plaintiff in error, in tresspass on the case, and recovered $200 damages. The injury charged is for entering upon the grounds of which he was renter for the year, for the construction of the road, and destroying his vegetables, houses, fences, &c.

Louisville and Nashville R. R. Co. *v.* James F. Faulkner.

Faulkner was the tenant of General Anderson, and had rented the land for the whole of the year 1853. During that year Anderson sold to the corporation, and executed his bond for title, which was accepted. In that it is expressly stipulated that Faulkner is to retain the possession until the 1st of January, 1854. But he was ousted by the company in October before, and forcible possession taken of the premises, and his property destroyed as before stated, in the construction of the road. Now, can he recover in this or any other mode of proceeding for this supposed injury?

The owner of the freehold can only proceed under the charter, and not by any other mode. But a termer is not embraced by the charter, and perhaps has no redress against a corporation of this description, for any injury he may sustain by the rightful entry upon his possessions, and necessary occupation of the same for the purposes of the charter.

The right of the State to appropriate private property to public use, is communicated to these corporations, and they may, in its rightful exercise, enter upon the lands of others in the construction of their roads, lawfully, and without liability as trespassers. So it could have entered upon Faulkner with impunity, unless by contract that right was lost. It was certainly competent for this artificial person to bind itself, by contract, as well as any other person. Its acknowledged right to enter upon this land, could be waived or postponed by contract. And in the present case this was done. The corporation bought of Anderson, and as a stipulation in that written contract, Faulkner was to retain the pos-

Louisville and Nashville R. R. Co. v. James F. Faulkner.

session unmolested for a fixed period. This was a postponement of an admitted right by contract. Surely both parties were bound to observe it. Though Faulkner was not a party to it, yet his landlord provided for his protection as a term in his sale. Here, then, is a case of entering upon another's possessions without authority, and against an express contract, and great damage is done. Can there be any doubt about the liability in such a case? It is not an injury embraced by the charter; the entry was in violation of a contract, and therefore, illegal; damage has resulted, and there is no other remedy given.

It was no defence to show that the title was out of Anderson, and in Maxey, or any one else. It was enough to show that Anderson had the possession, rightfully, by his tenant, and that the defendant acknowledged his right and contracted with him for it making the reservation stated, in favor of the plaintiff.

There is no error, and the judgment is affirmed.

A. D. Goss v. Moses Singleton et al.

1. TRUST AND TRUSTEE. *Gift. Acceptance. Benefit. Presumption of.* In general, any gift by deed, will, or otherwise, is supposed *prima facie*, unless the contrary appears, to be beneficial to the donee. Consequently the law presumes, until there is proof to the contrary, that every estate is accepted by the person to whom it is expressed to be given.

A. D. Goss v. Moses Singleton *et al.*

2. SAME. *Same. Not perfect until acceptance.* The gift is not perfect until ratified by the assent of the donee; and a disclaimer of the trust operates as evidence that such assent was never given.

3. SAME. *Same. Acceptance discretionary.* The law does not force the donee to accept the gift of an estate, whether made in trust, or otherwise, and therefore it is competent for the person appointed trustee to refuse both the estate and the office attached to it, provided he has done no act to deprive himself of that right.

4. SAME. *Same. Disclaimer. How made.* There is some conflict of authority as to whether a parol disclaimer is sufficient. But it is well settled that the renunciation may be by deed, by matter of record, or any written instrument, or by an answer in Chancery.*

5. SAME. *Same. Same. Relates back to the gift.* A disclaimer, or refusal to accept the trust will relate back, and be held to have been made at the time of the gift, if no act has been done to preclude the party.

6. SAME. *Same. Same. Effect of. Devise in trust.* The legal effect of a proper refusal or disclaimer of the trust is, that all parties are placed precisely in the same situation relatively to the trust property, as if the disclaiming party had not been named in the trust instrument, whether it be a deed or will. Hence, if all the trustees disclaim a devise in trust, the legal estate will vest in the heir of the devisor.†

7. SAME. *Trust does not necessarily pass with the property.* A trust is the mere creature of equity, and does not necessarily inhere in the property so as to be inseparable therefrom, but may remain in the trustee or elsewhere, wholly unaffected by an unauthorized sale of the property, the subject of the trust.

8. SAME. *Effect of the appointment of a trustee.* If, by reason of the disclaimer of the trustees, the property descends to the heir-at-law,

---

* The acceptance of a trust may be by acts and declarations; and, in the absence of proof to the contrary, it will be presumed. And it would seem that if the conduct and expressions of the trustee amount to an *unequivocal* refusal to accept the trust, it would be sufficient. *Thompson* v. *Tickell*, 3 B. & Al., 39; *Bingham* v. *Clanmorris*, 2 Moll., 253; Shep. Touch., 452; *Stacy* v. *Elph.*, 1 M.. & K., 195; 16 Conn., 291; 4 Leigh, 152.

† What would be the effect of a disclaimer by the trustee, if the *cestui que trust* and heir-at-law were not one and the same person? Would the title then be vested in the heir-at-law? and, if so, would it not be coupled with the trusts. in favor of the beneficiary? Would not the *heir* be, by operation of law, the trustee? *Field* v. *Arrowsmith*, 3 Hum., 442; *Hawly* v. *James*, 5 Paige C. R., 318; 8 Paige C. R., 295; *Lee* v. *Randolph*, 2 Hen. & M., 12; *Dawson* v. *Dawson*, Rice, ch. 243; 2 Story's Eq., 1058; *Saunders* v. *Harris*, 1 Head, 206.

A. D. Goss v. Moses Singleton *et al.*

who is also the *cestui que trust*, the legal estate is cast upon the *cestui que trust*, who applies to a Court of competent jurisdiction, and has a trustee appointed, in whom the legal estate is vested, coupled with the trusts, the legal estate is by necessary implication divested out of the *cestui que trust*.

9. SAME. *Same. Statute of limitations. Effect of.* If, from the time the legal title to real estate, the subject of the trust, is thus vested in the trustee, there is an adverse holding of the same for a period of seven years, the party's title becomes indefeasible by the act of 1819, as against the trustee, and equally so as against the *cestui que trust*.

10. SALE OF REAL ESTATE. *Vendor and vendee. When vendee bound to accept title.* In the absence of fraud, the purchaser of real estate is bound to accept a title which is perfect at the time it is to be made, although it may have been defective at the time of the sale.

11. SAME. *Same. Same.* The purchaser of real estate is compelled to accept the title if it has become *"indefeasible"* by operation of the first section of the act of 1819.

12. CHANCERY. *Decree. Effect of upon the rights of persons not parties.* Although a decree is not, in form, binding upon persons who are not parties, yet it is in effect, if the determination of the question presented by the record necessarily involves the determination of their rights and the validity of their title.

FROM DAVIDSON.

This cause was heard before Chancellor FRIERSON, at the November Term, 1858. Decree for the complainant. The defendant, Singleton, appealed. There is a clear and full statement of the facts in the opinion of the Court.

E. H. EWING and JOHN REID, for the complainant.

1. It was insisted in the Court below that Caroline Hagan was not a party to the bill filed by Henry Hagan under the act of 1837–8. That under that act the administrator could not file the bill in his own name and in behalf of the heirs. That Caroline Hagen should

A. D. Goss v. Moses Singleton et al.

have been made a defendant to the said bill, and personally served with process. And this not being done, the sale to Goss was void.

It is admitted by us that this principle was decided by this Court in the case of *Frazier and Tulloss, Ex'rs, v. Pankey et al.*, 1 Swan Rep., 75. That decision seems to have been made against the words, if not the spirit of the act. If the Court shall be disposed to reconsider this point, they will find, by examining the seventh section of the act of 1838, that the act declared, if the bill was filed by a creditor, it should be in his own behalf and all other creditors; that if filed by an executor or administrator, "*it may be on his own behalf, as well as the widow, heirs, and legatees or distributees of the estate, against such of the creditors as were named therein and sought to be enjoined, and all others interested and not named as complainants.*" We have understood that the lawyer who filed the bill in the case of *Hagen* v. *The Creditors of Sitler*, drew the act of 1838, and supposed himself to be complying with its provisions.

The case now before the Court seems to be a much stronger case than that reported in 1 Swan, and hereinbefore cited, inasmuch as Caroline Hagan subsequently filed a bill, and brought before the Court in a proper way all the parties interested, in which she referred to the proceedings of the suit in the said suit of *Henry Hagan, Adm'r*, v. *The Creditors of Sitler*, and ratified as far as she could all the proceedings of the Court. In fact her suit was the same in substance and design, and was but a continuation of the suit by Henry Hagan.

2. But be this as it may, we do not rest this case

A. D Goss v. Moses Singleton *et al.*

upon this point. We insist that Goss acquired a good title to this lot by *the statute of limitations.*

In the case of *Williams* v. *Otey,* 8 Hum. Rep., 563, this Court decided that "whenever a trustee *having the legal title* neglects to sue until he is barred by the statute of limitations, the *cestui que trust* is likewise barred, though an infant under twenty-one years of age."

In the case of *Susan Wooldridge et al.* v. *The Planters' Bank et al.,* 1 Sneed's Rep., 297, this principle is reiterated, and in a case, the facts of which bear a marked resemblance to the one now before the Court.

Yerger conveyed the lot in Pulaski to Walker in trust, to pay certain debts; and after their discharge, to hold the property, and apply the annual rents to the support of Susan, wife of John P. Wooldridge, and to the education and maintenance of her three children, until they should arrive at age or married, when each was to have one-third. Walker, the first trustee, resigned, and White was appointed trustee "in his room and stead." This lot was levied upon and wrongfully sold to satisfy an execution in favor of the bank. It was subsequently sold by the bank, and the united possession of those claiming under the bank was more than seven years. In this case it was decided by this Court that the statute of limitations gave a good title to the lot to the last purchaser, against Mrs. Wooldridge and her children. The trustee could sue, and was bound to sue or be barred.

In the case now before the Court, Edwin H. Ewing, Esq., and Dr. Jennings had the legal title to this lot from Isaac Sitler's death, in 1837, down to November, 1850. They could have sued John D. Goss, who was

A. D. Goss v. Moses Singleton et al.

in the actual possession from 1841, and claiming adversely all the time. But if it be objected that they only had the bare legal title and never consented to act, and that therefore the statute would not run, then we say, admitting this to be so for the sake of the argument, Isaac Litten was appointed trustee by the Chancery Court "in their room and stead," and accepted the trust. He was appointed at the November Term, 1850— more than seven years—and the statute certainly run against him; and barring his title, barred that of the *cestui que trust*.

It is believed the cases of *Smith* v. *Thompson*, 2 Swan's Rep., 386, and *Aikin* v. *Smith*, 1 Sneed's Rep., 304, do not apply. The statute of limitations could not be pleaded successfully in those cases, because, upon the termination ot the life estate, the legal title vested in the infants. The trustee was not clothed with the legal title for their use. The trustee was clothed with the legal title only for the life estate. Therefore both *the legal and equitable title* in the remainder being vested in the infants, the statute of limitations did not run against them. But in the case now before the Court, it is believed that the legal title in the remainder was in the trustees, and remained in them until the youngest child arrived at age. Between the time of the death of the mother, and when the youngest child arrived at age, the trustees were to collect the rents, and apply them to the support and education of the children.

JOHN TRIMBLE and T. D. MOSELY, for the defendants.

A. D. Goss *v.* Moses Singleton *et al.*

McKINNEY, J. delivered the opinion of the Court.

The bill seeks to subject a lot in Nashville, sold and conveyed by the complainant to defendant, Moses Singleton, on the 18th of August, 1852, to the satisfaction of the unpaid purchase money. This relief is attempted to be resisted on the ground of want of title in the complainant. The facts are briefly as follows:

Isaac Sitler, who died in the year 1837, devised said lot, together with other real estate, to E. H. Ewing and Thos. R. Jennings, in trust for his daughter Caroline Sitler, then an infant, to hold for her sole and separate use and benefit, and, in case of her marriage, free from the control of her husband, and of all liability for his debts or contracts. And in the event of the death of said Caroline, leaving issue living at the time of her decease, or children of such issue, in further trust, to hold said property for their use, until the youngest child of said Caroline should arrive at the age of twenty-one; and then to convey to her children, or the issue of such children, in such proportions as the law would give in case of intestacy. There are other limitations over, in certain events, and other trusts declared, which need not be noticed for our present purpose. Said Ewing and Jennings were likewise nominated executors of the will, but they declined to qualify; and at the term at which the will was offered for probate, they appeared in Court, and formally renounced the executorship of record. And thereupon Henry Hagan was appointed administrator, with the will annexed, of said estate.

In April, 1838, the administrator filed a bill in

Chancery, setting forth that the personal estate of the testator was insolvent, and had been so reported to the County Court, and praying a sale of so much of the real estate as might be required to pay the debts, and to have the estate administered pursuant to the statute applicable to insolvent estates. The bill set forth the provisions of the will, and alleged that Ewing and Jennings refused to accept the trust, and asked that a trustee be appointed by the Court in their stead. To this bill certain of the creditors were made parties by name. The nominated trustees, Ewing and Jennings, were likewise made parties. But the infant beneficiary, Caroline Sitler, was not made a party.

Ewing and Jennings answered the bill, and therein entirely renounced the acceptance of the trusts declared in favor of the testator's daughter; but no trustee was appointed in their place.

In October, 1838, a decree was made directing the sale of a portion of the real estate for the satisfaction of the debts reported due by the master; under which, the lot in controversy in this cause was sold by the master on the 18th of July, 1839. But the purchaser being unable to pay the purchase money when due, transferred the benefit of his purchase to the complainant, Goss. This was reported by the master, and approved by the Chancellor, and an order was made directing the master to convey said lot to the complainant; in pursuance of which, a deed of conveyance was executed to him by the master on the 28th of January, 1841. And under this conveyance the complainant held possession of the lot adversely to all persons until his conveyance to the defendant, in 1852—since when the possession has been continued in the latter in like manner.

Prior to the year 1849, the testator's daughter, Caroline, intermarried with Gilbert Hagan, and in December of that year (1849) she brought a bill, by her next friend, to which the administrator, her husband, and the issue of the marriage with him, as well as certain creditors and legatees, were made parties; the object of which was to have a full and final adjustment of her rights under the will, and to have the trusts declared therein executed.

In our view of the case, however, it becomes unnecessary to notice the purposes of that bill, or the proceedings that were had in the cause, further than to state, that, in her bill, she neither affirmatively sanctions nor impeaches the previous administration of the estate in any respect, although all the proceedings are circumstantially detailed; and, amongst other things, the renunciation of the trust by Ewing and Jennings, is stated, and the Court is called on to appoint a trustee in their stead, to carry out the trusts of the will. And in accordance with this prayer of the bill, by an order made on the 19th of November, 1850, Isaac Litton was appointed trustee, and invested with all the powers and duties conferred by the will upon the trustees therein nominated.

The present bill was filed on the first of May, 1855. Gilbert Hagan and his wife, (formerly Caroline Sitler,) and the children of the marriage—the *cestuis que trust* under the will—are not made parties.

Upon the foregoing facts, the question to be determined is, whether the defendant is *now* invested with a valid and indefeasible title to the lot in question, as against Mrs. Hagan and her children? For, although the title may have been defective at the time of filing the bill, yet, in the absence of fraud on the part of the vendor in making the sale, if the title be fully perfected at the time of the final decree, the purchaser will be compelled to accept it.

For the complainant it is insisted, that, admitting the sale to have been void, the title of the defendant is now absolutely perfect, and beyond the reach of impeachment, by operation of the statute of limitatio upon the established principle that the legal estate be vested in a trustee, whose right of action is for barred, the *cestuis que trust*, though under disability, are likewise barred.

To this, it is ingeniously replied by the defendant's counsel, that the conveyance of the legal estate in the lot, to the complainant, (after the disclaimer of the trust by Ewing & Jennings,) under the decree of the court, carried with it, not merely the legal title, but the *trust* likewise, so as, by implication, to constitute him a trustee; and that standing in this relation, he cannot denude himself of the trust, or set up an adverse claim.

This reasoning is not sound. The trust did not, nor could it, pass to the complainant with his purchase of the lot. The trust is the mere creature of equity, and does not necessarily inhere in the property so as to be inseperable therefrom, as the argument assumes, but may remain in the trustee, or elsewhere, wholly unaffected by an unauthorized sale of the property, the subject thereof.

And this leads to the consideration of matters connected with the creation of the trust, and the conse-

━━━
A. D. Goss v. Moses Singleton et al.
━━━

●●●●● of its renunciation by the persons nominated ●● trustees. It seems, in general, that every gift, by ●●●● or will, or otherwise, is supposed *prima facie*, ●the contrary appears, to be beneficial to the do- consequently the law presumes, until there is proof contrary, that every estate is accepted by the to whom it is expressed to be given. Hill on ●; (Ed. of 1854,) 304, top. But the law does ●force any one to accept the gift of an estate, made in trust, or otherwise; and, therefore, it ●tent for the person appointed trustee to refuse he estate and the office attached to it, provided done no act to deprive himself of that right. 312. The gift is not perfect until ratified by the ●● of the donee; and a disclaimer of the trust ● as evidence that such assent was never given. Id. 316. There is some difference of opinion as to what ●●●● be a sufficient disclaimer. There are authorities which seem to maintain that a parol disclaimer of a gift, either by deed or will, of a freehold estate, is sufficient. But, however this may be, it is well settled, that the renunciation may be by deed, by matter of record, or any written instrument, or by an answer in Chancery. Id. 316, 317. And such disclaimer or refusal to accept the trust, whenever made, will relate back, and will be held to have been made at the time of the gift, if no act has been done to preclude the party. Id. 318.

The legal effect of a proper refusal or disclaimer of the trust is, "that all parties are placed precisely in the same situation relatively to the trust property, as if the disclaiming party had not been named in the trust instrument, whether it be a deed, or will." Id. 318. Hence, in such case, if a sole trustee, or all the trustees, disclaim a devise in trust, the legal estate will vest in the heir of the devisor. Id.

From these principles, it follows that the legal estate never vested in Ewing & Jennings: they having properly renounced both the estate and the office of trustees; and, consequently, it descended to the heir at law of the testator, who was the *cestui que trust*, until, upon, her own application, it was vested in Litton, by the decree of a Court of competent jurisdiction, and, by necessary implication, divested out of her. In this novel state of the case, it might not be possible to hold that the statute of limitation could attach before the appointment of Litton, in November, 1850. The effect of the disclaimer of the trustees, being to cast the legal estate upon the *cestui que trust*, by operation of law, from the instant the will took effect; and thus to unite in her both the legal and equitable estates, (but without effecting a technical *meryer* of the latter estate in the former, under the peculiar circumstances; Id. 357,) it is difficult to perceive how the statute could have any operation against her so long, at least, as she remained under the disability of infancy; and when that ceased, whether before the appointment of Litton, is not shown. But, however this may be, we think it sufficient, for the determination of the case in hand, that Litton, the trustee appointed by the Court, is *now* forever barred of his action. By the decree of the Court, the legal estate was in him exclusively; and the trust was a continuing trust, until the youngest child of Caroline should arrive at full age. From the time of his appointment, the statute unquestionably began to operate; and having delayed more than seven years to bring suit for the recovery of the property, the defendant's title has become "indefeasible," by the express terms of the act of 1819, as against the trustee, and equally so as against the *certuis que trust*.

We have assumed, for the purpose of this decision, that the sale to complainant, under the decree, was void, as against the infant *cestui qae trust*, on the ground that she was not a party to the suit; but it is not thought necessary to discuss that question, as it is conceded that, by the decree, though void, the purchaser was clothed with such an apparent legal title, as brought him within the protection of the first section of the act of 1819.

As Mrs. Hagan and her children are not before us in the present case, we cannot, in form, make a binding decree against them; but we do so, in effect, as the determination of the question presented by the record, necessarily involves the determination of their rights, and the validity of their title. *Wooldridge v. Planters Bank*, 1 Sneed, 297.

The principle of the case of *Cunningham v. Sharp*, 11 Humph., 116, 119, that the purchaser will not be compelled to accept the title, if the *possessory right* of the legal owner of the land be merely barred by operation of the second section of the act of 1819, does not apply to this case. Here the rights of all adverse claimants are cut off, and their title absolutely extinguished by force of the first section of the act.

The decree will be affirmed.

W. S. WILLIAMS *v.* S. T. LOVE, EXR., &C. *et al.*

1. LIEN. *Equality among partners.* Partners in lands have an equity against each other, for the purpose of producing equality among themselves; and this equity fastens itself, and is a lien, upon their respective interests in the partnership lands, of which neither can be deprived by the other, or a creditor of his, or purchaser from him with notice.

2. SAME. *Same. Death of the partner having the lien.* It is immaterial whether the amount of the inequality is ascertained at the death of the partner in whose favor this inequality exists. If the indebtedness arise from transactions occurring in the lifetime of such partner, the lien may be enforced by his personal representative.

3. SAME. *For indebtedness to person holding the legal title to land.* If two persons are the joint owners of lands, but the legal title is in one of them, and the other, who has a mere equity in the land, is indebted to the one who has the legal title, the latter cannot be forced to part with the legal title, until the discharge of his indebtedness to him, and until he is freed from liability for him.

4. SAME. *Same. Rights of purchasers and creditors.* A purchaser of an equitable title must always abide by the case of the person from whom he buys. And if the person thus having an equitable interest in land, sell or mortgage the same, or his interest is attached by a creditor, the purchaser, mortgagee, or creditor, takes it incumbered with the equity existing against him.

5. SAME. *Same. Rights of the personal representative.* If the party thus holding the legal title, and an equitable lien on the land for satisfaction of indebtedness to him, dies before the enforcement of such equitable lien, the same right exists in favor of his personal representative, heirs and devisees.

6. SAME. *Same. When mortgagee becomes indebted to the person holding the legal title.* If a person who has an equity in land, mortgages the same to a third person, and the mortgagee becomes indebted to the person holding the legal title to the land, and then assigns his claim upon the mortgagor, together with his lien, the land, by reason of the indebtedness of the mortgagee, becomes subjected to an additional

equity against him, and his assignee occupies no higher ground, and must yield to the superior equity of the person holding the legal title.

FROM DAVIDSON.

This cause was heard at the November Term, 1858, before Chancellor FRIERSON. Decree against Williams, and he appealed.

WILLIAM THOMPSON, for the complainants.

F. B. FOGG, for the defendants.

WRIGHT, J., delivered the opinion of the Court.

On the 1st of September, 1837, John C. McLemore executed to William M. Gwinn, a deed of trust upon the one undivided moiety of two tracts of land entered in the name of Charles J. Love, situated in the county of Dyer, and State of Tennessee.

One of these tracts contained 5000 and the other 1700 acres, and the deed of trust recited that the other moiety belonged to Charles J. Love.

On the 10th of November, 1837, this deed of trust was registered in Dyer county, and purports to have been executed to secure *pre-existing* debts, due from McLemore to Gwinn.

On the 29th of November, 1847, Gwinn assigned to complainant, William S. Williams, the claim he so held upon McLemore, with the trust, to secure its payment.

These lands had been located by W. B. Jones, who

W. S. Williams *v.* S. T. Love, Exr. &c. *et al.*

was employed by Charles J. Love and McLemore for that purpose; and by a decree of this Court, rendered the 19th of February, 1846, one Woodfolk, as the assignee of Jones, recovered jointly against Samuel T. Love, as the executor of Charles J. Love, and also against said McLemore, the sum of $2,083.60, with interest from the 1st of January, 1846, as compensation to the locator, Jones, for locating said two tracts of land, and for other small amounts against them; and one-third of the costs of that suit—the whole of which Charles J. Love's executor paid—McLemore being unable to pay any part of it.

It further appears that Samuel T. Love, as the executor of Charles J. Love, on the 4th of March, 1843, obtained a decree in the Chancery Court at Franklin against John C. McLemore, for $3,867, upon which executions have been run, and returned no property found.

McLemore and Charles J. Love had been partners in the purchase and location of land warrants; and this last recovery grew out of matters pertaining to the partnership.

The amount due Charles J. Love's estate by McLemore, on account of these two recoveries, on the 22d of May, 1856, was $8,773.98, and the same remains unpaid.

Gwinn and Charles J. Love had been partners in the manufacture of iron; and the latter having died in July, 1837, a bill was filed on the 1st of September, of that year, by Samuel T. Love, as the executor of Charles J. Love, against Gwinn, for a settlement of the partnership; and on the 13th of June, 1851, a decree

W. S. Williams v. S. T. Love, Exr. &c. et al.

was had in his favor against Gwinn, for $30,994.00, and this also remains unsatisfied.

Charles J. Love, in his lifetime, had made a *covenant* with McLemore, to *convey him* the one undivided half of the 1700 acres, and had also made him a transfer of the one undivided half of the 5000 acres, upon a copy of the entry; but it was agreed between them that the grants should issue in Love's name.

The grants did, accordingly, issue to Charles J. Love, and the *legal* title to said lands stand now in the heirs and devisees of said Charles J. Love.

It is to be inferred from the record in this cause, that the two tracts of land aforesaid, belonged to the partnership lands of McLemore and Charles J. Love.

On the 3d of September, 1847, Samuel T. Love, as the executor of Charles J. Love, together with his heirs and devisees, filed a bill against McLemore, seeking to subject his interest in the said two tracts of land to the payment of his half of the Woodfolk decree, and, also, to the decree of the 4th of March, 1843, charging that they had a lien upon his interest in said lands.

On the 12th of April, 1849, William S. Williams filed his bill against Charles J. Love's executor, and heirs, and devisees, and, also, against McLemore and Gwinn, upon the mortgage debt assigned to him by Gwinn, claiming priority out of said McLemore's interest in said lands, and asking for an injunction against Charles J. Love's executor, heirs and devisees, and that the legal title of one-half of said lands be divested out of them, and sold to pay his debt.

The executor, and heirs, and devisees of Charles J. Love, insist that before they shall be compelled to part with the *legal* title to said McLemore's moiety of said lands, the debt due them from him, as well as the debt due from Gwinn, must first be paid.

And the question is, whether their rights and equities are not superior to the equity of Williams?

We think if it were necessary, it might fairly be deduced from this record, that the whole indebtedness of McLemore to Charles J. Love, arose out of transactions connected with their partnership in land warrants and lands, of which these two tracts were a part. If so, Charles J. Love, at his death, for the purpose of producing equality between them, had an equity against McLemore, which fastened itself upon his interest in these lands, and of which he could not be deprived by McLemore or any creditor of his, or purchaser from him with notice. *A forteori* would this be so as to McLemore's half of that part of the decree in favor of Woodfolk, which was given as compensation for the location of these very lands. *Sweat et al. v. Henson*, 5. Hum. 49; *Gee v. Gee*, 2 Sneed, 395.

And it can make no difference that at Love's death the amount of inequality between them had not been ascertained by a decree; and that the claim of the locator existed in the form of a joint *liability* which was not satisfied by the heirs and representatives of Charles J. Love until long afterwards.

They nevertheless arose from transactions occurring in the lifetime of Love, and the equity existed at that time.

But if we were to assume that the indebtedness to Charles J. Love by McLemore, and his liability for him to Jones or Woodfolk arose from independent transactions, unconnected with these lands, or with the partnership, he could not have forced him to a conveyance of his half of these lands, without paying his indebtedness to him, and freeing him from liability for him.

And the same rights, precisely, exist in favor of the executor, and heirs, and devisees of Charles J. Love. They have the *legal title* to these lands, and cannot be forced to part with it until the debt due from McLemore is paid.

And the same rule applies to Gwinn. If he had filed the bill he could not compel a sale by the executor, heirs and devisees of Love, who had the legal title until he would do equity by paying not only the debt due from McLemore, but also the debt due from himself to Love's estate, which has been ascertained by the decree aforesaid.

The transactions between Charles J. Love and Gwinn also occurred previous to July, 1837, the time of the death of the former, or the debt arose from transactions occurring prior to that time.

Gwinn, as we shall see, took his mortgage incumbered with the equity existing against McLemore; and in his hands it became subjected to an additional equity against him, because of his indebtedness to Love's estate, and the equity of the estate being at least equal to that of McLemore or Gwinn, and the executor, heirs and devisees of Love having the legal title in these lands, must, in a Court of Chancery, prevail. *Turner* v. *Pettigrew et al.*, 6 Hum. 438, 440; *Sweat et als.* v. *Henson*, 5 Hum. 49, 50; 10 Yer. 105.

Williams, in this case, is in no better situation than

Gwinn, and Gwinn in no better condition than McLemore.

There is no rule in equity better settled than this, that a purchaser of an equitable title must always abide by the case of the person from whom he buys. *Craig v. Leiper et al.*, 2 Yerg., 193.

The questions involved in this cause were decided by this Court in the late unreported case of *Johnston, Trustee, v. Napier et al.*

M. C. Napier was, in equity, entitled to certain lands, which had been entered and granted in the name of Thompson. The former sold these lands, with others, to E. N. Napier upon time, and bound himself to make a title. He made an assignment for the benefit of his creditors, by which Johnston, as trustee, became entitled to the debt for the purchase money of the land due from E. N. Napier. When Thompson was called on by M. C. Napier, or Johnston, his trustee, to convey, so that the title to E. N. Napier might be completed, he refused, unless M. C. Napier would indemnify him for his liabilities as surety and endorser, and also, pay him a debt due from M. C. Napier.

This Court decided he could not be compelled to convey unless indemnified and his debt paid.

Decree affirmed.

M. W. WOODRUFF v. NASHVILLE AND CHATTANOOGA RAILROAD COMPANY.

1. LIEN. *General and special.* Liens are of two kinds, general and particular, or special. A particular lien is the right to retain a thing for some charge or claim growing out of or connected with that identical thing. A general lien is the right to retain a thing not only for charges and claims specifically arising out of, or connected with the identical thing, but also for a general balance of accounts between the parties in respect to other dealings of a like nature.

2. FACTOR. *Lien upon goods consigned. Possession.* Where the consignor remains owner of the goods consigned, no special property can exist in the factor, or any lien general or special, unless he have possession, either actual or constructive, of the goods. If the goods are in *transitu,* or if the factor has only a right of possession, the lien does not attach.

3. SAME. *Same. Power of the owner.* If the factor has no property in the goods, and no lien upon them, the owner has a perfect right to dispose of them as he may please, and the factor cannot control him in this right.

4. SAME. *Question reserved.* Can a factor, who has neither the actual nor constructive possession of the goods, and no property in them, maintain an action against a mere wrong-doer, acting in opposition to the rights of both him and the owner?

5. SAME. *Same.* If a factor has made acceptances, or incurred liability upon the faith of the consignment of goods to him, but has no property in them, nor possession, either actual or constructive, do such acceptances or liability give him a lien upon or property in the goods consigned?

6. SAME. *Lien ceases when liability discharged.* If such lien exists, it ceases upon payment of the bills drawn, or liability incurred. And if the factor is under no liability for the consignor, or owner, at the time of the institution of his suit, it cannot be maintained.

FROM DAVIDSON.

On the 22d of May, 1856, one A. G. Henderson shipped by the defendant 123 casks of bacon, consigned to the plaintiff. By mistake of the agent of the defendant, the bacon was directed to Charleston, to the care of McCreery & Hook, at Chattanooga, Hook having been interested in some of the previous purchases of Henderson. Hook, considering himself interested in the bacon, sold it at Chattanooga. Henderson, about the time of the shipment of the bacon, wrote to Woodruff informing him that he had forwarded the bacon to him; and, on the faith of it, drew two bills of exchange on him, amounting to $2,800. Woodruff accepted the bills, and wrote to Henderson that the bacon had not been received. Henderson, on being informed of the change in the shipment of the bacon, and its sale, wrote to Woodruff explaining it. The bills were protested and returned to Henderson, who paid them, and obtained a credit, on account with Hook, for the proceeds of the bacon. Woodruff sued the company for not delivering the bacon to him, as specified in their receipt. Under the charge of Judge BAXTER, there was a verdict, and judgment for the defendant. The plaintiff appealed.

JOHN REID, for the plaintiff.

J. M. WILKIN, for the plaintiff, argued:

1. That the Court below erred in charging the jury "that the plaintiff, as factor of Henderson, would have a lien only upon the goods of the principal in the actual possession of the factor, and until they came into his actual possession the consignor could control them; that the delivery of the goods to the common carrier, and the taking a receipt or bill of lading from the carrier,

specifying the goods to be delivered to the factor, would not constitute such a possession as would support a lien for the balance due on account of previous dealings."

The law is, "that where a factor makes advances, and incurs responsibilities on account of consignments to him, the bill of lading vests such property in him that he may insure or sell the goods on the security and faith of the consignment. And the consignor cannot stop them without repaying what the factor has advanced, or is liable for." *Jordan* v. *James*, 5 Ham., 88, in United States Digest, p. 418.

If the bill of lading has been assigned over to the consignee, and he has actually come into possession of it, the bill of lading carries the title to the property, and is valid against the principal, especially if the consignor is indebted to the consignee. *Ryley* v. *Snell*, and *Walter* v. *Ross*, 2 Wash. C. C., 403 and 283, U. S. Digest, 414; *Currey* v. *Roulstone*, 2 Lem., 110, 113; 2 Kent, pp. 548, 549, &c. If this doctrine be true, then Henderson, the consignor, would not even have had the right to stop the bacon in *transitu*. But the proof clearly shows that the defendant's agent at Smyrna misdirected the bacon, without the knowledge, order, or consent of either the consignor or consignee, and that it was not until long afterwards that they learned the destination of the bacon.

Again, care must be taken by the common carrier to deliver the goods to the right person, according to the tenor of the bill of lading, else it is a conversion of the property. Story on Bailments, § 545.

Henderson intended to pass, and did pass all his right, title and property in and to the bacon, by delivering the defendant's receipt to the plaintiff, and plaintiff can only look to the defendant, either for the goods or damage for their loss, because he holds defendant's bill of lading, and it becomes his duty to see that the defendant complies with its original contract under it.

Henderson so regarded it, because he wrote plaintiff that he would send him other bacon of the same quality and quantity in lieu thereof, but which he failed to do.

2. The Court erred in charging that the onus was on the plaintiff to prove that the payment of the acceptances was not made until after he had instituted suit.

How could the plaintiff be presumed to know that the acceptances had been paid by the drawer, and were not outstanding against him?

The plaintiff, by accepting, had become the principal— the first payor—and therefore the presumptions are all in his favor that he was still bound; and it became the duty of the defendant to show no legal obligation of plaintiff on the drafts at the time of bringing suit.

3. The Court erred in refusing to charge, that if the bacon was wrongfully directed by the agent at Smyrna, in consequence of which misdirection the bacon was lost to the plaintiff, the defendant would be liable to the plaintiff, although the act of the agent was subsequently ratified by Henderson, the consignor.

If the plaintiff had acquired any interest or title in the bacon, by his acceptances and delivery to him of the bill of lading, upon which the acceptances were predicated, it was beyond the power of Henderson, the consignor, to ratify a conversion of the property by the defendant to the hazard, detriment, and damage of the plaintiff.

Ewing & Cooper, for the defendant.

His honor charged the jury, that if Henderson was the owner of the bacon, and Woodruff his factor or commission merchant, and Henderson consigned bacon to him for sale, and it went to another person, who sold it and paid the money over to Henderson, that Mr. Woodruff would have no right of action against the railroad, although Henderson was indebted to Woodruff. That the lien of a factor for a general balance, or previous indebtedness, only attached to property *in his possession;* and as he never had possession of this bacon, he acquired no lien for this purpose. If Mr. Henderson drew bills founded on this shipment of bacon, and Woodruff accepted them, even though the destination of the goods was changed before the drawing or acceptance, then, as long as Woodruff remained liable on these bills, he could have held the railroad liable; but when Henderson took up the bills and received the proceeds of his bacon from Judge Hook, then the action of Mr. Woodruff could not be maintained.

We insist this charge is, substantially, correct.

If a shipper of goods is the sole owner, and they are merely forwarded to a consignee for sale, the owner may change the direction of the goods, sell them before they reach their destination, or destroy them; and this

M. W. Woodruff *v.* Nashville and Chattanooga Railroad Company.

is a full answer to any action by the consignee. Story on Bailments, § 578; Angell on Carriers, § 495. In order to maintain a suit against the carrier, there must be a property in the goods, or a special agreement. Angell, § 499.

We know of no authority for an alteration of this rule in a case where the consignor intends to draw on the consignee for the proceeds of sale, and does in fact draw, and the consignee accepts the bills, more especially if the destination of the goods is changed before such draft and acceptance, and a right of action already accrued to the consignor. Angell, § 511; 11 Adolp. & Ellis, 260; 2 Kent Com. 831. If we are wrong, however, in this opinion, and the Circuit Judge was right, still, when these bills were paid by Henderson, and he received the proceeds of the bacon from Hook, the right accruing to Woodruff was gone, and fell with his interest acquired in the bacon.

The lien of a factor never attaches on goods in *transitu*, unless on account of money advanced, or bills accepted on their faith, and not even then, when the goods are never actually received. Story on Agency, 502, 486, 487; 3 Term. Rep., 119, 783.

WRIGHT, J., delivered the opinion of the Court.

We have been unable to find any error in the judgment of the Circuit Court in this case for which it should be reversed.

The plaintiff was not the purchaser or owner of this bacon. If he had been, the delivery to the defendant,

M. W. Woodruff *v.* Nashville and Chattanooga Railroad Company.

as a common carrier, for transportation to him, would have entitled him to its safe delivery; and neither A. G. Henderson or the defendant could lawfully have changed its destination, or diverted it from him.

But here is a different case altogether. Henderson was the owner of the bacon, and the plaintiff merely his factor to sell it on his account. It is not necessary for us to consider whether the plaintiff, standing in the relation which he did to this property, could maintain an action against a mere wrong-doer, acting in opposition to the rights both of him and Henderson, the owner. The case here is the same as a contest between him and the owner; for Henderson has sanctioned all that the defendant did, and has, in fact, received the proceeds of the bacon, and is satisfied.

If the factor have no property in the goods, and no lien, the owner has a perfect right to dispose of them as he may please, and the factor cannot control him in this right. *Walter et al.* v. *Ross et al.*, 2 Wash. C. C. Rep., 283; *De Forest* v. *The Fulton In. Co.*, 1 Hall's Rep., 84, 116; Story's Agency, § 372.

The case then resolves itself into this: Had the plaintiff, as against Henderson, any property in this bacon, or any lien upon it? That he had neither we think clear from the authorities.

Mr. Story, in his work on Agency, § 354, says: Liens are of two sorts, particular and general. A particular lien is usually defined to be the right to retain a thing for some charge or claim growing out of or connected with that identical thing; such as for labor, or services, or expenses bestowed upon that thing. A general lien is a right to retain a thing, not only for

M. W. Woodruff v. Nashville and Chattanooga Railroad Company.

charges and claims specially arising out of or connected with the identical thing, but also for a general balance of accounts between the parties in respect to other dealings of the like nature. It is less favored, and is construed somewhat more strictly by Courts of law than a particular lien; although, certainly, the tendency of late years in the commercial community has been rather to expand than to restrict the cases in which it is to be implied by the usage of trade.

But no special property can exist in the factor, or any lien, general or particular, unless he have possession, either actual or constructive of the goods. I speak of the case where the consignor remains the owner, as did Henderson in this case.

By constructive possession, is meant the possession of his servants or agents in the proper discharge of their duty. And it cannot be made to apply to the defendant in this case. For it seems to be well settled, that if the thing has not arrived to the possession of the factor, but is still in transitu, or, if he has only a right of possession, the lien does not attach. Story on Agency, sec. 361; 3 Kent, 638; *Kinlach* v. *Craig*, 3 Term. Rep., 119, 783; *Smet* v. *Pyne*, 1 East, 4; 2 Wash. C. C. Rep., 283.

Chancellor Kent says: That even though the factor may have accepted bills upon the faith of the consignment, and paid part of the freight; yet he can have no lien, unless the goods of the principal do, in fact, come to his hands; and for this, he cites the case in Term. Reports.

That case, when examined, will, we think, be found decisive of this:

M. W. Woodruff v. Nashville and Chattanooga Railroad Company.

The judgment of the Court of King's Bench, in that case, was affirmed in the House of Lords, by the unanimous advice of all the Judges. The Judge, in delivering the opinion of the Judges, observed, that the parties acted entirely upon the faith of the *agreement* between them; that they (the bankrupts) should accept the bills drawn on them by the Stienes, and should indemnify themselves out of the produce of the sales; and that the transaction between them, with respect to the consignments, was as between *principal and factor*, and not as between *vendor and vendee;* that, therefore, Laudiman and Graham, (the factors,) could have no *property* in the cargo; and the right of stopping in *transitu* was out of the question, that never occurring but as between vendor and vendee. And for this he relied on the case of *Wright* v. *Campbell*, 4 Burr., 2050. That the bankrupts could have no lien in the case, as the special verdict found that the goods never got into their possession. That though they might have given their acceptance on the faith that these consignments would be made to them, yet still it was *an executory agreement*, for the non-performance of which only a *right of action accrued*, but that no *property* in the goods was thereby vested in them.

In that case, the factors, Laudiman & Graham, who resided in London, had become liable for Stiene, the consignor and owner, who lived in Scotland, by acceptance made upon the faith of the consignments, to a large amount; and besides, there was a heavy balance due them on previous transactions, and they were without funds to meet it. They had been advised by letter of the shipment; had received the invoice and bill of lading; and before the arrival of the vessel, Stiene, the consignor had gone to London and conversed with them as to the cargo, giving directions as to its sale, and had caused them to have it insured, the premiums being charged to him. After his departure, the vessel and cargo reached London, and they paid a part of the freight, and were urged by the captain, to at once unload the ship and receive the cargo; but having stopped payment, they delayed until it was taken under a *writ of sequestration* against Stiene, the consignor, who never paid the bills, which were proved as debts against the consignees. And yet it was held they had no *lien* and no *property* in the cargo.

Judge Story, in section 377 of his work on Agency, says: "If goods come to the possession of the factor after a secret act of bankruptcy committed by the principal, the factor will not be entitled to retain them against the assignees for advances or acceptances made after such act of bankruptcy, upon the faith of the consignment of the goods to him, although such act was unknown to him at the time of the advances or acceptances; for the act of bankruptcy divests the property out of the bankrupt."

And he says: "Whether the like effect would be produced when the act of bankruptcy was committed after the advances or acceptances were made, and while the goods were in *transitu* to the factor, is a point upon which doubts have been entertained; but the weight of judicial opinion seems against the lien."

But it is unnecessary for us, conclusively, to decide here, that the *acceptances or liability* on the part of the plaintiff, gave him no lien, and no special property in the

W. R. Cornelius and D. W. Davis v. Joseph Merritt.

goods as against Henderson, because the Circuit Judge, in his charge to the jury, held the law upon that point to be for the plaintiff; and manifestly, if the lien existed at all, it could only be as to that transaction, and ceased upon the payment of the bills by Henderson. It could not be extended to the general balance remaining on account of previous dealings.

We do not think the Circuit Judge erred in charging the jury, that it lay upon the plaintiff to show he was under the *liability* for Henderson by these acceptances at the institution of his suit. How could he claim anything, or move the Court in his favor, unless he showed a lien; and could the lien exist if there was no liability? The bills were dishonored in August, 1856, and Henderson, who seems to be solvent, proves they were protested, and he paid them to the bank, but at what time, he does not say. The suit of the plaintiff was not brought till March, 1857. *Prima facie*, at least, they were paid before the institution of the suit.

Judgment affirmed.

W. R. CORNELIUS AND D. W. DAVIS v. JOSEPH MERRITT.

1. PRACTICE AND PLEADING. *Writ of Error. Plea not filed.* Act of 1852, ch. 152, §§ 4, 5. *Code*, §§ 2865, 2866, 2872, 2873. Since the passage of the act of 1852, ch. 152, §§ 4 and 5, the provisions of which are incorporated into the Code, sections 2865, 2866, 2872 and 2873, the want of a plea in a record brought up by writ of error, is

W. R. Cornelius and D. W. Davis *v.* Joseph Merritt.

regarded as a matter of form for which the judgment of the Court below will not be reversed.

2. SAME. *Account. Record. Bill of exceptions.* An account, unless made so by a bill of exceptions, is no part of the record in a cause, and cannot be noticed upon a writ of error, so as to raise the question whether there is a variance between the parties to the suit, and the account sued on.

FROM DAVIDSON.

This cause was tried at the May Term, 1858, BAXTER, J., presiding. Verdict and judgment for the plaintiff. There was no bill of exceptions filed, and the cause was brought up by writ of error.

A. L. DEMOSS, for the plaintiffs in error.

J. C. THOMPSON, for the defendant in error.

WRIGHT, J., delivered the opinion of the Court.

This was an action of debt in the Circuit Court of Davidson county, for goods, wares and merchandize, sold and delivered.

The record contains a declaration, which is in the usual form; and further shows, that the defendants were duly summoned to answer to the action. The writ and sheriff's return are in the transcript. The declaration was filed at the May Term, 1857, and the record shows, that the cause was continued at the September and January Terms, thereafter.

At the May Term, 1858, the cause was tried by a jury, who, as the record shows, were sworn to try the

W. R. Cornelius and D. W. Davis v. Joseph Merritt.

issue joined between the parties; and they find the same in favor of the plaintiff, and also find the debt due him to be $340.00, and assess his damages for the detention of the debt, to $71.40. Thereupon, the Circuit Court gave judgment upon the verdict against the defendants in favor of the plaintiff.

The record shows that, at the trial, the parties appeared by their attorneys.

No plea is found in the record, nor was there any motion for a new trial, or bill of exceptions filed; nor was there any appeal. Nothing appears to show that the defendants were, at the time of the judgment, at all dissatisfied with it.

They have since filed a transcript of the record in this Court, and obtained a writ of error; and now ask for a reversal of the judgment:

1st. For the want of a plea.

2d. Because the account upon which the recovery was had, was due to the firm of Merritt & Co.; whereas, the suit is prosecuted, and recovery had, in the name of Joseph Merritt.

There is nothing in these objections.

As to the first: Since the passage of the act of 1852, ch. 152, sections 4 and 5, the provisions of which are to be found in the Code of Tennessee, at sections 2865, 2866, 2872 and 2873, it must be regarded as a matter of form, for which we cannot reverse. We will, if need be, upon a record like this, presume that there was a proper plea and issue, and that its omission from the record is a mere clerical error, which does not touch the merits of the case. Unless a bill of exceptions be filed, how can we say that substantial errors exist? It is incumbent upon him who asks the reversal of a judgment to show that it is wrong. If this is not done, we must, in favor of the action of the Circuit Court, and in affirmance of the judgment, presume that all things were regular and proper.

In a case at Knoxville, at the last term, where there were no pleadings in the record, but only the writ, verdict and judgment, and no bill of exceptions; we refused to reverse upon the ground that we could see no errors.

It is useless to notice the action of the Circuit Court at the term subsequent to the judgment, in permitting a plea to be filed *nunc pro tunc*.

As to the second error assigned, the account is to be sure, copied into the record, but there is no bill of exceptions, and it is, therefore, no part of the record, and cannot be noticed; so that the fact upon which to raise this objection, does not exist.

Judgment affirmed.

JAMES L. ALLEN *v.* GEORGE C. BAIN *et al.*

1. REGISTRATION. *Law of the owners domicil prevails, in alienation of personal property.* The transfer of personal property is controlled by the laws of the owner's domicil, or the place of transfer, no matter where the property may be situated; but in ascertaining and giving preferences and priorities, the government where the property is situated will not extend this comity so far as to prejudice its own citizens, but will protect their interests.

2. SAME. *Assignments. Pennsylvania. Registry act of.* By the law of Pennsylvania, "all assignments, so as aforesaid to be made and

James L. Allen v. George C. Bain *et al.*

executed, which shall not be recorded in the office for recording deeds in the county in which such assignor resides within thirty days after the execution thereof. shall be considered null and void, as against any of the creditors of the assignor."

3. SAME. *Same. Same. What it embraces. Different in Tennessee.* This act is held to embrace assignments of legacies in payment of debts due from the assignor. But, by the construction given to the registry acts of Tennessee, they do not embrace legacies.

4. SAME. *Same. Attachment. Priority. Case in judgment.* B, to whom a legacy was coming in Tennessee, transferred it in Pennsylvania, the place of his domicil, in payment of a debt. The assignment was not registered in Pennsylvania, but was registered in Tennessee. A, a creditor of B, attached said legacy for the satisfaction of his debt. The attachment was levied after the registration of the assignment in Tennessee. Held, that the assignment not having been registered in Pennsylvania, it is void against the creditors of B, and the attaching creditor, A, has priority of satisfaction.

FROM DAVIDSON.

The bill of the complainant was dismissed by Chancellor FRIERSON, at the November Term, 1858. He appealed.

R. J. MEIGS, for the complainant.

1st. As to the validity and operation of the assignment, the *lex loci contractus* governs. Story Confl. 423; Burrell on Assignments, 336, 337, &c.

By the law of Pennsylvania, "all assignments of prroperty in trust made by debtors to trustees, on account of inability, at the time of the assignment, to pay their debts, to prefer one or more creditors—except for the payment of wages of labor—shall be held and construed to enure to the benefit of all the creditors,

James L. Allen *v.* George C. Bain *et al.*

in proportion to their respective demands," &c. Purdon's Digest, Tit. Assignments, A, 2.

By the same law, all assignments, so as aforesaid to be made and executed, which shall not be recorded in the office for recording of deeds, in the county in which such assignor resides, within thirty days after the execution thereof, shall be considered null and void as against any of the creditors of the said assignor. Purdon's Dig.; Tit. Assignments, B. 8, and notes *t* and *v*, from which it appears that the assignment must be recorded in the proper county, although the personal property be situated in another State; citing 7 Barr. 499.

The same thing is stated by Burrell on Assignments, ch. 21, p. 268, 269.

2d. By our own act of 1839, c. 26, § 1, deeds, powers of attorney, and other instruments for the transfer or conveyance of property or *effects*, real or personal, or appointing agents to transact any business whatever, and *all other deeds of every description*, may be proved or acknowledged, &c.; and when so proved, &c., may be read in evidence as other registered papers, and shall have the like force and effect.

This deed was registered, it is true, here, before the filing of the bill; but it is no notice of anything but what appears on the face of it, and nothing appears, on the face of it, to indicate that Bain was indebted to Bacon & Hallowell, or even to Bacon himself. And it certainly can be no notice of any indebtedness of Bain to Bacon & Hallowell, unless we interpolate into it what is stated in the answers.

3d. But the assignment is fraudulent on its face. It transfers to the trustee Bain's entire interest in Bell's estate: 1st. To pay an undefined amount to O. P. McRoberts. 2d. To pay over the balance to Charles Hallowell, "*to and for his own proper use and behoof.*"

S. L. FINLEY, for the defendants.

As to the necessity of registration—
This transfer or contract was made in Pennsylvania, but the proceeds were to be paid and settlement made in Tennessee, where the testator's property was, an interest in which was transferred.

" If a contract be made under one government, and is to be performed under another, and the parties had in view the laws of such other country in reference to its construction and force, it is to be governed by the law of the country or State in which it is to be executed." 2 Kent, 459.

Remedies upon contracts are regulated and pursued according to the law of the place where the action is instituted. *McKissick* v. *McKissick*, 6 Hum., 83; 2 Kent, 462.

The law of a place where a contract is made, is, generally speaking, the law of the contract, that is, it is the law by which the contract is expounded. But the right of priority forms no part of the contract itself. It is extrinsic, and is rather a personal privilege, dependent on the laws of the place where the property lies, and where the Court sits which decides the cause. 5 Cranch, 298, 302; 12 Wheaton, 362; Story's Conflict of Laws, sec. 287.

But I think the following is conclusive:

"But it does not follow that a transfer made by the owner, according to the law of the place of its actual *situs*, would not as completely divest his title."

And again: "If a person direct a sale of his property, or make a sale of it in a foreign country, where it is situate at the time, according to the laws thereof, either in person or by an agent, the validity of such a sale would scarcely be doubted. Story's Conflict of Laws, secs. 384, 396.

CARUTHERS, J., delivered the opinion of the Court.

Defendant, Bain, is a nephew and legatee of Montgomery Bell, late of Davidson county. His legacy, being one-fourth of the whole estate, after specific legacies, amounted to about $5000, and was in the hands of defendants, Roberts, Watkins and Bell, as the executors. The complainant, a citizen of Kentucky, is a creditor of Bain to the amount of $2,173.79, by two notes assigned to him by Peter Higgins.

Allen filed this bill the 22d of October, 1857, against the said Bain and the executors, and attached the said legacy in their hands. The answer of the executors admits the sufficiency of the fund in their hands, but allege that they had notice of an assignment by Bain of this legacy, to one Stephens, of Philadelphia, for the benefit of two other creditors—Hallowell and Roberts. By order of the Court, Stephens, the trustee, and these creditors, were made defendants. The Chancellor held that the assignment was valid, and that Allen was only entitled to what might remain after the satisfaction of the debts therein provided for, and ordered an account. The result was, that Allen had a decree only for $831 of his debt, that being the balance of the fund remaining after paying the debts of Roberts, Hallowell, and Bacon.

The question made in argument is, upon the validity of the assignment to Stephens, as against Allen's attachment. It is prior in date, having been made in the city of Philadelphia, the 30th of March, 1857, and purports to have been acknowledged before one "John Binns, Commissioner of Tennessee," on the next day, as appears by his certificate, and registered the 22d of June, 1857, in Davidson county. The parties lived in Philadelphia where the deed was made, but the executors and the fund were in Tennessee. It does not appear that the deed was recorded in Pennsylvania. It was, however, forwarded to the executors, who handed it over for registration, at the time stated, in Davidson county.

The assignment is for the expressed consideration of $2,500 to him in hand paid, by Lewis H. Stephens, of "all the right, title and interest, property, claim and demand, of whatever nature or kind, whether real, personal, or mixed, in possession, remainder, or expectancy, and wherever situate, coming to the said George C. Bain from the estate of Montgomery Bell, deceased, * * * which he is entitled to as one of the heirs of said Montgomery Bell, deceased." "In trust, nevertheless, to pay O. P. McRoberts, of Nashville," the amount of his indebtedness to him, and "afterwards, to pay over the balance coming into the hands of the said Stephens, to

James L. Allen v. Geocge C. Bain *et al.*

Charles Hallowell, of the city of Philadelphia, to and for his own proper use and behoof."

It turned out that the amount due to McRoberts from Bain, was only $548.57, which, together with other amounts paid out by the executors to Bain, and to his order, and the amount of his indebtedness to the estate, leaves a balance in their hands of $2,883.96. The report of the Master shows the debt of Hallowell & Bacon to be $2,052.69.

As there is not a sufficient fund to pay both, the question is one of priority between the complainant and Hallowell & Bacon.

It is insisted for Allen that the assignment is of no force as against his attachment, for two reasons: 1st. It is void as to creditors, if no other objection existed, because it was not registered or recorded, as required by the laws of Pennsylvania, where it was made and the parties to it resided.

It is the general rule that the alienation by assignment, or otherwise, of personal property, must be controlled by the laws of the owner's domicil, or place of the transfer, no matter where situated, with the exception that in ascertaining and giving preferences and priorities, the government where the property is situated, will not extend this comity so far as to prejudice its own citizens, but will protect their interests in preference. Burrell on As'gt., 336.

A transfer of personal property, good by the law of the country where made, will, with few exceptions, be good everywhere. 1 Swan, 399, citing Story's Conflict, secs. 380, 383 and 384. And the converse of this is generally true.

James L. Allen *v.* George C. Bain *et al.*

The validity and operation of this assignment must be tested by the laws of Pennsylvnia. Story on Conflict, § 423. This must extend to all the requirements there to make it binding; and whatever defects would avoid it there, will follow it here and everywhere. If for want of registration it be declared void there, as against creditors, so it would be here. By the Pennsylvania act, in Purdon's Digest, p. 53, it is declared that "all assignments, so as aforesaid to be made and executed, which shall not be recorded in the office for recording deeds, in the county in which such assignor resides, within thirty days after the execution thereof, shall be considered null and void, as against any of the creditors of the said assignor."

This statute has been held to apply to the assignment of property out of the State as well as in it. *Weber* v. *Samuel*, 7 Bar., § 499; Burrell, 268, 269.

But another question is, whether, by the laws of Pennsylvania, the assignment of a legacy is embraced by their acts to which we have referred.

It has been held in this State, in one or more unreported cases decided some years ago, that our registry acts did not apply to assignments of choses in action.

Whether this would be so under the statutes of Pennsylvania, would depend upon the construction given to them by their Courts. These would come to us with their statutes, having the same binding force as the law of that State, though it might conflict with our own construction of a similar statute of ours; the question being, not what the law of Pennsylvania should be, in our opinion, upon a proper construction, but what it is settled to be there. That is, we take their construction of their own statutes to be the correct one in questions of this kind.

But, after all, there may be no difference between us. Our registry act of 1831, or that of 1839, ch. 26, which is, perhaps, the broadest in its terms, in describing what may be registered, embraces "deeds, powers of attorney, and other instruments for the transfer and conveyance of property or effects, real or personal, or appointing agents to transact any business whatever, and all other deeds of every description."

In the case of *Marshall et al.* v. *Fields et al.*, decided by this Court in 1851, it was held that this did not embrace an assignment of a claim against a turnpike company, made in trust for the security of debts; and, consequently, the fact of registration did not operate as notice, because it was not required by the acts to be registered. Therefore such an assignment did not operate as against attaching creditors of the company, being incomplete without notice to the common debtor. This case was not reported, but it is in the recollection of the member of the Court, who was then on the bench, that the point was then distinctly decided and applied to other cases. The point settled was, that assignments of choses in action, and that would embrace legacies, was not intended by the Legislature to be included in the enumeration of instruments required to be registered. Whether the Code, in section 2030, enlarges the old acts on this subject, need not be examined now.

But it will be observed that "assignments" are not in terms included in any of our acts. Although it might seem that the words "instruments" or "deeds" would include them; yet the Pennsylvania Legislature appears to have thought differently, as it has provided for the two cases by distinct acts.

This word in its largest sense, at least in common parlance, signifies the transfer of all kinds of property, either absolutely or in trust. But in its more confined sense, and particularly in mercantile transactions, it is used in contradistinction to sales, and the sense in which it is treated of by "Burrell on Assignments" is as transfers by way of security for, or in payment of debts, and implies the existence of the relation of debtor and creditor. Burrell on Assignments, 3, 4. And this is evidently the sense in which they are regarded in the Pennsylvania acts before cited.

The decisions noted upon the act before extracted from Purdon's Digest, 53, at the foot of the same page, clearly show the scope given to their act to be such as to embrace assignments like this.

It follows, then, that by the laws of Pennsylvania, as the assignment to Stephens for the benefit of Hallowell was not recorded, as prescribed by the laws of that State, it is "null and void as against any of the creditors of the assignor," Bain. It would, however, be good between the parties.

This view of the case renders it unnecessary to notice the other questions made against the assignment, and the result is, that the complainant, Allen, by virtue of his attachment of the fund in the hands of the executors of Montgomery Bell, to which Bain is entitled as a legatee, is entitled to priority of satisfaction over Hallowell and Bacon.

The decree of the Chancellor to the contrary will therefore be reversed to that extent, and decree entered here in accordance with this opinion.

P. G. S. PERKINS *et al.* v. S. P. AMENT, FOR THE USE OF, &C.

BILLS AND NOTES. *Note executed to raise money. Surety.* If a party become surety on a note with the understanding that it shall be passed to a particular individual, and to no one else, he is not liable on said note unless passed to that person. But if he signed as surety with the general purpose to enable the principal to raise money on the note, without limiting him to the person to whom he should pass it, he would be liable, although the note was passed to another than the payee, and the holder thereof could maintain a suit in the name of the payee for his use.

FROM WILLIAMSON.

Verdict and judgment for plaintiff, at the March Term, 1858, BAXTER, J. presiding. The defendants appealed.

JOHN MARSHALL, for the plaintiffs in error.

It is insisted that the Circuit Judge should have granted a new trial, because the charge was erroneous in both branches of the charge.

In the first branch of the charge no weight is given to the fact that the note was payable to the *order* of S. P. Ament; and to defeat the plaintiff's action, not-

P. G. S. Perkins *et al* v. S. P. Ament, for the use of, &c.

withstandnig the form of the note, the burden of further proof is thrown on the defendant, to show the further fact that it was his intention that the note should be passed to Ament, and no one else.

The second branch of the charge intensifies the same idea. It throws the onus of proof on the defendant, of the further fact that he limited him to the person to whom he should pass the note, and says that the expectation of him and Bryan both, that Ament would take the note and pay the money would be insufficient to establish this further fact.

The expression in the charge, the general purpose of Perkins, to enable Bryan to raise money on the note, is too vague to relieve the charge from the remarks made, and might well have been understood by the jury to have meant nothing more than the purpose of raising the money on the note from Ament.

The charge, if not erroneous in other respects, is calculated to mislead the jury, and probably did mislead the jury, in finding their verdict; and to this extent is erroneous. It is insisted, upon the hypothesis that the charge of the Circuit Judge is free from all exceptions, that there is not any evidence in the record upon which the verdict can rest, showing, or tending to show, that Perkins consented or intended that the note should be used by Bryan, in receiving the money from any other person than Ament. A fair view of Bryan's testimony shows directly the contrary.

It is true that he received the $50 from Greenfield upon fraudulent representations; but Greenfield by no means became the holder of the note in due course of trade.

P. G. S. Perkins *et al.* v. S. P. Ament, for the use of, &c.

It is contended that, on this general ground, there should be a new trial.

FOSTER, for the defendant in error.

The defendant in error now insists that there was no error in the proceedings below, and judgment ought to be affirmed.

1. Because the charge of the Court, if erroneous, was in favor of the plaintiffs in error, of which error, if there be any, the defendant in error cannot complain.

2. Because there was no error in the admission to the jury of Bryan's deposition, as his interest was indifferent; for if Perkins pays the money, he, Bryan, is bound to pay to Perkins.

3. Because the law implies a good and valuable consideration in all promissory notes, between the original parties thereto and those who claim by endorsement or otherwise. Story on Promissory Notes, ch. 5, pp. 199–203.

4. Because, as Perkins signed the note, and gave it up to Bryan, and the note being negotiable, and Greenfield having upon the faith of that note, in the due course of trade, *bona fide*, and without notice, advanced the money to Bryan, Perkins is, by all rules of commercial law, liable for the same to the holder thereof.

5. Because any person is considered a *bona fide* holder, for value, of notes or bills, when he has advanced money or other value for them, or taken as collateral security, or has a lien on them. And from the proof in this cause, it is most apparent that Greenfield

P. G. S. Perkins *et al.* *v.* S. P. Ament, for the use of, &c.

was a *bona fide* holder of the note for money advanced, and, as such, has the right to enforce its payment by suit, in the name of the payee, for his use. Story on Promissory Notes, p. 215. And it is immaterial whether Ament knew anything of the suit, or knew anything of the transaction, for a Court of Chancery, if necessary, would have interposed to protect Greenfield.

It is insisted by the defendant in error that there is no error of fact in the record, and that the charge of the Court below was in favor of Perkins and against the defendant in error, as we conceive the law to be; and, therefore, this Court will not reverse, but affirm the judgment.

WRIGHT, J., delivered the opinion of the Court.

There is no error in this judgment. The proof makes it clear that T. L. Bryan, being desirous of raising money, made the bill single upon which the suit was instituted, and procured Perkins to execute and sign the same as maker with him—as his security, and for his accommodation.

The bill single, thus executed, was delivered by Perkins to Bryan. That this was done to enable the latter to sell it, and raise money upon it upon the faith of the name of the former, there can be no doubt.

It was, to be sure, made payable to Ament, because it was supposed—and, perhaps, they had good reasons so to think—that he would advance the money upon it. But there is no foundation for the belief that Perkins

P. G. S. Perkins *et al. v.* S. P. Ament, for the use of, &c.

placed Bryan under any restrictions as to the use to be made of it, or that it was his intention that it should be passed to Ament, and *no one else.*

Bryan thus having the possession of this note, passed it to Greenfield, and received of him, upon it, the sum of $50; and he has instituted this suit in the name of Ament, to his use, against Perkins, upon the note, to recover the amount for which it was given.

The Circuit Judge charged the jury, that if Perkins became surety upon the note, with the intention that it should be passed to Ament and *no one else.*, the plaintiff would not be entitled to recover. But if he signed as surety, with a general purpose to enable Bryan to raise money on the note, without limiting him to the person to whom he should pass it, then the plaintiff would be entitled to recover, although at the time defendant signed the note it was the expectation of him and Bryan both, that the note was to be passed to Ament, and the money obtained from him.

This charge is, we think, sustained by the principles laid down in *Kimbro* v. *Lytle,* 10 Yerg., 417, and the authorities there cited.

Judge Reese, in delivering the opinion of the Court, says: "The Chancellor, to sustain the principle determined in this case, refers to the cases of *The Bank of Rutland* v. *Buck,* 5 Wend., 66, and *The Bank of Chenango* v. *Hyde,* 4 Cow. Rep., 566. In the former of these cases the note was made by Spear and Everett, and signed by Buck, as surety, payable to the bank. It was made to enable Spear and Everett to raise money for their own accommodation. Upon its being offered at the bank for discount, the bank refused to discount it; and

P. G. S. Perkins *et al. v.* S. P. Ament, for the use of, &c.

it was subsequently, and before it was due, delivered over to House and others, as collateral security for the payment of a judgment in their favor against Spear and Everett. The suit was brought in the name of the bank, but for the use of House and others. It was objected that the object for which the note was made being to raise money from the bank, and the object having failed, it ought to have been returned to the surety. It was admitted, that if the Bank had refused to advance the money, and a third person had done so, as in the case of the *The Bank of Chenango* v. *Hyde*, 4 Cow. Rep., 567, the surety would have been bound, as the substantial object, the raising of money, would have been obtained. It was further objected that the note was not receieved in the ordinary course of commercial business, and so as to be governed by the law merchant. But Chief Justice Savage, delivering the opinion of the Court, says: I can see no well-founded objection to a recovery upon this note. It was drawn for the purpose of raising money for the accommodation of the two makers, Spear and Everett, who have had the benefit of it."

It is the same thing as if Perkins had expressly assented to the sale of the note to Greenfield. And the fact that it was payable to the order of Ament, and never endorsed or sanctioned by him, can make no difference.

Perkins must be regarded as having assented to the use of Ament's name for the benefit of Greenfield, in order to make the note available against him if a suit became necessary.

Mount Olivet Cemetery Company *v.* Charles Shubert.

We have been unable to discover that the charge of the Circuit Judge was open to the criticism made upon it, and think the verdict of the jury well warranted by the proof.

We therefore affirm the judgment.

MT. OLIVET CEMETERY COMPANY *v.* CHARLES SHUBERT.

1. PRINCIPAL AND AGENT. *Authority of general agent. Principal bound by contracts of agent.* If a general agent make a contract within the scope of his agency, the principal is bound by such contract, though in violation of instructions, unless the party with whom the contract is made knew that the agent was violating his instructions.

2. CIRCUIT COURT. *Charge to the jury.* A charge upon a question of law having no relevancy to any evidence in the cause, whether erroneous or not, is not ground of reversal, unless it is shown to have done harm to the party against whom the verdict is given.

3. ACCOUNT. *Assignment of. Practice.* The assignment of an account vests in the purchaser, only, an equitable interest in it and the promise of the debtor to the assignee to pay him said account is necessary to enable him to maintain an action in his own name for its recovery. Without such promise, the assignee would have to sue in the name of the assignor, for his use.

4. SAME. *Same. Promise by agent.* A promise made by the treasurer of an incorporated company to pay an account transferred to a third person, is sufficient to authorize the assignee to sue the company in his own name, unless it is shown that the treasurer had no authority to bind the company. Authority will be presumed unless the contrary is shown.

5. FRAUDS. *Statute of.* A promise by a company, or its agent, to pay an account due from said company, which has been assigned to a third person, is not within the statute of frauds, and need not be in writing.

6. EVIDENCE. *Payment. Receipt not conclusive.* A receipt of payment or delivery is only *prima facie* evidence of the fact, and not conclu-

sive, and, therefore, the fact that it recites may be contradicted by oral testimony.*

7. SAME. *Depositions. Competency. Objection to must be specific.* If a deposition contains matter that is relevant and competent, and that which is incompetent, an objection, to be available, must be specifically made to such parts as are incompetent. A general objection to the reading of the deposition will not do.

8. NON-SUIT. *Costs. Taxation of.* Act of 1794, ch. 1, § 74. *Code,* §§ 3197 and 3201. The plaintiff took a non-suit, which was set aside and he taxed with the costs of the Term. No exception was taken to the action of the Court. After verdict for the plaintiff, the defendant moved the Court to tax the plaintiff with all costs that accrued before the non-suit, which the Court refused. The Circuit Court did not err. The case is not embraced by the act of 1794, ch. 1, § 74, nor by §§ 3197 and 3201 of the Code.

FROM DAVIDSON.

This cause was tried at the May Term, 1858, BAXTER, J., presiding. Verdict and judgment for the plaintiff. The defendant appealed.

J. H. MCDONALD and A. H. HURLY, for the plaintiffs in error, cited and commented upon *Hill* v. *Childress,* 10 Yer., 516; Act of 1794, ch. 1, § 74; Code, §§ 3197, 3201; 5 Hum., 624; 3 Yer., 330—5.

REID and SHANE, for the defendants in error, relied upon the following authorities:

Chitty on Con., 613–14; 8 B. and C., 395; Addison on Con., 38, and authorities there cited; 8 Pick.,

---

* A receipt may also contain a contract to do something in relation to the thing delivered, and so far as it is evidence of a contract between the parties, it stands on the footing of all other contracts in writing, and cannot be contradicted or varied by parol.

Mount Olivet Cemetery Company *v.* Charles Shubert.

280; 21 Pick., 307; Act of 1856, ch. 192; 2 Yer., 260, 554, 559; 4 Yer., 202; 3 Hum., 490.

WRIGHT, J., delivered the opinion of the Court.

This was an action originally commenced before a justice of the peace, and carried by appeal to the Circuit Court, where the plaintiff below had judgment for $76 19; and the defendant below has appealed in error to this Court.

The Circuit Judge charged the jury, that if Stewart was the general agent of the defendant to superintend, control, and manage the cemetery grounds, and that the disposition, or renting of the house occupied by Shubert, come within the scope of that agency, and that Stewart, as such agent, had agreed with Shubert that he might occupy the house free of rent, in that case the defendant would be bound by the act of its agent, though in violation of his instructions, unless Shubert knew that Stewart was violating his instructions.

The counsel of the plaintiff in error insists that this charge is erroneous, not because, as an abstract proposition, it is not the law, but because it is based upon a suppositious state of facts which do not exist, and that it misled the jury.

He maintains that C. W. Nance was the general agent of the company, and that Stewart was *superintendent of the work*, and that there is not the slightest evidence of his general agency, or that he had authority to rent, or did rent the house of the company to Shubert.

Mount Olivet Cemetery Company *v.* Charles Shubert.

This exception to the charge is, we think, unfounded in fact. It is true, that Nance is shown to have been the general agent of the company, and Stewart the superintendent of *the work;* but there is also proof in this record, tending to show that Stewart was likewise the general agent of the company, and had authority to do, and did do many things not pertaining to the superintendency of the work, and from which his authority to rent the houses of the company might well be inferred. It is true that there is no proof that he did rent this house to Shubert, nor is it shown which one of the agents of the company did rent it. But it is proved positively, as a fact, both by Thomas and James Stewart, that Shubert was to have the house free of rent, and also firewood free of charge. He was a married man and labored as a hand for the company. It was to the interest of the company, that its other laborers and hands should be boarded near their work; and he was induced to open a boarding house for that purpose, in one of the houses of the company upon its grounds; and was to have the house, garden, water, &c., free of rent, and likewise firewood free of charge.

If the jury, therefore, rejected the set-off claimed by the company against Shubert, for rent and firewood, we think they were well warranted by the proof.

But if the charge were merely abstract, having no relevancy to any evidence in the cause, and were erroneous, much less if free of error, we do not understand it to be a ground of reversal; certainly not, unless it can be shown to have done harm to the party against whom the verdict is given. 2 Meigs' Dig., 775 and 776.

The next error assigned, is in relation to an item in

the plaintiff's account, of $27.75. It appears the company owed one Cunningham that amount, and he owed the plaintiff a less sum, and assigned to him in payment of the debt, the debt he held on the company, the plaintiff paying him the difference in money. He guaranteed the claim to the plaintiff, who afterwards presented it to the treasurer of the company, and he promised to pay it to the plaintiff, having then no funds in hand to pay it. This promise was manifestly made as treasurer for and on behalf of the company.

There is no attempt to show any want of authority in the Treasurer to make this promise, and if need be, we are authorized to presume it, unless the contrary be shown. Angell & Ames on Corporations, sections 290, 291, a, 292, 293, 298, 309.

By the purchase of the debt of Cunningham upon the company, the plaintiff acquired only an equitable interest in it, it being merely an open account, and, therefore, the promise of the company to the plaintiff to pay him, may, upon common law principles, have been necessary to enable the plaintiff, at law, to maintain the action in his own name. Vide, the note to *Nelson* v. *Marley*, 2 Yer., 576, and authorities there collected.

It is only in this aspect of the case that the promise of the company, or its treasurer, can be at all material, for, manifestly, the company owed Cunningham the $27.75, and the plaintiff had purchased the debt, and was entitled to collect it of the company.

It is manifest the statute of frauds can have nothing to do with this promise of the company, since it was simply to pay its *own debt to the plaintiff*, instead of to Cunningham, the original creditor, he having as-

Mount Olivet Cemetery Company *v.* Charles Shubert.

signed the debt to the plaintiff. It is alike manifest, that it can make no difference, that Cunningham remained bound, or guaranteed the debt to the plaintiff.

It is next assigned for error, that the Court received parol evidence to explain the receipts found in the record from the plaintiff, and from Cunningham to the company, and to show that the debts for which they were given had not been paid. There was no error in this. 1 Greenl. Ev., sec. 305; Angell & Ames on Corporations, sec. 294; 2 Meigs' Dig., 859.

Besides, it does not appear that any *specific objection* was made to this evidence. It is contained in the depositions of Thomas and James Stewart, and they contain much other testimony entirely competent. A general objection therefore, such as was made to the reading of these depositions, because of the alleged incompetency of the witnesses, they being competent, did not reach the particular part of the proof bearing on these receipts.

The record shows that on the 17th of February, 1858, the plaintiff took a non-suit, and on the next day, upon the application of the plaintiff, it was, by order of the Circuit Court, set aside, and the cause re-instated as before, and the plaintiff taxed with the costs of that term.

The record does not show the cause of the non-suit, nor the reason for setting it aside; and no exception is made to the action of the Court.

At the next term, and after the cause was tried, the defendant moved the Circuit Court to tax the plaintiff with all the costs of the cause up to the time of the non-suit. This the Court refused to do, and exception is taken to this action of the Circuit Court, and it is now assigned as error. But we are unable to say that the Circuit Court erred. We do not think the case is embraced by the act of 1794, ch. 1, sec. 74; nor by sections 3197 and 3201 of the Code of Tennessee, to which we have been referred.

Judgment affirmed.

J. A. ANDERSON *et al. v.* ALLISON, ANDERSON & CO.

1. PRACTICE AND PLEADING. *Profert. Demurrer. Oyer.* The plaintiff is bound to make profert of, and to produce in Court, the notes declared on, having them in possession. But the omission to file them with the declaration, is not a matter that can be reached by demurrer, profert being made in proper form. If the plaintiff fails to file the notes, the defendant may ask to have his demand of oyer entered, and have the judgment of the Court whether he is bound to answer until the notes are filed.

2. SAME. *Same. Same. Motion to take the demurrer from the file.* If the defendant demurs because the notes are not filed, it being an improper defence, the plaintiff may move the Court to order the demurrer to be taken off the file, and to enter up judgment by default, for want of a defence to the action.

FROM DAVIDSON.

This cause was heard at the September Term, 1858, before Judge BAXTER; and judgment final, by default, entered against the defendants, from which they appealed.

J. A. Anderson *et al.* v. Allison, Anderson & Co.

BRIEN & COX, for the plaintiffs in error

J. S. BRIEN, for the defendants in error.

McKINNEY, J., delivered the opinion of the Court.

There is no error in the judgment by default rendered in this case. The plaintiffs' declaration was filed at the appearance term. It makes profert, in the usual form, of the notes sued on; but it seems that at the appearance term, an informal demurrer was placed in the file of papers, assigning as cause of demurrer, that the defendants had craved oyer of the notes declared on, and they had not been produced. At the following term of the Court, the plaintiffs' counsel moved the Court to order the demurrer to be taken off the file, and to enter up judgment by default, for want of any defence to the action, and the motion was made absolute.

It is true that, by our law, the plaintiffs were bound to make profert of, and to produce in Court, the notes declared on—having them in possession. But the omission to file the notes with the declaration, was not a matter that could be reached by demurrer—profert being made in proper form.

If the plaintiffs failed to file the notes, the defendants might have asked to have their demand of oyer entered; which would have operated in the nature of a plea, and upon which the judgment of the Court might have been demanded, whether or not the defendants were bound to answer without it. The demurrer, for the cause stated, was an absurd practice, and it was properly taken from the file.

The facts stated in the bill of exceptions, do not better the case for the defendants. We see that the notes, though not filed with the declaration, were, in fact, filed on a subsequent day of the appearance term, and notice thereof given to defendants' attorney. We also see from the bill of exceptions, that, before judgment by default was entered, reasonable time was given the counsel of defendants to make defence. And, furthermore, it does not appear that the defendants have any substantial defence to the action.

Judgment affirmed.

JOHN HILL v. JAMES W. HINTON et al.

1. SUMMARY PROCEEDINGS. *Sheriff. Amendment of return.* The motion, and not the notice that it will be made, is the commencement of the suit; and the sheriff may be permitted to amend his return upon a summons at any time before the motion is made, even after service of the notice, that it will be made.

2. SAME. *Same. Evidence. Return of summons.* In a summary proceeding against the sheriff for the non-return of a summons, the enquiry is confined to the face of the return. Extrinsic evidence is not admissible.

3. SAME. *Same. Process. Non-return of. Act of* 1777, *ch.* 8, § 5. *Code,* § 3603. By the 3603 § of the Code. taken with some modifications from the act of 1777, a penalty of $125 is recoverable by motion of the party aggrieved against any sheriff or other officer who fails to execute and make return of any process issued from any Court of Record, and delivered to him twenty days before the return day.

John Hill *v.* James W. Hinton *et al.*

This means that he shall, not only hand in the writ, but return that he has executed it, or state a sufficient reason why he has not done so.

4. SAME. *Same. What sufficient return.* The return "not to be found in my county," would be more perfect and proper, but great strictness is not required when a motion is made for a penalty. Hence, the return "not found," although informal, is sufficient.

FROM DAVIDSON.

The motion was disallowed by the Court, BAXTER, J., presiding. The plaintiff appealed.

J. C. THOMPSON, for the plaintiff.

N. S. BROWN and MICHAEL VAUGHN, for the defendants.

CARUTHERS, J., delivered the opinion of the Court.

This was a motion against the sheriff of Davidson and his sureties, for a false return upon an alias summons in debt. The motion failed.

The process issued 10th of July, 1858, and come to the hands of the sheriff on the same day. The return was in these words: "Executed on McNairy Newell, July 12, '58, *Nathan Harsh not found in my county*, September 8, 1858.   K. BRANCH, D. Sheriff."

The entry of the motion at the return term, is as follows:

"The plaintiff by his attorney, moves the Court for judgment against the defendants for the sum of $125, penalty for the failure of the said James Hinton to

John Hill *v.* James W. Hinton *et al.*

execute and make return of an alias summons heretofore, to wit, on the 10th day of July, 1858, issued from this Court, at the suit of said John Hill against John B. Newell, McNairy Newell, trustee, and Nathan Harsh." The original had been served on J. B. Newell.

Two questions arise in the proceedings, upon which the Court is supposed to have erred:

1. The sheriff moved to amend his return by the insertion of the words, "to be." This was refused. An officer cannot be permitted to amend *after* a motion against him. 3 Hum. 396. But he may *before* the motion, even after notice. 6 Hum., 96–9. The reason of the distinction is, that the commencement of the suit is the motion, and not the notice that it will be made. It is the *lis pendens*, that precludes the right of the officer to amend.

2. The plaintiff proposed to prove that Nathan Harsh was a citizen of the county, and had a known place of business, where he is generally to be found. The Court rejected the evidence. This is alleged to be error. This ruling of the court was right. In *Fussell v. Greenfield*, 1 Sneed, 443, which was a *motion* for a "false return" upon an execution, it was held that no extrinsic evidence could be introduced, to show the falsity of the return, but that in this summary proceeding, nothing but the return itself could be looked to to determine its falsity. If the facts stated in the return were false, and injury resulted, that must be redressed by an action on the case. The remedy by motion can succeed only where the falsity appears on its face, as where he returns that the property levied upon could not be sold for want of time, and it appears in the return

John Hill v. James W. Hinton et al.

there was ample time. To these decisions we have uniformly adhered. But they were motions for "false and insufficient returns" of executions, under the act of 1835, adopted in the Code at section 3594.

The motion is founded upon section 3603 of the Code, taken, with modifications, from the act of 1777, ch. 8, sec. 5; C. & N. 664. That section gives a penalty of $125, to be recovered by motion of the party aggrieved, against any sheriff or other officer who " *fails to execute and make return of any process issued from any Court of Record, and delivered to him twenty days before the return day.*" The same reason would apply to confine the inquiry to the face of the return, and exclude extrinsic evidence, as in cases of executions. The motion is not for a failure to return in fact, but for a false or insufficient return. In order to give any pretence for the motion, the word "return" must be construed to mean, that he shall not only hand in the writ to the clerk at the proper time, and show by his endorsement upon it, his action has been such as the law commands. That is, he must show that he has done what the law requires of him, to-wit, that he has executed the writ, or state a good reason why he has not. This is perhaps the correct construction. This confines the enquiry to the return as endorsed upon the summons. Is that good in law? The only defect alleged is, that he states that the defendant, Harsh, "is not found in my county," when it should be, "not to be found," &c. That would be more perfect, because it might be true that he is not found, when in fact he might be, or is "to be" found by proper exertions. But such strictness will not be required where a motion is made for a *penalty*. In Peck's R., 196, it was held that such a defect, though an informality would not authorize a judgment by motion on the return of a *fi. fa.*

The judgment disallowing the motion, will be affirmed.

JEREMIAH CLEVELAND *v.* EDWIN MARTIN *et al.*

1. CHANCERY PRACTICE. *Bill of review. New matter.* A paper writing was mislaid. In the pleadings in the original cause, it was conceded by the parties to be a *title bond*, and the decree pronounced upon that hypothesis. The instrument was found after the decree passed. A bill of review was filed for new matter, charging that said paper writing was found, and was a deed of bargain and sale. Held, that the instrument was not a deed, and a bill of review will not lie.

2. SALE OF REAL ESTATE. *Lien. Assignment.* If the vendor of real estate retain the legal title as security for the purchase money, it has the effect of a mortgage for that purpose, and the assignment of the note given for the purchase money carries with it the benefit of the security.

3. SAME. *Same. Assignment by parol.* A debt or *chose* in action may be assigned, for a valuable consideration. by parol, and whatever passes the debt will carry with it the security for its payment. No deed or writing is necessary. A sale and delivery of the note is sufficient.

4. SAME. *Same. Extension of time. New note.* If the assignee of the note, given for the purchase money, and the creditor and his securities, extend the time of payment upon a new note, executed with an express stipulation that the lien or security should continue as before, the security for the note will remain as effective as if the time had not been extended and the new note given.

FROM FRANKLIN.

The bill of review was dismissed by Chancellor RID-

LY, at the November Term, 1858. The complainant, in said bill, appealed.

COLYAR, for the complainant.

ESTILL, for the defendants.

WRIGHT, J., delivered the opinion of the Court.

The decree of the Chancellor in this cause is affirmed.

There was no appeal from the decree upon the original bill, and that branch of the case is not before us, in any form, unless it be through the bill of review.

It is alone as to the bill of review that we are to consider the case; and we think the Chancellor acted very properly in dismissing it.

It was not filed for any errors of law apparent in the decree, but solely upon the ground of new matter, which, it was said, had arisen since the decree was made.

The new matter, as set forth in the bill of review, was this: that in the pleadings in the original cause it was conceded by all the parties, that the writing executed by Estell & Garner, to Curry McGreer, for the one-half of the two lots in Winchester, was only a *title bond*, and not a *deed of convyance;* and that they retained the legal title, as a security for the payment of the purchase money due from him to them; and that this writing had been left with Mr. Francis and lost, or mislaid, so that the same was not filed, or used on the trial of the original cause; and that the Chancellor's decree had been pronounced upon the supposition that these statements in the pleadings, to-wit, that the writing was only a *bond for title*, were true. Whereas, as the bill of review alleged, since the trial and decree, Mr. Francis, in the examination of some old papers, had found the writing, and it turned out not to be a title bond, but a *deed of bargain and sale*, wherein no lien in behalf of Estell & Garner had been retained.

The writing is copied into the bill of review, and filed in the cause, and it still plainly appears that it is not a *deed of conveyance*, but only the memorandum of a contract between Estell & Garner, and McGreer, by which they became bound to make him a title to their moiety of the lot, the legal title being still retained in them.

That this is the legal effect of the instrument is not denied in argument here, and cannot be. *Carnes* v. *Apperson & Co.*, 2 Sneed, 562.

This being so the bill of review, of necessity, failed, because, in point of fact, it contained no new matter; the pleadings and decree in the original cause embracing every fact contained within the bill of review.

But if this bill had been framed with a view to reach errors of law supposed to exist in the decree, or if the original cause were here by appeal, we think the equity of the case is against complainant, Cleveland. It is conceded in argument here by his counsel, that Estell & Garner retained the legal title to the half of the lots sold McGreer, as security for the purchase money, the legal effect of which was the same as a mortgage for that purpose. *Graham* v. *McCampbell*, Meigs' Rep., 52. In fact, in the very note executed to Estell for

Jeremiah Cleveland *v.* Edwin Martin *et al.*

his moiety of the purchase money, by McGreer, and Edwin Martin and John Fitzpatrick as his securities, it is expressly stipulated that the property is to remain a security for the debt. It is also conceded that the assignment of the note by Estell to Johnson, carried with it the benefit of the security; but it is denied that Daniel Champion, though he obtained the note by assignment from Logan, had the benefit of the security, because Johnson did not, in writing, assign the note to Logan, but only by sale and delivery without assignment. There is nothing in this objection. A debt or chose in action may be assigned, for a valuable consideration, by parol, and whatever passes the debt will carry with it the security for its payment. No deed or writing is necessary. A sale and delivery of the note is enough. *Craft* v. *Webster*, 4 Rawle, 242; *Prescott* v. *Hull*, 17 Johns. Rep., 285; 5 N. H. Rep., 420; *Hopson* v. *Hoge & Lester*, 8 Yer., 153; *Graham* v. *McCampbell*, Meigs' Rep., 57.

Nor do we think the position can be maintained, that the security, or mortgage, so to speak, upon the lot, was lost because Daniel Champion took a new note for the debt from the same parties, and extended the time of payment; because it is palpable, from the proof and the note, that the security upon the lots was continued and retained for the payment of the substituted note. At that time Cleveland had no interest in the property, and Estell & Garner were but trustees holding the lots as a security for the debt due Champion, and they were not necessary parties to the extension of the debt. Meigs' Rep., 57.

W. Champion, the creditor, and McGreer, the owner

Jeremiah Cleveland *v.* Edwin Martin *et al.*

of the lots in equity, with Martin and Fitzpatrick his sureties in the debt, chose to extend it upon a new note, as a mode or means of payment, with an *express stipulation* that the security, or mortgage, should continue as before. Why should this not be done? We confess we are unable to see why it may not. If so, the security for the debt remained as effective as before, and Cleveland could not afterwards purchase the property of McGreer so as to defeat or impair this security, any more than if the extension had never been made. If we establish the existence and continuance of the security as between Champion and McGreer and his sureties, this settles the case against Cleveland.

He is not an innocent purchaser, because if it were shown (it is not) that he had paid McGreer for the property, still he has no *legal title*, that remaining in Estell & Garner. And his answer fails, in other respects, to entitle him to the benefit of this defence. 10 Yer., 335; 1 Meigs' Dig., 244, 245.

It is argued that the substitution of the new note extinguished the debt, and the security, if it existed at all, was by *contract*, and not by *law*, and to be of any avail against Cleveland, should have been declared in writing and registered. But we have seen that the *original security* was never changed or given up, but expressly retained and continued upon the lots as before.

The case of *Gorden* v. *Johnson*, 5 Hum. 489, to which we have been referred, differs from this case in this: that the proof showed the note *had been paid by the bill*, and there *was, in that case, no express continuation of the debt and the security for its payment.*

It follows that Martin, the surety, having paid the

debt, was entitled to the benefit of the security upon the lots for his indemnity. *Uzzell* v. *Mack,* 4 Hum. 319.

Affirm the decree.

THOMAS PHILIPS *v.* HENRY & SCHACKLEFORD.

EVIDENCE. *Partner not a competent witness.* One of the copartners of a firm, in a contest between third persons and the firm, is not a competent witness to prove the existence of the partnership, or that the debt sued for was created for or on account of the firm.

FROM MONTGOMERY.

Verdict and judgment for the plaintiffs, at the September Term, 1858, PEPPER, J., presiding. The defendant appealed.

HOUSE and HORNBERGER, for the plaintiff in error, cited *Foster* v. *Hall,* 4 Hum., 346; *Vanzant* v. *Kay,* 2 Hum., 106; *Harvey* v. *Sweasy,* 4 Hum., 449; *Yancy* v. *Marriott,* 1 Sneed, 28; *Price* v. *Kearney,* 5 Hill, 82; *Marquand* v. *Webb,* 16 John. R. 89.

——— ———, for the defendants in error.

WRIGHT, J., delivered the opinion of the Court.

This was an action of assumpsit, commenced by the plaintiffs below, against Thomas Philips, as one of the members of the firm of H. H. Hollister & Co., to recover the amount of an account for professional services alleged to have been rendered the firm.

A recovery was had and Philips has appealed in error to this Court.

This firm, as was alleged, was composed of H. H. Hollister, Horace Hollister, W. E. Ellis, and the plaintiff in error, Thomas Philips, and Richard Jordan.

On the trial in the Circuit Court the question appears to have been, whether the plaintiff in error was a member of this firm, so as to be chargeable with this debt, and whether, in fact, the debt was created on account of the firm?

In this state of the case the plaintiffs introduced and read the deposition of H. H. Hollister, a member of the firm, who proved that in May or June, in the year 1853, he employed the plaintiffs to attend to the suit for the firm of H. H. Hollister & Co., at a fee of $200, and that they rendered the services for the firm.

To the reading of this deposition the defendant objected; but the Circuit Judge overruled the objection, and permitted it to go to the jury.

In this we think he erred. We understand the settled rule of law to be, that a co-partner of the defendant is not a competent witness for the plaintiff, either to prove the partnership or that the debt was contracted for, or on account of the firm. Here H. H. Hollister was, undoubtedly, liable for the whole of this debt, and was directly interested in fixing it upon the plaintiff in error, as one of the firm of H. H. Hollister & Co., so as to force him to share with him its payment. And such was the direct effect of his evidence.

It is true there is other evidence in this record tending to show that the plaintiff in error was a member of this firm, and that this debt, (which is admitted to be just as against H. H. Hollister,) was chargeable to the co-partnership. But still this does not obviate the difficulty, since it is impossible for us to say what influence the evidence of H. H. Hollister had with the jury in finding against the defendant. 2 Hum., 106; 4 Hum., 354–355; 4 Hum., 449; 1 Sneed, 28.

Reverse the judgment, and remand the cause.

THE STATE *v.* GEORGE BONNER.

CRIMINAL LAW. *Slaves. Purchase of liquor from. Aider and abettor.* The sale of liquor by a slave is a criminal offence, and a white man who tempts him to commit the offence, by purchasing liquor from him, is an aider and abettor, and as much guilty, as a principal offender, of a misdemeanor, as if the seller had been of his own color.

FROM WARREN.

Upon motion, the presentment was quashed by Judge MARCHBANKS, at the October Term, 1858. The Attorney General appealed.

SNEED, Attorney General, for the State.

J. L. SPURLOCK, for the defendant.

The State v. George Bonner.

McKinney, J. delivered the opinion of the Court.

At the June Term, 1858, of the Circuit Court of Warren, a presentment was made against the defendant by the Grand Jury, in which it is charged, in substance, that, on the 25th day of March, 1858, being the Sabbath day, in said county, a certain negro slave, the property of John H. Hopkins, did retail spirituous liquors to him, the said George Bonner; he, the said George Bonner, then and there aiding, promoting, and encouraging the said retailing, as aforesaid.

The Court, on motion of the defendant, quashed the presentment, and the Attorney General appealed.

Passing by objections to the form of the presentment, we proceed to inquire whether it substantially charges the defendant with any act indictable by our law. This is a new question, but we think it presents no serious difficulty.

If the acts charged had taken place *since* the new Code went into operation, the question would admit of no discussion. By section 2617 of the Code, slaves are absolutely forbidden to sell any spirituous liquors; and by sections 2672, 2673, it is made an indictable offence to purchase or receive from a slave any article, unless it be of the slave's own manufacture, without a written permit from the master, specifying the time when and the article to be sold.

To purchase or receive spirituous liquors from a slave would, clearly, fall within the prohibition and penalty of the latter section. And it may be observed, that, as slaves are positively disqualified to sell spirituous liquors by the section first referred to, a "permit" from the master to do so would be a nullity, and, of course, no defence to the person who may have purchased or received the liquor from the slave.

It remains to be seen whether the acts imputed to the defendant amount to an indictable offence, upon general principles of the common law, prior to the adoption of the Code.

In the case of a *white man*, we suppose it cannot be seriously controverted, that, upon general principles, the *purchaser* of spirituous liquors, in violation of the statutes passed to suppress tippling, is as much guilty of a violation of the law, and as much amenable to criminal prosecution and punishment, as the *seller*. They are, in all respects, *particeps criminis;* they are alike wilful violators of the law. The express prohibition to sell, upon every just principle of construction, must be considered as implying a prohibition to purchase. The purchaser—whether we regard his intent, or the effect and consequences of his act—is no less guilty, no less within the mischief intended to be suppressed, than the seller. It matters not that the former is not placed under the obligation of a bond or oath. This takes nothing from the force of the argument. He still stands guilty of wilfully participating in, and aiding and encouraging the commission of a criminal offence. Does not this, upon the soundest principles of criminal law, constitute him a *principal* in the offence? We think it does. And, perhaps, it would scarcely be going too far to say, that he ought to be regarded as less excusable than the seller. He has not the poor pretext of the latter, that the forbidden traffic is, in part, his means of procuring a living.

The State v. George Bonner.

If this conclusion be correct, as between citizen and citizen, is it not equally an indictable offence for a white man to purchase liquor from a *slave?* We think it is, with the qualification that it is, perhaps, a more aggravated, and, if possible, more mischievous wrong.

By the act of 1829, ch. 74, § 1, slaves are forbidden to sell spirituous liquors, (under the penalty of a limited number of stripes to be inflicted by order of a justice,) unless by the permission of the master. But the act of 1835, ch. 57, § 2, contains a prohibition upon the master to permit a slave to sell spirituous liquors. By these provisions, taken together, the sale of liquor by a slave is a criminal offence, absolutely prohibited, under corporal punishment. If so, is not a white man, who tempts the slave to commit an offence, and aids, abets and encourages him in doing so, as much guilty of a misdemeanor as a *principal* offender, as if the seller had been of his own color? The complexion and social condition of the slave does not enter into the gist of the offence; nor is it of any consequence, as we shall see presently, that the mode of prosecution and kind of punishment, in the case of the white man, are different from that prescribed for the slave.

It is well settled that a white man may be either an accessory, or principal, in a homicide committed by a slave, in like manner as if the crime had been committed by a white man. *State v. McCarn*, 11 Hum., 494. In that case it is said the offence is the same, though the punishment is different. That case proceeds upon the doctrine, that the Courts, to prevent a failure of justice and to secure the punishment of offenders, will so modify the rules and principles of the common law, as to adapt them to new offences created by statute, or to new cases as they arise. Hence, if a new felony be created, or if an act which, at common law, was only a misdemeanor, be made a felony, the rules and principles of the common law, as to principals and accessories, and in other necessary respects, will be applied to the new felonies, though the statute creating the felonies be silent on the subject. So, in McCarn's case it was held, that, although by the penal Code of 1829, principals and accessories are to be punished in like manner: yet, as under our law, white men and slaves are punished differently; a white man, convicted as accessory to a crime committed by a slave, must be punished in the same manner as if the principal had been a white man; and the slave, convicted as principal, must be punished as prescribed by the statute in such cases.

If the doctrine of McCarn's case be sound in respect to felonies, surely it is no less applicable to cases of misdemeanors. And if so, the principle of the case, in our opinion, warrants the conclusion, that the defendant in the case before us is liable to be prosecuted and punished in the same manner as if the offence charged upon the slave had been committed by a white man.

It follows that the judgment must be reversed, and the defendant be held to answer to the presentment.

J. B. Leetch v. The State.

1. CRIMINAL LAW. *Act of* 1831, *ch.* 103, §§ 1 *and* 2. *Slaves. Unlawful assemblage of.* Under the act of 1831, ch. 103, §§ 1 and 2, if the number of slaves assembled is *unusual*, or if the assemblage is at a *suspicious time* and *place*, the offence is complete. It is not necessary to show that the time and place are suspicious, and the number unusual. If either one is made out the offence is complete. But, in either case, it must be shown that the owner of the land on which the slaves meet, had *knowledge* of, and *permitted* the assemblage, without the *express authority* of their owners.

2. SAME. *Evidence. Onus of proof. Code,* § 2691. It devolves upon the defendant to show, by positive or circumstantial evidence, that the owners of the slaves gave permission to them to assemble. But this provision is not carried into the Code, and the question is not, now, of much importance.

FROM MAURY.

The plaintiff in error was convicted at the May Term, 1858, before Judge MARCHBANKS, and appealed, in error, to this Court.

J. M. HARRELL, for the plaintiff in error.

SNEED, Attorney General, for the State.

CARUTHERS, J., delivered the opinion of the Court.

This is an indictment under the act of 1831, ch. 103, secs. 1 and 2, and is the first which has come before us. The description of the offence is thus given in the act:

"Sec. 1. All assemblages of slaves in unusual numbers, or at suspicious times and places, not expressly authorized by the owners, shall be held and considered an unlawful assemblage.

"Sec. 2. Any person who shall knowingly permit any such assembly to be held on his or her land or premises, * * * shall be liable to presentment or indictment, and, on conviction, fined at the discretion of the Court."

The first section defines what is meant by an unlawful assemblage of slaves, that is, where the number is "unusual," or the time and place "suspicious," making two distinct cases. If there be nothing suspicious as to the time and place, still, if the number is unusual, the offence exists; and even if the number is not unusual, yet if the time and place are suspicious, the offence is complete. But in either case, the owner of the land on which they meet, is not criminated unless he "*knowingly permits*" it. Both his knowledge and permission must be established, to constitute the offence, in addition to the fact of the assemblage. But if all this be made out by the State, the statute provides an effectual defence; that is, that the slaves were "expressly authorized by their owners" to be there. A question is made as to the onus of proof upon the point of the owner's authority to their slaves to be at such assembly. We think this is matter of defence, and it devolves on the defendant to make it out by positive or circumstantial evidence, as held by His Honor, the Circuit Judge, in his charge. But this is not now of much importance, as this provision is dropped in the 2691st section of the Code, in the description of the same offence.

The argument is unsound, that to constitute the offence the slaves, when assembled, must do some other unlawful act. That is not made an element by the Legislature, and we are not authorized to add it. It is a police regulation, founded on sound policy. It cannot, however, be understood to apply to such cases as are put in the argument; such as congregations of slaves on occasions of funerals, preaching, and other ordinary lawful purposes, by permission of their owners, express or implied. The present case does not fall under any of those exceptions. It was an assembly of an unusual number, some forty or fifty, for social enjoyment, and without the permission or even the knowledge of the owners, from anything that appears. It is difficult to see to what sort of case the act would apply if not to this. The act does not make it necessary that there should be any appearance of suspicion to constitute the offence where the number is "unusual." If the "time and place" are calculated to excite suspicion, the number would not be material. What number would be regarded as "unusual," is not capable of any exact definition, but must be left for construction in reference to the facts of the particular case.

The defendant was convicted and fined fifteen dollars. We affirm the judgment.

George W. Lincoln *v.* William Purcell *et al.*

GEORGE W. LINCOLN *v.* WILLIAM PURCELL *et al.*

1. LIEN. *By contract, not in the nature of a mortgage or vendor's lien.* An express lien, created by contract and reserved on the face of the conveyance, is not, in all respects, equivalent to a mortgage, because the legal estate passes, by the conveyance, and vests in the purchaser. Neither is it, in all respects, in the nature of the vendor's lien. The latter, when the legal estate has been conveyed, exists only by implication of law, and is the mere creature of a court of equity. A lien created by contract, and reserved on the face of the conveyance, is regarded as a *specific lien*, forming an original substantive charge upon the estate thus conveyed, and as affecting all persons who may, subsequently, come into possession of the estate with notice, either actual or constructive, of its existence.

2. SAME. *Same. Statute of limitations.* This being the nature and effect of the lien, the presumption of law is that the purchaser of the land upon which the lien is reserved, holds under and consistent with the lien until the contrary is shown by him. And the statute of limitations will not run until he disclaims the lien, and assumes to hold adversely to it, with the knowledge of the party having said lien.

3. SAME. *Same. Same. Adverse possession.* Act of 1819, ch. 28, § 2. The debt of a mortgagee, or lien of a vendor, or other lien for the payment of money, is not barred, under the act of 1819, ch. 28, § 2, by the mere lapse of seven years before filing a bill to enforce them. To create the bar, under that section, the possession must be, in legal contemplation, adverse.

4. SAME. *Same. Same. Does not run until the money is due.* A cause of action must exist for the full period of seven years before suit brought in order to create the bar, and a note payable in stonework to be done at any time called for, cannot be sued on without a previous request to do the work, and the statute of limitations will not begin to run until such request is made.

5. SAME. *Release by trustee.* If a party hold, as a naked trustee, a lien, for another, a release, by him, of such lien to a person having a knowledge of the character of his claim, is a nullity.

6. SAME. *Same. Liability of the trustee. Estoppel.* If a naked trustee execute a release, under seal, of a lien for the payment of money, in which he acknowledges the reception of the money, he will be treated as holding the money in trust, and rendered liable for the same. And

George W. Lincoln *v.* William Purcell *et al.*

his acknowledgement would be an estoppel upon him, both at law and in equity, to deny the fact of having received the money.

7. CHANCERY PLEADING. *Demurrer. Presumption.* It is only in cases when it clearly appears from the face of the bill that the equity of complainant is barred, that the bill will be dismissed on demurrer, and every reasonable presumption is to be made in favor of, rather than against, the bill.

FROM DAVIDSON.

A demurrer to the bill was sustained by Chancellor FRIERSON, at the May Term, 1858, and the bill dismissed. The complainant appealed.

HOUSTON, for the complainant.

The demurrer was sustained and the bill dismissed upon the authority of the case of *Ray and others v. Goodman*, 1 Sneed, 586, in which it is held that "a possession of seven years by the vendee of land, claiming by virtue of his purchase, as evidenced by the bond for title under which he holds, gives him a right of possession that cannot be disturbed by the vendor by a bill to enforce his lien for unpaid purchase money, which has been due above seven years." Such lien is held to be barred by the 2d section of the act of 1819.

1st. Without questioning the correctness of this decision, I insist that it does not apply to this case. That case recognizes the principle that the vendor and vendee are trustees for each other, but holds that such trusts, in cases of ordinary title bonds, are not express but implied, and that express trusts may, certainly, be raised in the contract of the parties, but in the usual bonds, simply for title, the trusts are only implied by law.

George W. Lincoln v. William Purcell *et al.*

Now, in the case in hand, the parties were not satisfied with such lien or such trust as might be implied by law, but by express contract, they provide that the notes shall remain a lien upon the lot until paid, and when paid, Purcell is to hold the lot for himself, his heirs, &c. And I submit whether, as between the parties to the first deed, the statute of limitations ever operated at all. And I submit whether the transaction was not, in its effect, a mortgage, and if so, whether the statute would run in favor of Purcell, Northrop, or Cheatham, under the facts appearing in the cause.

2d. Again: I do not understand the case of *Ray* v. *Goodman* to go further than to decide that a sale, the execution of a title bond, and the possession of the vendee for seven years, claiming the land under his purchase, forms the bar of the statute. In such case, however, if the vendee were, all the time, acknowledging the existence and validity of the lien, the statute would not form the bar. For this effect the possession must be adverse, and this recognition of the lien removes the presumption of adverse holding which is raised by the sale, the title bond, and possession under it. There can be no bar of the statute in any case without an adverse holding. This is distinctly stated in the case of *Graham* v. *Nelson*, 5. Hum., 610, which case is recognized in the case of *Marr* v. *Chester*, 1 Swan, 416. The Court was construing the 2d section of the act of 1819, and its language is, that "It cannot be supposed that the bar was intended to apply to cases where there was no adverse claim to the party entitled to the land. If the party against whom suit is brought has been

George W. Lincoln *v.* William Purcell *et al.*

holding in subservience to the complainant's right, and his possession has been consistent therewith, it would be an absurd proposition to assume that such possession was a bar to the action." See, also, the case of *Nolen* v. *Larmon & Fenwick*, cited in the case of *Marr* v. *Chester*. Now, apply these principles to the facts stated in the bill, and it seems to me that the Chancellor, unquestionably, erred in sustaining the demurrer, for it is distinctly charged that both Northrop and Cheatham's possession was in subservience to complainant's rights, and that the possession of each was consistent therewith.

3d. Again: The deed to Purcell was made on the 1st of December, 1849; the deed of the sheriff to Northrop, on the 19th of January, 1850, and his deed to Cheatham was made on the 14th of January, 1851; and this bill was filed on the 11th of January, 1858, which was less than seven years from the time Cheatham acquired the title. Cheatham, then, did not himself hold the lot for seven years before this bill was filed, and unless he can connect his possession with that of Northrop, complainant's right is not barred. This he cannot do, because Northrop shows on the face of his deed to Cheatham, that he did not hold adversely to the lien for the unpaid purchase money.

4th. I insist further, that the contract between Northrop and Cheatham, as shown in the deed to the latter, raised, by contract, a trust in favor of complainant, against which the statute of limitations has not run, an would not, even if Cheatham had held it seven years. The language of the Court in the case of *Marr* v. *Chester*, is, "If a man receive a conveyance of a legal title of a tract of land, in which conveyance there is

George W. Lincoln v. William Purcell et al.

declaration that the bargainee is to be entitled to only three-fourths of the land, and that one-fourth is to be laid off for a third party, who has an equitable right to it; this is an implied undertaking, by contract, to lay off that one-fourth for the *cestui que trust*, and to hold the possession, not for himself entirely, but for himself and his co-tenant in equity."

Ewing & Cooper, for the defendants.

McKinney, J., delivered the opinion of the Court.

The complainant's bill was dismissed on demurrer. The bill seeks to subject a lot in the town of Nashville, to the satisfaction of a balance of unpaid purchase money, by force of an express lien reserved upon the face of the conveyance.

It appears, from the allegations of the bill, that, on the 1st day of December, 1848, the defendant, Kirkman, sold and conveyed the lot in question to the defendant, Purcell, at the price of $1500. At the time of said sale, Kirkman, the vendor, was indebted to the complainant; and it was mutually agreed between Kirkman, complainant, and Purcell, that the latter, in part discharge of the purchase money of the lot, due to Kirkman, should assume and become responsible for the debt due from Kirkman to complainant. And, in pursuance of this agreement, Purcell executed two notes, one for $525,00, and the other for $325,00, " payable in stone-work, to be done at any time called for, after the

1st of July, 1849." By this arrangement, and the payment of $650,00 in hand, by Purcell to Kirkman, the purchase money of said lot was fully paid to Kirkman, and the indebtedness of the latter to complainant was extinguished. The deed of conveyance from Kirkman to Purcell, which was executed at the time of the contract, recites the execution of said two notes by Purcell to complainant, in part discharge of the purchase money of the lot; and expressly provides that the sums of money specified in said notes, "shall be and remain a *lien* upon said lot or parcel of land, until said sums shall have been fully satisfied, discharged and paid; and the said William Purcell, upon the payment of said notes, is to have and to hold the aforesaid lot or parcel of land," &c. This deed appears not to have been proved or registered until January, 1852, which was after the sale and conveyance to Cheatham, hereafter to be noticed.

It further appears from the bill, that, on the 19th of January, 1850, said lot was sold at execution sale, as the property of said Purcell, and was purchased by one Northrop. The sheriff's deed to Northrop, in describing the lot, refers to it as "being the same conveyed by John Kirkman to the said William Purcell, by deed, (unregistered,) on the 1st day of December, 1848." On the 14th of January, 1841, Northrop sold and conveyed said lot to F. R. Cheatham, and in his deed of conveyance he covenants, amongst other things, that said lot "is unincumbered, with the exception of the balance of the purchase money due from one William Purcell, on the purchase of said lot of ground by said Purcell from John Kirkman, on the 1st day of December, 1848." And in the

George W. Lincoln *v.* William Purcell *et al.*

covenant of warranty, he warrants "against the lawful claim·of all persons, except such as may claim by virtue of the *lien* of said John Kirkman on said lot of ground, for the unpaid purchase money due from the said William Purcell on his purchase aforesaid from Kirkman."

The bill exhibits a copy of an instrument executed by John Kirkman to Cheatham, on the 17th of August, 1852, in which the former acknowledges the payment to him, by Cheatham, of the balance of the purchase money due on the two before mentioned notes, executed by Purcell to complainant, and in consideration thereof, he relinquishes to Cheatham all his interest in said lot.

The bill charges that, in fact, Cheatham paid nothing to Kirkman for said release, and denies that Kirkman had any interest in the notes, or in the lien reserved to secure their payment, or that he had any power to release or discharge said lien. It is further charged, in substance, that both Northrop and Cheatham purchased with full knowledge of the fact that a portion of the purchase money of the lot remained due to complainant, and, also, with knowledge of the existence of the lien, to secure the payment thereof; and that they, respectively, held said lot in subservience to, and consistently with the right of the complainant, and not adversely thereto; and that in the summer of 1857, Cheatham had promised to pay complainant the remainder of such purchase money.

It is further alleged that the note for $325,00 still remains unpaid; and complainant states that "he demanded payment of said note *long since*, and payment was refused."

The bill seeks to subject said lot to the satisfaction

of the amount of said note, by enforcing the lien, which, it is alleged, was reserved for the sole benefit of the complainant. Purcell, Cheatham and Kirkman, are made defendants to the bill. The demurrer to the bill is filed, on behalf alone, of Cheatham.

Taking the allegations of the bill to be true, for the present, we think the Chancellor erred in allowing the demurrer.

The pretended release of Kirkman might be left out of view, as entitled to no consideration in the determination of the main question intended to be raised by the demurrer. Upon the facts charged in the bill, the release is a mere nullity. Kirkman held the lien as a naked trustee for the complainant. No lien could, possibly, have existed in his own favor, for the simple reason that, by the arrangement stated in the bill, his claim for the purchase money of the lot was fully satisfied and extinguished at the time of the sale. And Cheatham, as is substantially charged, having knowledge of the facts, cannot avail himself of the release for any purpose. How it might be, if Cheatham occupied the footing of a *bona fide* purchaser without notice, need not be stated. It is clear, however, that Kirkman is a proper party defendant, either for the purpose of having the release annulled, or for the purpose of having a decree against him for the amount of the unpaid purchase money, which, by his deed, he acknowledges the reception of from Cheatham. For, although he had no right to receive the money, yet, having done so, he must be treated as holding it in trust for complainant. And his acknowledgement being under seal would be an estoppel upon him, at law, to deny the fact of having received the money; and he will be alike precluded in equity, for he cannot, in the latter forum, be heard to allege that he made the release without consideration, with a view to cut off the lien; for this would have been, on his part, a palpable fraud upon the rights of the complainant, which he will not be heard to insist upon, in exoneration of his liability.

But the Chancellor allowed the demurrer, as is stated in the argument, on the ground that the complainant's equity was barred by the statute of limitations. This conclusion is erroneous, we think, for several reasons.

That it was competent to the parties, by mutual agreement, to create the lien declared in the deed from Kirkman to Purcell, for the benefit of the complainant, admits of no doubt upon general principles of law. But the exact nature and legal effect of a lien thus created, seems not to be well defined, in any of the books to which we have had access. It certainly is not, in all respects, equivalent to a mortgage; because the legal estate passes by the conveyance, and vests in the purchaser, notwithstanding the lien reserved in the deed.

And yet it must be regarded as, in some respects, different from, and as possessing greater efficacy than the vendor's lien, properly so called. The latter, where the legal estate has been conveyed to the vendee, is the mere creature of a court of equity. It exists only by implication of law; and is in the nature of a trust only, and not a specific lien upon the land conveyed, until a bill has been filed to enforce it. 10 Hum., 371.

But an express lien, created by contract and reserved on the face of the conveyance, though not a mortgage, must at least be regarded as a specific lien, forming an

George W. Lincoln v. William Purcell et al.

original substantive charge upon the estate thus conveyed; and as affecting all persons who may subsequently come into possession of the estate with notice, either actual or constructive, of its existence. This must necessarily be so; for even the implied lien of the vendor exists not only against the purchaser and his heirs, but, also, against all persons claiming under him, with notice of it, though they be purchasers for a valuable consideration. But this implied lien does not exist against a *bona fide* purchaser, without notice; neither will it be allowed to prevail against a creditor who may have acquired a judgment, or execution lien upon the property, before a bill has been filed by the vendor to enforce his lien. 10 Hum., 371, 376. But not so of the lien created by contract, as in the present case. If the conveyance reserving the lien has been duly registered, such lien will be operative against creditors, *bona fide* purchasers, and all other persons, without regard to actual notice.

It is true, in the present case, that the deed from Kirkman to Purcell, reserving the lien, was not registered until after the sale by Northrop to Cheatham. But this is of no consequence, in this particular case, because the deed from Northrop to Cheatham expressly recognizes the existence of the lien declared in Kirkman's deed.

If this view of the nature and effect of the lien in question be correct, it certainly does not create between the parties a relation similar to that of a mortgage, as regards the application of the statute of limitations. The relation of the purchaser is more analogous to that of a trustee, by express contract, who may disclaim the trust; and after such disclaimer, and a knowledge thereof

George W. Lincoln *v.* William Purcell *et al.*

brought home to the *cestui que trust*, may claim and hold adversely to him. This is putting the case in the most favorable point of view for the defendant, Cheatham. But this will not avail him; as the presumption of law is, that he is holding under and consistently with the trust, until the contrary is affirmatively shown by him. Upon this presumption alone the complainant might have safely rested, in answer to the demurrer, without the aid of the affirmative allegation in the bill, that the defendant had held, and was holding, in subordination to his lien.

It is altogether a mistaken conclusion, that, under the second section of the act of 1819, the complainant's equity is barred by the mere lapse of seven years, before filing his bill, irrespective of the character of defendant's possession. To create a bar, under that section, the possession must be, in legal contemplation, adverse. Such has been the uniform course of decision since the case of *Dyche* v. *Gass*, 8 Yer., 397. And the case relied on, (*Ray* v. *Goodman*, 1 Sneed, 586,) when carefully examined, will be found to be in accordance with previous adjudications upon the statute.

But, again: The case of *Ray* v. *Goodman* settles, that the purchase money must have been *due* seven years, before the filing of the bill, to enforce the payment thereof, by a sale of the land.

In other words, a cause of action must have existed for the full period of seven years before suit brought, which might have been asserted at any time within that period, in order to create a bar. This cannot be predicated of the case under consideration, from the face of the bill.

George W. Lincoln v. William Purcell et al.

The notes were "payable in stone-work, to be done at any time *called for*, after the 1st of July, 1849." We take it to be too clear to require either authority or argument, that no action could have been maintained on these notes, without a previous request to do the work stipulated to be done. Until such demand, or request, made and refused, there was no default, or breach of contract, on the part of the maker of the notes; and, consequently, no right, or cause of action, on the part of the complainant. The principle, that in contracts for the payment of money, on demand, the bringing suit is all the demand required, has no application to a case like the present.

From the statement in the bill, that payment was demanded "*long since*," and refused, it cannot be inferred that it was demanded more than seven years before suit. This would be to reverse the rule, that, upon a demurrer, every reasonable presumption is to be made in favor of, rather than against the bill. It is only in cases where it clearly appears, from the face of the bill, that the complainant's equity is barred, that the bill will be dismissed upon demurrer, for that cause.

Decree reversed, and cause remanded.

John B. Bates *v.* S. K. Whitson.

John B. Bates *v.* S. K. Whitson.

1. PRINCIPAL AND SURETY. *Agreement to become principal. Consideration.* If an obligation is incurred by two, to raise money to discharge the debt of one, the other, who is in no way bound for the original debt, cannot, by agreement, become the principal, and the one whose debt is paid become the surety, so as to make him first liable on the obligation thus assumed, unless there is a legal consideration to sustain the promise made to become the principal.

2. SAME. *Same. Same. Case in judgment.* A bill of exchange was drawn by two partners. Money was retained by one partner to discharge the bill of exchange, but he appropriated $700 of the fund to his individual debts, and the bill, to that extent, remained unpaid. After the death of this partner, one of his administrators, together with the other partner, executed a note, in bank, in payment of the $700. This note was endorsed by the endorsers on the bill of exchange. The partner who was joint maker of the note paid it after judgment, at the request of the administrator, who promised to refund the amount paid. The estate of the deceased partner proved to be insolvent, and his administrator, who had jointly executed the note, refused to refund the money out of his individual means. The partner who paid the debt moved for judgment, as surety, against him. Held, that it does not appear that it was understood by the parties that the administrator was to be individually liable for the debt, and become the principal in the note; and, if it did so appear, there is no consideration to support the promise, and it cannot be enforced.

FROM BEDFORD.

This cause was tried at the August Term, 1858, BAXTER, J., presiding, by interchange with Judge DAVIDSON. Verdict and judgment for the defendant. The plaintiff appealed.

W. H. WISENER, for the plaintiff.

ED. COOPER, for the defendant.

John B. Bates *v.* S. K. Whitson.

CARUTHERS, J., delivered the opinion of the Court.

The plaintiff moved the Circuit Court of Bedford for judgment against the defendant, upon the ground that he was his surety in, and had paid off a judgment on the following note:

"$774.   ROWESVILLE, TENN., August 9, 1854.

"Four months after date, we, or either of us, promise to pay Jas. W. Johnson, or order, at the Branch of the Bank of Tennessee, at Shelbyville, seven hundred and seventy-four dollars, for value received. Witness our hands and seals, date above.

S. K. WHITSON, [SEAL.]
J. B. BATES,   [SEAL.]

Endorsed by Johnson, Knight, Stamps, and Elliot.

The bank sued the makers and endorsers, and Bates paid the judgment.

The Court submitted the question of suretyship to the jury, and they found the issue against Bates. The errors assigned are upon the charge of the Court. These will be better understood by a brief statement of the facts.

In the fall of 1853, Trigg and Bates were partners in buying and driving hogs to the South. Part of the funds employed by them in this business was raised by a bill of exchange upon Mobile for $3,500, drawn by them, and endorsed by the same men, perhaps, who endorsed this note, and discounted by the bank An amount sufficient to pay off this bill was retained out of the proceeds of the drove, and placed in the hands of Trigg, for that purpose. He paid all but the above balance, which he applied to his own debts, and left that unpaid. He gave assurances to the bank that he would soon discharge it, but died before it was done; and Whitson became his administrator. He applied to the bank for a further extension of the time, and the same was given by discounting the above note. The estate of Trigg was then thought to be good, but it turned out otherwise in the end; and the struggle now is upon whom the loss shall fall. This depends upon the issue submitted to the jury.

There is no controversy but the proceeds of this note were applied to the extinguishment of the balance due upon the bill of exchange of Trigg and Bates. But the question is raised upon the ground that Whitson, though not bound, when he became administrator of Trigg, in view of the fact that his intestate should have paid the debt, and considering the estate entirely solvent, made it his own debt, and procured Bates to become joint maker of the note in the character of surety, as between themselves, in order to obtain the same endorsers, and to satisfy the demand of the bank to have the same men on the note that they had on the bill of exchange; or, as appears by the proof of Johnson, one of the endorsers, that when the note was presented to him first to endorse, Whitson alone was maker, and he refused to endorse it unless Bates, who was bound before him on the bill as one of the drawers, or some other good man, would become joint maker of the note, after which it was returned with Bates' name, and he endorsed it. This application, first and last, was not by Whitson, but a man named Jett, who was joint administrator of Trigg.

John B. Bates *v.* S. K. Whitson.

After the note fell due, and was protested and sued upon, Whitson told Bates he did not intend for him to pay the note, or any part of it; that he should never pay "one dime of it," as he had become bound on it at his (Whitson's) request, and for his accommodation, to get the endorsers upon it. It appears further, that after the judgment and execution, upon application to Whitson for the money, he said he did not have the money of his own, or of the estate, but told the officer to request Bates to "advance the money for him, and he should be repaid out of or in the first note of the witness and Bates that fell due for the land and mill of Wm. H. Trigg, the intestate, which had been sold to pay debts." The witness advanced the money at the request of Bates, who has since refunded to him.

Upon these facts the Court charged, in effect, that the question of suretyship depended not upon the form, but the substance of the transaction. That if the money to be raised on the note was intended to be, and was applied to the payment of a debt for which Bates and not Whiston was bound, he would not be the surety of Whiston; and the fact that Bates had placed the money in the hands of Trigg, to pay the bill, would make no difference, as that would only be a question between the partners in their settlement. He further charged that if the debt was Bates' for which this money was raised, the understanding of the parties as to the relation they would occupy on the note, would not change the question; but that, from the fact that the note was made to pay a debt for which Bates was bound, and Whitson not, the law would fix the character of their relation, and Bates would be the principal, and not surety.

John B. Bates *v.* S. K. Whitson.

The Court was requested to charge that the parties might by contract change this relation, even if the money was used in discharge of Bates' debt; but this was refused. Whether the Court considered the proposition unsound in law, or not applicable to the facts of the case, and, therefore, a mere abstraction, does not appear. If the facts do not raise the question propounded, it was right to refuse to so instruct the jury even if such was the law. Indeed it would have been improper, though not error, to have done so. But it was, perhaps, declined upon the other ground, that the Court considered it not to be the law. Although there is no express contract or agreement to that effect, yet there is, perhaps, proof enough tending to establish that as the understanding of the parties to make it a proper question for the jury. So the questions made by the instructions asked is properly before us for decision. We are not aware of any authority on the exact point, but we think it presents no serious difficulty upon principle. It would seem to be a great absurdity to hold, that in an obligation incurred by two to raise money to discharge the debt of one, the other, who was in no way bound for the original debt, should become the principal, and the other, whose debt was paid, or for whose use and benefit the money was appropriated, should be surety. In such a case there would be no consideration for the agreement. There might be cases where such a contract would be enforced, but the facts would have to be very different from these.

Here was no consideration whatever. Whitson was in no way bound, in his individual capacity, for the debt to be paid or renewed by this note. All that he said and did in relation to the payment of it, was upon the idea that the estate of Trigg was good, and in that event he knew it was just that it should be paid by him, as representative of Trigg, who had used the firm money intrusted to him for that purpose, and he honestly intended that should be done, and Bates saved. But there is nothing to show that he ever intended to pay it out of his own means, without a certain prospect of reimbursement out of the assets. As soon as he ascertained that the estate would prove insolvent, he declined to take the loss upon himself for the exoneration of one of the original debtors. But then, if such had been his purpose, and he declined to execute a contract to that effect, our decision goes to the extent that he could not be compelled to do so without some consideration to sustain the promise.

This does not, of course, affect the question of the liability of the estate of Trigg, in the hands of Whitson, to Bates, for this debt, in the settlement of the partnership.

Let the judgment be affirmed.

WILLIAM B. WOOD *v.* JOHN H. THOMAS *et al.*

1. ATTACHMENT. *Verbal sale of real estate. Equitable interest. Creditor and debtor.* A creditor can be on no higher ground than his debtor, in attaching equitable interests of the latter. And if the debtor has done any act, or entered into any agreement which would preclude *him* from asserting an equity that he once had, his creditor would, likewise, be precluded from so doing.

2. SAME. *Same. Case in judgment* A. and B. entered into an agreement for the sale and purchase of real estate. The contract was in parol. A. paid B. $200, and executed his notes for the remainder of the purchase money, B. verbally agreeing to make him a title to the land when the purchase money should be paid. Subsequent to this agreement, the trade between A. and B. was cancelled, and the land sold to C., who refunded to A. the $200 paid by him, and executed his notes to B., in the place of the notes previously given by A., which notes were delivered up to A. After this latter agreement a creditor of A.'s attached his interest in the land and the fund. It was held that A. had parted with his equitable interest both in the land and fund, and it could not be attached at the instance of his creditors.

FROM WILLIAMSON.

Complainant's bill was dismissed by Chancellor FRIERSON, at the April Term, 1858. He appealed.

R. F. HILL, for the complainant.

E. C. COOK, for the defendants.

WRIGHT, J., delivered the opinion of the Court.

On the 15th of July, 1856, the complainant, Wm. B. Wood, who is a creditor of the defendant, John H. Thomas, filed his bill in the Chancery Court at Franklin against said Thomas and Thomas J. Gray.

The said Thomas, in the fall of the year 1855, had verbally purchased of said Gray a house and lot, in the town of Paytonsville, in Williamson county, for which he was to pay $400, to wit, $200 on the first of January, 1856, $100 on the first of August, 1856, and the remaining $100 on the first of January, 1857; and for

William B. Wood v. John H. Thomas *et al.*

which Thomas executed his notes to Gray, who never gave Thomas any deed, title bond, or writing of any kind, as to the house and lot.

A part of this purchase money, namely, the $200 due in January, 1856, had been paid by Thomas to Gray, and the object of the bill was to attach the interest of said Thomas in the house and lot, and in the $200 so paid Gray—the bill being framed in the alternative, so as to reach either the house and lot or the fund, and have the same applied in satisfaction of complainant's debt.

In May, 1856, prior to the filing of complainant's bill, Thomas had, with the assent of Gray, verbally sold his interest in the house and lot to Isaac Secrest for $450—of which sum he paid Thomas in cash, $250; and, as to the balance, he executed to Gray his two notes for $100 each, due the first of August, 1856, and first of January, 1857. These notes were accepted by Gray in lieu of Thomas' notes, which were surrendered to him by Gray, who agreed to make the title to Secrest instead of Thomas, upon receiving payment of the two notes.

All this took place prior to the filing of complainant's bill; and Gray, from thenceforward, held himself ready to make the title to Secrest as soon as he paid him, and had no claim on Thomas, who was let entirely out of the contract, and ceased all claim to the house and lot after the sale to Secrest.

The Chancellor decreed that Thomas had no attachable interest, either in the house and lot or in the fund, and that Gray, having waived the want of a writing,

William B. Wood v. John H. Thomas *et al.*

and submitting to make Secrest a title, should do so upon receiving of him the residue of the purchase money.

With this decree Secrest, Gray, and Thomas are satisfied, and do not appeal. An appeal is only taken by complainant, Wood.

We think the Chancellor's decree was right, and affirm it.

The complainant can be on no higher ground than John H. Thomas, his debtor. The latter had no claim or debt whatever against Gray, and could, in no aspect of the case, have any, for he had received back, of Secrest, all he had advanced. Neither had he any interest in this house and lot. How could he, if disposed, file a bill and assert any equity or claim to this property after what had taken place between him and Secrest? And complainant can be no better off. But he asserts no claim, and denies expressly he has any interest.

Even if Gray desired, (but he does not,) to abandon the contract with Secrest, and enforce the specified execution of the contract with Thomas, yet he could not do so against the will of Thomas. This could only be done by the voluntary consent of both parties. But here neither consents; but both aver that Secrest is entitled to the property, and express a wish that it be decreed him under the contract with him. And he also desires that this be done, and files a bill for that purpose.

How then can complainant interpose to prevent this? That he cannot is conclusively settled in the case of *Sneed et al. v. Bradley et al.*, 4 Sneed, 301. See, also, *Thacker* v. *Chambers et al.* 5 Hum., 313.

We affirm the decision, with costs.

MOORE SMILEY v. JAMES C. GAMBILL, EX'R, &c.

1. WILL. *Revocation of. Mistake. Fraud.* If the maker of a will burns a paper, which she thinks is her will, but by *mistake* or the *fraud* of others, burns a different paper, with the intention of revoking said will by its destruction, and honestly believed that she had done it, and continued in that belief, without any subsequent recognition, or even knowledge of its existence, it would amount to a revocation of the will.

2. SAME. *Same. Evidence.* Revocation is a question of intention, and the acts, conduct and declarations of the maker of the will, are admissible for the purpose of ascertaining whether it was revoked. Revocation may be established as other facts, by positive or circumstantial evidence.

3. SAME. *Same. Revocation a question of Law.* While it is the province of the jury to determine the facts, what amounts to a revocation is a question of law.

FROM BEDFORD.

The issue was found in favor of the will, at the August Term, 1858, DAVIDSON, J., presiding. The defendants appealed.

WISENER & CALDWELL, for the plaintiff in error.

BUCHANAN, KEEBLE & COOPER, for the defendant in error.

CARUTHERS, J., delivered the opinion of the Court.

This was a contest upon the will of Margaret Stewart. The issue was decided in favor of the will, and an appeal in error, by the contestant.

The error assigned is upon the charge of the Court on the question of revocation. He said:

"That if the alleged testatrix burnt a paper which she believed was her will, but in that was mistaken, it would be no revocation. Parol declarations that she had no will, amount in law to no revocation. Evidence that the alleged testatrix had, subsequent to the execution of the alleged will, made conveyances of a portion of the same property named in the will, was admitted only on the question of capacity, and if her capacity is not attacked, such evidence is irrelevant, and ought not to be considered."

The charge is applicable to the facts proved, and the question is, whether it is sound law. There is no doubt but that she made and executed the paper as her will, but there is just as little, that she thought she had destroyed it, and died in that belief. This is proved by her uniform declarations, and by her acts in disposing of some of the same property by deeds, and in applications made to friends to write another will for her, on the ground that she had destroyed her first. She became dissatisfied with the principal legatee, and determined to change her purpose. She disclosed to various persons, that she went to the drawer, where she caused her will to be deposited, took it out, and burnt it up —that she knew it was her will by a certain red ribbon that she had tied around it. There can be no doubt but that she believed the paper she burned was her will, and, perhaps, just as little, that some one had removed the paper without her knowledge, and thus de-

Moore Smiley v. James C. Gambill, Ex'r, &c.

ceived her. It seems afterwards to have been in possession of Gambill's son-in-law. She failed by *mistake* to accomplish her object, and it is more than likely that this mistake was caused by the fraud of others. She then lived at the house of her son-in-law, Gambill, the executor and main legatee whose interest it was to prevent its destruction.

Most of the States have statutes similar to that of the English statute of frauds on this subject, prescribing the acts that will revoke a. will. " Burning, cancelling, tearing or obliterating," are the words generally used. There are many nice distinctions drawn in the books, in the construction and application of these words, and some of the cases on those statutes seem to sustain the charge. But we have no statute of the kind. The only reference to the subject of revocation in our legislation, is that in the 14th section of the act of 1784, ch. 22, which provides that "no written will shall be altered or *revoked* by a subsequent nuncupative will, except the same be in the lifetime of the testator, reduced to writing," &c. But this is confined to that particular and single mode of revoking, and does not prohibit any other mode known to the law, independent of any statute regulation on the subject. It will not be controverted by any one, that where the maker of a will destroys it in any manner, or causes it to be done, with the intention that it shall no longer exist, that it is revoked, and can never be set up. This power over it results from its very nature. It is ambulatory, and has no vitality or binding force until the death of the maker—it only speaks from the death. It is a dead letter and binds no one until that time. It is the death of the testator which gives life to the testament. A simple determination of the mind, never executed, no matter how often declared or strongly made, however, cannot have the effect to avoid the writing, but this must be accompanied by some act designed to carry out the purpose of revocation.

All this is plain enough, but the question recurs, is the object accomplished in law, where, by *mistake*, or the fraudulent interposition of others, the thing intended to be done, was not, but the paper, contrary to the maker's intentions and belief, was still preserved? If this were so it would be an anomaly.

In *Ford* v. *Ford*, 7 Hum., 104, the Court say, that "if a testator, being of sound mind, told the witness to burn the will, and it was not done, although he supposed it to have been burned, it is a revocation," or rather, that the contrary, as held by the Circuit Judge, was not law. They say, in effect, if a man is deceived by the burning of another paper, which he supposed was his will, it would be sufficient to revoke. The Court admits, very correctly, in the same case, that a mere intention to revoke, however strong, without some act, will not be sufficient. The cases cited in 1 Jarman on Wills, 116 to 118, are in accordance, in principle, with the case of Ford. A Pennsylvania case, reported in 1 Smith, 41, cited by Jarman in a note, p. 117, holds, "that a will made many years before, and *believed* by the testator to be destroyed, but detained by one of the devisees to prevent its being cancelled or altered, was thereby avoided. This is correct, with the qualification that some act was done, or attempted to be done upon it, with the intention to revoke. Revocation is a question of intention, and evidence is admissible to show that intention, by any act done, or believed to have been done. The act done, or aimed to be done, as well as the purpose of the mind for which it was done, are matters of fact for the jury. *Burns* v. *Burns*, 4 Serg. & Rawle. And these may be established as other facts, by one credible witness, or convincing circumstances. But what facts amount to a revocation, is, of course, a question of law.

In this case, if the jury believed, as a matter of fact, that Mrs. Stewart burnt a paper which she thought was her will, although it was not, with the intention of revoking by its destruction, and honestly believed that she had done it, and continued in that belief, without any subsequent recognition, or even knowledge of its existence, the paper propounded would not be her will. As testimony bearing on this question, the excluded facts in relation to the sale of her property afterwards, were admissible as circumstances. Her declarations alone might not be sufficient, but they were competent, and it would be for the jury to determine whether they, together with other facts proved, made out the fact of burning, or intention to do so, by the act done.

For these errors in the charge of the Court, the judgment must be reversed, and a new trial granted.

JACOB STIPE v. THOMAS STIPE.

1. SALE OF REAL ESTATE. *Jurisdiction. Covenant of warranty. Fraud.* If there be no fraud in the sale of real estate, the purchaser, on failure of title, must rely, alone, on his covenants of warranty. And if there be no covenants of warranty, he has no remedy, either in law or equity, for his money.

2. SAME. *Same. Eviction. Breach of warranty.* The purchaser of real estate has no remedy on his covenants of warranty, either in a Court of Law or Equity, until there is a breach of the warranty; and there is no breach until eviction. But if there be a breach of the covenant, the remedy at law is plain and adequate, and a Court of Equity has no jurisdiction.

3. SAME. *Eviction. Question reserved.* Is the payment of a judgment which is an incumbrance upon the land, by a purchaser with covenants of warranty, an eviction *pro tanto?*

FROM WHITE.

The bill was dismissed upon demurrer by Chancellor VAN DYKE, and the complainant appealed.

SAMUEL TERNY, for the complainant.

COLMS, for the defendant, cited, M. & Y. R., 376–382; 10 Yer., 179–186; 3 Hum., 309–313; 1 Yer., 450–452; Story's Eq., §§ 298–306; 6 Hum., 455–458; 4 Yer., 270–297.

WRIGHT, J., delivered the opinion of the Court.

The bill, in this case, cannot be maintained, and the Chancellor acted very properly in sustaining the demurrer.

Jacob Stipe v. Thomas Stipe.

We think it very probable, from the facts shown in the bill, that in the purchase of the land by the complainant of defendant they were *particeps criminis* in a scheme of *fraud to defeat* the collection of the judgment afterwards had in the suit then pending against the defendant for slander. If so, the complainant can have no relief in a Court of Equity.

But if this be not so, the bill makes no case of fraud by the defendant upon the complainant, nor is any rescission of the contract sought. On the contrary, complainant, or his vendee, is in possession of the land, and seeks to maintain it. The settled rule is, that if there be no fraud, the purchaser of real estate, on failure of title, must rely, alone, on his covenants of warranty. And if there be none, he has no remedy, either in law or equity, for his money. *Maney* v. *Porter*, 3 Hum., 347.

The bill here alleges a covenant of warranty, but avers want of eviction. If this be so, there is no breach of the covenant, and how can complainant have relief in a Court of Equity any more than a Court of law? Neither the one Court nor the other can give any remedy until there is a breach of the warranty.

But if there be a breach of the covenant at all, the remedy of complainant in a Court of Law is plain and adequate, and equity has no jurisdiction.

If complainant's purchase were free of any taint of fraud, and he could, outside of the covenant of warranty, maintain the position, (as was done in *Winchester* v. *Beardin*, 10 Hum., 247,) that in paying the judgment in slander, he had discharged a debt of the defendant— an incumbrance upon the land—and had put himself in an attitude to have a recovery against the defendant for money paid to his use, still his remedy, in a Court of Law, is ample.

But we think, upon an examination of the authorities, it will be found that the payment by the complainant of the judgment in slander was an eviction *pro tanto*. 2 Green. Ev., § 244. Such is our recollection of the authorities, Rawle on Covenants for title, pp. 227–240.

But we do not now mean to decide this question.

It is palpable, that in whatever light this case may be viewed, a Court of Equity is not the proper forum.

The decree of the Chancellor, dismissing the bill, is affirmed.

JOHN COLCOUGH *v.* THE NASHVILLE AND NORTHWESTERN RAILROAD COMPANY.

1. RAILROAD COMPANY. *Statutory remedy exclusive.* The statutory remedy given to land proprietors, for land taken for the construction of railways, is, in general, exclusive of all other remedies, and not merely cumulative.

2. SAME. *Same. Damages.* The remedy prescribed in the charter of the Northwestern Railroad Company, embraces not only just compensation for the land taken, but likewise all such incidental loss, or damage, as must necessarily or reasonably result from the appropriation of the land and construction of the road in the manner authorized by the charter.

3. SAME. *Same. Same. Confined to the land taken.* This statutory remedy is confined to the land taken, and the damages incident thereto. It does not extend to, and embrace damage or injuries to adjoining land, not authorized by the charter to be taken; nor to damages resulting from carelessness, negligence, or wilful trespasses in the execution of the work.

John Colcough *v.* The Nashville and Northwestern Railroad Company.

4. SAME. *Same. Remedy not limited to the owner of the fee* This statutory remedy is not limited to the owner of the fee. A life interest, or a term of years may be carved out of the fee; and in such case the tenant for life, or lessee, as well as the remainderman, or lessor, is within the spirit and meaning of the charter, and they are entitled to recover compensation for the damage or injury by them respectively sustained.

5. SAME. *Practice. Proceeding may be joint or several.* The persons vested with the several interests which constitute the entire estate, may join in a proceeding under the statute to obtain compensation; or, as they have several interests, may proceed separately. In either mode of proceeding, the compensation for the entire damage must be apportioned according to the injury to their respective interests.

FROM DAVIDSON.

This cause was tried upon demurrer, at the May Term, 1858, BAXTER, J., presiding. The demurrer being sustained, the plaintiff appealed.

WOODS & MERRITT, for the plaintiff.

The plaintiff's right to compensation is admitted by the argument. The question is how it is to be enforced. If the act of incorporation had provided for the assessment of damages, it is admitted, that under our decisions, the mode pointed out by the State must be followed to the exclusion of the common law remedy. But it is insisted for the plaintiff that no mode is pointed out by the statute for anything but the freehold; (see Charter, Acts 1851–52, pp. 88, 89,) and, therefore, either the act is unconstitutional, as failing to provide for the payment of the "just compensation," as the New York decisions and many in the New England States decide, or else the party is to be permitted to look to the general principles of the common law for the enforcement of an admitted right. If this be so, assumpsit is the only remedy, as the company in the appropriation of this land was in the lawful exercise of a right delegated to it by the Legislature, and was in no sense a trespasser or wrong-doer. *Woodfolk* v. *Nashville and Chattanooga Railroad Company*, 2 Swan. The origin and history of the action of assumpsit show that this case is embraced in its principles, and is a fit one for their application.

EWING & COOPER, for the defendant.

The remedy given to persons for damages arising from the seizure of their land by the railroad is very broad, and, as explained in the case of *Woodfolk* v. *Nashville and Chattanooga Railroad Company*, reported in 2 Swan, —, embraces the value of the land seized by the road, as well as the incidental damages to the remaining portion. The Legislature evidently, by the provisions of that act, intended to give a full remedy to all owners of land who were injured by a *proper and legitimate construction of the road*, and, at the same time, give a right of way in fee simple to the railroad company when the damages were paid. If lessees for years are not embraced, then the railroad company could not legitimately seize land thus held—they can get no title to such land by any proceeding under their charter, and their whole enterprize would be balked. We insist,

John Colcough *v.* The Nashville and Northwestern Railroad Company.

on the contrary, that the words "owners of land" used in the statute, means all owners, whether in fee, for life or for years. That in a proceeding for damages by a seizure of land, all of these owners must, or at least *may* be included in the petition for relief, and separate damages given to each by the jury in their report, or they may be apportioned by the Court on final hearing.

Such is the construction given to similar statutes in other States of the Union. 5 Metcalf Rep. —; 22 Penn. Rep., 29; 15 Pick., 198; 2 Sandford, 506.

The Courts of other States of the Union have also decided that damages similar to those charged in this declaration are included under the word "owners" given in our statutes. Redfield on Railways, p. 180 and notes. It is hardly necessary to affirm, that if this plaintiff has any remedy given him under the charter of incorporation to defendants, that this remedy is necessarily exclusive, and that no other could be pursued.

McKinney, J., delivered the opinion of the Court.

This was an action of assumpsit. The case comes up upon demurrer to the declaration, which was sustained in the Court below.

The gravamen of the action, as alleged in the declaration, and in argument, is: That the plaintiff was seized, as owner for an unexpired term of years, of a lot of ground in West Nashville, which was taken by the defendant, under the authority of its charter, as part of the road bed; and that the defendant, in the proper construction of the road, and in the exercise proper and rightful power and authority under the charter, pulled down and removed the fences and part of the dwelling-house which had been erected and were standing upon said lot; and likewise used and destroyed the corn, potatoes, &c., growing thereon.

The supposed foundation of the action is an *implied promise* on the part of the company to make reasonable compensation to the plaintiff for the injuries sustained by him.

The current of authority seems to be, that the statutory remedy given to land proprietors, for land taken for the construction of railways, is to be regarded, in general, as exclusive of all other remedies, and not merely cumulative. Redfield on Railways, p. 173.

The remedy prescribed in the particular charter under consideration, embraces not only "just compensation" for the land taken, but likewise for all such incidental loss or damage as must necessarily or reasonably result from the appropriation of the land and construction of the road in the manner authorized by the charter. These are all proper elements of the damage to the owner, in taking the land, to be considered of in the assessment of damages; and as to these, in general, the assessment will be conclusive.

This statutory remedy does not, however, contemplate or extend to damage or injuries to adjoining land, not authorized by the charter, nor to damages resulting from carelessness, negligence, or wilful trespasses in the execution of the work.

The plaintiff's counsel does not controvert the general principle that the statutory remedy is exclusive. But the argument assumes that this remedy is confined to the owner of the fee; and that, consequently, the owner of a less interest, as a tenant for life or years, is without remedy, unless permitted to resort to a common law action adapted to the nature of the case; and that as the injuries complained of by the plaintiff were occasioned by the defendant, not by any wrongful act, but in the exercise of a lawful right conferred by its charter, the law in such case will imply a promise to compensate the plaintiff.

The fallacy of the argument lies in the assumption that the remedy given by the statute is limited to the absolute owner of the fee. This is not so. The word "owner," as used in the charter, is not to be taken in any such restricted sense. The ownership of the estate, so to speak, may be severed. A life interest, or a term of years, may be carved out of the fee. And in such case the tenant for life or lessee, as well as the remainderman or lessor, is within the spirit and meaning of the charter; and they are entitled to recover compensation for the damage or injury by them respectively sustained.

It would seem that, in such cases, the persons vested with the several interests which constitute the entire estate, might join in a proceeding under the statute to obtain compensation; or, as they have several interests, proceed separately. In either mode of proceeding, however, the compensation for the entire damage must be apportioned according to the injury to their respective interests.

We are of opinion that the demurrer was properly sustained, and the judgment will be affirmed.

W. B. LILLARD, ADM'R, v. REESE W. PORTER et al.

1. ATTACHMENT. *Parties. Corporation. Stockholders.* Stockholders are distinct parties from the corporation in which they are stockholders, and legal proceedings against them cannot reach it. Hence, if an attachment is sued out in a proceeding in which the stockholders are made parties, but the corporation not, and is levied upon the effects of the corporation, no *lien is acquired* by virtue of the levy of said attachment.

2. SAME. *Same. Amendment. Effect of.* If an attachment is sued out and levied upon the property of a party who is not a defendant in the suit, and the bill is subsequently amended, bringing such party before the court, the lien of said attachment takes effect at the time of the filing of the amended bill, and does not relate back and attach at the time of the levy of the attachment. And if, after the levy of said attachment, but before the filing of the amended bill, said property is attached by another, in a proper proceeding against the owner, a prior lien is, thereby, acquired.

3. ESTOPPEL. *By answer in Chancery. Corporation.* If a party, by his answer in Chancery, admits the existence of a corporation by a particular name, he cannot be heard to deny, in said suit, that admission.

4. CENTRAL BANK OF TENNESSEE. *Change of name. Act of* 1854, *ch.* 294, § 68. The act of 1854, ch. 294, § 68, chartered the Eastern Division Mining Company, with banking powers, and the privilege of changing its name and title whenever deemed necessary. Under the power thus conferred, the name of said corporation was changed to the Central Bank of Tennessee.

FROM DAVIDSON.

This cause was heard before Chancellor FRIERSON, at the November Term, 1857. A transcript of the record was filed with the Clerk of the Supreme Court, and a writ of error obtained by Porter.

W. B. Lillard, Adm'r, v. Reese W. Porter et al

BOSTICK, for the complainant.

J. S. BRIEN, for Porter.

WRIGHT, J., delivered the opinion of the Court.

The complainant, Lillard, as the administrator of Summerhill, and the defendant, Porter, are attachment creditors of the Central Bank of Tennessee—a corporation created under the laws of this State.

A fund belonging to said Bank was attached and placed in the hands of a receiver in the cause.

The only question made here is as to the priority of these two creditors in this fund. The Chancellor decreed in favor of complainant, and we think properly, and affirm his decree.

The bill of Porter was filed, and his attachment levied before that of Summerhill. But he failed to make the Bank, his only debtor, a party. His bill was filed, alone, against Edward Belknap, E. R. Tremain and Samuel L. Haven—the stockholders and owners of said Bank—treating them as his debtors.

It was not until more than eleven months afterwards that, under an order of the Chancery Court, he filed an amended bill, making the Bank a party.

In the meantime, and within two days after the filing of Porter's original bill, Summerhill had, by a bill with the proper parties, legally attached the *same fund*.

We hold it to be too clear for argument, that Porter, by virtue of his attachment, acquired no lien upon the assets of this corporation, until he made it a party by the amendment to his bill. The stockholders were totally distinct persons from the corporation, and legal proceedings against them, could, in no way, reach it, or attach upon any of its assets.*

It is difficult to perceive what authority an officer could have under a writ in such a case. How could he lawfully seize or attach the property or assets of the Bank? Angell & Ames on Corporations, sections 643, 665, 666, 667, 674, 675, 676. *Fay* v. *Reager, Exr., et al.*, 2 Sneed, 200, 203.

The amendment of Porter's bill cannot be made to relate so as to prejudice or overreach the lien previously acquired by Summerhill under his attachment. 2 Sneed, 492, 203.

It is also insisted by Porter's counsel, that there never was any such corporation as the Central Bank of Tennessee, and that Belknap, Tremain & Haven, merely took upon themselves that name under which to carry on their banking business—without any charter or act of incorporation—and that they are liable to him as partners; and, therefore, his attachment was properly sued out and levied, and entitled him to the prior lien.

This position has nothing in it; because, in the first place, the bill filed by Summerhill, and Porter's answer thereto, and his amended bill, admit the existence of

---

* The lien of an attachment takes effect from the time of the levy, and not from the time of its issuance. 1 S. & M., ch. 449; *Harvey & New* v. *Champion*, 11 Hum., 569; *Snell & McGavock* v. *Allen*, 1 Swan, 208; *Wallace* v. *Hanley*, 4 J. J. Marsh., 622; *Martin* v. *Dryden*, 1 Gilm., 187. It would seem, therefore, that if an amended bill is filed making a new party, and seeking to subject his property to the payment of a debt, an attachment must be prayed for in said amended bill, in order to acquire a lien on the property. The issuance and levy of an attachment, on the original bill, upon the property of a person not a party to said bill, would create no lien, although the bill is, subsequently, amended, and said party brought before the court.

the Central Bank of Tennessee as a corporation. Angell & Ames, sec. 635.

And we also find that this corporation was created by the 68th section of the act of 1854, chapter 294, under the corporate style of the "Eastern Division Mining Company," with banking powers, and the privilege of changing its name and title, whenever it deemed it necessary. And we have in this record, from the pleadings of the parties, sufficient evidence to warrant the conclusion that it did change its name, and do business under the corporate title of the Central Bank of Tennessee. 3 Sneed, 631–2.

Decree affirmed.

JAMES BROWN *v.* THE STATE.

1. CRIMINAL LAW. *Selling liquor to a slave. Code, § 4865.* By section 4865 of the Code, any person who sells liquor to a slave except in the *master's presence*, or upon his written order, is guilty of a misdemeanor. The law contemplates a *visible* presence of the master; such a presence as, necessarily, implies a knowledge of, and assent to the act of selling the liquor to the slave. If the master watch at a short distance, with a view to detect the party in the violation of the law, he is not present within the meaning of this provision of the law.

2. SAME. *Same. Presentment. Incapacity to obtain license.* It is not necessary to aver in the presentment or indictment, that the defendant is a licensed grocery keeper, to authorize the court to pronounce judgment of incapacity to obtain a license in future. It is sufficient to warrant such judgment if the fact appears in evidence on the trial, or is otherwise satisfactorily established, before rendition of the judgment.

James Brown v. The State.

3. SAME. *Same. Code* §§ 4865 and 2678. The offences defined in secs. 4865 and 2678 of the Code, however similar, are not the same, and the conviction, whether upon the one section or the other, must be followed by the prescribed punishment.

FROM RUTHERFORD.

The defendant was convicted at the January Term, 1859, TURNER, J., presiding. He appealed.

E. A. KEEBLE and J. J. PALMER, for the plaintiff in error.

SNEED, Attorney General, for the State.

McKINNEY, J., delivered the opinion of the Court.

The plaintiff in error was convicted upon a charge of selling liquor to a slave, and was sentenced by the Court to pay a fine of $50, and to suffer four months imprisonment in the county jail of Rutherford, and declared incapable of ever hereafter obtaining a license for the sale of spirituous liquors in Rutherford county.

Several exceptions are urged against the conviction. First: It is insisted that the facts proved on the trial do not make a case under sec. 4865 of the Code. That section is as follows:

"Any person who sells, loans, or delivers to any slave, except for his owner or master, and then only in such owner or master's presence, or upon his written order, any liquor, &c., * * * is guilty of a misdemeanor; and shall be fined not less than fifty dollars, and imprisoned in the county jail at the discretion of the Court."

Brown was a grocery keeper in the town of Murfreesboro', and being suspected of selling liquor to slaves, a plan was concerted for his detection. At an early hour in the morning, before daylight, one of the owners of the slave and another person, gave the slave an empty *flask* and a *dime*, and the owner directed him to go to Brown's grocery and get a dime's worth of liquor. The slave proceeded to the back door of the grocery, knocked, and was admitted by Brown, and immediately came out with the flask full of spirituous liquor. The owner and person in company with him, followed the slave, and took a position behind a fence within three or four feet of the back door of the grocery; where, unperceived by Brown, they could distinctly see, and did see him, open the door and admit the slave—heard him speak to the slave—and saw him let the slave come out with the flask of liquor. These facts are proved by the person who accompanied the owner. The defence is, that if this were not an unlawful conspiracy, and therefore inadmissible as evidence to ground a conviction upon, it was, at least, a sale of liquor to the slave "in the master's presence," and consequently no violation of the law. As this point has been gravely made, we suppose it ought to be answered; and the answer is easy. Although, in a certain sense, the master was present, yet he was not present in the sense of the law. The law contemplates a *visible* presence of the master—such a presence as necessarily implies a knowledge of, and assent to the act of selling the liquor to the slave. It is the master's assent, express or implied, that furnishes the only legal justification of the act; and the facts of this case directly negative and exclude the idea of such assent.

2d. It is insisted that the Court erred in pronouncing judgment of incapacity to obtain a license in future, because it is not averred in the presentment that the defendant was *a licensed* grocery keeper. This was not necessary. We have repeatedly held, that it is sufficien to warrant such judgment, if the fact appears in evidence on the trial, or is otherwise satisfactorily established, before rendition of the judgment.

3d. It is argued that the Court erred in not basing the judgment on section 2678 of the Code—which prescribes a *milder* punishment for such an offence. The offences defined in the two sections referred to, however similar, are not the *same;* and, of course, the conviction, whether upon the one section or the other, must be followed by the prescribed punishment.

Judgment affirmed.

V. F. FORSEY AND WIFE *v.* JESSE LUTON, EX'R, *et al.*

1. WILL. *Construction. Life estate.* If land and slaves, together with a sufficiency of all kind of stock for an ample support, household and kitchen furniture, are bequeathed by a testator to his wife for life, with a remainder in the land to his son—the residue of the property to be sold at her death or marriage, and the money to be equally divided between his children named in the will—the widow takes an estate for life in the property bequeathed, with the right *to enjoy and use this* property in *specie,* and the same cannot be sold by the executors.

V. F. Forsey and Wife *v.* Jesse Luton, Ex'r, *et al.*

2. SAME. *Tenant for life. Rights of.* The rents and use of the land, the hire and labor of the slaves, crops, young animals—the offspring of those originally given—new furniture, &c., and the entire fruits of the life estate, belong, absolutely, to the tenant for life, and make no part of the estate of the testator.

3. SAME. *Same. Liability of. Remaindermen. Rights of.* If the tenant for life wastes, or converts any part of the estate for life to unauthorized uses, her estate will be liable for the amount so wasted or converted. But if the property were consumed in the use intended to be made of it, or perished by time, or death of animals, or wear and tear of furniture and farming tools, the rights of the remaindermen are defeated, and they are entitled to nothing, except what remains of the original stock.

4. SAME. *Same. Executor. Liability of.* If an executor participate, with the tenant for life, in a breach of trust, in the sale of any part of the estate for life, he is jointly liable with her for the value of the property sold. If she received the proceeds of the sale, her estate is, primarily, liable to the remaindermen.

FROM HUMPHREYS.

This cause was heard before Chancellor PAVATT, at the March Term, 1858. Both parties appealed.

ROBB & BAILY, for the complainants.

KIMBLE, for the defendants.

WRIGHT, J., delivered the opinion of the Court.

The contest here arises upon the construction of the will of William Jones, who died in the year 1844.

The second clause of the will reads as follows: "That all my perishable property, such as cattle, horses, hogs, &c., with the exception of a sufficiency for the support of the family, be sold by my executors, and all my honest debts paid out of the proceeds by my executors; the balance of money arising from such sale to be applied to support and educate my minor children." And the first part of the third clause, as follows: "I give to my beloved wife, Zilpha Jones, during her lifetime or widowhood, the tract of land whereon I now live, together with one hundred acres entered by me, lying in the southwest corner of the home tract, together with a sufficiency of all kinds of stock for an ample support, household and kitchen furniture."

And in a subsequent part of the same clause, he gives to his son, William B. G. Jones, after the death or marriage of his wife, the tract of land devised to her for life or widowhood; and directs her to dispose of two mares—one a sorrel and the other a brown mare—as she might think right to settle debts due and shortly to fall due.

He then gives his wife, during life or widowhood, his two negro women, Creasy and Alley, and her child Lucinda, and their increase; and, finally, provides that *all* the property given to his wife, except the land given to his son William, shall, at her death or intermarriage, be sold, and the money equally divided between his children named in the will.

The wife of the complainant is one of these children and remaindermen, and brings this bill against the personal representatives of the executors of her father to recover her share in his estate under the will.

The testator, at his death, left a considerable family, consisting of his widow and several minor children, and three slaves of little value, together with the tract of land whereon he lived, some stock and personal estate of no great value. He left very little, if any, money.

V. F. Forsey and Wife *v.* Jesse Luton, Ex'r, *et al.*

His executors, after his death, met and examined the amount and condition of his estate, and determined that it was not more than sufficient to support his family and educate his children, and, therefore, left it with the widow for that purpose, and made no sale of anything, but reported that the debts of the estate had been paid. The widow and her family resided upon the land devised to her for life until her death, in 1853, and she has no personal representative before the Court.

We are of opinion that, under this will, Zilpha Jones, the widow, took an estate for life in the land, slaves, and other personal estate devised to her—including therein so much of the testator's cattle, horses, hogs, stock of every kind, household and kitchen furniture, and other personal effects as were then necessary, amply to support her and her family; that it was the intention of the testator that his widow should *enjoy and use* this property *in specie*, and that the same should *not be sold* by his executors during her life.

It results that the remaindermen are only entitled to such part of the property originally given as remained after the death of the tenant for life. If the tenant for life has wasted or converted any part of the chattels to unauthorized uses, her estate will be liable for the amount so wasted or converted.

But if it were consumed in the use intended to be made of it, or perished by time, or death of animals, or wear and tear of furniture and farming tools, the rights of the remaindermen are defeated, and they are entitled to nothing except what remained of the original tock.

The executors of the testator cannot be held responsible for this property while in the possession of the widow.

The rents and use of the land, the hires and labor of the slaves, the accessions, crops, young animals—the offspring of those originally given—new furniture, tools, &c., constructed by the labor of the property given, and the entire fruits of the life estate belong to the tenant for life, absolutely, and make no part of the estate of the testator. *Woods* v. *Sullivan,* 1 Swan, 507; *Henderson* v. *Vaulx and Wife,* 10 Yer., 80; 1 Hum., 498.

We are satisfied, from the proof in this record, that the testator left very little, if any, money, and that the stock and other personal effects left with the widow were not more than sufficient for the support of herself and family, and the education of her minor children. But if desired, complainants may have an inquiry before the master as to this matter, with a view to reach their share in any surplus—charging the surplus, however, if any exist, with the funeral expenses and such debts of the estate, and the costs and charges of its administration, as may have been paid by the executors or the widow, or as may be proper.

And any of the personal estate which may have been advanced or given off to any of the children will not be charged either to the widow or executors, but the same will be adjusted among the children.

No account will be taken as to the rents of the Gulledge tract of land, because we are satisfied nothing is due complainants as to that part of the estate.

In the account of the sales of the personal estate, made in 1853, after the death of the tenant for life, by Henry Luton, the executor of William Jones, care will be taken only to charge him with the proceeds of such of the *original property or stock* of the testator as remained after the death of the tenant for life, upon the principles of this opinion.

And the said executor, or his estate, shall have such credits or allowances as may be just and proper in taking the account of such sale.

As to the slave Vina, alleged to have been sold by the widow, her estate should only be held to account to the remaindermen for her value at and interest from the time of the widow's death; and her personal representative should be made a party, so that it may be decreed against Henry Luton, the executor, if he participated with her in the breach of trust in the sale of this slave, will be held liable, jointly, with her estate, for the value of the slave and interest. As to his liability, we leave the question open for the decree of the Chancellor, when the personal representative of the widow shall become a party, upon the proofs and principles applicable to the case. If she received the proceeds of the sale, her estate will be held, primarily, liable. And if applied to any extent in payment of the debts of the testator, her estate will, so far, be allowed credit in the account with the remaindermen.

As the decretal order of the Chancellor, and the report of the clerk and master in the Chancery Court, proceed upon principles in some degree differing from the above, the former will be reversed and the latter set aside, and the cause remanded to the Chancery Court at Waverley to be further proceeded in upon the principles of this decree.

Ira Connell *v.* The County Judge of Davidson.

IRA CONNELL *v.* THE COUNTY JUDGE OF DAVIDSON.

1. JAIL INSPECTORS. *Powers of. Costs. Physician's bills.* The power conferred upon jail inspectors, to "make rules and regulations for the preservation of the health and decorum of the prisoners," is confined to general sanitary and police regulations. It does not authorize them to charge the county with physician's bills for medical attention to the prisoners. Such bills do not form an item of costs provided for by law in prosecutions, either, for felonies or misdemeanors.

2. APPROPRIATIONS. *County Judge. Justices of the County Court.* The County Judge has no power to make appropriations of county monies. This power belongs to the Justices of the County Court. A proceeding, therefore, to compel an appropriation of money out of the county treasury, should be against the Justices, and not against the County Judge.

FROM DAVIDSON.

This cause was heard at the September Term, 1858, BAXTER, J., presiding. He refused the application for a *mandamus*, and the applicant appealed.

A. L. DEMOSS, for the appellant.

EWING & COOPER, for the County Judge.

McKINNEY, J., delivered the opinion of the Court.

This was an application to the Circuit Court of Davidson for a *mandamus*, to compel the County Judge of said county to audit, and issue a warrant on the Treasurer of the county, for the payment of an account

Ira Connell v. The County Judge of Davidson.

claimed to be due to Connell, as a physician, for medical services alleged to have been rendered to prisoners (confined in the jail of said county) at the request of the Jail Inspectors of said county.

The County Judge, it seems, allowed the claim so far as services were rendered to prisoners confined upon a charge of misdemeanor; but refused to do so, where the persons were charged with felony.

The Court properly refused the application, on various grounds:

1st. The power conferred upon Jail Inspectors, to "make rules and regulations for the preservation of the health and decorum of the prisoners," is confined to general sanitary and police regulations. It does not authorize them to charge the county with physicians' bills for medical attention to the prisoners. Physicians' bills do not form an item of costs, provided for by law, in prosecutions either for felonies or misdemeanors. For such services, the prisoner is personally liable, as other persons. If able to pay, the physician must look to him for his bill; and if not, he must go unpaid, unless the County Court, or some one from motives of humanity, voluntarily assumes to pay.

2d. From this view, it results, that the County Judge has no authority, in the absence of an express order made by a competent number of the Justices, to allow any such claim; and, therefore, the allowance of any part of the claim, from the statement in the record, was a void act.

3d. If the jail inspectors possessed the power to bind the County Court, the proceeding, upon their refusal to pay, should be against the Justices, and not against the County Judge, who has no power to make appropriations of county moneys.

Judgment affirmed.

J. BEASLEY v. H. JENKINS et al.

WILL. *Construction. Persons taking as a class..* The fifth clause of the will is as follows: "I give all the balance of my land to my brother Hiram during his natural life; and, at his death, my will is, that all my lands be sold—except what I have given above to my two nephews—and the proceeds of said lands to be equally divided between all my brothers' and sisters' children." Held, that the fund vests in the described class, as a class, as it exists at the time fixed for distribution of the same; and, under this clause, it goes to the children of the brothers and sisters of the testator, as a class, living at the termination of the life estate.

FROM RUTHERFORD.

This is an appeal from a decree pronounced by Chancellor RIDLEY, at the December Term, 1858. The facts are stated in the opinion of the Court.

E. A. KEEBLE, for the complainant.

JAMES M. AVENT, for the defendant.

McKINNEY, J. delivered the opinion of the Court.

J. Beasley *v.* H. Jenkins *et al.*

The questions in this cause arise upon the construction of the will of Nimrod Jenkins, who died in Rutherford county, in August, 1837.

The fifth "item" of the will is as follows:

"I give all the balance of my land to my brother Hiram, during his natural life; and, at his death, my will is that all my lands be sold—except what I have given above to my two nephews—and the proceeds of said lands be equally divided between *all my brothers' and sisters' children.*"

In the sixth "item" of the will, the testator directs his executors to sell, *immediately*, his house and lot in the town of Murfreesboro', his negro man Dembo, and stock of horses, cattle, &c., "and divide the money *equally amongst my brothers' and sisters' children, as soon as possible.*"

Hiram Jenkins, the devisee for life, under the fifth clause of the will, died in 1857.

At the [death of the testator, in 1837, twenty years prior to the falling in of the life estate, there were a large number of children of the brothers' and sisters' of the testator, residing, some in Tennessee, and others in four different States of the Union. Since *then*, other children of testator's brothers' and sisters' have been born; and some who were then living, have died—some leaving issue, and others without issue.

The complainant, who is sole surviving executor of the will, brought this bill to obtain the direction of the Court, as to who are entitled to take the proceeds of the lands, under the fifth "item" of the will.

The Chancellor held, that the case must be governed by the rule laid down in *Satterfield* v. *Mayes*, 11 Hum.

J. Beasley v. H. Jenkins et al.

58. It is attempted to exclude the present case from the rule in Satterfield's case, by force of the provision of the sixth "item" of the will. By the latter clause, the fund thereby created, was to be divided, *immediately* on the death of the testator; and, of course, to such children of his brothers and sisters as were *then in being*. And as the same class of persons are the objects of the testator's bounty, in the fifth as in the sixth clause, the intention is apparent, as the argument assumes, that the same persons who constituted the class, under the sixth clause, and in whom the interest vested under it, should take the remainder interest, under the fifth clause. The effect of which construction would be, that such of the "children," living at the death of the testator, as still survive, and the issue of such as have since died, would take the remainder interest under the fifth clause; but "children" born of brothers and sisters, *since the testator's death*, would be excluded.

This construction cannot prevail. The rule governs both clauses alike. The fund created by each, vests in the described class, as a class, as it exists at the time fixed for distribution of the fund.

There is nothing in any subsequent decision that militates with the rule in Satterfield's case, as properly understood and applied.

Decree affirmed.

JOHN G. BRAZELTON *v.* WILLIAM BROOKS.

1. SET-OFF. *When allowed.* A debt or demand, to be set-off, must be an existing debt or demand at the commencement of the plaintiff's suit. Otherwise, it cannot be allowed.

2. SAME. Same. *Insolvency of the party. Chancery jurisdiction.* If a party, who is insolvent, recovers a judgment against one to whom he is indebted, but who was not a creditor, so as to entitle him to his set-off at law, the latter may come into a Court of Chancery and be allowed to set-off his demand against the judgment thus recovered against him.

3. SAME. *Chancery jurisdiction. Waiver of a defence.* If a bill is filed seeking to set-off a demand against a judgment recovered against the complainant. and the defendant answers, virtually, submitting to the set-off, it is error for the Court to refuse the relief. The answer is a waiver of any objection to the jurisdiction of the Court.

FROM FRANKLIN.

This cause was heard at the February Term, 1858, before Chancellor RIDLEY, who dismissed the bill. The complainant appealed.

A. S. COLYAR, for the complainant.

JOHN FRIZZELL, for the defendant, said:

Brooks insists that the decree of the Chancellor should be affirmed—

1. Because there is no evidence whatever sustaining the allegations of fraud; and, that in the absence of this, the Chancery Court had no jurisdiction, and complainant's bill must be dismissed.

John G. Brazelton *v.* William Brooks.

2. The indebtedness on the part of Brooks to Brazelton, if any existed, was a defence of which complainant could have availed himself in the suit at law under his plea of payment, and there is no evidence in the record that he did not do so.

3d. It is a defence of which Brazelton could have availed himself at law, if he did not; and could not be considered in the Chancery Court, unless the evidence showed that he was prevented from so doing by accident, fraud, or some act of Brooks, and there is no evidence to sustain such a position. *Rice* v. *R. R. Bank*, 7 Hum., 39; *Gwinn* v. *Newton*, 8 Hum., 710.

WRIGHT, J., delivered the opinion of the Court.

On the 20th of November, 1848, complainant, as the endorser of a note made by Brooks, paid for him to Robert and John Edwards, the sum of $381.22; and on that day become his creditor for that amount. Brooks, in 1853, in the month of March or April, had obtained a judgment in the Circuit Court at Winchester, against complainant, for about $400.00.

The complainant, on the 8th of April, 1858, filed his bill in the Chancery Court at Winchester, to set-off the amount that Brooks owed him against the judgment, and alleged that Brooks was insolvent, and if allowed to collect his judgment against complainant, without abating for the set-off, the debt would be lost.

John G. Brazelton *v.* William Brooks.

He asked and obtained an injunction to stay defendant until the set-off was allowed.

The Chancellor, upon the hearing, refused to allow the set-off upon the ground that it was matter of defence of which complainant could have availed himself upon the trial at law; and that he was not prevented from so doing by the fraud of the defendant, by accident, or by any act of the defendant.

In this, we think, he erred. Because we have been unable to find anything in this record which shows that complainant was a creditor of the defendant, or had paid the money to Robert and John Edwards, *at the time of the institution of his suit* against complainant; and it devolves on defendant to show this, if he insists complainant could have made his defence at law.

. A debt or demand, to be set-off, must have existed at the time of the commencement of the plaintiff's suit. *Jefferson County Bank* v. *Chapman,* 19 John's Rep., 322.

It is plain that the set-off was not used upon the trial at law, for the defendant, in his answer, admits the existence of the debt to complainant, and assumes the position that his judgment at law is more than sufficient to pay off any demand that complainant may have against him; and that, therefore, he ought not to be restrained from the prosecution of another action at law, which he had then pending against complainant for a matter not embraced in said judgment.

He thus, virtually, submits to the set-off. In his answer, he makes no reference to, or reliance upon the matter, on which the Chancellor decided the case. He waives all that, if it ever existed.

We suppose, that in view of the facts of this case, no valid objection can be urged against the jurisdiction of the Court, or the relief proposed. Because defendant is alleged in the bill to be insolvent, and that is, in effect, admitted in the answer. *Smith* v. *Ross and Beeler*, 3 Hum., 220.

And if this were not so, and complainant had at first no ground to come into a Court of Equity, still the defendant did not demur, but filed an answer, and this, under the force of the act of 1852, ch. 365, sec. 9, was a waiver of any objection to the jurisdiction of the Court. Acts of 1851–2, pages 673 and 674.

We reverse the decree, and decree for complainant.

SCOTT, BAKER & CO. *v.* R. C. BANDY.

1. PARTNERSHIP. *Power of partners to bind the firm.* Each partner is the authorized agent of the firm, and may bind it in all matters within the scope of the partnership business, but not beyond this, except by authority, express or implied, from the other members of the firm.

2. SAME. *Same. Acceptance for accommodation.* It is not within the scope of the business of a mercantile firm to draw, accept, or endorse the paper of neighbors for accommodation. Hence, one partner cannot bind the other members of the firm, by note, endorsement, or acceptance, in any transaction unconnected with the partnership business, and known to be so by the party taking it; nor for the party's own debt.

3. SAME. *Same. Same. Evidence. Subsequent ratification.* An act of one partner, beyond the scope of his authority, may be rendered obligatory on the firm by antecedent or subsequent sanction by the other members of the firm. Proof of such sanction may be presumptive.

Scott, Baker & Co. *v.* R. C. Bandy.

That one member was in the habit of extending accommodations to others in the name of the firm, with approbation, or without dissent, would be sufficient evidence of authority, and the firm would be bound.

4. SAME. *Evidence. Competency of a partner as a witness.* A partner is not a competent witness to prove the existence of the partnership: but when proven, he is competent to prove the justice of the demand against the firm. This principle does not render a partner competent to prove that an obligation created by him in the name of the firm, and not within the scope of the partnership business, was authorized, or adopted, by the other members, so as to render the firm liable.

FROM DAVIDSON.

This cause was heard before Judge BAXTER, at the January Term, 1858. Verdict and judgment for the defendant. The plaintiff appealed.

FOSTER & McEWING and E. H. EWING, for the plaintiffs.

R. J. MEIGS, for the defendant.

CARUTHERS, J., delivered the opinion of the Court.

The defendant is sued as acceptor of a draft or bill, which reads as follows:

"$1,145.03. Nashville, August 10, 1854. Twelve months after date, pay to the order of Scott, Baker & Co., eleven hundred and forty-five and 03–100 dollars, value received, and place to account of
       "BOWLING & WHELESS.
"To Messrs. BOWLING & BANDY.
"Accepted August 19, '54."

Scott, Baker & Co. v. R. C. Bandy.

This draft was drawn by Robert P. Bowling, of the firm of Bowling & Wheless, and was accepted for accommodation by George S. Bowling, of the firm of Bowling & Bandy. It was drawn and used for the payment of a note, for that amount, then held by the plaintiffs against the drawers, for goods.

By the law of partnerships, each partner is the authorized agent of the firm, and may bind it in all matters in the scope and range of the business in which it is engaged, but not beyond this, except by some express or *implied* authority. In a mercantile partnership, one partner has not the power to bind the others by any note, endorsement, or acceptance, in any transaction unconnected with the partnership business, and known to be so by the party taking it; nor for his own debt. Story on Part., p. 208, note, cited in *Bank of Tennessee* v. *Saffarans*, 3 Hum., 610. Such fact itself raises a presumption of want of authority, and is a fraud upon the other members by both parties. See same authorities.

It is no part of the business of a mercantile firm, to draw, accept, or endorse the papers of neighbors, for accommodation; no such thing is presumed to be contemplated by the parties in the formation of a partnership for trade, and consequently the power to do such acts is not communicated to any of the members, without express stipulation, and the firm is not bound, except by antecedent or subsequent sanction. But the proof of approval and ratification may be presumptive. That one member was in the *habit* of extending these accommodations to others, in the firm name, with approbation, or without dissent, would be sufficient evidence of authority, and all would be bound. This does not result from the fact of partnership, but presumed assent, from such general course of dealing.

It will be readily seen from these general principles that the defendant is not liable in this case as a member of the firm of Bowling & Bandy, unless it can be established by proof, positive or presumptive, that the act of acceptance by his partner, was authorized or sanctioned by him.

This is attempted to be done by proving what he said, as to his authority from his partner, and also by his own deposition. This evidence was rejected by the Court as inadmissible, and that is the error relied upon for reversal. There is no question but that the action must fail, if this proof is incompetent. The acceptance was by Bowling, in the name of Bowling & Bandy, for the accommodation of Bowling & Wheless, not in the presence of Bandy, and without any evidence of his authority or sanction, either express or implied, except what is contained in the rejected deposition. There is no controversy as to the existence of the partnership at the date of the acceptance. To prove that, was not the object of introducing the partner, Bowling. For that purpose he would have been clearly incompetent, by all the authorities. But it is just as clear, that, if that was admitted or proved by others, he could be called to prove the "justice of the plaintiff's demand." *Vanzant v. Kay*, 2 Hum., 106. But what does that mean? The fact in that case, which it was held he was competent to prove, was that the note, to which he signed the name of the firm, was for a just amount against it, and so the demand against the firm was just, and should be a charge upon all the members, because it was made by a partner in the business of the firm. Whether even that position can be reconciled to the decision in *Foster* v. *Hall & Eaton*, 4 Hum., 354, may be questioned. The same rule would extend to proof of the justice of an account, or other proper demand, arising out of the firm business.

But the matter to be proved here by a partner was, that an act done outside of the firm business, and an obligation created by him in the name of the firm, was authorized or ratified by the other member. Not the "justice of the demand," but the existence of it as against his partner. Can he prove that? The case of *Vanzant* v. *Kay* does not extend to that question.

The proposition is to prove by one partner that an obligation created by him in the name of the firm, not within the scope of its business, was authorized or adopted by the other member, so as to create a joint and several liability. We are aware of no case that would authorize this. He is solely liable, and the effect of his evidence for the plaintiff, would be to cast it *all* upon the shoulders of another, in the first instance, and *one half*, ultimately, and in any event. There can be no principle that would authorize this. It is not to establish an existing demand against the firm, originating in the course of its legitimate operations, as in the case of Vanzant, but to establish a new and distinct authority for an unauthorized act of his own, deleterious to the firm, and binding *alone* upon himself, without this evidence.

This is more analogous to the case in 4 Hum., 449, where one joint maker of a note was held incompetent witness against the other to prove the making of the note.

Some other points are made upon the charge of the Court, but they are not seriously pressed as grounds for reversal, and need not be noticed. It is very manifest that without the excluded evidence the plaintiff could not have succeeded in making the defendant liable.

Let the judgment be affirmed.

ANDREW WOODS *v.* JOSEPH M. BURROUGH *et al.*

1. SLAVES. *Sale of under a will. Bill of sale or other writing not necessary, if possession delivered.* If a sale of slaves is made under a power created by a will, and is absolute, and possession delivered by the executor, no bill of sale, or other written evidence is necessary to transfer the title to the purchaser. The verbal sale accompanied by delivery of possession, is as operative to pass the title, as a bill of sale.

2. LIEN. *On slaves. Reserved by parol contract.* As respects personal property, no lien exists by implication of law, and in no other mode can a valid lien be created in favor of the seller of a personal chattel, when the legal title and possession have been parted with, than by express contract, which, at least, as against creditors and subsequent purchasers without notice, must be in writing, and duly proved and registered.

FROM FRANKLIN.

This cause was heard at the November Term, 1858, before Chancellor RIDLEY, who pronounced a decree for the complainant. The defendants appealed.

Andrew Woods v. Joseph M. Burrough et al.

P. TURNEY, for the complainant:

On a verbal sale and delivery of a slave at a fixed price, to be paid on a day certain; but until paid, the title to remain in the seller, the payment is a condition precedent; till the performance of which, the property does not become absolute in the buyer, nor liable to his debts. *Gambling* v. *Read*, Meig's Reports, 281.

Where a fund is secured by the principal debtor for the payment of a debt, the security will be entitled, in equity, to have it applied to the discharge of the debt. *Rodes & Kelly* v. *Crockett & Adams*, 2 Yer., 346.

The interposition of Courts of Equity is not confined to cases strictly of two funds and of different mortgages, for it will be applied in favor of sureties when the creditor has collateral securities or pledges for his debt; in which case the Court will place the security exactly in the situation of the creditor, as to the securities or pledges, whenever he is called upon to pay the debt. 1 Story Eq., sec. 638.

A. S. COLYAR, for the defendants:

The first question is, did the administrator with the will annexed make a valid sale of the negro? That a sale of a slave by parol, when possession accompanies or follows the sale, is valid, notwithstanding the act of 1784, there can be no doubt. 1 Hum. R., 466; 1 Haywood, 58; 2 Haywood, 66; 5 Yer., 282; 10 Yer., 507; Meig's R., 281.

Andrew Woods v. Joseph M. Burrough et al.

The act of 1831 applies, alone, to creditors and purchasers, and does not, in any way, change the law as it stood *between the parties.*

If the sale was a good one, and the title vested, was the lien of any binding force against an attaching creditor, being *in parol?* This case does not involve the question, whether a sale may not be made and the seller retain the title, *by contract,* to secure the purchase money, or rather, retain the title until the purchase money is paid.

No such question is raised. The bill alleges *a sale,* but sets up that a lien was retained. This cannot be done; to retain a *lien,* and to keep the title until the purchase money is paid, for the purpose of securing it, are very different things. The former must be done by writing, and it registered, to be good against creditors; but the latter may be done by parol. *Bradshaw* v. *Thomas,* 7 Yer., 497; *Gambling* v. *Read,* Meig's R., 281, and authorities cited; 2 Pick., 512; Story on Contracts, sec. 499.

Retaining a *lien* is not retaining the title, for a *lien* is not a property in the thing, nor does it constitute a right of action for the thing. 2 Story Eq. Jurisprudence, 1215. It is simply a charge upon the property. Same authority.

A lien upon personal property can only exist when connected with the possession, or right to the possession. 2 Story Eq., 1216, and note 2.

Andrew Woods v. Joseph M. Burrough et al.

McKinney J., delivered the opinion of the Court.

In the year 1856, the personal representative of the estate of William Duncan, deceased, in pursuance of a power in him vested by the will of the testator, sold certain slaves belonging to the estate, at public auction.

By the terms of sale, which were publicly announced at the time, a credit of twelve months was to be allowed, the purchasers giving bond with approved security; and it was further stated, that a *lien* would be retained upon the slaves sold, until the purchase money should be paid.

One Oldham became the purchaser of a negro man named "Dock," at said sale, at the price of $1053.00, for which he executed an obligation, with the complainant as his surety; and, thereupon, the slave was delivered into the possession of Oldham. No bill of sale was executed by the executor, to Oldham, nor does it appear that any such thing was thought of, or deemed necessary, by the parties. There was no reservation of the *title* to the slave; on the contrary, it is manifest from the proof, that it was the intention and understanding, on all hands, that both the right of property and possession should pass immediately to the purchaser; nothing more being contemplated by the reservation than a naked lien; and even of this, there was no notice in the written terms of sale, as set forth in the advertisement, nor in the obligation taken for the purchase money, it rested merely in *parol*.

It appears that on the 18th of November, 1857, suit was brought upon the obligation for the price of the the slave "Dock," against Oldham and complainant.

Andrew Woods *v.* Joseph M. Burrough *et al.*

Judgment was obtained thereon on the 29th of March, 1858, and said judgment was satisfied by the complainant, Woods, on the 17th of July, 1858, as the surety of Oldham.

It further appears, that a few days after the institution of said suit against Oldham and the complainant, to-wit: On the 24th of November, 1857, the defendants, who were creditors of Oldham, filed an attachment bill against him, whereon process of attachment was awarded by the Ceancellor; and, on the same day, they caused their attachment to be levied on the slave "Dock," together with other property of the said Oldham's.

The complainant, thereupon, filed this bill to enjoin the defendants from proceeding to subject said slave "Dock" to the satisfaction of their debt. The supposed equity of the bill is grounded upon the assumption, that the personal representative of Duncan retained a valid lien upon the slave to secure the payment of the purchase money; and complainant having been compelled to discharge the debt, as surety of the purchaser, is entitled to be substituted to the lien; and that, as against this equity, the defendants attachment is inoperative.

The Chancellor so decreed; and the defendants appealed.

The question is, can the decree be maintained? We think not. We take it to be too clear to admit of discussion, that the doctrine of an implied lien, in equity, in favor of the vendor of *real* estate (where the legal title has been conveyed to the vendee) to secure the unpaid purchase money, and no personal security has been given, has no application to sales of personal property: That, as respects the latter species of property, no lien exists by implication of law; and in no other mode can a valid lien be created in favor of the seller of a personal chattel, where the legal title and possession have been parted with, than by express contract, which, at least, as against creditors and subsequent purchasers without notice, must be in writing, and duly proved and registered. We do not controvert the principle laid down in *Gambling* v. *Read*, Meig's R., 281. That case establishes, that, on a verbal sale of a slave, though possession be delivered to the purchaser, an agreement between the parties at the time, that the right of property, or title, shall remain in the seller, as security for the purchase money, is valid; and that in such case, the payment of the money is a condition precedent to the passing of the right of property to the purchaser, and that such agreement is valid without registration, not falling within the description of any agreement required by our law to be registered. The same principle is recognized in *Houston* v. *Dyche*, Meig's R., 76, and other subsequent cases. But these cases are wholly unlike the one under consideration. They rest upon the simple fact that the right of property was never parted with by the owner, but by express contract was retained to secure the purchase money; the sale was only conditional. But, in the case before us, the sale was absolute and complete, and personal security taken for the purchase money. The sale was made under a power created by the will of the testator. No bill of sale, or other written evidence, was at all necessary to transfer the title to the purchaser. The verbal sale, accompanied by delivery, without any reservation of title,

Pilcher and Cataulis, Adm'rs, v. Richard Smith and Wife.

was as operative to pass the title to the purchaser, as would have been a bill of sale.

This principle is established by repeated decisions of this Court. 5 Yer., 282; 10 Yer., 507.

In this view it is clear, that no lien existed in favor of Duncan's representative; and, therefore, there is nothing to which the complainant can be substituted. The decree will be reversed, and the bill be dismissed, but without costs.

PILCHER AND CATAULIS, ADM'RS, *v.* RICHARD SMITH AND WIFE.

1. SPECIFIC PERFORMANCE. *Feme covert. Contract by.* A covenant to convey real estate, executed by a *feme covert*, who is not invested with power to sell and convey the same as a *feme sole*, is void, and will not be specifically executed by a Court of Chancery.

2. SALE OF REAL ESTATE. *Feme covert. Fraud.* The legal disability of coverture carries with it no license or privilege to practice fraud or deception on other innocent persons, nor will the disability be permitted to protect a person in doing so. Thus, if a married woman covenant to convey land, and, by reason of her coverture, the covenant is void, it would be a fraud for her to avoid the contract without restoring the purchase money, and it will not be permitted.

3. SAME. *Same. Rescission of contract. Refunding of the purchase money.* A married woman cannot avoid a sale of real estate made by her, without refunding the consideration money paid by the purchaser.

4. SAME. *Same. Chancery jurisdiction. Specific performance. Rescission of contract. Lien.* A purchaser of real estate from a *feme covert* whose covenant is void, has a right to come into a Court of Equity to obtain, either a specific execution, or rescission of the contract. And if the *feme covert* resist a specific execution, and the contract is re-

Pilcher and Cataulis, Adm'rs, v. Richard Smith and Wife.

scinded, as an incident to the rescission, the Court will order the repayment of the purchase money, and declare a lien upon the land to secure its payment.

FROM DAVIDSON.

At the November Term, 1858, Chancellor FRIERSON pronounced a decree in favor of the complainants. The defendants appealed.

JOHN REID, for the complainants.

WILLIAM THOMPSON, for the defendants, cited and commented upon Story on Con., § 95; 1 Story's Eq., § 243; *Jones* v. *Perry*, 10 Yer., 80; *Bird* v. *Pollard*, 4 Hum., 362; *Alston* v. *Boyd*, 6 Hum., 504; Code, §§ 2869, 3229, 3236, 2481.

McKINNEY, J., delivered the opinion of the Court.

On the 15th of July, 1846, the defendant, Hannah Smith, (being then a married woman,) bargained and covenanted to convey to Hannah Higgins (a free woman of color) a lot of ground in Nashville, for the consideration of $350. The bond for title recites that $200 of the purchase money was paid down, and a note executed for the residue, due on the 5th of September, 1847; upon payment of which, said Hannah Smith bound herself in the penalty of $700, to make the purchaser a good and sufficient title to said lot.

The lot in question was conveyed by Alfred Balch

to Hannah Smith, on the 22d of September, 1845—she being, at the date of the conveyance, a *feme covert.* It is intimated in the record that the purchase money was paid by the husband, and that the conveyance was to the wife, to protect the property from the husband's creditors.

It is admitted in the answer that the price of the lot was fully paid by the purchaser. And it is also shown, that, in pursuance to the title bond, the defendant, Richard Smith, husband of said Hannah Smith, executed a conveyance to the purchaser for said lot, but the defendant, Hannah, utterly refused to join therein. She distinctly admits the payment in full of the purchase money, but states that it was paid to her husband. The proof tends to establish that her husband received it as her agent, though the fact is not very clearly made out.

Hannah Higgins was put in possession of the lot at the time of the purchase, and continued in possession until her death, which took place in March, 1856. Complainant, Cataulis, is her sole heir-at-law, and the other complainant is the administrator of her estate.

In December, 1855, the defendant, Hannah Smith, caused an action of ejectment to be instituted to oust said Higgins of the possession of said lot; and, after her death, the suit was revived against the complainant, as her heir-at-law.

This bill was then brought to have a specific execution of the contract, or, if that be not allowable, to have the purchase money refunded, and compensation for improvements, with a prayer for general relief, and, in the meantime, to have the action of ejectment enjoined.

Pilcher and Cataulis, Adm'rs, v. Richard Smith and Wife.

The Chancellor refused a specific execution, but decreed that the purchase money should be refunded, with interest, and declared it a lien upon the lot; and also decreed, that improvements which had enhanced the permanent value of the lot should be set off against the rents.

We think the decree refusing to execute the contract was proper. It is not pretended that Mrs. Smith was invested with any power to sell or convey the lot as a *feme sole;* and being a married woman, her covenant to convey was, simply, void.

But though this be so, it must be borne in mind that the legal disability of coverture, or of infancy, carries with it no license or privilege to practice fraud or deception on other innocent persons; nor will the disability be permitted to protect them in doing so. *Barham* v. *Turbeville,* 1 Swan, 487; 1 Story's Eq., § 385, and note 3; 2 Kent's Com., 240.

The attempt, on the part of Mrs. Smith, to avoid the contract by resorting to a recovery in ejectment, without restoring the purchase money, was an aggravated fraud against an innocent purchaser, whose *caste* and condition entitled her to expect the observance of good faith on the part of those who had dealings with her.

It is well settled, in equity, that an infant cannot avoid a sale made by him during infancy, without refunding the consideration money. *Smith* v. *Evans,* 5 Hum., 70. And we understand the principle to be, alike, applicable to a married woman.

But it is assumed in the argument, that, inasmuch as Mrs. Smith is not actively invoking the aid of a Court of Equity to restore her to the possession of the lot, but has elected to resort to the legal forum, which is not possessed of the power to compel her to do equity, or to impose terms as a condition of granting relief, it is not competent to a Court of Equity, at the instance of the purchaser, to compel her to refund the purchase money; that the remedy of the purchaser, if any exists, is at law. The first answer to this objection is, that there being no demurrer to the bill, no exception can be taken to the jurisdiction on the hearing. But, this consideration aside, we think it would be sticking in the bark to hold, that, although a Court of Equity would not permit Mrs. Smith to recover the lot without restoring the consideration money, yet it is powerless to restrain her from doing so at law. If, upon an immutable principle of natural justice, the defendant be bound to refund the purchase money before being entitled to demand back the property sold, shall her fraudulent artifice of resorting to a Court of Law, in order to evade the repayment, debar a Court of Equity, on the application of the purchaser, from compelling her to do equity?

But if we were to admit the law to be so, though we do not, still, upon the facts of this case, we think the decree ordering the repayment of the purchase money, and making it a lien upon the lot, was proper, in a different view, and is maintainable upon a well established general principle. The purchaser had an undoubted right to come into a Court of Equity, without regard to the action of ejectment, to obtain either a specific execution, or rescission of the contract. The husband was willing that the contract should be executed, and if the wife had voluntarily assented thereto, there can be no question but the Court might have so decreed. But having refused, as was her right, there can be as little doubt that the Court might decree a rescission; and as incident to the latter relief, it was clearly competent to declare a lien upon the lot to secure the repayment of the purchase money—and this against a married woman, as much as against one free from disability, upon the principle that such disability cannot be a protection against fraud.

The decree will be affirmed.

TERRENCE MCMANNUS v. THE STATE.

1. EVIDENCE. *Privileged communication. Attorney and client.* Communications between a client and his attorney are under the seal of confidence, and cannot be disclosed in proof. It is not necessary to the application of this rule of evidence that a suit should be pending or anticipated, nor that there should be a regular retainer, or the payment of a fee. But the communication must be in a professional character, in relation to some act passed, or right or interest in existence.*

2. SAME. *Same. Same. Does not apply to abstract legal questions.* This rule of evidence relative to privileged communications, does not apply to cases where abstract legal opinions are sought and obtained on

---

* Can the party. or client himself be compelled, by a bill in Chancery, to produce a case which he has laid before counsel, with the opinion given thereon? *Radcliffe* v. *Fursman,* 2 Bro. P. C., 514; *Newton* v. *Beresford,* 1 You., 376; *Bolton* v. *Corp. of Liverpool,* 1 My. & K., 88; *Pearse* v. *Pearse,* 11 Jur., 52; 19 Ves., 267; 1 Green. Ev., § 240, and notes.

Terrence McMannus v. The State.

general questions of law, either civil or criminal. In such cases, no facts are or need be disclosed, implicating the client, and so there is nothing, of a confidential character, to conceal.

FROM MONTGOMERY.

The prisoner was convicted of manslaughter and sentenced to imprisonment for three years, at the January Term, 1858, TURNER, J., presiding. He appealed in error to this Court.

G. A. HARREL, for the plaintiff in error.

SNEED, Attorney General, for the State.

CARUTHERS, J., delivered the opinion of the Court.

This is an appeal in error from a conviction of manslaughter, in the Criminal Court at Clarksville.

The main question is as to the admission of the evidence of Thomas W. Wisdom, an attorney, which it is insisted was under the seal of professional confidence. The facts are thus stated by himself:

"The evening before the killing, the defendant came to his office, where witness, Johnson, Lindsey, and several other gentlemen were, and enquired for Mr. Quarles, his partner, who was the Attorney General; was told that he was absent. Stated that he wished to see him in reference to a contemplated suit against one Thurman, a railroad contractor, for whom the defendant had been at work, and with whom he stated he had an unsettled account. Witness talked to him some with regard to his suit with Thurman." Then said he had a difficulty with a man, got his finger cut, and wrested from him the knife, which he exhibited, and witness thinks it is the same shown on the trial. "He then asked the witness in regard to the law of self-defence—how far a party assailed could go in defending himself. The defendant was much intoxicated. Witness states that he did not regard the relation of client and attorney as existing between defendant and himself. He did not suppose the defendant knew him, or knew him to be a lawyer, but he was the partner of Quarles, the person enquired for by defendant; that both their names, on separate signs, were upon the office door. He advised him as desired."

Objection was made to him as incompetent, but the Court overruled it.

Are these facts sufficient to establish the relation of client and attorney? If so, a new trial must be granted, because we cannot tell what effect it may have had upon the jury, as it was a very pregnant fact occurring just the evening before the homicide. It showed that his mind was engaged on that subject, and he was desirous to know how far he could go and be safe under the law. That is the very defence set up in this case.

Sound public policy seems to have required the establment of the rule that facts communicated by a *client* to his *counsel*, are under the seal of confidence, and cannot be disclosed in proof. It is a rule of protection to the client, more than a privilege to the attorney. The latter is not allowed, if he would, to break this seal of secrecy and confidence. It is supposed to be necessary to the administration of justice, and the prosecution and defence of rights, that the communications between clients and their attornies should be free and unembarrassed by any apprehensions of disclosure, or betrayal. The object of the rule is, that the professional intercourse between attorney and client should be protected by profound secrecy. It is not necessary to the application of this rule, as was held in some of the old cases, now overruled, that a suit should be pending or anticipated, (1 Greenl. Ev., 240, note,) nor that there should be a regular retainer or the payment of fees. 1 Greenl. on Ev., § 241. But he must be applied to for advice or aid in his professional character, and that in relation to some act past, or right, or interest in existence. The rule has no reference to cases like the one before us, where abstract legal opinions are sought and obtained on general questions of law, either civil or criminal. In such cases no facts are or need be disclosed implicating the party; and so there is nothing to conceal, of a confidential nature.

If the defendant had perpetrated an act, and applied for legal counsel and advice in relation to it, secrecy would be imposed; but where no act had been done, or if done, not disclosed, and only a general opinion on a question of law was asked, there would be no *professional* confidence. It would be monstrous to hold, that if counsel was asked and obtained, in reference to a contemplated crime, that the lips of the attorney would be sealed, when the fact might become important to the ends of justice in the prosecution of crime. In such a case the relation cannot be taken to exist. Public policy would forbid it. We presume the rule has never been extended so far, nor will it be.

The State, then, was entitled to this testimony, whether it was entitled to much or little force in establishing the crime upon defendant.

The defendant's counsel also contend that the proof is insufficient to sustain the verdict. Upon weighing it carefully, we have come to a different conclusion, and concur with the jury in their opinion that the crime of manslaughter, at least, is fu'ly made out. The commencement of the fight was not seen, but the circumstances show that the fatal stab must have been given under a state of facts that would, at the lowest, amount to the crime of which he was convicted.

The judgment will be affirmed, and the sentence, of five years imprisonment from this day, enforced.

JAMES RIPPY *v.* THE STATE.

1. CRIMINAL LAW. *Homicide. Self-defence.* To excuse homicide on the ground of self-defence, the danger to life, or of great bodily harm, must be either real, or honestly believed to be so, at the time of the killing, and such belief of danger must be founded on reasonable grounds. There must, not only, be sufficient cause to authorize the fear of death or great bodily harm, but such fear must be really entertained, and the killing done under an honest and well founded belief that it is absolutely necessary in self-defence.

2. SAME. *Same. Same. Antecedent menaces.* The danger must be present and imminent. There must be some words or overt act at the time clearly indicative of a *present* purpose to do the injury. Previous threats, or even hostile acts, how violent soever they may be, will not, of themselves, excuse a homicide.

3. SAME. *Same. Same. Same. Evidence.* The character of the deceased for violence, as well as his animosity to the defendant as indicated by his words and actions, then and before, are proper matters for the consideration of the jury in ascertaining whether the defendant had reasonable cause to fear, and did fear, that his life would be taken, or great bodily harm done him.

FROM BEDFORD.

The plaintiff in error was tried and convicted in the Circuit Court of Bedford county, at the April Term, 1858, DAVIDSON, J., presiding. He appealed.

W. H. WISENER, for the plaintiff in error.

SNEED, Attorney General, for the State.

CARUTHERS, J., delivered the opinion of the Court.

James Rippy was indicted in the Circuit Court o Bedford county for the murder of Houston Porter, an convicted of murder in the second degree, and senten ced to twenty-one years confinement in the penitentiary

The verdict is well sustained by the testimony. Th defence, it seems, was rested upon the existence or ap prehension of danger to himself at the time of th homicide. It is now insisted there is error in th charge on that doctrine. The objection is confined t this clause.

"It is argued the deceased made violent threat against the life of defendant long before, and up to short period of the killing, and that these threats com ing to the knowledge of defendant, he had a right t

James Rippy v. The State.

kill the deceased on sight. Such is not the opinion of the Court; but to excuse the defendant, and therefore acquit him, the evidence ought to be such as to have reasonably satisfied the defendant that the deceased, at the time of the killing, was doing some overt act, or making some demonstration showing a present intention to carry such threats into execution, otherwise it would not excuse him."

The law, as thus laid down by the Court, is substantially correct. The doctrine of the Grainger case, as explained by that of Copeland, is undoubtedly the law. Yet no case has been more perverted and misapplied by advocates and juries. We have had one case before us in the last few years, in which the broad proposition stated in the first of the above extract was charged as law. But for this, and the indications that it has obtained to some limited extent in the legal profession, it would scarcely be deemed necessary to notice it. There is no authority for such a position. It would be monstrous. No Court should for a moment entertain or countenance it. The criminal code of no country ever has, nor, as we presume, ever will, give place to so bloody a principle.

The law on this subject is, that, to excuse a homicide, the danger of life, or great bodily injury, must either be real, or honestly believed to be so at the time, and upon sufficient grounds. It must be *apparent* and *imminent*. Previous threats, or even acts of hostility, how violent so ever, will not of themselves excuse the slayer, but there must be some words or overt acts at the time clearly indicative of a *present* purpose to do the injury. Past threats and hostile actions, or antecedent circumstances, can only be looked to in connection with present demonstrations as grounds of apprehension. To constitute the defence, the *belief* or apprehension of danger must be founded on sufficient circumstances to authorize the opinion that the deadly purpose then exists, and the *fear* that it will *at that time* be executed. The character of the deceased for violence, as well as his animosity to the defendant, as indicated by words and actions then and before, are proper matters for the consideration of the jury on the question of reasonable apprehension. Even if sufficient cause to fear does exist, but the deed is not perpetrated under the apprehension it is calculated to inspire, or the fear is feigned or pretended, the defence will not be available. So a case must not only be made out to authorize the fear of death or great harm, but such fear must be really entertained, and the act done under an honest and well founded belief that it is absolutely necessary to kill at that moment, to save himself from a like injury. It is scarcely necessary to remark that a real or apparent necessity, brought about by the design, contrivance, or fault of the defendant, is no excuse.

If any less injury than death or great bodily harm is feared or indicated by the circumstances, the plea of *self-defence* will not be sustained, but the degree of the crime may be reduced.

According to these principles, the guilt of the defendant was clearly made out—there was no error in the charge, and the judgment will be affirmed.

JAMES W. STARNES AND WIFE v. JAS. P. ALLISON et al.

1. SPECIFIC PERFORMANCE. *Not enforced if title defective.* A specific performance of a contract for the sale of land will not be enforced, unless the vendor can make the vendee a good and indefeasible title.

2. WILL. *Construction of. Settlement. Power of appointment.* The will contains the following clauses: "I give, devise and bequeath urto may daughter, Mary C. Rudder, all my estate or property of every description," * * * "of which I may die seized or possessed," * * * "to have and to hold all of said estate or property unto her, the said Mary C. Rudder, her heirs and assigns forever. But if the said Mary C. should marry, said estate or property is to be her own sole and separate estate, and the same, and every part and parcel thereof, as well as its increase and profits, shall remain free from the contracts and obligations of any person with whom she may intermarry, during her *coverture*, as though she had remained sole." * * * "In the event of the death of my said daughter without lawful issue, living at the time of her death, it is my will that all the estate and property, devised and bequeathed unto her, shall go as she may, by any instrument in the nature of a last will under her hand and seal, witnessed by three or more witnesses, direct; and the power to dispose of the same and its increase in the event of her death without issue, either before or after the age of twenty-one years, and either while single or covert, is hereby given her, to be exercised and executed in the manner just prescribed, and in no other manner; but in the event she leaves issue, she may provide for that issue in whatever manner she deems best, and in that event my intent is not to limit her power over her estate at her death, in any manner whatever." Held:

  1. That the property bequeathed to the said Mary C. Rudder, and its increase and profits are restricted to her separate use, and guarded against the contracts and obligations of her husband.

  2. She may, *at her death*, whether she be a minor or of age, single or covert, if she have no issue then living, dispose of her property, at discretion, by an instrument under seal in the nature of a will, with three or more witnesses. This power is to be exercised in the manner prescribed, and in no other. The daughter cannot dispose of the property by deed, gift, or sale.

  3. In the event she leaves issue, she may provide for that issue as she thinks best, not confining her to an equal distribution of the

James W. Starnes and Wife *v.* Jas. P. Allison *et al.*

property among them. Her power is to be unlimited, but it must be exercised at the time and in the manner pointed out by the testator.

4. If the daughter marry, and she and her husband sell the real estate, a specific performance of the contract cannot be enforced, because they cannot convey a good title to the purchaser.

FROM WILLIAMSON.

Decree for the complainants at the October Term, 1858, before Chancellor FRIERSON. The defendants appealed.

JOHN MARSHALL and W. F. COOPER, for the complainants.

E. C. COOK, R. HOUSTON and N. S. BROWN, for the defendants.

CARUTHERS, J., delivered the opinion of the Court.

This bill is filed for the specific performance of a contract made the 4th of May, 1858, for the, sale by the complainants, of a tract of 637 acres of land in Williamson county, for $30 per acre, to the defendants.

The defendants resist upon the ground that a good title cannot be made to them. This is the only defence to the prayer of the bill.

The title is in the complainant, Mary C. Starnes, formerly Mary C. Rudder, and was derived from her father, Richard H Rudder, under his will.

The two "items" upon which the question depends, are as follows:

James W. Starnes and Wife *v.* Jas. P. Allison *et al.*

"Item 1st. I give, devise and bequeath unto my daughter, Mary C. Rudder, al! my estate or property of every description, * * * * of which I may die seized or possessed, * * * to have and to hold, all said estate or property unto her, the said Mary C. Rudder, her heirs and assigns forever. But if the said Mary C. should marry, said estate or property is to be her own sole and separate estate, and the same and every part and parcel thereof, as well as its increase and profits, shall remain free from the contracts and obligations of any person with whom she may intermarry, during her coverture, as though she had remained sole."

"Item 2d. In the event of the death of my said daughter without lawful issue living at the time of her death, it is my will that all the estate and property devised and bequeathed unto her, shall go as she may by any instrument in the nature of a last will, under hand and seal, witnessed by three or more witnesses, direct; and the power to dispose of the same and its increase, in the event of her death without issue, either before or after the age of twenty-one years, and either while single or covert, is hereby given her, to be exercised and executed in the manner just prescribed, and in no other manner; but in the event she leaves issue, she may provide for that issue in whatever manner she deems best, and in that event, my intent is not to limit her power over her estate at her death in any manner whatever."

Mary C. was the only child of the testator, and he left to her all his large estate, except one tract of land devised in the third item of his will. She was then unmarried and quite young. His leading object seemed

James W. Starnes and Wife *v.* Jas. P. Allison *et al.*

to be, that she should not only be protected in the enjoyment of the property accumulated by a long life of labor and toil, but be entrusted with the discretion of making such disposition of it as her pleasure or sense of duty might dictate in any and all events. But he was, perhaps, a man of experience and observation, and contemplated the dangers that might arise in certain changes in her condition, that would probably come up in her pursuit of happiness when she reached the state of womanhood. So in case of her marriage, all the property given, and its increase and profits, were restricted to her separate use, and guarded against the contracts and obligations of her husband. No power of disposition would be obtained by the husband under his marital right. So far, no express restrictions are imposed upon her power of disposition, nor is any particular mode prescribed by which it may be done. That is reserved for the next item, and both have to be taken together in order to ascertain the extent of her rights and powers.

The time and mode of disposition is fixed in the second item:

She may, *at her death*, whether she be a minor or of age, "single or covert," if she have no issue then living, direct how her property shall go; but this must be done by some instrument under seal, in the nature of a will, with *three or more* witnesses. Here is an evidence of his solicitude to protect her against influence or imposition. This power, he says, shall be exercised in the manner prescribed, "*and in no other manner.*" She is not permitted to do it by gift, or sale, or deed. Since the case of *Morgan* v. *Elam*, 4 Yer., 374, where this doctrine is fully examined and settled, the law has

James W. Starnes and Wife *v.* Jas. P. Allison *et al.*

been understood in this State to be, that the power of a married woman over her separate estate does not extend beyond the plain meaning of the deed creating the estate, and that she is to be considered a *feme sole* in relation to it, only so far as the deed has conferred upon her the power of acting as such. When a particular mode is pointed out for the exercise of this power of disposition, she cannot dispose of it in any other way. But in this case the right to sell and dispose of it by deed, is claimed. Still more, the power to unite with her husband in the sale, it is said, is given by this will.

But the last clause in the second item provides for another state of facts: "In the event she leaves issue, she may provide for that issue in whatever manner she deems best, and in that event, my intent is not to limit her power over her estate at her death, in any manner whatever."

It is argued that this enlarges her power again to the extent given in the first clause of the first item; that is, that it removes the restrictions fixed in the preceding part of the second item, and makes it unlimited. But it will be observed that this power, no matter how large it may be, only arises upon the contingency that she *leaves* issue, and can only be exercised "at her death." Can it be exerted before she dies, and before it is known whether the "event" on which it depends will occur or not, and by deed instead of a will? When she comes to die, and has no longer any use for the property I have given her; when it ceases to be needed for her enjoyment and happiness, which is my great concern, she may make a will, and provide for her issue as she thinks best. I

James W. Starnes and Wife v. Jas P. Allison *et al.*

do not intend to compel her to make an equal division among them; or, perhaps, even to give it to them at all, if she chooses not to do so: her power is to be unlimited over the property, if she desires to exercise it in the mode indicated.

It is most manifest, that the leading object and controlling intent of the testator, was to secure all this property, and its proceeds and profits, to the use, control, and benefit of his daughter, as long as she might live, without any power, even in herself, and much less any one else, under whose influence a change in her condition might place her, to deprive herself of it. But when she should need it no longer, at her death, whether with or without children, he intended to give her the unrestricted power of selecting the objects of her bounty, and become the free and untrammelled benefactress of others, as her father had been to her. The whole arrangement presents the highest evidence of paternal love, and tender regard and confidence. His observation had taught him that his daughter might, without her fault, by over-confidence in others, be bereft of the ample provision made for her, if the power of disposition was not withheld. Her youth and inexperience at first, and after that her marriage, and the changes and new influences it brings upon the wife, made it wise and prudent to save her from herself. Then, after this first great object, her comfortable and ample support and happiness was fully accomplished, he places the whole power in her hands, and allows her to become the fountain of fortune and happiness to others.

The construction contended for by the counsel for complainants, would subvert the whole object and design of a settlement like this. If the husband can, by getting the wife to join him in a conveyance, dispose of her separate property, tied up and secured as this is by the limitations and restrictions of the will, what use would there be in the guards thrown around it, and the provision by which the power of disposition is withheld, even from herself, until her death?

We think this is the proper construction of the will. And the result is, that the complainants have no power to sell the land in question, and cannot, therefore, communicate a good title to defendants. The contract will, then, be annulled, the bill dismissed, and the decree reversed.

FRANCIS H. PUGH et al. v. THE STATE.

1. BAIL. *Recognizance. Power of justice of the peace to take. Act of 1715, ch. 16, § 1.* By the act of 1715, ch. 16, § 1, in all criminal offences that are bailable by law, the committing magistrate is required to "admit the party to bail." The act is silent as to the form in which bail shall be taken, but it may be done by bond or recognizance.

2. SAME. *Scire facias. Demurrer. Judgment nisi.* The judgment *nisi* must show that the recognizance was returned into Court, but it is not necessary that it should be expressly stated in the judgment. It is sufficient, if it is stated that it appeared to the Court that such a recognizance had been entered into before the committing magistrate.

3. SAME. *Same. Not necessary that it should show when the Court met.* It is not necessary that a writ of *scire facias*, issued upon a judgment *nisi* against bail, should show on what day the Court at which the judgment was rendered commenced. The Courts will take judicial notice of the terms of the several Courts within the territorial limits of

the State, and the days on which the terms commence. And if the day on which the forfeiture is taken is recited in the *sci. fa.*, the Court can see, without an express statement, whether it was on a day after the commencement of the term.

4. SAME. *Same. Need not recite that the prisoner was adjudged guilty.* A *scire facias* need not recite that the prisoner was adjudged guilty, by the justice, of the offence charged. No formal judgment of the guilt of the accused, by the committing magistrate, is required. The adjudication that the party shall stand committed, or give bail for his appearance to answer the charge before the tribunal having cognizance of the offence, is a sufficient performance of the duty imposed, by law, on the examining magistrate.

5. RECOGNIZANCE. *Lien of. When taken by a magistrate. Question reserved.* A recognizance entered into in a Court of Record, forms a direct and specific lien upon all the lands owned by the party at the time of its acknowledgment, or afterwards acquired by him. And from the force and effect of a magistrate's recognizance, upon its being returned into a Court of Record, the legal consequence, as respects the lien, must necessarily be the same; but whether the lien in the latter case shall be held to attach only upon the return of the recognizance into Court, is reserved.

FROM GILES.

Judgment final was rendered at the August Term, 1857, MARTIN, J., presiding. The sureties sued out a writ of error.

WALKER, for the plaintiff in error.

It is contended that the judgment in this cause is erroneous, and should be reversed for the following reasons:

The magistrates who tried the defendant, Pugh, when he was arrested, do not say, in their judgment or decision that the said Pugh has committed any crime or offence whatever. They merely say, "that having heard the evidence in this case, consider that the defendant give bail and sufficient security in the sum of three thousand dollars, conditioned to make his personal appearance at the next term of the Circuit Court of Giles county, to be held at Pulaski, on the second Monday in December." The magistrates had no right to require the defendant, Pugh, to give bail, unless they believed, from the proof, he had been guilty of some crime, and that that crime was bailable; and they should have said so in their judgment. The act of 1715, ch. 16, § 1, (Car. & Nich., 426,) says that "no person within this State shall be committed to prison for any criminal matter, until examination thereof be first had before some magistrate, which magistrate shall admit the party to bail, if bailable," &c. A magistrate has no right to require an innocent man to give bail, and there is nothing in the judgment of the magistrates showing that Pugh is not an innocent man, and nothing to show they had a right to require him to give bail, and a *scire facias* cannot be grounded upon a recognizance not authorized by law, nor can any judgment be pronounced upon it. *Owen* v. *Grundy and Rucks*, 8 Yer., 436–439. See, also, act of 1817, ch. 100, § 1, (Car. & Nich., 429,) which says: "If the justice shall be of opinion the defendant *is guilty of the offence*, he shall bind him over to Court."

Neither the *scire facias* or judgment *nisi* shows upon its face that the defendant, Pugh, has really forfeited his recognizance. His recognizance says, "he shall make his appearance at the Circuit Court of Giles county, on the second Monday in December, (being States day,) and the second Monday of the December

Term of said Court;" and the *scire facias* says, the said Pugh, on the 19th of December, 1856, a day of said term, was called to come into Court, and came not, without saying the 19th of December was the second Monday of said term or States day, or a day of said term after the second Monday or States day. The 19th day, from all that appears in said *scire facias*, may have been before the second Monday of said term, and before the defendant, Pugh, was bound to appear. And the judgment *nisi* merely says, "on this day the said Pugh was called to come into Court; came not;" without saying upon what day of said term he was called, and without stating any breach of said recognizance. The *scire facias* should recite upon its face a breach of the recognizance or bond. *McCombs* v. *Hall and Boddie*, 4 Yer., 455, 456; *Martin* v. *Gorden*, 3 Hayw., 173.

The Court cannot look outside of the *scire facias* in aid of its defects or omissions. *State* v. *Arledge*, 2 Sneed, 229, 231; *Knott* v. *Smith*, 2 Sneed, 246, 247.

It is contended that the *judgment nisi* is radically defective. It is a summary proceeding, and ought to assume every fact necessary to be proved to constitute the liability of the defendants. *Dickenson* v. *Kincaid*, 11 Hum., 72. Said judgment *nisi* does not show upon its face that the recognizance was returned into the office of the clerk of the Circuit Court of Giles county, or that said defendants signed, sealed, and delivered said recognizance, or that they acknowledged the same before a justice of the peace of Giles county, or any other judicial officer authorized to take the same. *State* v. *Arledge*, 2 Sneed, 229–231; *State* v. *Cherry*, Meigs' Rep. 236.

Francis H. Pugh *et al. v.* The State.

A *scire facias* is founded upon a record, and recites nothing that is not of record. *Nicholson* v. *Patterson*, 2 Hum., 448.

And it is contended that the *scire facias* in this cause should have recited nothing but the judgment *nisi*, or the facts set forth in said judgment. All the balance is merely a historical statement made by the clerk without any authority, and should not be looked to. And if the judgment *nisi* is defective and void, the historical statement of the clerk cannot cure it. The *judgment nisi* must embody such a statement of the facts as will show directly and certainly, and not by mere inference only, the liability of defendants. *Knott* v. *Smith*, 2 Sneed, 247; 3 Hum., 225; 11 Hum., 72.

The pretended recognizance in this case was not signed or sealed by any of the defendants, and the same is therefore void. Justices of the peace have no authority to take a recognizance. It can only be taken by a Court of Record, and a magistrate's court is not a Court of Record; and there is no statute that authorizes a magistrate to take a recognizance. They may take bail, if the case is bailable, but must do so by requiring bond and security, signed, sealed, and delivered.

If the justice had the power to take the recognizance, the defendant should have been recognized to appear at the next term of the Circuit Court, and not on the second Monday in the next term. The statute requires the justice to take bail for the appearance of the defendant at the *next term of the Court*, and not on any particular day of the term.

The final judgment states that two writs of *scire facias* had been issued against the defendants, and returned not found, when they show that they were executed upon all the defendants except F. H. Pugh. This is error for which the judgment should be reversed.

The act passed the 27th of February, 1852, has nothing to do with this case. See Acts of Assembly, 1851–52, p. 421, § 9, of said act. This act merely declares that bonds and recognizances good at common law, shall be good statutory bonds and recognizances.

The defendant cannot be required to appear at a time different from that stipulated, even if the Legislature changes the time of holding Court. *State* v. *Stephens*, 2 Swan., 308.

SNEED, Attorney General, for the State.

It is manifest that the words recognizance and bail are used in our statutes as convertible terms, and it has been the settled course of decision in this State for years past to recognize this form of obligation, when taken by a justice of the peace, as legal and binding. It was so understood by the compilers of the revisal of 1836, who, as the Court will see, have prescribed a form for such obligations, when taken by justices of the peace in criminal cases. See act of 1715, ch. 16, § 1, C. & N., 426, and note the word *recognizances*, as used in that act. See, also, the form of the bond predicated of said act, C. & N., 760.

And so, also, are these words used at common law. Thus it is said: "In all cases where the party is admitted to bail, the *recognizance* is to be returned to the

Court having jurisdiction of the offence." 1 Bouv. L. D., 153.

But it is said that the very definition of the word excludes the idea that a justice of the peace has authority to take that form of obligation. It is defined to be "an obligation of record entered into before a Court, or *officer duly authorized for that purpose*, with a condition to do some act required by law, which is therein specified." 2 Bl. Com., 341; 1 Chit. Cr. L., 90.

We say, then, that a justice of the peace is an officer duly authorized by law, and that the act of 1715, ch. 16, § 1, confers that authority.

A sheriff is not a "Court of Record," and yet he is authorized by the very words of the law to take a recognizance in certain cases. See act 1809, ch. 6, § 2, C. & N., 119.

But let us look at the reason of the thing, and see what magic there is in the terms "Court of Record," as used in this connection. What is the object of the record? Simply to preserve the evidence of the obligation. Why then is it more necessary to preserve the evidence of a recognizance than an ordinary bail bond in the common form? Are not both, in effect, precisely the same? Is not the only difference that one is signed by the justice and the other by the cognizor? And yet it is conceded that a justice may take a valid bail bond.

But we say that, aside from the act of 1715, and all other legislation upon the subject, this is not an open question in this State. It is true that the court of a justice is not a Court of Record; but the moment he files a recognizance taken by him in the Circuit

Court, it acquires the "dignity and verity" of a record. And, without further elaboration, this Court has, on two occasions at least, recognized the validity of a recognizance when taken by that officer. *Barkley* v. *State*, Meigs' R. 93; *State* v. *Cherry*, Ib., 232; and *Arledge* v. *State*, 2 Sneed, 229.

We insist, therefore, that the State is entitled to final judgment in this case.

McKINNEY, J., delivered the opinion of the Court.

Francis H. Pugh was arrested on a warrant issued by a justice, for the murder of J. P. Thompson, and was bound over to the Circuit Court of Giles to answer the charge. The plaintiffs in error entered into a recognizance in the sum of $3,000, jointly and severally, for the appearance of the prisoner on the second Monday of the December Term of said Court, 1856.

The prisoner failing to appear, a forfeiture was entered against him and his bail, upon the recognizance; and *scire facias* having been served on the bail, severally, they appeared and demurred. The demurrer was overruled, and final judgment rendered against them. From this judgment the bail have prosecuted a writ of error to this Court.

The first error assigned is, that a justice of the peace, by our law, has no legal authority to take a *recognizance;* and that, consequently, the entire proceedings are null, and of no effect.

The authority of a justice to take a recognizance,

seems to have been, always, *tacitly* conceded by our Courts from the earliest period of our judicial history. Numerous cases, necessarily involving the question, are to be found in our books—in none of which, nor, indeed, so far as we are aware, in any case before the present, was any point made as to the power of the magistrate to take bail in this form. If the question of power were a doubtful one, so long and universal an acquiescence in its exercise ought alone, perhaps, to be now held sufficient to have conclusively settled it. But we do not regard it as a doubtful question. We think it clear that the power exists by statutory enactments.

By the act of 1715, ch. 16, § 1, in all criminal offences that are bailable by law, the committing magistrate is required to "admit the party to bail." The act is silent as to the manner or form in which bail shall be taken, whether by bond or recognizance, for the appearance of the prisoner before the Court to which he is bound. But the same section makes it the duty of the magistrate to bind over the prosecutor and witnesses for the State, likewise, to appear at the Court to which the prisoner is bound; and in express terms prescribes the manner in which they shall be bound, namely, by "recognizance, with good and sufficient securities." The power being thus expressly given to take a recognizance from the prosecutor and witnesses, it would seem absurd to deny the authority to take a recognizance from the party accused.

There is certainly some plausibility in the suggestion, that, in some of our statutory enactments, the term "recognizance" has been used without regard to its strict legal import, and as obviously meaning a *bond*, rather than a recognizance properly so called; as in the act of 1805, ch. 37, § 1, which directs the sheriff, on executing a *capias* on an indictment, to take a *recognizance* for the appearance of the defendant; and so in other instances that might be mentioned. But notwithstanding this apparently loose use of the term in some instances, we are not prepared to admit that, in the act of 1715, it was not used, and intended to be understood, in its proper legal sense.

The strongest argument against the power of the justice, is the apparent incongruity of holding that a magistrate, whose court is not a *Court of Record*, may take an obligation, the legal efficacy of which depends upon the fact of its being *made of record*.

It is true that, in its technical sense, a recognizance "is an obligation of record entered into before a Court, or officer duly authorized for that purpose." 2 Bl. Com., 341; 1 Chitty's C. L., 90. But then, in the nature of things, there is no legal incongruity, or absurdity, in delegating the power to take bail, in this form of obligation, to a ministerial officer, or to a magistrate clothed with judicial power, though his Court be not a Court of Record. It is a matter of positive law, resting in the discretion of the Legislature, by whose will, a magistrate or officer, either judicial or ministerial, may, for a particular purpose, be invested with a power more properly appertaining to a Court of Record.

The manner of taking bail, in itself considered, is not very important; whether the obligation be in the form of a *bond* executed by the parties; or a recognizance, which need not be signed by the parties, the acknowledgment being reduced to writing by the magistrate, and attested by him, is merely a matter of form. But the legal consequences of these obligations are, in some respects, very different; and it is in view of these differences that the question derives all its importance.

It was settled by this Court, in the case of *Barkley* v. *State*, Meig's Rep., 93, that a recognizance taken by a magistrate when filed in the Circuit Court, becomes a part of the record of the proceeding in that Court, and is thereby invested with the dignity and verity which, by law, appertain to records; so that the party is precluded from availing himself of the plea of *non est factum* to such recognizance.

Again: A recognizance forms a direct and specific lien upon all the lands owned by the party at the time of its acknowledgment, or afterwards acquired by him. This is unquestionably so, of a recognizance entered into in a Court of Record, as held by this Court in the case of *The State* v. *Winn*, 3 Sneed, 393. And from the force and effect attributed to a magistrate's recognizance, upon its return into a Court of Record, in *Barkley* v. *The State;* the legal consequence, as respects the lien, must necessarily be the same; whether the lien in the latter case shall be held to attach, only, upon the return of the recognizance into Court; or, by relation, from its date, is a question upon which we need express no opinion at present.

The next error insisted on, is, that the judgment *nisi* is defective, in omitting to show that the recognizance was returned into the Circuit Court of Giles. This fact, it is true, is not expressly stated in the judgment, but it is stated that it *appeared to the Court* that such a recogniznce (the substance of which is recited in the judgment) had been entered into before the committing magistrates; and this, we think, is sufficient. From the statement, that it "appeared to the Court" that such a recognizance had been taken, it must be held, by necessary implication, that it had been returned, and was present before the Court when the judgment was entered, for the fact of its existence could not otherwise have appeared to the Court. The case of *The State* v. *Arledge*, 2 Sneed, 229, does not support this objection to the interlocutory judgment.

The third error relied on, is, that the forfeiture was entered on the 19th day of December, 1856, and the *scire facias* does not show that the day of the forfeiture was the *second Monday*, or a day subsequent thereto, of the December Term of the Court; and, therefore, it is argued it does not appear that the forfeiture was regularly entered. This objection is not well founded.

It is well settled, that the Courts will take judicial notice of the terms of the several Courts within the territorial limits of the State, and the days on which the terms commence. By this means we learn that the day on which the forfeiture was taken, was a day subsequent to the "second Monday" of the term to which the prisoner was recognized to appear. This is sufficient. Matters of which the Courts will take judicial notice need not, generally, be averred in pleading.

The fourth error alleged, is, that it does not appear from the magistrate's proceedings, as recited in the *scire facias*, that the prisoner was adjudged guilty, by the justices, of the offence charged; without which, it is argued, they had no power to bind him over to answer said charge. This is a mistaken conclusion. No formal judgment of the guilt of the accused, by the committing magistrate, is required. The adjudication, that the party shall stand committed, or give bail for his appearance to answer the charge before the tribunal having cognizance of the offence, is a sufficient performance of the duty imposed by law on the examining magistrate. More than this, on his part, would be nugatory.

The result is, that there is no error in the record, and the judgment is affirmed.

J. W. GEE et al v. H. GRAVES AND WIFE.

1. WILL. *Construction. Power of executor to sell property bequeathed.* The testator directed that his property, both real and personal, should be kept together and managed by his executor for the benefit of his wife, *during* her widowhood, and the maintenance and education of his children; but in case his wife married, she was to have the use and enjoyment of certain of the property during her natural life, and at her death, the same to be sold and equally divided between his, the testator's, children. The widow remained single, and, at her death, the executor sold and conveyed one of the slaves mentioned in the will. It is held, that the testator did not intend that his executor should sell any of his estate unless his wife married again, and the sale of the slave by him, was unauthorized and void, and communicated no title to the purchaser.

2. SLAVES. *Hire. Compensation for keeping, when allowed.* A party who purchases slaves from an executor who sells without authority, is a wrong-doer, and is not entitled to compensation for the support and raising of the slaves, and for physician's bills, taxes, &c., beyond the hire. And this relief is afforded him incidentally, by allowing him to *recoup* against the claim for hire.

3. POWER. *Referred to in the instrument executing it. Question reserved.* The rule, according to the weight of authority, seems to be, that although it is not necessary to the due execution of a power, that

J. W. Gee *et al.* *v.* H. Graves and Wife.

it should be recited or expressly referred to, yet, there must be something to show that the party intended to execute it. But since the act of 1827, an executor has no power to sell slaves under the will, unless the power is conferred therein; and it is difficult to see, if this power is conferred, wly, an absolute bill of sale, without reference to the power, is not a good execution of it. But the question is reserved.

FROM DAVIDSON.

This cause was heard at the November Term, 1858, before Chancellor FRIERSON, who pronounced a decree for the complainants. The defendants appealed.

R. J. MEIGS, for the complainants.

JOHN REID, for the defendants.

WRIGHT, J., delivered the opinion of the Court.

The complainants are the children and legatees of William W. Gee, who died in the year 1839; and file this bill to recover a slave Harriet, the property of their father at his death, and her increase.

These slaves, at the filing of the bill, were in possession of the defendant, Graves, who, about the year 1852, married Susan, the daughter of William Harris, and by the marriage, acquired Harriet and her child Houston, and, perhaps, others of her children. And certain other children of Harriet were born in his possession.

William Harris, in 1847, willed Harriet and Houston to his said daughter. He had purchased Harriet, on the

11th of September, 1840, of J. C. Gee, the executor of William W. Gee, by a bill of sale, as follows:

"Received of Wm. Harris, five hundred and twenty-five dollars for a negro girl named Harriet, aged twenty-one or two years, which I warrant to be sound, both in body and mind; and forever warrant the title of said girl to be a slave for life. This 11th of September, 1840. J. C. GEE."

It is contended by the counsel of Graves, that J. C. Gee had authority to make this sale under the will of William W. Gee; and that William Harris, upon the execution of the bill of sale, acquired a valid title to Harriet.

This is denied by the complainants.

The clause of the will under which the authority is claimed, is as follows:

"It is my will and desire that all my property, both real and personal, be kept together, and managed and controlled by my executor, for the use and benefit of my wife Mary, during her widowhood, and the maintenance and education of my children. And, in case my wife marry again, she is to have no use or benefit of my estate, but as follows, to-wit: I will and devise that she shall have and enjoy the rents, profits and increase of my tract of land in Wilson county, that I purchased of John Doke; my negro woman Harriet; my household and kitchen furniture; my barouche and mare; all which she is to use and enjoy during her natural life.

"At the death of my wife, the said last property, last mentioned, to be sold, and the same to be equally divided between my children, with this exception, that my son James Gee, when he comes of age, shall have to him and his heirs forever, one hundred acres of the said land that I purchased of John Doke, lying in Wilson county, to be laid off and apportioned at the discretion of my executor, and no other person. When my youngest child shall come of age, all my property, both real and personal, not herein given or bequeathed, is to be divided equally, that is, share and share alike, among and between my children. I hereby nominate and appoint my brother, Joseph C. Gee, executor of this my last will and testament, no security required of him."

The widow of the testator never again married, and died within a month after his death, leaving their children all infants of tender years.

Joseph C. Gee qualified as executor, and took upon himself the execution of the trusts of the will.

The first impression entertained by us upon reading this record, was, that Joseph C. Gee, as the executor of William W. Gee, under this will, did have the power to sell the slave Harriet, but that he had failed to execute it, so as to communicate to Harris, the purchaser, any title. And it is argued for the complainants, that conceding the power to exist, still the bill of sale, upon this latter ground alone, must be held wholly inoperative, because it contains no words indicating an intention to exercise the power; but, on the contrary, appears to be the *individual* and *personal* conveyance of Joseph C. Gee.

The rule, according to the weight of authority, seems to be, that although it is not necessary to the due execution of a power, that it should be recited or expressly referred to, yet there must be something to show that

J. W. Gee *et al. v.* H. Graves and Wife.

the party intended to execute it. *Probest* v. *Morgan*, 1 Atk., 440; *Matton* v. *Hutchinson*, do., 558; *Ex Parte Caswell*, do., 559; *Andrews* v. *Emmett*, 2 Bro. C. C., 297; *Bennett* v. *Abrenon*, 8 Ves., 609; Sugden on Powers, 284. And this intention becomes manifest by such description or notice of the estate or property, the subject matter of the power, in the conveyance, as shows that it includes something the party had not otherwise than under this power; and the conveyance would be wholly inoperative, unless applied to the power. *Ex-Parte Caswell*, 1 Atk., 559; *Bennett* v. *Abrenon*, 8 Ves., 615; Sugden, 282 to 294; *Bradish* v. *Gibbs*, 3 Johns. Ch. Rep., 551. Now it is palpable, that under the law of Tennessee, since the act of 1827, ch. 61, this bill of sale can be good in no other way than by virtue of the power in the will of William W. Gee. And if the power existed at all, it is difficult to see why this is not a good execution of it. But we do not mean to decide this now, it not being necessary to the determination of this cause, and because it is held in very respectable authorities that this principle has never been supposed applicable to the conveyances made by executors and administrators. *Griswold* v. *Bigelow*, 6 Con. Rep., 258; *Lockwood* v. *Sturdevant*, do., 373.

It is enough, that upon a critical examination of this will, we think the executor had no power to make the sale. Its meaning is not exactly clear. But we take it, upon the entire instrument, that the testator did not intend that his executor should sell any of his estate, unless his wife should marry again; in which event she was to have certain property, including the slave Harriet, set apart to her for her natural life; and at her death, the same, except the 100 acres of land which was to be laid off to his son James, was to be sold by his executor, and the proceeds divided among his children. Why was this *particular property*, and not the *entire estate*, to be sold? Evidently, because he contemplated that his wife might marry again, and still be alive when his youngest child should come of age, at which *time all his estate, except what is given to his wife for life and to James*, was to be divided, equally, among his children; but that given to his wife was not *then* to be divided, but was to await the event of her death, and *then* to be sold, and the *proceeds* equally divided among his children. No property is to be assigned to the widow, *separately*, unless she marries, and it is only the property that is assigned to her separately, in case of her marriage, that is to be sold. In this case no property was ever so assigned, because she died still living single, and so the case for assigning her property, separately, never arose; and, in like manner, the case for a sale never arose, and the power to sell never existed.

The controlling intention of this will is, that if the testator's widow does not marry, his *property*, the *property itself, real and personal*, is to be kept together for the use and benefit of his wife and the maintenance and education of his children, and not sold; and at the proper time divided among his children. Now that the widow has died, single, there can be no possible reason or purpose for the sale of Harriet and the land, the furniture, barouche and mare. On the contrary, we think the general intention of the will is against the exercise of any such power. 4 Term Rep., 87; *Jackson* v. *Veeder*, 11 Johns. Rep., 169.

The only remaining question is, as to the compensation claimed by Graves for keeping and raising the slaves while in his possession. Can this be allowed to exceed the value of their hires during the same period? We think not.

However innocent, in fact, he may be; in law, he can be viewed in no other light than as a wrong doer, who has intermeddled with the property of complainants without authority, and without their consent; and we know of no principle that entitles him to relief in such a case, beyond the hires. And this is afforded him *indirectly*, by allowing him to *recoup* against the claim of complainants, to that extent.

In the authorities to which we have been referred, by the counsel on both sides of the question, the rule seems never to have gone further than that, in the estimation of the amount to be paid for hire, the defendants should have credit for the support and raising of any of the slaves not worth their maintenance, and for physician's bills, taxes, &c., if any, to be deducted from the hires. *Fenwick* v. *Macey's Ex'rs*, 1 Dana, 286; *Newell* v. *Newell et al*, 9 Smedes & Marshall's Rep, 70; *Rhodes* v. *Hooper*, 6 Lou. An. Rep., 357.

The rule in this State, as to lands held under like circumstances as these slaves, is, that the defendant shall be allowed to *recoup* for any permanent and valuable improvements he may have made, so that such allowances do not exceed the rents and profits for which he is chargeable. *Jones* v. *Perry*, 10 Yer., 59; *McKinly* v. *Holliday*, do., 477.

The Chancellor took this view of the case, and we affirm his decree.

J. M. CONNER v. JAMES AND JEFFERSON CRUNK.

1. SLAVES. *Warranty. Fraud. Tender. Rescission of contract.* If, upon the sale of a slave, a warranty is made, and the vendor is attempted to be made liable upon the ground of fraud or deceit, for defects covered by said warranty, to authorize a recovery it must be shown that the vendee returned, or tendered the slave to the vendor in a reasonable time, or was prevented from doing so by the death of the slave.

2. SAME. *Same. Same. Same. Rule confined to cases of warranty.* This rule is confined to cases where there is a contract of warranty which covers the defects upon which the suit is based. But if redress is sought against a party, upon the ground of fraud, who has made no warranty, or for a fraud not covered by the warranty, the principle does not apply, and a tender of the slave is not necessary to entitle the vendee to recover for the fraud and deceit.

FROM BEDFORD.

Verdict and judgment for the defendant, at the December Term, 1858, DAVIDSON, J., presiding. The plaintiff appealed.

BUCHANAN, KEEBLE and BURTON, for the plaintiff.

COOPER and WISENER, for the defendants.

J. M. Conner *v.* James and Jefferson Crunk.

CARUTHERS, J., delivered the opinion of the Court.

On the 27th of December, 1854, the defendant, Jefferson, sold to the plaintiff, at Courtland, Alabama, two slaves; Lucretia, about 25 years old, and her son, Jordan, about six, for $1150, and executed *his* bill of sale warranting title and soundness.

The negro woman died in a very short time—but a few days after the purchase. This action is brought against the defendants upon the ground of deceit and fraudulent concealment of unsoundness known to them at the time.

The second count charges that the defendant James, being the owner of said slaves, and well knowing the said Lucretia to be unsound and worthless, sent her to Alabama by his brother, the said Jefferson, who was insolvent, to be sold, and under this combination and fraudulent contrivance they were sold, and a bill of sale made by the latter in his own name.

It is fully and clearly proved that they were bought by James, who was a physician himself, at a low price, as unsound. This is proved by his vendor, Dr. Burdett, who says they were very delicate; that he purchased them as "unsound property," and sold them with a full disclosure of that fact, about the 1st of December, 1854, for $600. The defendant, James, told witness, McMahon, before he bought them, and after, that he knew they were diseased, but that "he could make something on them by patching them up." Afterwards he told the same witness, and others, that "he had sent them to Alabama by his brother Jeff., and Jeff. had sold them." On being asked if he was not afraid they would come on him for damages, he said, "he was not, that he was not known in the bill of sale, that Jeff. had given it, and he was irresponsible." He boasted that he had made from *five* to *seven* hundred dollars upon the negroes.

There was some proof made by defendants, to the effect, that one Bobo was a partner in the purchase from Burdett, and that he sold out his interest to Jeff., and that the latter was not, in fact, insolvent. But this does not vary the case.

Dr. Crunk is the main actor in the fraudulent contrivance to impose upon some distant purchaser who might be ignorant of the diseased condition of the woman, and for that, he, and his brother whom he engaged to carry out his scheme, are sued. A case for recovery of full damages is made out against them, unless they are protected by some technical rule in their favor.

It is supposed that the principle of *Rosson* v. *Hancock*, 3 Sneed, 436, must defeat this action for want of a return, or offer to return the slaves, in a reasonable time. That case recognized and applied the principle, that where there is a warranty made by the defendant, who is attempted to be made liable upon the ground of fraud or deceit in relation to defects which are covered by an express warranty, that it must be shown that the property has been returned, or offered to the vendor, in a reasonable time. That is, if the contract of warranty is abandoned, and a rescission claimed for fraud, and the suit is for that, and not on the contract, the plaintiff must show, as a condition precedent to recovery, that he has proposed to rescind by tendering back the property. Yet, if the unsound slave should die within the reasonable time, that would excuse the return and remove the difficulty.

But that is not this case by any means, even if the slave had not died. That rule is expressly confined to cases where there is a contract of warranty against the same defects, upon which the suit may be brought, instead of the fraud, at the election of the plaintiff.

But if redress is sought against a party upon the ground of fraud, who has made no warranty, the difficulty is out of the way, and a tender of the property unnecessary, as a prerequisite. This is a case of that kind. James Crunk has not only failed to sign any bill of sale or written contract, but expressly and avowedly avoided it to escape liability and perpetrate a fraud upon an innocent stranger, for which he thought there would be no redress, because of the insolvency of the agent selected to *assume* the ownership and make title, with covenants.

There is no contract with him, in writing or otherwise, to sue upon, or rescind, but he is sued for fraud and deceit. It is no defence to him, that his brother is included in the action, and has otherwise bound himself. They are both liable, to be sure, but each is, separately, as well as jointly, responsible for the wrong.

We think his Honor erred in applying the principle of the case of *Rosson* v. *Hancock*, if the charge is to be so understood, as we think it was by the jury. But this was with reference to the first count, and properly qualified, by stating that the death of the slave within a reasonable time would excuse the tender. The Court, in that part of the charge which related to the damages, laid down the law correctly, to be, that where the sale was for a gross sum for both slaves, they must ascertain from the circumstances, what amount was allowed for the one proved and known to be unsound, and render their verdict for that alone, with interest. The whole charge, when properly understood, is, perhaps, substantially correct. But the verdict for defendants must have been produced by the closing remark of the Judge upon the request of defendant's counsel to instruct the jury to the effect that, upon a sale in gross, the plaintiff could not elect to keep the boy, Jordan, and recover for Lucretia, and that a suit could not be maintained for either on the ground of fraud, without a tender of both, or a sufficient excuse *as to both*. The Court refused to give this instruction, upon the express ground that he had so charged before. So the jury received that as the law, and of course were bound to render their verdict for defendants, as it was not pretended that Jordan had been returned, or offered to be. We think the Court had not so charged before, but the jury did not of course hesitate to act upon his Honor's construction of what he had laid down to be the law. There is no other way to account for the verdict, for surely a case had never been more fully made out. It was easy, from the evidence, to ascertain what had been given for the woman, as there was proof as to the value of the boy, as well as the woman, at the time of the sale.

There is no fraud imputed as to the boy, he having been bought and retained as sound; but the complaint is alone as to the mother. For the fraud in relation to her alone, the suit was brought, and the Court had correctly held, that if the proof was such as to enable the jury to ascertain what was the price given for her; the plaintiffs were entitled to a verdict for that, with interest. But then, when he afterwards said that could not be done, unless he had offered to return the boy, that ended the case. This was not one of the kind of cases where severance cannot be made of the property purchased.

We think this error was fatal to the plaintiff, and for it reverse the judgment.

JOHN W. ALLISON v. ELI H. STEPHENS et. al.

COSTS. *Liability of surety in the Chancery Court.* In a Court of Equity, where it is in the power of the Chancellor to award costs against either party without regard to the result of the suit, a person becoming security for costs undertakes with reference to that discretionary power, and is subject to its exercise whether his principal succeeds or not. And a bond conditioned that the complainant "shall successfully prosecute a bill of complaint this day filed by him," &c., "or pay all costs incident on failure thereof," will bind the surety for the costs, although his principal may succeed in the suit, if taxed to him by the Court.

FROM BEDFORD.

The final decree, in this cause, was made by Chancellor RIDLEY, at the August Term, 1857. For the reasons stated in the opinion of the Court, the surety of the complainant appealed.

John W. Allison *v.* Eli H. Stevens *et al.*

CARUTHERS, J., delivered the opinion of the Court.

This is an appeal from a decree for costs against a security for the prosecution of a suit in equity.

John W. Allison filed his bill in the Chancery Court at Shelbyville, against Eli H. Stephens and others, and R. B. Davidson signed the bond for costs. The condition is, "that J. W. Allison shall successfully prosecute a bill of complaint this day filed by him * * against Fisher & Stephens, or pay all costs incident on failure thereof."

This bill related, exclusively, to a partnership in the purchase and sale of a drove of mules. The defendants filed a cross-bill for discovery in that controversy, and also bringing up another transaction in relation to a joint purchase and sale of a lot of hogs, being a matter disconnected with the other.

An account was taken in reference to both transactions, and the result was that complainant obtained a decree for $76.50. But the Court taxed the complainant in the original bill, and *his surety* with half the whole costs.

The surety appealed, and insists that he was not liable under his bond for any costs, because his principal did "successfully prosecute his suit" according to the terms of his bond, and by which he was only to be liable for costs in case of failure, on his part, to do so successfully.

That argument would be sound, upon a bond for cost, in a Court of Law, where the costs are, by express statutory provision, to go with the cause, and necessarily fall upon the failing party. But in equity, where it is in the power of the Chancellor to award costs against either party, without regard to the result of the suit, a person becoming surety for costs undertakes with reference to that discretionary power, and is subject to its exercise whether his principal succeeds or not. This bond is in the ordinary form, and the obligation incurred by it renders the surety liable to the order of the Court in regard to costs, though the party for which he was bound may have obtained a decree for the full amount he claimed in his bill.

Affirm the decree.

ELIJAH HOPPER *v.* DAVID FISHER.

1. COURT, CHANCERY. *Is a Superior Court.* A Court of Chancery is a Superior Court within the sense and meaning of the term, as contradistinguished from an inferior one, and the validity of its decrees is not to be tested by the rules applicable to a Court of peculiar, special, and limited jurisdiction.

2. JURISDICTION. *Rule for, as to Superior and Inferior Courts.* The rule for jurisdiction is, that nothing shall be intended to be out of the jurisdiction of a Superior Court but that which specially appears to be so; and, on the contrary, nothing shall be intended to be within the jurisdiction of an Inferior Court but that which is so expressly alleged.

3. CHANCERY JURISDICTION. *Partition.* A Chancery Court has general power and authority to make partition of lands between tenants in common. This jurisdiction existed at the common law, and has since been declared and recognized by several statutory enactments.

4. SAME. *Same. Ejectment. Decree, when collaterally attacked.* If it appears that the Chancery Court, whose decrees are impeached in a collateral proceeding by ejectment, had jurisdiction over the subject matter of the decrees, and undertook to, and did declare the rights of the parties, there being infant defendants, who were represented by a

Elijah Hopper v. David Fisher.

guardian *ad litem*, it will be presumed that the defendants were duly served with process, or in some way had the proper notice, so as to give the Court jurisdiction of their persons; and the decrees will be held good, although it may not appear in the transcript of the record offered as evidence in the suit in ejectment, that the infant defendants were served with process, or had any notice of the proceedings, or that a guardian *ad litem* was appointed by order of the Court.

FROM DEKALB.

This cause was heard before his honor, Judge GOODALL, at the April Term, 1858. A transcript of the record of partition, from the Chancery Court at McMinnville, was offered as evidence. It was objected to upon the grounds stated in the opinion of the Court, and the objection overruled. Verdict and judgment for the plaintiff. The defendant appealed.

S. M. FITE, for the plaintiff in error, cited and commented upon *Robertson* v. *Robertson*, 2 Swan, 197; *Douglass* v. *Harrison*, 2 Sneed, 382; Act of 1851–52.

M. M. BRIEN, for the defendant in error relied on the following authorities to sustain the Court below: *Simmons* v. *Woods*, 6 Yer., 518; 1 Greenl. Ev., § 19; *Kilcrease* v. *Blythe*, 6 Hum., 389; *Thacher* v. *Chalmers*, 5 Hum., 313; *Robertson* v. *Robertson*, 2 Swan, 197.

R. CANTRELL, on the same side, cited, in addition, the Act of 1852, ch. 152, § 6; *Morris* v. *Richardson et al.*, 11 Hum., 389; *Greenlaw* v. *Kernahan*, 4 Sneed, 371.

Elijah Hopper v. David Fisher.

WRIGHT, J., delivered the opinion of the Court.

This was an action of ejectment, in the Circuit Court of DeKalb county, in which the plaintiff below had judgment, and the defendant has appealed in error to this Court.

In deraigning his title the plaintiff was compelled to use and rely upon certain decrees and proceedings had in the Chancery Court at McMinnville, to the reading of which the defendant objected; but the Circuit Court overruled the objection, and permitted the records to be read as a part of the plaintiff's title.

This is now assigned as error.

The land in controversy had been granted by the State of Tennessee to Thomas Hopkins. He died intestate, leaving a large estate in lands, in various tracts. His heirs-at-law, after his death, in the year 1838, by a decree in the Chancery Court at McMinnville, had partition made of these lands, and the tract in controversy, with others, was allotted to the heirs of Judith Vaughan, a sister of the intestate.

In the same year, and the year following, the children and heirs of Judith Vaughan, by a decree in the same Court, had partition made of the lands which had been allotted to them, and the tract of land in dispute was assigned to Thomas C. Vaughan, one of the children and heirs of Judith Vaughan.

In the bills and proceedings in both of these causes, certain of the heirs, who then appear to have been infants, were made defendants; and in the transcripts of the records used on the trial of this cause, no subpœnas were found, nor does it appear whether or not any

Elijah Hopper v. David Fisher.

ever issued or existed, or whether said infant defendants were ever served with process, or had notice by publication or otherwise, as required by law. As to this the records are silent. Nor is any order appointing a guardian *ad litem* found; and in one of the transcripts the answer of the guardian *ad litem* does not appear.

But in the decrees, in both cases, it is recited that the causes "came on to be heard, and were heard, before the Chancellor, upon the bill and answer of the minor defendants, by their guardian *ad litem*, John D. Lusk, when it appearing to the satisfaction of the Court," &c.: and after stating in the decree the rights and equities of the parties, the Court goes on and decrees the partition.

It is assumed that these decrees are now to be held void for the want of service of process upon these infant defendants.

The defendant, so far as we can see, is a trespasser, and has no interest in the land in dispute; and whether these decrees were, at the time they were made, formal and regular, in no way concerned him. The heirs themselves do not complain, but have acquiesced in these divisions for nearly, or quite twenty years.

The defendant seeks to attack and overturn them collaterally, in order to hold the possession of a tract of land to which he manifestly has no title.

We are of opinion this should not be permitted, and that, as to him, these decrees should be held valid.

A Court of Chancery is a Superior Court within the sense and meaning of the term, as contradistinguished from an Inferior Court. It has general power and authority to make partition of lands between tenants in common. This jurisdiction existed at the common law,

Elijah Hopper *v.* David Fisher.

and has been declared and recognized by many statutes since. It can in no just sense be claimed that the validity of these decrees shall be tested by the rules applicable to a Court of peculiar, special, and limited authority.

When we see, therefore, that the Court of Chancery at McMinnville had jurisdiction over the subject matter of these decrees, and undertook to, and did declare the rights of the parties—the infant defendants being represented by their guardian *ad litem*—we should now, in a mere collateral attempt to impeach them—especially after such lapse of time—presume that the defendants were duly served with process, or in some way had the proper notice, so as to give the Court jurisdiction of their persons.

The subpœnas in a cause are not required to be enrolled, and may not be, if they were; and they, with the evidence of notice to bring parties before the Court, may be, and often are, lost and cannot be copied into the transcript. And are we now, in a case like this, to say there were no subpœnas, or service, or notice of any kind?

The rule for jurisdiction, as laid down in *Peacock* v. *Bell and Kendal*, 1 Saund. R., 74, is, that nothing shall be intended to be out of the jurisdiction of a Superior Court but that which specially appears to be so; and, on the contrary, nothing shall be intended to be within the jurisdiction of an Inferior Court but that which is so expressly alleged.

This rule was adopted by Judge Reese, in delivering the opinion of the Court in the cases of *Brie Adm'r* v. *Hart*, and *Kilcrease* v. *Blythe*, 6 Hum., 1, 178.

And from these cases it will also appear that a Court of Chancery is a Superior Court within the sense of the rule.

The case of *Kilcrease* v. *Blythe*, involved a question of jurisdiction as to the person of infant heirs, and, in principle, seems to me to be very analogous to the present case.

From that case it would seem, that where, on the return of process not found, and affidavit of non-residence made, with prayer for the action of the Court to compel the appearance of the defendants, and the *record only shows* that the Court proceeded to take the bill for confessed, and determined the matter involved without setting forth that this was done *after due publication*, such decree, though reversible on appeal, is not void. 6 Hum., 378. And, on the same subject, *White* v. *Albertson*, 3 Dev., 242; *Brown et al.* v. *Wood*, 17 Mass., 72; *Britain* v. *Cowen*, 5 Hum., 318, 319; 1 Greenl. Ev., § 19.

We do not mean to question the rule that requires service or notice upon the parties, and that a decree taken contrary to the course of the Court is void. 1 Swan, 484; 2 Swan, 197; 3 Dev., 244.

But we take certain things in this case as evidence that the parties to these decrees were properly before the Court, and that all things were rightfully done.

Judge Resse, in *Britain* v. *Cowen*, 5 Hum., 318, 319, after speaking of the struggles of the Chancery Court against technical rules, and of its power, from its mode of practice, to see, from time to time, that necessary parties are brought before it, and of the crude and inartificial manner in which much of the public business is done, and how incautiously the papers and records pertaining to our Courts are kept, remarks: "We have strong motives of public policy to cherish substance more than forms, and to hesitate long, and insist upon a clear case, before we pronounce the decrees and judgments of our Courts of Record void, when brought collaterally in question."

It follows, of course, if the Chancery Court had the proper jurisdiction, that everything also will, in this contest, be taken to have been regular. 4 Sneed, 371.

The objections to the decree in the case of Harriet Vaughan and others, under which Harrison purchased, have nothing in them.

Judgment affirmed.

E. A. COLEMAN, by &c. *v.* JOSEPH SATTERFIELD, *et al.*

1. CHANCERY JURISDICTION. *Innocent purchaser. When protected.* If a deed is procured from a *feme covert* by fraud and coercion, and the conveyee sells and conveys the land to another person, for a valuable consideration, who has no notice of the circumstances under which the deed was procured from such *feme covert*, he is, in contemplation of law, an innocent purchaser, and will be protected in his right.

2. SAME. *Husband and wife. Fraud in sale of wife's land.* Although, in such a case, the wife is not entitled to relief against such third person, yet she is entitled to a decree against the party who fraudulently procured the deed from her, for the value of the land; for, in consequence of his wrong, the estate is irrecoverably lost to her.

3. HUSBAND AND WIFE. *Husband's right to the real estate of the wife.* By the common law the husband, by marriage, gains an estate of freehold in the lands of his wife, which he may convey by his own deed to another, and the wife can take no step, either at law or in equity, to regain the possession of the land, so long as the *coverture*

E. A. Coleman by &c., v. Joseph Satterfield, et al.

lasts. But her ultimate fee simple interest is not affected by her disability, and on its termination she will be remitted to her right of action to recover the possession.

4. SAME. *Same. When wife may sue. Cloud upon her title. Chancery jurisdiction.* Although the husband, by his own act may, by the principles of the common law, defeat the wife's enjoyment of the possession and profits of her land, yet he has no power over her title or interest in fee; of this she can, alone, be divested by her own *voluntary* act, in the form prescribed by law. And the attempt to deprive her of it by fraud, force, or undue influence, either on the part of her husband or a stranger, furnishes her in a suit by next friend, a clear ground for redress in equity, by having said deed declared null, and the cloud removed from her title, although she may not be entitled to the present possession of the land.

5. SAME. *Same. Same. Rights of the wife under the act of* 1849–50. The act of 1849–50 materially changes the common law. It not only protects the husband's interest in the lands of his wife from seizure and sale by his creditors *during* her life, but it likewise disables the husband to sell or dispose of such interest, without her joining in the conveyance. And if a conveyance has been procured from her by fraud, or other improper means, whether by her husband or a stranger, she may maintain a bill, by next friend; to have it set aside, and to have the possession restored to her—making the husband a defendant.*

FROM STEWART.

On the trial, at the October Term, 1858, Chancellor FRIERSON dismissed the bill. The complainant appealed.

W. LOWE, for the complainant.

KIMBLE and RICE, for the defendant, Satterfield.

McKINNEY, J., delivered the opinion of the Court.

The complainant, who is a *feme covert*, brought this bill, by her next friend, to recover a tract of land of

---

* The provisions of the act of 1849–50 are incorporated into the Code, §§ 2481, 2482.

E. A. Coleman, by &c., v. Joseph Satterfield, et al.

eighty-nine acres, in Stewart county; which, by a deed executed jointly by herself and husband, on the 29th of July, 1850, was conveyed to the defendant Cooly, who, shortly thereafter, sold and conveyed the same to the defendant, Satterfield, who is now in possession thereof. The land had been conveyed to the complainant when a *feme sole*, by her grandmother. The consideration paid by Cooly, to the defendant Coleman, complainant's husband, for said land, including the crop growing thereon, is stated in the deed, and shown by the proof, to have been $225 00, of which sum, one hundred dollars was the estimated value of the crop; making the price of the land but $125 00. The proof shows that the land itself, was then worth seven to eight dollars per acre; and in the deed from Cooly to Satterfield, the consideration is stated to have been $700 00.

The bill charges, that she was induced to sign the deed to Cooly, and to acknowledge its execution, by fraud and threats of violence made against herself, and against the life of her husband, by the defendant, Cooly; and also to surrender possession of the land, and remove to another State. It is further charged, that Satterfield, who purchased from Cooly, on the 2d of December, 1850, had full knowledge, at the time of his purchase, of all the facts respecting the manner in which the conveyance for the land had been extorted from her and her husband, by Cooly. The bill prays that the deed may be declared void; that she be restored to possession of the land; and for general relief.

The bill is taken as confessed against Cooly. The defendant, Satterfield, positively denies that, either at the time of his purchase, or of the payment of the purchase

E. A. Coleman, by &c., v. Joseph Satterfield, et al.

money, he had any knowledge or information whatever, of the alleged fraud or force, on the part of Cooly, in obtaining said deed; nor had he any knowledge or information thereof prior to this suit; and insists that he is a *bona fide* purchaser, for a full and valuable consideration; and therefore claims that he shall be protected in his purchase.

The charges in the bill, as to the defendant, Cooly, are very fully sustained by the proof. He was himself examined as a witness for complainant,—without exception, as it seems,—and makes out a stronger, and more aggravated case of fraud and coercion, than is charged in the bill. From his own showing, however, and from other testimony in the record, his statement is perhaps entitled to no consideration, except for the purpose of charging himself. But, his evidence aside, the allegations of the bill, as to him, are sufficiently established. But as regards the defendant, Satterfield, there is no sufficient evidence to overcome the substantial averments of the answer, that, at the time of the purchase and payment of the consideration money, and reception of the conveyance for the land he had no notice, or knowledge of the facts upon which the complainant's claim to relief is founded.

The Chancellor dismissed the bill as to all the defendants. We find, upon examination of the record, that the legal obstacles which were supposed, on opening the case, to lie in the way of complainant to relief against either defendant, do not exist. The bill was filed in less than six years from the date of the conveyance to Cooly; so that, both the statute of limitations of 1819, and the general statute applicable to money demands, in equity, are out of the case.

The decree of the Chancellor, as to Satterfield, was correct; and the only point to be considered is, whether the complainant is entitled to a decree against the defendant, Cooly, for the value of the land. The husband, it seems, declined to join with his wife in filing a bill to have the conveyance set aside, and to be restored to the possession of the land. And the first question is, can the wife, in such case, sue separately in equity? Whether or not the proof makes such a case as would entitle the husband to relief, so far as *he* is concerned, is a question not important to be considered. For, admitting that he might have maintained a suit in equity, in the joint names of himself and wife, to have the deed set aside, but refused to do so; or assuming, on the other hand, that, as to him, the deed was executed under such circumstances as would estop him, in equity as well as at law, from avoiding it; still, the question is, may not the wife, in either case, maintain a bill, by her next friend, to be re-invested with the title, and restored to the possession of her estate, of which she had been deprived by the exercise of fraud and coercion towards her personally? We think it clear that she may, under the act of 1849–50, ch. 36; and perhaps upon general principles of law.

It is true, that, by the common law, the husband, by marriage, gains an estate of freehold in the lands of his wife, in her right, which continues at least during their joint lives, and may possibly last during his own life. And this interest he may, by his own deed, convey to another, and the conveyance will operate to vest the pur-

E. A. Coleman, by &c., v. Joseph Satterfield, *et al*

chaser with the husband's estate; or the husband may voluntarily suffer a disseizin; or acquiesce in a wrongful ouster of the possession; and in neither case can the wife, separately, take any step at law or in equity to regain the possession; she is without remedy, by the common law, so long as the coverture lasts. But, still, her ultimate fee simple interest is not affected during her disability; and on its termination, she will be remitted to her right of action to recover the possession.

But though the husband, by his own act, may defeat the wife's enjoyment of the possession and profits of her land, by the principles of the common law, yet he has no power over her title or interest in fee; of this she can only be divested by her own voluntary act, in the form prescribed by law. And the attempt to deprive her of it by fraud or force, either on the part of her husband, or a stranger, furnishes her a clear ground for redress in equity, where a married woman may sue separately.

In this view, upon general principles, the bill might well be sustained so far, at least, as it seeks to have the deed set aside. But under the act of 1849–50, her right to relief is perhaps broader and more ample. By that act, the common law is materially changed. It not only protects the husband's interest in the lands of his wife from seizure and sale by his creditors, *during her life*, but it likewise disables the husband to sell or dispose of such interest, by his own act, during the wife's lifetime, without her joining in the conveyance. By the necessary construction of this act, the wife cannot be deprived either of the title, or possession of her lands, except by her own voluntary act. And if a conveyance

E. A. Coleman, by &c., v. Joseph Satterfield, et al.

has been procured from her by fraud or other improper means, whether by her husband or a stranger, she may maintain a bill to have it set aside, and to have the possession restored to her,—making the husband a party defendant. The object of the act, is the protection of the rights of the wife, rather than the husband's; and to deny her the right to sue separately in equity, in a case like the present, would be to defeat the obvious intention of the statute.

The remaining inquiry is, what relief is the complainant entitled to, under the peculiar circumstances of this case? It is clear that no decree can be made against the defendant, Satterfield. He acquired the legal title to the land, without notice of the complainant's equity, and for an adequate consideration, and must be treated as an innocent purchaser. The complainant cannot, therefore, regain the land itself. But we think it no less clear, that she is entitled to a decree against the defendant, Cooly, for the value of the land. This measure of relief results upon either of two distinct grounds. First, that in consequence of his *wrong*, the estate is irrecoverably lost to the complainant; and, secondly, that viewed as a *purchaser*, he fraudulently acquired the property, without any adequate consideration given for it.

The decree of the Chancellor will be modified accordingly.

William J. Alston, *et al. v.* Rebecca Davis, *et al.*

WILLIAM J. ALSTON *et al v.* REBECCA DAVIS *et al.*

1. WILL. *Construction. Limitation over.* When, by a will, an absolute gift of the property is made in the first instance, followed by a limitation over on the death of the devisee or legatee, the absolute gift is not taken away by the gift over, unless the gift over may itself take effect.

2. SAME. *Same. Same. Illustration of the principle.* The testator divided his estate among his children, of whom Rebecca Davis was one, and provided that her share should be vested in the hands of a trustee or trustees, for her use and benefit during her natural life, not subject to the control or obligations of her husband, and at her death, to be equally divided among her bodily heirs. By the proper construction of the will, in the event there are no "bodily heirs" (which in this connection means children) of the said Rebecca Davis, the gift becomes absolute. The testator did not, in that event, die intestate as to the remainder, so that the same would go to his heirs at law, under the statutes of distribution.

FROM WILLIAMSON.

The bill was dismissed upon the hearing at the October Term, 1858, FRIERSON, Chancellor, presiding. The complainants appealed.

——— ———, for the complainants.

——— ———, for the defendants.

McKINNEY, J., delivered the opinion of the Court.

The question for our determination is, what interest does the defendant, Rebecca Davis, take under the will of John Swancy; is it restricted to a life estate, or does she take the absolute estate, subject to a contingent executory limitation over, in the event of her leaving children at her death?

The will of the testator, after providing for the sale of all his property, and the payment of some specific legacies, directs that the executors "shall divide all the rest and residue of my estate, of every kind and description, whether the same be proceeds of the sale of real or personal estate, or debts coming to me, equally between the following named persons, each to receive, share and share alike, to-wit: My son, James N. Swancy; my three daughters, Sarah Vanzant, wife of ——— Vanzant; Nancy Palmore, wife of James Palmore; Rebecca Davis, wife of B. S. Davis; and my step-daughter, Elizabeth Hamilton, wife of Reuben Hamilton; also, my illegitimate son, John Swancy. But it is my will and desire that the shares of my daughters, Sarah Vanzant, Nancy Palmore, Rebecca Davis, and my step-daughter, Elizabeth Hamilton, shall be vested in the hands of a trustee or trustees, for their use and benefit during their natural lives; and at their death, to be equally divided among their bodily heirs." After providing for the appointment of trustees for the daughters and step-daughter, with power to vest the money of each in land or negroes, the bill proceeds, "which shares of money or property I wish my daughters and step-daughter to have and use during their natural life, not subject to the control or obligations of their respective husbands; and at their death, to be equally divided among their bodily heirs."

Rebecca Davis is still living, but has no child living, and having reached the age of about sixty years, in the

William J. Alston *et al. v.* Rebecca Davis *et al.*

ordinary course of nature, will have no child in future. Her share of the estate is still in the hands of her trustee, who resides in this State. But she and her husband being residents of Kentucky, an application was made to have the fund transferred to the possession of a new trustee appointed in the latter State. To prevent the removal of the fund, was the object of the present bill, which was dismissed on demurrer.

The bill assumes that it was the intention of the testator that Mrs. Davis should take nothing more than a life estate, and such, it is insisted, is the proper construction of the will. The argument is, that as the will makes no disposition of the remainder, in case of Mrs. Davis's death without child or children; and that event being now morally, perhaps absolutely, certain; the testator must be held to have died intestate as to the remainder interest; and, consequently, on her death, the heirs at law of the testator will be entitled to it under the statute of distributions. The Chancellor held otherwise, and we think correctly.

The general principle is well established, that where, by the will, an absolute gift of the property is made, in the first instance, followed by a limitation over, on the death of the devisee or legatee; the absolute gift is not taken away by the gift over, unless the gift over may itself take effect. And this principle is decisive of the present case. Here, by the first sentence of the residuary clause, taken by itself, an absolute gift is made to each of the several persons named therein; the three married daughters, and step-daughter, are placed on a footing of perfect equality with the sons—each is to have an equal share. The subsequent provisions of the

William J. Alston *et al.* v, Rebecca Davis *et al.*

will, vesting the shares of the married women in trustees, for their separate use during life, with a limitation over to their "bodily heirs" (which, in this connection, means children) in the event of leaving children at their deaths, do not affect the principle.

No provision is made for the contingency of the daughters' dying without children; and this must be taken as evidence of the testator's intention, that, in such event, the gift should be absolute, as it is not to be presumed that he intended to die intestate as to any part of his property. And such is the legal construction. The gift is not subject to any other contingency or limitation beyond that which is expressed, and if that cannot take effect, the gift remains absolute. For the limitation over, in a particular event expressly stated in the will, excludes all presumption of intention that the subject of the gift should go over in any other event.

The result is, that the absolute gift to Mrs. Davis, by force of the first operative words of the clause, remains in her, except so far as it is taken away by the executory bequest over, in favor of her children living at her death; and it is not taken away in the event of her dying without a child or children. *Hulme* v. *Hulme*, 16 Eng. Ch. R., 644; 2 Jac. & Walker, 279; *Whittell* v. *Derdin*, 15 Eng. Ch. R., 590; *Jackson* v. *Noble*, 8 Beav., 443; 1 Jarman on Wills, 782, marg. *et seq.*

Decree affirmed.

HARDY RYLAND v. WILLIAM BROWN et al.

1. BILLS AND NOTES. *Assignment. Consideration. Fraud. Notice of equity.* If a note is assigned to a party, before due, with notice, actual or constructive, that it is void, or subject to be impeached in the hands of the payee, either for fraud, or want, or failure of consideration, he will hold it subject to the same equities to which it was liable in the hands of the payee.

2. SAME. *Same. What sufficient notice of an equity against the note.* Whatever is sufficient to put a person upon inquiry, is equivalent to notice; and when a person has sufficient information to lead him to a knowledge of a fact, he will be presumed to be cognizant of that fact.

3. SAME. *Same. Same. What the recital of the consideration imposes.* The recital in a note, that it was given for land, does not require a person to examine, at his peril, the records, before taking such note, for the purpose of ascertaining whether, as between antecedent parties liens might not exist, growing out of unpaid purchase money. He would at most, only be required to know that the maker of the note was in the peaceable possession of the land under a title sufficient in law to invest him with a fee simple estate, accompanied with the usual covenants for his indemnity.

4. SAME. *Recital of consideration. Question reserved.* The recital of the consideration in negotiable paper is unusual, but its negotiability is not, thereby, affected. And if it be merely stated that the consideration of the note is the purchase of land or merchandise, is an innocent holder bound to know that the purchaser acquired a good title to the land, or that he received the goods bargained for?

5. SAME. *Equity against. Suit prematurely brought.* If a note given for land is transferred to an innocent party, it would be premature, on the part of the maker of said note, to commence suit to avoid payment thereof, on the ground of failure of the consideration, before there is an attempt, or a contemplated attempt, to subject the land to a prior equity, if such exists.

FROM BEDFORD.

This cause was heard before RIDLEY, Chancellor, at the November Term, 1858. Decree for the complainant. The defendants appealed.

Hardy Ryland v. William Brown *et al.*

W. H. WISENER and J. L. SCUDDER, for the complainants.

E. & H. COOPER, for the defendants.

MCKINNEY J., delivered the opinion of the Court.

This bill was filed to enjoin the collection of a note given for the consideration, in part, of a tract of land.

The substantial facts necessary to be stated, in order to present the question submitted for determination, are, that, on the 5th of April, 1856, the complainant purchased from the defendant, Thompson, two tracts of land, at the price of $2,000; and for a portion of the purchase money, not discharged at the time of the contract, he executed two notes—one for $833.33, and the other for $666.66. The consideration of said notes is expressed upon their faces, as follows: "The same being, in part, for an 85 acre, and 100 acre tract of land, this day bought of him." At the time of the contract, Thompson conveyed said lands to complainant by deed, with covenant of general warranty; and though the fact is not directly alleged or proved, the inference is irresistible, from the whole record, and is not denied in argument, that the complainant was put in possession of the premises by his vendor, and still continues in the undisturbed enjoyment of the same. It is shown that the 100 acre tract above-mentioned originially formed part of an entire tract of about 480 acres, purchased by said Thompson from one Gauntt, in February, 1854, and on the face of the deed from Gauntt to Thompson for said tract, (which was registered,) a *lien* is expressly reserved to secure the purchase money.

Hardy Ryland v. William Brown et al.

It appears, also, that Thompson had divided said tract, and sold it in separate parcels—the 100 acres purchased by complainant being *the last parcel sold*. It is further established, that about $1,500 of the consideration money still remains unpaid, from Thompson to Gauntt; for which, it is supposed, the said 100 acre tract is liable to be made subject—Thompson having, shortly before the filing of the bill, become wholly insolvent.

The two notes above-mentioned, executed by complainant to Thompson, were assigned to the defendant, Brown, before due, and without actual notice of any existing equity against them, as between the original parties. Upon the smaller note of the two, which was assigned to defendant, Brown, on the 23d of November, 1856, the latter had obtained judgment before a justice, to enjoin which this bill was filed. The ground of equity is the assumed liability of the 100 acre tract, for which said two notes were given (the price of the 85 acre tract having been discharged at the time of the contract) to the $1,500, unpaid purchase money, due from Thompson to Gauntt. This, it is alleged, constitutes a failure of the consideration of said two notes; and it is insisted that the defendant, Brown, is to be affected by this equity, by the constructive notice arising out of the recital, in the notes, of the consideration for which they were given. The complainant substantially alleges in the bill, that he was wholly ignorant of the fact that any portion of the purchase money of said land remained unpaid by Thompson to Gauntt, or that any such lien existed upon the 100 acres purchased by him, until the day preceding the filing of the present bill, which was the 2d of October, 1857.

Hardy Ryland *v.* William Brown *et al.*

It does not appear from the record, that Gauntt has taken any step to assert his supposed equitable lien upon said 100 acres of land, or that he contemplates doing so. This however is, perhaps, not important, as we do not intend to discuss the question, whether or not, upon the facts in this record, the lien could be made available against the complainant. But assuming, for the purpose of the present determination, that a valid lien exists, we will confine ourselves to the question, whether, upon that ground, the complainant can avoid the payment of the notes to Brown?

It is not pretended that the defendant is not a *bona fide* holder of the note for a valuable consideration, without notice of the facts upon which, according to the assumption, its validity may be impeached, unless the statement on the face of the note shall be held to be constructive notice of the facts.

It is conceded that whatever is sufficient to put a person upon inquiry, is equivalent to notice; and that where he has sufficient information to lead him to the knowledge of a fact, he shall be presumed to be cognizant of that fact. Upon this principle it is insisted that the defendant is chargeable with notice of the supposed equity in favor of complainant against the note in question; that information of the fact, derived from the face of the note, that it was given for specific tracts of land, was sufficient to put him upon a search of the register's books to see whether or not the lands were free from all liens and incumbrances which might, by possibility, affect the title of the complainant, and, by consequence, the validity of the notes given for the consideration money; and that it was likewise incumbent

Hardy Ryland v. William Brown et al.

upon him to inquire into the fact whether or not the purchase money had been fully paid to Gauntt, for the security of which a lien had been reserved, as before stated.

We fully assent to the legal proposition, that if Brown, at the time he took the note, had notice, either actual or constructive, that it was void, or subject to be impeached in the hands of Thompson, either for fraud, or want, or failure of consideration, he will hold it subject to the same equities to which it was liable in the hands of Thompson. But we are unable to concur with the complainant's counsel as to the extent of the duty or obligation imposed upon the defendant by the recital in the note. If the argument be sound, it will necessarily prove a very serious obstruction to the negotiation and free circulation of commercial paper.

The statement of the *consideration* is unusual in negotiable paper; but, still, its negotiability is not thereby affected. And if unnecessarily stated in a note, what effect can be predicated of it, as against a *bona fide* holder who received it before due, for a valuable consideration, and without actual notice of any equity existing against it in the hands of the original holder? If it be merely stated that the consideration of the note was the purchase of land, or merchandise, is an innocent holder bound to know that the purchaser acquired a good title to the land, or that he received the goods bargained for? We should hesitate to affirm that he was. But this point is not necessary to be decided in the present case. Admit, for the sake of the argument, that such a statement in the note imposes some sort of duty upon the person who takes it, in due course of trade, and under the circumstances before stated, what is the extent of that duty? In the present instance, was the defendant, at his peril, bound to examine the records of the register's office beyond the conveyance made to the complainant, for the purpose of ascertaining whether, as between antecedent parties, liens might not exist, growing out of unpaid purchase money, by which the title of the former might, by possibility, be affected? We think not. If any duty rested upon the defendant, the full extent of it was, simply, to know that the complainant was in the peaceable possession of the land under a title sufficient, in law, to invest him with a fee simple estate, accompanied with the usual covenants for his indemnity. If this view be correct, the bill is destitute of equity. But were it otherwise, the bill was prematurely filed. It would be introducing a new principle to hold, as the Chancellor did, that the complainant might avoid payment of the note given for the land, on the ground of failure of the consideration, when there is no intimation in the bill of any attempt, or even apprehension of an attempt, to subject the land to the supposed liability in favor of Gauntt.

The decree must be reversed, and the bill dismissed.

Robert D. Morgan *et al.* v. Robert Reed *et al.*

ROBERT D. MORGAN *et al.* v. ROBERT REED *et al.*

1. CONSTITUTIONAL LAW. *Sale of slaves. Act of* 1856, *ch.* 112, § 8. *Art.* 11, § 7, *of the Constitution.* The act of 1856, ch. 112, § 8, which declares, "That the title of all persons to any slave or slaves sold under proceedings in the Circuit, Chancery or County Court, under the act of 1827, and to which the heirs, distributees, or legatees were not made parties, shall be forever barred, unless suit to recover said slave or slaves shall be instituted within six months after the passage of this act," is in violation of Article 11, § 7, of the Constitution, and is void.

2. STATUTE OF LIMITATIONS. *When one capable of suing. Slaves.* If one of several parties who have a joint right to slaves is free from disability, and in a condition to be capable of suing, the statute of limitations will run against, and bar the right of all of said parties in case there is an adverse holding of the slaves for the period of three years.

3. SAME. *Same. Severance of the joint right.* A sale by one or more of the joint owners of slaves who are *sui juris,* of their interest in them operates as a severance of the joint interest, and leaves the parties under disability at liberty to sue separately for their slaves, as if there had never existed a unity of title or of interest between them and the other joint owners. And, consequently, the statute of limitations will not bar the right of those under disability, until after three years from the removal of the same, as to all.

4. SAME. *Same. Same. Estoppel* If two of the distributees of an estate, who are *sui juris,* administer, and in that capacity, petition and procure an order for the sale of the slaves of their intestate, in which they have a joint interest, but which proceeding is void against the other distributees, who are then minors, by reason of the latter not being made parties, such adult distributees are placed under an *estoppel,* and, thereby, disabled from suing; and the fact that they were co-distributees and *sui juris,* (the joint interest of the parties having been severed by the sale,) will not bar the right of the infants to sue and recover, at any time within three years after the youngest arrives at age.

FROM BEDFORD.

This cause was heard, and the bill dismissed, at the November Term, 1858, RIDLEY, Chancellor, presiding.

E. A. KEEBLE, for the complainants.

STEELE, on the same side, said:

As to the act of 1856; complainants insist it is *unconstitutional* and void. 2 Yer., 260, 554, 599.

As to the statute of limitations of three years, it cannot apply to this case.

When *all* are under disabilities at the time the action *accrued*, then none are barred until the disability is removed as to *all*.

The *widow* was a joint owner, but she was *estopped*, (and, therefore, under a disability,) by her act of joining in the sale to defendant, Reed.

The widow joining in the sale to Reed may be, *technically*, a *severance* of the joint estate; but that can have no effect upon the rights of the parties, so as to bar them as fast as the disabilities should be removed. In *joint estates*, either party *may* sue, but none are *compelled* to sue, or be barred until the disability is removed as to *all*.

The act of 1856, if constitutional, should be *strictly* construed in favor of those it was intended to operate against. The language of the act is, that in all cases where slaves have been sold under the act of 1827, ch. 51, *without making the heirs, &c., parties, &c.* The language of the act clearly imports, that when *all the other* requirements of the act of 1827 had been complied with, *except the making of the heirs parties* in *such* cases, the heirs shall sue within six months.

The act of 1827 requires the Court to hear *other evidence* than the petition; this was not done in this case, so that the sale was void for other reasons, besides not making the heirs parties.

There is no such act as 1827, ch. 51; the act of 1827, ch. 61, was, we suppose, meant.

W. H. WISENER, for the defendants:

The sale is conceded to be void, according to the case of *Elliott* v. *Cochran et al*, 2 Sneed, 468. But it is insisted that the complainants have no right to recover, because of the statute of limitations of 1856, ch. 112, § 8. If this act be constitutional, they are all barred. The statute of limitations only operates upon the remedy, and is no part of the contract. Meigs' Rep., 34, and 4 Hum., 13 to 21.

Then, if no part of the contract, they may be extended or shortened. 4 Hum., 13 to 21. And it is only a question of expediency which the legislative power must determine for itself, and having done so, Courts cannot interfere, because the Legislature may have, in the opinion of the other co-ordinate department of the government, shortened the time in a manner which might be considered too limited for the interests of the parties to be affected thereby. The authorities quoted, and references, sustain the position that these enactments, as to this point, are constitutional.

But it may be said, that this is not "the law of the land," that is a partial law, and, therefore, unconstitutional. It is true, there is a limit on the power of the Legislature contained in the constitution, to be found

Robert D. Morgan *et al.* v. Robert Reed *et al.*

in article 11, section 7. This, it is contended only applies to legislation, for particular individuals, and not to classes.

A clause in the Union Bank Charter, which made certain acts of its officers felony, was declared, in the case of *Budd* v. *The State*, 3 Hum., 483, unconstitutional, upon the ground that it was limited to officers of that corporation. But it was conceded in that case by the Court, if the clause had applied to the officers of all banks in the State, that it would have been constitutional. 2 Hum., 285, and 2 Yer., 260.

Suppose this section of the act of 1855, had been engrafted into the act of 1827, as a proviso, would it not have been constitutional? But suppose this law is unconstitutional, then, it is insisted, that the complainants are all barred by the general statute of three years. And if this is not so, they are all barred but the two youngest, who are not yet twenty-four years of age.

By the sale made by the administrators, they being distributees and joint owners with complainants, the joint ownership was severed, and each might sue for his or her share; as they might sue in regard to land; as they could do so they are each barred, unless they bring suit within the time limited by the statute, after arriving at age; and not having done so; the case of *Shute* v. *Wade*, 5 Yer., 1, does not apply.

The case of *Parker* v. *Elder*, 11 Hum., 546, settles the principle, that the sale to the defendant, by and of his joint interest, is a severance, and each may then sue for his share.

The decree obtained by the widow and Buckingham, and sale under it, and report thereof, will operate to convey their interest to the purchaser, Reed, and is, therefore, a severance of the joint ownership.

The complainants cannot recover the share of George Morgan; the statute will vest his interest in the purchaser.

If this latter view of the case be correct, only two of the complainants can recover; and their share is one-eighth each. Nor can the share of Mrs. Buckingham be recovered.

And in the event of a recovery of any portion of the slaves, to that extent, as they are asking equity, and the money of defendant went to pay their ancestors debts; the complainants, or such of them as succeed, must refund the purchase money with interest.

The Chancellor being of opinion that the act of 1855–6 was constitutional and governed the case, dismissed the bill; and we insist, here, his decree was right and must be affirmed.

McKinney, J., delivered the opinion of the Court.

The complainants, who are a part of the distributees of the estate of Moses A. Morgan, who died intestate in Bedford county, in the year 1845, brought this bill to recover certain slaves claimed by them, in the possession of the defendant, Reed. The intestate left a widow and seven children; the latter were then all infants under the age of twenty-one, and two of them are

Robert D. Morgan *et al.* v. Robert Reed *et al.*

still minors. The oldest daughter, however, had intermarried with one Buckingham, prior to the death of the intestate, during her minority. The widow and said Buckingham were appointed administratros of the estate. In that character they presented a petition to the Circuit Court of Bedford county, to which the distributees were not made parties, for the sale of two slaves, the property of the estate, Mary and Jeff.

At the August Term, 1845, the Court decreed a sale of said slaves, on *the statement of the petition*, that a sale was necessary "to pay debts, and to make distribution;" which statement, as the decree recites, was "believed by the Court." And, accordingly, the two slaves were sold, and purchased by the defendant, Reed, for $675.00. Two of the distributees are dead, to-wit: Malissa, the wife of Buckingham, who died some six years ago; and George, who died in 1855, during minority, and without issue.

This bill was filed on the 24th of August, 1858, by the five surviving children, the widow and Buckingham being made defendants. The Chancellor dismissed the bill.

It is conceded in argument, that the sale of the slaves was void, under the decision in *Elliott* v. *Cochran*, 2 Sneed, 468, and other decisions of this Court. But it is insisted, that the complainants right to recover the slaves, is barred by the act of 1855–6, ch. 112, sec. 8, which declares: "That the *title of all persons* to any slave or slaves, sold under proceedings of the Circuit, Chancery or County Court, under the act of 1827, and to which the heirs, distributees, or legatees, were not made parties, shall be forever barred, un-

Robert D. Morgan *et al.* v. Robert Reed *et al.*

less suit to recover said slave or slaves shall be instituted within six months after the passage of this act."

We feel constrained to declare this extraordinary enactment to be unconstitutional and void. There is much plausibility in the argument, that it violates the spirit of both the 8th and 20th sections of Art. 1, inasmuch as it attempts to deprive certain persons of their property, contrary to "the law of the land;" and is also a "retrospective law." But, perhaps, it is a still more palpable infringement of the provisions of sec. 7, Art. 11, which declares, that "the Legislature shall have no power to suspend any general law, for the benefit of any particular individual. Nor to pass any law for the benefit of individuals, inconsistent with the general laws of the land."

Can a more direct violation of the true spirit and meaning of these fundamental provisions be imagined, than is presented by the section of the act above cited? We think not. What does it propose? In some instances, prior to the passage of this act, sales had been made of slaves, under color of judicial proceedings, professing to have been founded upon the act of 1827, but which were, in fact, wholly contrary to law, and void; communicating no title to the purchaser, and divesting no title out of the former owner. By the general law of the land, as it existed at the time of these illegal sales, the persons who had thus been deprived of their property contrary to law, had the unquestionable right to bring suit for its recovery at any time within three years after the sale. And if the owner happened to be an infant, or under other legal disability, his right of action was saved for the period of three years after the disability ceased to exist.

Now, as a sort of "relief measure," in cases of such irregular and void sales as had been previously made, it is attempted by the act of 1856, in the very teeth of the constitution, (Art. 11, sec. 7,) "to suspend a general law for the benefit of (these) particular individual" purchasers; or, in other words, "to pass a law for the benefit of individuals, inconsistent with the general law of the land."

The act, it will be observed, does not contemplate any change of the existing "general law" in the future; it does not provide, that, in all similar cases of irregular sales of slaves, which may be made after its passage, suits shall be brought within six months, instead of three years.

It is altogether *retrospective* in its operation, refering, only, to *past cases*, and having no reference whatever to the future. In short, its whole scope and object, is simply to exempt "particular individuals," or special cases, from the operation of "the general law of the land;" or, "to suspend the general" law in their favor.

This conclusion, it seems to us, is so obvious, that argument is scarcely necessary to make it clearer.

There is no force in the argument, that the act affects, only, the *remedy*, and not the *right*. The remedy is sometimes so incorporated with the right, that it would be extremely difficult, if not impossible, to maintain, in any proper sense, that the former can be impaired without affecting the latter. But this is a point we need not stop to discuss, as it is clear beyond all doubt, that the prohibitions of the constitution, in letter and spirit, apply as much to *remedies* as to *rights*. It was thought proper and necessary that the rules regulating the *remedy* should be equal and uniform in their operation, as well as those regulating the *rights* of the citizens. And surely this is correct; for if the remedy may be frittered away, what is the right worth?

The act is likewise subject to the objection, as has been argued, of being a *partial* law. It does not profess to be applicable to *all* illegal sales of slave property, but only to judicial sales, under a particular statute; and not even to *all* irregular sales under that statute, but only to the special case, where "the heir, distributees, or legatees were not made parties." The act seems not to contemplate or provide for other irregularities in proceedings, under the act of 1827, which might avoid a sale; nor does it apply to an illegal sale of slaves by the sheriff, under the ordinary process of *fieri facias*.

If the act had been merely *prospective*, so as only to operate on sales to be made after its passage, whatever might be thought of its unreasonable severity and injustice, in extending indiscriminately to *all persons*, regardless of the rights of those laboring under legal disabilities; still, so far as regards the question of constitutional power, it might, perhaps, be sustained. But being of the character already stated, it is impossible to support it, without yielding to the Legislature the exercise of a power expressly denied by the constitution.

But, it cannot be necessary to reason upon this subject, as a simple comparison of the act with the provisions of the constitution, demonstrates at once their entire incompatibility.

But, it is argued for the defendant, that admitting the act of 1856 to be void, still, the complainants are barred by the general statute of limitations of three years. And this conclusion, it is assumed, results from the application of the principle of *Shute* v. *Wade*, 5 Yer., to the facts of the case. It is insisted, that inasmuch as the widow, who was a distributee, and Buckingham, in right of his wife another distributee, were free from disability, that the statute began to operate in favor of the defendant, Reed, and against *all* the distributees, from the time of the sale and purchase of the slaves in question. This reasoning is fallacious: and is an attempt to misapply the true principle of the case of *Shute* v. *Wade*, which is, that if one of the parties be free from disability, and in a condition to be capable of suing, the statute will run against all. But here, the widow and son-in-law, Buckingham, as administrators, had disabled themselves to sue, and were placed under an *estoppel* to do so, by the fact that the sale was made upon their own application, and by themselves; and because, the sale, though void as to the infants, not parties, was binding upon them, and operated to divest them of their respective interests, and to transfer the same to the purchaser. The reason of the rule in *Shute* v. *Wade*, does not, therefore, apply to the present case.

And the only question is, whether the fact, that two of the distributees, who were joint owners with the infants of the slaves and who were *sui juris*, having disabled themselves to sue, shall have the effect of destroying the right of recovery of the other joint owners, so

Robert D. Morgan *et al.* v. Robert Reed *et al.*

far as the interests of the latter are involved. We think not, upon well established principles. The effect of the sale, so far as the widow and Buckingham are concerned, was, as we have seen, to divest them of their interests, and vest the same in the purchaser. It was, in effect, by operation of law, a sale of their distributive shares to the latter. And in this view, it operated a severance of the joint interest, by their act; and, by legal consequence, left the infants who were not parties and had no participation in the matter, at liberty to sue separately for their distributive shares, as if there had never existed a unity of title, or of interest between them, and the other two distributees, to the slaves in controversy. *Parker* v. *Elder*, 11 Hum., 546. This being so, the five complainants in this suit, who were all minors when their right of action accrued, and of whom two are still minors, are within the saving of the statute, as expounded in *Shute* v. *Wade*; and, consequently, may well maintain the present suit, to recover *five-eighths* of the slaves in controversy. As to the minor who died in 1855, as there is no representative of his estate before the Court, no decree can be made in respect to his interest.

But, as the complainants seek equity, they must do equity; and, therefore, if it shall appear, upon an inquiry to be made before the master, that the proceeds of the sale of the slaves were applied by the administrators in discharge of debts due from the intestate's estate, in the proper course of administration, or otherwise properly applied to the benefit of complainants, the latter will be held bound to refund to defendant, Reed, five-eighths of the price paid by him for the slaves, with interest

Robert D. Morgan *et al.* *v.* Robert Reed *et al.*

thereon; and their interests in the slaves will be held liable for the same if not otherwise paid.

Decree of the Chancellor reversed, and a decree will be rendered conformable to this opinion.

CASES ARGUED AND DETERMINED

IN THE

SUPREME COURT OF TENNESSEE,

FOR THE

WESTERN DIVISION.

JACKSON: APRIL TERM, 1859.

G. M. BIRDSONG *v.* JOHN C. BIRDSONG *et al.*

1. CONTRACT. *Inadequacy of consideration. Fraud. Chancery.* The mere inadequacy of price, independent of other circumstances, when the parties stand on equal ground, and deal with each other without any imposition, or oppression, will not be sufficient to authorize a Court of Equity to set aside a sale. Inadequacy of consideration is only a badge of fraud.

2. SAME. *Same. Same. Same. When advantage is taken* If, however, advantage be taken, on either side, of the ignorance or distress of the other, it affords a new and distinct ground of equity; and a very great inadequacy of price will form a presumption of oppression.

3. SAME. *Same. Undue influence.* A contract will be set aside when it is obtained by undue influence over a person greatly under the power of another, if there is inadequacy of consideration, or a clear ground of inference that a confidence reposed had been abused, or advantage taken of incompetency, weakness of understanding, or clouded or enfeebled faculties.

4. SAME. *Same. Same.* It is not necessary that the influence should be due to antecedent or extraneous circumstances, it may have arisen in the course of the same transaction in which it was exerted. It is sufficient to show such a condition of dependency from any cause, as to raise the presumption that the party was unable to protect himself, and to justify the interference of the law to protect him.

G. M. Birdsong v. John C. Birdsong et al.

5. SAME. *Same Same. Drunkenness.* Contracts made by persons under the influence of liquor, without being completely intoxicated, are governed by the same principles which apply to other cases where one party is in a position to expose him to the exercise of an improper influence by the other. If carried so far that the reasoning powers are destroyed, the contract is void; but when it falls short of this, the contract will not be avoided, unless undue advantage has been taken, by one party, of the condition of the other.

6. SAME. *Same. Same. Same.* If a party, while excited by liquor, has been led into a hard and disadvantageous bargain, it will be set aside by a Court of Equity. And the same rule applies to persons whose minds are enfeebled by habitual intoxication, although not intoxicated when the contract is made.

7. SAME. *When not set aside if made under undue influence.* A contract will not be set aside on the ground of undue influence, apart from fraud, when proper in itself and for the advantage of the party who seeks to annul it. For example, the conveyance of a man habitually intemperate, but not actually drunk, of all his property in trust for his wife and children.

8. TRUST AND TRUSTEE. *Conveyance in trust for the wife and children.* If a person who is addicted to the excessive use of ardent spirits, and is a spendthrift, makes a conveyance of all his property in trust for the benefit of his wife and children, such conveyance will not be set aside by a Court of Chancery, although procured by the influence of another, and under such circumstances as would have authorized a Court of Equity to have annulled it, if the conveyance had been made to a stranger.

9. SAME. *Same. When conveyance absolute.* If such conveyance is absolute, a Court of Equity will execute the trust for the benefit of the wife and children.

10. CHANCERY PRACTICE. *Rehearing before the Supreme Court. Depositions. Evidence. Parties.* After the decree was pronounced by the Supreme Court, one of the defendants applied for a rehearing, upon the ground that the deposition of an incompetent witness was admitted; and the decree settled the rights of persons who were not parties to the suit. A rehearing was refused, and the Court held:

1. That there being no exception in the Court below to the reading of the deposition, the evidence was properly heard. And if the testimony was rejected, the result would be the same.

2. Although the beneficiaries are not parties to the record, the pleadings and proof establish the trust in their favor; the evidence *pro* and *con.* has been heard, and if the parties were turned loose to litigate anew, the depositions in this cause would be admissible in a suit by the *cestuis que trust* against the defendant, and in no aspect of the case could the latter be benefitted by another contest about the property.

G. M. Birdsong v. John C. Birdsong et al.

3. A Court of Chancery cherishes forms no further than they contribute to the main object of its existence, the attainment of substantial justice. It struggles against technical rules which merely impede this object.

4. The rule requiring all persons in interest to be made parties to suits in equity, is a rule of discretion, founded in the anxiety of those Courts to do justice among all the parties having an interest in the subject matter, or object of the suit. It is, in most cases, not a right of the parties brought before the Court, but rather a rule prescribed by Courts of Equity to themselves.

5. If persons whose interest is apparent are not made parties, they may be allowed, if they wish it, to bring forward their claim by petition, and have the benefit of the proof already taken, and will not be driven to a second contest.

FROM MADISON.

This cause was heard at the August Term, 1858, before Chancellor Williams, who dismissed the bill. Both parties appealed—the defendants upon the ground that the Court below excluded certain depositions taken by them.

TOMLIN, and STEPHENS & STEPHENS, for the complainant.

ALEX. MCAMPBELL, for Price.

M. & H. BROWN, for John C. Birdsong.

WRIGHT, J., delivered the opinion of the Court.

The complainant, and the defendant John C., are brothers; and the latter is the administrator upon the estate of William Birdsong, senior, who was their father, and who died *intestate*, the 26th of October, 1850.

G. M. Birdsong v. John C. Birdsong et al.

This bill was filed on the 3d of April, 1854, for the purpose of setting aside a conveyance of the share of complainant in the estate of his father, made to the defendant, John C., on the 2d day of November, 1850, and to obtain an account and decree against the administrator and heirs, for complainant's share in the estate in favor of his wife and children. Letters of administration were granted to the defendant, John C., on the first Monday in November, 1850—a few days after the date of said conveyance.

This conveyance is evidenced by a deed, absolute upon its face, from the complainant, of all his share and interest, real and personal in his father's estate; and the same purports to be for the consideration of $1,000. It appears that John C. executed to complainant his five notes for the sum of $200 each, due the 25th of December, 1851, 1852, 1853, 1854, and 1855, which have never been paid. And in his answer he insists that this was the only consideration for said conveyance, and all he was ever to pay complainant for his share in said estate; and that he is absolutely entitled to the same, freed of trusts of every kind; and he avers that his purchase of this interest was, in all respects, fair and free of fraud.

This deed was attested by T. R. Richardson and H. A. Welch, and proved by them, and immediately registered.

It is charged in the bill, that immediately after the death of their father, the said John C. proposed to complainant to make him a transfer of all his interest in his father's estate, with a view, as he said, to enable him, the said John, to hold it, and take care of it for

G. M. Birdsong v. John C. Birdsong et al.

the benefit of complainant's wife and children; representing to complainant that it would be wasted in his (complainant's) hands, and would do his family no good; and that, conscious of his own weakness, anxious to provide for his family, and confiding in the honor of his brother, and believing that he would act in good faith towards him and them, he agreed to the proposition, and executed the conveyance aforesaid—not knowing, and being incapable of knowing, that it was to have the effect of transferring his whole interest away from his wife and family, or that it would be used for that purpose.

This allegation, as before stated, is denied in the answer; but the defendant, in this connection, states that he may have said that complainant would waste the $1,000, and that he desired to secure *that* for complainant's wife and children—that this was his desire, and he supposes he said so; but again denies that he proposed securing the *interest* in the estate; admits that complainant was wasteful and intemperate at times, and poor; but insists he knew his rights.

The allegations in the bill are sustained by the deposition of M. E. Birdsong, a daughter of the complainant. She proves that John C. Birdsong came to her father on the same evening that the notes were executed, and said he intended we (meaning thereby, no doubt, the family of complainant) should have our part of the estate when it was wound up—that it was a trade made not to stand; that he intended to buy them some land, and place them upon it; and said, who could cheat the children out of a cent? And the reason he gave for doing this was, because he did not want his father's estate scattered about, and that if it was not for him it would soon be gone. As to the notes, he told complainant not to dispose of them, but that he wanted him to keep them until the estate was wound up, and he would lift the notes, and replace his part of the estate back to him; that the notes were not worth one-half or one-third his part of the estate; and that he intended to see that complainant's family should have their part of the estate.

She, at the time, was very young, but her story is a consistent and natural one, and she is strongly corroborated by most of the important facts in the case, and by the depositions of B. F. Bond, Jno G. Price, Wm. Knight, and others.

The defendant repeatedly said, for many years prior to his father's death, that complainant was a drunken fool, and that it would be wrong for his father to give him any part of his estate; that he would drink it up as soon as he could swallow it, and it would go out of the family.

Complainant is shown, when at himself, to have but ordinary capacity, and when drinking, to be incapable of business, and easily overreached at all times. The defendant spoke of him as a wretch, and that he would as soon rob a goose as to cheat him, &c. The proof shows him to have been poor, degraded, and destitute.

The estate of the intestate consisted of some twenty-three slaves, land, and other property, to say nothing of advancements.

As to its value, the answer of defendant admits, that, at the intestate's death, it was worth from $12,000 o $13,000, and the proof more than sustains it; th* making complainant's share, which was one-fifth of the value, at least, $2,500; which defendant assumes he purchased for $1,000, at one to five years' time—less than one-third of its value.

To countervail this proof, and much else of a like character to be found in this record, defendant proves efforts by complainant to sell to others before he bought, and that it is probable, if he had not taken it, others would; that he was not intoxicated on the day the deed was executed, though it appears he was just out of a debauch; and Richardson and Welch, the attesting witnesses—one of whom drew the deed—and McGregor, at whose house it was drawn, are examined, and the sum and substance of their proof are, that though they did not hear the conversation which preceded and led to the trade, yet the deed was executed in their presence, and by them attested; that it was read to complainant, who was sober and knew what he was about, and they regarded it as a fair trade; and that he stated he thought the $1,000 a fair compensation for his share in his father's estate, considering his situation, and the best he could do for himself and family; and that, when not drunk, he was capable of business. And it is further shown, that for some time afterwards he recognized the validity of the arrangement, and expressed himself satisfied with it, and that defendant would do right with him; and in a controversy with Price as to the notes, he notified defendant not to pay them to Price.

The Chancellor decreed for the defendant. We do not concur in this decree.

It is true that mere inadequacy of price, independent of other circumstances, where the parties stand on

G. M. Birdsong *v.* John C. Birdsong *et al.*

equal ground, and deal with each other without any imposition or oppression, will not set aside a sale. Inadequacy, of itself, is only a badge of fraud; and it is clear that if advantage be taken, on either side, of the ignorance or distress of the other, it affords a new and distinct ground, and a very great inadequacy may form a presumption of oppression. In equity a conveyance will be set aside where it is obtained by undue influence over a person greatly under the power of another, if there is inadequacy of price, or clear ground of inference that a confidence reposed has been abused, or advantage has been taken of incompetency, weakness of understanding, or clouded or enfeebled faculties.

It is not necessary that the influence should be due to antecedent or extraneous circumstances; it may have arisen in the course of the same transaction in which it was exerted. It is enough to show such a condition of dependency from whatever cause, as to raise the presumption that the party was unable to protect himself, and to justify the interference of the law to protect him.

A conveyance made by a man of weak mind and in necessitous circumstances, for an inadequate consideration, has been set aside; and where a man unacquainted with business and of feeble character, was induced to sell a legacy of $13,000 for $4,500, by means of the influence acquired over him by the purchaser, who took advantage of his ignorance of affairs and eagerness to obtain the money at once, to lead him to believe that the legacy was not worth a larger sum in hand, and might not be paid for many years—the sale was set aside.

G. M. Birdsong v. John C. Birdsong *et al.*

Contracts made by persons under the influence of liquor, without being completely intoxicated, are governed by the same principles which apply in other cases, where one party is in a position to expose him to the exercise of an improper influence by the other.

If carried so far that the reasoning power is destroyed, the contract is void; but when it falls short of this, the contract will not be avoided, unless undue advantage has been taken by one party, of the condition of the other.

If a party has been led into a hard and disadvantageous bargain, while excited by liquor, equity avoids it. And the same rule applies to persons whose minds are enfeebled by habitual intoxication, although not actually intoxicated.

But it seems a contract will not be set aside on the ground of undue influence, apart from fraud, where proper in itself, and for the advantage of the party who seeks to avoid it; as for instance, a conveyance by a man habitually intemperate—but not actually drunk —of all his property, in trust for his wife and children. *Chesterfield* v. *Josener*, and notes, White & Tudor, 420, 421; *Hugenenen* v. *Bosely*, and notes, White & Tudor, 64, 74.

These principles are decisive of this case. We are satisfied this conveyance was obtained in trust for complainant's wife and children, and upon no other condition can it be allowed to stand. The $1,000 in notes, were merely intended to put complainant off until the estate could be settled and property secured to his wife and children, and not intended to be paid, but to be restored and the estate fixed on them. Defendant knew

G. M. Birdsong *v.* John C. Birdsong *et al.*

he could not readily sell such notes, nor his share in the estate so entangled; and if he did sell the notes, he could still save something for his wife and children. We are, moreover, satisfied from this record, that defendant, in haste, and before administration, or complainant had time to know the debts or value of the estate, managed to become his *adviser* and *friend* as to the disposition of his share in the estate, to save it—not from his creditors, for we doubt if he had any credit —but from himself and his habits, and for his family and children. If so, his conduct was laudable. Why so anxious as to his brother's share—even before his father's death? And after his death, to keep off a sale to others? And in this view, the satisfaction expressed by complainant with the arrangement, and so much relied on by defendant, has no force. The attempt now to hold the property by defendant must be regarded as an after-thought.

The transaction with Price is not in the way—for he disclaims all interest in the notes—and complainant has them to surrender to defendant.

The Chancellor rejected the most material of defendant's proof, upon the ground of incompetency and illegality, and refused to reject certain of complainant's depositions, as to the character of Scarborough, and which are not deemed very material; but we have not thought it worth while to go into this, since we think if we allow defendant's proof so rejected,] and [reject the complainant's so excepted to, the result is the same.

The wife and children of complainant are not parties; but the bill sets up the trust in their favor, and without considering whether complainant might not file a bill for the specific *execution of the contract between him and defendant*, and to set up the trust in their behalf, it is enough that we have power to remand the cause, that they may become parties. Code, sec. 3170.

The decree of the Chancellor will be reversed—the $1,000 in notes surrendered to defendant, John C. Birdsong, and a trust of complainant's entire share in his father's estate, established in favor of his wife and children.

The cause will be remanded to the end the proper parties be made, and that an account of complainant's share in the estate of his father be had, in which will be embraced the increase since his father's death, hires, rents and interest—making defendant all just and proper allowances—and in this account an enquiry will be had as to advancements, and further proof taken on that subject; and as to this matter this Court now makes no decision.

Decree reversed.

The defendant, John C. Birdsong, since the decree was pronounced in this cause, has made application for a rehearing: 1st. Upon the ground that M. E. Birdsong—a leading witness—is one of the beneficiaries in the trust set up and established by the decree, and, therefore, is an incompetent witness, because of interest.

A conclusive answer to this is—that no exception, either general or special, to the reading of this deposion, was made in the Court below, and none can taken here. This rule of practice is settled in *Gunn et al.* v. *Mason et al.*, 2 Sneed, 637.

The reason of the rule and the authorities are there given, and it is founded in sense and sound policy.

A further answer to this objection is—that if we were to disregard the evidence of this witness altogether, the result must still be the same. The other evidence in the record demonstrates to our mind, that the conveyance to the defendant can only be allowed to stand as a trust for the wife and children of complainant.

2d. The next ground assumed for a re-hearing is, that the facts constituting the trust established by the decree, in favor of complainant's wife and children, were not alleged, or in issue in the pleadings; and, therefore, they cannot be noticed by the Court, or constitute the basis of the decree.

This assumption is founded in a misapprehension of the state of the pleadings between these parties. It will be seen that the existence of this trust is expressly alleged in the bill and denied in the answer, and proof *pro* and *con* taken upon it.

It is true the wife and children of complainant are not parties, but he sets up the trust in their favor; and the litigation, instead of being with them directly, is between complainant and defendant.

It may very well be made a question, if complainant had not the right to file a bill to enforce the *contract* between him and defendant, out of which was to arise a trust in behalf of complainant's wife and children. But passing this by, how does the case stand? Here, it is palpable, the defendant has been fully heard as to this trust and the rights of these parties. The proof, *pro* and *con*, has been exhausted. Then he has not suffered for want of an opportunity to adduce evidence of his defence. Then why, as to him, have a new litigation. If the wife and children of complainant were to file a second bill, or become parties by an amendment, the depositions and evidence already taken, could be used against defendant. It is not like the case of a judgment, which requires—to make it evidence—that there be mutuality between the parties. As to depositions the parties need not be the same. If the issue be the same, and the party against whom the proof is offered has been allowed a chance to cross-examine, that is enough. 1 Greenl. Ev., sec. 553.

It is clear, here, that as between complainant and defendant, the latter has no right to hold this estate. A stronger case against him, to our mind, can hardly be stated.

Then there can be no contest between complainant and his wife and children, because the bill itself sets up the trust in them; and as between him and them admits the right to be in them, and so is the proof. Then what ought a Court of Chancery to do in such a case? Put these parties out of Court and send them to a second and new contest over this estate? If such an objection as this were allowed, would it not be purely technical?

A Court of Chancery cherishes forms no further than they contribute to the main object of its existence, the attainment of substantial justice. It struggles against technical rules which merely impede this object. It is enabled from its mode of practice to see, from time to time, that necessary parties are brought before it; and

G. M. Birdsong v. John C. Birdsong *et al.*

this it can do, at almost any stage of a suit. 5 Hum., 318, 319.

The general rule, requiring all persons in interest to be made parties to the suit, is, in most cases, not, in any just sense, a right of the parties brought before the Court, but rather a rule prescribed by courts of equity to themselves in the exercise of their jurisdiction, founded upon their notions of public policy, or public convenience. It is, in a great measure, a rule of discretion, founded in the anxiety of those Courts to do justice among all the parties having an interest in the subject matter or object of the suit, whether that interest be mediate or immediate, present or future, for the purpose of suppressing future controversy and litigation. Story's Eq. Pl., sec. 135 *a*.

Accordingly, if the *cestuis que trust* or beneficiaries should not be made parties to the suit, and their interests are apparent, a Court of Equity will sometimes, as a matter of indulgence and to prevent further delay and expense, allow them (if they wish) to bring forward their claims by petition, in order that their rights may be protected. Story's Eq. Pl., sec. 208.

The plain meaning of the authority is, that they may be allowed to intervene and have the benefit of the proof already taken, and will not be put to a new bill and a second contest.

The ground upon which the decree goes, settles that defendant is the trustee to complainant's wife and children. He is a party, and the case is settled against him. The re-hearing is, therefore, refused.

Re-hearing refused.

R. P. MARR et al. v. JOHN MARR et al.

1. WILL. *Holographic. What meant by "valuable papers." Act of 1784, ch. 10, § 5.* Before the passage of the act of 1784, no devise of land was good unless it was signed and witnessed by two subscribing witnesses. This act made an exception in favor of holographic wills. The first requirement of the act is, that the will shall be found among the "*valuable papers or effects*" of the deceased, or shall have been lodged in the hands of some person for safe keeping. "Valuable papers," as used in this act, consist of such as are regarded by the testator as worthy of preservation, and, therefore, in his estimation, of some value. They are not confined to deeds for land, bills of sale for slaves, obligations for money, or certificates of stock. Any others which are kept and considered worthy of being taken care of by the owner of them, are *valuable* in the sense of the act of 1784.

2. SAME. *Same. What "found" implies.* To be "*found* among his valuable papers," implies that it must have been placed there by the writer, or with his knowledge and assent, not surreptitiously by some other person; and so deposited with the intention at the time, that it should be his will.

3. SAME. *Same. Not every paper thus deposited and found is a will.* All the requirements of the act of 1784 may be complied with, and the paper invalid as a testament. The paper thus found must be a *will*. And if a *will* it may be attacked, as other testamentary papers, for want of competency of the testator, for fraud and undue influence, or that it was never legally assented to by the maker, as a complete and finished act; not signed—with an attesting clause, but not witnessed, &c.

4. SAME. *Same. How revoked. Declarations of the testator.* When the requisites of the act of 1784 have been complied with, it amounts to a publication of the will, and gives it the same dignity as if it had been regularly executed and witnessed, and requires something more than verbal declarations to revoke it. There must be some act done, clearly indicating an intention of revoking the will—such as cancellation, destruction, removal from the place of deposit, or reclamation from the hands of the person with whom it may have been lodged.

5. SAME. *Same. Evidence. Declarations of the testator.* The declarations of the testator are admissible as evidence for the purpose of showing whether the requirements of the law exist, so as to establish

R. P. Marr et al. v. John Marr et al.

the paper propounded, as a will; but when these are established by proof, such declarations cannot have the effect to defeat the testamentary character of the paper, or to work a revokation of it, as a will.

FROM WEAKLEY.

The *venue* in this cause was changed from Obion to Weakley county, and a trial had at the October Term, 1858, FITZGERALD, J., presiding. Verdict and judgment against the will. The plaintiffs appealed.

I. G. HARRIS, FREEMAN, SOMERS, and COCHRAN & ENLOE, for the plaintiffs, relied upon the following authorities:

Act of 1784, ch. 10, § 5; *Crutcher* v. *Crutcher*, 11 Hum., 385; 1 Greenl. Ev., § 200; 3 Yer., 25; *Allen* v. *Huff*, 1 Yer., 409; *Young* v. *Crowder*, 2 Sneed, 156; *Tate* v. *Tate*, 11 Hum., 465; 1 Swan, 119; 1 Sneed 1.

M. R. HILL, ETHERIDGE and GARDNER, for the defendants.

CARUTHERS, J., delivered the opinion of the Court.

This case is now before us the second time. It is a suit for the probate of the will of G. W. S. Marr, deceased, upon an issue of *devisavit vel non* in the Circuit Court of Obion. This appeal in error is to reverse a judgment against the validity of the will, upon the new trial granted to the plaintiffs at our last term. We then reversed upon errors of law in the charge of the Court, in relation to the effect to be given to a label on the bundle of papers in which it was found, as may be seen by the report of the case in 5th Sneed. And now the error assigned, is supposed to be found in this clause of the charge: "But if you find that he kept it in a manner that satisfies you that it was a paper not cared for, but *repudiated* by him, or you are *otherwise* satisfied, than from the manner of keeping, that it was a *repudiated* paper, and not intended by him to operate or have effect as his will, then you will find for the defendant."

Again, in reply to a request by the plaintiff's counsel, to charge, that "if G. W. L. Marr, the deceased, prepared the paper in dispute, and placed it among his valuable papers before his death, that the law presumes it is his will, unless he revoked it." The Court said, "if the said paper was written by Marr, and placed among his valuable papers in his lifetime, it would be the will of said Marr, unless he afterwards revoked it, or *repudiated* it, and did not keep it with intent and purpose, that it should operate as his will, as before charged."

The Court rejected an application by the counsel, to instruct the jury that "G. W. L. Marr could not have revoked the paper writing here as his will, if he prepared it and placed it among his valuable papers or effects, unless he did so by a paper writing of the same dignity of the one propounded."

Much difficulty has been experienced by the Courts of this State and those of North Carolina, in the construction of the act of October, 1784, ch. 10, sec. 5, providing for holographic wills, and prescribing the requisites for their validity. Before that, no will for land, was good unless it were signed and acknowledged before two subscribing witnesses. This act made an exception in favor of wills of this description. The first requirement is, that "where any *will* shall be *found* amongst the *valuable* papers or *effects* of any deceased person, or shall have been lodged in the hands of any person for safe keeping," &c.

What is meant by *valuable* papers? No better definition, perhaps, can be given, than that they consist of such as are regarded by the testator as worthy of preservation, and, therefore, in his estimation, of some value. It is not confined to deeds for land or slaves, obligations for money, or certificates of stock. Any others which are kept and considered worthy of being taken care of by the particular person, must be regarded as embraced in that description. This requirement is only intended as an indication on the part of the writer, that it is his intention to preserve and perpetuate the paper in question as a disposition of his property; that he regards *it* as valuable. This is the only point in the requirements of the statute, about which there was any controversy in this case, all the others having been fully made out.

But the Courts have, however, properly held, that even if these requirements all concur, yet, the paper *may* not be valid as a testament. It is to be a "*will*" thus found; and not every *paper* so deposited, is, *necessarily* to be established, though it may be in proper form, in the hand writing, signed, &c. It is still open to attack on various grounds; such as, that the testator was of unsound mind, operated upon by undue influence, fraud, or duress, or that it was never legally assented to by the deceased as a complete and finished act to any extent. To be "found among his valuable papers," implies that it must have been placed there by the writer, or with his knowledge and assent, not surreptitiously by some other person, and so deposited with intent and purpose at the time that it should be his will. But when all *that* is done in conformity to the statute, it is equivalent to a publication; it requires something more than verbal declarations to revoke or defeat it. There must be some act done indicative of a change of purpose, such as the *cancellation*, destruction, or removal from the place of deposit, or reclamation from the hands of the person with whom it may have been lodged.

Chief Justice Best, in 15 Con. Law Rep., 491, in reference to a witnessed will, said: "It has been insisted that declarations of the testator were admissible in evidence, to show that the will he had executed was not valid; but no case had been cited to support such a position, and we shall not, for the first time, establish a doctrine which would render useless the precautions of making a will; for if such evidence were admissible, some witness would constantly be brought forward to set aside the most solemn instruments. Such a doctrine would be not only in the highest degree inconvenient, but contrary to the first principles of evidence, according to which the will itself is the best evidence which the nature of the case supplies." The writing and signing by himself, and the continued deposit among his valuable papers or effects, must have been intended by the Legislature to have the same effect as a signing, and acknowledgment before witnesses. Both amount to a publication in the legal sense, and the latter mode is certainly as solemn and deliberate. In both cases it is under his power till his death, and can only speak from that time. If he can alter, destroy, or change it in the one case, it can be as easily done in the other. It is more easy in the latter case to give effect to a change of mind, for by a simple removal from the place of deposit to a place where there are no *papers* or *effects*, or none of any *value*, it would be invalidated, if so "found" at his death. But in case of a witnessed will, it must be cancelled, destroyed or revoked, expressly or impliedly, by a writing of equal solemnity. A holographic will is of the same dignity when the things prescribed by the statute are done. Yet, on account of the requirement in relation to the place of deposit, the easy additional mode of rendering it invalid, exists, as it must not only be placed by him, but "found," after his death, among papers or things deemed valuable. This change of itself is a sufficient indication, under the statute, of a mind to revoke, or rather it displaces an essential ingredient in the solemnities required.

It is certainly not conclusive in favor of the paper that it is in the form of a testament, perfect in all its parts, written, signed, and found as prescribed. It may, after all that, not be his will, as before stated. It may be shown that he *never intended* it to be his will. But how is that to be shown? what kind of proof is admissible on that point? Upon the charge in relation to that question alone, extracted as a matter of law, our decision must turn in this case.

True, it is competent for the jury, in coming to a conclusion upon this question of fact, for the intent is an important fact in such a case, to look to all the circumstances, both "intrinsic and extrinsic;" but what kind of circumstances? Such as the general rules of law prescribe in such cases, as indicative of the intention that the paper shall be his will, and no others. Rights dependant upon the validity of wills should be as carefully guarded as those derived under deeds, or the statutes of descent and distribution, but not more so. In both cases they are questions of title to property, and are entitled to equal favor.

If it appear in the body of the instrument that it is incomplete, unfinished, not signed, with an attesting clause, but no witnesses, without testamentary form, these are *intrinsic* circumstances, against the intent that the paper should be a final disposition of his property, and tend to raise a presumption that it is not his will. But these circumstances may be rebutted.

But what is the character of *extrinsic* circumstances to which reference may be had in determining the question of intent, in cases falling under this statute, and where its requirements have been fully complied with? Some of them have been before stated as grounds of attack.

The declarations of the party with reference to the particular paper, would be proper to be considered, but entitled to very little, if any, weight, without some act showing an intention to change what he had deliberately done in full compliance with the statute. Having thus shown a settled purpose that such would be his will, there must be something more than simple declarations, if the paper, in his own hand writing, and under his own control, be still permitted to remain in the proper deposit, undisturbed by him, until his death. This law prescribes the requisites for a valid will, and when these are all performed in strict conformity thereto, can it be allowed, upon any proper principle, to countervail and defeat them by mere words and declarations, unaccompanied by any act?

It is not easy to ascertain by what motives a man may be influenced to make such declarations, or even to make overtures for the writing of another will, which was not carried out. All such facts must rest in the memory of witnesses, and are liable to be misunderstood; or, if not, they may have been done or said under some momentary impulse, or crude and unsettled purpose. But the deliberate acts of writing the paper himself in testamentary form, and depositing it with other things of value, with the act of assembly before him, prescribing the effect in law, of what he was doing, afford a safe ground for ascertaining his wishes in relation to his property after his death. If these solemn and deliberate acts can be frustrated by evidence of loose or casual declarations, that he had no will, or that he wanted some one to write a will, or that he had changed his purpose and intention, without any act done to carry out such purpose, which was so easy of accomplishment, if seriously entertained, there would be no certainty in this mode of disposing of a man's property.

The statute framed with so much care and precaution, if this were so, would have signally failed to answer the purpose for which it was designed.

We will not say that verbal declarations are not admissible as evidence in these cases for some purposes. In a case like this, they may be looked to as circumstances to aid in the determination of the question so much controverted; whether the paper was deposited and found among his valuable papers or effects, but not of themselves, to work a revocation. They may tend to illustrate the original intent, but not to show a change of that purpose which is established by the fact of a legal and continuing deposit of the paper. In the case of *Crutcher* v. *Crutcher*, they were proper, because the doubtful question there, was, whether the papers then found were even intended to be testamentary, as they were imperfect, unfinished, and not in the form of testaments, though written by himself.

When the jury were told by his Honor in this case, that "if they were otherwise satisfied than from the manner of keeping it, that it was a *repudiated* paper, and not *intended* to operate or have effect as his will," they should find for the defendants; that is, that it was not his will, what else could they have understood, but that they were at liberty to rely upon his subsequent declarations, that he had no will as sufficient to defeat it, although it remained till his death, properly deposited and unrevoked by any *act* of his? The tendency of the whole charge, is to authorize the jury to recognize a mere parol revocation by a simple change of intent, without any act done to evince that such was his settled purpose.

The word repudiated, in the connection in which it was used, was not very appropriate to convey the legal idea to the jury, and was well calculated to give them a wrong conception of their duty upon the issue submitted to them. Wills, which should be the most solemn act of a man's life connected with his property, are not to be thus lightly regarded when made in conformity to the law.

John Drewry v Lemuel R. Vaden et al.

It may be that this will is in conflict with public sentiment, and against our ideas of equality and justice among his children, or that it was made under a state of feelings towards them, which was afterwards changed; but still the case must be governed by general rules in its investigation and determination. The danger is, that a wrong principle established to accomplish what seems to be right in one case, may defeat right and justice in many others. All cases, therefore, must be governed by the same general rules and principles.

We feel constrained by these considerations, to again reverse the judgment in this case, and grant a second new trial.

JOHN DREWRY v. LEMUEL R. VADEN et al.

SUMMARY PROCEEDING. *Jurisdiction. Circuit Court. Justices of the peace. Acts of* 1801, 1823, *and* 1835. *Code,* § 3591. By the provisions of the acts of 1801, 1823, and 1835, and the 3591 section of the Code, the Circuit Court and justices of the peace have concurrent jurisdiction of motions against officers for failing to pay over money collected by them, and for the non-return of executions within thirty days. But justices of the peace are confined to cases where the amount is within their jurisdiction. The Circuit Court is not limited as to amount.

FROM WEAKLEY.

The motion was made, and disallowed, at the June Term, 1858, FITZGERALD, J., presiding. The plaintiff appealed.

John Drewry *v.* Lemuel R. Vaden *et al.*

CARUTHERS, J., delivered the opinion of the Court.

A motion was made in the Circuit Court of Weakley, at February Term, 1857, by Drewry, against Vaden, a constable of that county, and his sureties, "for failing to return within the time prescribed by law, and paying over the money upon an execution which was issued and placed in his hands for collection on the first day of September, 1853, for $22.72, besides costs, in favor of the said John Drewry, and against S. L. Williams and S. Williams, and stayed by W. Faust."

The motion was refused, as appears from the record, upon the ground of want of jurisdiction in such a case, as the money had not been collected. We do not so understand the statutes.

By the act of 1801, (Car. & Nich., 180,) the motion is given against the constable before the County Court, for failure to render the moneys on executions in twenty days, if not staid, and in thirty if there be a stay, after its expiration, "unless by his return it shall appear no property can be found." Cook's Rep. 267.

By the act of 1835, (Car. & Nich., 211, § 10,) "all judgments by *motion*, now cognizable in the County Court, shall be cognizable *only* in the Circuit Courts."

Now, by the act of 1801, as we have seen, the County Court had this jurisdiction, not only where the money was collected, but even where it was not, and he failed to show, by his "return," that it could not be made. Consequently the same jurisdiction passed to the Circuit Court in such cases, and has never been taken away.

In cases where the money was collected and not

paid over, the act of 1823, (Car. & Nich., 182,) conferred jurisdiction for the first time upon justices of the peace to give judgment by motion. In 1835, the same was given to a justice for failure to return in thirty days. But this did not oust the Circuit Court of the jurisdiction it then had of the same matter, but it was concurrent.

The Code (§ 3591) *continues* this concurrent jurisdiction over these motions. Of course this is confined, as to the justices of the peace, to cases within their jurisdiction, but in the Court to any amount.

Taking these acts altogether, we conclude, contrary to our first impression, that the Circuit Court had jurisdiction to render judgment for *a failure to return* an execution in proper time, whether the money was collected or not.

But not having the facts fully before us, we reverse the judgment, and remand the case for the action of the Circuit Court.

JACOB F. FISHER *v.* WILLIAM POLLARD.

WARRANTY. *When it embraces visible defects. Evidence.* A general warranty of soundness, whether in writing or by parol, does not extend to an unsoundness or defect which is plain and obvious to the purchaser, or of which he had cognizance. But to exclude a defect or disease from the operation of the warranty, it must be of such a character or description as to disclose to the vendee, not only the *existence*, but the *extent* of the defect or disease, and if this is not so, it is

Jacob F. Fisher *v.* William Pollard.

covered by the warranty. And parol evidence to show that the defect was obvious, or that the seller disclosed the unsoundness at the time of the sale, is admissible, notwithstanding the warranty may be in writing.

FROM DECATUR.

This cause was heard at the July Term, 1858, WALKER, J., presiding. Verdict and Judgment for the plaintiff. The defendant appealed.

M. & H. BROWN, for the plaintiff in error.

MAXWELL and DOHERTY, for the defendant in error.

CARUTHERS, J., delivered the opinion of the Court.

In August, 1857, Pollard sold to Fisher a slave named Bill, for $800, and a certain iron gray horse, provided the slave, then runaway, could be obtained in possession by the vendee. In that event the money was to be paid, and the horse delivered, and "said Fisher agrees to make all things right as to the horse above spoken of, *as to soundness in every respect."* Such is the contract as set forth in a writing that day signed by both parties. The events contemplated, all, very soon after, happened. The money was paid, the horse delivered, and a bill of sale executed for the slave. In March, 1858, this action was instituted for unsoundness in the horse, and a verdict and judgment for $150 against the defendant.

There is nothing in the objection, that as this trade

was conditional, that is, only to take effect in the event the slave was reclaimed, the written warranty of the soundness of the horse was not obligatory. The contingency having happened, it took full effect as if it had been at first without condition. So, the contract of warranty was binding.

The main controversy in the case, upon the trial, was as to the extent of the warranty. It was conceded that the horse was unsound in one or both of his eyes; but this, it was insisted was visible to the most casual observer, and was, in fact, well known to the vendee, and consequently not covered by the warranty. How the facts were in that respect is not so material now, as the jury have passed upon them, but the question before us is, whether the law was correctly charged by the Court on that doctrine.

It is well settled that a *general* warranty of soundness, whether in writing or parol, does not extend to an unsoundness or defect which is plain and obvious to the purchaser, or of which he had cognizance. 1 Par. on Con., 460, (top,) and *n. i.;* 2 Hum., 308. This is upon the ground that it will not be presumed that the parties intended to embrace in the general terms employed in the contract, imperfections well known to both, or so plainly visible and obvious as that they must be presumed to have been known by the vendee. This rule is always applied for the purpose of restricting the general words used, to the manifest intention and understanding of the parties. It would be absurd to suppose that the seller intended to make, and the vendee supposed he was receiving, a warranty against defects well known to both parties, or so apparent and visible as to be obvious to ordinary observation.

The case of *Long* v. *Hicks*, 2 Hum., 305, decides, that "a written warranty does not extend to defects which are visible, or of which the vendee is informed at the time of sale." The case before the Court, to which this principle was applied, rested upon the correctness of the charge to the jury, in these words: "That if the negro was unsound at the date of the warranty, there was a breach, and that *they were to disregard the testimony* as to the knowledge of the plaintiffs in reference to the unsoundness." The Court had rejected all proof of the knowledge of the purchaser of the unsoundness. It is stated in the opinion, in that case, that the proof shows "that the unsoundness was so obvious, that any one who had ever seen a negro might discover it by casual view;" and the purchaser, in reference to it, said he did not care, as the woman was worth the money he was paying for both. That decision was certainly correct, and so is the rule laid down in reference to it. That case was fully recognized in the charge now before us.

But the character of the *known* or *patent* defects, which, according to this principle, are excluded from the warranty, is another question. The want of a tail, or ear, or limb, are certainly excluded, but any other *permanent* defect or unsoundness known or visible, would likewise be embraced by the rule. But if it is made known, or seen, that there is some defect in the eye, or a *splint* on the leg, without present lameness from it, but afterwards the eye went out from the injuries, or the horse became lame from the effects of the *splint*, yet the warranty of soundness would cover those defects, because the extent of the disease or defect was not known. The principle seems to be, that to exclude a defect from the operation of a general warranty of soundness, upon the ground that it is known to the purchaser, or might have been because of it being plain and obvious, it must appear that the vendee was not misled as to its character or extent. The fact that a slave has a cough, or doubtful indications of a cancer, white swelling, dropsy, or any other disease, and this known to the buyer, does not save the seller from the obligations of a *general* warranty of soundness, if these appearances and indications should turn out to be the incipient stages of a permanent disease. 1 Par. on Con., 460, *n*. (i), and cases there cited. To exclude a defect or disease from the operation of the warranty, it must be of such a character or description, as to disclose to the vendee not only the existence, but the extent of the defect or disease, and if this is not so, it is covered by the warranty.

To illustrate by the case in hand. Some defect in the eye of the horse was not only made known, but was visible; but it was said by the vendor it resulted from an injury recently received by a blow, and its extent was not declared, nor could it be discovered. This sort of case is covered by the warranty, even though there be no fraud.

The part of the charge particularly objected to is this, "if a horse is sold with a written warranty of soundness, the vendor could not protect himself from an action by introducing parol proof to show that he disclosed the unsoundness at the time of the sale, and that the vendee took the horse at his own risk." Proof to show these facts was offered and rejected. We are not able to reconcile this position in the charge to the general rule, that defects *known* to the vendee are not covered by the warranty. The rule stated in *Long* v. *Hicks* is, that a written warranty does not extend to "defects of which the vendee is *informed at the time of sale.*" If the writing specified that the eyes or the limbs were sound, or that the animal was free from the glanders or any other specified disease, then it would not be admissible to prove in the face of the writing, that such disease was made known or excepted; the rule would be the same if the warranty was in parol. But when the warranty is in general terms, we think the law is too well settled to be now disturbed, that defects known or visible, are not covered; and, consequently, proof to establish these facts must be competent. The object of the rule is, not to defeat or contradict the contract, but to define and explain it; not to frustrate the intention of the parties, but to ascertain what was meant by them to be covered by the undertaking of the vendor. The rule itself would seem, at first view, to infringe upon other established principles, but with this explanation of it, perhaps it does not. At all events, it is fixed and settled, whether it be consistent with other rules, or an exception to them.

In this particular we think his Honor erred, though his charge is, in other respects, very able and correct on the doctrine involved.

From what we see of the case, it is by no means certain, that a correct charge, on this point, with the proof rejected, would have changed the result; because,

E. R. Egnew et al. v. S. W. Cochrane et al.

it may be that all which was said and made known at the time, would only amount to the disclosure of a blemish or injury that might not have been understood by the parties to be permanent, in which case it would not be exempted from the warranty, but be covered by it, in the event that it turned out to be more serious and fatal than the information communicated, or the appearance indicated. In other words, the *extent* of the disease, or defect may not have been obvious or made known, and if not, as we have seen, it would still fall under the warranty of soundness.

But the defendant was entitled to the benefit of his proof on this point, before the jury, on a correct charge.

For this error, the judgment will be reversed.

E. R. EGNEW *et. al. v.* S. W. COCHRANE *et al.*

1. LAWS IN FORCE. *What portions of the law of North Carolina in force. Cession act. Constitution of* 1796, *and* 1834. By the cession act, the laws in force and use in the State of North Carolina at the time of its passage, were to be and continue in force within the ceded territory until repealed or altered by the Legislature thereof. And by the Constitution of 1796, it was declared that all the laws then in force and use in said territory, not inconsistent with it, should continue to be in force and use in this State until they should expire, be altered, or repealed by the Legislature. The Constitution of 1834 has a clause to the same effect.

2. LAND LAW. *Entry and entry taker. Act of* 1777, *ch.* 1, § 18 By the Act of 1777, ch. 1, § 18, if any entry taker is desirous of making any entry of lands in his own name, such entry shall be made in its

E. R. Egnew et al. v. S. W. Cochrane et al.

proper place before a justice of the peace of the county not being a surveyor or assistant, which entry the justice shall return to the County Court at its next sitting, &c.; and every entry made by, or for such entry taker, in any other manner, is illegal and void, and any other person may enter, survey, and obtain a grant for the same land.

3. SAME. *Same. Same. Not repealed.* The 18th section of the act of 1777 has not expired or become obsolete by non-user, nor changed by practice and usage; neither has it been repealed by the act of 1796, or by the 6th section of the act of 1801, ch. 3, or by the act of 1806, ch, 1, or by the act of 1819—said section of the act of 1777 is in full force.

4. SAME. *Same. Same. Applicable to lands south and west of the Congressional Reservation Line.* The 18th section of the act of 1777 is applicable to, and embraces that portion of the State south and west of the Congressional Reservation Line.

5. SAME. *Same. Common law.* Upon common law principles, the entry taker cannot make an entry in his own name, before himself, because it is against public policy.

6. SAME. *Same. Question reserved.* Is a grant obtained by the entry taker, upon an entry before himself, to be regarded as void and open to attack in a Court of Law, or only voidable at the suit of the party aggrieved in a Court of Equity?

7. SAME. *Same. Same.* What would be the effect of a purchase from the grantee thus obtaining a grant upon his own entry, and can a person holding a younger entry and grant call in question the prior grant of the same land to the entry taker?*

FROM OBION.

The bill was dismissed upon demurrer, by Chancellor WILLIAMS, at the February Term, 1858. The complainants appealed.

---

*It will, perhaps, be found, upon a close examination of the opinion, that this case was decided upon the principles settled in the case of *Fogg et al. v. Hill;* and the *syllabus* contains principles that are not, authoritatively, settled by the Court.

W. P. SMITH, for the complainants.

JAMES DAVIS and A. B. ENLOE, for the defendants, the latter of whom said:

It will be seen that complainant's entries were made under the act of 1819, ch. 1, and subject to the limitations of the act of 1823, ch. 35; and that defendant's entries were made in the intervening time, between the expiration of the extending act of 1850, ch. 138, and the enacting of the extending act of 1851, ch. 326, and, therefore, the defendant has a good title to said lands. *Vaughn & Brown* v. *Hatfield*, 5 Yer., 236; *Williamson* v. *Throop*, 11 Hum., 265; *Sampson* v. *Taylor*, 1 Sneed, 600.

But it is alleged that defendant, Cochrane, was, at the date of his entries, entry taker of Obion county, and said entries were made without complying with the provisions of the act of 1777, ch. 1. The 18th section of said act prescribes the mode of making entries by entry takers. 2 H. & Cobb, p. 17, &c.

The act of 1777, ch. 1, is an act of the North Carolina Legislature, and only in force in this State by virtue of the eighth condition of the Cession Act of 1789, ch. 3, § 1, (H. & Cobb, 7,) and only remained in force until repealed, or otherwise altered.

The Constitution of 1796, art. 10, § 2, provides that all laws and ordinances now in force and use, &c., &c., should continue until they shall expire, be altered, or repealed. The Constitution of 1834, art. 11, § 1, makes the same provision. N. & C., p. 59.

Hence, it will be seen, that the laws of North Carolina were only temporarily in force and use in this State.

The Tennessee Legislature, by the act of 1801, ch. 3, § 6, prescribes entirely a different mode of making entries by entry takers, than the mode prescribed by the 18th section of the act of 1777, ch. 1. Scott's Revisal, p. 761.

The act of 1777, ch. 1, requires the entry taker to make his entry before a justice of the peace, and it was made his duty to return said entry to the County Court, &c. The act of 1801, ch. 3, required the entry taker to make oath that the claim, &c., &c., was just, &c., before a justice of the peace, and said justice of the peace was required to subscribe his name officially to said entry. The entry taker performed every other duty in relation to said entry, as he did in case of other entries.

It is insisted that the act of 1801, ch. 3, repealed the act of 1777, ch. 1; and being a foreign law only in use temporarily, when once repealed, is forever gone, without special enactment reviving said law.

Again, it is insisted that the act of 1777, ch. 1, is repealed by the act of 1806, ch. 1, which act prescribes another and different mode of entering lands. Said act of 1806, abolishes the offices of county entry taker and surveyor, and establishes in their stead the office of principal surveyor, who acts as entry taker, and makes no distinction, in the mode of entering, between the entry taker and other enterers; and the 37th section of said act in terms repeals the act of 1801, ch. 3, § 2. H. & Cobb, 2d vol., 44, &c.

E. R. Egnew *et al.* v. S. W. Cochrane *et al.*

The modes of entering lands in this State, since 1801, are in conflict with the act of 1777, ch. 1. A repeal or alteration of any of the North Carolina laws introduced into this State, is a satisfaction of the Cession Act and Constitution.

The office of entry taker, separate from the office of principal surveyor, was wholly unknown to the laws of this State from 1806 to 1836, when the office of county entry taker was established.

The act of 1819, ch. 1, introduces a system of land laws applicable, alone, to the lands lying in that portion of this State south and west of the Congressional Reservation Line; and the titles south and west of said line have to be procured upon the plan and terms prescribed in said act and the subsequent acts of the Legislature. *Sampson* v. *Taylor*, 1 Sneed, 602.

The mode of entering land prescribed in the act of 1819, is inconsistent with the act of 1777. 2 H. & Cobb, 85.

The act of 1842, ch. 34, prescribes still a different mode of entering lands. The 10th section of said act prescribes the form of making entries; the 18th section prescribes a penalty for embezzling money received by the entry taker. Nicholson Sup., 199, &c.

There is no act of the Legislature, since 1801, that contemplates or requires the intervention of a Court or justice of the peace in case an entry taker should desire to make an entry for himself. The act of 1844, ch. 8, N. Sup., 211, provides still another mode of procuring titles to the vacant lands in this State, and makes no provisions for the operation of the act of 1777.

E. R. Egnew *et al.* v. S. W. Cochrane *et al.*

If the act of 1777 is unrepealed, it had become obsolete by reason of the non-user of said act.

It has been the constant practice of the principal surveyors, since the opening of the county office, for the entry takers to make entries in their names, and for themselves, without pursuing any other mode than was usual and practiced by other enterers; which shows the understanding and judgment of the officers of the law upon that subject, and shows that the act of 1777 was not used.

The legislation for half a century, in relation to the making of entries of land, nowhere requires the intervention of a Court or justice, as prescribed by the act relied on by complainants; which shows that the Legislature did not consider the act in force, and the universal practice of another mode of entering lands by the officers (if proper to be considered) shows the same interpretation of the law, &c.

WRIGHT, J., delivered the opinion of the Court.

The complainants, George R. Egnew and Eleanor Maxwell are the heirs of George M. and Jesse W. Egnew, deceased.

On the 24th of May, 1843, they caused an entry to be made in their names, in the entry taker's office of Obion county, for 166 acres of land, in that county, by virtue of a certificate warrant issued to them on the 27th of August, 1842.

On the 3d of June, 1843, they caused two other entries to be made in their names, in the same office, for lands lying in Obion county—one for 200, and the other for 153½ acres.

These entries were also founded upon certificate warrants, issued to them by John S. Young, secretary and commissioner of West Tennessee—the one on the 29th of August, 1842, and the other the 20th of April, 1843.

All these entries were *special*, and a valid appropriation of the land.

It seems that no grants were issued upon these entries; and, on the 15th of September, 1851, the defendant, Cochrane, by virtue of the fees paid into the office, entered the same lands in his name, in the office of the entry taker of Obion county, he, at the time, being the entry taker for said county.

In making said entries, he did not pursue the requirements of the 18th section of the act of the State of North Carolina, passed in the year 1777, ch. 1. Grants have issued to him upon his entries.

In October and November, 1857, complainants, George R. and Eleanor, caused their entries to be surveyed, and the plats and certificates of survey, with the proper fees, were tendered by them to W. P. Hill, then the entry taker of said county, for the purpose of obtaining grants upon said entries; but he refused to receive the fees, or permit complainants to obtain grants, because of the entries in the name of defendant, Cochrane.

The object of this bill is to divest the legal title to these lands out of defendant, Cochrane, and to vest the same in complainants, George R. and Eleanor.

In making his entries, the defendant acted upon the assumption that the lands had become vacant by reason

E. R. Egnew *et al.* v. S. W. Cochrane *et al.*

of the *hiatus*, between the last of August and the 13th of November, 1851—a period of two months and thirteen days—in the law, extending the time for making surveys and obtaining grants upon entries.

It is manifest, from reading the bill and exhibits, that when he made these entries, he had both actual and constructive notice of the prior entries of complainants, George R. and Eleanor.

The Chancellor dismissed the bill upon demurrer.

This decree is erroneous. The entries of complainants, George R. and Eleanor, being founded upon *North Carolina land warrants*, the case comes directly within the decision of this Court, made at the present term, in *Fogg et al.* v. *Hill and Williams*.

We need only refer to the opinion of the Court in that case, as decisive of this, without again stating its principles.

Another question is, whether Cochrane, being the entry taker, could, legally, make these entries for himself. The act of 1777, ch. 1, § 18, above referred to, provides that if any entry taker be desirous to make any entry of lands in his own name, such entry shall be made in its proper place before a justice of the peace of the county—not being a surveyor or assistant—which entry the justice shall return to the County Court at their next sitting; and the County Court shall insert such entry, and every entry made by or for such entry taker in any other manner than is herein directed, shall be illegal and void, and any other person may enter, survey, and obtain a grant for the same land.

It is argued that this section of the act of 1777—if it ever was the law of this State—has become obsolete, or been repealed, and, in any event, is inapplicable to that portion of the State which lies south and west of the Congressional Reservation Line. It seems not to have been considered as repealed or obsolete, by Messrs. Haywood & Cobb, and is preserved in their Revisal of the Statutes of Tennessee, and not embraced in the "table of repealed and obsolete laws." 2 Haywood & Cobbs' Rev., 20, 190.

It is clear that it originally applied to the entire vacant territory of the State of North Carolina, extending as far west as the Mississippi river, and including these very lands. Acts 1777, ch. 31; 1783, ch. 2, § 3, (1 Scott's Rev., 221, 267;) 2 Meigs' Dig., 662. And it is equally plain that it was in force and use in the State of North Carolina at the time of the passage of the Cession Act of 1789. *Tyrrell* v. *Mooney*, 1 Murphey, 375, 401; *Terrell et al.* v. *Logan*, 3 Hawks., 319. And, therefore, became a law of the ceded territory, and of the State of Tennessee upon the adoption of the Constitution of 1796.

The Cession Act provides that the laws in force and use in the State of North Carolina at the time of its passage, shall be, and continue in full force within the ceded territory, until the same shall be repealed, or otherwise altered by the legislative authority of the said territory. And in the Constitution of this State, in 1796, it was declared that all the laws then in force and use in said territory, not inconsistent with the Constitution, should continue to be in force and use in this State until they should expire, be altered, or repealed by the Legislature. The Constitution of 1834 has a clause to the same effect.

E. R. Egnew et al. v. S. W. Cochrane et al.

We are not able to perceive that this section of the act of 1777 has expired, or become obsolete. It is, upon the face of it, perpetual, without limitation or time fixed when it shall cease to be in force; and we are bound to give it effect, in every case which falls within its provisions, until it is repealed by the Legislature. *Brice* v. *The State*, 2 Tenn. R., 255, 256. It may be that no entry has been made under its requirements, even for half a century. But how are we to know that? The record does not inform us how the fact is. And if it were so, we do not understand that a statute can be repealed by non-user. The want of individual cases under it, or the existence of a series of cases in violation of it, ought not, we apprehend, to destroy the law. Dwarris on Statutes, 9 Law Library, 29, top page; *Brice* v. *The State*, 2 Tenn. Rep., 255, 256, 257, 258.

Then has it been repealed, or so altered by the Legislature, as to enable us to dispense with its provisions? It is insisted it has upon various grounds.

First. It is said the act of 1777, if ever of force, being so only by the Cession Act and the Constitution of 1796, any *alteration* of it by the legislative authority of the territory or State, *though it did not touch the* 18*th section* would satisfy the Cession Act and the Constitution, and put an end to the *entire act;* and that such an alteration having been made as early as 1799 and 1801, this section is not now in force in this State, nor has been for half a century. This position is untenable. The repeal of a statute may be total, or only partial, according to the will of the Legislature; and we know of no difference, in this respect, between the statute of the State of North Carolina, made of force here by the

Cession Act and Constitution, and one of our own enacting. And that there is no such difference, will appear from the authority of *Brice* v. *The State*, 2 Tenn. R., 258, 259. See, also, *State* v. *Patterson*, 2 Ird. R., 356. Unless the *section itself* has been repealed, or altered, it must be declared in force.

Secondly. It is said to be repealed by the 6th section of the act of 1801, ch. 3, (1 Scott, 672,) which provides that no entry taker in this State shall receive or admit any entry or location to be made in his or their office, unless the person applying to make such entry first make oath that the claim or warrant on which such entry or location is founded, is equitable, just, and legal, to the best of his knowledge and belief; which oath the entry taker is empowered to administer. Nor shall any entry taker, for himself, make any entry but on oath as aforesaid, before some justice of the peace of his county, which justice shall subscribe his name officially to such entry. We perceive no conflict between these two sections, and are of opinion they may both stand together. Dwarris, 9 Law Lib., 31. It certainly was not the intention, as we think, by anything in this act, to supersede the requirements of the 18th section of the act of 1777. And if it had been, the former act is expressly repealed by the 37th section of the act of 1806, ch. 1, (1 Scott, 305,) and thereby the 18th section of the act of 1777 is revived. Dwarris, 9 Law Lib., 32.

Third. The system of obtaining grants to land through the offices of county entry taker and surveyor, established by the act of 1777, was changed by the act of 1806, ch. 1, to the district system, and the office of principal surveyor created; and he required to perform the duties of both the entry taker and surveyor. This continued to be the case until 1836, when the system of county offices was restored, and an entry taker and surveyor for each county again elected. Act 1835-6, ch. 48. It is now insisted that *this change* was a repeal of the 18th section of the act of 1777. We do not assent to this argument. The necessity for this law is the same under either system. It was immaterial in whose hands might be confided the duties of the entry taker, so long as lands remained to enter the propriety of this law could not be questioned, unless an entry, by the entry taker or surveyor, for himself, were altogether prohibited.

In an examination of the changes and modifications which the land law of this State has undergone, we have not been able to discover anything in the act of 1819, or other legislation of the State, which either repeals or alters this section of the act of 1777; but much to the contrary. And the fact that during all this time, while many portions of the system have been amended, altered and repealed, even the oath required in the act of 1801, a thing closely connected with the subject, being expressly repealed, no notice, whatever, has been taken of this section—so far from being an argument against it—is evidence that the legislature was content with it, and purposely omitted its repeal. Dwarris 9 Law Lib., 50. And it would certainly be going a great way to hold that the repeated legislation of this State, defining the duties of entry taker in general terms, and, evidently, as we think, in regard to entries to be made by *others*, should have the effect of repealing the *special and particular provision* in regard to

E. R. Egnew *et al. v.* S. W. Cochrane *et al.*

entries to be made by *himself*, to be found only in the act of 1777. Dwarris, 9 Law Lib., 86.

Finally. It is argued that it has been the constant *practice* of surveyors and entry takers south and west of the Congressional Reservation Line, to make entries in their own names and for themselves—without the intervention of a court, or justice of the peace, and it is believed that not a single instance can be found in the reservation, in which the requirements of the 18th section of the act of 1777, have been complied with, although hundreds of entries have been made by said officers in their own names, and many thousand acres of land thus appropriated. And it is insisted that this *practice* and *usage of these officers*, called into action when the statutes were new, and acquiesced in for so long a time by the whole community, furnish *contemporaneous construction* of them binding upon the courts, and that serious would be the consequences to hold differently at this day.

But how do we know anything of the existence of this practice and usage? It is not alleged in the bill, or anywhere shown in the record. We cannot judicially know it. It is not embodied in any judical opinion or public record of which we can take cognizance. Like any other fact it must be alleged and proved. 2 Greenl. Ev., secs. 248 to 252; 1 Id., secs. 4 to 6; *Smith* v. *Wright*, 1 Caine's R., 43.

In the cases in 1 Yer., 376, and 1 Cranch., 299, to which we have been referred, the evidence of interpretation was drawn from *judicial decisions*. But if we had evidence of this practice, is it true that repeated violations of a law through a series of years, by the very parties interested in its infraction, can be received by the courts as material for the application of the doctrine of contemporaneous construction? I will not say, without further argument, that usage may not, in some cases, be pleaded to assist the Court in the construction of a doubtful statute. But certainly it must be received with great caution and care taken not to transgress the limits of the law. *The King* v. *Miller*, 6 T. R., 269. The principle of contemporaneous construction has been considered applicable to statutes where the words are obscure, or doubtful, and generally, we believe, has been founded upon the judicial determinations of the country. An eminent judge has said, that great regard ought, in construeing a statute, to be paid to the construction which the sages of the law, who lived about the time, or soon after it was made, put upon it; because they were best able to judge of the intention of the makers at the time when the law was made. Dwarris, 9 Law Lib., 42.

We are, therefore, driven to the conclusion that the 18th section of the act of 1777, is not inapplicable to that portion of the State south and west of the Congressional Reservation Line, and that it is to be regarded by us as in force and use. But it is not necessary, in this case, conclusively so to adjudge, though we do not see how it is to be escaped.

Upon common law principles, the entry taker cannot, as we think, make an entry in his own name, before himself, because it is against public policy. No such thing was contemplated, as we are satisfied, any where in our landed system. His interest would, in many cases, conflict with his duty. Not that there has been anything intentionally wrong in this particular case. The high character of the gentleman who filled the office forbids any such supposition. But as a rule of law founded in public policy, for wise reasons, it cannot be allowed in any case. It is upon the same reasoning that a sheriff is not permitted to buy at his own sale, or execute his own writ—nor a surveyor to make his own survey—nor a clerk to take the probate of his own deed. *Avery* v. *Walker*, 1 Hawks, 140; *Greenler* v. *Tate et al.*, 1 Dev., 300.

That the principle is applicable here, we have only to examine our legislation. By the act of 1836, restoring the office of county entry taker, he is to be governed by the same law as the surveyors, while acting as entry takers, had been, under the act of 1819 and other acts. How could he select arbitrators to value improvements, under the 12th section, to be paid for by himself, in case *his own entry conflicted with the settler?* Or conduct the drawings for priority of entry under the 16th section? Or, if one or more persons offer to enter the same land, at the same time with himself, how could he have the priority between them determined by lot under the 17th section? He is to demand and receive fees. Sec. 47. Does this mean of himself? By the 10th section of the act of 1842, ch. 34, the enterer is to *tender to the entry taker* his location, and the same is to remain on file twenty days before he records it; and if then no person files *just reasons* in writing against it, the entry taker shall record it; but should *just reasons* be filed with the *entry taker why such entry should not be made*, he shall not record the same until the dispute shall be settled. How could he, *in his own case*, determine as to the reasons against the entry?

Under the act of 1843, the entry taker had to dispose of the public land to the highest bidder, through offers to be made him, and the person paying the most for the land become the enterer, and obtained the grant. How is it possible here to suppose that the entry taker could, himself, be permitted to take and enter any of the lands so offered? *Maxwell* v. *Wallace*, 3 Ird. Eq. R., 593.

But it is useless further to multiply instances. The whole current of our legislation, it seems to me, demonstrates that he was not to make his own entry before himself.

What is to be the effect upon a grant thus obtained by the entry taker—whether it is to be regarded as void, and open to attack in a court of law, or only voidably at the suit of the party aggrieved in a court of equity—we need not here decide, because complainants have the oldest entries, and standing as they do, in a court of equity, have a right to have the defendant, Cochrane, declared a trustee for them, and a legal title decreed to them. 1 Mur., 401; 4 Dev., 417, 596; 2 Dev. and Batt, Law Rep. 246.

It seems, however, to have been decided in North Carolina to be only voidable. *Tyrrell* v. *Mooney*, 1 Mur. 401.

Nor are we called upon to decide as to the case of a purchaser under such a grantee, nor whether one holding a younger entry and grant can call in question the prior grant of the same land to the entry taker. These are questions not necessarily in this case, and we do not intend now to determine them. 1 Mur., 401; 1 Hawk., 140; 2 do., 231; 3 do., 319; 1 Dev., 300; 2 Mur. 375; 4 Dev., 417, 596; 2 Dev. and Batt. Law R., 246; *Jackson* v. *Lawton*, 10 Johns. R., 23; 4 Hum., 203; 1 Sneed, 134; 2 Sneed, 674.

And it is alike unnecessary for us to put a construction upon the second section of the act of 1853, ch. 24—since it is palpable it does not help the defendant in the present controversy.

The decree of the Chancellor will be reversed, and the cause remanded for an answer.

Martha J. Clark v. Hugh M. Clark et al.

1. WILL. *Construction. Estate tail. Rule as to realty and personalty.* As a general rule, whenever the words of a will, if applied to real property, would create an estate tail, they will, when applied to personalty, vest the absolute property in the first taker.

2. SAME. *Same. Same.* The testator, by his will, bequeathed to his daughter, who was a *feme sole*, certain slaves and sums of money, with directions to his executor to invest the money in young negroes for her benefit. The bequest is subject to the following provision, namely: "The said negroes with their increase shall be *entailed* on my said daughter Martha J., and her children, and not be taken for the debts of her husband." It is held, that the above rule has no application to this clause. That by the use of the word *entailed* it was not the intention of the testator to create an *entail* in the technical sense of that term. And the daughter took the negroes and money to her sole and separate use for life, free from the marital right of any future husband, with remainder to her children.

FROM HAYWOOD.

A decree was pronounced for the complainant at the

Martha J. Clark v. Hugh M. Clark et al.

February Term, 1859, by Chancellor WILLIAMS. The defendants appealed.

L. M. CAMPBELL and M. & H. BROWN, for the complainants.

T. G. & W. M. SMITH, for the defendants.

McKINNEY, J., delivered the opinion of the Court.

The bill seeks to have the rights of the complainant declared, under the will of her deceased father, Jacob Wilson. The testator, by his will, bequeathed to the camplainant, who was then a *feme sole*, certain slaves and sums of money, with direction to his executor to invest the money in young negroes for her benefit. The bequest is subject to the following provision, namely: "The said negroes, with their increase, shall be *entailed* on my said daughter, Martha J., and her children, and not be taken for the debts of her husband."

In 1848, sometime after testator's death, the complainant intermarried with John C. Clark, who died in 1855, leaving two infant children, the issue of said marriage.

It appears that sometime after the marriage, the executor purchased two slaves, with the money of the complainant, and delivered them to her husband. And afterwards, the executor having in his hands $1800 of the money bequeathed to complainant, instead of investing it in negroes himself, paid it over to the husband, to be by him invested pursuant to the direction of the will. In the receipts and acquittances executed by the husband to the executor, for the slaves specifically bequeathed to complainant by the will, and the two slaves purchased by the executor, and also for the money above mentioned, the former, either expressly or impliedly, acknowledges the property and money to have been received by him, subject to the provision of the testator's will, and the rights of the complainant.

The question now is, whether, under the before recited provision of the will, said slaves and money were the separate property of the wife, for life, with remainder to her children, or vested in the husband upon his marriage with complainant.

The Chancellor decreed for the complainant, and we think correctly. It is certainly true, as a general rule, that whenever the words of a will, if applied to real property, would create an estate tail, they will, when applied to personalty, vest the absolute property in the first taker. 7 Yer., 519, 525; 9 Yer., 242.

But this rule has no application to the present case. By the use of the word "entailed," in the clause of the will under consideration, it is not to be supposed that it was the intention of the testator to create an *entail*, in the technical sense of that term. The object and intention of the testator manifestly was, to make a settlement on his daughter, to her sole and separate use, for life, free from the marital right of any future husband, with remainder to her children, in the event of a future marriage and issue. This is, beyond all doubt, the proper construction of the will. And in this view, the slaves remaining in specie will be settled accordingly, and the executor of Clark will account for the value of such, if any, as may have been converted by his testator during the marriage; and, also, for the amount of money by him received, belonging to the complainant. The cause will be remanded for taking the account ordered by the Chancellor.

Decree affirmed.

Joseph Croone v. N. W. Bivens et al.

1. PARTNERSHIP. *Sale, by one partner, of his interest in the firm. Lien.* Where a partner sells his interest in the partnership concern, either to his co-partners or strangers, he has no lien on the partnership property for the payment of partnership debts for which he is liable. He cannot pursue specifically, or have an account of the effects of the late firm of which he was a partner, to the end that they may be subject to the satisfaction of claims existing against the firm.

2. SAME. *Same. Same. Contract to pay the debts of the firm.* The fact that when such partner retired, his co-partners stipulated to pay the debts of the concern, and indemnify him, can make no difference, he having trusted to the personal covenants of his assignees; unless he retains an interest in, or lien upon, the effects transferred, or stipulates that they shall be applied in payment of the partnership debts.

3. CHANCERY JURISDICTION. *When surety entitled to relief.* A surety has a right to bring his principal and the creditor into a Court of Chancery, to compel the payment of the debt for which he is bound.

4. SAME. *Same. Partnership. Question reserved.* If one partner, who is bound for the firm debts, sells his interest in the firm to his co-partners, who agree to pay the debts and release him, can he be regarded in the light of a surety for them, and come into a Court of Chancery to compel payment of the debts?

5. SAME. *Fraudulent conveyances, may be attacked without judgment. Code, § 4288.* Under section 4288 of the Code, a creditor may, without first having obtained a judgment at law, come into Chancery to

set aside fraudulent conveyances of property, or other devices resorted to for the purpose of hindering and delaying creditors, and subject the property, by sale, or otherwise, to the satisfaction of his debt.

FROM MADISON.

The bill was dismissed on demurrer by Chancellor WILLIAMS, at the February Term, 1859. The complainant appealed.

M. & H. BROWN, for the complainant.

M. BULLOCK, TOMLIN, and STEPHENS, for the defendants.

WRIGHT, J., delivered the opinion of the Court.

The Chancellor dismissed the bill, and amended bill, upon demurrer, and in this we think he acted properly.

The case is governed by *Smith* v. *Edwards et al.*, 7 Hum., 106. It is there held, that where a partner sells his interest in the partnership concern, either to his co-partners or strangers, he has no lien on the partnership property for the payment of partnership debts for which he is liable, any more than those against the private property, or effects of his former partners. He cannot pursue specifically, or have an account of the effects of the late firm of which he was a partner, to the end, that they might be subject to the satisfaction of claims existing against the firm. And the fact, that when he retired, his co-partners stipulated to pay the debts of the concern, and indemnify him, can make no difference, he having trusted to the personal covenants of his assignees.

Here, the case made is, that complainants, Nathaniel W. Bivens and William H. Stone, were, at first, partners under the firm name of N. W. Bivens & Co., after which they took in one Emmerson, and the business progressed under the firm name of Bivens, Croone & Co. After this, complainant and Bivens purchased out the interest of Stone and Emmerson, and the concern was carried on under the partnership style of Croone & Bivens, until the 8th of January, 1857, when complainant transferred all his interest in said firms, to said Bivens and one Bryan, and placed the assets, of every kind, in their possession, in consideration of which, they, in writing, stipulated to pay all the outstanding debts against said firms, and to release complainant therefrom.

He retains no interest in, or lien upon, the effects so transferred; nor is there any stipulation that they shall be applied in payment of the partnership debts.

Bivens & Bryan have failed to pay said debts, or to have complainant released, and he has been sued and forced to pay a part of them, and is liable to pay the residue; and the said Bivens and Bryan are insolvent, and are applying the assets so transferred to their own private use.

The object of the bill is to obtain an account of these assets, specifically, to have the firm debts paid, and complainant released.

But, as we have seen, upon the authority of *Smith* v. *Edwards et al.*, and the cases there cited; the bill can-

Joseph Croone v. N. W. Bivens *et al.*

ot be maintained, and complainant must look to the personal covenants of Bivens & Bryan.

Neither is there any other aspect in which the case can be maintained. It is a rule, to be sure, that a surety has a right to bring his principal and the creditor into a Court of Chancery, to compel the payment of the debt. But if we were to concede that complainant occupies—towards the creditors of these firms, and the defendants—the relation of a surety, yet the bill makes no case under this head of equity. The creditors are not parties, and the case is, in other respects, perhaps, defective. 5 Hum., 66.

It is true, that complainant has been compelled to pay a part of these debts, and is, therefore, a creditor, to that extent, of Bivens & Bryan; and that now, under section 4288 of the Code, he may, without first having obtained a judgment at law, come into Chancery to set aside fraudulent conveyances of property, or other devices resorted to for the purpose of hindering and delaying creditors, and subject the property, by sale, or otherwise, to the satisfaction of the debt. But the bill also fails to make a case under this section of the Code. It alleges no fraudulent conveyance, or other device to hinder and delay creditors, and no relief is claimed upon that ground.

Decree affirmed.

Lownes, Orgill & Co. v. Augustus Hunter.

LOWNES, ORGILL & CO. *v.* AUGUSTUS HUNTER.

1. STAY OF EXECUTION. *Justice's docket. Act of* 1835. The fact that the name of the stayor is not written in the most appropriate place on the justice's docket, or that the docket is not made out with all the formality prescribed by the act of 1835, will not vitiate the security, or discharge the stayor from his liability.

2. SAME. *Irregularities in the judgment.* If the judgment upon which a party undertakes to stay execution remains in force, the stayor cannot go behind it in search of irregularities upon which to be discharged from his liability. If the party prejudiced by the supposed irregularity submits to it, it does not lie in the mouth of the surety for the stay of execution to complain.

3. CERTIORARI AND SUPERSEDEAS. *Judgment. Interest. Costs. Procedendo. Code* §§ 3124, 3188. Prior to the adoption of the Code, the practice, upon dismissing a petition for a writ of *supersedeas*, was to discharge the *supersedeas* and award a *procedendo* to the justice to issue execution. But, by the proper construction of §§ 3124, 3138 of the Code, judgment is to be rendered in the higher Court for the amount of the justice's judgment with interest thereon, at the rate of twelve and one-half *per cent. per annum* against the principal and sureties in the *certiorari* bond, and also for costs of suit.

FROM HAYWOOD.

At the September Term, 1858, the execution issued by the justice was quashed, READ, J., presiding. The plaintiffs appealed.

E. J. READ, for the plaintiffs, cited: *Atkinson* v. *Rhea,* 7 Hum., 59; *Roberts* v. *Cross,* 1 Sneed, 233; *Carmichael* v. *Hawkins,* 2 Sneed, 405; *Hennegar* v. *Mee,* 4 Sneed, 33; *Newman* v. *Rogers,* 9 Hum., 121; *Winches-*

ter v. *Beardin*, 10 Hum., 247; *Johnson* v. *Billingsley*, 3 Hum., 152.

B. J. LEA, for the defendant, said:

The defendant contends that he is not liable as stayor:

1. Because the judgment rendered by the justice of the peace is void; void because the summons which was issued the 26th day of May, 1857, against "E. R. Midyett and J. L. Henry, late partners under the firm and name of Midyett & Henry," was only executed, as will appear by reference to the record, upon J. L. Henry, and returned before W. Saryster, who gave judgment against Midyett & Henry; the said Midyett never having been summoned to appear, nor did he appear; and, therefore, the judgment against Midyett & Henry, was void, and the defendant, Hunter, is not, therefore, liable as stayor.

Again: The judgment is void by reason of irregularity, as will be seen by the leaf of the docket here exhibited. There is no caption to the docket, nor is it in any way, shape, or form, a compliance with the 17th section of the act of 1835, ch. 17. (N. & C., 435.) In the case of *Johnson* v. *Billingsley*, 3 Hum., 151, this Court say, that a substantial compliance with the act of 1835, is sufficient; but, as will be seen, the judgment is not only irregular, but the entry upon the docket is in no manner an *approach* to the form given in the act of 1835.

2. There is nothing on the docket to show that the defendant, Hunter, ever was stayor to said judgment; and it is contended that his name must be in the

column where stayors are entered, or the word stayor opposite to his name, or, in other words, the docket must show that he is stayor.

In view of these facts, we contend that there was no error in the ruling of the Court below, in quashing the execution as to defendant.

McKinney, J., delivered the opinion of the Court.

In quashing the execution, on the ground that Hunter was not legally bound as *stayor*, we think the Court erred. The case is within the principle of *Carmichael v. Hawkins*, 2 Sneed, 405. It is fully proved, that Hunter voluntarily applied to the justice to become stayor of the execution in this particular case, and accordingly wrote his name on the justice's docket, with the express intent of binding himself as surety for the stay of execution, and was accepted by the justice as such. The fact that the name was not written in the most appropriate place on the docket; or that the justice's docket was not made out with all the formality prescribed by the act of 1835, will not be allowed to vitiate the security, or discharge the stayor from the liability, on the ground of the supposed irregularity in the judgment upon which he assumed to stay execution. Admitting it to be true, that the warrant was served on only one of the two joint defendants named therein and that the judgment was rendered jointly against both; this is a matter of which the party not served with process might complain; or, he might waive service of the warrant, and acquiesce in the judgment, as he seems to have done. But this is a matter with which the stayor has no concern. The judgment upon which he undertook to stay execution remains in full force, and he cannot go behind it in search of irregularities upon which to seek to be discharged from his liability. If the party prejudiced by the supposed irregularity, submits to it, it does not lie in the mouth of the surety for the stay of execution to complain.

In this view of the case, the judgment must be reversed. Prior to the adoption of the Code, the practice in such cases was, to discharge the *supersedeas*, and direct a *procedendo* to the justice to issue execution. But, by the proper construction of sections 3124 and 3138 of the Code, judgment is to be rendered here for the amount of the justice's judgment, with interest thereon, at the rate of twelve and one-half per cent. per annum, against the principal and sureties in the *certiorari* bond; and also for the costs of suit. Judgment will be rendered accordingly.

L. MAYER & Co. et al. v. J. L. PULLIAM et al.

1. DEED OF TRUST. *Not void if creditors are required to present their claims within a specified time.* A deed of trust was executed on the 12th of May, 1857, providing for the payment of the "home creditors," by name, of the bargainors, and then directed that the remainder of the fund in the hands of the trustee be divided *pro rata* among their New York and Philadelphia creditors, to whom they owed $21,000; but said creditors were not otherwise referred to than by this

general description. The benefit of this provision was confined to such of those creditors as would present their claims to the trustee on or before the 25th day of December, 1858, and they were to be notified by him. Held, that this was a just and prudent provision, and did not render the deed void.

2. SAME. *Assignment of choses in action. Probate. Registration.* An assignment of *choses in action* is not embraced by the registry acts, and such assignment is as good without as with registration. If made to a third person, as trustee, for the benefit of creditors, it is good against subsequent attaching creditors without probate and registration.

FROM FAYETTE.

Decree pronounced by Chancellor WILLIAMS, at the November Term, 1858. The defendant appealed.

J. W. & J. A. HARRIS and CALVIN JONES, for the complainants.

THOMAS RIVERS and J. L. PULLIAM, for the defendants.

CARUTHERS, J., delivered the opinion of the Court.

Thomas & Greenway, merchants in Somerville, being largely indebted, even to insolvency, on the 12th of May, 1857, made an assignment for the benefit of their creditors, of cash notes on Washer & Rose, for $12,000, and all their other notes, accounts, officer's receipts and judgments, to Joel L. Pulliam, as trustee, to collect and pay out. The deed provided for the payment of their "home creditors," and endorsers by name, and the balance to be divided *pro rata* among their New York and Philadelphia creditors, to whom they owed $21,000, but were not otherwise specified than by this general description. But the benefit of this last provision was confined to such as might present their claims to the trustee on or before the 25th of December, 1858, and they were to be all notified by the trustee. The trustee was put into possession of the notes, &c., thus assigned, on the 15th of May—three days after the assignment.

This deed of trust, as it is called, was regularly proved by the subscribing witnesses on the day of its date, as to Thomas, and at the same time acknowledged by Greenway; but the clerk failed to state, in his certificate, that *he was personally acquainted with him.* It was on the same day filed and noted for registration.

On the 28th of October, 1857, this bill was filed in the Chancery Court at Somerville, by a large number of the Philadelphia creditors, who had obtained judgments, and had executions returned, "no property found," on their respective claims, amounting to a large sum, against Pulliam, the trustee, Thomas & Greenway, and all the beneficiaries in the trust deed, to reach the effects in the hands of the trustee, and make them liable to their debts. They claim the interest of Greenway, at all events, if they cannot reach the whole, on account of the defect in the certificate of acknowledgment, as to him. They impute no fraud whatever, but contend that the deed is void on account of the provision excluding such eastern creditors as do not file their claims in the specified time.

The Chancellor overruled the demurrer to the bill, and after answers and proof, decreed that the assignment was good as to Thomas, but not as to Greenway, and subjected his one half of the property in the hands of the trustee, to the payment of the debts of complainants. From this decree the defendants appealed.

His Honor erred in his final decree, as well as upon the demurrer.

The bill is based upon but two grounds. 1st: That the deed is void on account of the provision in relation to the New York and Philadelphia creditors; and 2d: That the half interest of Greenway does not pass under the deed, because of the defect in his acknowledgment before stated. If the complainants be wrong in both their positions, then, there is no equity in their bill, as they make no other objection to the assignment, and the demurrer should have been allowed, and the bill dismissed.

1. We are aware of no decision of this, or any other Court, that will sustain the first position. It was a just and prudent provision. Twenty months were given to them to present their claims. It was proper to prescribe some time for the distribution of the fund in justice to those that might be vigilant; otherwise, as there was not enough to pay all, and the distribution among them was to be equal, according to the amount of their claims, the delay might have been unreasonable, on account of the supineness of a few, and the trustee would never have been able to act with safety to himself and justice to them, in the discharge of his trust. They were *not prohibited from suing under a penalty of forfeiture*, nor were they *required to remit part of their debts in order to get the balance*. This provision, then, does not invalidate the deed upon any established principle, or sound reason.

2. Waiving the question as to the power of one member of the firm to make an assignment of the joint effects for the payment of demands against the firm, after the dissolution, and also the question as to the effect of the insufficiency of the acknowledgment, if it were an instrument required to be registered, the case is still without difficulty on this point. We have recently decided in the case of *Allen* v. *Bain and others*, to be reported, that an assignment of *choses in action* is not embraced by our registry acts, and it is as good without, as with registration. Therefore, this deed was as effectual to pass and vest rights as if it had been registered upon a valid probate, there being no other objection to it. We need not now re-open that question, or enter into an argument to fortify our conclusion. It was decided upon full consideration, and must stand as the law.

The question upon the necessity of notice to Thomas & Greenway's debtors, of the assignment, in order to make the right of the assignee complete and perfect, though presented in the argument, does not arise. The bill does not attack the conveyance upon that ground, nor does it make the debtors, but only the trustee and beneficiaries in the deed, defendants. The attachment is only asked and issued against the defendants, and not the debtors in the claims assigned. Therefore, we are relieved from the consideration of that question, also.

The result is, that the bill is destitute of equity, and should have been dismissed upon the demurrer.

Let the decree be reversed, and the bill dismissed with costs.

C. D. VENABLE & CO. v. LEVICK, BROTHER & CO.

1. PARTNERSHIP. *Agency of each partner.* Each partner is the agent of the partnership, and, therefore, the act of each in transactions properly relating to the partnership business, is regarded as the act of all, and binds all. But it is only in the capacity of an authorized agent of his co-partners, that he has power to bind them. Hence, in order to bind the firm the act must, ordinarily, be done in the name of the firm, otherwise, it will only bind the individual partner as his own private act.

2. SAME. *Same. Sale of goods to one partner presumed to be for the firm.* A sale of goods to one partner within the scope and course of the partnership business, is in judgment of law, a sale to the partnership, and the seller of the goods will not be affected by any fraudulent intention of the purchasing partner in buying them, or by his subsequent misapplication of them, if the seller be clear of the imputation of collusion.

3. SAME. *Same. Same. Negotiable securities.* The same principle applies to negotiable securities drawn, endorsed, accepted or negotiated by one partner within the scope and course of dealing of the partnership in the absence of fraud on the part of the person receiving such securities.

4. SAME *Same. Same. Same. When the firm not bound. Fraud. Constructive knowledge.* But if goods be sold to one partner on his private account, and for his individual benefit, or, if partnership security be taken from him for a debt which the creditor knew at the time was the private or individual debt of the particular partner, without the previous knowledge or consent of the other partners, it would be a fraudulent transaction as to them, and clearly void. So, if from the subject matter of the contract, or the course of dealing, or the circumstances of the transaction, the creditor was chargeable with constructive knowledge of the fraudulent purpose, or intended misapplication on the part of the particular partner, the partnership cannot be made liable.

5. SAME. *When a fraud for a person to take a partnership engagement without the authority of the firm.* If the public have the usual means of knowledge given them in regard to the existence and business of a partnership, and no acts have been done or suffered by the partnership to mislead or deceive, every one is presumed to know the nature and extent of the partnership with whose members he deals; and where a person takes a partnership engagement without the knowledge or authority of the firm, for a matter that has no reference

to the business of the firm, and is not within the scope of its authority, or its regular course of dealing, he is, in judgment of law, guilty of a fraud, and cannot enforce such engagement.

FROM HENRY.

Verdict and judgment for the plaintiffs, at the September Term, 1858, FITZGERALD, J., presiding. The defendants appealed.

MCAMPBELL and DUNLAP, for the plaintiffs in error.

B. F. LAMB, for the defendants in error.

MCKINNEY, J., delivered the opinion of the Court.

This was an action of assumpsit brought by Levick, Brother & Co., on a bill of exchange drawn in their favor by B. H. Badwell, for $803.15, on the firm of C. D. Venable & Co., and purporting to have been accepted by said firm.

The defendants pleaded: First, non-assumpsit; and, secondly, a special plea, on oath, denying the acceptance of said bill. Judgment was for the plaintiffs.

From the bill of exceptions, it appears that C. D. Venable & Co., of which firm B. H. Badwell, the drawer of said bill, was a member—carried on the mercantile business in Henry county, Tennessee. Badwell resided in Angelo in the State of Kentucky, where he carried on a separate, individual mercantile business.

On the 19th of April, 1855, said Badwell was in the city of Philadelphia, and called at the house of

Levick, Brother & Co., merchants of that city, and represented to them that he was a member of the firm of C. D. Venable & Co., and was buying goods for them. The plaintiffs, thereupon, sold him a bill of goods, amounting to $803.15. The goods were purchased by Badwell, in his individual name, and were so entered on the plaintiff's books; and were shipped to him at Angelo, Kentucky; the bill of lading was likewise made out in his name. Badwell stated to the clerk of plaintiffs, "that he would prefer to give his own obligation for the bill of goods, but that he was a member of the firm of C. D. Venable & Co., and as such, was authorized to use the firm name if necessary." But objection being made to this, Badwell drew the bill of exchange before mentioned, and immediately wrote an acceptance thereof, in the firm name of Venable & Co.

The charge of the Court assumes, that, as Badwell was a member of the firm of Venable & Co., he had authority, as such, to bind the firm for the bill of goods purchased from the plaintiffs, although the purchase was not in the name, or for the use of said firm, but in his own name, and for his individual benefit; unless it were shown that the plaintiffs had knowledge of the fraudulent purpose of Badwell.

This is a mistaken view of the law of the case. It is true, that each partner is the agent of the partnership, and, therefore, the act of each, in transactions properly relating to the partnership business, is regarded as the act of all, and binds all. Each one may enter into any contract, on behalf of the firm, in the ordinary business thereof, which, according to the common course and usages of such partnerships, is incident or appropriate to the business. But it is only in the capacity of an authorized agent of his co-partners, that he has power to bind them. Hence, in order to bind the firm, the act must ordinarily be done in the name of the firm; otherwise, it will only bind the individual partner as his own private act. Story on Part., sec. 102; 3 Kent's Com., 41, 45; 3 Hum., 209; 1 Hum., 28, 29.

It is certainly correct, as a general proposition, that a sale of goods to one partner, within the scope and course of the partnership business, is, in judgment of law, a sale to the partnership, and the seller of the goods will not be affected by any fraudulent intention of the purchasing partner in buying them, or by his subsequent misapplication of them, if the seller be clear of the imputation of collusion. 3 Kent's Com., 44. Colyer on Part., sec. 392.

And the same principle applies to negotiable securities drawn, endorsed, accepted, or negotiated by one partner, within the scope and course of dealing of the partnership, in the absence of fraud on the part of the person receiving such securities. But, if goods be sold to one partner on his private account, and for his individual benefit; or, if partnership security be taken from him for a debt which the creditor knew at the time was the private or individual debt of the particular partner, without the previous knowledge or consent of the other partners, it would be a fraudulent transaction as to them, and clearly void. So, if from the subject matter of the contract, or the course of dealing, or the circumstances of the transaction, the creditor was chargeable with constructive knowledge of the fraudulent purpose, or in-

C. D. Venable & Co. *v.* Levick, Brother & Co.

tended misapplication on the part of the particular partner, the partnership cannot be made liable. 3 Kent's Com., 42. If the public have the usual means of knowledge given them in regard to the existence and business of a partnership, and no acts have been done or suffered by the partnership to mislead or deceive, every one is presumed to know the nature and extent of the partnership with whose members he deals; and when a person takes a partnership engagement, without the knowledge or authority of the firm, for a matter that has no reference to the business of the firm, and is not within the scope of its authority, or its regular course of dealing, he is, in judgment of law, guilty of a fraud. 3 Kent, 48.

These principles are decisive of the case before us. The purchase of the goods and the partnership security given for their payment, did not purport to be for the partnership, but for Badwell, as a private individual. And of this fact, from the very nature and circumstances of the transaction, the plaintiffs were chargeable with knowledge. It was the folly and the wrong of the plaintiffs to accept a partnership security for a debt, not created in the name of the firm, or for its benefit, on the faith of the statement by the particular partner, which, *prima facie*, was untrue, as they were bound to know.

The judgment will be reversed.

THE STATE v. W. B. GREEN.

1. CRIMINAL LAW. *Costs. Taxed to the prosecutor. Certiorari and supersedeas. Justices of the peace.* The power given to magistrates to tax the prosecutor, in criminal cases, with the costs, when the prosecution is frivolous or malicious, is discretionary; but it is a legal and not an arbitrary discretion, and is subject to revision by the Circuit Court by virtue of the constitutional writ of *certiorari*.

2. SAME. *Same. Same. In what cases the prosecutor should be taxed with the costs.* To authorize a taxation of the costs in a criminal proceeding to the prosecutor, the proof should be clear and conclusive that the prosecution was frivolous or malicious, and known to the prosecutor to be without foundation. It may, and often does happen, that sufficient apparent cause exists, when, upon investigation, it turns out to be otherwise.

3. SAME. *Same. Same. Judgment. Certainty of.* If a warrant is taken out, upon the oath of the prosecutor, for a criminal offence, and upon the trial judgment is rendered by the justice, on the warrant, discharging the defendant, and taxing the prosecutor with the costs, without stating in the judgment the name of the prosecutor, it is not void, and should not be quashed for uncertainty. To hold that such a judgment was void for uncertainty, would be too technical for justices proceedings.

4. SAME. *Same. Same. Evidence. Question reserved.* If the evidence is not taken down by the committing magistrate, would his judgment taxing the prosecutor with the costs be subject to the revisory power of the Circuit Court, or does it apply, alone, to cases where the proof is reduced to writing by the justice, as required by law?

FROM PERRY.

At the June Term, 1858, WALKER, J., presiding, the judgment of the justices was held to be void, and the execution quashed. The State appealed.

CARUTHERS, J., delivered the opinion of the Court.

This is an appeal in error by the State, from a judgment of the Circuit Court quashing an execution against Green for the costs of a prosecution instituted by him before a justice of the peace against Thomas W. Palmer, for the crime of malicious shooting, from which the defendant was discharged by the magistrates who sat upon the case, and the prosecutor taxed with the costs, because they found that the prosecution was *malicious*.

Upon the petition of Green, and the fiat of the Judge, the case was brought into the Circuit Court by writs of *certiorari* and *supersedeas*. The Court refused to entertain the case for an investigation of the grounds of the magistrate's judgment, holding that no appeal, or *certiorari*, will lie to remove the judgment of a justice taxing a prosecutor with costs, into the Circuit Court; but held that the judgment against the petitioner was void, and therefore quashed the execution.

The warrant recites that it was issued upon the oath, and at the instance of W. B. Green; and upon the back of this is the judgment, which is, that the defendant, Palmer, was not guilty, and then proceeds, " and that the prosecution was a malicious one, and we do order that the prisoner be, and he is hereby released from the charge, and that the prosecutor pay all costs of suit for which execution may issue." One of the three justices who sat upon the case dissented, in writing, on both points, believing that the defendant was guilty, and should be bound over to Court to answer the charge.

We think his Honor erred in quashing the execution upon the ground that the judgment was void for uncertainty. It is true that the judgment does not show on its face that Green was prosecutor, nor is his name inserted in it; but the warrant shows that, and cures the defect, as it is entered upon the same paper. There is no uncertainty, when reference is had to the whole paper, and the rule applied is too technical for proceedings before a magistrate. It is not like a case of a judgment by motion, where everything necessary to give jurisdiction and establish liability must appear in the judgment, for, in those cases, there is nothing with which to connect and help out the judgment.

But we think the Circuit Court had jurisdiction to revise the judgment, by *certiorari*, upon the facts as recorded by the justices in the discharge of their duty as a committing tribunal. This was offered to sustain the allegations of the petition that the prosecution was not frivolous, or malicious, and rejected by the Court upon the ground that a judgment for costs against the prosecutor was final and conclusive. If this were so, the cause of public justice would often be defeated by deterring citizens from prosecuting offenders. There is, in many cases, too much reluctance, on the part of citizens, to undertake the performance of this disagreeable and, often, thankless duty, for other reasons; but if, in addition to these, they are put in danger of having the costs thrown upon them by an *irreversable* decree of the committing Court, the guilty will too often go unpunished, and even unarraigned. The prosecution should be very clearly without foundation, and that known to the prosecutor, so as to show that his motives were malicious, and not for promotion of public justice, in instituting the prosecution, in order to subject him to the costs.

It may, and does often happen, that sufficient apparent cause exists, when, upon investigation, it turns out to be entirely groundless. This law was intended only for strong and clear cases of malicious prosecution, unmixed with the proper motive, which is to bring offenders to justice for the public good. In such a case the law is right, and ought to be enforced, as the process and forms of the law ought not to be used *solely* to gratify personal animosity, nor recklessly, where there is no grounds for the charge. It is of very doubtful expediency to extend this power to a committing Court, where the cases must of necessity, as a general thing, be imperfectly examined. But as it has been done, it is almost indispensable that their judgments should be subject to revision. Such a power the Circuit Court, as a Court of general jurisdiction, has over all inferior jurisdictions, even courts martial, by virtue of the constitutional writ of *certiorari*, analogous to the King's Bench in England. *Duggan* v. *McKinney*, 7 Yer., 21.

The practice of re-examining the facts in the Circuit Court would, certainly, be inconvenient in cases where the evidence had not been written down by the justices, as they are required to do by law. Where that is not done, we will not say how the law would be, as that is not the question now before us. But in this case the petitioner proposed to show by the proof, as written down, that the judgment against him for the costs was erroneous. We think the Judge should have examined it, and determined the question of the liability of the prosecutor under the law. The power given to the magistrate is discretionary, but it is a legal, and not an arbitrary discretion. It may be very much abused, and should be subject to revision in the Circuit Court. The ground upon which it may be exercised, is fixed by the law—that is, where the prosecution is frivolous or malicious, not otherwise. By *certiorari* the case may be brought before the Circuit Court, to determine whether the judgment of the committing Court was correct on that question; and if not, to reverse it.

We reverse the judgment dismissing or refusing the *certiorari* as to that point, as well as the judgment quashing the execution, and remand the case, with directions to examine the evidence as recorded, and decide the question upon its merits. If the Court should find that the facts authorize the judgment against the prosecutor for the costs, it will be proper to see that no illegal costs are charged in the execution.

WILLIAM GRAY et al. v. JAMES DAVIS et al.

1. LAND LAW. *Occupant claim. Act of* 1848, *ch.* 8, § 4. *Administrators and executors.* The act of 1848, ch. 8, § 4, provides that in all cases where an occupant claimant south and west of the Congressional Reservation Line, "may have heretofore died, or may hereafter die, without having perfected his title to his occupant claim, it shall be the duty of the administrator, or executor, by the use of the first money which shall come to his hands, to perfect the title to the occupant claim of his testator or intestate, in the name and for the use of the heirs at law, of such decedent claimant." This act is retrospective, and applies to all cases occurring before its passage, when the administration has not been settled up, and the administrator or executor discharged of the trust.

William Gray *et al.* v. James Davis *et al.*

2. SAME. *Same. Same. Same. Application of the principle. Trust and trustee.* The testator died in 1834. He was the owner, at his death, of an occupant claim south and west of the Congressional Reservation Line, the title to which had not been perfected. His widow was duly qualified as his executrix. She received money and assets of the estate, but had made no settlement of her administration at the time of the filing of the bill in this case. In 1846 the widow caused said lands to be entered, and she procured a grant therefor, in her own name; and afterwards, by her will, devised the land to two of her children. Held, that not having closed her administration, and been discharged of the trust prior to the passage of the act of 1843, she was bound to carry out its provisions, and must be held to have taken the legal title as trustee for the heirs, and her devisees can stand in no better condition.

FROM OBION.

Decree for the complainants, at the July Term, 1858, WILLIAMS, Chancellor, presiding. The defendants appealed.

COCHRAN & ENLOE, for the complainants.

DAVIS, for the defendants.

McKINNEY J., delivered the opinion of the Court.

Benjamin Hubbard died in 1834. He was the owner, at the time of his death, of an *occupant right*, to 160 acres of land in Obion county.

His widow was duly qualified as executrix of his will. She received money and assets of the estate, but up to the filing of this bill, in 1857, failed to settle her administration account, and discharge herself of the trust. It appears that said executrix, on the 7th of March, 1846, caused said lands, to which the testator

William Gray *et al.* v. James Davis *et al.*

had an occupant right, to be entered in her own name, and procured a grant in her own right, and afterwards, by her will, devised the same to two of her children— the defendants, Evelina and Catharine.

This was a direct violation of the act of 1843, ch. 8, sec. 4. By this act it is provided, that in all cases where an occupant claimant, south and west of the Congressional Reservation Line, "may have heretofore died, or may hereafter die, without having perfected his title to his occupant claim, it shall be the duty of the administrator or executor, by the use of the first money which shall come to his hands, to perfect the title to the occupant claim of his testator or intestate, in the name and for the use of the heirs at law of such decedent claimant," &c.

This act, it will be observed, is *retrospective;* and, therefore, there is nothing in the argument, that the testator had no transmissible interest in the occupancy claim at the time of his death—the statute not having been passed until some eight years after the qualification of the executrix. If she had closed her administration, and been discharged of the trust, prior to the passage of the act, of course she would have been free from the duty imposed by the statute. But she failed to do so—the trust remained—and having funds of the estate in hands, it was her imperative duty to have perfected the title, as provided by the act of 1843. The attempt to appropriate the land to her own use, was a gross breach of trust, and a fraud upon the rights of the heirs. She must, consequently, be held to have taken the legal title as trustee for the heirs, and her devisees stand in no better condition. The decree divesting them of the title to eight-tenths of the land, was, therefore, proper. The decree is also correct in declaring, that, under the fourth item of the will, the widow took only a life interest.

Decree affirmed.

R. T. ADAMS v. MAYOR AND ALDERMEN OF SOMERVILLE.

1. CONSTITUTIONAL LAW. *Art.* 2, §§ 28, 29. *Taxation.* An important and fundamental distinction is made by the Constitution, between *property* and *privileges*, in regard to the power of taxation delegated to the Legislature. The rule laid down as to the former, is, that "all property shall be taxed according to its value;" and "no one species of property from which a tax may be collected, shall be taxed higher than any other species of property of equal value." But the rule as to privileges, is the discretion of the Legislature: the latter are to be taxed in such manner as may, from time to time, be directed by the Legislature.

2. SAME. *Same. Same. Corporations. Act of* 1854, *ch.* 17, § 6. *Negro traders.* Hence, the act of 1854, ch. 17, § 6, incorporating the town of Somerville, and conferring power on the Mayor and Aldermen, by ordinance, "to license, tax, and regulate auctioneers, grocers, merchants, retailers, brokers, coffee houses, confectioneries, retailers of liquors, hawkers, pedlers, negro traders, and tavern keepers," is constitutional. And an ordinance passed by the Mayor and Aldermen, by virtue of said charter, requiring, "That all negro traders who shall expose negroes for sale within the corporate limits of the town of Somerville, he or they shall pay a yearly license tax of twenty dollars," is not in conflict with the Constitution, and may be enforced.

FROM FAYETTE.

This cause was heard, on an agreed case, at the October Term, 1858, HUMPHREYS, J., presiding. Judgment in favor of the corporation. Adams appealed.

R. T. Adams *v.* Mayor and Aldermen of Somerville.

J. D. GOODALL, for the plaintiff in error.

L. P. JONES, for the defendant in error.

McKINNEY, J., delivered the opinion of the Court.

This suit was commenced before a justice, to recover the sum of $40.00, the forfeiture imposed by the corporation, for a breach of one of its ordinances by the plaintiff in error. The case was removed, by appeal, to the Circuit Court, where, on an agreed case, judgment was rendered for the corporation. The case is this:

By the act incorporating the town of Somerville, (see act of 1854, ch. 17, sec. 6,) express power is conferred on the Mayor and Aldermen, by ordinance, "to license, tax, and regulate auctioneers, grocers, merchants, retailers, brokers, coffee-houses, confectioneries, retailers of liquors, hawkers, pedlers, livery stable keepers, *negro traders*, and tavern keepers."

In pursuance of this power, an ordinance was passed, which provides, among other things, "That all *negro traders* who shall expose negroes for sale within the corporate limits of the town of Somerville, he or they shall pay a yearly license tax of twenty dollars."

The ordinance requires, that a license shall be procured from the Recorder, "by paying the tax thereon, and his fee of one dollar and a half for issuing the same." And it is further provided, that if any person shall exercise the privilege, without first obtaining a license, "he shall forfeit and pay *double* the amount of the license, and all costs incident to the collection of the same."

R. T. Adams *v.* Mayor and Aldermen of Somerville.

It is admitted in the agreed case, that Adams, the defendant, was a "negro trader," and that he exposed negroes for sale, and sold one within the corporate limits of the town of Somerville, in October, 1856, without obtaining a license, as required by the ordinance.

The argument for the plaintiff in error assumes, that, if it were competent to the Legislature, to confer such a power upon a municipal corporation, still, the ordinance is invalid, because the mode of exercising the power provided therein, is different from, and incompatible with, the principle and mode prescribed by the general law of the State, in regard to this particular "privilege." In other words, the argument is, that the corporation cannot adopt a different principle, or mode, of taxing "privileges" from that adopted in regard to State taxation.

We think this argument is unsound. By the second article of the Constitution, sec. 28, the power is given to the Legislature to tax "privileges, in such manner as they may, from time to time, direct." And by the 29th section, the power is given to authorize counties and incorporated towns, "to impose taxes for county and corporation purposes, respectively, in such manner as shall be prescribed by law; and all *property* shall be taxed according to its value, upon the principles established in regard to State taxation."

It must be borne in mind, that, in regard to the power of taxation delegated to the Legislature, an important and fundamental discrimination is made between *property* and *privileges*, by the Constitution. The rule laid down as to the former, is, that "*all property* shall be taxed according to its value," and, "no one species of property from which a tax may be collected, shall be taxed higher than any other species of property of equal value." But the rule, as to privileges, is the *discretion* of the Legislature; the latter are to be taxed *in such manner* as may, from time to time, be directed by the Legislature.

It will be observed, too, that the 29th section, which authorizes a delegation of the power of taxation to incorporated towns, for corporation purposes, is very broad in its terms; it does not mention "privileges" at all; *property* alone is embraced; and in reference to *that*, the only restriction is, that the principle established in regard to State taxation, shall be observed by corporations.

But, in respect to *privileges*, the corporation is left to the exercise of a sound discretion in imposing a tax thereon, unless restricted by the Legislature, in the charter of incorporation, or by some general law of the State.

In the charter before us, the power of the Mayor and Aldermen "to license, tax, and regulate" negro traders, is general and unrestricted. It is no valid objection, therefore, that the Board, in the exercise of this discretionary power, has proceeded upon a different principle, or in a different mode, from that adopted by the Legislature in respect to State taxation. *Mayor and Aldermen of Columbia* v. *Beasly*, 1 Hum., 232, 240.

The principle of taxation applicable to property, is altogether impracticable in regard to privileges. It is obviously necessary and proper, that the exercise of the power to impose a tax on privileges, should be left to a sound discretion; because no definite rule, based upon a supposed equality in value, can be prescribed, as respects what are denominated privileges; and if such a rule were practicable, reasons founded in public policy might demand, that privileges of certain kinds should be taxed upon a very different principle from others. This is peculiarly proper in regard to town corporations. The power to the latter, to tax privileges, was not intended as a source of *revenue* merely. It was likewise designed as a means for imposing restraints upon the exercise of certain privileges, whose tendencies were of a nature to encourage vice or disorder, or were contrary to public policy.

It follows, then, that the validity of the ordinance (not being in itself oppressive) must depend upon the grant of power in the particular charter of incorporation. In the present instance, the express grant of power is ample; and the ordinance is consequently valid.

The judgment will, therefore, be affirmed.

M. DEMENT, GUARDIAN, &c., v. W. S. SCOTT.

1. EVIDENCE. *Hearsay. Admissions of guardian.* The statements of a guardian relative to a contract for the hire of a slave, made by him as guardian, in a suit to which he is not a party, are not admissible. First, because it is mere hearsay evidence. If admissible, the guardian must be called on as a witness. Second, the evidence is inadmissible on the principle that the admissions by a guardian, though the plaintiff, or a party on record, is not evidence against the infant.

M. Dement, Guardian, &c., v. W. S. Scott.

2. SLAVES. *Contract of hire. Liability of the hirer.* To work at digging a race, which, in some cases, might require the blasting of rock and standing in water, is not properly embraced by a contract to work on or at the mill. The race, though necessary to the mill, is distinct from it, and might demand exposure to extra hazardous employment.

3. SAME. *Same. Same. Voluntary exposure by the slave.* The hirer having power to control the slave, is bound to restrain him from wilful exposure, by the obligations which the law impose on him. And he is responsible for the consequences of any exposure of which he has knowledge and does not prevent, although it may be voluntary by the slave, and against his orders.

4. SAME. *Same. Same. Same. Previous disease of the slave. Rescission of contract of hiring.* If a hired slave is diseased at the time of the contract, and this fact is not communicated to the hirer, either from fraud or ignorance of its existence, the hirer has the right, upon coming to a knowledge of the fact, to abandon the contract, and return the slave; but he is not justified in requiring the slave to perform a kind or amount of labor for which he has not the physical capacity, and which, of necessity, must destroy his life more speedily.

FROM WEAKLEY.

This cause was tried at the October Term, 1858, FITZGERALD, J., presiding. Verdict and judgment for the defendant. The plaintiff appealed.

ROGERS, SOMERS, and CALDWELL, for the plaintiff.

EDWARDS and ETHERIDGE, for the defendant.

MCKINNEY, J., delivered the opinion of the Court.

This was an action on the case, to recover damages for the loss of a slave, the property of the plaintiff, hired to the defendant for the year 1856, and who died during the year. Verdict and judgment were for the defendant.

M. Dement, Guardian, &c., v. W. S. Scott.

The declaration contains counts both in trover and case. The slave was hired out at public auction by one Valentine, who was then the regular guardian of the plaintiff, a minor, but who ceased to be guardian before the institution of this suit.

The contract of hiring is admitted on all hands to have been special; but there is a disagreement in the testimony as to the extent of the restrictions imposed on the hirer. The auctioneer states that the terms proclaimed were, that the slave was "not to work on railroads, mills, rivers, boats, or public works." But there is testimony going to show, that while the bidding was progressing, the defendant stated that he desired to hire the slave, but the terms precluded him. Valentine then inquired of him what he wanted the negro to do; and the defendant replied that he was about to build a new mill, and he wanted the boy to work part of the time on the mill, part in getting timber, and part on the farm; and Valentine then told him to bid on. There is other testimony in conflict with this, and tending also to establish that the boy was not to work in mud or water.

The ground of the action is, that the slave was put to digging a mill-race and foundation for the mill, in doing which he was exposed to standing in mud and water, whereby his sickness and death were caused.

For the purpose of presenting the questions submitted for our determination, it is not necessary that we should do more than state this mere outline of the proof.

The first error assigned is, the admission of the statements of Valentine, the former guardian, made long after the hiring, and after the death of the slave, to

M. Dement, Guardian, &c., v. W. S. Scott.

the effect that it was useless for the plaintiff to sue for the loss of the slave, that she could not recover, for he had hired the slave to defendant to work at the mill.

In admitting this evidence, the Court erred. First, because it was mere *hearsay* evidence. If admissible, Valentine, who was not a party on record, must have been called as a witness. But the evidence was inadmissible, in the second place, on the principle, that the admission by a guardian, though the plaintiff, or a party on record, is not evidence against the infant. 2 Stark. Ev., (ed. of 1828,) p. 40, and cases cited in note *o*.

The other errors relied on are in the charge of the Court. In expounding the contract, the Court stated to the jury, that "if the contract was, that he (defendant) might work the negro in building a mill, he had a right to put him at any work necessary and proper for the construction of the mill." We are unable to assent to the correctness of this proposition. To work at digging a race, which, in some cases, might require the blasting of rock, and standing in water, is not properly embraced by a contract to work on or at the mill. The race, though "necessary" to the mill, is distinct from it, and might demand exposure to extra hazardous employment.

Again, the Court further said to the jury, that "if the negro went into the mud and water of his own accord, against the orders of the defendant, and when it was not necessary for him to do so in order to perform the labor at which he was put, this being voluntary on the part of the slave—he being a reasonable creature—would not make the defendant liable for his loss."

M. Dement, Guardian, &c., *v.* W. S. Scott.

This would be correct, perhaps, if the slave thus exposed himself without the knowledge of the defendant. But if the defendant had knowledge thereof, the fact that the slave exposed himself voluntarily, without necessity, and against orders, would be no excuse for the defendant. The latter having power to control the slave, was bound to restrain him from wilful exposure by the obligations which the law imposed on him.

The error seems to be in attributing to a slave that freedom of will and power of self-determination which belong, only, to a freeman.

The Court likewise stated to the jury, in substance, that if the slave was diseased at the time of the hiring, and Scott was not informed of it, and worked the slave in such a way as he had hired him to work, and in a reasonable manner, and the slave became sick and died of his original disease, the defendant would not be liable.

This position, we think, is not quite accurate. If the slave were in fact diseased at the time of the contract, and this fact was not communicated to the defendant, either from fraud, or ignorance of its existence, it would have clearly entitled the defendant, upon coming to a knowledge of the fact, to have abandoned his contract, and to have returned the slave; but he would not have been justified in requiring the slave to perform a kind or amount of labor for which he had not the physical capacity, and which, of necessity, must destroy his life more speedily.

Without noticing other matters in the case, the judgment must be reversed on the grounds before stated.

Newman Haynes *et al.* v. W. Jones *et al.*

NEWMAN HAYNES *et al.* v. W. JONES *at al.*

1. STATUTE OF LIMITATIONS. *What will arrest it. Descent cast.* If a parent place a son in possession of land under a verbal gift and the possession is held by the son adversely to the father and all other persons, the death of the father will not arrest the running of the statute. By the *descent cast* the heirs are placed exactly in the shoes of their ancestor. And the statute having attached and commenced running against him in his lifetime, it continues to run without intermission against his heirs. Its operation can, in such case, be arrested, only, by a suit at law, or in equity, effectually prosecuted.

2. SAME. *Same. Same Saving of the statute.* The ancestor being free from disability when the adverse possession is taken and the running of the statute commenced, there is no saving or exception in the statute in favor of his heirs; and they, though infants or *femes covert*, are bound to sue just as much as their ancestor would have been had he lived, before the expiration of seven years from the adverse possession.

3. SAME. *Possessory right. Act of* 1819. *Advancement.* If a child is placed in the possession of land, by the parent, under a parol gift as an advancement, and such child holds said land adversely to the parent and the other heirs for a period of seven years, he will be protected under the second section of the act of 1819, to the extent of his enclosure, for which he must account at the estimated value put upon the land at the time of the advancement.[*]

FROM GIBSON.

At the June Term, 1858, Chancellor WILLIAMS pronounced a decree, from which the defendants appealed.

HILL, for the complainants.

---

[*] The parol gift of the land, as an advancement, is void. The possessory right to the land is perfected, only, by operation of the statute of limitations. Now, is the land to be valued at the time the possession is given, or at the time the title is perfected by the running of the statute?

T. J. & J. T. CARTHEL, for the defendants, argued—

The course of decision, both in England and in this country, has established the rule, *beyond doubt*, that when the statute of limitation has commenced running, it runs over *all* subsequent disabilities and intermediate acts and events. 2 Greenl. Ev., § 439; Angel on Lim., ch. 36, and page 520.

The question of joint tenancy has nothing to do with the case, because the parties had no joint interest at the time the adverse possession of J. W. Jones commenced. That possession having commenced in the lifetime of the father, his death did not arrest the operation of the statute, although some of the heirs upon whom the estate was cast may have been *infants*, or *femes covert*.

J. W. Jones having acquired a title to the land by operation of the statute of limitations, we insist that it relates back to, and he is only chargeable with the value of the land at the time he was placed in possession.

MCKINNEY, J., delivered the opinion of the Court.

The complainants are a portion of the heirs at law

The former seems to be the ruling of the Court. Yet, such has not been the universally received opinion of the Bar, nor the uniform course of decision in the inferior Courts. The rule is different in Kentucky. There every advancement is to be charged at its value at the time when the gift becomes complete and irrevocable, in law or equity. And where a father advances a child by a verbal gift of land, which cannot be enforced and may be revoked, but is afterwards confirmed by a conveyance, the value of the land at the date of the conveyance is the value at which it is to be brought into *hotchpotch*. *Barber* v. *Taylor's heirs*, 9 Dana., 84; *Hook* v. *Hook*, 13 B. Monroe, 528. See, also, *Stallings* v. *Stallings*, 1 Dev., ch. 298; *Robinson* v. *Robinson*, 4 Hum., 392: *Cawthon* v. *Coppedge*, 1 Swan. 487.

and distributees of the estate of John Jones, who died intestate in Gibson county, in 1853, and the defendants are the administrator and remaining distributees and heirs.

In addition to an account of the administration, the complainants seek distribution and partition of the slaves and real estate.

The case is brought here upon a single question, in relation to part of the real property. Some time previous to the year 1846, the intestate made a parol gift to the defendant, Joshua, his son, of two hundred acres of land, part of the tract on which the intestate resided. The only written evidence of the gift is a memorandum made in a book kept by the intestate, showing the advancements made to his several children, which is as follows: "Gave to my son, Joshua, 200 acres of land, to be taken off of the west side and north end of the tract I now live on, at $450.00." The land was not run off or set apart by metes and bounds, to the donee; but about the first of the year 1847, and nearly seven years before the death of his father, he entered into possession of a tenement on the land intended for him, and has resided thereon ever since, and has made valuable improvements on the same. Before the filing of this bill, he had been in possession for more than seven years, claiming it as his own, with the knowledge and approbation of his father during his life; and since the death of his father, he has, in like manner, claimed it against the other heirs, to which no objection has been made, except by the complainants—his brothers-in-law. The proof shows that some thirty acres or more were enclosed and adversely held by the defendant, Joshua, for a period of more than seven years before this suit. The Chancellor was of opinion that the defendant would only be protected in the possession, under the second section of the act of 1819, of so much of said land, if any, as he had in actual possession, by enclosure, for the full space of seven years, prior to the death of the intestate; and that on the death of intestate, and consequent descent of the title to his heirs at law, the operation of the statute was arrested.

In this view, his Honor erred. By the descent cast, the heirs were placed exactly in the shoes of their ancestor. And the statute having attached and commenced running against him in his lifetime, it continued to run, without intermission, against his heirs. Its operation could only have been arrested by a suit at law, or in equity, effectually prosecuted. The ancestor being free from disability when the adverse possession was taken, and running of the statute commenced, there is no saving or exception in the statute in favor of his heirs; and they, though infants or *femes covert*, were bound to sue just as much as their ancestor would have been had he lived, before the expiration of seven years from the commencement of the adverse possession.

The idea that the title descended to *all* the heirs jointly, and, therefore, the possession of the defendant, Joshua, was the possession of all, and, consequently, the statute ceased to operate from the descent of the title to the heirs, is altogether fallacious. The exclusive and adverse character of the defendant's possession, upon which the operation of the statute depended, was, in no respect, changed or affected by the descent of the title to the heirs.

The result is, that the defendant, Joshua, has acquired a possessory right to so much of said tract of land as may have been held and occupied, by actual enclosures, for the period of seven years *before the commencement of this suit;* for which he must account at the estimated value put upon the land at the time of the advancement.

The decree will be modified accordingly.

MARY W. BOWERS *v.* A. H. DOUGLASS.

PARTNERSHIP. *Contract with one partner. When illegal. Usury.* If one partner borrows money for the benefit of the firm, and executes the firm note for the amount borrowed, but at the same time enters into a *verbal contract* with the lender to pay usurious interest for the use of the money, such independent parol agreement will not bar the right of recovery on said note. This contract, though illegal and void, is, in legal contemplation, separate and distinct from the contract evidenced by the note, and does not fall within the principle in the case of *Hutchins* v. *Turner.*

FROM SHELBY.

At the November Term, 1858, there were verdict and judgment for the defendant, CARUTHERS, J., presiding. The plaintiff appealed.

SMALL & FOUTE, for the plaintiff, referred to *Smithwick & Co.* v. *Anderson,* 2 Swan, 573; *Bailey* v. *Cooper,*

5 Hum., 401-2; 2 Greenl. Ev., §§ 206-7; *Hutchins* v. *Turner*, 8 Hum., 415.

YERGER & FARRINGTON, for the defendant.

MCKINNEY, J., delivered the opinion of the Court.

This was an action of debt, founded on a promissory note for $1200.00, purporting to have been made by the firm of Douglass & Witherspoon, payable to A. J. Montgomery, and by him endorsed to the plaintiff. This suit is against Douglass alone. The defendant pleaded: First, *nil debet;* and, secondly, a plea in the nature of *non est factum.* Judgment was for the defendant, and the plaintiff prosecuted an appeal in error.

The proof establishes, that the note was made by Witherspoon, in the absence of Douglass, and without his knowledge; that the consideration of the note was $1200.00, in money, borrowed on the credit, and applied to the use of said firm, which was composed of the defendant and Witherspoon. The loan was really made, and the money advanced by the plaintiff, through her agent. At the time of the loan and the execution of said note, a *verbal* agreement was made, that interest at the rate of two and a half per cent. per month should be paid on the amount of the note; but the note was taken only for the amount of money actually advanced to Witherspoon.

The Court instructed the jury, that the verbal agreement of Witherspoon with the plaintiff, in the absence, and without the knowledge of his co-partner, the defendant, to pay two and a half per cent. per month, for

Mary W. Bowers v. A. H. Douglass.

the use of the $1200.00, made the whole contract illegal and void; and the plaintiff could not, therefore, recover on the note against Douglass.

This instruction, we think, is erroneous. The case of *Hutchins* v. *Turner*, 8 Hum., 415, does not sustain the charge. In that case, the usurious interest agreed on was incorporated in, and formed part of the nominal amount of the note sued on. Such is not the present case. Here, the note was for the actual amount of the loan. And, inasmuch as, by our law, the effect of usury is only to avoid the contract to the extent of the excess beyond the legal rate of interest, it follows, that there can be no valid objection to a recovery on the note. The collateral, independent, verbal agreement, for usurious interest on the loan, does not, in any way, affect the validity of the note. This latter agreement, though illegal and void, is, in legal contemplation, separate and distinct from the contract evidenced by the note. The case, therefore, is wholly unlike the case of *Hutchins* v. *Turner*. In the one case, the note itself was tainted with usury; in the other, the note is free from any such taint.

As regards the competency of Montgomery, the payee and endorser of the note; for anything appearing in the record before us, we perceive no objection to his competency. 2 Greenl. Ev., sec. 207.

Judgment reversed.

JAMES BOND *v.* JNO. W. CLAY *et al.*

1. JUDICIAL SALES. *County Court. Jurisdiction in setting aside sales after confirmation.* The jurisdiction of the County Court, under the law authorizing the sale, by that tribunal, of the property of decedents, for partition, &c., is limited, alone, to the making and completion of the sale. After such sale has been completed, by the confirmation of the report, if any matters of equity exists, or should arise, entitling the purchaser to be relieved against the payment of the purchase money, resort must be had to a Court of Equity.

2. SAME. *Same. Same. Code, §§ 4204, 4205, does not enlarge the jurisdiction.* Sections 4204 and 4205 of the Code are merely declaratory of the law as it previously existed in regard to the jurisdiction of the County Court in sales of property for partition, &c. No new and enlarged jurisdiction is conferred upon that Court by the Code.

FROM HAYWOOD.

The petition was dismissed by the County Court, and Bond, the purchaser, appealed.

E. J. READ, for the appellant.

H. J. LIVINGSTON, for the defendants.

McKINNEY, J., delivered the opinion of the Court.

Bond presented his *ex-parte* petition to the County Court of Haywood, to be discharged from his purchase of certain lands, sold under a decree of said Court for the purpose of partition, on the alleged ground of defect of title, by reason of the irregularity of the proceedings and decree of the Court.

James Bond *v.* Jno. W. Clay *et al.*

The sale took place in March; and at the April session, 1858, of said Court, the sale was confirmed, and the title to the lands divested out of Clay's heirs and vested in Bond, the purchaser.

This petition was filed in March, 1859, nearly twelve months after confirmation of the sale.

The Court properly dismissed the petition. The case falls within the principle laid down in *Young* v. *Shumate*, 3 Sneed, 369, and other cases, that, after confirmation of the sale, the Court had no jurisdiction to administer the relief sought by the petition.

The assumption that, by the provisions of sections 4204, 4205 of the Code, a new and enlarged jurisdiction, in this respect, was intended to be conferred upon the County Courts, is, we think, altogether unfounded.

These sections, in our opinion, are merely declaratory of the law as it previously existed in regard to the jurisdiction of the County Court upon the subject, without vesting in that tribunal any new or more extended power or authority. If, in respect to a matter of such vital importance to the community, it had been intended to clothe that tribunal with an enlarged equity jurisdiction, we are bound to suppose that such intention would have been explicitly declared. For obvious reasons the jurisdiction is not to be extended upon doubtful implications.

Decree affirmed.

J. W. HASSELL *et al. v.* SOUTHERN BANK OF KENTUCKY.

1. EXECUTION. *Levy of. What property to be levied on first.* It is the duty of the officer into whose hands an execution is placed, first to levy on the personal property of the defendant or defendants, before making a levy on land. If there be several defendants, all primarily liable, the officer may proceed against the goods and chattels of either one to levy the whole debt, leaving the question of contribution to be settled among the defendants. And if some of the defendants have personal property liable to the satisfaction of the debt, and others have not, it is the duty of the officer to proceed against the former, or either of them, until property sufficient is found to discharge the debt.

2. SAME. *Return of. Summary proceeding. Case in judgment.* The officer cannot screen himself from liability for an insufficient return, by returning that one of several defendants had no property subject to execution. To protect him, his return must show that the money could not have been made out of either defendant. Thus, a return on an execution against several defendants, "no personal property to be found in my county, of E. W. Tipton," (one of the defendants,) "on which I can levy for said debt and cost," is an insufficient return, and the officer is liable therefor, upon motion.

FROM DYER.

Judgment was rendered against the sheriff and his securities, at the October Term, 1856, READ, J., presiding. They appealed.

T. F. BRADFORD, for the plaintiff in error, cited and relied upon the following authorities: Act of 1794, ch. 1, § 23; *Crowder* v. *Sims*, 7 Hum., 257–260; *Trigg* v. *McDonald*, 2 Hum., 386; *Miller* v. *Moore*, 2 Hum., 421; 1 Tenn., 228.

COCHRANE & ENLOE, for the defendants in error.

J. W. Hassell *et al.* v. Southern Bank of Kentucky.

McKINNEY, J., delivered the opinion of the Court.

This was a motion for judgment against the plaintiff in error, as sheriff of Dyer county, and his official sureties, for an "insufficient return" of an execution.

The execution issued on the 11th of August, 1856, on a judgment in favor of the bank, against T. F. Bradford and four other defendants, returnable to the October Term of said Court, and was received by him four days after its issuance, to wit, the 14th of August.

The following return was endorsed on the execution:

"No personal property to be found in my county, of E. W. Tipton," (one of the defendants,) "on which I can levy for said debt and cost. This 16th of August, 1856."

"J. W. HASSELL, Sheriff."

Then follows the statement of a levy, of the same date, "upon one tract of land of one thousand acres," but not showing whose land it was. And the execution was returned with an endorsement that the "land was offered for sale, on the 6th day of October, 1856; and there being no bidders, the execution returned to the office."

It is argued for the plaintiffs in error, that the Court erred in sustaining the motion, and the case of *Crowder* v. *Sims*, 7 Hum., 257, is relied on as an authority. That case does not apply to the present. We are not now inquiring whether or not, if the tract of land levied on had been sold, the title of the purchaser could have been successfully impeached, on the ground that the personal property of all the defendants in the execution had not been exhausted, before proceeding against the real

J. W. Hassell *et al.* v. Southern Bank of Kentucky.

property of one of them. Be this as it may, it does not touch the present question. The inquiry now is simply this: Does the return show a sufficient reason, in law, why the money was not made according to the command of the writ? That it does not, is too obvious to admit of any discussion. Without controverting, for the present, any position assumed in *Crowder* v. *Sims*, it may be observed, that it is the duty of the sheriff, by positive law—whether the statute be construed to be imperative or merely directory—first to levy on the personal property of the defendant or defendants, before making a levy on land. If there be several defendants, all primarily liable, as in the present case, the sheriff may proceed against the goods and chattels of either one, to levy the whole debt, leaving the question of contribution to be settled among the defendants. And if some of the defendants thus liable have personal property liable to the satisfaction of the debt, and others have not, it is the duty of the sheriff to proceed against the former, or either of them, until property sufficient is found to discharge the debt. He cannot screen himself from liability by returning that one of the several defendants had no property subject to execution. To protect him, his return must show that the money could not have been made out of either defendant.

The present return is, therefore, insufficient, as, *prima facie*, the money might have been made out of either of the four other defendants. From the silence of the return, it cannot be presumed that they had no personal property; and if the fact were so, it was incumbent on the sheriff to return that fact affirmatively.

Judgment affirmed.

J. M. FLETCHER *v.* MARTHA A. COLEMAN *et al.*

1. WARRANTY. *Husband and wife. Liability of the wife on joint warranty with the husband. Estoppel.* If land is conveyed to the wife, with authority to her by joint deed with her husband to dispose of the same, and she join her husband in a deed for the land, with covenants of warranty, such warranty can only affect her by way of *estoppel*, if she attempts to assert any title in opposition to the one thus warranted. She would not be liable on her covenants in the joint deed. And it would not prohibit others from acting as trustees for her, and thereby secure her a benefit.

2. SAME. *Same. Same. Case in judgment.* A tract of land was conveyed to the wife, with authority to her to dispose of the same by joint deed with her husband. She joined her husband in a conveyance of the land to a third person, with covenants of warranty. After the execution of this deed, the original vendor filed a bill, and procured a decree for the sale of the land, to pay the purchase money. The trustee of the *feme covert* bid off the land for her, and gave bond and security for the purchase money. Subsequent to the sale, and before any title was vested in the *feme covert*, the parties and the sureties entered into an agreement by which the sureties paid the trustee $1,000, and were substituted as the purchasers. Held, that the warrantee of the wife could not be substituted to the title, the wife having acquired none, and not being liable on her warranty; nor could he be indemnified out of the $1,000 paid by the sureties.

FROM SHELBY.

At the November Term, 1858, CARUTHERS, J., presiding, the bill was dismissed on demurrer. The complainant appealed.

POSTON & SCRUGGS, for the complainant.

The demurrer admits the truth of the several allegations of complainant's bill.

J. M. Fletcher v. Martha A. Coleman et al.

The allegations of the bill admitted, the case stands as though Martha A. Coleman was the present holder of the estate acquired at the sale by the clerk and master, and the only question presented for the adjudication of the Court, is, whether that estate, the estate of a married woman, acquired subsequently to her conveyance with warranty, enured to the benefit of her vendee, whose title, under her previous deed, had failed. *Mark* v. *Willard*, 13 N. H., 389.

It is said that it will not, because a married woman cannot be held liable for damages after the death of her husband, upon the breach of a covenant of warranty; and that, therefore, the reason of the rule which causes the subsequently acquired title to enure to the benefit of the vendee, does not apply. Such is not, however, the course of decision in this country.

The Courts in this country have holden " that, although by a married woman's joinder with her husband in a covenant of warranty, she cannot be held liable in damages after his death; yet the covenant will estop her, and those claiming under her, from setting up any claim to an after acquired title. Rawle on Cov. for Title, p. 429; *Fowler* v. *Shearer*, 7 Mass. R., 21; *Colcord* v. *Swan*, 7 Mass. R., 291; *Nash* v. *Spofford*, 10 Metc. R., 192; 2 Kent, 167, (4th Ed.;) *Hill's lessee* v. *West*, 8 Ohio R., 226.

In the latter case it is said: "These decisions (referring to the cases cited above, which are referred to and approved,) may not seem to be founded upon the reasons which are usually assigned why the covenants in a deed should operate by way of estoppel, that is, to prevent circuity of actions; still they seem to us reasonable, and such as tend to the furtherance of justice; and when a married woman undertakes, in conjunction with her husband, to convey his land with covenants of warranty, it is sufficient to protect her from the payment of damages for the breach of these covenants. For all other purposes they should be held operative."

See, also, the case of *Massie* v. *Sebastian*, in 4th Bibb's (Ky.) R., 436, in which the Court held that "it is perfectly clear that neither Breckinridge or his wife, after the acknowledgment of the deed to Sebastian, would be permitted to claim in opposition to their deed, by alleging that they had then no estate in the premises; and as their heirs claiming through them, and any stranger to whom they might sell, can be in no better situation, they must be, also, equally estopped." And cases cited in 4 Bibb, 436.

The case cited in 17 Johns. R., 167, *Jackson* v. *Vanderheyden*, has been followed by the case in 6 Wendell, 9, *Martin* v. *Dwelly* and they were decided without argument or authority submitted. The case of *Wight* v. *Shaw*, 5 Cush. R., 65, is not a case in point. There the conveyance embraced "all the right, title and interest which the wife then had," being one-sixth of a certain estate, and the effort was to make a subsequent interest, descended to her by death of other parties, possessed at the date of her covenant, pass by her conveyance.

W. G. THOMPSON and SULLIVAN, for the defendants.

J. M. Fletcher v. Martha A. Coleman *et al.*

CARUTHERS, J., delivered the opinion of the Court.

Vance sold to Hanna lot 230, in Memphis, and took his note for the purchase money, in 1847, reserving in the deed a lien. In 1849 Hanna sold and conveyed part of the lot to Antwine, who in 1853 conveyed the same to Martha A., wife of Walter Coleman, with authority to her, by joint deed with her husband, to dispose of the same. This power was exercised by her, with her husband, in 1854, by sale to complainant, Fletcher, for the consideration of $750, with covenants of warranty. After this, the original vendor, Vance, filed a bill to enforce his lien for the purchase money. A decree was made in his favor, the whole lot sold and purchased by E. M. Yerger, as trustee for Mrs. Coleman, at $1,175. Defendants, Pitman and Taylor, became the sureties, in a note at seven months, for the amount of the bid. By an arrangement between the parties, the sureties were substituted as the buyers, and upon payment of the note obtained the title.

It is charged that they gave Mrs. Coleman a *bonus* of $1,000 for the privilege of substitution.

This bill is filed by Fletcher to assert his right to the title obtained by Mrs. Coleman at the Chancery sale, by way of enurement, as the title conveyed by her and her husband, to him, by their deed with warranty, in 1854, has thus failed. It is charged that the intervention of a trustee, and the substitution of Pitman and Taylor, were all fraudulent contrivances to defeat the complainant in his right to the benefit of the title acquired by her, as the best bidder, at the Chancery sale.

J. M. Fletcher v. Martha A. Coleman *et al*.

The demurrer to this bill was sustained, and we think correctly.

The wife was not liable on the warranty in the joint deed to Fletcher. It could only affect her by way of estoppel if she attempted to assert any title in opposition to the one thus warranted. It would not prohibit others from acting as trustees for her, and thereby securing her a benefit. *She* did not, in any view, by the facts stated, become invested with a title that could enure to others for any purpose. The incipient step by bidding off the property, had only been taken, and without having paid anything towards the consideration, the benefit passed to those who were bound as sureties for the bid, and *they*, by paying it, properly became invested with the title. That she obtained a *bonus* of $1,000 in the transaction, can make no difference whatever. The only ground upon which the complainant can go in this case, is that the best title was obtained by his vendor under this sale, and that it should, in equity, enure to him, in aid of the defective title before acquired from her. That principle is, certainly, correct when it applies. But no title ever accrued to her, or any one for her benefit, nor did she ever pay any thing for it. She preferred the $1,000 to getting the title by paying the $1,175. The true title then passed to Pitman and Taylor, and the complainant must rely upon his warranty for his loss.

It is also objected that the sale is not good under the Chancery decree as to the complainant, because he was not a party. That was not material. The vendor's lien is fixed upon the *land*, and he can enforce it without making all who may have bought it from or under his vendee, parties. He has only to do with the thing sold, and his debtor for the price. It is not necessary to incumber such cases with intervening purchasers, and, thereby, increase the burthen by an accumulation of costs.

Affirm the decree.

JOHN CROMWELL et al. v. SARAH WINCHESTER et al.

1. LAND LAW. *Words of inheritance.* "*Heirs*" *necessary to create a fee.* At common law, the word "*heirs*" is indispensable to convey an estate of inheritance. Without the use of that term in deeds an estate for life only, is created. But this rule has been changed in Tennessee, by statutory enactment.

2. CHANCERY JURISDICTION. *Mistake. Correction of.* If, by *mistake*, a writing contains less or more, or something different from the intention of the parties, and this is made to appear by clear and satisfactory proof, a Court of Equity will reform the writing, so as to make it conform to what the parties intended.

3. SAME. *Same. Same. Case in judgment.* A lot in Memphis was conveyed, in 1843, to a trustee, for Mrs. Elizabeth Armour and "her children forever." In addition to the *intrinsic* evidence in the deed, parol evidence was introduced to show that it was the intention of the conveyor to create an estate in fee. Held, that it was a proper case for the interposition of a Court of Equity, to reform the deed, so as to make it convey an estate of inheritance, and thereby carry out the intention of the parties.

FROM SHELBY.

At the November Term, 1858, Judge CARUTHERS, pronounced a decree for the complainants. The defendants appealed.

John Cromwell *et al.* v. Sarah Winchester *et al.*

W. K. POSTON, for the complainants.

WICKERSHAM & BEECHER, HAYS & MORRILL, for the defendants.

CARUTHERS, J., delivered the opinion of the Court.

In 1843, David Winchester, who is now dead, leaving the defendants, his widow and children, sold and conveyed to Cromwell in trust, "for Mrs. Elizabeth Armour and children," a lot in Memphis, for the consideration of $300. This bill is filed to correct an alleged mistake in the deed, by the omission of the words of inheritance. The words used are "to the said John Cromwell, trustee of Elizabeth Armour, and her *children forever.*"

The rigid and well established rule of the common law, 4 Kent, 4, 5, &c., that the word *heirs* is indispensable to convey an estate of inheritance, and without it, only, an estate for life is created in deeds, is recognized by this Court in *Hunter* v. *Bryan*, 5 Hum., 47. This rule, though of feudal origin, has been too long established to be changed, except by the Legislature. This has been done by several of the States, and recently by our own. But this deed was before our statute. This deed is not before us, however, for construction, but upon a bill to reform it, because of a mistake in not inserting words of inheritance, in conformity to the understanding of the parties at the time.

That this power has been always exercised in proper cases by Courts of Chancery, there can be no doubt. 1 Story Eq, sec. 152. If, by *mistake*, the writing contains less or more, or something different from the intent of the parties, and this be *clearly* made out by proof *entirely* satisfactory, a Court of Equity will reform the contract so as to make it conform to such intent. But if the mistake is not made *entirely* plain, and put beyond all reasonable controversy, the Court will not interpose. It is not easy to reconcile this doctrine to the common law rule, which excludes all parol evidence to vary or control written contracts, and that it is liable to abuse is obvious. But where terms and stipulations are inserted, or omitted, by *fraud* or *mistake*, greater frauds and injustice would be perpetrated by closing the door against any relief, than the rule is designed to prevent. Let this be as it may, the jurisdiction of a Court of Equity on this subject is well settled. The presumption always is strong, that a writing contains the whole contract, and sets it forth accurately; but, if it can be *clearly* and *indisputably* shown, that by *fraud* or *mistake* it does not, the presumption fails, and it will be reformed.

The question is, whether, according to these rules, the complainants have made out a case for the relief they ask. It is proved by two witnesses that they saw the vendor on the day he made the sale, and he said he had sold the lot to Cromwell for a certain price, which is proved to have been a full and fair one for the *fee* at that day. He made no reservation, said nothing about a life estate or a reversion, or the reservation of any interest. But we are not left to parol proof to ascertain the intention of the parties, because the *internal* evidence is conclusive upon the point. In a perfectly formal deed in other respects, he conveys the lot to John Cromwell, as trustee for Elizabeth

John Cromwell *et al. v.* Sarah Winchester *et al.*

Armour, and "her *children forever*." Although that may not be, according to the authorities, equivalent to the word "heirs," so as, of itself, to create a fee, yet it is enough to show that it was the intent of the parties at the time, that an estate of inheritance was bought and sold, but, by mistake, the proper *technical* word was omitted. It is not possible to suppose that the vendor reserved a life estate in the face of the words, "and children *forever*." No room is left for conjecture, and the presumption or rule of law, that a life estate, only, is intended to be conveyed, because the word *heirs* is omitted, is entirely rebutted and overthrown. Story in sec. 162, says, that this relief is not only granted where the mistake is expressly established, "but also where it is fairly implied from the nature of the transaction." There can be no doubt whatever left upon the mind, but that it was the object and intent of the parties that a fee was conveyed in this deed, and that it was by mistake so written, as not to carry out that intent. Perhaps the proof would not be sufficient for the purpose, independent of this intrinsic evidence, but with that, it is beyond all controversy.

We have not thought it necessary to decide the question of the competency of the husband of Mrs. Armour, but decide the case without reference to his testimony.

We think there is no doubt of the correctness of the Chancellor's decree granting the relief, and affirm it.

J. C. BAKER v. PETER AMMON.

PRACTICE AND PLEADING. *Pleas sworn to. Code,* §§ 2886, 2887. By the provisions of the Code, the plaintiff, in his pleading, may require the answer of the defendant to be given under oath, and the answer of the defendant thus put in, has the same force as an answer in Chancery requiring two witnesses, or one with corroborating circumstances, to overturn it. And this applies to every description of plea, or defence, to any civil action at law.*

FROM SHELBY.

The defendant having failed to put in his defence under oath, as required by the plaintiff, judgment by default was rendered up against him at the January Term, 1859, HUMPHREYS, J., presiding. He appealed.

TREADWELL and VOLLENTINE, for the plaintiff in error.

SMITH & STOVALL, for the defendant in error.

CARUTHERS, J., delivered the opinion of the Court.

This was an action of debt upon a note for $1,000, in the usual form. The pleas are, *nil debet*, payment, set-off, and statute of limitations. These pleas were not sworn to, as required in the declaration. For that reason they were disregarded by the Court, and judgment by default given against the defendant for want of any defence.

---

* This provision of the Code is repealed by the Act of 1859, ch. 5, § 1.

J. C. Baker v. Peter Ammon.

Whether this was erroneous, is the only question; and to settle that, the case is brought up, as it seems different opinions are entertained, by the Circuit Judges, upon it.

In chap. 9, art. 1, of the Code, this subject is regulated. The subject is introduced by section 2880, in these words: "The pleadings treated of in this chapter apply to all actions at law."

Section 2886 provides that "the plaintiff, in his pleadings, may require the answer of the defendant to be given under oath."

Section 2887 gives to such pleading the same force as an answer in Chancery, requiring two witnesses, or one with corroborating circumstances, to overturn it.

We see no possible way to avoid the conclusion, that every description of plea, or defence, to any civil action at law, must be under oath, if expressly required in the declaration.

It is a great innovation, but such is the legislative will, and we must obey it. The object, doubtless, was to prevent expense and delay in reaching a man's rights wrongfully withheld. The defendant, it was thought, should not be allowed to rely upon any plea, general or special, unless he is willing to swear that he believes it to be true. He is not permitted to plead that he does not owe, did not assume, has paid, is not guilty, or interpose any other defence upon which to claim an issue, unless it be verified by oath.

On the one hand it will, doubtless, lead to much perjury, but on the other it will prevent unreal or false defences, and thereby cut off the law's delay, and expedite the administration of justice, where there is no true and real defence. It will prevent much recorded falsehood in untrue pleas, but may increase false swearing. It was for the Legislature to decide between these evils; and as they have done so, it is only for us to enforce their declared will.

Judgment affirmed.

GEORGE THREADGILL et al. v. RICHARD TIMBERLAKE et al.

USURY. *When it may be recovered back in equity.* The rule in equity is to apply the excess of interest to the satisfaction of the principal, and when that is paid in this way, all that is paid afterwards may be recovered by the borrower as so much money had and received by the lender to his use. And this may be done although the party has been sued at law, and failed to make the defence.

FROM HENDERSON.

This cause was heard before Chancellor PAVATT, at the February Term, 1859. Decree for the defendants. The complainants appealed.

M. & H. BROWN, for the complainants.

W. E. PENN, for the defendants.

WRIGHT, J., delivered the opinion of the Court.

The bill in this case is filed to be relieved against the payment of a usurious judgment.

George Threadgill *et al.* v. Richard Timberlake *et al.*

The facts are these: On the 19th of February, 1853, complainant, Threadgill, borrowed of defendant, Timberlake, $500.00, and executed his note of that date, with the other complainant as his security, for said sum, due at the time of its execution.

They, also, at the same time, executed to Timberlake their note for $70, due at one year from that date; and, also, on the 14th of July, 1854, complainant, Threadgill, with W. C. Threadgill as his surety, gave Timberlake another note for $70, due the 20th of February thereafter.

These last mentioned notes are admitted to be for illegal interest, reserved upon the loan of the $500.00 above mentioned.

On the 30th of November, 1855, Timberlake took judgment against complainants for $583.32, the same being the amount of the $500.00 note with legal interest.

They have paid him $566.66, in a note on Bell and McHenry, due the 25th of December, 1856, and, also, in March, 1857, the sum of $85, out of which the sheriff took the costs of the suit at law, leaving $61 to be credited upon the judgment.

Timberlake claims the right to apply, as far as necessary, the Bell and McHenry note in discharge of the two notes of $70, and to credit the judgment with the balance, and in this way, insists that complainants yet owe him about $275,00; and has caused their property to be levied on to pay it.

The complainants failed to plead or rely upon the defence of usury at law.

The bill is for an injunction and relief against the

George Threadgill *et al.* *v.* Richard Timberlake *et al.*

judgment, and a decree for any over payment. The Chancellor dismissed the bill, and gave a decree against complainants for $274.89 and the costs of this suit and of the suit at law.

This decree is erroneous. The note upon Bell and McHenry, and the $61, should have been applied, entirely, as a credit upon the judgment, and not upon the notes for $70. If this had been done, the judgment would have been extinguished.

The rule in equity is to apply the excess of interest to the satisfaction of the principal, and when that is paid in this way, all that is paid afterwards may be recovered by the borrower, as so much money had and received by the lender to his use. *Boyers* v. *Boddie*, 3 Hum., 666.

As to the abatement claimed by Timberlake, of $16\frac{3}{4}$ per cent. discount upon the Bell and McHenry note, upon the ground that he purchased and took it of complainants at that rate—the same cannot be allowed, because it is new matter, set up in the answer by way of avoidance, and not proved. It is not pretended that every dollar of the note was not realized.

As to the costs of the suit at law, they appear to have been paid. It was error, therefore, to decree complainants to pay them.

The decree of the Chancellor will be reversed, and the injunction made perpetual.

The complainants will have a decree for an account upon the principles of this opinion, and a recovery for any balance due them.

Decree reversed.

J. H. CRINER *v.* JACOB PIKE.

1. TRESPASS *Exclusive possession sufficient to support this action* An actual and exclusive possession by a party, even though it be by wrong, is sufficient to support an action of trespass against a mere stranger or wrong-doer, who has neither title to the possession in himself, nor authority from the legal owner.
2. SAME. *How possession lost.* The fact that the property in suit, a mare, was in her usual *range* in the woods, or had gone to the defendant's, in the neighborhood, if this be so, where he killed her, did not destroy the plaintiff's possession, so as to prevent him from sustaining the action.
3. SAME. *Measure of damages.* Ordinarily, in such cases, the party in possession is either the owner of the property, or answerable over to the owner; and in either case he is entitled not only to damages for the taking, but also for the value of the same.
4. SAME. *Same. Mitigation.* The defendant may prove, in mitigation of damages, that the goods did not belong to the plaintiff, and that they have gone to the use of the true owner, either by being restored to him in *specie*, or taken upon legal process in payment of his debts.

FROM HENDERSON.

At the July Term, 1858, before Judge WILLIAMS, there were verdict and judgment for the plaintiff. The defendant appealed.

BROWN and PENN, for the plaintiff in error.

H. WRIGHT, for the defendant in error.

WRIGHT, J., delivered the opinion of the Court.

This is an action of trespass, *vi et armis* for killing a mare, alleged to be the property of the plaintiff.

J. H. Criner v. Jacob Pike.

She was raised on his premises, and there is proof tending to show that she belonged to him, and that the defendant frequently requested him to keep her up, she being in the habit of getting into the defendant's wheatfield. He shot and killed her.

On the other hand, there is proof tending to establish that this mare did not belong to the plaintiff, but to Mrs. Fowler.

She was a witness for defendant, and proved that she and plaintiff were brother and sister, and lived together—their father living with them—until her marriage, in April, 1855, when she went away, and desired to take the mare with her, but the plaintiff would not permit her to do so. And it is to be inferred from the record that she left the mare in possession of the plaintiff, and never afterwards exercised any further acts of ownership over her. The proof discloses none. It is further to be inferred, from the evidence, that the plaintiff retained the possession and control of this mare until she was killed.

Upon these facts, the defendant requested the Court to charge the jury, that if the plaintiff was not the owner of the mare, to enable him to recover, he must show the actual possession of her, which he could not do if she were running at large in the woods, and that less than three years adverse possession would not give him a title as against Mrs. Fowler; and that even if he had the actual possession, and the right of property was not in him, or was in Mrs. Fowler, then he could only recover nominal damages, or not more than the damage done him by defeating his possession, and could not recover the full value of the mare.

J. H. Criner *v.* Jacob Pike.

These instructions the Circuit Judge refused to give; but charged the jury, that if the plaintiff and his sister lived together with their father for several years, and had raised the mare on the premises, and each of them claimed her until the marriage of Betsy, the sister, when she went home with her husband, leaving the mare in the possession of the plaintiff, and she remained in his possession and was claimed by him ever after the marriage until she was killed; and that, since her marriage, the sister had not claimed the mare by suing for her, or taking her in possession, or doing any act of ownership, then the plaintiff would be invested with such title as would authorize him to maintain a suit against a trespasser having no claim to the property, and to recover the value of the mare at the time she was killed. But that if these facts did not exist, he could not recover. That a person who has had a horse beast in possession for several years, claiming it, can maintain trespass against a person destroying the property while in the range, who has no claim to it.

The jury, under these instructions, rendered a verdict in favor of the plaintiff for 'the full value of the mare, and the defendant has appealed in error to this Court.

We think the instructions to the jury were proper, and that the Circuit Judge did right in pronouncing judgment upon the verdict.

It is well-settled that an actual and exclusive possession by the plaintiff, even though it be by *wrong*, is sufficient to support this action *against a mere stranger* or wrong-doer, who has neither title to the possession in himself, nor authority from the legal owner. 2 Greenl. Ev., § 618. Therefore, if we were to canclude that

J. H. Criner *v.* Jacob Pike.

Mrs. Fowler was the owner of this mare, yet it is manifest the plaintiff had such a possession as enabled him to maintain the action; and, certainly, the evidence warranted the jury in so finding. The fact that the mare was in her usual range in the woods, or had gone to the defendant's field in the neighborhood—if this be so—where he killed her, did not destroy the plaintiff's possession, especially when we consider she had been left with him by Mrs. Fowler for so great a length of time.

As to the measure of damages, the reason given why a party having possession should maintain trespass is, that he may have sustained injury by being deprived of the goods; nor should his claim to damages be construed strictly. Ordinarily, he is either the owner, or answerable over to the owner; and, in either case, he is entitled not only to damages for the taking, but also for the value of the goods. *Squire* v. *Hallenbeck*, 9 Pick., 551. This is the general rule. A defendant has been allowed to prove, in mitigation of damages, that the goods did not belong to the plaintiff, and that they have gone to the use of the true owner, either by being restored to him in specie, or taken upon legal process, in payment of his debts; for, in such case, the plaintiff is not answerable over. 9 Pick., 551; Sedgwick on the Measure of Damages, 548.

But Mr. Sedgwick thinks the principle of these decisions has been carried quite far enough, and that it is of importance to draw the line between good and bad faith. Where the party acts with pure motives, and endeavors, as soon as possible to repair his mistake, it may, says he, be very proper to construe his conduct favorably; but it will not do to permit acts of wilfu

J. H Criner v. Jacob Pike.

or wanton trespass to be excused by the defence of outstanding titles in third persons. It would lead directly to that reckless interference with the property of others, which the law always sedulously seeks to prevent. This distinction, he maintains, is well laid down in a case in New York, where it was held, that where property tortiously taken by one person from the possession of another, is subsequently levied upon, whilst in the hands of the tortfeasor, by a third person, under a warrant of distress for rent due by the owner, such last taking may be shown in mitigation of damages in an action by the owner against the tortfeasor, *if the latter took the property under an honest belief that he had a title to it, and not for the purpose of subjecting it to the landlord's warrant.* Sedgwick, 548, 549.

Without stopping to consider of the validity of this distinction, it is enough for our purpose, that here the defendant is a mere wrong-doer, having no sort of claim upon the mare, and that he wantonly destroyed her; and that the plaintiff is either the owner, or had such possession as made him answerable over to the true owner.

In such a case, we have been unable to find any authority in support of the argument that the plaintiff shall not have full damages.

Judgment affirmed.

Henry J. Maley v. N. Tipton.

HENRY J. MALEY v. N. TIPTON.

1. REGISTRATION. *Vacancy in the office of Register. Deputy Register. Act of* 1851-2. By the act of 1851-2, each county register is authorized to appoint one deputy; and all deeds previously registered by *deputies* are declared to be valid. The act also provides that when the register shall die, the deputy may continue to act until the appointment of a successor; and all instruments registered by a deputy during a vacancy in the office, by death, are declared as effectual as if made by the principal register. Although a vacancy occasioned by the *removal* of the register is not embraced by the words of the act, it is within the spirit of the law, and conveyances registered by a deputy during such a vacancy are as effectual as if the vacancy had been occasioned by death.

2. SAME. *Same. Register de facto.* The acts of an officer *de facto* are valid as respects third persons who have an interest in them, and as concerns the public, in order to prevent a failure of justice. Hence. if the office of register becomes vacant by the removal of the incumbent, and his deputy continues to act, the acts of such deputy, being an officer *de facto,* are valid and effectual without the aid of any statutory enactment.

FROM TIPTON.

This cause was heard before Judge HUMPHREYS, at the January Term, 1858. The defendant appealed.

SMALL & FOUTE, for the plaintiff in error.

I. M. STEELE, for the defendant in error.

MCKINNEY, J., delivered the opinion of the Court.

This was an action of replevin brought by Tipton against Maley, to recover certain goods, wares and mer-

Henry J. Maley v. N. Tipton.

chandise conveyed to Tipton, as trustee, by one Smith, for the benefit of creditors. Judgment was for the plaintiff; and the case is brought to this Court, upon an exception taken to the registration of the deed of trust. The deed purports to have been registered on the 14th of January, 1858. The certificate of registration is signed thus: "Ben. Sherrod, Register, by J. Morrison, D. R." The record shows that Sherrod, the register of Tipton county, removed to Texas a day or two before the registration of said deed; whereby the office became vacant, and, therefore, it is argued, the registration of said deed, by the deputy, was a nullity.

It is true, that the act of 1823, ch. 5, sec. 1, declares, that by the removal of a county register out of the bounds of the county in which he may have been elected, the office shall become *vacant;* still, we think, the registration of the deed is not vitiated on this ground.

A deputy register is an officer known to the law. By the act of 1852, ch. 175, sec. 4., each county register is authorized to appoint one deputy; and all deeds previously registered by *deputies*, are declared to be sufficient. By ch. 48, of the same session, it is provided, that when the register shall die, the deputy may continue to act until the appointment of a successor; and all instruments previously registered by a deputy, during a vacancy in the office, by death, are declared as effectual as if made by the principal register.

The case of a vacancy, by the removal of a register, is not embraced by the words of the foregoing enactment, but it is within the spirit of the law. And in this view, the registration might well be considered valid; as it cannot be regarded as of the essence of the thing how the vacancy happened—whether by the death or removal of the register. But, without the aid of any statutory enactment, the registration would be valid and effectual, upon the principle, that it was the act of an officer *de facto*, acting under color of office. It is a well established principle, that the acts of such an officer are valid as respects third persons who have an interest in them, and as concerns the public, in order to prevent a failure of justice.

The judgment will be affirmed.

Duncan Thompson *v.* Sallie Thompson.

1. PAYMENT. *Presumption of, after the lapse of sixteen years.* If a bond or note under seal, be suffered to lie dormant for the space of sixteen years, without demand being made, or payment of interest, or other explanatory circumstances to show that it is still in force, payment will be presumed upon the mere fact of lapse of time.

2. SAME. *Same. Effect of.* This presumption of payment, like other legal or artificial presumptions, derives from the law a certain technical force and effect, which courts and juries cannot disregard. Until rebutted, or displaced by evidence, it has all the force and effect of plenary proof of the fact of payment, and the jury are bound so to regard it.

3. SAME. *Less than sixteen years.* The fact of payment may be inferred by the jury from the circumstances of the particular case, in a shorter period than sixteen years, but the presumption of law does not attach until the full expiration of that time.

FROM CARROLL.

Verdict and judgment for the plaintiff, at the April Term, 1858, FITZGERALD, J., presiding. The defendant appealed.

Duncan Thompson *v.* Sallie Thompson.

A. HAWKINS, for the plaintiff in error.

S. M. JONES, for the defendant in error.

MCKINNEY, J., delivered the opinion of the Court.

This suit was commenced before a justice, on the 24th of July, 1857. The foundation of the suit is a note under seal, executed by Duncan Thompson to Sallie Thompson, on the 22d of March, 1824, for one hundred and ten dollars, on which a credit is endorsed for $60.50, under date of November 30th, 1826.

The case was taken, by appeal, to the Circuit Court, and on the trial the plaintiff recovered judgment for $49.50, the balance due upon said note, with the further sum of $93.30, the accruing interest.

The defence relied on was the presumption of payment. And it is difficult to see why it did not prevail, if the facts be correctly stated in the record before us. The jury were probably misled by some things needlessly thrown into the charge of the Court, tending to weaken the presumption, and to place the *onus* upon the defendant.

The evidence is very brief. The note was made in North Carolina, where both the parties (who are brother and sister) then resided. Duncan Thompson removed to the Western District of Tennessee in the fall of 1826, about the time, perhaps, of the date of the payment credited on the note. His means were very limited at the time of his removal. But the proof fully establishes that he has been solvent, and possessed of considerable property, ever since his removal to this State, and that he has always been "remarkably punctual" in the payment of his debts. The plaintiff remained in North Carolina, and still resides there. It is not pretended that she was not fully aware of the place of residence of the defendant from the time of his removal. It does not appear that from the defendant's removal, up to the institution of this suit—a period of more than *thirty years*—said note was ever spoken of, or payment thereof demanded.

The rule so often recognized by this Court, that if a bond, or note under seal, be suffered to lie dormant for the space of *sixteen* years, without demand being made, or payment of interest, or other explanatory circumstances to show that it is still in force, payment will be presumed, upon the mere fact of lapse of time, is not now to be questioned. The fact of payment may be inferred by the jury, from the circumstances of the particular case, in a shorter period; but the presumption of law does not attach until the full expiration of sixteen years.

This presumption of payment, like other legal or artificial presumptions, derives from the law a certain technical force and effect, which courts and juries cannot disregard. Instead of being of "but little force," as the Court said to the jury, the presumption, until rebutted, or displaced by evidence, has all the force and effect of plenary proof of the fact of payment; and the jury are bound so to regard it.

We are not called on in the present case to say what circumstances would be sufficient to repel the presumption. It is enough, for the decision of the case, to

Levi C. Bullock v. E. W. Tipton et al.

express our opinion, that the circumstances relied on are not sufficient.

The only facts entitled to any consideration, are, the near relationship of the parties, and the removal of the defendant, and his permanent residence in a different State from the plaintiff.

These circumstances, after the lapse of nearly double the time required to raise the presumption, weigh but little.

It is scarcely necessary to remark, that the evidence relied on to displace the legal presumption, ought to be more satisfactory in proportion to the length of time that may have been suffered to elapse before suit.

The judgment will be reversed.

LEVI C. BULLOCK v. E. W. TIPTON et al.

1. LAND LAW. *Grant. Hiatus between the expiration of the act of* 1850, *and the passage of the act of* 1851. *Abandonment of an entry.* If land was entered previous to the expiration of the act of 1850, but no grant issued until after that time, and a third person, during the *hiatus* between the 30th of August, 1851, the time the act of 1850 ceased, and the passage of the act of the 13th of November, 1851, entered the same land; but, upon discovering the conflict with the older entry, he abandoned his entry, which, being left in the entry taker's office, was recorded by the deputy without his knowledge, such subsequent enterer could not hold the land in opposition to the older entry.

2. SAME. *Entry. Assignment of.* If, upon a promise made prior to the discovery of said conflict, the second enterer of the land assigns

his entry to a third person, without consideration, and with a full knowledge of the prior claim, and the abandonment of the second entry, the assignee can have no higher equity than his assignor, and could not, by virtue of such second entry, defeat the title of the older enterer.

3. SAME. *Legal title. Valuable consideration. Prior equity. Question reserved.* If a party procures from the State the legal title to a tract of land, and has paid a valuable consideration therefor, will a Court of Equity take it from him at the instance of one who, with a full knowledge of his previous rights, seeks to come in under an *hiatus* in the extension law upon an entry made upon a mere nominal consideration?

FROM OBION.

The bill was dismissed by Chancellor WILLIAMS, at the July Term, 1857. The complainant appealed.

SOMERS, for the complainant.

It is insisted: First. That Tipton, by his failure and neglect to procure a grant upon his entry, No. 95, prior to the 1st of September, 1851, forfeited his right to the land, and that the same was then vacant, and subject to general entry.

The act of the General Assembly, passed Jnauary 24th, 1850, extends the time for making surveys and obtaining grants, on *all entries before that time made in any of the land offices of this State,* until the 1st day of September, 1851. The language of the act is general, and includes *all entries,* without any reference to the law under which they may have been made. Such being the case, the act includes the entry, No. 95, in question, if the legislature had a right to pass it, or, in other words, if it is constitutional. In the case of *Williamson and Wife* v. *Throop and Luna,* 11 Hum., 265, it was decided, that, in case two individuals enter the same land, and the younger enterer procures a grant before the expiration of the time allowed for that purpose, and the elder enterer neglects to procure a grant before the expiration of such time, the younger enterer will hold the land, the other having forfeited his right by his neglect. To the same effect is the case of *Sampson* v. *Taylor,* 1 Sneed, 600. The entry of the plaintiff in that case was made on the 1st of September, 1851, the same day upon which entry No. 216, in question, was made. But in both these cases grants had been obtained by the younger enterers, and the law under which the elder ones were made, required that grants should be obtained within a specified time, or the entry should be void, or the land vacant, and subject to appropriation as other lands. In these respects those cases differ from the one under consideration; and it is argued that the law under which entry No. 95 was made, does not contain any such condition, or does not provide that the entries made under it shall be void, or the land covered by them shall be vacant, unless grants are obtained within a certain specified time; and that, therefore, the act of 1850, giving until the 1st of September, 1851, to procure grants upon all entries does not apply to said entry, No. 95; or, it was intended to apply to entries made under the law, by virtue of which said entry, No. 95, was made, it is void for want of constitutional sanction. If this is so, an entry under these laws would be as good a title as a grant, which is surely not law. These acts were passed for the bene-

Levi C. Bullock *v.* E. W. Tipton *et al.*

fit of the citizen; the one under which entry No. 95 was made, passed November 2d, 1847, requires nothing to be paid by the enterer but the fees of office. The State is not divested of the legal title to land simply because it is entered; and it is the duty of all enterers to perfect their title, so that the land may be subject to taxation; and we insist the State has a right to compel them to do so, or forfeit their entries. This entry, No. 95, was made on the 4th of August, 1849, prior to that time, (viz,) the 25th of January, 1848, the legislature passed an act, giving until the 1st of September, 1849, to perfect title to all lands and entries in the State. We insist that all those acts respecting lands, from 1837 to the present time, are to be construed in *pari materia;* and that the act giving time until the 1st of September, 1849, to perfect titles, is engrafted upon, and constitutes a part of the act passed 2d of November, 1847; and that a proper construction of them makes it inoperative upon enterers, to procure grants within that time, or forfeit their entries. And we further insist, that the act of January 24th, 1850, giving further time until the 1st of September, 1851, must be construed in the same way. 3 Sneed, 152.

That the complainant has a right to have the legal title to the land, wrongfully obtained by Tipton, divested and vested in himself, in virtue of his entry, No. 216, there can be no doubt. *Reese* v. *Crockett*, 8 Yer., 129. This case decides, that where two persons claimed the same land as occupants, and the one having no title, wrongfully procured a grant, the other might file a bill, and have the title illegally obtained by the other, vested in himself. There is no difference in principle between that case and

Levi C. Bullock *v.* E. W. Tipton *et al.*

this. Bullock did all within his power to get a grant. He tendered the fee required by law, to the proper officer, within the time allowed by law for perfecting his title. He has been in no default, and has incurred no forfeiture of his rights.

The act passed January 20, 1850, is in the nature of a statute of limitations, and the effect of it was to revest the entire title to land which had been entered, unless the enterer procured his grant by the time allowed, viz, the 1st of September, 1851.

COCHRAN & ENLOE, for the defendants.

The act of 1823, ch. 35, secs. 9 and 10, (2 H. & C., p. 104,) limiting the time in which entries should be perfected into grants, has no application to Tipton's entry.

The system of land law introduced by the act of 1819, ch. 1, was closed by the act of 1842, ch. 34.

Up to the date of Tipton's entry, No. 95, there was no law limiting the time in which entries made under the act of 1842, ch. 34, and the subsequent amendatory acts, should be perfected into grants.

Tipton's entry was made under the act of 1847, ch. 20, (Nich. Sup., p. 30,) which requires the fees of the entry taker, surveyor, register, and Secretary of State, all to be paid to the entry taker. (See sec. 1.)

The act of 1845, ch. 8, secs. 2 and 3, requires the entry taker to procure the grant; and the act of 1847, ch. 20, does not repeal that provision of the act of 1845, ch. 8, but rather confirms it, by the absence of any repealing clause, and more especially by the requirement that all the fees shall be paid to the entry taker.

Thus, Tipton, by his entry, stood in the attitude of a purchaser for a valuable consideration, and it was the duty of the State to make the title.

These circumstances repel the idea, that any of the acts limiting the time for the issuance of grants, were intended to apply to this character of entries.

Any act passed subsequent to the date of Tipton's entry, could not affect his right.

His entry was a contract between him and the State, and he had a free-hold estate in the land. No subsequent conditions could be annexed to the contract, nor could he be divested of his free-hold by subsequent legislation, if there be any such intended to apply to the case. *Terrell* v. *Murray*, 2 Yer., 386, 387; 4 Kent, 23, (8th edition); Bill of Rights, sec. 8, (C. & N., 46); Constitution, sec. 10, Art. 1, (C. & N., 12).

WRIGHT, J., delivered the opinion of the Court.

This is a bill to divest out of the defendant, Tipton, the title to 730 acres and 30 poles of land in the county of Obion, claimed by complainant.

The facts of the case are these: On the 4th of August, 1849, Tipton made a consolidated entry for 1200 acres, under the provisions of the act of 1847, ch. 20.

In October, 1840, six individuals, whose names are given in the record, being, separately, the owners of

Levi C. Bullock *v.* E. W. Tipton *et al.*

small certificate warrants issued by the register of West Tennessee, amounting in the aggregate to 141 and 4-9th acres, caused several entries to be made of the same, in their respective names, in the entry taker's office of Obion county; and being thus the owners of these small tracts, they caused the same to be enlarged to 200 acres each—under the occupant laws of the State, providing for extension rights—and, also, had the same entered in their respective names. These tracts constitute the 1,200 acres before mentioned.

Tipton became the assignee of these warrants and extension entries, and for the purpose of obtaining a grant, made the consolidated entry aforesaid—having paid to the entry taker the fees that were allowed by law, to the entry taker, surveyor, register, and Secretary of State, in obtaining grants. But the State did not issue the grant to him till the 1st day of January, 1856.

On the 1st day of September, 1851, S. W. Cochrane made an entry of the land claimed by complainant, and which, in part, conflicts with Tipton's entry and grant; but being subsequently informed of the conflict, he determined to abandon his entry, but the same being left on file in the entry taker's office, was recorded by the deputy entry taker without his knowledge.

It seems, that prior to the discovery of the conflict, Cochrane had proposed to *give* this entry to the complainant; and, as we take it, from the record, without any consideration. At all events, none appears, and we are satisfied none was paid. Complainant does not allege or pretend there was any. But, notwithstanding these facts, and with a full knowledge of Tipton's prior claim, he insisted that Cochrane should permit him to have the benefit of the entry; and Cochrane did, accordingly, on the 13th of August, 1855, assign it to him, without consideration—informing him at the time of Tipton's prior right—and of his determination not to claim the entry.

Afterwards, and on the 12th of December, 1855—complainant caused this entry to be surveyed, and tendered the plot and certificate of survey, with the fees of office, to the entry taker, who refused to receive the same, because of the existence of Tipton's prior right.

The complainant insists that Tipton's right to obtain a grant, by force of the act of the 24th of January, 1850, expired on the 30th of August, 1851, and that in consequence of the *hiatus* in the law—extending the time to obtain grants—between that time and the act of the 13th of November, 1851, Tipton's entry became vacant, and subject to his entry, and that he now has a right to divest the legal title out of Tipton.

The Chancellor decreed otherwise, and we think his decree was right. It is manifest complainant has no equity to move a court, actively, in his behalf. This is so upon general principles. It is not necessary for us to decide the question debated here, whether after Tipton—under the act of 1847, ch. 20—had paid the fees allowed by law to the entry taker, surveyor, register and Secretary of State, and had done every thing required at his hands in order to obtain a grant, leaving nothing but the simple *duty* upon the State, and its officers, to issue it—the Legislature intended, by the subsequent legislation, to impair his rights—or if so intended, could do so—because we think it is enough that Cochrane himself, having abandoned his entry, and yielded

Levi C. Bullock v. E. W. Tipton *et al.*

to Tipton's prior title, could have no equity against Tipton; and comp inant is, necessarily, in his shoes, having- no higher equity.

There has been no *hiatus* in the law, securing Tipton's rights, since the 13th of November, 1851—and if no right remained in Cochrane during the *hiatus* of that year, which he could enforce against Tipton—and we have seen that none did—how can complainant, by the assignment to him in 1855, when Tipton's title had perfect vitality, by relation to the entries in 1840—acquire any equity? We are unable to see.

It may, also, be remarked, that as to the 141 and 4-9th acres held by Tipton under the certificate warrants, the same were protected from Cochrane's entry upon the principle of the case of *Fogg et al. v. Williams and Hill*, decided at the present Term of this Court.

There are other grounds, possibly, placing the equity of this case with defendant, Tipton. He has the legal title, and has paid a valuable consideration for it; and it may well be questioned—consistent with the case of *Sampson v. Taylor*, 1 Sneed, 600—whether a Court of Equity could be moved to take it from him, at the instance of one who—with a full knowledge of his previous rights—seeks to come in under a *hiatus* in the extension law, upon an entry made upon a mere nominal consideration. In such a case, are not the equties of the defendant, at least equal to those of complainant, and having the legal title, ought he not, in a Court of Chancery, to prevail? But we do not mean to settle this now, being enabled to put this case on other grounds.

The decree of the Chancellor will be affirmed.

James B. Seay et al. v. E. G. Young et al.

James B. Seay et al. v. E. G. Young et al.

1. WILL. *Construction. Life estate. Remainder.* The testato queathed certain property to his wife, during her widowhood, and then provided: "And at her death or marriage the said land and negroes, with their increase, to be equally divided among my children and surviving heirs of the body of those who may have deceased before that period, except the children of my daughter Nancy." * * "It is my will and desire that my wife keep possession of the property of such of my children as may be under age, without paying hire, as a compensation for maintaining and educating said children; and as they arrive of lawful age, or marry, my executors are authorized and required to allot to such child or children an equal part," &c. "And at the death or marriage of my wife, I desire that my whole estate be equally divided among the following children: I mean and wish it clearly understood before I name them, viz: It is my express meaning and wish that all my children share alike in my general estate, and all those who have not received any part thereof, are to be made equal with my children beforementioned, viz:" * * "to them and their lawful issue, or the survivors of them, as before stated, forever. And if any of my children should die before they come of age, or marry, (or, in that case, leave no child,) it is my will and desire that their part or parts be equally divided among the survivors of them, or their lawful issue, except the children of my daughter Nancy, to whom I have given all I intend." The widow survived the marriage of her daughter Jemima, but died first. A negro girl, Leah, was allotted to Jemima upon her marriage or arrival at age. This suit is by the children of the daughter, Jemima, to recover said slave Leah and her increase, she having been sold by the husband. It is held:

1. That the widow took an estate for life or widowhood in the land and slaves given her, and, at her death or marriage, the same, with its increase, was to be equally divided among such of the testator's children as may *then* be living, and the surviving issue of such of his children as may have died before that period, except the children of his daughter Nancy.

2. That if a child died before the period of division, viz, the death or marriage of the widow, leaving children who remained alive until the period of division, then they took the share of the deceased child; but if such child left no children living at the time of the division, the share of the child went to the surviving children, and the surviving issue of such as may have died before that period.

James B. Seay *et al* *v.* E. G. Young *et al.*

3. That no remainder was created in favor of any of the grandchildren cf the testator whose parents were living when the particular estate of his widow ceased; and the daughter, Jemima, took an absolute estate in the woman Leah and her increase, and the title to them passed by the marriage to her husband, who might sell or otherwise dispose of them.

FROM HAYWOOD.

This cause was heard before Chancellor WILLIAMS, at the February Term, 1859. Decree for the defendants. The complainants appealed.

RAINS and BLACK, for the complainants.

T. G. & W. M. SMITH, for the defendants, cited 2 Wills. on Exr., 927, 928, 929, and 932; *Simpson* v. *Smith*, 1 Sneed, 394; *Randolph* v. *Wendel*, 4 Sneed, 646; *Thompson* v. *McKisick*, 3 Hum., 635; 2 Yer., 557; 2 Jar. on Wills, 328 *et seq.*; 2 Wills. on Exr., 951 *et seq.*; 7 Yer., 519; 8 Edwards' Ch. R., 1; 15 Pick., 104; 2 Lomax on Exr., 19; *Pastell* v. *Pastell*, 1 Bailey Ch., 390.

WRIGHT, J., delivered the opinion of the Court.

This is a bill filed by the complainants, James B. Seay and Joseph S. Seay, who are infants, to recover of the defendants, Young and Cowan, a slave by the name of Leah, and her children, five in number.

The title supposed to exist in complainants is derived from the will of their grandfather, William Peatrass, of Caroline county, in the State of Virginia, who died in the year 1808.

James B. Seay *et al* v. E. G. Young *et al.*

They allege, that under said will, their mother, Jemima, who was a daughter of the said William Peatrass, the testator, took a life estate in the slave Leah, with remainder to them, as her only children; and that the other slaves being the offspring of Leah born since the will took effect, they are now entitled to recover the whole of them, their mother being dead.

The said will was made and took effect in the State of Virginia, where the testator lived and died, somewhere between the years 1826 and 1829; Jemima Peatrass then having, as it is probable, arrived at the age of twenty-one years, intermarried in said county of Caroline with William B. Seay, the father of the complainants, who are the only issue of that marriage, and either shortly before or after the marriage, received into possession the slave Leah, under said will; after which she and her husband, with said slave, removed to the county of Haywood, in this State, where the said Jemima departed this life, in the year 1842.

The defendants claim said slaves by purchase, made of the said William B. Seay, the father of complainants and husband of Jemima, in the year 1846.

They deny that complainants took any remainder under said will, and insist that the slave Leah, by the force of said will, became the absolute property of the said Jemima; and that, upon her marriage with William B. Seay, the slave became his, and that he might lawfully sell her to them, and that they acquired a perfect title. And the question is, whether complainants or defendants have the better title?

The clauses of the will, upon the construction of which this contest depends, are as follows, to wit:

James B. Seay *et al.* *v.* E. G. Young *et al.*

"To my beloved wife, Amy Peatrass, I lend the land and plantation whereon I reside, together with Randal and Milly, also her choice of one fellow and one woman of my estate, during her widowhood; and, at her death, or marriage, the said land and negroes, with their increase, to be equally divided among my children and surviving heirs of the body of those who may have deceased before that period, except the children of my deceased daughter, Nancy Haden, to whom, in her lifetime, I lent two negroes, to wit: Abram, a man, and Jerusse, a girl; and it is my will and desire that those two negroes and their increase be equally divided among my grandchildren, by my daughter Nancy, deceased, when they come of age or marry, or when either of them marry or come of age. To this branch of my family I leave no more of my estate.

"*Item.*—It is my will and desire that my wife keep possession of the property of such of my children as may be under age without paying hire, as a compensation for maintaining and educating said children; and as they arrive of lawful age, or marry, my executors are authorized and required to allot to such child, or children, an equal part with my son Richard, who has received a negro boy, Jerry, and a girl, Amy, horse, saddle, and bed and furniture; also, my daughter Jane, who has received a negro woman, Rachel, and a child, Hulda, horse and saddle, bed and furniture; also, my daughter Polly, I give a negro boy, Moses, and a girl, Judy, horse and saddle, bed and furniture—none of which she has received, except a bed and furniture. But if, when such allotment or division is made, there should not be enough to give to each of those children who may be of age, or marry, an equal portion with my beforementioned children, Richard, Jane, and Polly, in that case they will only receive a proportion of what may be, exclusive of the part left my wife, at whose death, or marriage, I desire that my whole estate be equally divided among the following children: I mean and wish to be clearly understood before I name them, viz: it is my express meaning and wish that all my children share alike in my general estate, and all those who have not received any part thereof, are to be made equal with my children beforementioned, viz: Richard, Jane, and Polly, to whom I have lent and given already, near, or quite as much, except my daughter Polly, who has only received the bed and furniture beforementioned, to wit: Richard, Matthew, William, Jane, Amy, Polly, Barbara, Walter, Sally, Samuel, Betsy, Susannah, Rebecca, and Jemima, to them and their lawful issue, or the survivors of them, as before stated, forever. And if any of my children should die before they come of age, or marry, (or, in that case, have no child,) it is my will and desire that their part or parts be equally divided among the survivors of them, or their lawful issue, except the children of my deceased daughter Nancy, to whom I have given all I intend."

The testator then, in order that there might be no difficulty in making an equal division among his children, when the period for the final division should come, empowers his executors to assess the value of the property already given off to his children, or to select three disinterested men to do so. And, lastly, he gives to his wife, during life or widowhood, certain chattel property,

James B. Seay *et al.* v. E. G. Young *et al.*

and provides, that at her death or marriage, the same be divided "as before stated."

It is probable, from this record, that Amy Peatrass, the widow of the testator, survived the marriage of her daughter Jemima, but died long before the death of said Jemima. At all events, it is shown that the slave, Leah, was allotted to the said Jemima, under the second clause of the will, upon her coming of age, or marriage, and not in the general division of the estate.

There can, we think, be no doubt, upon a proper construction of this will, that complainants took no interest whatever in the slave Leah; and that, in the events that have happened, she became the absolute estate of their mother, the said Jemima, and passed, by the marriage, to her husband, William B. Seay, who had a right to sell her and her offspring to defendants.

In the construction of this will, all its parts are to be taken with reference to each other, and the intention of the testator collected from the entire instrument. 1 Sneed, 394.

The true meaning of the first clause of the will undoubtedly is, that the widow of the testator is to have an estate for life, or widowhood, in the land and slaves given her; and, at her death, or marriage, the same, with its increase, is to be equally divided among such of the testator's children *as may then be living*, and the surviving issue of such of his children as may have died before that period, except the children of his daughter Nancy.

If a child died before the period of division, viz: the death or marriage of the testator's widow, leaving children who remained alive until the period of division, then

James B. Seay *et al* v. E. G. Young *et al.*

they took the share of the deceased child; but if the child left no children, or there were none at the time of division, the share of that child went to the surviving children, and the surviving issue of such as may have died before that period.

It is manifest no remainder was intended to be created in favor of any of the grandchildren of the testator whose parents were living when the particular estate of his widow ceased; and that under this clause complainants can claim nothing, their mother having survived the widow of the testator.

And it is equally plain the second clause of the will hath this extent and no more. The devise to all his children in that clause, and the words "to them and their lawful issue, or the survivors of them, as before stated, forever," have precisely this meaning.

The words "as before stated," refer expressly to the first clause, and can have no other meaning than that the children alive at the period of the final division, and the children then living of such as may have died, (except the children of Nancy,) are to take an absolute estate.

These words controlled the estate to be divided at the death or marriage of the widow, and then to provide for the care of children who might be under age or unmarried at the period of general division, (the death or marriage of the widow being possible at any time,) and who might die before they came of age or married, or the case of married children who should die without child; and to cover the entire share of each child in the estate, the will further provides: "And if any of my children should die before they come of age, or marry, (or, in that case, have no child, *i. e.* in case of marriage,) it is my will and desire that their part or parts be equally divided among the survivors of them and their lawful issue, except the children of my deceased daughter Nancy, to whom I have given all I intend."

It will thus be manifest that Jemima's share was an absolute interest, unless she died under twenty-one, unmarried, or without issue, upon which events there was an executory devise in favor of her surviving brothers and sisters, and the issue of those deceased. But there was no remainder or interest to her children in the events that have happened, and the ulterior interests, *as to her share*, are all defeated, because the events on which they depended never occurred.

The Chancellor so held, and we affirm his decree.

JOHN J. MATTHEWSON *et al.* *v.* W. J. SPENCER.

LAND LAW. *Ejectment Construction. Trust deed. Notice of sale.* H. sold a tract of land to R. and J., and executed a bond for title on payment of the purchase money, for which notes were executed. Afterwards H. made an assignment of these notes and his title to the land to A., for the benefit of creditors, reciting in the deed his previous sale to R. and J., and his obligation to make them a title upon payment of the purchase money The deed provided that if the notes were not paid within a reasonable time, the trustee, A., should dispose of them to the highest bidder, at public auction, the sale to be made at the court-house, after giving notice thereof for the space of twenty days by public advertisement at three or more public places. The trustee sold the notes of R. and J., to M., at public auction, and ex-

John J. Matthewson *et al.* v. W. J. Spencer.

cuted to him a deed in fee to the land. Afterwards R. and J. paid the purchase money to M., who, thereupon, conveyed said land, in fee, to them. In the conveyance from the trustee to M, and from him to R, and J., the covenant to convey, on payment of the purchase money, executed by H. to R. and J., is specially recited. *Held,*

1. That, by the proper construction of the deed from H. to A, the lands previously sold by A. to R. and J. were not intended to be sold by the trustee, but the object was merely to enable the trustee, on collecting the notes from R. and J. to transfer to them the title, in pursuance of the bond before mentioned; or, if they failed to pay in a reasonable time, and a sale of the notes at public auction should become necessary, that the trustee might be in a condition to transfer the title to the purchaser, as a security to him for the payment of said notes. And, by the conveyances thus made, R. and J. acquired a valid title to the land.

2. That a stranger to the title thus derived from H., and a trespasser upon the premises, cannot be heard to set up, as an objection to the validity of the title of R. and J., that it does not appear that the twenty days' notice of the sale of their notes was given by the trustee, even if the title could be successfully assailed on this ground, by a party in interest.

FROM MADISON.

This cause was tried at the September Term, 1858, before Judge READ. Verdict and judgment for the defendant. The plaintiff appealed.

McLANAHAN, for the plaintiffs.

STEPHENS, BULLOCK, and BROWN, for the defendant.

McKINNEY, J., delivered the opinion of the Court.

This case is brought here, for the third time, upon a question not before presented for our consideration.

John J. Matthewson *et al. v.* W. J. Spencer.

The point now is, another supposed chasm in the plaintiff's chain of title. The facts upon which the objection rests, are these:

James Hart, of North Carolina, being the owner of the tract of land in controversy, on the 31st day of March, 1830, bargained and sold said tract, with several other tracts, situated in the western district of Tennessee, to John Ray and John Jenkins, and executed a bond for title, binding himself to convey said lands to them when the purchase money should be paid; the same being payable in four annual instalments, for which their bills-single were executed to him.

Afterwards, on the 15th of December, 1830, said James Hart made a conveyance to Andrew Hart, by which he assigned to the latter, in trust for the benefit of creditors, all his bonds, bills, notes, and other evidences of debt, including the notes of Ray and Jenkins, given for said lands; also, all his personal property; also, eight tracts of land in Carteret county, North Carolina: And in said deed, James Hart likewise conveyed to said trustee, all his right, title, and interest in and to said lands previously bargained and sold to Ray and Jenkins; and reciting particularly in said trust deed his previous sale of said lands to Ray and Jenkins, and his obligation to make title to them on payment of the purchase money due on the before mentioned notes assigned to said trustee.

In the deed of trust it is provided, that if the bonds, notes, and other evidences of debt therein specified and assigned, were not collected within a reasonable time, the trustee should dispose of them to the highest bidder, at public auction.

John J. Matthewson *et al.* v. W. J. Spencer.

The deed likewise provides for the sale of the real and personal property therein conveyed, and directs that the sale shall be at the court-house of Carteret county, and that notice thereof, for the space of twenty days, shall be given by public advertisement at three or more places in said county.

Afterwards, on the 18th of July, 1831, the trustee sold said notes of Ray and Jenkins to one Thomas Marshall, at public auction: And, on the same day, the trustee executed to him a deed of conveyance, in fee, for said lands bargained and sold by James Hart to Ray and Jenkins. And on the 20th of September, 1831, Thomas Marshall conveyed said lands in fee to said Ray and Jenkins. In both of said last mentioned conveyances, the covenant to convey, on payment of the purchase money, executed by James Hart to Ray and Jenkins, is specially recited.

In this way, Ray and Jenkins, having paid the purchase money, acquired the legal title to the lands covenanted to be conveyed to them by James Hart, as before stated.

And the question to be determined is, whether or not the title thus acquired by them is a valid one. Its validity is denied by the counsel of the defendant, on the ground that the trustee did not pursue the power conferred upon him by the deed of trust. The specific objections are, first, that the trustee conveyed the lands to Marshall *without a sale at public auction;* and, secondly, that it does not appear that twenty days' notice of the sale of the notes of Ray and Jenkins was given by the trustee.

The first objection is founded upon a misconstruction

John J. Matthewson *et al.* *v.* W. J. Spencer.

of the deed. It is manifest, from the whole instrument, that the lands previously bargained and sold by James Hart to Ray and Jenkins, were not intended to be sold by the trustee. No such thing was contemplated. It is obvious that the object of James Hart, in conveying the legal title to said lands to the trustee, was merely to enable him, on collecting the notes from Ray and Jenkins, to transfer to them the title, in pursuance of the bond for title before mentioned; or, if they failed to pay in reasonable time, and a sale of the notes at public auction should become necessary, that the trustee might be in a condition to transfer the legal title to the purchaser as a security to him for the payment of said notes. The instrument admits of no other reasonable or sensible construction.

As regards the second objection, it would not be going too far to say, perhaps, that as more than twenty years elapsed from the time of the sale of the notes before the institution of the present action, it might properly have been left to the jury to presume that the twenty days' notice had been given by the trustee. But, for the sake of the argument, let this presumption be rejected, and let it be admitted that the notice was not given; still, we are of opinion, that the defendant, who is a stranger to the title derived from James Hart, and a trespasser upon the premises, cannot be heard to set up this objection to the validity of the title acquired by Ray and Jenkins, if, indeed, it be an objection at all.

We do not intend, by any means, to question the correctness of the general principle, that where a specific mode of executing a power is prescribed, that must be pursued. Nor do we stop to inquire whether or not the title in question might be successfully assailed, by a party in interest, on the ground of the supposed omission of the trustee to give notice. It is sufficient for the present determination, to say, that the defendant does not occupy such a relation to the transaction as entiltes him to raise any such question.

Ray and Jenkins acquired precisely the title they had contracted for with James Hart, and they acquired it, substantially, in the mode stipulated in the covenant for title. True, James Hart did not, in proper person, execute the conveyance to them; but it was made with his consent and by his authority, through the medium of others, in a mode approved by him; and in reason, as well as in law, this was equivalent, to every intent and purpose, to an execution of the contract by himself.

From this view it results that the judgment is erroneous. It will be reversed, and the case will be remanded for a new trial, on the merits.

Thomas S. Philips *v.* Isaac Sampson.

1. FORCIBLE ENTRY AND DETAINER. *Three years possession.* The uninterrupted possession of the premises in controversy, by the defendant, continuously, for the space of three years immediately preceding the commencement of the action, is, if the estate of the defendant has not determined within that time, a bar to any proceeding by writ of forcible entry and detainer.

2. SAME. *When title may be enquired into.* As a general rule, the title cannot be enquired into, in this form of action; yet it is admissible

Thomas S. Philips *v.* Isaac Sampson.

to look to the title to define the boundaries ; or, in view of the question of damages, or rents to be recovered in an action brought by a mere intruder against the rightful owner of the land; or, where the claimant by fraud induces another to take a lease, or to enter under him, upon a false representation as to his title. In such cases, and, perhaps, others, the title may be looked to, in the determination of the question, whether the case made out constitutes, in law, a wrongful entry or detainer.

3. SAME. *Evidence. Case in judgment.* Both claimants derive title from the same source—one dating back to 1795, and the other to 1838. The premises were rented by the agent of the older claimant to a tenant for the years 1847 and 1848. At the end of 1848 he rented it to the defendant, who held under that title until this suit was instituted. The other claimant procured an instrument of writing, purporting to have been executed on the 18th of November, 1848, from the person in possession that year, recognizing his tenancy under him, and agreeing to deliver the possession to him on the first of January, 1849. *Held*, that the instrument of writing thus executed, the party being a competent witness, is inadmissible as evidence of the character of his holding ; and the three years continuous possession of the tenants under the elder claimant, is a bar to the action of the plaintiff.

FROM DYER.

This cause was heard before Judge WILLIAMS, at the February Term, 1859. Verdict and judgment for the plaintiff. The defendant appealed.

RAINS and CARTHEL, for the plaintiff in error.

M. R. HILL and F. G. SAMPSON, for the defendant in error.

MCKINNEY, J., delivered the opinion of the Court.

This was an action of unlawful detainer, brought by Sampson against Philips, the tenant of Henry W. Con-

Thomas S. Philips v. Isaac Sampson.

ner, on the 19th of September, 1850, to recover possession of a tract of land lying in Dyer county, containing five hundred and ninety-five acres. The plaintiff recovered, and the defendant prosecuted an appeal in error to this Court.

It appears from the record, that Sampson and one H. W. Conner both claim title to the land under one Henry Rutherford. The latter conveyed to James Conner, on the 28th of September, 1795, and he to Henry W. Conner, on the 25th of April, 1834. Sampson claims under a deed dated 25th of January, 1888.

It is proved by Philips, a witness for plaintiff, that in the year 1839, Sampson put a tenant in possession of part of said land, who remained thereon till the close of the year 1841, when the witness rented from Sampson, and held possession under him up to the last of the year 1845. Soon after witness left, one Pettyjohn went into possession, who told' witness that he had rented from Sampson, but afterwards said he had not rented either from Sampson or Conner. Philips further stated, that in the latter part of the year 1848, before Christmas, Pettyjohn quit the place; and his wagon, "that carried out his property, moved in the defendant, Philips," who still continues in possession.

Miller, the agent of Conner, (who is a resident of Charleston, South Carolina,) proved that, at the end of the year 1846 or first of 1847, he, as the agent of Conner, rented the land to Pettyjohn (who was then in possession) for the years 1847 and 1848; and, at the end of the year 1848, he rented to the defendant, Philips, who went into possession when Pettyjohn left.

Thomas S. Philips v. Isaac Sampson.

The plaintiff produced and read to the jury a paper executed by Pettyjohn, of which the following is a copy:

"On or before the first day of January, 1849, I do promise to deliver to Col. Isaac Sampson, the place where I now live, which I have had possession of for the last three years. This 18th November, 1848. Up to that time under him.
JOHN F. PETTYJOHN."

The Court, among other things, said to the jury, that "if Pettyjohn went on the land by virtue of a renting from Sampson, and continued to rent from him until the end of the year 1848, and Sampson had no knowledge that he had been renting of Conner's agent, and he then moved out to let in defendant, in that event plaintiff ought to recover in this action. It would be such collusion as would place defendant in an attitude that he could not resist plaintiff's claim."

This case is very imperfectly presented in the proof, yet enough appears to show that the judgment is against the law and evidence; and it would seem, from what we see of the title, equally against the right and justice of the case.

The title of Conner dates back upwards of sixty years, and the proof establishes an actual possession under it—though not of the exact spot in controversy—for more than thirty years; while the conveyance to Sampson, which is *prima facie* fraudulent and invalid, goes back only to 1838, under which there has been no possession, except for the short period before stated, and *that* by an apparently wrongful intrusion upon the prior existing possession of Conner.

Thomas S. Philips *v.* Isaac Sampson.

This aspect of the case demands that the plaintiff's case should be clearly made out, to support the recovery in his favor.

It is true, as a general proposition, that the title cannot be inquired into in this form of action. The *gist* of the action is, the alleged wrongful entry or detainer. That is the issue properly involved, and not the state of the title, or which of two conflicting titles is the valid or better title. Yet it is admissible, in this action, to look to the title for some purposes; as to define boundaries, or in view of the question of rents or damages to be recovered in an action brought by a mere intruder against the rightful owner of the land: So, where the claimant, by fraud, induced another to take a lease, or to enter under him, upon a false representation as to his title, and, consequently, the contract is vitiated by fraud. *Shultz* v. *Elliott*, 11 Hum., 183, 186. In such cases, and others that might be stated, the title may be looked to in the determination of the question, whether the case made out, constitutes in law, a wrongful entry or detainer.

The case before us, however, turns rather upon the facts for the present. The fact is distinctly proved by Miller, that from the first of the year 1847—a period of more than three years before the commencement of this suit—the possession of the premises was held for Conner; and, in opposition to this proof, there is no admissible evidence in the record. The paper produced by Sampson, and allowed to go to the jury, executed by Pettyjohn, was not admissible evidence against Conner or his tenant. The paper is discredited upon its face. It has the appearance very much of having been manufactured for the purposes of this suit. It purports to be a mere declaration made by Pettyjohn when quitting the premises, or, probably, after his removal, that he had held possession for the three preceding years under Sampson, and promising to surrender possession to him on the first of January, 1849. If this paper were to be supposed genuine, still Conner, or his agent, had no connection with it—as to him, it is the *ex-parte* hearsay declaration of Pettyjohn, and ought not to have been received. Except this paper, there is not the color of evidence in the record that Pettyjohn professed to hold under Sampson for the years 1847 and 1848: And, therefore, upon this paper alone, the hypothesis of the Judge, in that portion of the charge above quoted, must have been based, as there is nothing else in the record to which it can be referred. The legal proposition of the judge, if admitted in the abstract to be correct, was calculated to mislead the jury. The objection is, that it impliedly recognizes the facts stated in said paper as legal evidence for the consideration of the jury.

Pettyjohn is an admissible witness, and ought to have been called, though his credibility is, perhaps, impaired by the statement of the witness Philips, and very seriously damaged by the execution of the paper above referred to. ...

If the possession was held for Conner for three years before the commencement of this suit, the action must fail. There is no legal evidence in the record of a collusive attornment by Pettyjohn to Conner's agent or tenant. But if the fact were even so, it would avail the plaintiff in the action nothing if he had knowledge of it and acquiesced.

Without going into other questions for the present, the judgment must be reversed, for the reasons before stated.

Thomas Ford *v.* J. Grieshaber.

DEPOSITIONS. *Effect of release after deposition taken. Witness.* If the deposition of a witness is taken, who is incompetent at the time his testimony is given, the subsequent release of the interest, on the trial, will not operate to remove the objection existing at the time the deposition is taken. The witness must be competent at the *time* his testimony is given.

FROM MEMPHIS.

Verdict and judgment for the plaintiff, at the November Term, 1858, CARUTHERS, J., presiding. The defendant appealed.

WICKERSHAM & BEECHER and SULLIVAN, for the plaintiff in error.

SMALL & FOUTE, for the defendant in error.

McKINNEY, J., delivered the opinion of the Court.

The error assigned in this case, is the refusal of the Court to reject the deposition of the witness Wheatley.

Thomas Ford *v.* J. Grieshaber.

At the time the deposition was taken in the case, Wheatley stood bound as security for the prosecution of the suit, and the deposition was taken by the plaintiff, for whom he was surety.

When offered on the trial, the objection was urged, that the deposition was incompetent evidence on the ground of interest in the witness. Thereupon the plaintiff was allowed to release the deponent, Wheatley, by substituting other security; and this being done, the deposition was again offered, and admitted to go to the jury, though still objected to by the defendant.

This was erroneous. The objection to the deposition was, that it was the statement of a person incompetent, by law, to give evidence in the suit at the time it was made. The subsequent release of the interest, on the trial, could not operate to remove the objection existing at the time the deposition was taken. The deposition remained as objectionable after the release as before. It was still, notwithstanding the release, the statement of one disqualified to give evidence by reason of interest.

Judgment reversed.

JAMES H. GIBBS *v.* W. R. ROSS, ADM'R, &c.

SALE OF REAL ESTATE. *Rent. When it passes by the sale.* The sale of land passes the right to the rents that subsequently become due as incident to the reversion, but not the rents then in arrear. Rent is not due, where the contract for renting is by the year, until the end of the year, and the rent is not in *arrear* until due. Rent, therefore, not due at the time of the sale, passes with the reversion, unless there is a stipulation to the contrary, in the contract.

FROM WEAKLEY.

Verdict and judgment for the plaintiff, at the October Term, 1858. FITZGERALD, J., presiding. The defendant appealed.

ROGERS and SOMERS, for the plaintiff in error.

The charge of the Court is manifestly erroneous in more than one particular. It is nearly all wrong.

An estate for years is a contract for the possession of land for some determinate period, and the lessee is tenant for years, although the lease be for less than a year. 2 Bl. C., 99.

A reversion is an estate left in the grantor, after a particular estate, either for life or years, is granted by him. 2 Bl. C., 175; 4 Kent C., 853.

Then Gibbs was tenant for years of the land, and the intestate, Parnetta Thompson and her brothers and sisters, were reversioners.

James H. Gibbs v. W. R. Ross, Adm'r, &c.

Rent is one of the incidents to a reversion, and passes by a general grant of the same to the grantee. It may be reserved by *special words*. 2 Bl. C., 176, margin; 4 Kent C., 356. Rent not due is an incorporeal hereditament, and goes to the heir of the landlord in case of his death. 3 K. C, 464; 1 Hilliard's Abridgement, 155.

But in this case the rent must necessarily have passed to Gibbs when he purchased the land and became the owner of the reversion, from the way in which it was to be paid. Gibbs was tenant for years, and was to pay the rent in improvements upon the place rented, and before the expiration of the time within which he was allowed to make the improvements, he buys the reversion, and gets an absolute conveyance. Of course his particular estate was *merged* when he became owner of the reversion. And it was surely a matter of no interest to the intestate, Parnetta Thompson and her brothers and sisters, whether Gibbs improved the place after they had sold it to him. They had not the right to complain if he did not improve it; and it was no concern of theirs if he did.

This case is nothing more nor less than a suit against Gibbs for an alleged failure to improve his own property. His purchase of the reversion could not have the effect to abrogate the contract for the rent of the place, so far as to change the terms relative to the way in which Gibbs had the right to pay the rent. He was not thereby deprived of his right to pay the rent in improvements, if bound to pay at all. And the proof is clear that he did make improvements worth as much or more than the rent of the place within the time for

James H. Gibbs *v.* W. R. Ross, Adm'r, &c.

which, according to the plaintiff's proof, he had rented it. This was a perfect compliance with the contract of rent, which the plaintiff below insists was made.

CARDWELL and ROULSTON, for the defendant in error.

CARUTHERS, J., delivered the opinion of the Court.

Parnetta Thompson, the intestate of Ross, rented a tract of land to Gibbs, in March, 1855, for that and the year 1856. The rent of the first year was to be paid in improvements, as the weight of the evidence shows. Before the expiration of that year, viz: in October or November, 1855, Gibbs became owner of the land by purchase from said Parnetta Thompson and her sisters by deed. There was no reservation of rent or any other stipulation in relation to it, but the sale was general, without reference in any way to the pending contract of renting. Some improvements were made by Gibbs, but mostly after the date of his purchase.

This suit is instituted upon this state of facts to recover the rent of 1855. The charge to the jury was—

"That the rent in the case did not pass as an incident to the reversion when defendant purchased the land; that if the purchase had been made soon after, or in a few days after the contract for renting, then the rent would have passed as an incident; but in this case the rent was nearly due when the purchase was made, and therefore did not pass."

James H. Gibbs v. W. R. Ross, Adm'r, &c.

We apprehend his Honor misconstrued the law in the distinction taken by him as to the importance given to the time of the year at which the reversion was purchased from the lessor. Kent says a sale "passes the right to the rents that subsequently become due as incident to the reversion, but not the rents then in arrear." 4 Kent, 354. Rent is that which is to be paid for the use of the land, whether in money, labor, or other thing agreed upon. It is not due until the year is out, where the renting is by the year. The rent is not in 'arrear" until after it is due. If not, it passes with the sale of the reversion without regard to the time of the year it was made, unless there had been some stipulation to the contrary.

We think the finding was contrary to the law as charged on another question. The Court charged that if the contract was that the rent of 1855 was to be paid in improvements, there could be no recovery in this action. That is so clearly established that it may be said there is no proof to the contrary, and the verdict should have been for the defendant on that ground. The supposed promises of the defendant to pay something, after the year had passed, were not such as to bind him, if any were made. What was said on that subject was in view of a compromise, and if not, was void for want of consideration. The recovery was small—only $19—but the law should be correctly administered without regard to amounts.

Judgment reversed, and a new trial granted.

WM. H. THOMPSON v. COLLINS, KELLOGG & KIRBY.

1. CONTRACT. *Illegal. Effect of. Note.* A contract containing on its face an illegal stipulation cannot be enforced either at law or in equity. Therefore, no suit can be maintained in the Courts of Tennessee on a note executed in this State stipulating *on its face* for usurious interest, if no other place of payment is designated where a greater rate of interest is allowed.

2. SAME. *Same. Plea.* If a note purports on its face to have been executed beyond the limits of the State, and the declaration avers that fact, and contains a stipulation for the payment of *ten per cent.* if not paid at maturity, it is competent for the defendant to put in issue, by a proper plea, the fact as to whether it was executed in Tennessee, or not. If executed in Tennessee, it would be illegal on its face, and the plaintiff would be repelled from the Court.

FROM HENRY.

On motion of the plaintiff's counsel the plea that the note sued on was executed in Tennessee and not in Missouri, was stricken out, and judgment rendered at the September Term, 1858, for the plaintiffs, FITZGERALD, J., presiding. The defendant appealed.

McAMPBELL, for the plaintiff in error.

Where a contract is made in one place to be executed in another, it is to be governed, as to usury, by the law of the place of performance, and not by the law of the place where it is made. So that if the transaction is *bona fide*, and the law of the place of performance allows a higher rate of interest than that

Wm. H. Thompson v. Collins, Kellogg & Kirby.

permitted at the place of the contract, the parties may lawfully stipulate for the higher interest. Story's Conflict of Laws, § 304-5.

The law of the place where the contract is made is to determine the rate of interest, where the contract specifically gives interest, and this will be the case, though the loan be secured by the mortgage of lands in another State, unless there be circumstances to show that the parties had in view the law of the latter place in respect to interest; when that is the case, the rate of interest of the place of payment is to govern. 2 Kent Com., 460, 461, 3d ed.

The rule is that the law of the place where a contract is made governs its construction, unless it be to be performed in a different place—in which case the law of the place of performance governs. If, therefore, a contract stipulate for a rate of interest which is illegal at the place where it is made, it will be void for usury, unless its terms contemplate the performance thereof at a different place, where the rate of interest secured is legal. Story on Contracts, § 599, 2d ed., 5-7.

Where a contract is made in one place, to be executed in another, it is to be governed, as to usury, by the law of the place of performance, and not by the law of the place where it is made. 13 Peters, 65, 77, 78.

A contract to pay more than *six per cent. per annum* is illegal, and a Court will not lend its aid to enforce it. 6 Hum., 277.

The note declared upon is illegal, and cannot be recovered without the averment that it was executed in St. Louis, Mo. This is a material and necessary averment to make it a legal contract. The plea denies the averment, and presents the issue upon which the validity of the contract depends.

Dunlap & Porter, for the defendants in error.

Caruthers, J., delivered the opinion of the Court.

This is an action of debt brought in the Circuit Court of Henry, upon a promissory note for $1,314.67, by the defendants against the plaintiff in error. The declaration alleges that the note was made in St. Louis, Missouri. The note is dated, "Saint Louis, May 13, 1859," and due six months after date. It contains this stipulation on its face; "if not paid at maturity, with interest at ten per cent. per annum." There are two pleas in defence.

1. That the note sued upon was not made in Saint Louis, Missouri, but in Paris, Tennessee.
2. Payment.

The plaintiffs took issue upon the last plea, but moved the Court to strike out the first. This motion was sustained, and verdict and judgment on the other for the plaintiffs below.

The only question here is, whether there was error in the action of the Court in striking out the first plea. If it was a perfect defence to the action, if true: it was a good plea, and issue should have been taken upon it.

It is not controverted in the argument that by the

law of Missouri ten per cent. interest by contract is allowed, and may be reserved and taken. But in Tennessee, such a contract is illegal and usurious; it is an indictable offence by our law to take more than six per cent. A contract containing on its face this, or any other illegal stipulation, cannot be enforced in a court of law or equity. No court will give its active aid upon such a contract. *Isler* v. *Brunson*, 6 Hum., 278, applies this universal principle to contracts stipulating for usurious interest *on their face*. Then it cannot be controverted if this note were made in Tennessee, and no other place of payment designated where a greater rate of interest is allowed, no suit could be maintained upon it in our courts.

But it is averred in the declaration that it was made in Missouri, and must be governed by the law of that State, and consequently they have not only a right to sue upon it here, but to recover the ten per cent. That is certainly true if the fact be so, as the law of the place where the contract is made, unless some other place is fixed for its porformance, must govern on this question. Story on Con. of L., § 304–5; 2 Kent Com., 460, 461; 13 Peters, 65, 77, 78; 2 Parsons on Con., 96.

This being the law, why is it not material, in view of the question, not so much of usury, but to test the legality of the contract, to ascertain where it was made? If in Missouri, it could be enforced here as well as there, but if in Tennessee, it is illegal on its face, and the plaintiffs would be repelled from our courts. It is averred to have been executed in Missouri. May not that averment be met by plea, and an issue made up to try the fact? It is certainly an important fact. If the plea be found true the action is barred and defeated. It is clearly, then, a good and effectual defence. Upon what principle, then, can it be rejected, and its benefit denied to the defendants?

It is most likely that the plea is not true, and was only put in for delay. But this we cannot know. If that be the case, it will be easy for the plaintiffs to take issue upon it, and appeal to the proof.

The conclusion is that the court erred in striking out the plea in question, and for this the judgment must be reversed, and the cause remanded for further proceedings.

JOHN OVERTON *v.* BENJAMIN PHELAN.

1. CONTRACT. *Recoupment. Damages. Act of* 1856, *ch.* 71, § 1. In a suit upon a contract, if the defendant has sustained damages by reason of the plaintiff's non-performance of his part of the agreement sued on, such defendant has the right to abate the plaintiff's recovery by the amount of such damages, and have judgment over against him for any amount or balance for which he may be found liable.

2. SAME. *Same. Measure of damages.* The amount of damages to which the defendant is entitled, in abatement of the claim against him in such case, is the damages which he would be entitled to recover in a cross-action by him against the plaintiff for the non-performance of his part of the contract.

3. WARRANTY. *When implied.* When goods are ordered and supplied, or manufactured for a particular purpose, there is an *implied warranty* that they are reasonably fit and proper for that purpose. And this rule especially applies in a contest between the manufacturer and purchaser of the articles.

John Overton *v.* Benjamin Phelan.

4. EVIDENCE. *Settlement. Receipt.* The fact that the defendant had paid, in part, for articles or work, and taken a receipt therefor, or taken receipts from the plaintiff and another person, before the same were found to be defective, does not change the rule as to damages, or lessen the plaintiff's liability, or preclude the defendant from showing that the plaintiff is the person really liable to him.

FROM MEMPHIS.

This cause was tried at the November Term, 1858, before Judge CARUTHERS. The defendant appealed.

B. M. ESTES and COOPER & WHITE, for the plaintiff in error.

YERGER & FARRINGTON, for the defendant in error.

WRIGHT, J., delivered the opinion of the Court.

This action is brought to recover the value of work and labor performed and materials furnished by Phelan, a foundry-man, for Overton, in building certain houses in the city of Memphis.

Upon the trial, the defendant offered to prove that the plaintiff furnished the iron-work, including fronts, &c., in the construction of certain buildings of defendant in Memphis; that the items in the account sued on in this action were a part of the iron-work so furnished; that all the work which plaintiff had performed, and the materials which he had furnished for defendant, were to these buildings and under the same contract; and that the said iron-work was so unskilfully manufactured and put in said buildings by the said plaintiff and his agents,

John Overton *v.* Benjamin Phelan.

that before all of said work was done, and after said buildings were partially erected, the said iron fronts, supporting the brick-work, gave way and fell by reason of the imperfect and unskilful manner in which the plaintiff had manufactured and erected said iron-work. And that, after giving plaintiff an opportunity to repair the same, defendant was compelled to pay out $2,500 to have the same repaired; and that said iron-work and materials, so done and furnished by the plaintiff, were unsuited to the purposes for which they were sold and used. But the Circuit Court refused to allow this evidence to go to the jury.

In this we think he erred. It is well settled, upon common law principles, that where the defendant has sustained damages by reason of the plaintiff's non-performance of his part of the agreement sued on, such defendant has the right to abate the plaintiff's verdict and recovery by the amount of such damages. *Porter v. Woods, Stacker & Co.*, 3 Hum., 56; *Whitaker v. Pullen*, 3 Hum., 466. In these cases it was held that the amount of damages to which the defendant is entitled, in abatement of the claim against him in such case, will be the damages which he would be entitled to recover in a cross-action* by him against the plaintiff for the non-performance of his portion of the agreement.

Not only so, but now by force of the Act of 1856, ch. 71, § 1, the defendant may not only avail himself of these damages to abate or extinguish the plaintiff's demand against him, but will also be entitled to judgment and execution against the plaintiff for any amount or balance for which he may be found liable.

It is settled that where goods are ordered and sup-

John Overton *v.* Benjamin Phelan.

plied, or manufactured for a particular purpose, there is an *implied warranty* that they are reasonably fit and proper for that purpose. This rule especially applies in a contract between the manufacturer and purchaser of the article. *Donelson* v. *Young & Clements*, Meigs' Rep., 155; Chitty on Contracts, 450; 5 Bing., 533; Story on Contracts, § 835.

We think, then, the proof should have been received.

We are not able to perceive from this record that any part of the defective work was performed by Isaac Phelan.

If it shall turn out that he did any portion of it upon a contract unconnected with the plaintiff, of course to that extent the plaintiff will not be held answerable.

The fact that Overton had settled with the plaintiff for a good part of the work and taken his receipts, before it gave way and fell, does not change the rule or lessen the plaintiff's liability. 10 Yer., 160; 1 Greenl. Ev., § 305. Nor does the fact that these receipts were signed or executed by both the plaintiff and Isaac Phelan preclude the defendant from showing that the work and materials referred to were really performed and furnished by the plaintiff. 1 Greenl. Ev., § 305.

The judgment will be reversed, and a new trial granted.

RICHARD NORED v. ROBERT T. ADAMS.

EVIDENCE. *Statement of slave. When admissible.* The principle admitting as evidence the representations of a slave made to a physician, or other person, is confined to statements made as to the nature, symptoms, effects, and duration of the malady under which he is laboring. A representation to a person, by the slave, without any question being asked, to the effect that she had become diseased after the plaintiff purchased her, and in consequence of ill-treatment, is not admissible.

FROM HENRY.

The plaintiff failed in his suit, which was tried at the January Term, 1859, before Judge FITZGERALD. He appealed.

A. McAMPBELL, and J. J. LAMB, for the plaintiff.

B. F. LAMB, FITZGERALD, and BROWN, for the defendant.

McKINNEY, J., delivered the opinion of the Court.

This was an action of covenant for breach of warranty of the soundness of a female slave, named Minerva, conveyed by the defendant to the plaintiff, on the 28th of March, 1857. Verdict and judgment for the defendant.

The proof is conflicting; and it being admitted upon the record that the charge of the Court (which is not set out in the bill of exceptions) was unexceptionable, we should not feel at liberty, under the rule of this

Richard Nored v. Robert T. Adams.

Court, to disturb the verdict, but for the statement of the witness Pryor, which, though objected to by the plaintiff's counsel, was admitted to go to the jury as competent evidence.

The witness stated, that in October, 1858, after the institution and during the pendency of this suit, he had a conversation with the girl Minerva in the street, in the town of Paris, in substance as follows: "The girl wanted him to buy her; he told her that she was diseased: She replied that she was sound when she went to plaintiff's; that she had become diseased since she went there, from carrying wood and water, and meal and flour from the mill; that plaintiff's was a hard place to get along at; that she had been whipped by plaintiff, and bore the marks upon her back; and that she would go anywhere in preference to living with plaintiff."

This entire statement of the witness ought to have been rejected. Its admission was not sanctioned by any determination of this Court of which we are aware—certain'y not by either of the cases referred to—*Yeatman* v. *Hart*, 6 Hum., 375; *Jones* v. *White*, 11 Hum., 268. It does not fall within the principle that the representations of a sick person, made to a physician, or other person, of the nature, symptoms, effects, and duration of the malady under which he is laboring at the time are admissible. Such representations are received upon the principle that they aid in forming a correct judgment of the character of the disease, and are part of the *res gesta*. In the present instance, no question was asked or representation made as to the character of the alleged disease—its nature, symptoms, or effects. The slave simply stated the fact that she had become diseased after the sale to plaintiff, and in consequence of ill-treatment.

It is easy to imagine what influence such a statement, recognized by the Court as legitimate evidence, would have on the minds of jurors in a case at all doubtful. As the case must be again submitted to a jury, we forbear to comment upon the proper force of the testimony.

Judgment reversed.

WILLIAM PARK *v.* GEORGE W. CHEEK.

1. DEED. *Consideration. Covenant of seizin.* The defendant executed a deed to the plaintiff in 1851, for a lot of ground in the city of Memphis, for the consideration of four thousand dollars. The deed contained, simply, a covenant of general warranty in the usual form. About eighteen months after the execution of said deed, the defendant executed to the plaintiff another deed for the same lot, without any new consideration. This deed was made to bear the same date and to recite the same consideration of the first deed, and in no respect differed from it, except that it contained a covenant of seizin, and that the lot was free from all incumbrances *Held,* that, if in the absence of fraud the defendant voluntarily and understandingly executed the second deed with the intent and for the purpose of carrying out the original agreement between the parties at the time of making the contract, and to supply the omission in the first deed : or, if the original contract were *silent* as to the covenants incorporated in the second deed, and the vendor, at the instance of the vendee, and with knowledge that the first deed was defective, in respect to the proper and necessary covenants—fairly and voluntarily executed the latter conveyance as a farther and better assurance of title to the purchaser, intending that the former deed should be abandoned and the latter substituted in its stead, the second deed would be valid and binding without any new or additional consideration

William Park v. George W. Cheek.

2. SAME. *Same. Estoppel.* In such a case the vendee would be estopped to question his liability on the covenants of the second deed, on the score of want of consideration.

FROM MEMPHIS.

There were verdict and judgment for the defendant, at the November Term, 1858, CARUTHERS, J., presiding. The plaintiff appealed.

TURNAGE & MASSEY, for the plaintiff.

VANCE & ANDERSON, and SULLIVAN, for the defendant.

McKINNEY, J., delivered the opinion of the Court.

This action was brought for an alleged breach of a covenant of seizin.

In December, 1851, the defendant, Cheek, conveyed to the plaintiff a lot of ground in the city of Memphis. The deed purports that the consideration of four thousand dollars was paid for said lot by the plaintiff to the defendant. This deed contains simply a covenant of general warranty in the usual form. The plaintiff was let into possession of the lot—on which a mill had been erected—and still remains in the undisturbed possession of the same.

About eighteen months after the execution of the before mentioned deed, the defendant executed to plaintiff another deed for the same lot, upon the representation of plaintiff, as is stated in the proof, that the first deed was "formally defective." The last deed was made

William Park *v.* George W. Cheek.

upon no new consideration. It was made to bear the same date, and to recite the same consideration, of the first deed; and in no respect differed from it, except that it contained a covenant of seizin, and that the lot was free from all incumbrances, and that Cheek had a lawful right to sell and convey the same.

Upon this latter deed the present action is based. The breaches assigned, negative the several covenants above mentioned, especially the covenant of seizin.

The proof shows that Cheek derived title to the lot by conveyance from one Varnum Ozment, bearing date the 5th day of November, 1849. And it is further shown, that prior to the time of said conveyance, namely, on the 11th of May, 1847, Ozment had divested himself of the legal title to said lot, by an ante-nuptial marriage settlement, under which the title was vested in one James A. Banks, in whom it still remains.

It is proved that the consideration of the conveyance from Cheek to Park, was not four thousand dollars in money, as the deed imports; but that the true consideration was a steamboat, called the "St. Cloud," given in even exchange by the latter to the former for said lot.

The jury were instructed by the Court that the latter deed, containing new and additional covenants, if made without any new consideration to support it, would, for that reason, be inoperative and void.

In this instruction, it is said, there is error.

In the proof as set forth in the bill of exceptions, there is no intimation of *fraud* in the procurement of the second deed. It is not made to appear whether the additional covenants in the latter deed were incorporated therein in fulfillment of the original agreement, and to supply an unintentional omission in the first deed; or whether they were inserted upon some new agreement between the parties, subsequent to the execution of the first deed; or whether, without any new contract, the execution of the second deed was an act merely voluntary and superrogatory on the part of Cheek.

If, in the absence of fraud, Cheek, voluntarily and understandingly, executed the second deed, with the intent, and for the purpose, of carrying out the original agreement between the parties at the time of making the contract, and to supply the omission in the first deed; or, if the original contract were *silent* as to the covenants incorporated in the second deed, and the vendor, at the instance of the vendee, and with knowledge that the first deed was defective, in respect to the proper and necessary covenants, fairly and voluntarily executed the latter conveyance, as a farther and better assurance of title to the purchaser, intending that the former deed should be abandoned, and the latter substituted in its stead; then, upon either hypothesis, it seems to us, the second deed would be valid and binding on Cheek. As regards the consideration, the latter conveyance would, in either view, be referred to the original consideration of the contract, and be sufficiently supported by it. No new or additional consideration would be requisite to give effect to the deed. The vendor, we think, would be estopped to question his liability on the covenants of the deed, on the score of want of consideration.

How it would be, if it were shown that the execution of the second deed was superinduced by fraud, or artifice, on the part of the vendee, or in other supposable aspects of the case, we need not now inquire, as no such questions arise upon this record.

The question, as to the proper measure of damages in the present case, cannot be regarded as properly before us. Upon that subject, we refer to *Kincaid* v. *Brittain*, 5 Sneed, 119, 123; Sedgwick on Damages, 176, *et. seq.*

The judgment must be reversed for error in the instruction given to the jury. The case will be remanded for a new trial.

LEONARD OWENS *v.* THE STATE.

1. CRIMINAL LAW. *Gaming. Witness examined before the Grand Jury Act of* 1824, *ch.* 5. *Code,* § 5089. By the act of 1824, ch. 5, incorporated in the Code, § 5089, any person who is summoned and examined as a witness before the grand jury, as provided in said act, is not liable or bound to answer to any criminal proceedings for any offence about which he may have been so examined as a witness; but this statute was intended to relieve such persons, only, in cases, although guilty with others, where they had informed against them for the identical offence, and not in all cases of like offences.

2. SAME. *Same. Same. Plea in abatement.* If a party wish to avail himself of the benefit of the protection of the act of 1824, ch. 5, by a plea in abatement, he must aver, specifically, in his plea, that he was examined before the jury as to the particular offence charged

Leonard Owens v. The State.

against him in the indictment. An averment that he was summoned and went before the grand jury to testify as to unlawful gaming, &c., is not sufficient.

FROM HARDEMAN.

This cause was tried before Judge HUMPHREYS, at the October Term, 1858. The defendant appealed.

WOOD & SMITH, for the plaintiff in error.

SNEED, Attorney General, for the State.

CARUTHERS, J., delivered the opinion of the Court.

The plaintiff in error was presented, for gaming, in the Circuit Court of Hardeman. He filed a plea in abatement, setting up the protection afforded to all persons summoned before the grand jury as informers in relation to that offence. The plea is, that he was subpœnaed and went before the grand jury to testify as to unlawful gaming, &c., and that "he did, before said grand jury, testify in relation to said offence * * * all the facts within his knowledge or recollection."

The act of 1824, ch. 5, Car. sec. 359, after conferring upon the grand jury the power to send for witnesses, &c., provides for their protection, thus: "Nor shall any such witness be liable or bound to answer to any criminal proceedings for any offence about which he may have been examined as a witness, by virtue of this act." Code, 5089.

Leonard Owens v. The State.

The demurrer to the plea was sustained by the Court, and the defendant convicted on the general issue.

This was certainly right, as the plea does not aver that he was examined before the jury as to the particular offence charged against him in this indictment.

The statute was only intended to relieve him, though guilty, with others, in cases where he had informed against them for the identical offence. The object was to save him from self crimination so far as he was used as a witness to bring others to justice, but no farther. It was not intended that the mere fact of summoning a man before the jury, under the act, should operate as a pardon of all his crimes of the same nature. To have this effect, the offence charged against him must be the same about which he actually testified before the jury against others. If this were not so, evasion or perjury, in behalf of others, might be made to screen him from liability.

The judgment will be affirmed.

ISAAC (A SLAVE) v. THE STATE.

CRIMINAL LAW. *Juror. Power of the Court when juror refuses to be sworn.* The Court has the power, in a criminal case, before the jurors are sworn, to discharge one of the number upon his persistent refusal to take the oath; but after the juror has been actually discharged for this cause, the court has no power to recall him and force him upon the prisoner without his consent.

FROM MEMPHIS.

The prisoner was convicted at the October Term, 1858, McKIERNON, J., presiding. He appealed.

BROWN, KING, and BARNETT, for the plaintiff in error.

SNEED, Attorney General, for the State.

McKINNEY, J., delivered the opinion of the Court.

The prisoner was convicted in the Criminal Court of Memphis, of the murder of a white man, named Gideon Bauden, and sentenced to be hung. From this judgment an appeal in error was prosecuted to this Court.

Of the several errors assigned, the only one thought necessary to be considered for the present, arises out of the action of the Court in regard to one of the jurors.

After the full number of twelve jurors had been regularly tried and elected, and were about to be sworn, W. W. Ritchie, one of the number, refused, repeatedly, to take the usual oath, on the ground, as was pretended, "of conscientious scruples in regard to capital punishment." And, thereupon, the other eleven jurors were sworn; and Ritchie was ordered by the Court to be imprisoned one month, and was accordingly committed to jail forthwith.

There is some confusion and apparent contradiction in the statements, in the bill of exceptions, as to what followed, but from the whole record, the probable truth of the case is, that after ordering the juror, Ritchie, to jail, the Court further ordered that he be "discharged as a juror," and directed the sheriff to summon a panel of nineteen jurors by next morning. On the next morning, before the return of said panel of jurors, and after fifteen hours' imprisonment, the sheriff announced that Ritchie was *then* willing to be sworn as a juror. Upon this information Ritchie was brought into Court, and the Court directed that he be sworn as a juror in the case. The Attorney General thereupon challenged him for cause, but the Court overruled the challenge; to which exception was taken on behalf of the State. The Court again ordered him to be sworn as a juror, to which the prisoner then objected; but the objection was overruled, and said Ritchie was then sworn, and served as a juror on the trial of the prisoner.

This was an exercise of power on the part of the Court, which, in our opinion, cannot be sanctioned.

That the Court possessed the discretionary power, before the jurors were sworn, to discharge one of the number upon his persistent refusal to take the oath, admits, perhaps, of but little doubt. The question, however, is not whether the discharge of Ritchie was proper, under the circumstances, or not. Be this as it may, we think it clear that, after having been actually discharged, the Court had no power to recall him and force him upon the prisoner, or even upon the State. Without the consent of the prisoner, and likewise, as we incline to think, of the Attorney General, he could not have been reinstated as a competent juror in the case. The effect of the discharge of Ritchie necessarily was, so far as respects the power of the Court over him, to place him exactly in the same situation as if he never had been elected as a juror in the case. In principle, the Court might as well have ordered a bystander, never put to the prisoner, to be sworn as a juror.

On this ground, without noticing other objections, the judgment must be reversed, and a new trial granted.

THE STATE v. CRAWFORD, McNEILL & CO.

CONSTITUTIONAL LAW. *Code, § 545. Tax on articles manufactured of the produce of this State. Merchants.* Section 545 of the Code, which provides that "salt, sugar, coffee, spun cotton, garden seed, iron, and articles manufactured in this State, may be sold without paying a tax, but these articles are not exempt in the hands of any person who sets himself up as a merchant or grocer," is not in violation of article 2, § 30, of the Constitution. This section not only refrains from taxing the articles mentioned, but saves the producer or manufacturer from any tax for the privilege of selling them. But when they become articles of merchandise and profit in the hands of a merchant by occupation, they direct that reference shall be had to them as well as foreign articles, in estimating the amount to be paid for exercising the occupation or privilege of a merchant. It is only a different mode of taxing the privilege, and not a tax upon the articles.

FROM HENRY.

This was an agreed case, submitted to the Court at the January Term, 1859, FITZGERALD, J., presiding. Judgment was rendered for the defendants. The State appealed.

SNEED, Attorney General, and B. F. LAMB, for the State.

A. MCAMPBELL, for the defendants.

CARUTHERS, J., delivered the opinion of the Court.

This agreed case, between the clerk of the County Court of Henry, on the part of the State, and the defendants, who are merchants in that county, raises the question of the liability of a merchant to pay a tax for selling things manufactured in this State.

The statute is, that "salt, sugar, coffee, spun cotton, garden seeds, *iron*, and articles manufactured in this State, may be sold without paying a tax; but these articles are not exempt in the hands of any person who sets himself up as a merchant or grocer." Code, § 545.

The Constitution provides that "no article manufactured of the produce of this State shall be taxed, otherwise than to pay inspection fees." Article 2, § 30.

But in section 28 of the same article, it is provided that "the Legislature shall have power to tax *merchants*, pedlars, and privileges, in such manner as they may from time to time direct."

In the exercise of this power, the Legislature at one time taxed the merchant a specific sum for the privilege of selling merchandise, without regard to the extent of his business; but afterwards the more just and equitable mode was adopted, to graduate the amount of the tax by the quantity of goods sold. And the question made in this case is, whether, in this estimate of sales made by them, iron, castings, spun cotton, and other things manufactured in this State, must be included, and in that way enhance the amount of the tax to be paid by them. This involves the construction of the sections of the Constitution above cited.

The power to tax merchants in such manner as they may think proper, is expressly given in section 28; and they have "directed" that the "manner" shall be to settle the amount to be paid by the extent of their business, or the quantity of goods, wares, and merchandise sold in each year, including things made or produced in this State. Is this prohibited by section 30? We think not. This is not a tax upon the article, but the occupation of the merchant. There would have been no question if the old mode of taxing the occupation of the merchant a gross sum had been continued. But what difference can it make? The change is only as to the "manner" of settling the amount to be paid for the privilege. It is not the article which is taxed, but the occupation or privilege.

The Legislature may tax a man's land, slaves, plate,

jewelry, stocks, and almost every other kind of property, but not his flour, tobacco, cotton, iron, &c., "otherwise than to pay inspection fees," when there are laws requiring or allowing inspection of such products, as was once, if not now, the case, in this State, as to tobacco, flour, and other articles to be exported. This exemption was intended to encourage domestic manufactures, and stimulate production. It is a wise prohibition. The Legislature, in this case, have not attempted to violate or evade it. They have not only refrained from taxing such articles, but saved the producer or manufacturer from any tax for the privilege of selling them. But when the reason of that protection fails, and they become articles of merchandise and profit in the hands of a merchant by occupation, they direct that reference shall be had to them as well as foreign articles in estimating the amount to be paid for exercising the occupation or privilege of a merchant. There would be a great absurdity in any other construction. If a merchant got his iron or cotton yarns on one side of the State line, they would be taken into the account, but if in sight, on his own side, they would not be, according to the doctrine contended for.

But it is enough to say that we think the Legislature were not prohibited by the Constitution from providing that, in ascertaining the amount of tax to be paid by "*merchants*" for the exercise of their privilege, the articles in question should be included; that not being a tax upon the article in the sense of the Constitution, (sec. 30,) but upon the occupation, under sec. 28.

The judgment will be reversed, and entered here according to this opinion on the agreed case.

Francis Frazer *et al.* *v.* Newton Ford, Adm'r, &c., *et al.*

FRANCIS FRAZER *et al. v.* NEWTON FORD, ADM'R, &C., *et al.*

1. SALE OF REAL ESTATE. *Frauds, Statute of. By whom agreement to be signed.* To make a contract for the sale of real estate valid, it must be in writing and signed by all the owners, by themselves or by some person lawfully authorized to sign their names.

2. SAME. *Same. Same. Must be binding upon all.* The language in the statute of frauds, "the party to be charged therewith," means the persons who sell the land. The filing of a bill by all the owners, in the absence of a memorandum or writing as required, with an express ratification of the contract and a tender of title, will not remedy the defect and compel the purchaser to take the land. To make the contract obligatory it must be mutual.

FROM MEMPHIS.

Decree for the complainants at the November Term, 1858, CARUTHERS, J., presiding. The defendants appealed.

BROWN & FRAZER, WICKERSHAM & BEECHER, and E. M. YERGER, for the complainants.

WILLIAMS & MCKISICK, and WATSON, for the defendants.

CARUTHERS, J., delivered the opinion of the Court.

The bill was filed to enforce a specific execution of a contract for the sale of lots in Memphis, and the question is, whether the contract is binding under the statute of frauds, so as to be enforced by a court of equity. The Chancellor thought it was, and decreed a specific performance. This is the writing:

"This agreement of sale entered into 21 May, 1857, between C. W. Frazer, for himself, and the heirs of John A. Frazer, deceased, of the one part, and Thomas Mull, of the other part, witnesseth, that said Frazer agrees to sell all the land now owned by himself and said heirs on Adams street, between Main and Second streets, south side of Adams, say 124 feet more or less, fronting on Adams street, and running back to an alley, say 148 feet; and said Mull agrees to buy the same and pay for it the sum of $250 per foot front; $6000 of said sum to be paid on 1st Nov., 1857, the balance" (of about $24,000) "in equal payments of one, two and three years from that date, with interest. A lien to be retained on said property for the payments.

Witness our hands and seals the day and date above written. C. W. FRAZER, [SEAL.]
THOMAS MULL, [SEAL.]
Test: E. L. JONES,
W. H. WYNNE."

The statute of frauds of 1801, requires that "no action shall be brought, * * * * upon any contract for the *sale* of lands, * * * * unless the promise or agreement upon which such action shall be brought, or some memorandum or note thereof shall be in writing, and signed by the *party to be charged therewith*, or some other person by him thereunto lawfully authorized."

This property belonged to C. W. Frazer and his brothers and sisters, as the children and heirs of John

Francis Frazer *et al.* *v.* Newton Ford, Adm'r, &c., *et al.*

A. Frazer, deceased, by descent. To make the contract of sale good and valid, it must have been signed by all the owners, by themselves, or some one lawfully authorized to sign their names for them, not by one of them alone. C. W. Frazer had no legal authority from the other owners at that time, and if he had, it was not executed, as he did not sign their names. The argument is that, as the action is against Mull, and he signed it, that is a compliance with the statute, as he is the party attempted "*to be charged therewith.*" This is not the meaning of the act—it means the persons who *sell* the land shall sign the writing,—the vendor, and not the vendee. The filing of the bill by all the vendors, with an express ratification of the contract therein, and tender of title, does not remedy the defect, of failure to sign the writing, by the vendor, as is contended by counsel. That principle would make the contract binding on one party and not the other—on the purchaser, and not the seller. Whereas, to make it obligatory, it must be mutual.

The article leaves it entirely uncertain who are the vendors. They are the heirs of Jno. A. Frazer, deceased. But how many of them are there, and what are their names and condition? Are they adults, infants, or *femes covert?* Then there is no title or right to a title obtained in the contract.

We will say nothing as to the sufficiency of the description of the property, because the other point is decisive, and a further multiplication of cases on that subject in our books, is not desirable, as it would tend to produce confusion, and by our own cases, to which reference has been made in argument, the rules by which contracts are to be tested, under the statute of frauds, are sufficiently explicit.

The decree must be reversed, and the bill for specific performance dismissed.

MEMPHIS AND LITTLE ROCK RAILROAD COMPANY v. SAML. P. WALKER.

1. SET-OFF. *Obligation to be discharged in bonds.* An obligation for money to be paid in the bonds of a railroad company, by a given day, may, if not complied with, be the subject of set-off in a suit against the original holder of said obligation, or his assignee, for money due said company. And this is so, whether the obligation fixes the value at which the bonds are to be received or not, the law having established a rule by which the value may be ascertained and rendered certain.

2. DAMAGES. *Measure of. Obligation for railroad bonds.* If an obligation is executed for a sum of money, to be paid in the bonds of a railroad company, and said obligation is not complied with, the measure of damages in an action thereon, or when offered as a set-off is the nominal value of the bonds, and not the value at which they might be rated in the market.

FROM SHELBY.

This cause was tried before Judge HUMPHREYS at the September Term, 1858. Under the charge of the Court the jury sustained the plea of set-off, and the plaintiff appealed.

ESTES, WICKERSHAM & BEECHER, for the plaintiff.

Memphis and Little Rock Railroad Company *v.* Saml. P. Walker.

E. M. YERGER and W. T. BROWN, for the defendant.

MCKINNEY, J., delivered the opinion of the Court.

This was an action of assumpsit upon a promissory note for $7,168.00, made by W. F. Barry, payable to the defendant, Saml. P. Walker, and by him indorsed to the plaintiff.

Among other matters of defence, was that of set-off. The evidence of set-off relied on by the defendant, was the following obligation, which had been transferred to, and was owned by defendant, prior to the institution of this suit: "Six months from date, or sooner if practicable, the Memphis and Little Rock Railroad Company promise to pay to the order of H. R. Austin, five thousand dollars, in the bonds of said company, at par; of equal character with any bonds issued by said company; to bear interest from the first day of January, 1857; in part payment of the award made on the 26th day of November, 1856, by the arbitrators to whom was referred the matters in controversy between said company and the assignees of the contract for the construction of said road." Then follows a stipulation to the effect, that said bonds are not to be of the class of bonds which entitled the holders thereof to take the lands of the company, at three dollars per acre, or at the appraised value, in satisfaction of their bonds.

The plaintiff objected to the admission of said obligation, as evidence in support of the plea of set-off, but the objection was overruled. After it had been read to the jury, the plaintiff proposed to prove the market value of the description of bonds mentioned in said ob-

Memphis and Little Rock Railroad Company v. Saml. P. Walker.

ligation, and propounded a question to that effect to a witness on examination; but objection being made to the evidence proposed, the court refused to allow the question to be answered.

The court instructed the jury, in substance, that said obligation was competent and sufficient evidence to support the plea of set-off; and that the failure of the company to issue and deliver the bonds, according to the terms of the obligation, entitled the defendant to claim the full amount of the five thousand dollars, with interest thereon from the first day of January, 1857, as a set-off to the note sued on. The jury found accordingly.

An earnest and ingenious argument is made for the plaintiff in error, to show that both of the propositions asserted in the instructions to the jury, are erroneous.

The argument assumes, that the obligation for five thousand dollars in the bonds of the company, is not the proper subject of set off, because an action of debt could not be maintained thereon, for the reason that the value of the bonds is uncertain, and must be fixed by a jury on proof of their value in the market. In this reasoning we are unable to concur. If it were to be conceded that the value of the bonds is not the nominal amount stated in the obligation, but their market value, still, upon the authority of *Moore* v. *Weir & Smith*, 3 Sneed, 46, this would be no objection to the set-off; the law having established a rule by which the value may be ascertained and rendered certain.

But we dissent from the position, that the value of the bonds is uncertain. Upon the proper construction of the instrument, we think the plaintiff is precluded

Memphis and Little Rock Railroad Company *v.* Saml. P. Walker.

from insisting that the bonds should be estimated as of less value than that stated in the obligation. By the stipu'ation, the plaintiff—within a limited time—was bound to deliver, and the defendant to receive, five thousand dollars of the bonds of the company, not at the value at which they might be rated in the market, but "*at par*." In the negotiations between the parties, the bonds were treated as being of their nominal value—five thousand dollars. To the plaintiff they were equivalent to that value, because their delivery was to extinguish a fixed indebtedness of the company to that amount. And to the defendant they were, *prima facie*, of equal value, because they were to bear interest at the legal rate until paid.

We think it clear, therefore, that in a cross-action against the company, founded on the obligation, for failing to deliver the bonds, the proper measure of damages would be their nominal value of five thousand dollars, with interest thereon; and the same rule must prevail where the claim is set up by way of set-off.

This conclusion is not in conflict with any recent determination of this Court of which we are aware. It results from the peculiar nature of the obligation in question, and is without an exact parallel in any of our own cases.

There is no error in the record.

Judgment affirmed.

JAMES H. BAKER *v.* JOHN B. COMPTON.

ABATEMENT *Plea of. When proper, and what it must aver. Writ. Code, § 3828.* A party may plead, in abatement of a summons, that it was served on him while in attendance as a witness upon the Circuit Court; but great strictness and accuracy is required in a plea of this character; and to be good, it must set out the Court which he was attending, the suit in which he was a witness, and that it was then pending in the Court, the parties to the suit, and the party for whom he was summoned.

FROM MADISON.

A plea in abatement was filed and demurred to by the plaintiff. The demurrer was overruled, and the writ abated, at the January Term, 1859, W. H. STEPHENS, S. J., presiding. The plaintiff appealed.

M. BULLOCK, for the plaintiff, cited and commented upon the Code, § 3814; Act of 1794, ch. 1, § 28; *Martin* v. *Ramsey*, 7 Hum., 260.

TOMLIN, for the defendant.

CARUTHERS, J., delivered the opinion of the Court.

This was an action of debt, brought upon a note, under seal, for $500, in Madison Circuit Court. At the appearance Term a plea in abatement was filed upon the ground that the summons to answer was served on the defendant while in attendance as a witness, under sub-

James H. Baker v. John B. Compton.

pœna, in the Circuit Court. The demurrer to this plea was overruled, and the writ abated. The plaintiff appealed to this Court.

It is conceded that the Code, § 3828, copied from the act of 1794, ch. 1, § 34, makes the matter of this plea good in abatement, but it is insisted that it is not well pleaded. The reason why any process not against the person may not be served upon a witness, is not very manifest to our minds. But the language of the act is too plain for construction; and if it were doubtful, the case of *Martin* v. *Ramsey*, 7 Hum., 260, has settled it. That was the case of the service of a subpœna to answer in Chancery, and was held to fall under the act, subject to plea in abatement.

So the only question here is, whether the matter is well pleaded. All the authorities agree that great strictness and accuracy are required in pleas in abatement, and "no latitude in practice is extended to them." 9 Yer., 10; 10 Yer., 527. They must be in the "right form." If they commence and conclude in bar, the defect is fatal. 10 Hum., 506.

The plea, in this case, is in these words:

"The said John B. Compton, in proper person, comes and defends the wrong and injury, &c., and says that he ought not to be compelled to answer the said original writ sued out in this cause, because he says that he, the said Compton, was, on the day of suing out the said original writ and execution of the same, a witness in said Circuit Court, duly subpœned, &c.; that he was, at the time of the execution of said writ, attending his duty in said Court as a witness, and that, according to the privilege granted to him during his attendance on said

James H. Baker *v.* John B. Compton.

Court as a witness, by statute made and provided in such cases, he ought not to be compelled to answer against his will any person in any civil action prosecuted against him by original writ in said Circuit Court, sued out against him at the suit of any person whatever. And the said Compton in fact saith that he is impleaded by said original writ as aforesaid, against his will and against the privilege granted to him by the statute made and provided in such cases; and this he is ready to verify. Wherefore he prays judgment of said original writ sued out in this cause, and that the same may be quashed."

We think this plea is fatally defective. Without noticing other objections, it does not show in what suit or for which party he was attending as a witness, nor, indeed, whether any suit was then pending, or in what Court he was giving his attendance. This is certainly too vague and indefinite for a plea in abatement, where no latitude of construction is allowed, because its object is to delay or defeat right and justice, upon a strict legal privilege against or aside from the merits. In such a case, the rule that requires the greatest strictness in making out this defence is just and reasonable. They should be certain to every intent. Bouv. Dic., 17.

In *Martin* v. *Ramsey*, 7 Hum., 260, where the plea was held to be good, it will be seen that the Court at which he was attending, the parties to the suit, and the one for whom he was summoned, are all particularly set forth. All this, we think, is necessary to make a good plea in such a case.

The judgment overruling the demurrer will be reversed, and the case remanded for plea to the merits.

F. B. Fogg et al. v. Samuel Williams et al.

F. B. Fogg et al. v. Samuel Williams et al.

1. LAND LAW. *Cession Act. Constitution, art.* 1, § 31. The validity of North Carolina land claims is recognized by the Constitution of Tennessee, art. 1, § 31. It is, in substance, declared that the sovereignty and right of soil of Tennessee are subject to the conditions and provisions of the "Cession Act," and shall not "extend to affect the claim or claims of individuals to any part of the soil which is recognized by the aforesaid Cession Act."

2. SAME. *Same. North Carolina land claims. State a trustee for the claimants.* The relation between the State of Tennessee and the owners of North Carolina land warrants, or other claims, is that of *trustee* and *cestui que trust*. The State, as trustee, cannot divest the claimants of their right, either directly or indirectly. And this trust is so incorporated with the claims and the land appropriated by them, as to affect all subsequent enterers of the same land.

3. SAME. *Same. Same.* Independent of the exercise of any power or authority in Tennessee, the owners of land appropriated under North Carolina land warrants, may be regarded as invested with an estate in fee-simple, merely by force of the Cession Act and the acts of Congress and of the General Assembly of Tennessee, passed in pursuance thereof.

4. SAME. *Same. Same. Power of the Legislature to annex conditions. Act of* 1850, *ch.* 138. The Legislature, therefore, does not possess the power to annex subsequent conditions, by which the failure of claimants, under North Carolina land warrants, to apply for a grant within a limited time, shall work a forfeiture of their estates.

5. SAME. *Power of the Legislature to annex conditions to the procuring of grants. Question reserved* Has the Legislature the power to annex subsequent conditions and limitations in regard to the time within which the enterers of land, deriving their right from the exclusive sovereignty and right of soil in Tennessee, shall perfect their titles?

FROM DYER.

At the July Term, 1858, Chancellor WILLIAMS dismissed the bill of the complainants, and they appealed.

F. B. Fogg et al. v. Samuel Williams et al.

COCHRAN & ENLOE, for the complainants.

F. B. FOGG, for the complainants, said:

The Cession Act, the Compact, the acts of Congress from 1818 to 1846, our Constitution of 1834, all recognize the validity of North Carolina land claims, and provide for their satisfaction § 2, Meigs' Digest, pp. 689–691, § 1212. And the last act of Congress, passed the 7th of August, 1846, surrendered to Tennessee their right and title to all lands south and west of the Congressional Reservation Line which then remained *unappropriated;* but the lands thus released, and the proceeds thereof, were to remain subject to all the same claims, incumbrances, and liabilities in relation to North Carolina land warrants, or other claims of North Carolina, as if the lands still remained in the hands of the United States. The State of Tennessee had no title to the lands south and west of the Congressional Reservation before this act of Congress passed. She had no domain thereon—only the sovereignty, and the agency to satisfy the North Carolina land claims. Immediately after the passage of this law, on the 2d of November, 1847, by ch. 20, § 4, the act of Tennessee provided, "that any of the *vacant* lands, not claimed by occupancy or preemption rights, may be entered in the same way that *vacant* lands are now entered north and east of the Congressional Reservation Line." How was that done? By the acts of 1823, ch. 49, vacant lands could be entered at twelve and a half cents per acre; 1825, ch. 64, at one cent per acre, and 1829, ch. 85, upon paying twenty-five cents for making the entry and the other fees necessary for obtaining a grant. In other words, a gratuity from the State to any individual who would enter vacant and unappropriated land. Was it intended to provide, or did it provide, that where land had been entered by a valid North Carolina claim, and the warrant satisfied thereby, and the entry surveyed, and the plat and certificate recorded in the surveyor's office, that because from some mistake, owing to deaths of parties, no grant had issued, that such land was liable to be entered? Until 1823, the non-issuance of a grant had no effect, and the non-survey of the land entered had no effect, except as between those in *equalis gradu*. If two North Carolina claimants were bound to have their claims satisfied by Tennessee, and this State provided the mode and time, and one party complied and the other not, the diligent one would secure his land entered, surveyed, and granted, but no obligation of the contract to satisfy the claim in land remained unimpaired, the claimant being at liberty to make an entry elsewhere. *Huntsman* v. *Randolph*, 5 Hay., 263–271; 4 Yer., 170; 5 Yer., 236. These cases refer to claims that are equally meritorious, and that the State of Tennessee was bound to satisfy.

The defendants having notice of the previous entry, survey, and appropriation of a North Carolina certificate, was it right, just, and conscientious in them to enter the same lands for nothing except fees of office, &c.; deprive the former owners of their rights on account of a mistake in not getting out their grants, even if it had been the law that the grant should issue in a limited time. Equity will not recognize such proceedings.

I refer to a case of *Ornick & Gregory* v. *Hickman*

& McEwen, decided in the Supreme Court at Nashville in 1828, for some principles analogous to those now contended for. The case has never been reported.

T. J. FREEMAN, BRADFORD, and HILL, for the defendants, cited and commented upon 2 Hay. & Cobb, 16, 36, 37, 58, 73, 74, 78; Acts of 1798, 1807, 1813, 1815, 1819, 1823, 1835, 1850; 5 Yer., 236; 3 Peters' R., 280; 1 Sneed, 604.

McKINNEY, J., delivered the opinion of the Court.

This bill was filed to enjoin the defendants from prosecuting an action of ejectment, brought by them against the complainant, Tipton, who claims under Fogg, for the recovery of a tract of land of one hundred and seventy-five acres, lying in Dyer county, and to have the legal title to said land divested out of the defendants, and vested in the complainant.

The Chancellor, on the hearing, dismissed the bill, and the cause is brought to this Court by an appeal.

The decision depends entirely upon the question of title.

The complainant, Fogg, as assignee, claims under an entry made by John McIver, on the 20th of March, 1821, founded on *certificate warrant*, No. 3792, issued by the register of West Tennessee, for one hundred and seventy-five acres, entered in the office of the thirteenth surveyor's district; which entry was surveyed on the 1st of January, 1831, and the plat and certificate of survey were returned and recorded in said surveyor's office, on the 12th of February, 1831. But *no grant was ever issued on said entry.*

The defendant, on the 1st day of September, 1851, made an entry of said land, in the entry-taker's office of Dyer county, and procured a grant thereon on the 1st day of October, 1852, with constructive notice, and, as is necessarily to be inferred, with actual knowledge that the land had been previously appropriated by McIver's entry, in satisfaction of a valid North Carolina land claim.

The defendants insist, that by said entry and grant, they acquired a valid title; and the ground on which they rest their claim is, that by the failure of complainant to obtain a grant before the 1st day of September, 1851—the time limited by the act of 1849-50 "for making surveys and obtaining grants on all entries heretofore made in any of the land offices in this State"—his entry became void, and the land was subject to entry as other vacant land. And of this opinion was the Chancellor. Upon a careful consideration of the principles involved in the case, we are led to a different conclusion.

It is obvious, that entries based upon valid North Carolina land claims, recognized and provided for by the *Cession Act*, stand on very different ground from entries deriving their entire efficacy from the acts of the General Assembly of Tennessee.

The right of the claimant to the land appropriated under a North Carolina land warrant, is not derived from Tennessee, but from North Carolina, under the provisions of the Cession Act. By solemn acts of legislation, prior to the Cession Act, North Carolina had constituted herself a trustee for the officers and soldiers of her continental army, for the quantity of land to which they were respectively entitled. *Pinson* v. *Ivey*, 1 Yer., 297, 360. By the provisions of the Cession Act, the lands ceded were to remain subject to the satisfaction of all *bona fide* claims, of every description, which had been derived before the cession from the laws of North Carolina. This trust was devolved upon Tennessee, and was solemnly recognized by her compact with North Carolina, ratified by the act of 1804, ch. 14, and by the act of Congress of 1806, ch. 31, and other acts of Congress, up to the act of 1846, whereby the right and title of the United States, under the Cession Act, to all lands south and west of the Congressional Reservation Line, *which then remained unappropriated*, was surrendered to Tennessee; but upon the express condition, that the lands thus released, and the proceeds thereof, were to remain subject to all the same claims, incumbrances, and liabilities, in relation to North Carolina land warrants, or other claims of North Carolina, as if the lands still remained in the hands of the United States.

It has been settled by repeated decisions of this Court, that the relation between the State of Tennessee and the owners of North Carolina land warrants, or other claims, was that of *trustee* and *cestui que trust*. The State is regarded as having become bound to give the owner a complete legal title, vesting him with an estate in fee simple in the quantity of land to which he is entitled. The claimant is considered as having acquired an absolute vested right to the specific land appropriated by his warrant; and the State, as trustee, cannot divest him of this right, either directly or indirectly. And this trust became so incorporated with the claim, and the land appropriated by it, as to affect all subsequent enterers of the same land—upon the familiar principle of equity, that where a purchaser has notice of the trust, though he pay a valuable consideration, he shall be subject to the trust. *Pinson* v. *Ivey*, 1 Yer., 309, 324, 359; 6 Yer., 190, 193.

The validity of these North Carolina land claims is emphatically recognized by the Constitution of Tennessee, art. 1, § 31. It is in substance declared, that the sovereignty and right of soil of Tennessee are subject to the conditions and provisions of the "Cession Act," and shall not "extend to affect the claim or claims of individuals to any part of the soil which is recognized to them by the aforesaid Cession Act."

The right to the land appropriated by these "claims," as before remarked, is derived, not from Tennessee, but from North Carolina. The former was merely invested with the naked power of issuing a grant to the *bona fide* claimant. And even the power to issue the grant is a delegated power, not emanating from her own independent sovereignty, but from the sovereignty of North Carolina. 5 Hay., 113, 117.

Independent of the exercise of any power or authority in Tennessee, the owner of the land appropriated under a North Carolina land warrant, may be regarded as invested with an estate in fee simple, merely by force of the Cession Act, and the acts of Congress, and of the General Assembly of Tennessee, passed in pursuance thereof.

F. B. Fogg *et al.* v. Samuel Williams *et al.*

If these principles be correct, it follows that the Legislature does not possess the power to annex a subsequent condition, by which the failure of the claimant to apply for a grant, within a limited period, shall work a forfeiture of his estate.

Tennessee voluntarily took upon herself the positive, active obligation to perfect the titles, by the issuance of grants upon all *bona fide* claims originating under the provisions of the Cession Act. This duty could have been easily discharged, consistently with her own obligations and the rights of the claimants, by causing the grants to be in fact issued, and, if thought proper, making the necessary expenses incident to their issuance a charge upon the lands of the respective owners. But clearly, the Legislature, by merely providing for the issuance of a grant, on the application of the owner of the land within a limited time, could not, on the ground of his neglect to demand a grant within the time, destroy the right vested in him by his entry: This is a right which Tennessee did not give, and could not, in this manner, take away.

This point is, perhaps, now directly decided for the first time in this State. It might have been raised upon the facts of the case of *Sampson* v. *Taylor*, 1 Sneed, 600; but neither in that case, nor in any other known to us, was the question presented for determination.

We do not deem it proper, at present, to discuss the question as to the power of the Legislature to annex subsequent conditions and limitations in regard to the time within which the enterers of land, deriving their right from the exclusive sovereignty and right of soil in Tennessee, shall perfect their titles. The question, in this aspect, is not before us, and we intimate no opinion upon it.

We likewise pass by the position assumed for the complainants, that their entry being prior to the act of 1823, ch. 35, the case does not fall within the provision of the ninth section of that act—choosing, rather, to rest the determination of the case on the more general ground before stated.

The result is, that the defendants must be regarded as holding the legal title, acquired by their grant, in trust for the complainants; and it will be so decreed.

Decree reversed.

JAMES LASHLEY et al. v. T. WILKINSON.

1. SUMMARY PROCEEDING. *Motion. Constable. Notice.* In a summary proceeding, by motion, against a constable, the notice is sufficient if it describes the note placed in the constable's hands for collection—the date and amount—the date and amount of the judgment rendered upon it, and the execution issued to him in the case—that the execution had not been returned into the office from which it issued within thirty days thereafter, nor the money due thereon paid over according to law; and that, therefore, judgment is demanded against the officer and his securities for the amount of the judgment of the justice of the peace, with legal interest from the rendition thereof, and twelve and one-half *per cent.* interest on the same from the time it was demanded, by way of damages.

2. SAME. *Same. Same. Same.* The validity of a notice, for the non-return of an execution, is not affected by the fact that it demands, as a legal conclusion, more or less by way of interest, or damages, than the plaintiff is entitled to. The law fixes the officer's liability upon the case stated, and it is the duty of the court to give judgment for the proper amount.

James Lashley *et al.* v. T. Wilkinson.

3. SAME. *Same. Same. Same. Variance.* If the notice is, in other respects, good, a *variance* between the date of the execution produced on the trial and the one described in the notice will not be fatal.

FROM FAYETTE.

At the February Term, 1859, HUMPHREYS, J., presiding, judgment was rendered for the plaintiff. The defendants appealed.

J. A. ANDERSON, for the plaintiffs in error.

The first point contended for by the plaintiffs in error is, that the notice does not sufficiently state the grounds of the motion, that is, whether for the *non-return* of the *execution*, or for collecting money and not paying it over. The language of the statute authorizing the motion for *non-return* of an execution, is as follows: "Provided the plaintiff, his agent or attorney, give to the constable or other returning officer, five days' notice, at least, of the time and place of *such motion*." Nicholson & C., page 299. The statute requires notice of *such* motion. That is, it requires that the notice shall state the *grounds* of the *motion*. The notice in this case states that the constable had not returned the execution; and, also, that he had not paid over the money due thereon. It says that the motion will be made for "the amount of the judgment and legal interest from the execution thereof, and twelve and a half per cent. interest thereon from the time it was demanded, by way of damages." That is clearly a notice of motion for *collecting* and failing to pay over. The motion given by

James Lashley et al. v. T. Wilkinson.

statute for failure to *return* an execution, is for the amount of the execution, and twelve and a half per cent. damages thereon, *absolute*. The motion for money collected, is for the amount collected and *twelve and a half per cent*. per annum, from the time demand is made. Nicholson Sup., 105. There is, therefore, a fatal variance between the grounds of motion mentioned in the notice, and the motion actually made. The constable had not five days notice of "*such*" motion as was made.

The second point is this: The notice speaks of an execution issued on the 5th of June. The execution offered in evidence issued on the 5th of *April*. Plaintiffs in error objected, at the trial, to the reading of said execution, as being a different one from that mentioned and described in the notice. The variance is, clearly, fatal. The notice certainly ought to state the ground of action. The failure to return *every* execution is a *distinct* cause of action, and the party should have notice of the *exact* execution, so that he may be prepared for defence. The authority relied on by the defendant in error, is *McMullen* v. *Goodman*, 4 Hum., 239. That is a case where the execution mentioned in the notice was described as an execution against J. L., and the execution offered in evidence was against J. L. and A. L. The court held that not to be a fatal variance.

The distinction between the two cases is this—in the case recited the *same* execution is merely *mis-described*, in the case before the court the executions are necessarily *different*. In the case recited, the court says: "The execution was certainly against J. L., and in that particular complies with the notice; but it is, also, against

James Lashley *et al. v.* T. Wilkinson.

Almond Lowry, the stayor. *Does this necessarily make it a different paper?"* The court said not. But is not an execution described as issuing on the 5th of June, *necessarily a different* paper from one issuing on the 5th of April? Clearly so.

This case, therefore, comes up to the test laid down by the court. The ground of the motion made before the magistrate for non-return of *one* execution—the proof before the Circuit Court is non-return of *another*—an entirely separate cause of action. 1 Sneed, 201.

PULLIAM, for the defendant in error, insisted that the notice given in this case was in substantial compliance with the law, and sufficient; and to sustain this position, cited the act of 1835, ch. 17, § 4; act of 1842, ch. 37, § 1, Nich. Sup., 105; *Cook v. Smith*, 1 Yer., 148-9.

He also contended that the *variance* between the date of the execution mentioned in the notice—the 5th of June, 1856—and the date of the execution produced on the trial—the 5th of April, 1856—was an immaterial one; and, therefore, not fatal. *McMullen v. Goodman*, 4 Hum., 239-40; *Marshall v. Hill*, 8 Yer., 101-3; *Howard et al. v. Union Bank*, 7. Hum., 26.

WRIGHT, J., delivered the opinion of the Court.

Judgment was rendered, upon motion, against James

James Lashley *et al. v.* T. Wilkinson.

Lashley, a constable of Fayette county, and his sureties in office, for the non-return of an execution placed in his hands. He and his sureties have appealed in error to this Court, and ask for a reversal of the judgment.

The first error assigned is, that the notice does not sufficiently state the grounds of the motion—whether for the non-return of the execution, or for collecting and failing to pay over the money.

We think the notice is, in this respect, sufficient. It describes the note placed in the officer's hands for collection—the date and amount of the judgment rendered upon it, and the execution issued to him in the case; and then states that the execution had not been returned into the office whence it issued, within thirty days from its issuance, nor the money due thereon paid over as the law directs; and that, therefore, judgment was demanded against the officer and his securities for the amount of the judgment of the justice of the peace, with legal interest from the rendition thereof, and twelve and a half per cent. interest on the same from the time it was demanded, by way of damages.

It is said the motion and judgment for the non-return of the execution, differ from the case where the money has been collected and not paid over; the former being for the amount of the execution, and twelve and a half per cent. damages thereon, and the latter for the amount collected, with twelve and a half per cent. per annum interest, from the time demand is made of the officer. If we were to concede this difference to exist, still, we think, the notice was sufficient upon which to base a judgment for the non-return of the writ. It distinctly states the fact, that the execution had not been returned, and that, for that reason, a judgment would be demanded. The validity of the notice could not be affected by the fact, that it, also, asked for judgment for the non-payment of the money, nor by the fact, that it demanded, as a legal conclusion, more, or less, by way of interest, or damages, than the plaintiff was entitled to. The law fixed the officer's liability upon the case stated, and it was the duty of the Court to give judgment for the proper amount. This was done.

The next objection to the judgment is, that the execution, for the non-return of which the motion was made, when produced, appeared to have been issued on the 5th of April, 1856, whereas, the notice describes it as having been issued on the 5th of June, in that year. This variance is said to be fatal. We do not think so. As we have seen, the notice fully described the note, and the judgment rendered upon it, and the execution, with great particularity, giving the amounts and dates, with the names of the parties, with the exception, only, that the 5th of June was, by mistake, or clerical omission, substituted for the 5th of April.

It was shown that no other execution issued upon the judgment, and that there was no other judgment between the parties to this judgment, in any way, to correspond with it. It is impossible, therefore, that this officer could have been misled by this notice, or that he could, for a moment, have hesitated, as to the execution, for the non-return of which he and his sureties were sought to be held liable. It could have applied to no other, for none other existed. If so, the object of the law is attained, as he could have come prepared to make his defence.

The judgment of the Circuit Court will, therefore, be affirmed.

J. H. DEAN et al. v. A. VACCARO & Co.

1. CARRIER. *Common. Delivery of goods. Notice.* Carriers by railroads, or steamboats engaged in the internal coasting and river trade, in the absence of a contract for a particular mode of delivery, must deliver freight received by them to the owner, consignee, or some authorized agent, or safely land it upon the wharf at the place of destination, or deposit it in their depot houses, and promptly notify the consignee. If delivered to a drayman, cartman, or any other person not authorized by the consignee, to receive it, it is at the risk of the carrier.

SAME. *Same. Same. Same. Effect of usage or custom.* The usage or custom of a port cannot dispense with delivery, or notice of the landing of the goods. Nor will the fact, that the consignee and others, had submitted to a delivery of goods to a drayman, before, when no loss occurred, bind him to yield his legal right to notice when it is to his interest to assert it.

3. SAME. *Same. Measure of damages if goods not delivered.* Upon failure to deliver goods, by a carrier, as required by law, the net value of the goods at the place of delivery is the measure of damages.

FROM MEMPHIS.

Upon an agreed case his Honor, Judge CARUTHERS, rendered judgment for the plaintiffs, at the November Term, 1858. Defendants appealed.

J. H. Dean *et al.* *v.* A. Vaccaro & Co.

E. M. YERGER, for the plaintiffs in error.

MASSEY, for the defendants in error.

CARUTHERS, J., delivered the opinion of the Court.

This suit was instituted to recover the value of several boxes of cigars, forwarded by the steamboat Glendale, from Cincinnati, to the defendants in error, who resided and did business in Memphis. They were landed on the wharf at Memphis, and delivered over to one of the city draymen, by the clerk of the boat, to be carried to the consignee, Vaccaro, but never delivered to him. On the arrival of the boat, the bill of lading was handed to Vaccaro, but no other notice given to him on the subject, and it does not appear by the case agreed, that he, in fact, had any notice of the arrival of the boat, further than it might be implied from the receipt of the bill of lading. The boat landed at the port on Sunday, and on the next day she was unloaded, and the cargo turned out upon the wharf at the usual place of landing, and the goods in question placed in charge of a drayman, as before stated. There is no evidence that Vaccaro was cognizant of any of these facts, or that any authority was given by him for that mode of delivery, except it may be implied from the usage of the port.

The case was presented by agreement to the court below upon the facts and the law. About the facts there is no dispute, as they are clearly set forth by the parties in the form of an agreed case, and are substantially, so far as they are material to raise the questions of law, stated above.

J. H. Dean *et al. v.* A. Vaccaro & Co.

What shall be a sufficient delivery to discharge a common carrier, by water, has given the courts some difficulty in all commercial countries.

The general rule as to carriers is, that they shall deliver goods entrusted to them, to the bailor, or consignee, his agent, or as he may be otherwise directed. 1 Parsons on Con., 658, 660.

As to the most important class of carriers by land—railroads—it is the usage, founded on necessity, as they cannot leave their rails, to deposit freight intrusted to them, in their station warehouses; but the owner or consignee must be notified. Id., 663.

Upon the same necessity, to some extent, as the steamboat or ship cannot leave the water, a usage has ripened into law, that a delivery upon the wharf at a public port, with notice to the consignee, will excuse the carrier by water. When there is a contract for any particular mode of delivery, that will, of course, govern. But when the place and consignee are designated, and nothing more, the rule is, that the delivery must be made to the owner, consignee, or some authorized agent, or safely landed upon the wharf at the designated place of destination or delivery, and prompt notice to the consignee. Id., 669 and note z. If the goods are delivered to a drayman, cartman, or any one else not authorized by the consignee to receive them, it is at the risk of the carrier.

The rules prescribed by the commercial and maritime code for ocean trade and foreign ports may be different, and more favorable to the carrier as to the mode of delivery, but for the internal coasting and river trade of our country, the rule stated above must govern and regulate the liability of the common carrier. 8 Louisiana Rep. 224, cited by Parsons in note z.

The authorities are not in harmony in relation to the duty of the carrier in the coast or river trade. The case of *Ostrander* v. *Brown*, in 15 John. 39, seems to require an actual delivery to the consignee to discharge the carrier from responsibility. But the conclusion of Mr. Parsons, that a delivery at the usual place at the port to which the goods are directed or consigned, with the knowledge of the consignee, by notice or otherwise, we think most reasonable, and better supported by authority. To require personal delivery would, in many cases, be impracticable, and if not so, would operate seriously on the general interests of trade and speedy transportation. There can be no injury to the consignee with proper diligence and attention to his interest, where the goods are delivered at the proper wharf or landing, if he has knowledge of the fact. But without this, the goods would be put in jeopardy, with great danger of loss.

But even upon this relaxed rule of accountability, how does this case stand? There is no sufficient evidence that the consignees had any knowledge of the arrival of the boat, and the landing of the goods. The delivery of the bill of lading by the agent afforded no evidence that the boat had arrived, or the time when it would arrive. It would not amount to notice of the time, or raise any reasonable presumption of it. To excuse the carrier, and relieve him of his legal responsibility, notice must be given, or knowledge otherwise fixed upon the consignee; not only that the goods have been shipped, or are on the way, but that they are at the wharf, so that they may be taken charge of at once, and secured from hazard by the person interested. This important fact is not made out in the case before us, and, therefore, the defendants were properly held liable. The usage or custom of that port cannot be allowed to excuse notice; it is enough to give it the effect of dispensing with actual delivery to the consignee. Nor can the custom of delivering goods to public draymen have the effect of superseding the requirements of the law on this subject. That this consignee, and many others, had submitted to it before, when no loss occurred, would not bind them to yield their legal right to notice when it became their interest to assert it. Such a custom cannot change the law in that respect.

A question is made as to the measure of damages. The Court allowed the value of the goods at Memphis instead of their cost at Cincinnati. There was a difference of $100. At the latter place it is agreed they were worth or cost $500, and at the former $600. Where a carrier makes a wrong delivery, or *fails to deliver*, so as to become liable, "the net value of the goods at the place of delivery is the measure of damages." 2 Par. on Con., 468; 8 John., 213; 15 John., 24. The case in 4 Hay., 114, is not in conflict. That case prescribes the measure of damages to be the value at the place of reception, and not delivery, where there is no fault or *neglect*, but admits it would be different where these exist.

The judgment will be affirmed.

Charles A. Stockley *v.* Rowley, Ashburner & Co.

CHANCERY JURISDICTION. *Waiver. Act of* 1852, *ch.* 365, § 9. Prior to the passage of the act of 1852, it was the settled rule that if a party neglected to make his defence at law, whether the defence were purely legal, or, from its nature, both legal and equitable, and no obstacle in the way of such defence existed in the legal forum, he could not afterwards avail himself of it in a Court of Equity. But this rule is so far changed by the act of 1852, that, at least, in all cases not unfit for the investigation of a Court of Equity, if the defendant neglect to avail himself of the objection to the jurisdiction, by demurrer, and answers to the merits of the bill, the objection is *waived* and cannot afterwards be insisted on.

FROM MEMPHIS.

The bill was dismissed by his Honor, Judge CARUTHERS, at the May Term, 1858. The complainant appealed.

E. M. YERGER, for the complainant.

Fraud being originally and properly cognizable in equity, is a ground for coming into a Court of Equity for relief against a judgment, although the complainant attempted, unsuccessfully, to avail himself of it in the trial at law. Thus, a party sued on a bill single for hire of a slave, represented to be sound, but really unsound, and known to be so by the obligor, will not be repelled from a Court of Equity when asking for relief against the judgment, though he attempted to bar the suit at law by relying on the fraud. Cooke, 242, 245; 1 Meigs' Dig., p. 243, sec. 3, of title 404.

Fraud, to say the least, is of both legal and equitable cognizance, and the defendants having answered to the merits, a Court of Chancery will take jurisdiction.

There is another objection to the defence of former judgment. The defendants rely upon it in their answer. This cannot be done. It can only be available by plea. 1 Meigs' Dig., p. 244.

T. S. & S. W. AYRES, for the defendants.

Where a Court of Law having jurisdiction of the parties and subject matter, has heard and determined the facts and rendered judgment, a Court of Chancery will not afford any relief.

A Court of Chancery can give no relief against a judgment at law, on the ground of a defence which the *party could have made at law*, unless he was prevented from so doing by *accident, fraud, or some act of the opposite party*. *Gwinn* v. *Newton*, 8 Hum., 710; *Rice* v. *R. R. Bank*, 7 Hum., 39.

In this case, the matters set up in the bill of complainant shows a defence *purely legal*, which was made at law, and heard and determined by the Court of Law, and a Court of Chancery will not afford relief. *White* v. *Cahal*, 2 Swan, 550; *Bumpass* v. *Reams*, 1 Sneed, 595.

Charles A. Stockley *v.* Rowley, Ashburner & Co.

McKINNEY, J., delivered the opinion of the Court.

This bill was filed to enjoin a judgment recovered by the defendants against the complainant, on a promissory note for $413.17, made by the latter to the former on the 14th day of April, 1854, payable six months from date.

The consideration of the note was a quantity of oil sold by the agent of defendants to complainant, in the city of Memphis. The bill alleges that the agent of defendants, at the time of the sale, represented the oil to be what is called "machine oil," and to be of good quality, and suitable for that purpose. But that it was found, on examination, to be entirely unfit for the use for which it was purchased, and of little or no value.

The answer denies that the oil was unfit for the use for which it was purchased; and it is also denied, that the defendants' agent made any representation to the complainant whatever, in respect to the kind or quality of the oil.

The proof of two witnesses establishes very fully the representations of the agent as to the description and quality of the oil as charged in the bill. The witness, Guthrie, proves that he purchased some of the oil from the complainant, and sent a barrel of it to the Memphis and Charleston Railroad; but it was returned to him as of no value, and the superintendent stated that it "nearly ruined his engines."

The Chancellor dismissed the bill on the ground, it is said, of want of jurisdiction to interpose after a trial and judgment at law.

The decree ignores the effect of the act of 1851-2,

ch. 365, sec. 9. Before the passage of that act, it was the settled rule, that if a party neglected to make his defence at law, whether the defence were purely legal, or, from its nature, both legal and equitable, and no obstacle in the way of such defence existed in the legal forum, he could not afterwards avail himself of it in a Court of Equity. But this rule is so far changed by the act above referred to, that, at least, in all cases not unfit for the investigation of a Court of Equity, if the defendant neglect to avail himself of the objection to the jurisdiction, by demurrer, and answers to the merits of the bill, the objection is waived, and cannot afterwards be insisted on.

Such is the present case, the defendants having answered without exception to the jurisdiction, and they are now precluded from doing so.

The case must be remanded for an account. From the allegations of the bill, the oil was not entirely worthless; and, therefore, the failure of consideration was only partial; consequently, the complainant must account for its reasonable value, with interest thereon.

Decree reversed.

ISABEL B. BRADFORD v. R. CALDWELL et al.

LIMITATIONS. *Statute of. When it will bar a life estate.* If a person own a life estate in a slave, which he can sell and transfer, or which can be sold by execution; and such person, for a valuable consideration, sells and transfers said slave to another, who takes possession thereof

Isabel B. Bradford v. R. Caldwell et al.

and holds and claims the slave, adversely, for a period of three years, the statute of limitations will perfect his title and protect the possession, so far as the life estate is concerned, against the person from whom the slave was purchased, his creditors, and all other persons, except the owner of the remainder.

FROM MEMPHIS.

Upon the hearing, at the November Term, 1858, CARUTHERS, J., presiding, the bill of complainant was dismissed. She appealed.

W. K. POSTON, for the complainant.

It cannot be questioned that, so far as the life estate is concerned, Mrs. Bradford's possession was adverse to the widow's.

"Adverse possession of a slave for three years bars the former owner's remedy to recover the slave, and vests the right of property in the possessor." *Kegler* v. *Miles*, M. and Y., 426, 430.

"A possession acquired by means of a verbal gift and delivery of a slave, if continued three years without interruption, will vest the possessor with title by operation of the statute of limitations, though the gift alone be inoperative in law or equity." 4 Yer. R., 507–9; 8 Yer. R., 145–9; Meigs' R., 427, 434–6; 6 Hum. R., 75, 84.

Mrs. Cowden, surely, could not have recovered in an action against the complainant, Mrs. Bradford, whatever of interest she had passed to Mrs. Bradford by her bill of sale; and if registration had been necessary, to make the sale good, still, three years uninterrupted possession perfected the complainant's title. If Mrs. Cowden had no right or remedy, those claiming under her are in no better condition.

The case of *Turner* v. *Turner*, 2 Sneed, 27, is essentially different from this. The principle there decided is, that a person cannot, under a loan from the true owner, set up a claim to a life estate, and by holding under that claim, acquire, by operation of the statute of limitations, this qualified estate. In that case, as in this, there were not two distinct and separate estates upon which the statute could operate; and the court held that the estate could not be divided and a less estate carved out by operation of the statute.

E. M. YERGER, for the defendants.

McKINNEY, J., delivered the opinion of the Court.

The bill seeks to enjoin the sale of certain slaves, upon the following state of facts.

The defendant, Ellen F. Cowden, was lawfully vested with an interest, during her own life, in the slaves mentioned in the bill. On the 23d of December, 1851, in consideration of the sum of $1600, to her paid by Mrs. Bradford, the complainant, the former sold and conveyed her said life interest in said slaves to the latter, to her sole and separate use: the complainant then, and still,

Isabel B. Bradford v. R. Caldwell *et al.*

being a married woman—wife of the defendant, Simon Bradford.

In pursuance of said sale, the slaves were delivered to the complainant, who retained the undisturbed possession of them for a period of more than three years before the filing of this bill, claiming the life interest in them conveyed to her as above stated. The bill of sale for the slaves, from Mrs. Cowden to complainant, was never registered.

The defendants, Caldwell & Co., on the 14th of March, 1856, recovered a judgment against Simon Bradford, (the husband of complainant,) and said Ellen F. Cowden, jointly, for the sum of $3268.57, upon which execution issued and was levied upon said slaves. And the question is, whether or not said slaves are subject to the satisfaction of the judgment.

It is clear, that so far as regards the creditors of the husband of complainant, registration of the bill of sale was not essential.

But as respects the creditors of Mrs. Cowden, it is equally clear, that by reason of the non-registration of the bill of sale, the slaves remained subject to the satisfaction of their debts. Admitting this to be so, it is insisted for the complainant that her title was perfected by operation of the statute of limitations, before the date of the defendant's judgment; and this position, it seems to us, cannot be successfully resisted. The case of *Turner* v. *Turner*, 2 Sneed, 27, is not an authority against the correctness of this conclusion. That case holds, that a life estate cannot be created by operation of the statute, against the acknowledged owner of the reversion, from whom the possession has been obtained. The case

Isabel B. Bradford *v.* R. Caldwell *et al.*

is a peculiar one, and was correctly decided upon the facts of the particular case. But the principle is not applicable to the facts of the case before us. Here, it is admitted, that a valid life estate in the slaves existed in Mrs. Cowden. This was an interest which she might sell and transfer to another, or it might have been sold upon execution by her creditors. She did, in fact, sell it, for a valuable consideration, as is admitted in the agreed case in the record. The sale was not by parol, but by a conveyance in writing, in proper form; and under this bill of sale, the complainant held the slaves, claiming an estate for life in them, for a period of more than three years before the defendants obtained their judgment, or caused the slaves to be levied on.

Upon these facts, we are at a loss to perceive any reason why the statute of limitations should not inure to perfect the title, and protect the possession of the complainant, so far as her life estate is concerned: at least, as to all persons against whom she might, by law, set up an adverse possession: that is, against the person from whom she purchased, her creditors, and all other persons, except the owners of the remainder interest in the slaves; as against the latter, she could not, of course, set up an adverse possession.

From this view of the case, it follows that the decree is erroneous; and it will be reversed, and a decree be made in favor of the complainant.

C. J. ROBERTS v. THE STATE.

1. CRIMINAL LAW. *False pretence. Code, § 4701.* The Code, § 4701, provides that "every person who by any false pretence, or by any false token, or counterfeit letter, with intent to defraud another, obtains from any person any personal property *on* the signature of any person to any written instrument, the false making of which is forgery, shall, on conviction," &c. The word *on*, in the third line, after "property," is, by misprint, or clerical error, substituted for *or*, and it should read, "or the signature of any person to any written instrument," &c.

2. SAME. *Same. Passing counterfeit coin.* The offence of passing counterfeit coin is a distinct, substantive felony, of higher grade from that of obtaining goods by false pretences, created by the act of 1842; and if the false pretence be the passing of counterfeit coin, the indictment cannot be sustained.

3. SAME. *Same. Same.* To constitute the offence of passing counterfeit coin, the spurious coin passed must be a representation of genuine coin on both sides. If it be a piece of spurious metal, about the size of current coin, representing it on one side, but merely an advertisement on the other, and not purporting to be coin, the passing of it (the other requisites existing) is a false pretence, under the statute.

FROM MEMPHIS.

The plaintiff in error was tried and convicted in the Criminal Court of Memphis, at the February Term, 1859, MCKIERNON, J., presiding. He appealed.

BROWN & KING, for the plaintiff in error.

SNEED, Attorney General, for the State.

CARUTHERS, J., delivered the opinion of the Court.

The indictment and conviction in this case was for obtaining twenty dollars in bank notes by false pretences, under the Code, art. 5, p. 844. The term of imprisonment was fixed at seven years.

Code, § 4701: "Every person, who by any false pretence, or by any false token, or counterfeit letter, with intent to defraud another, obtains from any person any personal property, *on* the signature of any person to any written instrument, the false making of which is forgery, shall, on conviction," &c. The difficulty made upon the section is entirely obviated by changing the word *on* to *or*, in the third line after the word "property," which was evidently intended, and must be regarded as a clerical error or misprint. It would be nonsense as it stands, and must be read with the change suggested. It would then so read as to make the "obtaining" of property, including money, or "obtaining" the name of any one to an instrument, by false pretences, tokens, or counterfeit letters, felony. This last branch of the offence is not in the act of 1842, but is certainly an improvement of it. This reformation of the language of the act, by changing the word "*on*" to "*or*" is indispensable to make it intelligible.

It is insisted, that if the plaintiff in error, and his accomplice, Smith, whose case is not now before us, are guilty of any offence, it is that of passing counterfeit coin, and not the offence charged. This position is correct, if it applies, as we have heretofore held. It was not intended by the act of 1842, or the Code, § 4701, to cover or give a new name to the then existing and long established offence of passing counterfeit money, but to create a new felony. So if the crime here consisted of passing counterfeit coin for goods or bank notes, the conviction would be erroneous, because that is not the charge in the indictment.

These are the facts, as stated by the prosecutor, Stephen Gibson:

"On the 10th of February, 1859, he was at a boarding-house, near the Memphis and Charleston Railroad depot, in company with two gentlemen from Arkansas; that while conversing with them, the defendant, Roberts, came up to them and joined in the conversation. He told defendant, Roberts, that he was from Alabama, and a stranger in Memphis. Roberts spoke of the danger to be apprehended by strangers from pickpockets, thieves, and swindlers who infested the depot and city; that they all walked over to the depot, still talking about thieves, &c.; that soon after they reached the depot, and were standing near the lamps, Wm. Smith, who is jointly indicted, came up to where they were standing, and asked Roberts if he could change for him a twenty dollar gold piece. Roberts said he did not know, but would look and see, and pulled out his *port-monnaie* and examined it, and said that he could not, but perhaps the gentleman from Alabama could give him the change. Witness then said he believed he could, and walked to the light with Roberts and Smith, where he pulled out his pocket-book and took therefrom two five dollar bills, one on an Alabama and the other on a South Carolina bank, and a ten dollar bill on the Bank of Tennessee, and handed the same to Smith, who thereupon handed witness what he, at first, took to be a twenty dollar gold piece, but which was in fact a piece of spurious metal, about the size of a twenty-dollar gold piece, which was the color of gold; and upon one side could

C. J. Roberts v. The State.

not be distinguished, without close inspection, from genuine gold coin; but on examination of the other side, it could be easily and readily discovered to be but an advertisement, and *did not purport to be gold coin.*" Smith immediately made off with the bank bills, before the witness had inspected the metal, which he at once discovered to be base metal, but could not overtake Smith. The defendant denied having any acquaintance with Smith; but made his escape while the prosecutor went after a policeman. They were both soon after arrested, and found to be well acquainted, and both had in possession the same kind of metal pieces passed to defendant. The proof leaves no doubt of the complicity of Roberts with Smith, or the guilt of both.

This was not counterfeit coin, as it did not purport to be a representation of gold coin, when examined, but a false imitation of it only on one side. It was a trick, and base contrivance, and false pretence to obtain money or property fraudulently. This is the offence charged against them. This objection, then, cannot be maintained.

Again, it is insisted that the imposition could have been easily detected by ordinary care, and therefore it does not constitute the offence charged. This does not fall within that class of cases contained in the books referred to. It was calculated to deceive, and did deceive under the circumstances. The time, place, and circumstances are all to be taken into view in determining this question. Only one side of the metal was presented, and that by a dim light, and in the hurry and confidence of the moment, was calculated to deceive and accomplish the fraudulent purpose. We are not disposed to carry this defence to the extent of some of the cases relied upon, to screen the guilty thief from the penalty of the law for this most detestable species of larceny. The trick must be obvious and palpable to ordinary observation—the circumstances all considered—to constitute this defence.

The conviction is well sustained by the law and evidence, and the judgment is affirmed.

ZACHARIAH DEMENT *v.* THE STATE.

CRIMINAL LAW. *Passing a counterfeit Bank note. Rule as to resemblance.* If a party is indicted for passing a counterfeit resemblance or imitation of a genuine bank note, to authorize a conviction, the imitation or resemblance must be such as to be capable of imposing on persons of *ordinary observation.*

FROM OBION.

The plaintiff in error was tried and convicted at the February Term, 1859, WILLIAMS, J., presiding. He appealed in error.

——— ———, for the plaintiff in error.

SNEED, Attorney General, for the State.

McKINNEY, J., delivered the opinion of the Court.

The prisoner was convicted in the Circuit Court of Obion, and sentenced to three years confinement in the

Zachariah Dement v. The State.

penitentiary, for the supposed offence of passing a counterfeit bank note.

The indictment charges, that the note was the counterfeit resemblance or imitation of a genuine ten dollar bank note issued by the Bank of Tennessee.

The proof shows, that the note passed, a copy of which is set out in the indictment, was in fact a genuine note, issued by the president, directors and company of the Bank of East Tennessee; but altered by the erasure of the word "East."

The Court instructed the jury, in substance, that it would be sufficient to support the charge in the indictment, if the note passed by the prisoner was such a resemblance of a ten dollar note of the Bank of Tennessee, "as might probably be passed off on a *careless and negligent* person," although it might not be, "in many respects," exactly like the genuine note. This was stating the rule applicable to such cases too strongly. The correct rule is, that the imitation or resemblance must be such as to be capable of imposing on persons of "*ordinary observation.*"

Such is not the character of the note in question. In a legal sense, it bears no resemblance to a genuine note of the Bank of Tennessee, and no one of "ordinary observation" could be deceived or imposed on by it.

The indictment contains no count for *forgery*.

The judgment is erroneous, and it will be reversed, and the prisoner be remanded for a new trial.

J. M. Patrick v. S. O. Nelson & Co.

J. M. PATRICK *v.* S. O. NELSON & CO.

1. WRIT OF ERROR. *Bond. Code,* § 3177. The bond to be given upon suing out a *writ of error,* whether the application be to the clerk of the court, or a judge thereof, or to the court itself, and whether a *supersedeas* issue or not, must, by § 3177 of the Code, be the same as in an appeal in the nature of a writ of error.

2. SAME. *Same. Upon an appeal in the nature of a writ of error. Code,* § 3162. By the Code, § 3162, in actions founded upon liquidated accounts signed by the party to be charged therewith, bonds, bills single, &c., upon an appeal in the nature of a writ of error, the bond shall be taken, and the securities bound for the payment of the whole debt, damages and costs, and for the satisfaction of the judgment of the superior court, where the cause may be finally tried and determined. The bond must be the *same* if a case is brought up by a *writ of error.*

3. SAME. *Same. Motion to dismiss for want of. What may be looked to.* Upon a motion to dismiss for want of a sufficient bond, the court cannot look to, or decide whether there be error in the record or not. It is sufficient to authorise the dismissal of the writ if it appear that the proper bond has not been executed by the party.

FROM MEMPHIS.

At the July Term, 1858, a judgment was rendered against the defendant, CARUTHERS, J., presiding, and he filed a transcript of the record with the clerk of the Supreme Court, who, upon a bond being executed for costs, issued a writ of error.

T. S. & S. W. AYERS, for the plaintiff in error.

————— —————, for the defendant in error.

J. M. Patrick v. S. O. Nelson & Co.

WRIGHT, J., delivered the opinion of the Court.

This is a motion by S. O. Nelson & Co., to dismiss the writ of error for want of a sufficient bond.

The plaintiff in error, a merchant at Memphis, doing business under the style of J. M. Patrick & Co., was sued in debt by S. O. Nelson & Co, in the Common Law Court of Memphis, upon an account, and judgment had against him.

The account appears to have been created in New Orleans, in 1855; and at the foot of it is the following acknowledgment, signed by J. M. Patrick & Co.:

"We acknowledge the correctness and justness of the above account of nine thousand and eighty-eight dollars and ninety-three cents, bearing interest at the rate of eight per cent. per annum, since the 8th of June, 1855.

J. M. PATRICK & CO."

This account was specially declared upon, and profert made of it in the declaration.

The plaintiff—within twelve months after the rendition of the judgment—has filed, with the clerk of this court, a transcript of the record, and obtained from him a writ of error, upon giving a bond for costs only. No *supersedeas* was asked for or issued, and the question now is, whether this bond is sufficient. And we hold it is not.

Section 3162 of the Code provides that in actions founded upon liquidated accounts, signed by the party to be charged therewith, upon an appeal in the nature of a writ of error, the bond shall be taken, and the sureties bound, for the payment of the whole debt, damages and costs, and for the satisfaction of the judgment of the superior court, where the cause may be finally tried and determined; and in such case the appellant shall pay interest at the rate of twelve and a half per cent. per annum.

In the same section certain other enumerated instruments—such as bonds, bills single, &c.—are put upon a like footing. And in section 3163, in all other cases of appeal in suits at law, not mentioned in the previous section, the bond shall be for damages and costs, only, and the rate of interest shall be six per cent. per annum.

Section 3177 provides that a writ of error may be moved for, and obtained, in the appellate court, or issued by the clerk of the appellate court in vacation, upon the transcript of the record being filed in his office, and bond given as required by law.

Sections 3180 and 3181 prescribe the time within which a writ of error shall be prosecuted, namely: to the clerk within one year, and to the appellate court, or a judge thereof, within two years after the judgment or decree.

And, finally, section 3184 provides that the bond required from the applicant for the writ of error, and the proceedings in the appellate court thereafter, shall be the same as those upon an appeal as therein before provided in that chapter.

It will thus be seen, that by the express provisions of the statute, whether the application for the writ of error be to the clerk of this court, or a judge thereof, or to the court itself; and whether a *supersedeas* issue or not, the bond must be the same as in an appeal in

James N. Wilson v. B. G. Beadle et al.

the nature of a writ of error. From this we cannot escape, because the statute is general, and makes no exception of the case where no *supersedeas* is had.

We, also, think the account upon which the judgment in this case was rendered, must be held to be a liquidated account within the meaning of section 3162 of the Code, and the bond must be as there directed.

We are not permitted, upon this application, to decide whether there be error in this record or not, nor upon the effect of the stipulation in the acknowledgment at the foot of the account, to pay eight per cent. per annum interest; nor whether this was executed in New Orleans or not. These matters can only come up for decision when a proper bond is given, and the case is regularly before us.

It is enough that we can see that the writ of error is sought to be prosecuted from a judgment rendered upon a liquidated account, signed by the party to be charged therewith. We are bound to require the bond before we proceed further.

The result is, the motion must be sustained.

JAMES N. WILSON *v.* B. G. BEADLE *et al.*

1. ATTACHMENT. *Act of* 1843, *ch.* 29, § 1. *In what cases an attachment will lie.* By the act of 1843, ch. 29, § 1, in all cases where a debtor shall be absconding or concealing himself, or his property or effects, a creditor may sue out an attachment against the property

James N. Wilson *v.* B. G. Beadle *et al.*

debts, *choses in action*, and effects of such debtor, in the same manner that such process may be obtained against absconding or non-resident debtors under the different statutes in force in this State.

2. SAME. *Same. Judgment not necessary before suing out the attachment. Chancery Jurisdiction.* The act of 1848 confers upon the Chancery Court jurisdiction for the recovery of demands purely legal in attachment cases, and no previous suit or judgment, on the part of the creditor, is necessary before suing out the attachment.

3. SAME. *Act of* 1852, *ch.* 365, § 10. *Fraudulent conveyances.* By the act of 1852, ch. 365, § 10, a creditor is authorized to file a bill for an attachment, without a judgment at law and an execution with a return of *nulla bona*, in all cases where a conveyance is made by a debtor, of property, either real, personal or mixed, of any description to which he has a legal or equitable title, for the purpose of hindering, delaying, or defrauding his creditors.

4. SAME. *Same. Same. Embraces choses in action.* This act not only embraces conveyances of what is, strictly, termed property, but also fraudulent assignments of claims, and every species of *choses in action*.

FROM MEMPHIS.

The bill was dismissed by his Honor, Judge CARUTHERS, upon demurrer, at the May Term, 1858. The bill and amended bill, in substance, charged that the defendant, Beadle, was indebted to the complainant in the sum of $500; that Beadle and his wife sold a tract of land, jointly, to their co-defendant, W. L. Delany, for the sum of $2500, he executing his notes for the purchase money; that the note first due was payable to and endorsed by the defendant, Finnie, and the others were payable to his wife, Dorcas C. Beadle; that the notes payable to Dorcas C. Beadle were executed to her and endorsed to the defendant, Payne, to defraud the creditors of the said B. G. Beadle, and that he was concealing his property and effects.

James N. Wilson v. B. G. Beadle *et al.*

YERGER and SULLIVAN, for the complainant.

VANCE and ANDERSON, for the defendants.

WRIGHT, J., delivered the opinion of the Court.

The Chancellor dismissed the bill and amended bill upon demurrer.

This decree is erroneous.. The act of 1843, ch. 29, sec. 1, provides (among other things) that in all cases where a debtor shall be absconding or concealing himself, or his property or effects, it shall be lawful for the creditor to obtain an attachment against the property, debts, choses in action, and effects of such debtor, in the same manner as such process may be obtained against absconding or non-resident debtors under the different statutes now in force in this State. In the case of *Isaacks and wife* v. *Edwards*, 7 Hum., 465, it was held, that this act of Assembly conferred upon the Chancery Court jurisdiction for the recovery of demands purely legal in attachment cases, and that no previous suit or judgment on the part of the creditor was necessary.

This embraces the present case. The amended bill, if the original does not, alleges that the defendant, B. G. Beadle, is concealing his property and effects, and was concealing the same at the time of filing the original bill.

But it is said the amended bill contains no prayer for an attachment. This was unnecessary. The original bill did, and the amended bill incorporated itself with, and become a part of it. Moreover, we think, the original bill itself made a proper case for an attachment

James N. Wilson *v.* B. G. Beadle *et al.*

under the act of 1852, ch. 365, sec. 10, if it did not under the act of 1843.

Under that statute it was not necessary for the creditor to come into Chancery with a judgment at law, and an execution with a return of no property. He was authorized to file a bill in all cases where a conveyance is made by a debtor, of property, either real, personal or mixed, of any description, to which the title was legal or equitable, for the purpose of hindering, delaying, or defrauding his creditors.

It is argued here, that the word conveyance used in the statute, does not comprehend the fraudulent assignment of a chose in action. We think it does. It is true, that in its more restricted sense it is often limited to conveyances of what is strictly termed property; but, in its more enlarged meaning it embraces assignments of claims, and every species of choses in action. Here the words of the act are very comprehensive, and statutes made to suppress fraud are to be liberally expounded.

Again, it is argued that the notes on Delany, whether made payable to B. G. Beadle, the debtor, and by him assigned to his wife, D. C. Beadle, or made payable to her directly, would, as between them, they being husband and wife, be a mere nullity, and leave the title to the notes still in the husband, and that such an assignment could not be considered as standing in the way of creditors within the meaning of the act of 1852.

If we were to concede this to be so, (1 Bac. Ab. Baron and Fame D., 705; *McNeilage* v. *Halloway*, 1 Born. and A., 218,) still the bill and amended bill go further. They allege that the defendant, B. G. Beadle, had made, or caused his wife to make, a fraudulent assignment and deposit of these notes with the defendant Payne, to hinder and delay his creditors.

The decree will be reversed, and the cause remanded for an answer.

HUGH LESLIE *v.* JOSEPH JOYNER.

FRAUDULENT CONVEYANCES. *Debtor and creditor. What liable to creditors.* A conveyance of an interest not liable to creditors, though fraudulent, is not within the provisions of the statute of frauds. Neither can the creditor coerce the debtor to labor for his benefit. If, therefore, a debtor, by an agreement with his son, permit him to have the use of his horse and the services of two other sons, who are minors, to raise a crop, and furnish the family with provisions for that year out of the crop—reimbursing himself for the supplies thus furnished, and also to retain reasonable wages, and whatever beyond this remained of the proceeds of the crop was to go to the payment of the father's debts—such agreement is not a fraud upon the creditors of the father, and the crop raised is not liable to execution.

FROM HENDERSON.

This cause was heard before his Honor Judge FITZGERALD, at the April Term, 1858. Verdict and judgment for the defendant. The plaintiff appealed.

No counsel appeared for either party.

MCKINNEY, J., delivered the opinion of the Court:

Hugh Leslie *v.* Joseph Joyner.

This was an action of trover, for the alleged conversion of a quantity of tobacco. Verdict and judgment were rendered for the defendant, and the plaintiff appealed in error.

The plaintiff, as constable, had levied on the lot of tobacco, as the property of William Joyner, the father of defendant, Joseph Joyner; after which the defendant, claiming to be the proper owner of the tobacco, obtained possession thereof, and refused to deliver it to the plaintiff.

The facts respecting the ownership of the tobacco appear to be, that the old man, Joyner, who was in debt, and had a large family of ten children, which he was unable to support by reason of his poverty and physical disability, entered into a contract with his son, the defendant, by which the latter agreed to take two of his brothers—boys of the respective ages of eleven and thirteen years—and a horse beast belonging to his father, and to raise a crop, and furnish the family with provisions for that year, (1857.) Out of the crop he was to reimburse himself for the supplies furnished to the family, and also retain reasonable wages; and whatever beyond this remained of the proceeds of the crop, was to go to the payment of his father's debts. William Joyner, the father of defendant, was examined on the trial as a witness for defendant, and admitted that the object of the above arrangement was to provide a support for his family, and to prevent the crop from being seized by creditors—being unable himself to supply his family with the necessaries of life.

The tobacco in controversy is part of the crop raised by the defendant under the above arrangement.

Hugh Leslie v. Joseph Joyner.

For the plaintiff it is contended that this was a fraud upon the old man's creditors, and that, in law, the crop raised was the property of the father, and liable to the satisfaction of his debts.

We do not think so. We have said in a recent case—*Hamilton* v. *Zimmerman*, 5 Sneed, 39, 45—that every man is under a positive obligation, both in law and morals, to support and maintain his family; that this is his first and most imperative duty. An unfortunate debtor is not bound to appropriate the proceeds of his daily labor to the benefit of creditors, leaving his own family to suffer hunger and want.

The position assumed for the plaintiff has no foundation in our law. The general principle is well established, that a conveyance, though fraudulent, of an interest not liable to creditors, is not within the prohibition of the statute of frauds. It is equally well settled that the creditor cannot coerce the debtor to labor for his benefit. If, in the case before us, the old man, even without any consideration, had relinquished the use of his horse (which the law protects to him) and the labor of his two minor sons, to the defendant, upon what principle could any creditor of the former have complained of it? He might use his horse himself, or give the use to another, at pleasure; and so in regard to the labor and services of his minor children. In the arrangement that was made, there was no transfer of property, or of anything of which, in the absence of such arrangement, the creditors of the father could have availed themselves, by law, for the satisfaction of their debts. Consequently their rights were in nowise prejudiced thereby.

Judgment affirmed.

Memphis and Charleston R. R. Company v. O. F. Jones.

MEMPHIS AND CHARLESTON R. R. COMPANY *v.* O. F. JONES.

CONTRACT. *Construction. Railroad Company. Liability of. Slaves.* The defendant in error hired to the plaintiff in error, for the year 1856, two slaves. The contract of hiring contained the following stipulation: "And all risks incurred, or liability to accidents, whilst in said service, is compensated for and covered by the pay agreed upon: the said railroad company assuming no responsibility for damages from accident, or any cause whatever." This stipulation does not relieve the company from liability for any injury or loss resulting from the wilful wrong or gross negligence of said company, or its agents, but it is responsible for the same.

FROM FAYETTE.

This cause was tried at the October Term, 1858, before Judge HUMPHREYS. Verdict for the plaintiff. The defendant appealed.

PULLIAM and RIVERS, for the plaintiff in error.

JONES, and J. W. & J. A. HARRIS, for the defendant in error.

MCKINNEY, J., delivered the opinion of the Court.

This was an action on the case, brought by Jones against the company, to recover damages for the loss of a slave, run over by a train of cars, and killed. The plaintiff recovered judgment for $1232.

The record shows that Jones, the plaintiff, hired to the defendant, for the year 1856, two negro boys to work on the railroad, at twenty-three dollars per month, for each. The contract of hiring contained the following stipulation, namely:

"And all risks incurred, or liability to accidents, whilst in said service, is compensated for and covered by the pay agreed upon; the said railroad company assuming no responsibility for damages from accident, or any cause whatever."

The slave, it seems, was lying on the track of the road, as a freight-train of some fourteen cars approached; whether or not he was asleep, or sick, or intoxicated, does not appear certainly, though it is most probable that he was under the influence of liquor. The engineer on the locomotive saw the boy, as he stated, at the distance of one hundred and fifty yards, "but thought it was a carpet-sack, or an old bag of clothes." The train was stopped, but not until all the cars, except one or two, had run over the body of the slave.

The proof shows that the road, for a distance of upwards of two miles from the spot where the slave lay, was straight, and a slight up-grade. There is some disagreement as to the distance at which the body might have been seen, as the train approached. We do not think it necessary, however, to notice the testimony, particularly, as the question for our determination arises upon the charge of the court, though it may be proper to state that, in our opinion, the verdict is sufficiently supported by the evidence.

The judge instructed the jury, that, under the before recited stipulation of the contract of hiring, "the defendant would not be responsible for the loss of the slave, unless it appeared from the evidence that his loss was in consequence of the *wilful misconduct, or gross negligence,* of defendant's agents; and that the burden of the proof was upon the plaintiffs."

This instruction is supposed, by the counsel for the plaintiff in error, to be erroneous. It was argued with great earnestness, that, admitting the loss of the slave to have been caused by the wilful misconduct, or gross negligence of the defendant's agents in charge of the train, still, the defendant cannot be held responsible for the loss; that the contract is an absolute exemption of the company from liability for any injury to the slave, or for his loss, no matter how occasioned. We think differently. It might be somewhat difficult to define the exact meaning and effect of the foregoing stipulation; this, however, is not necessary for the present determination. But there is no sort of difficulty in determining what it does not mean. It is true the language of the instrument is very strong, but it must receive a reasonable and sensible construction. It would be most absurd to suppose, that it was the intention and understanding of the parties, that the company should be protected from liability, not only against all the ordinary casualties to which the slave might be exposed in working on the road, and, also, against injuries caused by third persons in which the company had no participation, but likewise against injury or loss occasioned by the wilful wrong, or gross negligence, of the company itself, or its agents!

Such a construction of the agreement is altogether inadmissible. The stipulation is not available for the defendant, against its own wilful wrong, or culpable negligence. The charge of the court concedes to the defendant the utmost benefit that can be claimed upon any just construction of the instrument.

There is no error in the record.

Judgment affirmed.

JAMES NOLEN *v.* THE STATE.

1. CRIMINAL LAW. *Discharge of jurors.* Pending the selection of the jury, and before the jurors had been charged with the trial of the prisoner, two of them were discharged by the Court, with the consent of the Attorney General and the prisoner In this there was no error.

2. SAME. *Statement made by one juror to his fellow jurors. New trial.* A new trial will not be granted in a criminal case upon the unsupported affidavit of the prisoner, to the effect that after the jury retired from the bar, one of the number made a statement as of his own knowledge, that the prisoner was a violent, dangerous man. And the jurors are not bound to appear in court and convict themselves of a violation of duty.

FROM HARDEMAN.

The plaintiff in error was tried and convicted at the February Term, 1859, HUMPHREYS, J., presiding. He appealed.

L. M. BROWN, for the plaintiff in error.

SNEED, Attorney General, for the State.

James Nolen *v.* The State.

McKinney, J., delivered the opinion of the Court.

The prisoner was convicted of murder in the second degree, and sentenced to ten years in the penitentiary. There was a motion for a new trial, and, also, in arrest of judgment—both of which were overruled.

The proof is not set forth in the bill of exceptions. Two errors are alleged to have intervened in the progress of the trial. The first is, that the court discharged two of the jurors, after they had been regularly elected and chosen by the prisoner, and had taken their seats in the jury-box. It appears from the record, that during the process of impaneling the jury, and after six jurors had been selected, it was discovered that one of the six was *intoxicated;* and thereupon it was suggested by the court, that he be excused from serving on the jury; and the counsel for the prisoner and the Attorney General assenting to his discharge, it was ordered, accordingly, by the court. On the next morning, and before a jury was made up, one of the six jurors selected on the preceding day, was, at the request of the counsel for the defendant and the Attorney General, excused by the court from serving on the jury, for the reason that his wife had been taken very ill.

It is now objected, that the court had no power to discharge said jurors. This objection is not tenable. The jurors had not been charged with the trial of the prisoner. Their discharge was with the consent of the prisoner's counsel; and, as the record shows that the prisoner was present, in proper person, it must be taken to have been with his consent also. It is not pretended that the prisoner was in anywise prejudiced by the release

James Nolen v. The State.

of said jurors; and he cannot now be heard to impeach the regularity of the proceedings on that ground.

The second error assigned is, that after the jury had retired from the bar, to consider of their verdict, one of the number made a statement, as of his own knowledge, to his fellow jurors, to the effect that the prisoner was a violent, dangerous man; that he had stabbed other persons, and should not be turned loose upon the community. This statement is verified by the affidavit of the prisoner alone. Upon this unsupported affidavit, an application was made to the court to award compulsory process, to bring before the court certain of the jurors, to testify as to the matter alleged in said affidavit—the jurors refusing, as is stated, to appear voluntarily. The court refused the application. In this there is no error. What might have been the effect of the statement alleged to have been made by the juror, if the fact had been established, we need not now declare. It is sufficient to say, that the jurors were not subject to be called on to convict themselves of a palpable violation of duty; for which, if guilty, they were liable to be punished by the court.

The exceptions taken to the indictment are merely technical, and not available after verdict.

There is no error in the record.

Judgment affirmed.

JOAB PARKS v. J. B. M. ALLEN, EX'R, et al.

SURETY. *Recognizance. How far surety liable.* Pending the suit in the Circuit Court, the former securities were released, and the following recognizance entered into by the new surety: "Joab Parks comes into open court and acknowledges himself the defendant's security in the sum of $1000, in the room and stead of M. D. Cardwell and John A. Rogers, their former securities, conditioned that they defend their suit successfully, or in case of failure to pay all costs." *Held*, 1: That an undertaking, by recognizance, for costs, is as binding as if by bond, and is good, although the party to whom bound is not named, if the parties to the suit are named, and the party agrees to be the defendant's security for costs. 2: That the act prescribing the sum for which bond is to be taken in cases of contested wills, is directory, and the bond may be for a larger sum; and the fact that the former sureties were only bound in the sum of $500, does not change the undertaking of the new security.

FROM WEAKLEY.

At the February Term, 1859, application was made to his Honor, Judge FITZGERALD, for a writ of *supersedeas*, which being refused, the applicant appealed.

ROGERS and SOMERS, for Parks.

———— ————, for Allen and others.

CARUTHERS, J., delivered the opinion of the Court.

This is a case of some novelty, and it is difficult to know what disposition should be made of it. It comes before us by appeal in error from the action of

Joab Parks v. J. B. M. Allen, Ex'r, et al.

the Circuit Court, on the petition of Parks for a writ of *supersedeas* to an execution issued against him upon a judgment of the Circuit Court of Weakley, for $1086 cost, as the security of the contestants of the will of one James Turner, deceased.

The contest commenced in 1856, when Cardwell & Rogers were the sureties, who continued until August Term, 1858, when they were released, and Parks became bound. The entry of record is in these words, as set forth in the petition, viz: "Joab Parks comes into open court and acknowledges himself the defendant's security in the sum of $1000, in the room and stead of M. D. Cardwell and John A. Rogers, their former securities, conditioned that they defend their suit successfully, or, in case of failure, to pay all costs." The case was then continued by the defendants, at the costs of the term. It was tried the next October, and decided in favor of the will and against the defendants. Whereupon, the execution now complained of was issued on the 3d of November, for the costs, amounting to $1086 The Circuit Judge granted his fiat out of court on 23d of February, 1859, for a *supersedeas* as to the cost of August Term, 1858, but refused it as to the balance. At the next term, it appears that an application was made in open court upon the same petition for a *supersedeas*, and the court refused it, except to the extent before stated. From that judgment the appeal is taken to this court.

It is impossible for us to pass upon the correctness of the judgment of the Circuit Court in granting the *supersedeas* as to the costs of August Term, 1858, because the record is not before us, and without that we cannot know against whom that judgment was rendered, or whether after or before the petitioner entered into the recognizance for cost. The petition does not even disclose that fact.

But the appeal is not from that, but from the refusal to go further. It is probable that the main object of the appeal is to test the question of his liability at all, and if liable, to reduce it to $500. These questions are made by the petition, and if with the plaintiff would entitle him to the *supersedeas*.

1. Is he bound at all? There can be no doubt that an undertaking, by recognizance, for costs, is as good and binding as if by bond, which is the ordinary mode. But it is insisted that if that be so, yet this is not good because it does not bind the surety to the other party in the suit, or name any one to whom he is to be bound. That would have been more formal, but it is only a defect in form, and not in substance. It is upon the records in the suit of *Allen* v. *The Turners*, and he agrees to be the *defendants'* security for cost, to the plaintiff, of course, to whom else could it be? It is too easily rendered certain to be void for uncertainty.

2. It is argued that he could only be bound for $500, for two reasons: 1. That is the sum prescribed by statute for contestants of wills; and 2. They enter in the "room and stead" of the former securities, and they were only bound to that extent. Neither of these grounds are available. The statute is only directory as to the sum of $500, and the courts may exercise a proper discretion in view of the magnitude of the suit, and the probable cost, in regulating the amount. And so, in taking other or additional security, the amount

may be changed. The fact that the former sureties were bound in $500, is no reason why the latter might not be bound for more. He took their places as to the suretyship, not the amount,—he agreed in his recognizance that might be raised to $1000.

We do not see why the Circuit Judge did not supercede the execution as to the $86. He could not be liable beyond his obligation.

All we decide now is, that the grounds assumed in the petition are not sufficient to exonerate him from the costs, or to reduce his obligation one-half; and, therefore, the Circuit Court did right in refusing the *supersedeas* to the extent demanded. The case is affirmed, and remanded where justice will be done by correcting and limiting the bill of costs as may be right and proper.

WILLIAM S. SMITH *v.* MARY J. COZART.

1. SLAVES. *Warranty. Fraud. Evidence.* Where the contract for the sale of a slave is in writing, and contains no warranty, or a refusal to warrant, parol evidence is inadmissible to superadd a warranty. But if the contract is induced by an oral warranty, which the seller knows to be false, and is made for the purpose of throwing the other party off his guard, and fraudulently obtaining his consent to the bargain, evidence of such verbal warranty is admissible to show that the assent of the party to the contract was obtained by falsehood and fraud, and therefore has no legal existence. The same principle applies in the case of false and fraudulent representations made under like circumstances.

2. SAME. *Same. Same. Effect of stipulation that the slave is sold as unsound.* A stipulation in the bill of sale that the slave is sold as

William S. Smith v. Mary J. Cozart.

unsound property, is, in itself, an exclusion of all warranty; but such a stipulation will be of no avail where the seller has been guilty of a wilful and intentional false representation or concealment, or has resorted to any contrivance to deceive and mislead the purchaser.

8. SAME. *Same. Same. Measure of damages.* If there is a breach of the warranty of the soundness of a slave, or a fraudulent representation or concealment of her unsound condition—the slave not having been returned or offered to be returned—the proper measure of damages is the difference in value between the slave, if in the condition in which she was *represented* to be at the time of the sale, and her then *actual* condition, and not the value of the slave or the price paid for her.

FROM MADISON.

At the September Term, 1858, READ, J., presiding, a verdict was rendered in favor of the plaintiff. The defendant appealed.

H. E. JACKSON and W. H. STEPHENS, for the plaintiff in error.

HERVEY BROWN, for the defendant in error.

McKINNEY, J., delivered the opinion of the Court.

This was an action on the case for fraud in the sale of a female slave. There was a recovery for $1,112.50.

The case is peculiar in some of its features, and by no means free from difficulty.

It appears that the negotiation between Mrs. Cozart, the plaintiff below, and the defendant, Smith, for the purchase of the girl in question, was conducted through one Lightfoot, the brother and agent of plaintiff.

William S. Smith *v.* Mary J. Cozart.

It further appears that Mrs. Cozart had raised the girl, and owned her until some time in the year 1853, when she sold her to Smith. Not long after said sale, Mrs. Cozart became anxious to re-purchase the girl, and, through her agent, frequently importuned Smith to assent to a re-sale. But up to the month of June, 1856, he uniformly refused to do so, saying that he was pleased with the girl. At the period just mentioned, in a conversation between Smith and Lightfoot, in regard to a house and lot in Jackson, of which Mrs. Cozart was a part owner, Smith proposed to purchase said property, if Lightfoot would take said negro girl at $1000, to which the latter assented; and a bill of sale was made to him, in his own name, for the slave. But the purchase being made for Mrs. Cozart, it was agreed between Lightfoot and Smith, a day or two after the contract, that said bill of sale should be cancelled, and that Smith should convey the girl directly to Mrs. Cozart, which was done accordingly. Lightfoot was examined on the trial, and proved that the proposal of Smith to sell the girl excited his suspicions that something was the matter with her, and he inquired of him if she was sound. Smith replied that "she had had a cough, and suppressed menstruation for some short time, which might possibly be caused by pregnancy; and spoke of it as not being a serious matter, and that it was temporary only." Witness further stated, that upon this representation, on which he relied, the trade was made.

It is proved, that shortly after the purchase of the girl—within a week perhaps—Mrs. Cozart procured a physician to examine her; and he stated to the jury that he found the girl had consumption, and, in his opinion, had been laboring under that disease for six or twelve months; that he so informed Mrs. Cozart, and expressed the opinion that the girl could not be cured, and was worthless. The slave died in the summer of 1857.

The memorandum, or bill of sale, executed by Smith to Mrs. Cozart, is as follows:

"Received of Mrs. Mary Cozart one thousand dollars in payment of a negro, Maria, she being the negro I purchased of her in 1852, or 1853. I consider the negro unhealthy, and sell her as unsound property, and do not warrant her sound. I convey to the said Mrs. Cozart such title as was vested in me by my purchase of the said girl from her.

JUNE 30, 1856.　　　　　　　　　WM. G. SMITH."

It might seem, at first view, that the jury acted rashly in finding a verdict for the plaintiff in the face of the foregoing bill of sale; but an attentive consideration of the whole case will lead to a different conclusion.

The jury must have believed (and we cannot say that the belief was unwarranted) that Smith knew of the diseased and unsound condition of the slave at the time of the sale, and was therefore guilty, not only of suppression of the truth, but also of intentional misrepresentation. The circumstances of the case must also have satisfied the jury that the sale of the slave to Mrs. Cozart was a meditated scheme of fraud. He was fully aware of her desire to re-purchase the slave. He must have known, or at least had sufficient reason to suppose,

William S. Smith *v.* Mary J. Cozart.

that Mrs. Cozart, who had raised the slave, believed her to be sound, and therefore would be careless in respect to anything that might be inserted in the bill of sale as to her soundness. And the conviction forces itself upon the mind, that, in this view, the foregoing bill of sale was concocted and imposed on the plaintiff as a fraudulent artifice to shield the defendant against the consequences of a deliberate and detestable fraud. In this aspect of the case the verdict is well warranted.

It is admitted to be true, as a general proposition, that where the contract of sale is in writing, and contains no warranty, or a refusal to warrant, parol evidence is not admissible to superadd a warranty. But this statement of the general rule implies the absence of fraud in the transaction. For, as is said by an intelligent author, if it can be shown that the contract was induced by an oral warranty, which was false, to the knowledge of the party making it, and was made for the purpose of throwing the other party off his guard, and fraudulently obtaining his consent to the bargain, evidence of such verbal warranty is admissible. This is no infringement of the rule which forbids the introduction of parol evidence to contradict, vary, or add to a written instrument. The evidence is received not for that purpose; but, admitting the terms of the written contract, to show that the assent of the party to the contract was obtained by falsehood and fraud, and has therefore no legal existence. Addison on Contracts, 129, 130. The same principle applies in the case of false and fraudulent representations, made under like circumstances.

The stipulation that the slave was sold as "unsound

property," was, in itself, an exclusion of all warranty, and, in the absence of fraud, would protect the defendant from all liability. But such a stipulation is no protection against fraud, nor will it prevent the sale from being avoided on proof of fraud. The seller will not be permitted to make use of such an artifice to cover the perpetration of a fraud, and exonerate himself from the consequences. Such a stipulation will be of no avail where the seller has been guilty of a wilful and intentional false representation or concealment, or has resorted to any contrivance to deceive and mislead the purchaser. Ibid., 132, 133; 1 Parsons on Contracts, 473.

It follows, therefore, that the statements of the bill of sale, that the slave was sold as *unhealthy*, *unsound*, and *without warranty*, must be regarded as avoided by fraud; and the case must stand upon the false and fraudulent representations, on the faith of which the purchase of the slave is proved to have been made.

On the subject of damages, the Court stated to the jury, "that the criterion of damages, if the slave was entirely worthless, was the value or sum paid for the negro, and interest, if the jury thought proper to allow it."

This is a confused and inaccurate statement of the rule of damages applicable to the case.

The slave not having been returned, nor offered to be returned, the proper measure of damages was the difference in value between the slave, if in the condition in which she was represented to be at the time of the sale, and her then actual condition; and not, as the Court assumed, either the value of the slave or the price paid for her. But we think this error of the

R. F. Scott *et al. v.* Price and Bell.

Court does not so "affect the merits of the judgment" as to justify us in reversing it under section 4516, of the Code.

The verdict would, perhaps, have been the same upon a correct charge. It being proved that the slave was really valueless at the time of the sale, it was the duty of the jury to inquire, as the proper criterion of damages, what would have been the value of the slave if merely laboring under the slight temporary indisposition represented by the defendant. And it is certainly true, that the price paid by the plaintiff was by no means conclusive evidence of what the value of the slave would have been if in the condition represented. Yet, as it was the value as estmiated by the parties at the time, the jury were at liberty to regard it as at least persuasive, perhaps it might be said as sufficient, evidence of the value, in an action against the defendant grounded upon intentional fraud.

In this view, we think the error does not affect the judgment, and it is affirmed.

R. F. SCOTT *et al. v.* PRICE AND BELL.

1. LAND LAW. *Act of* 1851, *ch.* 826. *Occupant claim. Time to perfec title.* By the act of 1851, ch. 826, it is unlawful for any person to enter land on which another resides, or which is cultivated, or has been previously entered by him, until such person gives at least thirty days notice in writing to the person residing on or cultivating said land, or to the previous enterer or his assignee, of his intention to

enter the same Any entry made, or grant obtained contrary to the provisions of said act, are void. And time is given until the first of March, 1854, to have surveys made and grants issued.

2. SAME. *Same. Same.* The language of the act of 1851 is general, and embraces all land which had been previously entered under authority of law, no matter when, and without any distinction as to the origin or nature of the right of entry. It applies to an occupant enterer, and protects him as fully as it does the general enterer.

8. SAME. *Descent. An occupant right descends to heirs.* Upon the relinquishment of the pulic lands, by Congress, to the State, the occupant laws previously enacted, conferred upon those who complied with their provisions, an inheritable interest in the lands. And upon the death of any person having an occupant right, or of his assignee, such right is cast by descent upon his heirs.

4 SAME. *Act of* 1851, *ch.* 326. *Assignee protected.* The right of the assignee of an original occupant claim is protected by the act of 1851, without an actual residence on the land by such assignee, or his heirs.

FROM WEAKLEY.

Verdict for the defendant at the February Term, 1859, FITZGERALD, J., presiding. The plaintiffs appealed.

ROGERS, SOMERS and ROSS, for the plaintiffs.

ETHERIDGE, for the defendants.

WRIGHT, J., delivered the opinion of the Court.

This is an action of ejectment for the recovery of two tracts of land in Weakley county: one for 170 acres, and the other for 51¾ acres.

The plaintiffs concede they have no title to the latter tract, and the contest is, as to the title of the 170 acres.

R. F. Scott *et al.* v. Price and Bell.

The Circuit Judge held, that the defendants, also, had the better title to this tract.

In this we think he erred. We are satisfied that one Howard, under the act of 1829, ch. 22, and prior to the year 1831, had an occupant right to this land; and that in February of that year, he entered the same in the proper office by a special occupant entry, as required by that act and the act of 1826, ch. 7; that said occupant right was preserved by said Howard and his assignees until the year 1838, when James H. Moran, the ancestor of the plaintiffs, become the owner thereof by assignment; and that upon his death, the same came by descent to the plaintiffs, who are his heirs at law; and that they caused the said tract of land to be granted to them, by the State of Tennessee, on the 1st of May, 1854.

The defendants claim under a general entry made the 20th of October, 1852, and a grant thereon by the State, of date the 1st of February, 1853; and if it were not for the existence of the occupant right of the plaintiffs, would have the better title. But we think the grant and entry under which the defendants claim, so far as they conflict with the entry of Howard, absolutely void, because made in violation of this occupant right.

The act of 1851, ch. 326, gave to the enterers of land in any of the land offices in this State, and to their assignees, time, until the 1st day of March, 1854, to have their entries surveyed and granted, and made it unlawful for any person to enter any land on which another resided, or which was cultivated by another, or which had been previously entered, until such person had given, in writing, at least thirty days previous notice to the person residing on or cultivating said land, or to the previous enterer, or his assignee of his intention to enter the same; and any entry made, or grant obtained contrary to the provisions of the act are declared void. Etheridge, who made the entry and obtained the grant relied on by the defendants, did not give any notice to the assignees of the previous enterer. And it is now assumed for the defendants, that this act of Assembly has no application to an entry founded upon an *occupant right*, and which could never be the foundation of a grant; but was only intended to protect *general entries*, founded on military warrants, or entries made after the vacant lands in Tennessee were ceded to the State, by Congress, in 1841, by the payment of the fees of office, or such other consideration as the Legislature, in the disposition of these lands, had from time to time required. That a grant could issue upon no other class of entries, and none other could have been intended. We do not assent to this argument. The language of the act is general, and embraces all land which had been previously entered under authority of law, no matter when, and without any distinction as to the origin or nature of the right of entry; and we are satisfied it applies to an *occupant enterer*, and protects him as fully as it does the general enterer. It embraces all entries. And unless it can be shown that the location made by Howard is not, in any legal sense, an entry, the plaintiffs' rights are secured.

The act of 1826, ch. 7, sec. 8, provides that where any of said occupants may wish to have their lands laid down on the general plan, as directed in the act, they shall file with the surveyor, a *location* in legal form for the same, and it shall be the duty of the surveyor to record it in a book to be kept by him for that purpose. And what is a *location* thus filed, received and recorded, but an entry? 2 Meigs' Dig. 669, 670. It was recognized by the Courts, at an early day, as an entry. *Pettyjohn* v. *Akers*, 6 Yer., 448.

It is true, that prior to the Cession Act of 1841, a grant could not issue unless based upon a warrant; and since that act, upon the payment of the fees of office, or such other consideration as had been prescribed by law. But this does not prove that a new or second entry is necessary, any more than that an additional survey is required where a sufficient one has already been made. Act of 1829, ch. 22, sec. 16. Why make an additional or second entry on the *same land*, when the one already made is *special* and valid? But, if the second entry be necessary, the case is still within the act, because it gives further time to procure grants upon *all entries*, and of necessity includes everything proper or requisite to be done, in order to obtain the grant.

We are to observe, also, that the act not only prohibits an entry and grant upon lands appropriated by a *previous entry*, but also upon land on *which another resides*, or which is *cultivated by another*. This provision is to be found in the act of 1824, ch. 22, sec. 6, and is noticed in *Den* v. *Nixon*, 10 Yer., 518; and there can be no question, that the draftsman of the act of 1851 was familiar with the course of legislation and decision in the State upon this subject. This being so, it can hardly be supposed that an *occupant entry* was not to share in the protection afforded by the act. These rights have always been guarded by the Legislature with much care. They included some of the most valuable property in the State, and since the year 1819, at least, it has been unlawful for a general enterer to interfere with them, unless it be during some *hiatus* in the law by which they were secured.

It is obvious, that these considerations are not reckoned by the fact that the plaintiffs, as the heirs of James H. Moran, upon the payment of the fees of office, for the purpose of procuring their grant, on the 22d of October, 1858, caused a second entry to be made of this land. And they are fortified by the fact, that in 1846, the survey then made of this land, recites that it was made for the plaintiffs *as the heirs of James H. Moran, assignee of Littleton Howard, as their occupant claim;* and this survey is recited in the plaintiffs grant. *Kelly* v. *Hare*, 1 Hum., 163, 166.

The provisions of the act of 1851 are extended in the act of 1853 to the 1st of April, 1856; and the protection has been continued by subsequent legislation; so that at no time since the 13th of November, 1851, could said Etheridge have made an entry, or have obtained a grant for this land. The plaintiffs' grant, therefore, in 1854, gave them a perfect legal title, the entry and grant of Etheridge being void. *Kelly* v. *Hare*, 1 Hum., 163, 166; *Patterson et al.* v. *McCutchen et al.*, 5 Hum., 322, 828.

The right of James H. Moran and his heirs to this occupancy, was protected without actual residence, he being the assignee of the original occupant. Act of 1837, ch. 1, secs. 17 and 18.

Neither is there anything in the argument, that James H. Moran had no such interest in this land, as that it could be transmitted by inheritance to his heirs. There can, we apprehend, be no question that so soon as the public lands were relinquished to this State by Congress, the occupant laws, previously enacted, conferred upon those who had complied with their provisions an inheritable interest in the land. *Knox* v. *Thomas*, 5 Hum., 573. It has been decided since that act, in an unreported case, by our predecessors, to be such an *equitable estate* as could be subjected, in equity, to debts. The case of *Brown* v. *Massey*, 3 Hum., 470, arose before the relinquishment. But if this were not so, an inheritable quaikty was imparted to these lands by the act of 1845, ch. 8, sec. 4. And there can be no doubt, as we think, that the plaintiffs stood in the shoes of their ancestor and were as fully secured and protected as he was.

The judgment of the Circuit Court is reversed, and a new trial granted.

JAMES M. TOMLINSON et al. v. WILLIAM DARNALL.

1. PATROLS. *Pleading. What a general replication to a plea justifying an act upon the ground of being a patrol puts in issue.* All matters which confess and avoid, whether alleged by the plaintiff or defendant, must be specially pleaded. Therefore, if a person justify a battery upon a slave upon the ground that he was a patrol, and acting in discharge of his duty, the plaintiff must, if he wishes to rely upon excessive punishment, plead it specially: It is not admissible under a general replication to the plea of the defendant.

James M. Tomlinson *et al* v. William Darnall.

2. SAME. *Public officers. What prima facie evidence of appointment.* Proof that a person has notoriously acted as a public officer, is *prima facie* evidence of his official character, without producing his commission or appointment.

3. SAME. *Same. Pleading. Slave. What replication of excess admits.* If a party justify a trespass upon a slave upon the ground that he was a patrol, and the plaintiff replies that the punishment was excessive, the replication admits the justification as alleged, and precludes the plaintiff from offering any evidence to disprove it.

FROM MADISON.

This cause was heard at the September Term, 1858, before Judge READ. Verdict for the plaintiff. The defendants appealed.

H. E. JACKSON and S. MCLANAHAN, for the plaintiffs in error.

STEPHENS & STEPHENS, for the defendant in error.

CARUTHERS, J., delivered the opinion of the Court.

This action of trespass was brought against the plaintiffs in error to recover damages for an injury done to a slave. The defence relied upon was, that the acts complained of were done in the exercise of the duty of a patrol, by Tomlinson, with the assistance of the others. The slave was found from home without a pass, and attempted to escape, when he was pursued, knocked down, and whipped. The pleas were not guilty, and a special plea setting up the authority of a patrol. The jury found against the pleas, and assessed the damages at

James M. Tomlinson *et al.* *v.* William Darnall.

fifteen dollars. The errors assigned are upon the charge of the Court upon two points:

1. His Honor instructed the jury that they might find the defendants guilty for excessive punishment, although they may have been vested with the authority of a patrol, without a new assignment in the replication to that plea, or under a general replication, as the case was.

2. The Court refused to charge, that proof that Tomlinson was acting as patrol was sufficient, *prima facie*, to entitle him to that defence, without the record evidence of such appointment, but, in substance, held the contrary to be the law, or evaded the question.

On both points we are of opinion his Honor erred.

The plea justifies the act complained of upon the ground that Tomlinson was a patrol. The general replication only puts that fact in issue. If the plaintiff intends to rely upon the fact that the chastisement was so excessive that it was not justified by the authority of the office, that must be put in issue by a special replication, in the nature of a new assignment. 2 Green. Ev., § 634. Unless this is done, there is no notice of the fact to be tried. The pleadings present nothing to be tried but the fact of the defendant's official character; and if that be established, the verdict must be for him, and there is no other matter in issue. If the plaintiff chooses to rely upon excessive punishment, or improper exercise of authority by the defendant, he must make an issue upon that point by a special replication to that effect. This would confess the plea, but avoid its effect as a defence. In the section of 2 Greenleaf, cited above, several pertinent instances are given in illus-

James M. Tomlinson *et al. v.* William Darnall.

tration of this rule. In the preceding section, 633, it is stated as a general rule of pleading, that all matters which confess and avoid, whether alleged by the plaintiff or defendant, must be specially pleaded; otherwise the proof of them is not admissible. We are not aware that this rule has ever been changed.

But on the second point the Court held, that although the question of excessive punishment was raised by the replication, yet the plaintiff could controvert the official capacity of the defendant, as set up in his plea. This is contrary to the authorities, which hold that "the replication of excess admits the justification as alleged, and precludes the plaintiff from offering any evidence to disprove it." 1 Stark. Rep., 56; 4 Camp., 219, cited in § 634, 2 Green. Ev. The two positions in the charge are, therefore, contradictory. One or the other must be erroneous. But they are both wrong as stated by the Court. We understand the law to be well settled, that when the official character of a party comes in question, proof that he has been in the undisturbed exercise of such office, raises a presumption that he has been duly appointed, until the contrary is made to appear by the party contesting it. This is an established exception to the rule that the best evidence of a fact, and none other, is admissible. 1 Green. Ev., §§ 88 and 92; 1 Philips' Ev., 226; 2 Philips', 544, notes. This exception is founded on general convenience, and is universally recognized. Proof, then, that a party has acted notoriously as a public officer, is *prima facie* evidence of his official character, without producing his commission or appointment. His Honor deprived the defendant of the benefit of this rule, by refusing to charge it as requested; but

James M. Tomlinson *et al. v.* William Darnall.

stated that if defendant believed he was a patrol, that should only save him from vindictive damages. This was not meeting the point at all, but virtually evaded it. Yet the effect was a rejection of the instructions requested on that point.

It is of great importance to society that these police regulations connected with the institution of slavery should be firmly maintained. The well being and safety of both master and slave demand it. The institution and support of the night-watch and patrol, on some plan, are indispensable to good order, and the subordination of slaves, and the best interests of their owners. But the authority conferred for these important objects must not be abused by those upon whom it is conferred, as it sometimes is by reckless persons.

In this case we give no opinion upon the conduct of defendants. If they exceeded the bounds of moderation in the injury inflicted, and transcended the limits prescribed by the law for the office of patrol, if it be found that they were entitled to that justification, then they will be liable under a verdict to that effect, on the proper issue to be raised by an amendment of the pleadings.

Judgment reversed.

Caleb Cope & Co. v. E. J. McFarland, Adm'r, &c.

CALEB COPE & CO. v. E. J. MCFARLAND, ADM'R, &c.

1. ADMINISTRATOR AND EXECUTOR. *Devastavit. Scire facias. Debt.* When an administrator or executor has been guilty of a *devastavit* he becomes personally responsible, and his liability may be enforced, either by an action of *debt* on the judgment obtained against him suggesting a *devastavit;* or, by *scire facias,* founded on such judgment, suggesting, in like manner, a *devastavit.*

2. SAME. *Same. Judgment conclusive.* In either form of proceeding on a judgment against an administrator or executor, suggesting a *devastavit,* he will not be allowed to plead any plea which assumes to place his defence merely on the want of assets. The judgment is, in general, conclusive upon him.

3. SCIRE FACIAS. *Administrator and executor. Judgment. What the scire facias must aver.* A scire facias against an administrator or executor, to render him personally liable on a judgment rendered against him in his representative character, must allege a *devastavit*; and, also, the fact of a judgment obtained against him in his character of executor or administrator; for a *scire facias* will not lie on a judgment against him individually, or against his testator or intestate.

FROM HAYWOOD.

This cause was heard upon demurrer to the *scire facias,* before W. H. LOVING, S. J., at the July Term, 1858. The demurrer was allowed, and the plaintiff appealed.

E. J. READ, for the plaintiff.

T. G. & W. M. SMITH, for the defendant.

MCKINNEY, J., delivered the opinion of the Court.

Caleb Cope & Co. *v.* E. J. McFarland, Adm'r, &c.

The demurrer to the *scire facias* was properly sustained. Where an executor or administrator has been guilty of a *devastavit*, that is, a wasting or misapplying of the assets, contrary to the duty imposed on him by law, he becomes personally responsible; and his liability may be enforced either by an action of debt, on the judgment obtained against such executor or administrator, suggesting a *devastavit*, or, as is the usual course in our practice, by *scire facias* founded on such judgment, suggesting, in like manner, a *devastavit*. Whichever mode of proceeding is adopted, the averments and proof are the same, and the defence is also the same; in both, a *devastavit* must be distinctly averred and proved. The foundation of this proceeding, in either form, is the judgment obtained against the executor or administrator. And if he has allowed judgment to go against him, without pleading *plene administrarit*, or want of assets, such judgment will, in general, be conclusive upon him to show that he has assets to satisfy the judgment. So that, in an action of debt, or *scire facias*, on such judgment, suggesting a *devastavit*, he will not be allowed to plead any plea which assumes to place his defence merely on the want of assets, for such plea would be contrary to what is impliedly admitted by the judgment against him.

The *scire facias* in the present case does not sufficiently allege a *devastavit*. The statement that the defendant "converted to his own use" the assets of the estate, is not of itself sufficient; it is not equivalent to a charge of a *devastavit*. On the contrary, the authorities fully establish that a disposing of the goods of the testator to the executor's own use, is no *devastavit*, if he pays the testator's debts, to their value, with his own money. 1 Saund., 307; 1 Williams on Ex'rs, 543; Com. Dig. Admin., (J. 2.) Another objection to the *scire facias* is, that it does not distinctly allege the fact of a judgment obtained against the defendant, as administrator of the intestate. This is indispensably necessary, for no action of debt, or *scire facias*, founded on a *devastavit* by the executor or administrator, will lie against him upon a judgment obtained against his testator or intestate; at least, not until after the executor or administrator shall have been made a party to such judgment. 2 Williams on Ex'rs, 1700. Neither can this proceeding, in either form, be supported against the executor or administrator upon a judgment against the latter in his individual, and not in his representative, capacity. Id., 1699, note 1.

Upon the foregoing grounds, without noticing other informalities in the *scire facias*, the judgment must be affirmed.

WILLIAM MOORE *v.* SAMUEL C. SIMMONS *et al.*

CONSTRUCTION OF WRITINGS. *Deed. Made to separate use of wife and children.* Property was conveyed, by deed, to trustees, to be sold and divided "in equal shares between Elizabeth Frierson, Solomon H. Shaw, *Sally Simmons,* Clara Brown, and Caty Grady's children ; that portion that may belong to *Sally Simmons,* and the children of Emily Shaw and Caty Grady, (the two last being dead, leaving children,) to be held by said trustees in trust, for the only proper use, benefit, and

William Moore *v.* Samuel C Simmons *et al.*

behoof of the said *Sally Simmons and her children*, and the children of Caty Grady and Emily Shaw, not to be subject to the control or debts of any other person, either their husbands or otherwise, the same being intended to be held in trust by said trustees, for the use and benefit of the said last-named children of the said Simpson Shaw, and their heirs." *Held* that the children of Sally Simmons are not vested with an equal interest with the mother, as joint owners. That it was the intention of the donor to give the entire estate to the daughter, to her separate use, by which she would be enabled to support herself and children, as a family, and the children take no interest that can be reached by their creditors.

FROM GIBSON.

At the December Term, 1858, Chancellor WILLIAMS dismissed the bill. The complainant appealed.

T. J. & J. T. CARTHEL, and WILLIAMS, for the complainant.

HILL, for the defendants.

CARUTHERS, J., delivered the opinion of the Court.

This case turns upon the construction of a deed of gift made by Simpson Shaw to *his* children, in 1842.

The complainant, is a judgment creditor of Samuel C., who is a son of Sally Simmons, one of the daughters of Simpson Shaw. This bill is filed to reach a supposed interest of said Samuel C., under said deed of gift; and the question is, whether, by a proper construction of it, he has any interest which can be subjected to his debts by his creditors? The Chancellor thought not, and the case is brought up by complainant to reverse his decree.

The property, consisting of land, a number of slaves, and other personal property, is conveyed by the deed to Solomon Shaw and John M. Frierson, as trustees, to pay all his debts; a portion of it for his wife for life, and at her death to be sold, and the proceeds, together with the balance of the property *in presenti*, to be divided "in equal shares between Elizabeth Frierson, Solomon H. Shaw, *Sally Simmons*, Clara Brown, and Caty Grady's children; that portion that may belong to *Sally Simmons*, and the children of Emily Shaw and Caty Grady, (the two last being dead, leaving children,) to be held by said trustees in trust, for the only proper use, benefit, and behoof of the said *Sally Simmons and her children*, and the said children of Caty Grady and Emily Shaw, not to be subject to the control or debts of any other person, either their husbands or otherwise, the same being intended to be held in trust by said trustees for the use and benefit of the said last-named children of the said Simpson Shaw, *and their heirs.*"

In the first clause the gift of the use is to his daughter, Sally Simmons, and in the last it is to her *and her heirs.* Both these clauses give to her the sole and entire right. But in the same section, where he aims to protect the property from the husband, and settle it to her separate use, he employs the words, "to the use and benefit of the said Sally Simmons *and her children.*"

Upon this clause the argument is based that the three children she then had, of whom the said Samuel C., complainant's debtor, is the oldest, were vested with an

William Moore v. Samuel C. Simmons *et al.*

equal interest with the mother, as joint owners. We think this construction, though plausible, cannot be maintained. Taking the whole instrument together, and in view of the considerations by which it was prompted, we entertain no doubt but that the intention was to give the entire estate to the daughter, to her separate use, by which she would be enabled to support herself and children, as a family. If that were not so, but a joint interest was vested in the children, the object intended could be defeated by any creditor of the children, as is now attempted. If he intended to give the property to the latter, would he not have protected it in them, as he did that of their mother, against creditors? Surely the same reason existed for doing so. Another absurd consequence, subversive of the apparent intention, would result from that construction. If any interest passed to the children, it must be a present one, and, as such, might be demanded by a guardian, or by any child on coming of age or marrying, with an account perhaps, and thus defeat the prominent object of keeping all together for the support of the family, as a unit.

Again: why are not the children coupled with the mother in the first and last clauses, where the estate is measured and given, if they were intended to have any title to the donation? The true intention, and palpable construction is, that the property was given to the daughter alone, protected from the control of her husband, and all others, to enable her to support herself and children, as members of her family. This advantage the children would perhaps have a right, under the deed, to enforce, if withheld, so long as they might constitute a part of the family.

W. M. Henry *et al. v.* J. B. Compton *et al.*

The children, then, have no rights by virtue of the deed, which can be reached by their creditors, and the bill was properly dismissed.

The decree will be affirmed.

W. M. HENRY *et al. v.* J. B. COMPTON *et al.*

1. SURETIES. *Entitled to substitution before payment of the debt.* Sureties are entitled to the benefit of all securities which the creditor obtains against the principal debtor; and this is so, whether the debt has been paid by the surety, or not, if the principal has become insolvent.[*]

2. SAME. *Same. Case in judgment.* A slave was sold under a decree of court, which decree retained a lien on the slave for the payment of the purchase money. The purchaser gave bond and security for the price. He became insolvent, and the slave was levied on by his creditors. The surety of the purchaser, not having paid the debt, filed a bill to enjoin the sale of the slave by the creditors, and to be *substituted* to the *lien* retained by the decree. It is held that the surety is entitled to the relief asked for.

FROM MADISON.

The bill was dismissed upon demurrer by Chancellor WILLIAMS, at the August Term, 1858. The complainants appealed.

---

[*] There is an apparent conflict between this and the case of *Gilliam* v. *Esselman*, 5 Sneed, 86; but it will be seen that the question, as to the *solvency* of the principal, was not, as in this, raised in that case.

W. M. Henry et. al. v. J. B. Compton et al.

HAYES & MORRILL, for the complainants.

M. & H. BROWN, for the defendants.

CARUTHERS, J., delivered the opinion of the Court.

This case comes up by an appeal from a decree of the Chancellor, sustaining a demurrer to the bill.

The object of the bill is to protect a slave, for the price of which the complainants are sureties, from execution creditors of the purchaser, upon the ground that by the decree of the court under which he was sold, a lien was reserved, and the purchaser has become insolvent without discharging the note for the consideration.

The facts, as stated in the bill, are, that at the March Term, 1855, of the Chancery Court for Madison county, a decree was made upon the petition of Thomas Ingram, as administrator of John Ingram, deceased, against the distributees, to sell, among other property, a negro woman named Susan, who was struck off to defendant, Drake, at $501, for which he executed his note at twelve months credit, with the complainants as his sureties; that a lien was retained by the decree upon the slave for the payment of the purchase money: that the note has not been paid, and that, although the sale was confirmed at February Term, 1857, yet no title has yet been vested, by decree, in the purchaser, Drake. That Drake is utterly insolvent, and they will have the money to pay, unless the slave is held liable under the lien reserved. It is further stated that defendant, Compton, who is a constable of Madison county, has levied sundry executions, in his hands against Drake, upon the slave, Susan, and has taken possession of her, and appointed a day for her sale by public advertisement. The prayer is for the sale of the slave for the payment of the note in which they are bound as sureties, and for an injunction and attachment.

There would be no doubt but that this bill would be entertained, if the complainants had paid up the purchase money, and thereby raised an equity to be substituted to the rights of the creditor, (*McNairy* v. *Eastland*, 10 Yer., 310; Meigs, 172; 1 Story's Eq., 502,) and just as little that no such right would exist, even if the money had been paid by them, but for the lien retained in the decree. But the question here is, whether, when the money has not been paid by the sureties, they can claim the benefit of the lien reserved. We have no decision upon this precise point, and can only be guided by principle. The vendor has no lien upon slaves, or other personalty, as upon land, for the security of the purchase money. When the sale is made, either by the owner himself, or by a Court, the right to the property passes, unincumbered, to the purchaser. It can only be held liable for the consideration, in the former case, by express contract, by mortgage, or reservation of the title; or in the latter, by a provision in the decree. This last mode is in the nature of, and equivalent to, the former. It binds the property, and limits the rights and power of the vendee over it, until the price is paid, for the benefit and security of the vendor. But the question here is, have the sureties of the vendee a right to enforce or compel an observance of that lien for their benefit; or, in other words, to be substituted to the rights of the creditor in regard to the property before they have discharged the debt.

The case of *Green* v. *Crockett*, 2 Dev. and Bat., 390, is upon this doctrine, and commends itself to our approval by its reason and justice. The rule in equity, which has ripened into a maxim, that sureties are entitled to the benefit of all securities which the creditor obtains against the principal debtor, is there extended to a case where the debt has not been paid, but the principal has become insolvent. That was a case of land sold under a decree of Court where the title was retained until the purchase money should be paid. It is there held, that, as the principal debtor had become insolvent, the sureties, by virtue of their liability to suffer, had "a right, before paying the debt, to file their bill to restrain the conveyance of the land, and have it applied to their relief." *Bunting* v. *Ricks*, in the same volume, page 130, and *Williams* v. *Helme*, 1 Dev. Eq., 151, are cited as accordant decisions.

Without looking further, we approve the principle of these cases, and adopt it. There can be no difference in the equity of the sureties, between a case of real estate and that of slaves with a lien, or the title expressly reserved by the decree for the sale.

The property is bound for the debt to the creditor, and when the principal debtor, or purchaser, becomes insolvent, his sureties have an interest in it, so far as to be authorized to compel its application to their discharge and exoneration, in preference to the general creditors of their principal, or purchasers from him.

We think, then, upon these principles, that the bill should have been entertained, and the prayer granted. The decree sustaining the demurrer will be reversed, and the case rem.nded for answers.

W. E. CATHAM *v.* THE STATE.

ESCHEATS. *What necessary to establish an escheat.* To entitle the State to recover lands alleged to have escheated, it must appear that the owners were *foreigners*, that they died without *issue*, and left no relations within the United States entitled, by law, to succeed to said land. If there is an omission to prove these facts, a verdict in favor of the State will be set aside, and a new trial granted.

FROM PERRY.

This cause was tried at the June Term, 1858, before Judge WALKER. Verdict and judgment for the State. The defendant appealed.

DOHERTY and HUBBARD, for the plaintiff in error.

SNEED, Attorney General, and MAXWELL, for the State.

McKINNEY, J., delivered the opinion of the Court.

W. E. Catham *v.* The State.

This was an action of ejectment to recover a tract of land in Perry county, supposed to have escheated, by reason of the want of heirs, on the part of the person last seized, capable of inheriting. Verdict and judgment were for the plaintiff, and the defendant brought the case to this court.

The evidence, as presented in the record before us, fails to make out a case entitling the plaintiff to a recovery. It appears that the land was conveyed to D'Entraigne and wife, jointly, on the 13th of October, 1852. The proof shows that D'Entraigne, the husband, died in 1853, and his wife in 1854; "and that they were *foreigners;*" whether or not they left *issue*, is not stated in the bill of exceptions. Neither is it shown, whether or not they left any relations within the United States entitled, by law, to succeed to said land under the provisions of the act of 1848, ch. 165, sec. 4; or, 1852, ch. 128, sec. 2.

For this omission in the proof, the verdict cannot be maintained. On the return of the case to the Circuit Court, the first count of the declaration will be struck out. It is repugnant and absurd, to lay a demise in the names of persons as *heirs* of the person last seized, when the action is brought upon the assumption that the land escheated *for want of such heirs.*

From the fact proved, that the parties were "foreigners," the legal presumption in the absence of all evidence would perhaps be, that they were *unnaturalized*. But from the mere fact that D'Entraigne and wife were unnaturalized foreigners, it cannot be presumed that they died without issue, or without any relative entitled, by the provisions of the before recited acts, to succeed to said land.

For this failure in the proof, the judgment must be reversed, and the case remanded for a new trial.

D. M. TUCKER AND N. OAKS v. THE STATE.

CRIMINAL LAW. *Costs. How taxed when the defendant is acquitted.* Code, § 5581. If the defendant, in a State prosecution, is tried for a public offence, and acquitted on the merits, his costs cannot be taxed to, and paid by the State. The State, or the county, according to the nature of the offence, pays, only, the costs accrued on behalf of the State in the cases specified in § 5585 of the Code.*

FROM GIBSON.

The court below, WILLIAMS, J. presiding, refused to tax the witness fees of Oaks, a witness summoned by Tucker, who was tried and acquitted, to the State. Tucker and Oaks appealed.

M. R. HILL and R. P. RAINS, for the appellant.

SNEED, Attorney-General, for the State.

---

*By the act of 1860, ch. 76, § 1, any person tried and acquitted of a public offence, shall be liable for his own costs, unless the court trying such person shall adjudge the same against the prosecutor, State, or county. And the court is empowered to so adjudge it. Acts of 1859–60, page 57.

D. M. Tucker and N. Oaks v. The State.

WRIGHT, J., delivered the opinion of the Court.

This is a motion to retax costs.

Tucker was indicted for murder, and, upon the plea of not guilty, was acquitted upon the merits of the case at the July Term, 1858, of the Circuit Court of Gibson county.

Upon the trial, Oaks was examined as a witness for the defendant, having been summoned for him. His fees amounted to $25.00; and the clerk having taxed them against the defendant, he and Oaks moved that they be taxed against the State, which the Circuit Court refused to do.

This judgment of the Circuit Court was, we think, correct. It is an established principle of the common law, that costs are not to be recovered by the prisoner from the government. This principle hath always prevailed in this State. Even a statute which directs the county or State to pay costs, is to be expounded as limited to the costs of the prosecution, unless a further intention be shown to embrace the costs of the defendant. The State cannot be taxed with the prisoner's costs by implication or conjecture. To do so, the intention must be clear. *State* v. *Barton*, 3 Hum., 13; *Prince* v. *The State*, 7 Hum., 137.

There is nothing in section 5581 of the Code, nor in any other section of that or the subsequent article, which changes this principle. It is true, that sections 5581 and 5582 do provide that any person tried for a public offence, and acquitted on the merits, shall pay no costs; and that in all other cases, the defendant shall pay the costs of witnesses summoned by him. And by section 5583, if the defendant is convicted of a criminal offence, he shall pay all the costs which have accrued in the cause.

It may not be very clear, from these sections taken alone, whether it was meant that where a person was tried for a public offence and acquitted on the merits, no *judgment* shall go against him for his own costs, leaving the parties to their remedies at common law; or whether judgment shall be rendered against the State or county for the same; or whether they shall remain unpaid altogether.

We are now only to decide as to the liability of the State. And section 5585 of the Code, and subsequent sections of that and the next article plainly show that the common law principle remains unchanged.

There is not only an entire absence of any provision to charge the State, but it is obvious no such thing was intended.

To demonstrate this, we need only refer to section 5585, which provides that the State or county, according to the nature of the offence, pays the *costs accrued on behalf* of the State in the following cases:

1. When the defendant is acquitted by the verdict of the jury upon the merits.

2. When the prosecution is dismissed, or a *nolle prosequi* entered by the State.

3. When the action has abated by the death of the defendant.

4. When the defendant is discharged by the Court or magistrate before indictment preferred or found, or after indictment and before verdict.

5. When the defendant has been convicted, but the

execution issued upon the judgment has been returned "*nulla bona.*"

This legislation, and indeed the entire legislation of these two articles of the Code, when all the sections are considered, are at war with the idea that the State is to be taxed with the defendant's costs.

We are bound to suppose the doctrine so well established in 3 and 7 Humphreys, was familiar to the Legislature. If so, and the State was to be made liable to the defendant's costs, how easy to have so said in express terms.

The judgment of the Circuit Court will be affirmed.

J. M. RELFE & Co. *et al.* v. DAVID McCOMB *et al.*

LIEN. *Judgment. Priority of, when several have been rendered.* If several judgments are rendered against a party at different terms of the Court, and he, thereafter, acquires the legal title to real estate, the *liens* of the several judgments attach, together, upon the property, at the same instant; and all stand upon the same footing, as respects the proceeds of the sale of the same.

FROM MEMPHIS.

This was an agreed case in the Court below. At the July Term, 1858, CARUTHERS, J., presiding, judgment was rendered in favor of the parties according to the priority of their respective judgments. Relfe & Co., appealed.

· J. M. Relfe & Co. *et al.* v. David McComb *et al.*

AYRES, YERGER, and ELDRIDGE, for the plaintiffs in error.

J. G. FINNIE, for the defendant in error.

McKINNEY, J., delivered the opinion of the Court.

This was an agreed case, made in the Court below. The facts are these:

The plaintiffs are the separate judgment creditors of the defendant, McComb.

The judgments were all rendered in the Common Law Court of the City of Memphis, but at different terms of the Court. The judgment of Johnson was obtained at the March Term, 1857, for $364.

The judgment of Roberson & Dennett, for $1199.24, and also the judgment of Macy & Sons, for $902.30, were obtained at the November Term, 1857.

And the judgment of Relfe & Co., for $269.87, and the judgment of Greenwood, for $649.80, were obtained at the March Term, 1858.

At the respective dates of these several judgments, the defendant, McComb, it seems, had no property subject to execution at law. He was the owner, however, of an equitable interest in certain real property, which, prior to the rendition of any of said judgments, had been conveyed by deed of trust for the benefit of other creditors. And on the 25th of April, 1858, he procured a re-conveyance to himself of the legal title to said real property. Immediately thereafter executions upon the several judgments before mentioned, all tested of the same

J. M. Relfe & Co. et al. v. David McComb et al.

term—March Term, 1858—were issued and levied on said real property; and the same was sold by the sheriff, on the 26th of June, 1858, for the sum of $1360.54.

This fund being inadequate to the satisfaction of all the above mentioned judgments, the question is, how shall it be applied?

It was held by the Circuit Judge that the creditors were entitled to the fund according to the priority of their respective judgments.

This was not the correct principle. No lien upon the property existed at law in favor of either creditor previous to the re-conveyance of the legal title, on the 25th of April, 1858. And the moment the legal title was re-invested in McComb, the liens of the several judgments attached, together, upon the property, at the same instant. This being so, no priority of satisfaction can be claimed by either over the others; all stand upon exactly the same footing, as respects the proceeds of the sale of said property; and the plain principle of reason, and of law, in such case, is, that the fund shall be distributed amongst them all *pari pasu*. Neither is entitled to any preference; and it is ordered accordingly. 2 Sneed, 665.

Judgment reversed.

WILLIAM A. SWAILS *et al.* *v.* JOHN BUSHART.

CONSTRUCTION OF WRITINGS. *What requisite to constitute a deed.* A deed must take effect *in præsenti*, but this may be so without the present enjoyment or possession passing, either in fact, or in right. It is sufficient if a vested right to the present or future enjoyment passes. But it must be a right to some specific thing *then* owned by the person executing the conveyance; and the conveyee designated in the instrument. An instrument possessing these requisites, and wanting nothing in form, substance, or legal ceremonies to give it effect, as a title, *in presenti*, is a deed, and not a testamentary paper.

FROM HENRY.

This cause was heard by his Honor, Judge FITZGERALD, sitting as Chancellor, at the March Term, 1859. A decree was pronounced for the complainants. The defendant appealed.

WILLIAMS & GREER, for the complainants.

A. MCAMPBELL, for the defendant.

CARUTHERS, J., delivered the opinion of the Court.

Richard Forrest, on the 20th of February, 1837, executed an instrument under seal, in the following words:
"Know all men by these presents: that I, Richard Forrest, of Pike county, for and in consideration of my natural love and affection, * * * * * * * do, for myself, my heirs, executors, administrators and assigns, give, * * * * * sell and deliver, * * * *

William A. Swails et al. v. John Bushart.

* * * unto my daughter, Elizabeth Shelling, and Mathew B. Forrest, my son, to their heirs and assigns forever, *after my death*, the following described property, viz: To my daughter, Elizabeth Shelling, my negro boy named Aaron, and negro girl named Mariah, with all their increase. To my son Mathew B., my negro boy Daniel, and girl Rose; upon this condition, that the said Elizabeth and Mathew B., or their heirs and assigns pay, or cause to be paid to my daughter Mary Ann, at my death, the sum of $250, each; * * * * * * and then to have and to hold said negroes, * * * * * * to them, their heirs and assigns forever. In testimony hereof, I have this 20th February, 1837, set my hand and seal."

This was, on the same day, duly acknowledged for registration in Pike county, Mississippi; and on that day endorsed, as "received for record," by the proper officer.

Whether this is to be regarded as a deed, or testamentary paper, is the question upon which the case turns. The Chancellor held it was not testamentary, but took effect as a deed to pass the title at the date, subject to the reserved life estate. We are unable to perceive any difference in principle between this case and that of *Caines and wife* v. *Marley*, 2 Yer., 582, and *Walls* v. *Ward*, 2 Swan, 653.

It is true, that in both those cases there was an *express* reservation of a life estate, or possession for life; but in this it is only reserved by implication, and also with a condition, or rather an incumbrance attached. The conveyance here is formal and complete, but it is to operate upon the use and possession only after his death. The clause in the case of Walls was, "to take effect after the termination of my natural life; I retaining the property of said slaves during my life." Here the conveyance is to his daughter "*after my death.*" There can be no difference between them in this respect. In both cases the plain meaning is, that the title is passed, subject to the enjoyment of the donor while he lives. That is rendered just as certain and distinct by the words here employed, as it was by the express reservation in the case of Walls, or that of Marley. If this be so, the same construction must be given as to the question of *will* or *deed*, so far as that point is concerned.

The condition in this case annexed to the gift, that the donee should pay at the death of the donor, $250 to another daughter, cannot affect the question. The failure to do that would not make the conveyance void, but would be an incumbrance or lien upon the property. We cannot see how this fact can have any effect upon the question in hand. Whether a deed or testament, its force and effect would be the same as to that incumbrance.

It is true, that a will is a disposition of property, to take effect after the death, as argued; but that definition of a will does not exclude the conclusion that a deed may be the same in effect in that particular. The former is necessarily so, but not the latter. This assumed criterion, then, cannot aid us much in reaching a conclusion. It is true, that a deed must take effect *in præsenti*, but this may be so without th epresent ment or possession passing either in fact or n right. If a vested right to the present *or futur* enjoyment passes, that will do to make the paper a d. But

William A. Swails *et al. v.* John Bushart.

must be a right to some specific thing *then* owned by the donor, and to a designated person. Not as in the case of *Watkins* v. *Dean*, 10 Yer., 827, where the instrument conveyed one-half of the estate he might own at his death; nor like the case of *Taylor* v. *Taylor*, 2 Hum., 597, where the paper, though in the form of a deed, had never been delivered, so as to give it vitality as such, although it specified the property.

The paper in this case, as in that of Walls, was acknowledged by the donor and placed on the records. It lacked nothing in form, substance, or legal ceremonies to give it complete effect as a title to the remainder in this slave, *in præsenti;* and therefore it is a deed, and not a will, which might be revoked, and if not, would require probate to give it effect as a title. There was then nothing remaining in him but the life estate reserved, and that, alone, passed to his son Armistead, the testator of defendant, by the absolute bill of sale made to him by Richard, after the execution of the former deed.

The result is, that the paper was not testamentary, but a valid deed, and sustains the title of complainant to the slave, with the right to possession at the death of the donor.

The decree of the Chancellor is, therefore, right, and must be affirmed.

ROBERT H. TAYLOR et al. v. E. R. JONES.

CIRCUIT COURT. *Charge to the jury.* The verdict of a jury will not be set aside if there is any proof to sustain it; and the jury should be left to the free and fair exercise of their judgment, and not subjected to threats or coercion to induce them to surrender their honest convictions. Hence, it is error in the Circuit Judge for which a new trial will be granted, to say to the jury that he must keep them together until they can agree, and that it would be better for them to find a wrong verdict than not to agree at all, as any error that might be committed could be corrected by the Supreme Court.

FROM HAYWOOD.

Verdict and judgment for the plaintiff, at the September Term, 1858, READ, J., presiding. The defendants appealed.

T. G. & W. M. SMITH, and STEPHENS, for the plaintiffs in error.

CAMPBELL & LEA, SCURLOCK, and E. J. READ, for the defendant in error.

CARUTHERS, J., delivered the opinion of the Court.

We are constrained to reverse the judgment in this case, without looking into the merits or examining the legal questions presented, upon the single ground that the verdict was obtained under circumstances that it

Robert H. Taylor *et al. v.* E. R. Jones.

cannot be permitted to stand even if no other errors existed. The matter is thus stated in the bill of exceptions:

"The jury were charged by the Court on Thursday morning. After they had been out some time, they returned and reported they could not agree. The Court, after giving them some instructions, went on to tell them of the importance of their agreeing, and of the expense to the parties of prolonged litigation. The Court also told them that he must keep them together until they could agree, telling them that he could remain here until the fourth Monday in next month, as he had no other court till then. The Court also made the following remark to them: 'There are some cases in which I have been sometimes, in case of hung juries, almost constrained to tell the jury that it would be *better for them to find a wrong verdict than not to agree at all*, as any error *we* may commit may be corrected by the Supreme Court.' The Court also told them they must be governed by the law and the facts of the case."

We would not for a moment suppose that his Honor intended these suggestions to have any improper effect upon the jury, but doubt not that they were prompted by an anxious desire to terminate in his Court a troublesome and expensive suit, and avoid a mis-trial. Yet the effect of such remarks from so high a source were well calculated to mislead them as to the proper grounds and considerations upon which they should found their verdict and settle the rights of the parties. The danger that such would be the effect, whether it was so or not, would be sufficient to vitiate the verdict. Some of them state in their affidavits, filed on the motion for a new trial, that they were influenced by these suggestions from the Court to surrender their opinions and concur in the verdict.

The almost conclusive effect given by the law to the finding of juries, as settled in various adjudications in this Court, upon questions of fact, renders it indispensably necessary that they should be properly instructed in the law, and placed under no improper influence; or in any way misguided in coming to correct conclusions. With all possible precautions on the part of the Circuit Judge, we have sometimes seen that they find against the preponderance of evidence. This we cannot correct, if there be any evidence to sustain them. It was, therefore, a mistake in his Honor to tell them, as he did, that this Court could correct any errors *they* might commit.

It was also calculated, perhaps, to have an undue influence upon them to threaten to keep them confined after the business of the Court was over, and until it would be necessary to hold another Court, some weeks off. It is the duty of a jury to make every possible effort to agree upon a verdict, and not improper in the Court to urge them to do so, that the litigation may be speedily terminated, and the ruinous expense of mis-trials avoided. But these considerations should not influence them to violate their consciences by uniting in a verdict believed by them, upon the law and facts, to be wrong. The harsh and unreasonable, if not cruel, treatment of juries once tolerated in England, to force their consciences and judgments, and coerce a concurrence in a verdict, has long since been condemned and repudiated there and here. They should be left to the free and fair exercise of their judgments, and not subjected to threats or coercion to induce them to surrender their honest judgments.

Let the judgment be reversed, and a new trial granted.

W. S. WELLS v. W. L. GRIFFIN & Co.

1. EXECUTION. *When it may be collaterally attacked.* An execution cannot be attacked, collaterally, except by showing a total want of jurisdiction to render the judgment upon which the execution issued, so as to make it void. It cannot be done for mere errors that may exist in the proceedings and judgment, which do not render the judgment void.

2. SURETY. *Bound by the litigation of his principal.* A surety in a replevin bond is bound by the result of the litigation with his principal. And, if the Court had jurisdiction of the subject matter and of the parties, he is bound by the orders and judgment.

3. SAME. *Judgment. Form of.* A judgment "that the plaintiff recover of the defendant and of William S. Wells, the security on the replevin bond, the said sum of $1427.28, the damages so by the jury aforesaid assessed, and the costs of the suit, and that execution issue, to be levied of the proper goods and chattels, rights and credits of the said intestate, in the hands of the said administrator to be administered," is, in legal effect, a judgment against Wells in his own right and against the administrator in his representative character.

FROM MEMPHIS.

A motion was made by Wells, at the July Term, 1858, CARUTHERS, J., presiding, to quash an execution issued against him as surety in a replevin bond. The motion was disallowed, and Wells appealed.

W. S. Wells v. W. L. Griffin & Co.

HAYES & TURNAGE, for the plaintiff in error.

W. T. SWAYNE and B. M. ESTIS, for the defendants in error.

WRIGHT, J., delivered the opinion of the Court.

There is no error in this judgment.

It is an attempt, on the part of Wells, to attack, collaterally, an execution issued against him from the Common Law Court of Memphis. This cannot be done for mere errors, if they exist, in the judgment and proceedings of that Court. It can only be done by showing a total want of jurisdiction, to render the judgment upon which the execution issued, so as to make it void. No such thing can be shown here.

W. L. Griffin & Co., caused the property of one Horsely, their debtor, to be attached, by proceedings, returnable to the Common Law Court of Memphis, and Wells became his surety in a replevin bond, taken by the sheriff and filed in the cause. Horsely, afterwards, died, and the suit was revived against Bettis, his administrator.

At the November Term, 1857, of said Court, the plaintiffs recovered judgment in said cause against Bettis, the administrator of Horsely, and Wells, the surety in the replevin bond. He does not appeal, or in any way complain of the judgment, though, we apprehend, he had a perfect right to do so, if he had deemed it assailable, but lies by until June, 1858, when his property is levied on, and he executes a delivery bond, and, at the July Term of the Court, in 1858, moves to quash the execution, upon the ground that the judgment, as to him, was void; and, also, upon the ground that the form of the entry of the judgment upon the records of the Court, did not warrant any execution against him. This motion was overruled, and he has appealed to this Court.

A reversal is asked here upon two grounds:

1. The record shows that the writ of attachment, affidavit, attachment bond, and the replevy bond, with the sheriff's levy, were lost or mislaid during the pendency of the suit, and copies were supplied, and substituted, by order of the Court, upon the affidavit of one of the plaintiffs, of their attorney, of Horne, the justice who issued the attachment, and of Gilmore, the sheriff. This affidavit seems to be regular, save that it is not authenticated by the clerk before whom it was made. But the parties, by their counsel, in a writing signed and filed in the cause, agree that an order of Court may be made in the suit, supplying the lost papers, and that the affidavit be taken as sufficient to authorize said order, without more.

Upon this the order was made; and it is now said that this agreement being between the plaintiffs and Horsely, and not with Wells, his surety, he is not bound by it, and that it renders all subsequent proceedings void, as to him.

This position cannot be maintained. He, as surety, must be held bound by the result of the litigation with his principal. The Court had jurisdiction of the subject matter and the parties; and an order supplying lost papers upon insufficient or improper evidence, could not displace that jurisdiction. It could, at most, only be error. But in this case we are satisfied that it was not even error. So far from exception being taken to it, it was agreed to.

The next objection is to the form of the judgment. It reads "that the plaintiffs' recover of the defendant, and of William S. Wells, the surety on the replevin bond, the said sum of $1427.23, the damages so by the jury aforesaid assessed, and the costs of the suit, and that execution issue, to be levied of the proper goods and chattels, rights and credits of the said intestate, in the hands of the said admistrator to be administered."

This is, in legal effect, a judgment against Wells in his own right, and against Bettis in his representative character. It may not be after the most approved precedents, and scarcely any entries of judgments now are. But we cannot, even if the parties had appealed, notice such an objection; and surely Wells cannot, collaterally, do so. 5 Hum., 318, 315, 319.

Judgment affirmed.

SAMUEL ELROD *et al.* v. SAMUEL LANCASTER.

1. ADMINISTRATION. *Settlement of executor, effect of. Infants.* Settlements made by an executor or administrator, if the legatees or distributees are infants, are not in the nature of settled or stated accounts, so as to require them to surcharge and falsify the same before they can be opened. Such settlements are only *prima facie* correct, and may be opened for a general account. They are, however, *prima facie* evidence for the executor or administrator in taking the general account·

Samuel Elrod et al. v. Samuel Lancaster.

2. SAME. *Same. Same. When a decree between defendants conclusive.* A decree between defendants will be conclusive and binding upon them where an antagonism exists, so as to make them actors against each other; but if a part of the defendants are minors, and have no regular guardian, and a person is appointed guardian *ad litem* for them, who is a defendant, and whose interest in the suit is in conflict with theirs, the decree pronounced in the cause will not bar a subsequent suit by said minors against said defendant.

3. SALE OF REAL ESTATE. *Guardian. Parties. Form of the petition.* In a proceeding for a sale of the real estate of minors, it is immaterial whether the petition is filed in the name of the guardian, for the minors, naming them, or in the names of the minors, by their guardian. If all the other steps taken are regular, the fact that the petition is filed in the name of the guardian, for his wards, will not vitiate the sale.

4. SAME. *Same. When guardian may purchase.* In sales of the real estate of infants, made by a Court of competent jurisdiction, the guardian of the infants may purchase, if he act fairly, with the utmost good faith, and the transaction is free from any imputation of design on his part to gain a benefit to himself, to the prejudice of the interests of his wards. Yet his conduct will be watched with jealousy.

FROM MADISON.

A decree was pronounced at the December Term, 1858, by Chancellor WILLIAMS, in favor of the complainants. The defendants appealed.

M. & H. BROWN, for the complainants.

STEPHENS & STEPHENS, for the defendants.

CARUTHERS, J., delivered the opinion of the Court.

The father of complainants died in Jackson, in 1839, leaving a will, with defendant his executor, and a large estate. The will was proved and executed by the defendant. The deceased had been a merchant for a number of years, and had succeeded in accumulating an estate of fifty or sixty thousand dollars. The most of his fortune consisted in money and choses in action, and the settlement of the business was, necessarily, slow and troublesome. There were a vast number of small debts, and the ultimate loss by insolvencies was very great, probably thirty or forty thousand dollars. The testator left a wife and six children, all of whom were then, and four of them yet, under age. The widow married Barr, and, on the 24th of January, 1845, they filed their bill in the Chancery Court against the executors and the children, the latter all then being minors, for the settlement of the estate, so far as to obtain the part to which they were entitled under the will, which was one equal seventh in the event of marriage. In that suit an account of the estate was taken, and the part of the complainants paid over, and the balance retained by the executor in his new character of guardian, which he assumed at the request of the mother of the children soon after the decree. After that he made his reports and settlements, as guardian, in the County Court.

In 1850, certain real estate was sold upon the petition of Lancaster and Lyon, who had then become guardians of the oldest son. Some, and perhaps most of the property, was bought by one or other of the guardians. This bill was filed on the 3d of March, 1854, for two main objects:

1. To have a general account and settlement of the estate, both as executor and guardian, against Lancaster, charging various specific abuses of his trust.

Samuel Elrod *et al.* *v.* Samuel Lancaster.

2. To set aside the sale of the lots in Jackson, and recover them back, with rents.

As to the first ground, in addition to the general and specific denial of the charges, the defendant relies upon the settlement and decree in the Chancery suit of 1845, as a bar to this bill, so far as it seeks to re-open his accounts as executor. We are not prepared, under the circumstances, to give it that effect, except as to Barr and wife. The other complainants were all infants, and the object of the proceeding was not to assign to them their parts of the estate, but only to obtain the one-seventh of the complainants, and leave that of the minors where it was. A settlement of the whole administration was only necessary for that purpose. It is true that a decree between defendants will be conclusive under certain circumstances and in proper cases, where an antagonism exists between them, so as to make them actors against each other. But we do not regard this as such a case. Against all the rules of propriety, the executor was appointed to act as guardian *ad litem* for the infants, they having no general guardian at that time. Their interests and his were directly in conflict, and the substance of it was that he assumed to act for them against himself. The fact that his appointment was recommended in the bill can make no difference. It all seems to have been a hurried proceeding, got up by himself. The bill was filed on the 24th of January, 1845, on which day he was appointed by the clerk and master, guardian *ad litem*. But his answer, as executor, was prepared and sworn to on the 23d; and on the same day, *prior* to the filing of the bill, and *before* his appointment, his answer as guardian referring to, and admitting to be correct his answer as executor, was drawn up and sworn to. All this by the same solicitor. Great confidence existed between the parties, and it may be that no wrong was intended. But we cannot permit a decree, made under such circumstances, to compromit the rights of the infants.

That is not, therefore, in the way of the relief now sought. It may be further observed that this defence is not set up in the answer with that precision and particularity which seems to be required by the rules of equity pleading on this subject. But whether that objection alone would prevail under the present relaxation of the rules of pleading, we need not say, as we consider the other ground sufficient.

Much proof has been taken to show that independently of the settlement in the chancery suit, upon the merits, there is no grounds for the account demanded in the bill. That is a matter to be determined by reference to the Master. We think the principle settled, and ever since acted upon, in the case of *Turney* v. *Williams*, 7 Yer., 212, must govern this. The construction given in that case, and the case of *Burton* v. *Dickinson*, 3 Yer., 112, of the act of 1822, ch. 31, we think correct. The settlements made by the proper authorities, when *infants* are concerned, are not in the nature of settled or stated accounts, so as to require surcharging and falsifying before they can be opened, but only *prima facie* correct, and may be opened for a *general* account. They are, however, *prima facie* evidence for the executor in taking the general account, but nothing more.

We are of the opinion that that part of the Chan-

Samuel Elrod *et al.* v. Samuel Lancaster.

cellor's decree ordering a general account of the administration, is correct, and affirm it to that extent.

But on the second question, we think he erred in setting aside the sale of the lots in Jackson. There are but two objections made to it.

1. That the petition is in the name of the guardian and not the minors. It is in these words: "Your petitioner, Samuel Lancaster, as guardian for Samuel, James, Mary Eliza, and Sarah Jane Elrod, and Jas. S. Lyon, guardian for Austin Elrod, minor heirs of James Elrod, deceased," &c. The case is fully set forth, with the reasons for the sale, in the petition signed by an attorney. The reference, proof, reports and decrees are in strict conformity to the requirements of our decisions. The heirs were all then under age, but two of them, after arrival at age, by petition and orders of the Court, fully recognized this proceeding, and took benefits under it. We think there is nothing in this objection to avoid the sale, and, simply, refer to the recent case of Winchester, decided at the last term at Nashville, and reported in 1 Head, for the principles which govern it.

There is nothing in the second objection, as held by this Court in the case of *Blackmore* v. *Shelby*, 8 Hum., 489. The Court there say, that in sales made by a Court of competent jurisdiction, "the guardian may purchase, and although his conduct will be watched with jealousy, yet if it be manifest that he acted fairly, with the utmost good faith, and the transaction is free from any imputation of design on his part to gain a benefit to himself, to the prejudice of the interests of his wards, such purchase will be held valid." In this case there is every evidence of fairness and good faith. After the report of the sale, a reference was made and proof taken upon it, and the Court held it was fair, the price full, and promotive of the interest of the heirs.

So much of this decree as annuls the sale of the lots, will, therefore, be reversed, and that ordering a general account affirmed.

The case will be remanded for taking the account, according to the rules of law and the principles stated in the decree, both as to the executorship and guardianship. Barr and wife will only be entitled to an account for matters since the decree of 1845.

ELIZA J. SAUNDERS, EXECUTRIX, &c., *v.* JAMES B. WILDER *et al.*

1. PARTNERSHIP. *Death of a partner. Remedy of Creditors. Act of 1789, ch. 57, § 5.* By the act of 1789, ch. 57, § 5, modifying the common law doctrine, all "obligations or assumptions of co-partners" are declared to be joint and several, and to survive against the personal representative of a deceased partner, as well as against the surviving partner. The effect of which is to give the joint creditors the same remedies *at law* against the estate of the deceased partner which they were entitled to in equity.

2. SAME. *Same. Same. Judgment.* Creditors may, therefore, ob'ain judgment against the survivor and the representative of the deceased partner, jointly; or, at their election, against either, separately; an proceed to enforce satisfaction against either. Of this, neither the representative of the deceased partner, nor the survivor can complain, but they have their remedy over against each other.

3. SLAVES. *Pass to the distributees. Sale of, by execution. Act of 1827.* Slaves pass to distributees in like manner as lands go to the heirs, and

Eliza J. Saunders, Executrix, &c. v. James B. Wilder et al

cannot be seized and sold upon an execution at law against the personal representative. The representative, or creditors, must, to subject them to the payment of debts, proceed under the act of 1827.'

FROM DYER.

The bill was dismissed, upon demurrer, by Chancellor WILLIAMS, at the January Term, 1859. The complainant appealed.

RICHARDSON, for the complainant.

———— ————, for the defendants.

MCKINNEY, J., delivered the opinion of the Court.

The bill was dismissed on demurrer. The substance of the bill is, that complainant's testator, F. L. Saunders, died on the 17th of June, 1857: That for some time previous to his death, a mercantile business had been conducted by him and one J. A. Pierce, in copartnership, under the firm of Saunders & Pierce: That after testator's death, the defendants, as creditors of said firm, severally recovered judgments against the surviving partner and the complainant, as representative of the deceased partner, jointly, for about the sum of $1500: That executions, upon said judgments, had been issued, and were levied on six slaves, the individual property of the testator at his death, and were the property of the legatees under his will.

The bill further charges, that the assets of the firm

Eliza J. Saunders, Executrix, &c. *v.* James B. Wilder *et al.*

have not been exhausted, and that more than sufficient remain to discharge said judgments and all the liabilities of the firm.

The ground of equity assumed in the bill is, that the individual property of the estate of Saunders, or of his legatees, is not subject to the satisfaction of said judgments, until after the partnership effects shall have been exhausted. And the prayer of the bill is, that the sale of said slaves shall be enjoined, and the creditors be restrained from proceeding against the separate property of the deceased partner's estate; at least until after the firm assets shall have been exhausted.

The bill is brought against the creditors alone, the surviving partner, and the legatees under the will of the deceased partner, are not made parties.

The bill is extremely defective. It is framed upon an erroneous conception of the rights of the parties, and passes by the only point of equity that could be made, upon the facts stated.

It is true, that, by the common law, upon the death of a partner, the *legal* remedies against him, in respect of partnership contracts and liabilities, are extinguished. The partnership creditors cannot sue his personal representative, and have no remedy, except against the surviving partner, for their debts. But it is otherwise in equity, according to the modern decisions. In equity, partnership debts are looked upon as joint and several liabilities; and, consequently, the joint creditors have, in all cases, an election, either to proceed at law against the survivor, or in equity against the estate of the deceased partner. And this is so, whether the survivor be solvent, or bankrupt. Hence, the joint creditors

Eliza J. Saunders, Executrix, &c. *v.* James B. Wilder *et al.*

are not required to wait until the partnership affairs are wound up, and a final adjustment thereof is made, but may proceed at once, as upon a joint and several contract, in equity, against the separate estate of the deceased partners, leaving it to the representative of the deceased partner and the survivor, to adjust the partnership accounts between themselves. Story on Part., sec. 362; 1 Mylne and Keen, 582.

The common law doctrine upon this subject, however, was modified by the act of 1789, ch. 57, sec. 5. By that statute, all "obligations or assumptions of co-partners" are declared to be joint and several; and to survive against the personal representative of the deceased partner, as well as against the surviving partner. The necessary effect of this enactment is, to give the joint creditors the same remedies, *at law*, against the estate of the deceased partner, which they were entitled to in equity. They may proceed to obtain judgment against the survivor and the representative of the deceased partner, jointly, or, at their election, against either, separately. So, they may proceed to enforce satisfaction against either. And of this neither can complain. If the representative of the deceased partner is subjected to the payment of firm debts, he can call upon the surviving partner to reimburse him out of the joint fund, if upon an adjustment of the partnership accounts a balance shall be found in his favor; and so, if the surviving partner has been subjected beyond his just proportion, he may require the representative of the deceased partner to contribute. But neither can require a joint creditor to wait for an adjustment of the partnership accounts.

Thus far, there is no equity in the bill. But it has been repeatedly determined by this Court, that, since the passage of the act of 1827, ch. 61, the title to slaves does not, as formerly, pass to the personal representative, but vests directly in the distributees or legatees, as the case may be, subject, however, to be made liable for the debts of the estate, by the personal representative. *Savage* v. *Hale & Coggin*, 1 Sneed, 365; *Elliott* v. *Cochran*, 2 Sneed, 468. In the former case, it is laid down that slaves pass to the distributees, in like manner, as lands go to the heirs. From this it of necessity results, that the slaves cannot be seized and sold upon an execution at law against the personal representative.

It is equally well settled, that in proceeding to subject slaves to the satisfaction of the debts of the estate, the personal representative must pursue the act of 1827. And, although the act does not, in terms, extend to *creditors*, yet we think that, upon an equitable construction of the statute, the creditors, in the present case, might proceed to subject the slaves to the satisfaction of their debts. But in doing so, they must make the distributees or legatees, together with the personal representative, parties to such proceeding.

In any aspect of the case, however, the bill cannot be maintained in its present shape. As a bill merely to enjoin the sale of the slaves, upon executions at law, the legatees, in whom the legal title is vested, ought to have been parties; and as a proceeding, by the personal representative, to subject the slaves to the payment of debts, the legatees were likewise necessary parties.

The decree allowing the demurrer must, therefore, be affirmed; but the cause will be remanded with leave to make all such amendments as may be deemed proper and necessary.

C. D. VENABLE & CO. v. CURD AND WHITE.

1. OFFICERS, DE FACTO. *Acts of, when binding.* The acts of officers *de facto* are valid when they concern the public, or the rights of third persons who have an interest in the act done. But a different rule prevails where the act is for the benefit of the officer, because he is not permitted to take advantage of his own wrong.

2. SAME. *Same. Circuit Court. Judgment. Times of holding the Court. Illustration of the rule.* By an act of the Legislature the times of the sitting of the Circuit Court for Henry county were changed. This change was not known to the officers of the Court, the act having been passed but a short time before a term of said Court was to be held. The Court was held by the presiding Judge at the time before fixed by law, but at a different time from that required by the law *then* in force. A judgment was rendered by the Court thus sitting, the justice of which was not controverted. Held, that the judgment is valid; that the judgments and decrees of a judge regularly in office are valid, if he hold his Court under color of law, although the law may be repealed, or invalid.

FROM HENRY.

A writ of error was prosecuted to reverse the judgment rendered at the May Term, 1858, FITZGERALD, J., presiding.

J. P. Dunlap, for the plaintiffs in error.

Dunlap & Porter, and B. F. Lamb, for the defendants in error.

McAmpbell, on the same side, said:

It is insisted under the law as it existed, that the Court had no jurisdiction.

If it needed authority to sustain this position, the case of *Gregg* v. *Cooke*, Peck's Reports, 82, directly decides the principle. In this case the Court was opened at the time required by law, but rendered the judgment at a day when, by law, the judge was required to be at another Court. This is a much stronger case than the one at bar. In the one at bar, the Judge had no authority to open and hold the Court, by virtue of any law.

The same principle is announced in the case of *Brown* v. *Newby*, 6 Yer., 395.

Wright, J., delivered the opinion of the Court.

This is a writ of error prosecuted to this Court by the plaintiffs in error, in which they seek to reverse a judgment rendered against them in the Circuit Court of Henry county, on the 25th of May, 1858.

The ground upon which the reversal is asked, arises upon the following facts:

C. D. Venable & Co. *v.* Curd and White.

The times of holding the Circuit Courts for Henry county were changed, from the third to the fourth Mondays of January, May and September, by an act of the Legislature, passed the 25th of January, 1858, which act took effect from and after its passage.

On the 1st day of March afterwards, at the same session of the Legislature, the act of the 25th of January, 1858, fixing the times of holding the Circuit Courts for said county, was repealed, and the time changed from the fourth to the third Mondays of January, May and September; and which act, also, took effect from its passage.

No alteration was made in the time prescribed by the act of March the 1st, 1858, for holding the Circuit Courts of Henry county, either by the act passed March the 20th, 1858, or by the Code. So that the proper time to hold said Court in May, was the third, instead of the fourth Monday.

The Circuit Judge not being able to keep pace with these sudden changes in the legislation of the State; and not being aware of the existence of the act of the 1st of March, 1858; but supposing as he well might, and as no doubt did the other officers and suitors of the Court, that the proper time to hold it, by law, was the fourth Monday in May, proceeded to open and hold said Court at that time, as required by the act of the 25th of January, 1858, and during that term rendered the judgment aforesaid.

The act of the 25th of January, 1858, was printed in the general and public laws of that session, while the act of the 1st of March, only appeared among the private acts.

C. D. Venable & Co. v. Curd and White.

It is true, that in the act of the 20th of March, printed among the public laws, the sessions of the Circuit Courts of said county were permanently fixed upon the third Mondays of January, May and September; but, in the same act, it was expressly provided, that no alteration made by that act in the time then prescribed by law for holding said Court, should take effect until after the first term of the Court after the expiration of forty days from the end of that session of the General Assembly.

It will thus be seen that this course of legislation was well calculated to mislead, and did mislead the officers and suitors of the Court as to the true time of holding it; and that scarcely any amount of vigilance could guard against it.

The plaintiffs in error, after the adjournment of the term, having discovered that the Court had been holden at the wrong time, have obtained a writ of error; and now allege that said judgment is erroneous and void.

We do not think so. The Circuit Judge in this case, acted under color of legal authority, and no objection was made to the jurisdiction of the Court, or the power of the Judge to act, at the time the judgment was rendered.

It is not pretended the judgment is not just, or that they were in any way surprised upon the trial; but, on the contrary, the record shows that the parties appeared by their counsel, and no exception whatever was taken, either to the authority of the Court, or the course of proceeding in the case.

The public acts of officers, *de facto*, are often valid, though the authority under which they act is void

C D. Venable & Co. *v.* Curd and White.

Public convenience, as well as public justice, requires that they should be supported.

Indeed, no principle is better settled in the English and American law, than that the acts of officers, *de facto*, are valid, when they concern the public, or the rights of third persons, who have an interest in the act done, and the rule has been adopted to prevent a failure of justice. But a different rule prevails, where the act is for the benefit of the officer, because he shall not take advantage of his own want of title, which he must be cognizant of; but where it is for the benefit of strangers, or the public, who are presumed to be ignorant of such defect of title, it is good. *Taylor* v. *Skaine*, 2 South Ca. Rep., 696; *People* v. *Collins*, 7 Johns. Rep., 549; *McInstry* v. *Tanner*, 9 Johns. Rep., 135.

The same rule is laid down by this Court in *Pearce* v. *Hawkins*, 2 Swan, 87.

The consequences of holding a contrary doctrine would be alarming, and it is very easy to see the most serious results would follow.

In England, upon a writ of error, the question whether the judges in the Court below are properly judges or not, can never be decided; it being sufficient if they were judges *de facto*, 2 Term. Rep., 87, 6 Bac. Ab. (Title offices and officers K.) 36.

We have been referred by the counsel of the plaintiffs in error, to *Gregg* v. *Cooke*, Peck's Rep., 82, and *Brown* v. *Newby*, 6 Yer., 395. But it is manifest that in these cases, as also in *Smith* v. *Normant*, 5 Yer., 271, the doctrine as to the force and effect of judgments and decrees pronounced by judges *de facto*, was not considered.

There can be no doubt whatever, upon reason and authority, that a judgment given by a judge *de facto*, sitting and holding a Court at the proper time and place, is as valid and free of error as a judgment pronounced by a judge rightfully in office.

If so, upon what reason shall we hold that the judgments and decrees of a judge regularly in office are erroneous, because he held his Court under color of a law that turned out to be repealed or invalid?

In the case referred to from South Carolina (2 S. Ca. Rep., 696) the judge who pronounced the decree sought to be reversed, had been appointed by the Governor, pursuant to the act of 1790 of that State; and after the decree, the act was, by the Supreme Court of that State, declared unconstitutional and void; and yet the decree was held valid upon the principle laid down in 2 Swan, 87, and the other authorities to which I have referred.

The Circuit Judge has not been put to answer for any illegal exercise of power, and the plaintiffs in error cannot, in this collateral way, call in question his authority.

We, therefore, think the judgment of the Circuit Court must be held valid, and affirm it.

W. H. CRITTENDEN v. A. S. TERRILL et al.

1. SUMMARY PROCEEDINGS. *Constable. Sureties of, when liable.* When a constable executes his receipt for a claim, placed in his hands for collection, he assumes the double relation of *private agent* and *officer*. When his term of office expires, all his authority, as an officer, ceases. His agency continues until revoked by the principal. His sureties are liable, *alone*, for his official misconduct. They are not liable for his negligence as a *private agent*.

2. SAME. *Same. Liability as agent*. When a constable thus becomes the agent of a party, he is personally liable to him for any negligence in failing to sue on the claim, or to take out execution, or to do any other unofficial act. But for these his sureties are not liable.

3. SAME. *Same. Case in judgment*. A note was placed in the hands of a constable for collection. He executed his receipt therefor, and obtained judgment on the note. After the expiration of his term of office, he took out an execution on the judgment, and placed it in the hands of his successor in office, who collected the money and paid it over to him. He failed to pay it over to the plaintiff, who proceeded, by motion, against him and his sureties. Held, that after the expiration of his term of office, the constable could do no official act that would bind his sureties, and they were not liable. That the plaintiff's remedy, if any, was against him as his agent.

FROM HAYWOOD.

This case was heard at the January Term, 1859, before W. H. STEPHENS, Special Judge, who rendered judgment in favor of the defendants. The plaintiff appealed.

W. F. TALLEY, for the plaintiff, cited *Sherrell* v. *Goodrum*, 3 Hum., 419; *Pate* v. *Parks*, 4 Sneed, 330; *State* v. *Gilmore*, 3 Sneed, 503.

C. C. BATTLE, for the defendants.

W. H. Crittenden v. A. S. Terrill *et al.*

WRIGHT, J., delivered the opinion of the Court.

This was a motion for judgment against a constable and his securities, for the non-payment of money collected by him.

The Circuit Judge gave judgment against the plaintiff, and he has appealed to this Court.

The facts of the case are these: The defendant, Terrill, was elected a constable for the fourth civil district of Haywood county, in March, 1852; and at the next term of the County Court thereafter, was qualified, and remained in office during his term of two years. While so in office, and on the 6th of January, 1854, the plaintiff placed in his hands for collection a note upon one Jones, for $97.16, and took his receipt as an officer, in which he promised to collect, or return it, as the law directs. On the 14th of the same month, he took judgment upon the note against Jones, and it remained without the issuance of any execution until the expiration of his official term, when he moved into the fifth civil district of said county, where he was again elected a constable, in March, 1856, having been out of office two years.

He qualified under this last election on the 7th of April, 1856, and gave bond, with the other defendants as his securities, and remained in office until July, 1857, when he resigned.

On the 9th of September, 1854, Terrill, who was then out of office, caused an execution to be issued upon said judgment, and placed in the hands of one Brantley, who had succeeded him as constable in the fourth district. Brantley collected the money on the 21st of

April, 1856, and on the 9th of October of the same year, paid it to Terrill, who has never paid it to the plaintiff.

The collection by Brantley was upon a levy made by him while in office.

We think the judgment of the Circuit Court was correct. It is clear there is no liability on Terrill and his securities in his first bond, as no *official default* occurred during that term. He had no execution in his hands, made no levy, and collected no money; and when he ceased to be an officer, the liability of his sureties, for any other misconduct, also ceased. 3 Hum., 419; 7 Hum., 447.

It is true that he, by the receipt for the note in this case, became the agent of the plaintiff for its collection; and for any negligence in failing to sue on the note, or to take out execution, or any other *unofficial* act, he would be, *personally*, answerable in an action; but for these things his sureties are not responsible, the same not constituting *official* misconduct, but merely the violation of the duties of a *private agency*, which, it has been held, he is not forbidden by his official station to assume. 3 Hum., 218; 6 Hum., 20; 6 Yer., 502.

It will thus be seen, that this officer stood to the plaintiff in the double relation of private agent and constable at the same time. When his official term expired, all authority over this claim, as an officer, of necessity, was at an end. Not so with his *private agency*. That continued unrevoked and in full efficacy to the period of the reception of the money from Brantley. And he could not legally, we apprehend, have received it in any other character than that of *agent* for the plaintiff. A payment in any other sense would have been no discharge to Brantley, as was held by this Court, in *Pate et al.* v. *Parks et al.*, 4 Sneed, 330. An officer cannot, by virtue of his office merely, without warrant or authority from the creditor, take money belonging to him in the hands of another officer, and which he had collected upon claims or executions in favor of that creditor. It is true that the *official duty* of constables has been so enlarged by statute, as to render them and their sureties responsible for a failure to pay over money collected by them, as constables, by *virtue of their office*, but without process in their hands; but that is not this case. 3 Hum., 406.

Judgment affirmed.

WILLIAM TRICE v. THE STATE.

1. CRIMINAL LAW. *Evidence. Parol, to establish the existence of Free Banks. Act of* 1851-2, *ch.* 118. Upon an indictment for fraudulently keeping in possession the counterfeit resemblance or imitation of the note of a Free Bank, created by the act of 1851-2, ch. 113, parol evidence is not admissible to establish the existence of said Bank. The memorandum required by said act, or a copy thereof, duly certified, either by the Register or Secretary of State, must be produced.

2. SAME. *Fraudulently keeping in possession the counterfeit note of a Free Bank. When note described of a different denomination from any issued by the Bank.* By the 3d section of the act of 1851-2, ch. 118, the Banks organized under its provisions are empowered to issue and circulate notes of the different denominations authorized to be issued by the incorporated Banks of the State. And, therefore, the

fact that the counterfeit note, for having possession of which a party is indicted, is of a denomination different from any issued by the Bank, will not defeat the prosecution. It is sufficient that the Bank had lawful authority to issue notes of the denomination of that described in the indictment.

FROM SHELBY.

The plaintiff in error was convicted in the Criminal Court of Memphis, at the June Term, 1858, and appealed.

G. W. BAYNE, for the plaintiff in error.

SNEED, Attorney General, for the State.

McKINNEY, J., delivered the opinion of the Court.

The prisoner was indicted and convicted, in the Criminal Court of Memphis, under the 82d section of the penal code, for fraudulently keeping in his possession the counterfeit resemblance, or imitation, of a bank note, of the denomination of ten dollars, of "The Merchants' Bank of Nashville, State of Tennessee,"—"a corporation established by law, and authorized as a Bank in the State of Tennessee."

The note—a copy of which is set out in the indictment—purports to have been issued by "The Merchants' Bank," and to be payable at Nashville, and bears date August 12th, 1857.

Parol evidence was admitted, though objected to, to show that "a corporation existed, and was located in

Nashville, Tennessee, the style of which was the "Merchants' Bank." It seems from the proof, however, that this bank had never issued any notes of the denomination of *ten* dollars.

The bank spoken of in the proof, seems to have been one of the "Free Banks," organized under the act of 1851-2, ch. 113.

By said act, "any person, or association of persons," on complying with the conditions and requirements therein prescribed, is authorized to engage in, and "carry on the business of banking." The act requires, however, "that before commencing said business, such person or association make, and, after the manner of a deed of conveyance, acknowledge and cause to be registered in the office of the register of the county where said business is to be carried on, a written memorandum, specifying, 1: The name by which the bank is to be distinguished, &c.; 2: The place and county where the operations of said bank are to be carried on; 3: The amount of capital stock, &c.; 4: the names and places of residence of the share-holders, &c.; 5: the period at which said bank shall commence and terminate, &c., "a copy of which memorandum from the register's office, duly certified by him, shall be filed by such person or association, in the office of the Secretary of State; and said memorandum, or a copy thereof duly certified, either by the Register or Secretary of State, may be used as evidence in all courts and places, for and against such person or association." And, "on complying with the conditions aforesaid, such person or association, by the name stated in the momerandum aforesaid, shall be a body politic and corporate, and have succession," &c.

William Trice v. The State.

The mode of organization of a bank, under the statute, being thus provided for, the first question for our determination is—can parol evidence, if objected to, be received to show the organization and existence of a bank under the law?

We think not. We can take judicial notice of the statute authorizing such banks to be established, but we cannot take judicial notice of the books of the County Register, or of private papers lodged in the office of the Secretary of State; and only from one or other of these sources can it be judicially known that such a corporation legally exists. The statute has made the "memorandum, or a copy thereof, duly certified, either by the Register or Secretary of State," the proper evidence of the creation and existence of the bank. We are of opinion, therefore, that the parol evidence was improperly admitted.

The objection, that no notes of the denomination of *ten dollars* had been put in circulation by the "Merchants' Bank," if the fact were admitted to be so, has nothing in it. By the third section of the act, the banks organized under its provisions, are empowered to issue and circulate notes " of the different denominations authorized to be issued by the incorporated banks of this State." It is quite sufficient to sustain the prosecution, that the bank had lawful authority to issue notes of the denomination of *ten* dollars; whether, in fact, any such notes were issued, is an immaterial inquiry; the artifice of varying the denomination from that of the genuine notes in circulation, cannot avail the offender.

The misnomer of the bank, in the indictment, is,

perhaps, cured by setting out the note in words and figures—the name of the corporation being substantially correct—in the forged note.

Judgment reversed.

R. P. NEELY v. MORRIS, TANNER & CO.

1. BILLS AND NOTES. *Protest. Notary public. Act of* 1835, *ch.* 11. As a general principle, protest of a bill or note must be made by a a notary at the *place* of *payment.* And the authority of a notary public is confined to the county for which he was appointed and commissioned. He has no power to do an official act in another county. Hence, a protest of a bill or note must be made by a notary of the county in which the place of payment is fixed.

2. SAME. *Indorsement. Evidence. Proof of joint interest in plaintiffs.* When several persons sue as indorsees of a bill, if the bill is indorsed *in blank,* there is no necessity for their proving that they were in partnership together, or that the bill was indorsed or delivered to them jointly. The indorsement in blank conveys a joint right of action to as many as agree in suing on the bill.

3. SAME. *Same. Same. Same.* But when a bill is payable or indorsed *specially* to a firm, it must be proved that the firm consists of the persons who sue as plaintiffs on the record.

FROM HARDEMAN.

This cause was heard at the October Term, 1858, before HUMPHREYS, J., when there were verdict and judgment for the plaintiffs. Neely, the indorser, brought the cause up by writ of error.

R. P. Neely v Morris, Tanner & Co.

J. R. FENTRESS, A. T. & J. R. ROBERTSON, and H. BROWN, for the plaintiff in error.

PAYNE & UNTHANKS, for the defendants in error.

MCKINNEY, J., delivered the opinion of the Court.

This was an action of assumpsit, founded on a promissory note for $3805.35, made by the Mississippi Central and Tennessee Railroad Co., payable to R. P. Neely, and by him indorsed to the defendants in error. The suit is against the maker and indorser jointly. Pleas, non-assumpsit and payment. Judgment in favor of the plaintiffs against both defendants. To reverse which judgment, Neely, the indorser, for himself, has brought the case to this Court by writ of error.

The principal error insisted on is, the admission of the protest and certificate of the notary, as evidence to the jury.

The note was indorsed in blank, and the address of Neely, the indorser, was written underneath his name, thus: "Bolivar, Tennessee."

The protest shows on its face, that A. Woodward, the notary, was a notary public for the county of Shelby. That, at the request of Morris, Tanner & Co., he presented the note for payment at the office of R. P. Neely, president of said railroad, in Bolivar. And he certifies that he left a written notice of protest at said office, addressed to Neely, who was absent.

This protest was a nullity. Under our statute, the authority of a notary public is confined to the county for which he was appointed and commissioned. Act of

1835, ch. 11. He has no more power or authority to do an official act in a different county, than a justice of the peace, or other county officer.

It is well settled, as a general principle, that protest of a bill or note must be made by a notary *at the place of payment*. In the present case, the place of payment was Bolivar, in the county of Hardeman— the address of the indorser on the face of the note, and the place of his residence. The protest should, therefore, have been made by a notary of Hardeman county. The protest purports, on its face, to have been made in the city of Memphis, the residence of the notary. But whether made in Memphis or in Bolivar, is unimportant; in either case it is alike void. 3 Kent's Com., 120; Story on Bills.

The next error assigned, is the refusal of the Court to instruct the jury, that it was incumbent on the plaintiffs to prove that they were partners, as alleged in the declaration, or had a joint interest in the note sued on. The Court held that this was not necessary, as that matter had not been put in issue by the pleadings.

The rule upon this subject seems to be, that where several persons sue as indorsees of a bill, if the bill appears indorsed *in blank*, there is no necessity for their proving that they were in partnership together, or that the bill was indorsed or delivered to them jointly. Chitty on Bills, (7th Am. ed.,) 393. The indorsement in blank conveys a joint right of action to as many as agree in suing on the bill. 3 Camp., 239. And it is not incumbent on the plaintiffs, in such case, to prove their joint title to sue on the bill, by showing that they were partners, or proving a transfer to them jointly. 1 Starkie's Rep. 446.

But when a bill is payable or indorsed specially to a firm, it must be proved that the firm consists of the persons who sue as plaintiffs on the record. Chitty on Bills, 394; 1 Stark. Rep, 499; 10 Hum., 493.

There is some confusion in the bill of exceptions upon the point, whether the indorsement of the note in question was made in blank, or specially to the firm of Morris, Tanner & Co. But, from the whole record, it is apparent that it was in blank, and, most probably, was filled up during the trial. This point was therefore decided correctly. But on the other ground, the judgment must be reversed.

WILLIAM R. HAYNES *v.* WILLIAM H. GATES *et al.*

1. CHANCERY JURISDICTION. *Garnishment. Judgment by motion. What it must show.* In a summary proceeding by motion, enough must appear upon the record to show that the court before which the proceeding is had, has jurisdiction, and likewise all the facts necessary to authorize the judgment must be assumed therein. If these requisites do not exist, the judgment is a nullity, and a proceeding by garnishment founded upon such a void judgment, is likewise a nullity, and money received thereon by the garnishing creditor, will be ordered to be refunded, by a Court of Chancery.

2. SAME. Same. *Effect of notice to the garnishing creditor that the fund has been assigned* Notes were placed in the hands of an attorney for collection, and his receipt taken. These notes were assigned to another party, the receipt of the attorney handed over to him, and a guaranty of the solvency of the notes indorsed on the receipt. After the money was collected by the attorney, a garnishment was served

on him at the instance of a creditor of the assignor. Before this process was taken out, both the creditor and the attorney had notice of the transfer of the notes and fund. The attorney appeared and answered to the garnishment, and judgment was rendered against him, and he paid the money over to the creditor. In the view of a Court of Equity, this is a manifest fraud upon the assignee of the notes, and the garnishing creditor must be regarded as having received the money, and as holding it for the assignee; and, in a Court of Equity, will be required to refund it. And this, perhaps would be so, even though the creditor had obtained possession of the money in ignorance of the fact that it belonged to another.

FROM MADISON.

At the August Term, 1858, Chancellor WILLIAMS dismissed the bill as to the defendant, Gates. The complainant appealed.

M. BULLOCK and W. H. STEPHENS, for the complainant.

H. BROWN and J. M. MORRILL, for the defendants.

McKINNEY, J., delivered the opinion of the Court.

This bill was brought to recover a sum of money belonging to the complainant, alleged to have been wrongfully received by the defendant, Gates, from McElrath, under color of a void proceeding before a justice of the peace. The Chancellor decreed for the complainant, against McElrath, but dismissed the bill as to, Gates, and from the latter part of the decree, the complainant appealed.

William R. Haynes *v.* William H. Gates *et al.*

The facts appear to be: That on the 28th of March, 1855, one William Croom placed in the hands of the defendant, McElrath, (an attorney at law,) for collection, three promissory notes on W. B. Bright and others, each for the sum of $162.00; and took his receipt for the same in the usual form. Shortly afterwards, to-wit, on the 2d of April, 1855, Croom sold said notes, for a valuable consideration, to the complainant; and underneath the receipt of McElrath, made the following assignment: "For value received, I assign the within claims to W. R. Haynes, and do guarantee the solvency of the same. April 2d, 1855. . WM. CROOM."

It is alleged in the bill, that McElrath was notified of the assignment of the notes by Croom to the complainant. This allegation is denied by McElrath in his answer; but the fact is fully proved by Croom, that he, in person, gave notice to McElrath of the transfer of the notes, and directed him to pay the money, when collected, to complainant; and that he promised to do so. And the testimony of Croom is corroborated by a letter from McElrath to complainant, under date November 5th, 1856, a copy of which is set forth in the record.

It appears, that after the money due upon said notes had been collected by McElrath, a garnishment process was served on the latter, on the 9th of March, 1857, at the instance of defendant, Gates, who claimed to be a judgment creditor of Croom. And on his examination, as *garnishee*, McElrath stated that he had received, as attorney of Croom, and had in his hands, the sum of $491.91; and that he had received from Croom no written or verbal order to pay the same to any person.

William R. Haynes *v.* William H. Gates *et al.*

Upon this statement the Justice rendered judgment against the defendant, McElrath, as *garnishee,* for $320.25, the amount of Gates' debt; and, thereupon, McElrath paid, over said amount to Gates.

For the defendant, Gates, it is insisted, that, all other questions aside, the judgment on the garnishment, so long as it remains in force, is a protection to him against the relief sought by the complainant. This is denied by the complainant's counsel; and it is argued that the defendant is liable to refund the money: first, upon the ground that the garnishment proceeding was void; and, secondly, that even if it were admitted to be otherwise, still, that inasmuch as the proceeding was *ex-parte,* and was set on foot with full knowledge on the part of Gates, that the money belonged to the complainant, and not to Croom, that he cannot be permitted to retain it.

The basis of the garnishment is a supposed judgment obtained by Gates against Croom and Russell, by motion, before a justice of the peace, for money paid by the former as security of the latter. The so-called judgment is as follows: " In this case, I give judgment in favor of W. H. Gates for $314.00, on his motion, as security for William Croom and James F. Russell; founded on a judgment, No. 4364." According to the settled course of decision of this Court, the foregoing judgment is simply void. It has been uniformly held, that, in these summary proceedings, enough must appear upon the record to show that the tribunal has jurisdiction; and, likewise, all the facts necessary to authorize the judgment, must be assumed therein. 10 Yer., 310, 314. According to this rule, the judgment in ques-

William R. Haynes *v.* William H. Gates *et al.*

tion is destitute of all the necessary requisites to a valid judgment. It is a mere nullity, and of course can afford the defendant no protection.

But even if the judgment were valid, the defendant, Gates, could not, under the circumstances of this case, resist the decree sought against him. It is sufficiently established, by the allegation of the bill and the admission of the answer, that very shortly before taking out the process of garnishment, the defendant, Gates, acquired information from a conversation with the complainant, of the fund in the hands of McElrath; and that complainant claimed said fund as belonging to him, by purchase from Croom.

With knowledge of this fact, thus acquired, as appears from the record, Gates resorted to the proceeding before mentioned, in order to appropriate the fund to the satisfaction of his demand against Croom and Russell. This he cannot be permitted to do. It would be, in the view of a Court of Equity, a manifest fraud on the rights of the complainant. The money belonged to the complainant; Croom had no claim to it; and no creditor of his had any right, under color of legal process, or otherwise, to possess himself of it: And in doing so, the defendant, Gates, must be regarded, in equity, as having received it, and as holding it as the money of the complainant. He is, therefore, clearly liable to refund it. And the result would, perhaps, be the same, even though he had obtained possession of the money in ignorance of the fact that it belonged to the complainant.

The decree will be reversed, and a decree rendered for the complainant.

George M. Birdsong v. Jno. C. Birdsong.

GEORGE M. BIRDSONG v. JNO. C. BIRDSONG.

STATUTE OF LIMITATIONS. *Bar of two years, as to administrators and executors. Act of* 1789. *Code,* §§ 2279, 2280. The delay necessary to remove the limitation of two years, provided by the act of 1789, (Code, § 2279,) must be a delay at the request of the administrator or executor, for a *definite time,* or to an *event which may occur,* and thereby render the period *certain.* A payment of part of the claim, and a promise to credit a note due the estate for so much of the balance as may be just, will not take the case out of the statute.

FROM MADISON.

This cause was heard, upon an appeal from a magistrate's judgment, at the September Term, 1858, READ, J., presiding. Verdict and judgment for the defendant. The plaintiff appealed.

TOMLIN, for the plaintiff.

M. & H. BROWN, for the defendant.

CARUTHERS, J., delivered the opinion of the Court.

The plaintiff had an account against his father, the intestate of defendant, for $82, which he presented to the latter, as administrator, for payment. One-half of it was paid, and a promise made by the administrator to credit a note due the estate for so much of the balance as might be just—not admitting it all to be so. More than two years were permitted to elapse, before

George M. Birdsong *v.* Jno. C. Birdsong.

this suit was instituted, and the limitation of two years provided by the act of 1789, Code, section 2279, relied upon as a bar. To avoid this, it is insisted that the delay was at the request of the administrator. Code, 2280. The suit was commenced before a magistrate, and there are no pleadings; but the questions arise in the case as above stated.

In the construction of this statute it has been held by this Court, that the delay agreed upon at the request of the administrator, to avoid the bar, must be for a definite time, and such is the express language of the Code, 2280, or to an event which may occur, and thereby render the period certain. 11 Hum., 515; 1 Sneed, 470. In this case, nothing of the kind appears. The proof shows nothing like a request for delay for any time, or until any event; but establishes a settlement of the claim by the payment of one-half, and a discharge of the other, so far as it might be just, by a credit on an adverse claim. Whether, in fact, the credit was entered upon the note due the estate, or what was the amount of that note, if it existed, does not appear, nor is it material in the aspect in which the questions are presented.

It was the folly of the plaintiff not to have attended to that, and sued in the prescribed time for the balance of his claim, if justice was not done to him in that matter by the administrator. But all that, let it be as it may, has nothing to do with the questions of law presented in the case. The fact is admitted that the claim was not asserted by suit within the two years from the qualification of the administrator, and the only inquiry is, was this delay excused, and the bar saved, as required by the act and the decisions referred to. There can be no pretence that such a case is made out, and the judgment against the plaintiff was proper, and will be affirmed.

NANCY COOLEY v. GEORGE R. STEELE et al.

ESTOPPEL. *Feme covert. Sale of slaves. Coverture* confers no privilege or license to commit either fraud or falsehood under sanction of an oath; nor protection from the consequences. And if a married woman makes a solemn disclaimer on oath, in a deposition or otherwise, of title to slaves which are legally hers, she is estopped from thereafter claiming them.

FROM WEAKLEY.

Decree for the complainant, by Chancellor WILLIAMS, at the July Term, 1858. The defendants appealed.

J. R. & J. C. HAWKINS, and ROSS, for the complainant.

ROGERS and SOMERS, for the defendants.

ETHERIDGE, on the same side, argued:

1. The bill should have been dismissed on demurrer, because it shows that, at the time of the death of the

tenant for life, Sarah Wells, the defendants were in possession of the slaves. *Caplinger* v. *Sullivan*, 2 Hum., 548; *Bugg* v. *Franklin*, 4 Sneed, 130.

2. The proof shows that this possession of the defendants had been adverse, and had existed and continued for many years before the death of the tenant for life, under their purchase from the husbands and wives of some of the complainants, who claim in remainder.

Further, that this possession of the defendants had been decreed to them many years ago, by the decree of the Chancery Court at Dresden, in the suit of Sarah Wells (the tenant for life) against these defendants. To this, the last-mentioned suit, the complainant was a party. See authorities above cited.

3. The complainant was a party to the said Sarah Wells' suit, and disclaimed all interest in the property, because *she* had sold it. This fact appears in her answer and *in her deposition*, which was taken in the suit.

4. The complainant was guilty of a fraud on the defendant, Steele, and is not to be heard in opposition to her own fraudulent acts. *Crittenden* v. *Posey*, 1 Head, 311.

5. If the complainant is entitled to relief, the defendant, Steele, is entitled to his money which he paid, and which was received by Mrs. Cooley. *Coppedge* v. *Threadgill*, 3 Sneed, 577.

7. As *Mrs. Wells*, the tenant for life, died *before George Cooley*, the husband of complainant, the sale by George Cooley and the complainant, his wife, to the defendant, Steele, becomes good, upon the principle that

this Court, regarding as performed that which ought to be done, will force the husband to convey to his purchaser when he had the power so to do. George Cooley had the power after the death of the tenant for life. 2 Hum., 548.

McKINNEY, J., delivered the opinion of the Court.

The complainant, who is a *feme covert*, brought this bill, by her next friend, to have her share of certain slaves, claimed under the will of her deceased father, William Hubbard, settled upon her.

The testator bequeathed the mother of the slaves in question to his widow for life, with remainder to his children. The widow afterwards married one Robert Wells; and, on the 18th of January, 1828, she and her husband, by an instrument executed by both, relinquished and transferred the life interest in said slaves to certain of the defendants to this bill. In 1841, after the death of her second husband, the widow filed a bill to set aside the relinquishment of her life interest in said slaves. To which bill the complainant and her husband, George Cooley, and all the other persons claiming the remainder interest in said slaves, were made defendants.

Shortly after the filing of said bill, and before putting in an answer to the same, to wit, on the 12th of February, 1841, the complainant and her husband, by an instrument, under seal, sold and transferred all their interest in remainder, in said slaves, to the defendant,

Nancy Cooley *v.* George R. Steele *et al.*

Samuel Steele. And in their answer to said bill, they state this fact, and say that Steele is the *bona fide* owner of the same. But it seems this answer was not sworn to by the wife, and therefore it can only be treated as the husband's answer, and is no estoppel as to the wife. In the progress of said cause, however, the complainant's deposition was taken, in which she repeats that she had sold all her right and interest in said slaves to Steele, and considered that she had no interest in the matter.

The life interest of the widow being at an end, by her death, the complainant now claims, that, as no division of said slaves ever took place, the marital right of her husband never attached upon her interest in them; and that as her relinquishment to the defendant, Steele, of said interest, was not binding on her, by reason of *coverture*, and the want of her privy examination, she is entitled to recover her share of said slaves, and have the same settled upon her by a decree of the Court.

To this measure of relief the complainant would be clearly entitled, upon well established principles, but for the *estoppel* created by her solemn *disclaimer on oath*, in the before mentioned deposition. From this she can not escape. *Coverture* confers no privilege or license to commit either fraud or falsehood, under sanction of an oath; nor protection from the consequences. The complainant has offered no explanation of the sworn statement in her deposition, and she must abide by it. On this ground she must be repelled. *Hamilton* v. *Zimmerman,* 5 Sneed, 39, 48.

Decree reversed, as to the complainant, Mrs. Cooley.

GEORGE G. WARE v. JAMES A. STREET & Co.

1. PAYMENT. *In bank notes. Effect, if genuine, though worthless.* A payment of indebtedness in *genuine* bank notes, supposed by both parties to be good, though in fact worthless, is binding, and the loss must, in the absence of fraud, fall upon the party receiving them. It is otherwise if the bank notes are not genuine—not what they purport to be.

2. SAME. *Same. Demand and notice, and tender of worthless bank notes.* A payment in bank notes is not upon the same footing as a payment in promissory notes, or bills, so as to avoid the payment by presentation and refusal to pay. If a payment is made in *genuine* bank notes, circulating and received as money, such payment cannot, in the absence of fraud, be avoided by demand, refusal, and notice or tender to the payor.

3. DEMAND AND NOTICE. *Bank notes.* When, for any purpose, demand of payment of bank notes is necessary, the demand must be made at the place where the notes are, *upon their face*, made payable.

FROM MEMPHIS.

Verdict and judgment, upon the facts stated in the opinion, for the plaintiffs, at the November Term, 1858, CARUTHERS, J., presiding. The defendants appealed.

W. P. WILSON, for the plaintiff in error.

WICKERSHAM & BEECHER, for the defendants in error.

CARUTHERS, J., delivered the opinion of the Court.

Street & Co. commenced suit by warrant before a

George G. Ware v. James A. Street & Co.

a justice of the peace against Ware, on an account of $191.00 for merchandise. The only controversy, was upon a payment of $100 upon the 12th of July, 1858. This is not disputed, but it is insisted it should not have been allowed, because the payment was made in notes upon the Citizens' Bank, which suspended on the next day, and the notes became worthless.

The proof is not sufficient to fix upon Ware any knowledge that the bank was broke, or that it had suspended, or was about to suspend. He lived forty miles from Memphis, and it is not probable he knew as much about the condition of the banks as the plaintiffs, who were merchants in that city. The facts relied upon to fasten knowledge upon him, are not at all sufficient for that purpose; and so the question of fraud is out of the case.

The proof shows that the bank did business on that day to the close, and did not suspend until the next day. It seems by the evidence of the clerk, that it was resolved upon that evening, but not made known. The payment in question was made by the agent, and son-in-law of the defendant, late in the evening of the 12th, and a receipt taken. The plaintiffs made demand at the bank, in Memphis, next day, and notified the defendant that the payment should not stand, and the credit was cancelled upon the books. The notes were tendered in a few days to the defendant, and he refused to receive them, but insisted upon the credit.

The loss must fall on one of two innocent men, and the law must control it. At the time the payment was made the notes were circulating as currency, and considered good by the community. But they were in fact of no value at the hour they were paid out, although a few hours before, they were convertible into specie.

A payment in *genuine* bank notes, supposed by both parties to be good, though in fact worthless, will be binding, and the loss must fall upon the receiver, in the absence of fraud. It is otherwise if the notes be not genuine—not what they purport to be. So, a payment in forged or counterfeit paper would be void, and have no effect as a credit or payment for property or pre-existing debts.

But it is contended that by the same case, a payment good under the above rule, may be avoided by presenting them to the bank where they are payable, and a refusal to pay, with notice to the person from whom they were received. But even if that were the law, the Court erred in relation to the proper place for the demand. The notes were payable at the Branch of the Citizens' Bank at Knoxville; but they were presented at the principal bank at Memphis. The charge made this sufficient, and that was fatal to the defendant by avoiding the payment. To this the defendant excepts, as error. We have heretofore held in a recent unreported case, that where a demand for any purpose is necessary, it must be made at the place where the notes, upon their face are made payable. So there was no legal demand here, and the payment was binding upon the parties on the principle first stated.

This is decisive of the case, and other objections might not be noticed. But another error exists in the charge, equally fatal to the case, and is one of practical importance, and, perhaps, ought now to be decided as it fairly arises. That is as to the effect of a pay-

George G. Ware *v.* James A. Street & Co.

ment made in bank notes under the circumstances stated. His Honor, in his charge, adopted the *obiter dictum* of the Court, in the case of *Suggs* v. *Gass*, 8 Yer., 175, and placed a payment in bank notes on the same ground as ordinary promissory notes or bills, so that recourse could be had upon them, or the payment avoided, in case of presentation and refusal to pay, &c.

We think such is not the law; but that a payment without fraud, in bank notes circulating and received as money, cannot be avoided by demand, refusal, and notice or tender to the payor. It would be most unreasonable and inconvenient to hold otherwise.

The supposed commercial interest of our country, and the general convenience of the people, have produced a course of legislation by which the bank paper has become the circulating medium and the standard of value, instead of specie. True, it has not been made a lawful tender, and cannot be without a change of the Constitution.

But by almost universal consent, it has become the medium of exchange and the representative of property. It has taken the place of the precious metals, and is regarded as money. This, however, is by consent, and not by law. No man is *bound* to receive it in payment of debts, or for property. But if it gets into his hands by consent, and a loss comes by the failure of the bank the misfortune must and should be his in whose hands it happens to be at the time. The risk must follow the paper, and not the former owners. It passes from hand to hand without recourse, except in cases of fraud or concealment, as before explained. Upon no other ground can the payment be avoided.

The judgment must be reversed, and a new trial awarded, when the law will be charged as laid down in this opinion.

JOSEPH MITCHELL et al. v. W. G. BURTON et al.

1. SURETIES. *Release of, by erasure of name of one. Covenant.* If two or more persons become the surety of a third person, to a bond, and the obligees and principal obligor erase the name of, and release one of the sureties, without the knowledge or consent of the co-securities, or their subsequent ratification of the same, they are not bound on said bond.
2. SAME. *Same. Same. Signed by others after erasure.* But if the obligation, after such erasure, is presented to other persons, who sign the same as sureties, they are bound by their undertaking, although they may be ignorant of the circumstances of the erasure and of the fact that the other sureties on the bond are released thereby. The erasure was visible, and they should have ascertained all the facts in reference thereto, before signing the obligation, and not having done so, are bound by their act.

FROM DYER.

The presiding Judge, WILLIAMS, being incompetent to try the cause, the parties selected R. P. RAINS, who presided; and the cause was submitted to a jury at the June Term, 1858. Verdict and judgment for the plaintiffs, against Bradford, the principal obligor, but in favor of the other defendants. The plaintiffs appealed as to the sureties.

Joseph Mitchell *et al. v.* W. G. Burton *et al.*

LATTA and RICHARDSON, for the plaintiffs.

SCURLOCK, for the plaintiffs, assumed that, the covenant was never altered in any respect after Sampson and Burton had signed it. Now, what have they to complain of? As a question of fact, they saw, when they signed the paper, that the name of E. W. Tipton was erased.

An alteration of a note, before it is delivered or issued, is of no importance; for up to the time of issue (in this case delivery) it is in *fieri*. Smith's Leading Cases, 1st vol., top page 709; *Downs v. Richardson*, Baily on Bills, 116; *Johnson v. Duke of Marlborough*, 2d Starkie, 313.

A bill or note is not issued until it is in the hands of some person entitled to make a claim upon it. *Downs v. Richardson*, Baily on Bills, 116.

An alteration of a deed, however, in a material part, may be made after execution, if it is proved, or may be presumed to have been done by consent of all the parties. Smith's Leading Cases, 1st vol., 712, top page, and authorities there referred to. This consent may be implied from all the circumstances.

HILL, and COCHRAN & ENLOE, for the defendants.

CARUTHERS, J., delivered the opinion of the Court.

Bradford entered into a covenant with the plaintiffs as Commissioners of the Forked Deer River, to make

Joseph Mitchell *et al.* v. W. G. Burton *et al.*

certain improvements in the river, therein designated, and the other defendants became his sureties in his penal bond, for the faithful performance of his undertaking. A large amount was advanced to him, and he failed to perform the work. This action of covenant was brought to recover back the amount paid to him on the contract.

The suit is defended by most rare and voluminous pleadings, joint and several. But the case is presented to us upon a few simple questions. There was a recovery against Bradford, but all his sureties were discharged by the verdict of the jury and the judgment of the Court. From this the plaintiffs appealed, except as to Bradford.

The facts, so far as they are necessary to be stated for the questions before us, are, that the bond of Bradford was signed by himself, E. W. Tipton, P. M. Tipton, and S. G. Gillespie, and presented to the commissioners, then in session, for acceptance, when it was agreed that E. W. Tipton could not properly be a surety, as he was one of the commissioners; whereupon they erased his name, without the knowledge or consent of the other two sureties, P. M. Tipton and Gillespie. After that, Bradford procured the defendants, Sampson and Burton, to enter their names to the same bond, as his sureties.

P. M. Tipton and Gillespie join in a plea setting up the above facts. The Judge properly charged the jury that if the joint obligor, E. W. Tipton, had been discharged, by the erasure of his name, without their approbation or any subsequent acknowledgment or ratifica-

Joseph Mitchell *et al.* *v.* W. G. Burton *et al.*

tion on their part, they were not bound. This is too plain for argument.

But as to Sampson and Burton, the case is very different. They, also, join in a plea setting up the defence that they signed the bond "after the other defendants, and upon the faith of their being bound, and without any knowledge or information that they were not bound, or that the writing obligatory had been altered by the plaintiffs, and they aver that said bond had been altered by plaintiffs after the signature of the other defendants, and without their consent, by striking out the name of E. W. Tipton, and which fact was concealed from them."

Upon this part of the case, the Court laid down the law to the jury thus: "As to the case of Sampson and Burton, the jury should examine the proof and see if they signed the contract *upon the belief* that P. M. Tipton and Gillespie were bound," and if not, but they had been discharged by the act of the plaintiffs, in the erasure of the name of E. W. Tipton, and they did not inform them of that fact before they signed the paper, *as it was their duty* to do, it would be a fraud upon them, and they would not be bound.

In this we think there is manifest error. The obliteration occurred before the bond was signed by them. It was palpable to their observation. They knew the the fact, for it was before them. They signed with that knowledge. The plaintiffs concealed nothing from them; all that they had done, and the fact complained of, was visible. It may be true that they did not know by whom it was done, nor that the circumstances were such as to discharge the joint obligors before them—P. M.

Tipton and Gillespie. But that was their own fault; they were, or should have been, put upon the inquiry by the obliteration of the name, and should have satisfied themselves before they signed, as to all the circumstances. It may be true, also, that even if they knew all the facts and circumstances correctly and fully, still, they may not have been aware, as a matter of law, that the effect of the release of one obligor would discharge the others, then on the bond. If they did not know the law on this subject, it was their misfortune, not the fault of the plaintiffs. There was no fraud, concealment, or mistake of facts, and ignorance of the law is no defence in such a case.

So, we think, Sampson and Burton were improperly discharged, because of the error in the instruction of the Court, and, therefore, reverse the judgment, and grant a new trial.

ALEXANDER R. RUCKER *v.* JAMES T. WYNNE *et al.*

CHANCERY JURISDICTION. *Gaming securities.* Act *of* 1789, *ch.* 8 § 1.
The act of 1789 makes all gaming contracts, and all gaming securities, absolutely void, at law, as well as in equity; and it provides a new remedy in the legal forum for the recovery of "money or goods" lost at gaming, and paid or delivered. This act was not designed, nor does it interfere with the previously well established jurisdiction of Courts of Equity to compel gaming securities to be delivered up

Alexander R. Rucker v. James T. Wynne et al.

and cancelled. In transactions contravening public policy, relief may be given in equity to a *particeps criminis;* but the relief is given, always, in aid, not in subversion, of the public policy.

FROM MEMPHIS.

At the November Term, 1858, Judge CARUTHERS dismissed the bill. The complainant appealed.

B. B. WADDELL, and WILLIAMS & McKISICK, for the complainant.

THOMPSON, SULLIVAN, HIGGINS, and YERGER & FARRINGTON, for the defendants.

McKINNEY, J., delivered the opinion of the Court.

This bill was brought to have a gaming security delivered up and cancelled. The bill was dismissed on demurrer.

The case made in the bill is briefly this: In the summer of 1858, the complainant, who is a resident of Louisiana, made a visit to Hardin Springs, in this State, for the benefit of his health, which was then bad.

On his arrival at the Springs, his condition was such as to require the aid of a physician. The defendant, Dr. Creighton, a physician of Memphis, who was at the Springs, was called in. After some days, complainant's health began to improve; and his physician advised him that exercise at rolling ten-pins, and the use of champaigne wine as a tonic, would be of benefit to his health. Accordingly, a game was made up, at which it was arranged that complainant and his professed friend and physician, Dr. Creighton, should play against the defendants, Wynne and Worsham. They at first played for wine; but after complainant had become much excited by the free use of wine, it was proposed to play for money, at twenty dollars a game; this was assented to, and the playing and drinking were continued until it was announced that complainant and his partner, Creighton, had lost one thousand dollars; five hundred of which, complainant was told, he must pay to defendant Wynne. Complainant while incapable, from his condition, of attending to business, was induced to sign a draft, written by Wynne, for $500.00, on the defendants, Webb & Ruffin, of Memphis. After the draft was given to Wynne, Creighton pretended that he was compelled to return to Memphis, and abandoned complainant, though urged to continue his attentions as a physician.

Wynne, on reaching Memphis, presented the draft to Webb & Ruffin, and procured their check on a bank in Memphis for the amount. But, before the check was paid, complainant learned that the advice of his physician, to exercise at ten-pins and drink wine, was part of a meditated scheme between him and his confederates, Wynne & Worsham, to ensnare complainant and swindle him out of his money; and that in playing, Creighton colluded with Wynne and Worsham, so as always to make them win the game. Upon being satisfied of this fact, complainant sent a dispatch to Webb & Ruffin, directing them not to pay said draft; on the reception of which they notified the bank to withhold payment of their check, and payment was accordingly

Alexander R. Rucker v. James T. Wynne et al.

refused. Wynne, thereupon, had the check protested, and commenced suit upon the same.

To enjoin this suit, and to have said check surrendered up and cancelled, is the object of the bill.

The jurisdiction of a Court of Equity to grant this relief is denied, on the authority of the case of *Weakly* v. *Watkins & Ferguson*, 7 Hum., 356. That case, it is apparent, was hastily considered; and there is no reference to any authority in support of the decision. It is in direct opposition to the case of *Johnson* v. *Cooper & Crosswhite*, 2 Yer., 524, in which, upon an elaborate examination of the question on principle and authority, the contrary doctrine was established.

The case of *Weakley* v. *Watkins*, might well enough be distinguished from the present case, by the element of a most atrocious fraud which characterizes the latter.

We are not inclined, however, to rest our determination upon this distinction, but upon the distinct principle announced in *Johnson* v. *Cooper & Crosswhite*, which, in our opinion, is the sound doctrine, and well sustained by authority.

The act of 1789, ch. 8, sec. 1, declares, that every promise, agreement, bill, bond, or other contract, to pay, deliver, or secure money or other thing, won or obtained by any species of gaming; likewise, every sale, conveyance or transfer of land, slaves or other personal property, shall be void. And by the 4th sec., a remedy is provided for the recovery, within a limited time, of any money or other valuable thing, so lost and paid or delivered, in any Court of Record having cognizance thereof.

This statute makes all gaming contracts, and all

Alexander R. Rucker *v.* James T. Wynne *et al.*

gaming securities, absolutely void, at law as well as in equity; and it provides a new remedy in the legal forum, for the recovery of "money or goods" lost at gaming, and paid or delivered. This limited remedy at law is not adequate in all cases. It is not adapted to the relief necessary in some instances, nor to the carrying into full effect the great public policy intended to be established by the Legislature. It was not designed, nor can it be construed, to interfere with the previously well established jurisdiction of Courts of Equity on this subject. And at the date of the passage of the act, perhaps no head of equity jurisdiction was better established than that of compelling gaming securities to be delivered up and cancelled.

This is, perhaps, sufficiently demonstrated by Judge Whyte, in his elaborate opinion in *Johnson* v. *Cooper & Crosswhite*. In that case, Johnson conveyed to Crockett, a tract of land, lost by the former at a game of cards, and the latter sold and conveyed the land to Crosswhite, who was found to have had knowledge of the illegal consideration of the deed to Crockett; and the Court decreed the deed to be delivered up and cancelled.

The Court held, that, in view of the public policy of the law to suppress all manner of gaming, the complainant would not be repelled merely on the ground that he was a *particeps criminis*. The Court said, in the language of Lord Hardwick, that in cases of violations of public policy, it is indifferent who stands before the Court, because the Court does not regard the state and condition of the parties so much as the nature of the contract and the public good. 2 Hov. Sup., 122.

Alexander R. Rucker *v.* James T. Wynne *et al.*

The Court likewise adopted the language and sentiment of Lord Thurlow, in *Neville* v. *Wilkinson*, (18, ves. 382,) that if courts of justice mean to prevent the perpetration of crimes, it must be, not by allowing a man who has got possession to remain in possession, but by putting the parties back to the state in which they were before. Numerous cases, of the highest authority, are cited by Judge Whyte, to the effect, that, in transactions contravening public policy, relief may be given in equity to a *particeps criminis;* but the relief is given always in aid, not in subversion of the public policy. The Court interferes for the sake, not of the party, but of the public. See cases referred to.

This doctrine of the jurisdiction of a Court of Equity to declare gaming securities void, and to order them to be given up and cancelled, is sustained by numerous other authorities. Mr. Story (1 Eq. Juris, § 303) regards the principle as not to be doubted, that a bill in equity may be maintained to have any gaming security delivered up and cancelled. And, furthermore, that money paid upon a gaming contract may be recovered back, in furtherance of a great public policy, independently of any statutable provision.

In the case of *Partarlington* v. *Saulby*, (3 Mylne & Keene, 104; 8 Cond. Eng. Ch. Rep, 298,) the complainant had accepted a bill of exchange for £1000, for money lent by him at gaming, payable to one Aldridge, by whom it was indorsed to Brook, and by him to the defendant; and the bill was brought to restrain the defendants from suing thereon, in Ireland. The Lord Chancellor refused to dissolve the injunction, on the

Alexander R. Rucker v. James T. Wynne et al.

ground that the consideration of the bill was not denied to be illegal, and the circumstances leading to the belief that the defendants took the bill with knowledge of the facts as to the consideration. The only point of doubt in the mind of the Chancellor, arose out of the fact that the suit had been brought, and was pending in a court of law, in Ireland; and this was obviated on the ground that the person of the party, on whom the injunction was served, was within the jurisdiction and power of the Chancellor.

So in *Winne* v. *Callander*, (1 Russell's Ch. Rep., 293,) the complainant accepted bills of exchange for money lost at gaming. Several of these bills were not paid when due, and other bills were substituted in their stead. Afterwards the complainant went to reside in France, and in the latter country accepted other bills of exchange, on French stamps, to the amount of the principal and interest due on the unpaid bills, and delivered them in lieu of the bills which the parties held before, which were given in England. And the Master of the Rolls held, that the consideration of the first bills being a debt contracted by gambling in England, and the French bills substituted for them being founded on the same consideration for which the original securities were given, the complainant was entitled to have the French bills delivered up and cancelled, notwithstanding the objection that he was *particeps criminis*.

Authorities might be multiplied to the same effect, but we deem it unnecessary.

We concur in the view, that the only effectual method of discouraging gaming, and carrying out the policy of the law, is to remove the temptation, by denying to the offender the profits of his violation of the law. The contrary principle is rather an encouragement to the commission of the offence.

Decree reversed, and demurrer disallowed, with costs.

MARIA O. BIGELOW v. THE MISSISSIPPI CENTRAL AND TENN. R. R. CO.

RAILROAD COMPANY. *Construction of charter. Lands taken. Act of 1853.* The eighth section of the charter of the Mississippi Central and Tennessee Railroad Company, which does not materially differ from most of the other railroad charters, provides that where the company and owner of the soil required for the road fail to agree upon the terms of purchase and sale, the Court shall appoint commissioners to value the land taken, &c. It is not necessary, under this charter, that the parties should make an effort to agree, and fail, before the Court has jurisdiction to appoint commissioners to assess the value of the land.

FROM MADISON.

The petition for a writ of error *coram nobis* was dismissed upon demurrer by Judge READ, at the September Term, 1858. The petitioner appealed.

McLANAHAN and STEPHENS, for the petitioner.

M. & H. BROWN, for the defendant.

Maria O. Bigelow *v.* The Mississippi Central and Tenn. R. R. Co.

CARUTHERS, J., delivered the opinion of the Court.

On the 28th of September, 1855, the plaintiff moved the Circuit Court of Madison, for the appointment of commissioners to assess the damages of defendant for the land necessary to be taken for the railroad. The application was granted, and the commissioners in the performance of their duty, assessed the damages of Mrs. Bigelow to $800, for one acre and a fraction taken from her. No appeal was taken by her, and the report was made to the Court at the January Term, 1857. No objection having been made in her behalf, the report was confirmed, and the title to the land divested out of her and vested in the plaintiff, "so soon as the value aforesaid is paid or tendered." After one year had elapsed from this judgment of the Court, a petition was filed for a writ of error, *coram nobis*.

The grounds relied upon in the petition, among others not necessary to notice, is, that the Court had no jurisdiction of the case, because the eighth section of the charter, act of 1853, required that an effort to agree upon the value must be first made, and fail, before the application could be made to the Courts. It is further stated that, at the time of this proceeding, an agreement existed to settle and adjust the matter between themselves, by negotiation, or reference. This is the main error of fact relied on to revoke and annul the judgment of the Court, by the use of the writ of error *coram nobis*. The Circuit Court sustained a demurrer to the petition, or rejected the application, and from that judgment this appeal was taken. The same question, and no other, is now before us; that is, does the case stated

Maria O. Bigelow v. The Mississippi Central and Tenn. R. R. Co.

authorise the issuance of the writ and the relief demanded? We cannot now examine into and correct any errors that may exist in the original proceedings. It is said that no judgment was given for the $800 damages, and that should be corrected. The case is not before us in a form to reach that question, or any error of law that may exist in the case. We are confined to the scope of this particular remedy. Nor need we make any remarks upon it, or the mode by which it may be recovered from the company; but certainly there can be no difficulty about that. The only question properly before us is, whether the Circuit Court erred in refusing to grant the prayer of the petition, and dismissing the same. We may, also, waive the question, whether if the position assumed in the petition and argument here be correct, this is the proper mode to obtain the advantage of it. For it is clear, that if the matter would be no defence, that the application was properly rejected. Considering, then, the question properly presented, we have no difficulty in deciding it.

The provision of the eighth section of this charter, which is not different from most, if not all, the railroad charters in this State, is, substantially, that where the company, and owner of the soil required for the road, fail to agree upon the terms of purchase and sale, the Court shall appoint commissioners to value the land taken, &c. The position assumed is, that this is a condition precedent, and until it is complied with, that is, until an effort to agree is made, and fails, that the Courts have no jurisdiction. We do not think this is the proper construction of the act. It has never been so understood in any of the numerous cases which have been

Maria O Bigelow v. The Mississippi Central and Tenn. R. R. Co.

before us, under various charters containing similar provisions—no such question has ever been made.

The company have a perfect right to take the land for their road, without consent or negotiation, and are guilty of no trespass. There accrues to the owner of the soil a right, just as perfect and unquestionable, to just compensation. The reference in the charter to the probability that the parties might agree, without a resort to the Courts, was not intended to make it a condition to the jurisdiction. It was barely a recognition of the right of the parties to settle the matter without litigation, which they would have enjoyed just as fully without it, in that, as well as any other case. It was surplusage in the act, and no legal effect can be given to it. The construction contended for would be exceedingly inconvenient, and, in some cases, impracticable. The owners of the soil might be non-residents, unknown, or under disability.

The fact stated, that there was an understanding between the parties, that the matter was to be settled by agreement, at the time the report was made, does not alter the case as to this proceeding. The party had proper notice, and should have attended to the case at the right time. There was no appeal from the action of the commissioners to the Court, nor any writ of error from that Court to this; but a year was permitted to pass before this peculiar remedy is resorted to. The Circuit Court was right in refusing it, and we affirm the judgment.

GAUGH AND WIFE v. ANDREW HENDERSON et al.

1. SALE OF LAND. *Fraud. Infancy. Improvements. Rents.* A lot was purchased in the city of Memphis with a fund raised by contribution. The title was made, by direction of the contributors, to A, an infant of tender years. The creditors of A's father obtained judgments against him—levied upon said lot, and had it sold under a writ of *venditioni exponas;* and H, one of the creditors, purchased the same. The sheriff executed a deed to H. H sold and conveyed the lot, and there were several intermediate conveyances, before the defendant, Greenlaw, acquired the title. Subsequent to the sale, and purchase of H, a bill was filed in the Chancery Court against A, the minor, and others, to set aside the deed made to her, upon the ground that the father had paid the purchase money, and the conveyance was executed to the infant daughter to protect the lot from his creditors. This suit was conducted, collusively, by the complainant and *next friend* of the infant, and a decree was pronounced divesting her of her title. *Held,* that said sale, by virtue of the *venditioni exponas,* and the proceedings in the Chancery Court—together with the conveyances made by H and those claiming under him—were void; and A is entitled to the lot, with the accruing rents—she accounting for such improvements as may have enhanced the value of the property.

2. SAME. *Venditioni exponas. When lost.* A sale of land under an order of condemnation and a writ of *venditioni exponas,* is not void if the writ cannot be found, provided it appears by the testimony of the clerk, the memorandum on his execution docket, and the recitals in the sheriff's deed, that the writ did issue and the sale was made by virtue of the same.

3. SAME. *Fraudulent conveyances. Question reserved.* If land is purchased and paid for by a father, but the deed made to his infant daughter, (the legal title never having vested in him,) for the purpose of protecting the property from the creditors of the father, can said land be seized and sold by execution at law at the instance of the creditors; or, must it be done by a decree of a Court of Equity?

4. SAME. *Voluntary conveyance. Advancement. Question reserved.* If a father, not being indebted at the time, purchase a tract of land and have the title made to an infant daughter, it being done *bona fide,* will it not be regarded as an advancement, or a voluntary settlement upon the child; and can subsequent creditors of the father impeach the conveyance merely upon the ground that it is voluntary?

5. EVIDENCE. *Onus probandi. Recitals of a deed. Consideration.* The burden of proof, when a party attacks the consideration of a deed, and

Gaugh and Wife v. Andrew Henderson *et al.*

attempts to prove that it was paid by another than the person recited in the deed, is upon the party attacking the same; and he must disprove, by clear and satisfactory evidence, the truth of the fact recited.

6. SAME. *Disability. Infancy. Presumption from lapse of time.* So long as a party is under a disability, or within the saving of the statute of limitations, lapse of time furnishes no presumption against her, and does not operate prejudicially to her rights.

7. *Depositions. Taken before issue, or by collusion.* If a deposition is taken in a cause, to which an infant is a party, before the same is at issue, and it does not appear to have been taken *de bene esse*, and there is reason to believe that there was collusion between the complainant and the *next friend* of the infant, the deposition will be rejected.

FROM MEMPHIS.

Decree for the complainants by Judge CARUTHERS, at the November Term, 1858. The defendants appealed. The facts are stated in the opinion of the Court.

YERGER, BLYTHE and WICKERSHAM, for the complainants.

BAILY, SMITH & STOVALL, and WILLIAMS & McKISICK, for the defendants.

McKINNEY, J., delivered the opinion of the Court.

The complainants brought this bill to regain the possession of a lot in the city of Memphis, alleged to be the property of Mrs. Gaugh, and to have the title of the defendants declared void for fraud. The Chancellor decreed for the complainants, and the defendants appealed.

The material facts of the case are as follows: On

the 18th of December, 1840, the lot in question, which was then wholly unimproved, was conveyed by W. L. Vance to the complainant, Alicia, then Alicia Ann Kernahan, an infant about six years of age, and daughter of one Andrew Kernahan. The consideration of the conveyance is stated to be $850, paid by said Alicia. This deed was duly proved and registered on the 6th of February, 1841.

Shortly after the date of this conveyance, Andrew Kernahan, complainant's father, proceeded to erect a frame dwelling house on said lot; and in April, 1842, five several judgments were rendered against him before a justice of the peace of Memphis, in all amounting to some $900, for the carpenters' and brick-masons' work done on said house. Executions on these judgments issued, and were returned levied upon said lot, being lot, No. 358, in the city of Memphis, on the 18th of April, 1842, as the property of Andrew Kernahan; and at the June Term of the Circuit Court of Shelby county, the papers being returned into Court by the justice, judgments of condemnation were rendered, and said lot ordered to be sold.

The lot was sold by the sheriff, on the 2d of October, 1842, and was bid off by William Henderson, at the price of $950; and on the 12th day of December, 1842, the sheriff executed a deed to said Henderson for said lot. On the day after the sheriff's sale, to-wit, on the 3d of October, 1842, William Henderson, the purchaser, sold and conveyed said lot to said Andrew Kernahan, at the price of $2000, for which Kernahan executed four notes, each for $500, payable at one, two, three and four years, and to secure said purchase money,

Kernahan, at the same time, by deed of trust of even date with the conveyance to him, conveyed said lot to Seth Wheatly and Jas. R. Williams, as trustees, vesting the legal title in them, with power to sell, if said notes were not paid at maturity, (which deed of trust seems still to remain in force.)

Afterwards, on the 23d day of June, 1843, Kernahan, for the consideration of $750, sold and conveyed all his interest in said lot,—being his equity of redemption under the trust deed—to the defendant, Andrew Henderson; and afterwards, on the 28th day of February, 1844, William Henderson assigned and transferred all his interest under said deed of trust, and the debt of $2000, thereby secured, to defendant, Andrew Henderson. Shortly after this, to-wit, on the 4th of March, 1844, Andrew Henderson, (who was a resident of New Orleans,) by his agent, said William Henderson, filed a bill in the Chancery Court at Somerville, against the infant, Alicia Ann Kernahan, to have the foregoing deed made to her by Vance, for said lot, declared void, and the title divested out of her and vested in said Henderson.

The ground of the relief, assumed in the bill, is that the consideration money of $850, paid to Vance for the lot, was paid by said Andrew Kernahan, out of his own money, and that he caused said conveyance to be made by Vance to his infant daughter, to protect the property from his creditors—he being then insolvent, and indebted to a large amount—therefore, said conveyance was "voluntary as against his creditors, and void."

On the 23d day of May, 1845, a decree was made in said cause for the complainant, declaring the conveyance to Alicia to have been made to defraud the creditors of A. Kernahan, and divesting the title out of the said Alicia Ann, and vesting the same in complainant, Henderson.

Soon after the filing of said bill, namely, on the 16th day of June, 1844, the complainant, Andrew Henderson, by his attorney in fact, William Henderson, sold and conveyed said lot to one John Delafield, of whom notice will be taken presently.; and after various intermediate sales and conveyances, said lot was purchased by the defendants, the Messrs. Greenlaw.

The said Alicia intermarried with the other complainant, and on the 8th day of May, 1858, and within less than three years after complainant, Alicia, attained her full age, this bill was filed, to have said sheriff's sale, the decree before mentioned, and the various conveyances, including that to defendants, Greenlaw, declared illegal, fraudulent, and void.

Several important and vexatious questions of law and fact have been discussed in the argument.

For the complainants it is insisted, that the execution sale was void, and communicated no title to the purchaser for various reasons:

1. It is insisted, that if it were admitted to be true, that the lot was purchased and paid for by Andrew Kernahan, with his own money, and the title made by his procurement to his infant daughter, for the avowed purpose of protecting the property against his own creditors, that still the lot could not be seized and sold by execution at law by his creditors; but only by decree of a Court of Equity. See 10 Hum., 13; 7 Yer.,

Gaugh and Wife *v.* Andrew Henderson *et al.*

155, 159; 1 Iredell's L. Rep., 553; contra 1 Hum., 491; 6 Hum., 93; 19 Wend., 414.

There is a serious conflict of judicial opinion upon this point, and as its determination is not necessary to the present decision, in the view we have taken of the case upon the facts, we pass it by.

2. It is further urged, that taking it as established, that the consideration money was paid by the father, still, as it is not proved that there were any judgment creditors of his existing at the time of the conveyance, the investment must be regarded as an advancement by the father for the benefit of his child; or a voluntary settlement upon her, which subsequent creditors cannot challenge or impeach, merely on the ground of its being voluntary. With reference to the facts of this case, this proposition is by no means free from difficulty. But we lay it aside, and proceed to consider the case upon the facts.

3. It is insisted that the sale was void, because there is nothing in the record to show that writs of *venditioni exponas* ever issued to authorize said sale. The proof shows that no such writs can now be found by the present clerk—not that such writs were not in fact issued; but the clerk states, that in the column of the execution docket, set apart to note the date of the issuance of writs of *fi. fa.* and *venditioni exponas*, he finds this memorandum, "July 7th, '42;" which, from his knowledge of the manner of keeping the docket, he understands to represent the date of the issuance of the writs of *venditioni exponas* in said cases. This date would suit, as the writs must have been tested of the June Term, 1842, the date of condemnation of the lot, and

Gaugh and Wife v. Andrew Henderson et al.

were executed on the return day of the following October Term. The sheriff's deed, made soon after the sale, recites the writs in his hands; but this recital is not evidence of the fact. Without more, however, we think this objection must fail.

4. But the fact that Andrew Kernahan paid any part of the consideration money of said lot is utterly denied by the complainants. And this is the turning point of the case. If the truth be not so, then it follows, of course, that the sheriff's sale, and the proceeding in equity, are alike inoperative and void to affect the title of the complainant, Alicia.

And upon this point, it must be borne in mind, that the burden of proof is upon the defendants, to disprove, by clear and satisfactory evidence, the truth of the fact recited in the deed. And it must likewise be remembered, that lapse of time, under the circumstances, furnishes no presumptions in favor of the defendants, or prejudicial to the complainant, who all the while, from the time of the sale, has been within the saving of the statute of limitations.

The proof mainly relied on to establish the fact of the payment of the purchase money of the lot by A Kernahan, is his deposition taken in the Chancery suit of Andrew Henderson, against complainant, Alicia, before mentioned.

If exception had been taken to this deposition on the hearing, we incline to the opinion that it ought to have been rejected; and, on the objection made here, we are by no means satisfied that it ought not to be regarded as inadmissible evidence. The objections to it are numerous, and some of them of a very grave character.

It was taken on the 19th of March, 1844, just fifteen days after the filing of the bill, which was an appearance to the May Term, following, and three months before the cause was put at issue, by filing a replication; and was not, so far as can be seen from this record, taken *de bene esse*. For this reason it was liable to have been suppressed, and would have been, doubtless, but for the culpable neglect of the next friend of the infant to take exception to it. But another objection, of a more serious nature, arises out of the conduct of the next friend of the infant in taking said deposition. And here it is proper to exonerate from all censure, the highly respectable gentleman who appeared as counsel for the plaintiff, in taking said deposition. He did nothing more than his professional duty seemed to demand of him, and was doubtless wholly ignorant of the fact, too apparent from all the circumstances of this case to be denied, that a combination existed between the agent of complainant and the next friend of the infant, to obtain a decree divesting the infant of her title by artifice and fraud. The next friend of the infant was a lawyer, and was appointed next friend on the application of the agent of complainant; and from all the circumstances of the case, the conclusion cannot be resisted, that he was so appointed to aid in the accomplishment of the object sought by the bill. The law partner of the next friend was counsel for the complainant; and the next friend could not, perhaps, have better subserved the purposes of the complainant, if he himself had stood in the same relation. And in less than three months after taking said deposition, and pending the suit, the next friend became himself the absolute purchaser of said lot; thus putting

Gaugh and Wife v. Andrew Henderson *et al.*

himself in an attitude of open hostility to the interests of the minor, which he had undertaken to protect. This act of the next friend furnishes almost conclusive evidence of the charge in the bill, that he was procured to accept that office by collusion with the agent of the complainant, not to protect, but the more effectually to aid in destroying her rights, under color of the decree of a Court of Equity. And it may be here remarked, that the very fact of resorting to a Court of Equity to divest the title of the infant, is persuasive evidence of the belief, on the part of the complainant and his confederates, that the execution sale was ineffectual for that purpose, and cannot but tend to discredit the truth of the hypothesis upon which it is now attempted to sustain the validity of that sale. It furnishes a clue likewise to the hasty, extraordinary, and irregular proceedings which characterize the management of the suit in Chancery.

But, to return to the deposition of Andrew Kernahan, and the circumstances under which it was taken. It seems that the next friend was intrusted to write both the questions and answers. And what is most worthy of notice is, that after writing down the answers to all the questions put by the complainant, and finding a strong *prima facie* case made out against the infant, the next friend seemed satisfied to dismiss the witness without even attempting to break the force of his statement by a single question, by way of cross-examination. If this be explicable, or excusable, it cannot be on the score of ignorance of duty on the part of the next friend, for he is shown to have been a lawyer of some experience. Nor does it appear that a single deposi-

Gaugh and Wife v. Andrew Henderson *et al.*

tion was taken in the cause, or a question asked of any witness, on behalf of the infant.

But waiving the foregoing objections to the deposition of the witness, the objection that he was an incompetent witness by reason of interest in the result of the suit, is at least very plausible. His notes for $2000 remained unsatisfied to Henderson, the complainant, in the event of the determination of the suit in favor of the title of the infant. If this be not sufficient to render him incompetent, it certainly tends to impair his credit. His claims to credit must also be somewhat impaired by the fact, that the deposition was taken at a time when he was just recovering from a state of mental and physical derangement, the result of excessive intoxication, to which he was subject. This fact is established not only by the proof of Mrs. Burns, but also by the deposition of Mrs. Logan.

If, however, we overlook all exceptions to the testimony of A. Kernahan, does it sustain the assumption that the lot was paid for by him with his own money?

The witness states the fact to be, that he paid for it, except the sum of twenty-five dollars, paid by Thos. Patterson, and that he obtained the money from the Farmers' and Merchants' Bank.

This is the only proof in support of the allegation that the lot was paid for by Kernahan. It is true, Titus proves that he indorsed a note for Kernahan, about the year 1840, for about the sum of $350, to be used, as he understood, in building a house, or in purchasing a lot for his family. But whether or not the money was actually received on the note thus indorsed, is not proved; or if received, there is no proof that it was applied to the payment of the price of the lot, except the uncorroborated statement of Kernahan; in opposition to which there is an overwhelming weight of evidence, direct and circumstantial. The whole testimony in the case, however, is perfectly reconcilable. The fact that Kernahan received $350 from the bank, may be admitted as proved; but how was it applied? Titus says, it was to be used *in building a house*, or *in the purchase of a lot*—he does not know which. Now the fact is shown, that immediately after the sale of the lot by Vance, Kernahan commenced the erection of a house on said lot; and it is not questioned but that all that ever was paid towards the expenses of building the house, was paid by Kernahan.

And from the whole record, the conclusion is forced upon the mind, that the $350 procured from the bank must have been expended in paying for the materials and the building of the house. This view reconciles the testimony of the witnesses with each other, and with what appears to be the truth of the case. And, at most, it merely involves Kernahan in a mistake as to the fact of the appropriation of the money; or rather, perhaps, that in taking his deposition, he was, by misapprehension or otherwise, made to say that the money was applied to the payment of the price of the lot, instead of to the purchase of lumber and the expenses of the building, which, it is admitted, he put upon the lot.

In any other view of the case, it is impossible to give credit to Kernahan's statement.

The proof establishes positively that the purchase of the lot was negotiated by Joseph Henderson, on behalf of the wife and infant daughter of Kernahan, who were reduced to the necessity of going into a *shanty*, by the intemperance and improvidence of the husband and father.

Top proves that Henderson paid the money for the lot; that it was made up, as he understood, by the friends of Mrs. Kernahan, who had high esteem and affection for her, and deeply sympathized with her and her infant in their abject poverty. He further proves, that he and Vance (who owned the lot) estimated its value at five to six hundred dollars; but at the importunity of Henderson, Charles Lofland, and other friends of Mrs. K., agreed to take $350, intending the difference between that sum and the value of the lot, as a contribution on their part to Mrs. K. and her infant. And Top likewise proves that the title was made to the infant daughter by the direction of the persons who made up the money to pay for the lot.

The witness, C. D. McLean, proves that he was called on by Joseph Henderson, as a friend of the family of Kernahan, to assist in making up the money to purchase a home for them; and that an appeal was made to him, as a brother mason, to assist, in the ante room of the lodge, in the presence of Fraser Titus, E. Titus, Charles Lofland, and others, whose names he had forgotten—all of whom contributed, and handed the money over to Joseph Henderson, the witness himself paying ten dollars; and said money, as he understood, was appropriated to pay for the lot for Kernahan's infant daughter.

Other testimony, of a circumstantial character, goes to place the truth of this fact beyond all reasonable doubt; and the allegation of the bill that the lot was thus purchased and paid for, we regard as sufficiently proved.

This single matter of fact is decisive of the case. The consequence is, that the sale of the lot, upon an execution against Andrew Kernahan, was simply a nullity, and in no way affected the title of the infant daughter. And for this the auxiliary proceeding in Chancery was alike inoperative and void; and if necessary to the decision of this case, we should likewise declare it void on the ground that it was, in its inception, as well as in its progress and final consummation, a meditated scheme of fraud between the next friend of the infant and the agent of Andrew Henderson, to take from her the bounty intended to be secured to her by the friends of herself and mother.

The decree of the Chancellor will therefore be affirmed, so far as it goes. But the complainants are seeking equity, and must do equity, by accounting for the enhanced value of the lot, by reason of the permanent improvements erected thereon, exclusive of the improvements made by Andrew Kernahan. But the extent of this liability will be left open. until the final hearing.

Decree for complainant.

Mary A. Parker *et al.* *v.* Jesse D. Hall.

MARY A. PARKER *et al.* *v.* JESSE D. HALL.

1. INNOCENT PURCHASER. *Notice. Chancery pleading. Registration. Case in judgment.* If a party have either actual or constructive notice of title, he cannot avail himself of the plea of an innocent purchaser, for value, without notice. A bill of sale, evidencing the title of the complainants, was registered in the county where the bargainor and bargainees resided. The bargainees, subsequently, removed to another county with the slaves, where they were sold by the trustee to the defendant. *Held,* that the defendant was bound to trace the residence of the parties and the history of the title of the slaves, by a search of the Register's books. That the registration of the bill of sale was constructive notice to him, and if he failed to make such search, he was guilty of gross negligence, and could not rely upon the plea of being an innocent purchaser.

2. STATUTE OF LIMITATIONS. *Trust and trustee. When the statute runs against the title of a trustee. Infants.* The principle that when the trustee is barred all the beneficiaries are barred, whether under disability or not, applies, only, when the trustee can sue, but fails to do so. If the trustee estops himself from suing by a sale of the property—thus uniting with the purchaser in a breach of trust—the wrong is to the beneficiaries, not to him. He cannot sue, and the beneficiaries, if under disability, are not affected by the statute.

3. SAME. *Same. Same. Time given persons, under disability, to sue.* In such case, if the beneficiaries are all under disability at the time the adverse possession commences by the sale of the trustee, they are allowed the time, within which to sue, given in the statute, after the disability is removed as to all of them. If any one is capable of suing at the time of the sale, the bar will be perfected within the time allowed by the statute, from that date.

FROM TIPTON.

The bill was dismissed by Chancellor WILLIAMS, at the November Term, 1858. The complainants appealed.

BATE & MORRISON, for the complainants.

Mary A. Parker *et al.* v. Jesse D. Hall.

H. D. SMALL, and J. W. & J. A. HARRIS, for the defendant.

WRIGHT, J., delivered the opinion of the Court.

The bill in this case, is filed to recover of the defendant, Jesse D. Hall, a slave, Judy, and her child Henry.

The bill alleges, and the proof shows, that the defendant, very soon after he came into possession of said slaves, for the purpose of defeating the claim of complainants, whatever it was, removed said slaves to another State. The prayer of the bill is, that complainants may have a decree, in specie, for said slaves and their hires, and the increase of Judy; and if defendant has rendered such a decree impossible, that then they may recover the value of said slaves and hires and interest, as shall be found just and proper.

The decision of this case rests upon the following facts, to-wit: In October, 1842, George H. Parker, the father of complainants, George A., Mary and Alvin D. Parker, and of their deceased sister, Malvinia M. Parker, was duly qualified as their guardian in the County Court of Weakley county, in this State; and as such, received into his possession a fund belonging to them.

This fund was derived by them under the will of Alonzo P. Smith, a deceased relation.

On the 6th of May, 1843, the said George H. Parker, the guardian, with a portion of said funds, purchased of C. McAlister, the slave Judy and her son Robert, and took of him a bill of sale, in the words and figures following, viz:

APRIL TERM, 1859.

Mary A. Parker *et al. v.* Jesse D. Hall.

"State of Tennessee, Obion county: For six dred dollars to me in hand paid, by George H. Parker, guardian of his minor children, George Parker, Mary Parker, Malvinia M. Parker, and Alvin D. Parker, and in right of his wards and of their money: I hereby bargain and sell, and by these presents do bargain and sell, and deliver to said Parker, guardian as aforesaid, for the purposes aforesaid, the following named slaves, for life, Judy, a woman aged about twenty years, and Robert, her child, aged about two years. To have and to hold, in trust, for his wards forever; and I hereby warrant them sound and slaves for life, and the title to them clear and indisputable.

Troy, May 6th, 1843.   C. McALISTER, [L. S.]"

This bill of sale was, on the same day of its execution, duly acknowledged by McAlister, the vendor, before the clerk of the County Court of Obion county, and on the same day properly registered in that county.

At the time of the execution and registration of said instrument, the said McAlister, and the said guardian and his wards, resided in said county of Obion.

The slave Henry is a child of Judy, born after the execution of the bill of sale.

Some two years after its date, the said George H. Parker, with his wards and their mother, and said slaves, removed from Obion, to Tipton county, in this State; and on the 26th of May, 1845, while he was yet a stranger in said county, sold and conveyed Judy and Henry to the defendant, Hall, by bill of sale, on that day duly registered in that county, and which bill of sale is in the usual form, and recites the consideration as 600.00.

Judy is there described as aged about twenty-three years, and Henry as about six months; and the proof shows that Judy's was correctly described in both of these bills of sale.

George H. Parker, the guardian, was insolvent, and had in possession, only, these slaves, and the boy Robert and two others, Dick and Briss, the latter of no value, and both had been purchased, also, with funds of his wards; and the bill of sale to Dick is precisely similar to the one for Judy and Robert, taken from McAlister, of same date, and registered as the other.

At the time of these transactions, these wards were infants of tender years, and one of them, viz., Alvin D., a complainant, is yet an infant under twenty-one years of age.

They were all infants under twenty-one, in May, 1845, when their guardian sold Judy and Henry to Hall, and when he took possession of them, and for sometime thereafter.

George H. Parker, the guardian, died soon after the sale to Hall; and since his death, Malvinia M., one of the wards, died; and complainant, Mary A., her mother, is her administratrix.

The defences relied upon, are that of an innocent purchaser for value, without notice and the statute of limitations.

Neither of these defences can be allowed to avail the defendant. If he had not actual, he had constructive notice, which is equally fatal to him.

The bill of sale from McAlister was duly registered

in Obion county, the residence of the parties at the time, as required by the act of 1831, ch. 90; and by the 12th section of this act, the instrument so registered is declared to be notice to all the world from the time of its registration. Upon its face it disclosed the title to Judy to be in complainants; and the defendfendant's own bill of sale showed that Henry was a child of Judy, born since the execution of the bill of sale. The removal and sale of the slaves in a different county, cannot displace the notice afforded by the registry. To so hold, would be ruinous in its consequences, and a virtual repeal of the registry laws.

The defendant, before buying, was bound to trace the residence of these parties, and the history of the title of Judy, by a search of the Register's books. Not to do so, was gross negligence. If he had done so, and the law holds that he did, he could not have failed to see that his vendor had no title. 4 Hum., 212; 1 Swan, 896; 2 Johns. Rep., 510, 523.

As to the statute of limitations, it can have no operation in the case. When the cause of action accrued, the owners of these slaves were *all* under the disability of infancy, and *one* of them was still an infant, at the institution of this suit; and upon the principles of *Shute* v. *Wade*, 5 Yer., 1, all are saved from the bar.

The position, that when the trustee is barred all the beneficiaries are barred, though they may be under disability, has no application here. That doctrine only applies where the trustee could sue, but fails to do so, as where a stranger intrudes himself into the trust estate and holds wrongfully, and *adversely, both to the trustee* and *the beneficiaries.* In such a case, if the trustee fail to sue and is barred, the beneficiaries, though infants, &c., are also barred. But here, George H. Parker, the trustee and owner of the legal estate, had estopped himself from suing by his bill of sale. He had turned against his wards, and united with the defendant in a breach of trust. The wrong *was to them, not to him.* He could not sue for, or represent them. In such a case it has been repeatedly held, by this Court, since *Herron,* v. *Marshall,* 5 Hum., 443, that the beneficiaries can alone sue, and if they are under disability when the cause of action accrues, they will not be barred until they are allowed the time given in the statute after the disability is removed.

The record entirely fails to disclose any fraud, or other act on the part of complainant, towards defendant, when he purchased this property which will estop, or repel them from a Court of Equity. 4 Hum., 212; 1 Swan, 437.

The decree of the Chancellor will be reversed, and complainants will have a decree for the slaves Jude and Henry, and increase of Judy, born since the defendant's purchase, with hires and interest; but if the slaves have been so disposed of that they cannot be had, then a decree will go for their present value, hires and interest. 10 Yer., 217.

Decree reversed.

GEORGE W. REEVES *et al.* v. JOSEPH M. STEELE *et al.*

SURETIES. *Administrators and executors. Judicial sales. When sureties liable on administration bond* The bond given by an administrator only binds the sureties for the faithful performance of his duties in his capacity as administrator, and not for the performance of any duty imposed by an appointment of the Court. And if, upon the petition of an administrator and the distributees of his intestate, a slave is ordered to be sold, and the adminstrator appointed commissioner to make the sale, his sureties in the administration bond, are not liable for the proceeds of such sale, in the event he sells the slave and fails to pay over the proceeds to the distributees.

FROM FAYETTE.

At the June Term, 1858, HUMPHREYS, J., presiding, there were verdict and judgment for the plaintiffs. The defendants appealed.

SHELTON, and J. W. & J. A. HARRIS, for the plaintiffs in error.

CALVIN JONES, for the defendants in error.

CARUTHERS, J., delivered the opinion of the Court.

Henry F. Steele died intestate in Fayette county in 1852. Appleberry was appointed his administrator, who died in 1854, before the estate was fully settled up, when Wm. Campbell was appointed administrator *de bonis non*. He also died, and was succeeded by Stanly Campbell, of whom the plaintiffs in error were sureties in his administration bond, joined with defendants in error, who are all the distributees of Henry F. Steele, deceased, and were then all of age, in an *ex-parte* petition to the County Court of Fayette, for the sale of a negro man, slave, for distribution, he being the only slave belonging to the estate. The petition was granted, and the slave sold by Campbell under the decree of the Court, for $1000, of which he failed to distribute about $700, and died insolvent. This action of covenant was instituted in the name of the State, for the benefit of the distributees, upon the administration bond, against his sureties, for the amount not distributed. And the only question is, whether they are liable for that defalcation. The Circuit Judge thought they were, and gave judgment against them, from which they have appealed in error to this Court.

We have heretofore held, when the case was before us upon the suit of Stanly, as successor of Campbell in the administration, that they were not liable to him, upon the ground that neither a prior administrator nor his sureties are liable to a succeeding administrator *de bonis non*, for things administered. But this is entirely a different question.

It is not easy to see why it was necessary to call in the aid of a Court to make the sale, when all the distributees were of age, and the title was complete in them, and the debts of the estate all paid. There were no infants, and a proceeding in Court was not necessary to give the purchaser a good title.

But still that course was adopted, and we have to consider its effect as to the responsibility of the sureties of Campbell for his administration.

George W. Reeves et al. v. Joseph M. Steele et al.

We have several times held, that since the act of 1827, the title to slaves passed directly to the distributees of the deceased, subject, only. in the hands of the administrator, to the payment of debts. He has no power to sell them even for that purpose, as he had before that act, but this could only be done by the Courts, so as to divest title out of the distributees. By the act of 1849, this jurisdiction was given to the County Courts concurrently with the Circuit and Chancery Courts. The Court could order the sale to be made by their clerk, he having given a general bond to cover such cases, or by a commissioner, from whom bond and security was required to be taken to secure the fund.

In this case, the decree for sale was made by the County Court, empowering Campbell, the administrator, to make the sale, and pay out the proceeds to those entitled, who are the plaintiffs in this action. No bond was ever given by him, and only a part of the proceeds paid out, and the balance lost by his insolvency, as before stated. Upon whom shall the loss fall, is the question now presented.

The bond of his sureties as administrator, only binds them for the faithful performance of his duties in that capacity, not for anything that might be done by him under an appointment by the Court for a different purpose. The sale of the slaves of the estate was not embraced in his functions as administrator, even if sold for distribution. It was not contemplated by his sureties, that any fund would come into his hands of that kind. They knew the law forbid him to convert them into money. If then, the Court by a distinct appointment clothed

James E. Felts, Sheriff, &c. *v.* The Mayor and Aldermen of Memphis.

him with this power, it is exercised in his new character of commissioner, and not administrator. If the Court failed to secure the fund thus to come into his hands under the decree, it is not the fault of his sureties, as administrator, and the loss should not fall upon them.

The present plaintiffs were parties with him in the Court, and should have attended to their interests by demanding the proper bond. They united in the petition for the sale, and upon their prayer he was appointed. They were the real parties to the proceeding, and he, perhaps, entirely an unnecessary party, as there were no debts to pay. The slave was taken out of his hands as administrator, upon that petition, by the Court, and returned to him in his new character of commissioner, to sell. The liability of the defendants then terminated, because he was not acting as administrator.

We think that his Honor erred in holding the plaintiffs in error liable on the administration bond, and reverse the judgment.

James E. Felts, Sheriff, &c. *v.* The Mayor and Aldermen of Memphis.

1. MANDAMUS. *When the proper remedy.* In general, where a man is refused to be admitted, or wrongfully turned out of any office, or franchise that concerns the public, or the administration of justice, he may be admitted or restored by a writ of *mandamus.*
2. SAME. *When prosecuted by a public officer the suit enures to the benefit of each successor. Sheriff. Abatement.* When a suit for a writ of

James E. Felts, Sheriff, &c. *v.* The Mayor and Aldermen of Memphis.

mandamus is prosecuted by a sheriff, or other public officer, in his official capacity, for the public benefit, the law regards the name of the office, and not the adjunct name of the individual, and in it are implied all the successors that shall ever be to it—each successor, for the time of his term, being the real plaintiff to support the action, whether described by name or not. And, if one dies, or his term of office expires before the determination of the suit, it will not abate, but shall be continued by his successor.

3. JAILS AND JAILORS. *How jails are built, and are public prisons.* Jails are usually built by the County Courts, out of the funds in the County Treasury, but the Legislature may authorize them to be constructed by the towns and cities; and, unless restricted by law, they, *all*, become the public prisons of the State, to be used for the safe custody of offenders. And it does not lie in the power of any county, town, or city, to exclude the State, or its officers, from the custody and control of them.

4. SAME. *Sheriffs entitled to the custody of the jails.* At the common law the custody of jails, of right belonged, and was annexed, as an incident, to the office of sheriff. He was amenable for escapes, and subject to amercements if he had not the bodies of prisoners in Court; and, therefore, had the appointment of jailers and the custody of the jails. These common law rights of the sheriff have not been abridged by the Legislature; and they have the right to the custody and control of the public prisons of their respective counties.

5. SAME. *Same. When the sheriff may be restored to the custody of the jail, by mandamus.* If a jail, built by authority of law, is placed in the possession and under the control of another, than the sheriff, by the County Court, or the Mayor and Aldermen of a town or city, and the sheriff of the county virtually refused all legal authority and control over it, he may be restored to his rights by a writ of *mandamus.*

6. SAME. *Jail in Memphis.* The acts creating the Court in, and amending the charter of the city of Memphis, clearly imply that there should be a jail within the jurisdiction of said Court, as well for the safe-keeping of offenders against the State laws, as the city ordinances. Hence, the jail built by the corporate authorities is a prison of the State, under the care and control of the sheriff of the county.

FROM SHELBY.

A petition was filed by the sheriff of Shelby county, in the Circuit Court, at Raleigh, for a writ of *man-*

James E. Felts, Sheriff, &c. *v.* The Mayor and Aldermen of Memphis.

damus, to be restored to the custody and control of the jail built by the Mayor and Aldermen of Memphis. At the January Term, 1857, HUMPHREYS, J., dismissed the petition. The sheriff appealed. The facts are stated in the opinion of the Court.

JAMES WICKERSHAM, for the sheriff.

S. P. BANKHEAD and H. D. SMALL, for the Mayor and Aldermen.

WRIGHT, J., delivered the opinion of the Court.

On the 19th of December, 1853, the Legislature established a Court in the city of Memphis, to be composed of one Judge, to be elected by the qualified voters of the 5th, 13th and 14th civil districts of Shelby county. He was to hold his office for eight years, and reside in said civil districts.

The style of said Court was the Criminal Court of Memphis. It was to be held *in said city*, and have exclusive original jurisdiction of all crimes and misdemeanors committed against the laws of the State within said civil districts; all authority over said offences being taken away from the Circuit Court of Shelby county, and the Common Law and Chancery Court of the city of Memphis.

It was made the duty of the sheriff of Shelby county to attend the said Criminal Court, and perform all the duties required of him in relation to such criminal business as might come before said Court—he being en-

James E. Felts, Sheriff, &c. v. The Mayor and Aldermen of Memphis.

titled to the same fees and compensation therefor as for like services in other Courts.

The said Court was to have no jurisdiction beyond the limits of said civil districts; and the expenses of providing a house in which to hold the same, and of the jurors in said Court, were required to be paid by the corporation of the city of Memphis.

Afterwards—at the same session of the Legislature—the charter of said city was amended, and the collector of the county revenue for the county of Shelby, was required to pay to the Mayor and Aldermen of said city, the county tax thereafter collected within the limits of said city; and they were to have the fines and forfeitures of the Common Law and Chancery Court of the city of Memphis, and of all other Courts which might thereafter be held in said city; and the said Mayor and Aldermen are required to defray all the expenses incident to the holding of all such Courts.

They have power given them to provide for the erection of all buildings necessary for the use of the city, for the arrest and confinement until trial of all vagrants, rioters, or disorderly persons within the limits of the city; and to authorize the arrest and detention of all persons violating any ordinance of the city.

The City Recorder is declared to have exclusive original jurisdiction of all offences arising under any violation of the provisions of the city charter, or breach of any ordinance of the city.

In September, 1855, William D. Gilmore, then being the sheriff of Shelby county, filed his petition in the Circuit Court of said county, stating that said Mayor and Aldermen of the city of Memphis, had built a

James E. Felts, Sheriff, &c. v. The Mayor and Aldermen of Memphis.

good jail in said city, out of the common public funds of the city, and had set apart the ground floor, or basement story, of the west end of said jail, for a calaboose to imprison offenders against the city laws and ordinances, and the remainder of said jail—including all above the entrance floors on the east end—was, by them, set apart for the imprisonment of persons charged with crimes and misdemeanors against the laws of the State, and for the accommodation of the jailer; and that there was no other jail, or safe place, to keep the prisoners committed to his charge, as sheriff, within the jurisdiction of said Criminal Court.

It was further stated, that the said Mayor and Aldermen of the city of Memphis, and Thomas B. Mynott, City Marshall, and J. S. Dyer, Deputy Marshall, held possession of said jail and all parts of the same, adversely to the petitioner, and his right to the possession and control of the same; and that they have confined in said jail persons for offences against the State, and hold them without any authority from the petitioner, or responsibility to him or the State for their safe-keeping; and that they have ousted petitioner of his possession and control of said jail, for the safe-keeping of prisoners committed to his charge, and assume to act as jailer in his stead, against his wish, and in violation of his right and franchise as sheriff.

The prayer of the petition was for a writ of *mandamus*, and that the petitioner, as sheriff, might be restored to the possession of all that part of said jail so set apart for the safe keeping of offenders against the laws of the State, and for the accommodation of the jailer.

James E. Felts, Sheriff, &c. *v.* The Mayor and Aldermen of Memphis.

An alternative *mandamus* was issued and served upon the defendants.

In their answer, the facts stated in the petition are, in substance, admitted. They, to be sure, state, and the proof shows, that the sheriff has at all times, been allowed free access to the jail and the prisoners confined there for offences against the laws of the State, and to use the said jail for the confinement of said prisoners, and to remove them at pleasure; but this is stated and claimed as matter of favor to the sheriff, and not of *right* in him; and that the Mayor and Aldermen of the city of Memphis are the absolute owners of said jail, and the keepers of the same; and as such, have the right, at their will, to exclude the sheriff and the State's prisoners therefrom. And the record shows they have, accordingly, appointed the jailer, and have the entire control of the jail and the keys thereof.

The Circuit Judge dismissed the petition, and the plaintiff has appealed in error to this Court.

If this be regarded as a legal prison, and the sheriff has the right claimed by him, it will hardly be denied that the writ of *mandamus* is the proper remedy. It is laid down as a rule, that, in general, where a man is refused to be admitted, or wrongfully turned out of any office, or franchise, that concerns the public, or the administration of justice, he may be admitted, or restored by *mandamus.* 5 Bac. Ab. (Title Mandamus C.,) 261. The rule has been applied to the case of a constable. 5. Bac. Ab., 264.

Neither can it be maintained that, in this particular case, the injury to the sheriff is insufficient to authorise the writ, since he has been, virtually, refused all legal

James E. Felts, Sheriff, &c. v. The Mayor and Aldermen of Memphis

authority and control over the jail; and the custody and keys thereof have, by the Mayor and Aldermen of the city of Memphis, been placed in the hands of a jailer of their own appointment.

The next question is, whether anything has transpired since the institution of this suit to abate it? The official term of Gilmore, who was then the sheriff, has expired, and though Felts, his successor, became a party by an amended petition, yet his term has also expired, and his successor been elected. The record does not disclose any personal or individual interest, either in Gilmore or Felts; but the suit appears to have been prosecuted by them in their *official character of sheriff*, for the time being, for the public benefit, and not as individuals.

In such a case, the law regards the name of the *office*, and not the adjunct name of the individual; and in it are implied all the successors that shall ever be to it, each successor, for the time of his term, being the real plaintiff to support the action, whether described by name, or not. And if one die, or his term of office expire, before the determination of the suit, it shall be continued by his successor, and will not abate. 1 Hay., 144; *Polk* v. *Plummer, et al.*, 2 Hum., 500.

We are of opinion, therefore, that the present sheriff of Shelby county may take the benefit of this suit.

We are next to inquire whether this is a legal prison for the safe custody of all persons charged with offences cognizable in the Criminal Court of Memphis; and whether the State has not the right so to regard and use it?

In England, jails are said to be of such universal

concern to the public, that none can be erected by any less authority than by act of Parliament. All prisons, or jails, belong to the King, although a subject may have the custody or keeping of them. This is so, *pro bono publico;* and, therefore, they were to be repaired at the common charge. A subject was not allowed to have a prison of his own. And, therefore, where the Lord of a franchise, or some other than the sheriff, as was sometimes the case, by special custom or grant, had the custody of a prison, it was the King's prison. Even a house of correction, is a jail, to which a prisoner charged with high treason may be committed. 4 Bac. Ab., (Title Gaol and Gaoler, A. and B.,) 28, 29; 4 Com. Dig.; (Title Imprisonment, A.,) 619; 8 Term A., 172.

In Tennessee, jails are usually built by the County Courts, out of funds in the County Treasury; but the Legislature may authorize them to be constructed by the towns and cities; and unless they be, by law, restricted to the confinement of a particular class of offenders, it cannot, we apprehend, be questioned, that, upon common law principles, they will become the public prisons of the State, to be used for the safe custody of offenders; and it does not lie with any county, town, or city, to exclude the State and its proper officers therefrom.

Here there is no such restriction. On the contrary, it seems to me, from the scope and language of the acts creating this Court and amending the city charter, it was intended that there should be a jail in the city of Memphis, as well for the safe custody of offenders against the State laws, as the city ordinances. How else could public justice be administered, or the Criminal

James E. Felts, Sheriff, &c. v. The Mayor and Aldermen of Memphis.

Court be held with any safety or convenience? It can not be supposed that the multitude of criminals whose offences might come within the cognizance of that Court, were to be kept without a jail, or be confined in the county jail at Raleigh—a distance of nine miles from the city—and from thence taken, and restored, as they should be needed, from day to day, during the sessions of the Court.

It is true, it is not said, in so many words, that the Mayor and Aldermen of Memphis shall build a jail; but what is sufficiently implied need not be expressed.

The Court is to sit in the city. Its jurisdiction is confined to the three civil districts above mentioned, which embrace the city. The sheriff of the county is the sheriff of that court. The Mayor and Aldermen of Memphis are to furnish a court-house, and be at all the expenses of that and the other Courts of the city: may erect all buildings necessary for the use of the city, and provide for the arrest and confinement of all offenders against the city laws and ordinances; and are to have the county tax collected within the city—the fines and forfeitures of its Courts, and the revenue from license granted to its inhabitants.

We are not at liberty, therefore, as we think, to hold this to be any other than a public jail—to be used as other prisons. The Mayor and Aldermen have so interpreted the law, and, as we think, properly. They have erected the jail out of the public funds of the city, and have dedicated it, chiefly, to the use of the State, in the confinement of offenders against its laws.

The only remaining question is, whether the sheriff

James E. Felts, Sheriff, &c. *v.* The Mayor and Aldermen of Memphis.

of Shelby county, by law, is entitled to be the keeper of this jail? And we are of opinion he is. At the common law, the custody of jails, of right belonged, and was annexed, as an incident, to the office of sheriff. The safe keeping of prisoners involved much peril and responsibility, and it was esteemed unsafe to commit them to the care of any less a personage than the sheriff himself, whose office was one of very ancient date, and of great trust and authority, and who might bring to his assistance the *posse comitatus*, or power of the county.

He had the appointment of the keepers of jails, and was to put in such for whom he would answer; for being an immediate officer of the King's Courts, and amenable for escapes, and subject to amercements if he had not the bodies of prisoners in Court, it was esteemed against all reason, that another should have the keeping and custody of the jail. His right was favored, and could only be abridged by act of Parliament. Even the King's grant to another, of the custody of prisoners, was, after 5 H., 4, void. The care of Gaols, cited in Milton's case, 460, 34 *a*; 4 Bac. Ab., (Gaol and Gaoler, A.,) 29.

These rules of law and principles govern the present case. The sheriff's common law right cannot be abridged, or given to another, unless the purpose so to do be clearly expressed by the Legislature; and this is not done here. The intendment of the law is in favor of the sheriff's right; and public policy requires that he should be the keeper of all prisons. It would be unsafe to commit so important a trust to another, unless for some imperative reason.

Benj. A. Rogers *et al.* v. Jeptha T. Rogers *et al.*

As to that portion of the jail set apart for the confinement of offenders against the city laws and ordinances, we say nothing, the case calling for no remark as to that.

The judgment of the Circuit Court will be reversed, and a *peremptory mandamus* will issue according to the prayer of the petition.

BENJ. A. ROGERS *et al.* v. JEPTHA T. ROGERS *et al.*

WILL. *Construction of. Power. Implied gift over, in default of appointment. When persons take per capita.* In the second clause of his will, the testator bequeathed seven slaves to his wife, during her life, or widowhood, and at her death, or marriage, to be disposed of as he should afterwards direct in his will, unless she died his widow; in which event he gave her the privilege of giving said slaves to whom she pleased, among his children or grandchildren. In the fourth clause he makes his four sons his residuary legatees. In the fifth clause he directs that, in case of the marriage of his wife, said slaves shall be equally divided among his children, if living; and if any of them be dead, leaving issue, that issue to receive the share of its parent. His wife died without having again married, and without disposing of said slaves under the power given her. Upon the construction of this will it is held:—

1. That the testator did not intend to die *intestate* as to these slaves. That the legal presumption is, that he did not so intend, and that presumption is not overturned by anything contained in the will.

2. From the context, it is apparent that said slaves were not intended to, nor do they pass to the four sons under the residuary clause. Nor do they go to his children under the fifth clause of the will.

3. Under the second clause of the will there is a gift, by implication, of the slaves to the children and grandchildren of the testator, subject to the power of appointment by the widow, at her death,

among them. And the power not having been exercised by the widow, the shares go, under said clause, to the children and grandchildren.

4. When the donee of a power has a life interest in the subject of the power which is to be exercised by will, or at the death of the donee, or at or before that time, the objects will be considered to be those who answer the particular description at the time the power is to be exercised. And, therefore, the children and grandchildren of the testator, living at the death of his widow, are entitled to the slaves.

5 The grandchildren of parents living at the death of the widow are not embraced. Grandchildren are mentioned merely as substitutes for children, and to take only in the event of the parents being dead. And the slaves go to the children living, and the grandchildren whose parents are dead, living at the time of the death of the widow.

6. The children and grandchildren, living at the death of the widow, take the slaves *per capita*, and not *per stirpes*.

FROM WEAKLEY.

Decree for the defendants, by Chancellor WILLIAMS, at the January Term, 1859. The complainants appealed.

SOMERS, for the complainants.

J. A. ROGERS, for the defendants.

WRIGHT, J., delivered the opinion of the Court.

This is a bill for a construction of the will of Jubilee Rogers.

In the second clause, he bequeathed to his wife, Harriet, during her life, or widowhood, seven slaves, by name, and at her death, or marriage, to be disposed of as he should afterwards direct in said will, unless she died his widow; in which event he gave her the privilege of giving said negroes to whom she pleased, among his children or grandchildren.

The fourth clause of the will is a general residuary one, to his four sons, John A., Peleg M., Benjamin M., and Jubilee W., or their legal representatives.

In the fifth clause he directs, that in case of the marriage of his wife, Harriet, the said slaves shall be equally divided among his children, if living; and if any of them be dead, leaving issue, that issue to receive the share of its parent.

The testator died in June, 1855, and the said Harriet died the 15th of February, 1858, without disposing of said slaves, under the power given her in the second clause of the will, and without having again married.

The question to be decided is, what becomes of these slaves? Do they go to the testator's children and grandchildren under the second clause, or to his four sons under the residuary clause, or to his children under the fifth clause, which only directs to whom they shall go in case of the second marriage of said Harriet; or did the testator die *intestate* as to them?

The Chancellor held, that, as to these slaves, the testator died *intestate*.

In this we think he erred. From an examination of this will, we cannot believe the testator intended to die intestate as to any of his property; and the legal presumption is, that he did not so intend. Such is the rule in all cases where a man engages in an act so important as the execution of his will. *Williams* v. *Williams*, 10 Yer., 25. Nor do we think they pass under the residuary clause to the testator's four sons, it being apparent, from the context, that they were not intended so to pass. And it is clear they do not go to his children under the fifth clause, for that could only be in the event his widow married again, and she never did marry.

We have had much difficulty in arriving at what we supposed to have been the meaning of the testator in this will. At one time we were inclined to concur with the Chancellor's decree. But a more careful examination of the will and the authorities, lead us to the conclusion, that under the second clause of the will, these slaves, upon the death of the testator's widow, went *per capita* to his children and grandchildren then living.

It is a well established principle, that where a trust is created for a certain class of objects, and the discretionary power applies only to the selection from, or distribution amongst those objects, the Court, while it disclaims the exercise of the discretion reposed in the trustees, will, if necessary, enforce the performance of the trust by decreeing a distribution of the property amongst all the objects equally. Hill on Trustees, 486; *Brown* v. *Higgs*, 4 Ves., 708; 5 Ves., 495; 8 Ves., 561; 18 Ves., 192.

The difficulty here is, to determine whether Harriet, the widow of the testator, had a power, simply as such, or a power in the nature of a trust; or if it be not a power in the nature of a trust, whether it is not to be considered as a power with a bequest over to the objects of it in default of any appointment by her. In many instances it is difficult to distinguish the cases upon these questions. Sugden on Powers, 394–397.

If the testator intended it to be a condition precedent to the gift of these slaves to his children and grandchildren, that his widow should exercise her power in their favor, then no interest could vest in them until the power was duly exercised; and she having died without executing it, the gift cannot be enforced. Hill on Trustees, 490. And so if it were simply a power. Hill on Trustees, 67; *Brown* v. *Higgs*, 8 Ves., 570. But if it be a power in the nature of a trust, which it was her duty to execute, or a power with a bequest over to the objects of it in default of any appointment by her, and of her failure to marry again, then, though she might, by the exercise of the power, at her death, have given these slaves to whom she pleased, among the testator's children or grandchildren—being confined to that class—yet having omitted to exercise it, the entire class will take. Hill on Trustees, 67–70; 5 Ves., 595; 8 Ves., 561; *Jarnagin* v. *Conway*, 2 Hum., 50.

In some of the cases decided on this subject, there appears to be a material distinction between those cases where the *absolute interest* is given to the donee of the power, and where, consequently, the exercise of the power can take effect only out of that interest, and where the person by whom the power is to be exercised, takes only a previous *estate for life*, to which the power is only collateral.

In the former case, the donee of the power himself would be entitled beneficially, upon his refusal or omission to exercise it; and the intention or wish of the testator to qualify the gift to him would thus be disappointed. Consequently, in such cases, the Court has always endeavored to give effect to the apparent intentions of the testator, by treating the donee as a trustee for the objects of the power.

But where the execution of the power is not to take effect out of the interest of the person by whom it is to be exercised; as where it is given to a tenant for life, to be exercised after the detrmination of his life estate, or *a fortiori*, where the party to whom it is given takes no beneficial interest, the same argument on behalf of the objects of the power does not hold good, and the decisions in favor of their taking, in default of the exercise of the power, are said not to be so uniform. And it is said that indeed where they have been held entitled, in default of appointment, the decision has proceeded, not on the ground that the power was in the nature of a trust in their favor, but that the bequest operated as a direct gift to the objects, in default of the exercise of the power. Hill on Trustees, 67, 68.

But the above distinction between an *absolute* or *less interest* in the donee of the power, seems now not to be attended to; and at the present day, the Courts will endeavor, if possible, to construe a bequest of this description into a gift, by *implication* to the objects of the power, in default of its being exercised. Hill on Trustees, 69; Sugden on Powers, 397, 398; *Walsh* v. *Wallinger*, 2 Rus. & Mylne, 78; *Kennedy* v. *Kingston*, 2 Jac. & Walker, 431; *Brown* v. *Pocock*, 6 Sim., 257; *Croft* v. *Adam*, 12 Sim., 639; *Burrough* v. *Philcox*, 5 Myl. & Cr., 72; Notes to *Harding* v. *Glyn*, in White and Tudor's Equity Cases, reported in 72 Law Library, 844-852, top pages.

In *Brown* v. *Higgs*, the words "authorize and empower" were held to create an imperative trust, or gift, in favor of the objects of the power in default of its exercise. So in *Burrough* v. *Philcox*, the words "shall have power to dispose of by will" had this effect. Notes to *Harding* v. *Glyn*, 72, Law Library, 338-344. And so, also, in *Brown* v. *Pocock*, 6 Sim., 257, a bequest to one for life, *with the power of leaving* a moiety of the same property to and for the benefit of his wife and children, in such manner as he should, by will, duly executed, give and bequeath the same; in default of appointment, was held a gift to the wife and children by *implication*. The Vice-Chancellor said: "The codicil contains no express gift over in default of appointment; but it is clear that the testatrix intended the wife and children to take the fund, and, therefore, I am of opinion, that there is a gift to them, by implication, subject to the power." And in *Kennedy* v. *Kingston*, 2 Jac. & Walker, 431, upon a bequest to "Ann Rawlings, for her life, of £500, and, at her decease, to divide it in portions, as she shall choose, to her children," the Master of the Rolls held, that a power to appoint the proportions in which definite objects are to take, *tacitly includes a gift to them, in default of appointment*. And in *Burrough* v. *Philcox*, the same rule applies where there is a power of selection from a class, or from one class of persons, or *another* in the alternative. Hill on Trustees, 70; *Jones* v. *Torin*, 6 Sim., 255; *Longmore* v. *Broom*, 7 Ves., 125.

With these authorities, how are we to construe the present will? Here is no *express* gift over in default of appointment; but only upon her second marriage, which never having taken place, neither the fourth or fifth clause touched these slaves; for, if she died his widow, they were disposed of in the second clause, or not at all. Now, can there be a doubt, if we look to the entire will, that the testator intended, in the events that have happened, to dispose of them: and that, upon the death of his wife, his children and grandchildren, should take them? We think not. And that it must be held a gift to them by implication, subject to the power which the testator, for wise and obvious reasons, intended she, at her death, might exercise among his children or grandchildren.

Here the subject of the power and of the gift—the seven slaves—admits of no uncertainty. And so, as to the objects or persons to be benefitted, to wit: children or grandchildren of the testator. Not *his* children and grandchildren at *his death*, but at *his wife's death;* for the rule is, that when, as in this case, the donee of the power has a life interest in the subject of the power which is to be exercised by will, or at her death, or at or before her death, the objects will be considered to be those who answer the particular description, at the death of the donee, and there will be no uncertainty. Notes to *Harding* v. *Glyn*, White and Tudor's Eq. Cases, 72, Law Lib., 338–346; 2 Jac. & Walker, 431; 2 Rus. & Mylne, 78; 6 Sim., 257.

But who are the objects of the power and of the testator's bounty here? What is the meaning of children or grandchildren, as used in the second clause of this will? Are the grandchildren to take with their parents; or are the grandchildren mentioned merely as substitutes for children, and to take only in the event of the parents being dead? The latter is, we think, the rule by which this will should be construed. This is,

Benj. A. Rogers. *et al.* v. Jeptha T. Rogers. *et al.*

we think, the intention upon the whole will, and upon the authority of *Jones* v. *Torin*, 6 Sim., 255, and *Garthwaite* v. *Robinson*, 2 Sim., 43, though it may seem to be against *Longmore* v. *Broom*, 7 Ves., 125. We take it, as well upon this, as upon the other clauses of this will, that the testator did not intend the parents and the children to take at the same time; but only that grandchildren were to take, if the parent is not living. 2 Sim., 43.

Then how do they take? And are the children and grandchildren (those who take) to take *per stirpes* or *per capita?* It seems, upon authority, they take *per capita*—though I am not sure this was the testator's meaning. But I have been unable to find that, in this will, he has sufficiently expressed a different intention, to authorize a departure from the rule. Notes to *Harding* v. *Glyn*, 72 Law Lib.. 346, 347; 7 Ves., 125; *Davenport* v. *Hanbery*, 3 Ves. Jr., 257; 3 Hawk's R., 604; 2 Dev. Eq. R., 509; *Seay, adm'r,* v. *Winston et al.*, 7 Hum., 472.

Reverse the decree, and decree for the children and grandchildren, upon the principles of this opinion.

GAGE, DATER AND MASSEY *v.* E. M. EPPERSON *et al.*

1. FRAUDULENT SALES. *Liability of purchaser from vendee with notice of the fraud.* If goods are procured by fraud under color of a contract of purchase, and the same are received by a third person with notice of the fraud in obtaining them; or under circumstances sufficient to put him on inquiry; or such third person fails to put himself on the footing of a *bona fide* purchaser for a valuable consideration; then, by the mere act of receiving the goods and appropriating them to his own use, he is guilty of a conversion, for which the original owner of the goods may maintain an action of *trover.*

2. SAME. *Same.* Such third person is thus liable, although he may have received the goods *before* the owner took any steps, or made known his determination to reclaim them. Being affected with notice of the fraud, he is chargeable with all the legal consequences of the same. He cannot excuse himself upon the ground that the owner might acquiesce in the fraud, and abandon his legal right to treat the sale as a nullity and reclaim the goods.

FROM SHELBY.

Verdict and judgment for the defendants at the May Term, 1858, HUMPHREYS, J., presiding. Plaintiffs appealed.

H. G. SMITH, for the plaintiffs, contended:

That when a sale of goods is obtained by fraud, the title or right of property does not pass as between vendor and fraudulent vendee. Chitty on Con., 406; Low. on Sales, 167–8; 2 Green. Ev., § 638; Parsons Merc. Law, 56.

As against fraudulent vendee and a purchaser from

Gage, Dater and Massey v. E. M. Epperson *et al.*

him, with notice, trover will lie without demand and refusal, because no title passes, and the original taking is tortious, and itself is a conversion. 1 Hill, 302; 1 Hill, 311; 13 Wend., 570; 1 Metc., 557: 22 Pick., 18; 24 Pick., 241.

WICKERSHAM & BEECHER, for the defendants, said:

The Court charged the jury, that the defendant would not be protected if he had knowledge of the fraud supposed of Davis, or was cognizant of such facts as would ordinarily induce a reasonable man to believe or suspect the goods had been fraudulently obtained; nor would he be protected if he took them in payment, or as security for a pre-existing debt, or to sell or pay such debts; but if he did not have such information, or he made advances of money or other thing of value, in purchase of them; or to sell and repay such advances, then he would be entitled to hold them against the plaintiffs.

And further, the Court charged the jury, that if at the time of the attempt of the plaintiffs, or their agents, to reclaim the goods from the defendant he had sold them, and no longer had control of them, or possession of them, he would not be liable, &c.

1. As to the protection of innocent purchasers, or one who advances on goods fraudulently obtained, see 15 Wend., 20; 15 Wend., 16; U. S. D., 556 and 7; 34 Eng. Law and Eq. Reps., p. 607.

The case, in 5 Sneed, of *Arendale* v. *Morgan*, p. 703, fully settles this doctrine.

2. As to the action of trover against a person taking the goods of a fraudulent purchaser after they have been disposed of, see 10 U. S. Dig., 416; 2 Green. Ev., Trover, sec. 642, latter part; 13 Pick., 294; 11 Meeson & Welsby, 866.

E. M. YERGER, for the defendants.

McKINNEY, J., delivered the opinion of the Court.

This was an action of *trover*, to recover the value of a quantity of goods, wares and merchandise, specifically described in the declaration, amounting in value to upwards of $2000, as procured from the plaintiffs, in the city of New York, by fraud, under color of a contract of purchase made by one Davis; and afterwards received from him, at Memphis, by the defendant and others, with full knowledge, as is alleged, of the fraudulent means by which they were obtained from the plaintiffs. Judgment was for the defendant in the Circuit Court, and an appeal in error to this Court.

The principles of law applicable to this case, except as to one point, were recently laid down in *Arendale* v. *Morgan*, 5 Sneed, 703.

The new point presented in the case under consideration, arises upon the instruction of the Court, to the effect, that if the defendant had sold the goods, and had not the possession or control of them, at the time the plaintiffs elected to avoid the sale to Davis, and to reclaim the goods, he would not be liable in an action of *trover*.

In one aspect of the case, this instruction was erroneous. If the defendant, in good faith, made a valid purchase of the goods from Davis, in ignorance of the fraudulent means by which the latter had gained the possession of them from the plaintiffs, then, upon the principle of the case of *Arendale* v. *Morgan*, no action could be maintained against him by the plaintiffs. But, if he received the goods with notice of the fraud of Davis in obtaining them; or, under circumstances sufficient to have put him on inquiry; or failed to place himself upon the footing of a *bona fide* purchaser, for a valuable consideration paid for them; then, by the very act of receiving the goods, under such circumstances, and appropriating them to his own use, he was, in law, guilty of a conversion. And this is so, although his pretended purchase may have been *before* the plaintiffs took any step, or made known their determination to reclaim the goods. Being affected with notice of the fraud of Davis, he was chargeable with knowledge of all the legal consequences of such fraud, and cannot excuse his wrong upon the flimsy pretext, that, perchance, the plaintiffs might acquiesce in the fraud, and abandon their legal right to treat the sale as a nullity, and reclaim the goods.

If it were admitted to be true, that a purchase of goods, in good faith, from one who had no right to sell them, is not of itself a conversion of them, as against the rightful owner, until his right has been made known and resisted; the admission would be of no avail in the present case.

The case of *Edwards* v. *Hooper*, 11 Meeson and Welsby's Rep., 362, does not touch the question in this case. That was a case under the bankrupt laws. The conversion had, in fact, taken place *before* the bankruptcy, but the plaintiffs in the declaration alleged a conversion *after* the bankruptcy, assuming that the property in the goods, and not the right of action merely, was vested in the assignees. And it was correctly held that the plaintiffs could not recover; and that, as the conversion was before the bankruptcy, a demand and refusal of the goods after the bankruptcy, and after the possession of them had previously been parted with by sale, would not entitle the plaintiffs to recover; that it would not support the allegation of a conversion subsequently to the bankruptcy.

It might be conceded, that, in a case where the party had not become chargeable with a conversion, either by the act of receiving or disposing of the goods; that a demand and refusal, after they had been parted with, would not be sufficient evidence to support an action of trover. In such case, the presumption of a conversion, arising ordinarily from refusal to deliver on demand, might be repelled by showing that, at the time of demand, the goods were not in the defendant's possession, or subject to his control. But this principle can have no application to a case, where, by the act of receiving and appropriating the goods to his own use, the party was guilty of a conversion of them. It would be absurd to hold, that his own voluntary act of parting with the goods, before demand by the lawful owner, should operate to discharge him of the liability with which he had become previously fixed.

For the error of charge upon this point, the judgment must be reversed.

L. A. WEISINGER *et al.* v. E. M. MURPHY *et al.*

1. STATUTE OF LIMITATIONS. *Land law. Tenants in common. Deed by one co-tenant. Adverse possession.* If real estate is held in common, and one tenant assumes to convey the entire land, or any specific part of it, by metes and bounds, his deed will be a *color of title*, and possession under it for seven years, will be adverse to the title of the co-tenants, and bar their right to recover the land conveyed.

2. SAME. *Same. Same. Notice. Ouster.* Such deed and possession of the land is an actual ouster, and disseizin of the co-tenant, which he is bound to notice. In order to create this adverse relation, no formal or other notice, from the vendee in possession, is necessary.

3. SAME. *Husband and wife. Joint estate of. Tenancy by the curtesy.* By marriage, the husband derives an estate of freehold in the real estate of the wife. He is jointly *seized* with his wife, and during the existence of the *coverture* he is not tenant by the curtesy; and cannot be, unless he survive her. If there be a disseizin during the coverture, it is a disseizen of the entire joint estate, and the husband and wife must, jointly, bring suit to recover the possession. If they neglect to sue for seven years, during which period there is an adverse possession of the land, their joint right of action will be barred.

4. SAME. *Same. Same. Same. Extinguishment of husband's interest.* If the joint right of husband and wife is barred by the statute of limitations, the husband's interest is extinguished. And if he survive his wife, he has no right to, or interest in her real estate as tenant by the curtesy.

5. SAME. *Same. Same. Wife surviving. Must sue within three years.* If the wife survive her husband, she has, by the *proviso* of the statute, only three years next after their coverture shall cease, within which to sue; and if she neglects to sue within that time her right is barred.

6. SAME. *Same. Same. Husband surviving. Heirs of wife must sue within three years.* If the husband survive the wife, his interest in the estate having been extinguished, her heirs, though under the disabilities of infancy, coverture, &c., must sue within three years next after her death, or their right of action will be barred. Cumulative disabilities are not allowed to suspend or arrest the statute after it has commenced running.

7. SAME. *Same. Same. If severed by the deed of the husband, when the bar of the statute is formed.* The case is different where there is no joint right of suit in husband and wife, as when the husband makes a conveyance of the lands of the wife, she not joining therein. In such case the husband, by his deed, has estopped himself from suing, and the wife cannot sue alone, nor can she or her heirs sue the husband's vendee until after the death of the husband. The estate becomes one of remainder in the wife or her heirs, with the right to sue therefor at any time within seven years next after the husband's death.*

FROM WEAKLEY.

This cause was heard at the October Term, 1858, FITZGERALD, J., presiding. Verdict for the defendant. The facts are, sufficiently, stated by the Court.

W. R. ROSS, and RAINS & BLACK, for the plaintiffs.

GARDNER and CARDWELL, for the defendants, cited: Act of 1828, ch. 31, § 1; 2 Green. Ev., §§ 430, 557; *Waterhouse* v. *Martin*, Peck's R., 392, 411; Angell on Lim., 98; *Guion* v. *Anderson*, 8 Hum., 298.

---

* This case removes some of the difficulties heretofore *supposed* to exist, growing out of the case of Guion v. Anderson. It will be observed that the principles decided, are founded upon a state of facts existing prior to the acts passed protecting the real estate of the wife. Act of 1850, ch. 36, §§ 1 and 2; Code, §§ 2481 and 2482.

L. A. Weisinger et al. v. E. M. Murphy et al.

WRIGHT, J., delivered the opinion of the Court.

This is an action of ejectment brought by the plaintiffs, as the heirs of Frances W. Porter, to recover the one undivided half of 715 acres of land in Weakley county.

Verdict and judgment being against them, upon the statute of limitations; they have appealed in error to this Court.

This case is governed by the principles of *Guion* v. *Anderson*, reported in 8 Hum., 298. It is there held, that by marriage the husband gains an estate of freehold in the inheritance of his wife, in her right, which may continue during their joint lives; and may, by possibility, last during his own life. He is not, however, solely seized, but jointly with his wife. During the existence of the coverture he is not tenant by the curtesy, and cannot be, unless he survive his wife; and, therefore, has no particular interest or estate, separate from the fee simple estate in his wife. If there be a disseizin during the coverture, it is a disseizin of the entire joint estate, and they must jointly bring suit to recover the possession. And if they fail to do so, their joint right of action will be barred by seven years adverse possession; and the husband's interest barred and extinguished, so that if he even survive his wife, he has no estate or interest; and if she survive him, she has, by the proviso in the statute, only three years next after their coverture shall cease, within which to sue. And if he survive her, her heirs, though under the disabilities of infancy, coverture, &c., must, by the same statute, sue within three years next after her death, or be forever barred. Cumulative disabilities, or other event, not being allowed to arrest or suspend the statute after it has commenced running.

The case is entirely different where there is no *joint right of suit* in husband and wife, as where the husband makes a conveyance of the lands of the wife, she not joining therein. Where the husband, by his deed, has estopped himself from suing, and the wife cannot sue alone; nor can she, or her heirs, sue the husband's vendee, until after the husband's death, and the case becomes one of particular estate and remainder, with the right of seven years, in the wife, or her heirs, to sue next after the husband's death. *Guion* v. *Anderson*, 8 Hum., 327; *McCorry* v. *King's Heirs*, 3 Hum., 267; *Miller* v. *Miller*, Meig's Rep., 484.

These rules applied to the present case, are decisive of it.

The tract of land in dispute, belonged to the said Frances W., and her sister, Helen M., in equal moities, as tenants in common in fee simple. In 1822, the former intermarried with James B. Porter, by whom she had, in the year 1829, an only daughter; and she and her husband, with the three other children of the said Frances W., by Mr. Bond, her first husband, are plaintiffs in this action.

The said Frances W. died February the 4th, 1850, and her husband, the said James B. Porter, died in October, 1854.

At her death, all her children, save her son William, were *femes covert*, and have so continued ever since.

The said Helen M. intermarried, in 1808, with David Yarbrough, and he died in 1841. Prior to his death, and in the years 1838 and 1839, the said David Yarbrough, and wife, Helen M., by their joint deeds, and in some cases, the said David by his deeds, assumed to convey, and did convey, by their attorney in fact, the *entire tract* of land in dispute, to the defendants, who immediately took actual possession, and have held it ever since, claiming the entire and whole interest in said land as their own.

These deeds were absolute conveyances in fee simple, by metes and bounds, and with full covenants of warranty; and they, and the power of attorney, were immediately registered.

This suit was commenced the 9th of January, 1857, *more than three years after* the death of the said Frances W. Porter, the ancestor of plaintiffs.

Neither the said James B. Porter, or the said Frances W., his wife, had anything to do with the conveyances by Yarbrough, and Yarbrough and wife. The effect of these deeds, and the possession under them, was an actual ouster of Porter and wife; and they had a joint right of action at once, against the vendees of Yarbrough and wife, to recover their half of this land; but having failed to sue until the joint right was barred; and the plaintiffs having also failed to sue until more than three years after the death of the said Frances W., it follows they are barred.

It is true, as argued, that the legal effect of the deeds of Yarbrough and wife, and Yarbrough, upon the title, was only to pass such interest and estate as they had in this land, and to leave untouched the title of Porter and wife to the other moiety. Meig's Rep., 484.

But it is not true that the possession of defendants,

under these deeds, was not adverse to Porter and wife. On the contrary, it seems to be well settled in this State and elsewhere, that if one tenant in common assume to convey the entire land, or any specific part of it, by metes and bounds, his deed will be a color of title; and possession under it for seven years, will be adverse to the right and title of the co-tenants, and bar their action to recover the land conveyed. It is an actual ouster and disseizin of the co-tenant, which he is bound to notice; and in order to create this adverse relation, no formal, or other notice from the vendee in possession, is necessary. *Waterhouse* v. *Martin*, Peck's Rep., 392, 411; *Thurman* v. *Shelton*, 10 Yer., 383, 388; Angell on Lim., 97, 98; *Higber* v. *Price*, 5 Mass., 352: 5 Cowen, 483; *Cullen* v. *Matzer*, 13 Serg. & R., 356; 2 Green. Ev., secs. 430, 557.

The cases from North Carolina to which we have been referred, we do not understand to differ, in principle, from the doctrine of our own Courts, as above laid down. 3 Dev., 317; 4 Dev., 290.

If, however, there be the difference supposed, our own decisions furnish the rule by which we must be guided.

Judgment affirmed.

Benjamin H. Sandeford *v.* James A. W. Hess.

BENJAMIN H. SANDEFORD *v.* JAMES A. W. HESS.

1. SALE OF PERSONALTY. *Judgment. Execution. Trover. Replevin. Evidence.* A purchaser of personal property at a sheriff's or constable's sale, cannot maintain an action of *trover* or *replevin* against a party who subsequently causes the same property to be sold by virtue of a judgment and execution in his favor, without producing in evidence the judgment, as well as the execution under which his purchase was made.

2. SAME. *When made after the teste of an execution issued from the Circuit Court.* The owner of personal property cannot sell and make a good title to the same after the teste of an execution issued from the Circuit Court.

3. SAME. *Private sale of property after levy of an execution. Question reserved.* Can an officer sell property levied on, at private sale with the consent of the debtor, especially after he has taken a delivery bond, and before the restoration of the property to him?

4. SAME. *Same. Same.* If property is levied on by an officer, and is sold at private sale by him and the debtor, (the debtor conveying the title,) is it to be regarded, in a contest with a third person as to the validity of the title, as a sale made by the officer?

FROM GIBSON.

Verdict and judgment for the defendant, at the March Term, 1859, WILLIAMS, J., presiding. The plaintiff appealed.

BLACK, FREEMAN and TOTTEN, for the plaintiff.

M. R. HILL, for the defendant.

WRIGHT, J., delivered the opinion of the Court.

Benjamin H. Sandeford v. James A. W. Hess.

This is an action of replevin for a slave, Mary, in which the defendant had judgment, and the plaintiff has appealed in error to this Court.

The facts of the case are these: One Landis, a constable of Gibson county, had in his hands for collection, three executions, issued by a justice of the peace, against R. P. Raines; and on the 14th of June, 1858, he levied two of them on the slave, Mary—as the property of Raines—and took delivery bonds, for the forthcoming of the property for sale, on the 5th of July, afterwards. Afterwards, he also levied the remaining execution.

Landis proved that on Saturday, the 26th of June, 1858, James Blakemore, a constable of said county, came to his house in Trenton, late in the evening, and requested him to walk down to Mr. Raines' office—that the plaintiff had agreed to purchase the slave, Mary— but that Mr. Raines refused to sell her unless Mr. Landis would agree to it. Landis then went down, and found the plaintiff was willing to purchase the slave at $800, but that he, Raines, would not sell her, unless he, Landis, was willing. To this Landis replied that he was of opinion that he had no right to say anything about it, until the delivery bonds were forfeited; that, after some conversation, Landis wrote a bill of sale, conveying the slave to plaintiff, at the price of $800—which Raines signed and executed, and Landis attested it as a witness, and it was duly registered; that plaintiff received the slave, and two days afterwards paid Landis $550 of her price, which was applied by him to the three executions in his hands—satisfying one, and leaving some balance on the other two—and the residue of the money went to Blakemore, the other constable, who had executions against Raines, and to plaintiff himself, who, also, had a judgment against Raines.

Landis further proved that he told Raines he had no right to consent or object to the sale to plaintiff; that he was afraid if he did consent, it would discharge the security in the delivery bonds for the balance of the debts. Raines then asked him how much money would do him at that time, and he replied $525. Raines then told him to write the bill of sale—which he did—and plaintiff agreed to pay him, and did pay him, the $550, and the same was applied as before stated.

Landis made the following endorsement on one of the executions, and signed the same officially, to-wit:

"June 28, 1858. Satisfied in full by proceeds of negro girl sold B. Sandeford.
B. LANDIS, C. G. C."

And on the same day he placed the proper credits on the other executions, showing that the money had come from plaintiff, and was the proceeds of the sale of said slave; and also signed the same officially.

It further appears that sundry judgments were rendered against said Raines in the Circuit Court of Gibson county, upon which executions were issued and placed in the hands of the sheriff of that county, on the 20th of April, 1858, tested on the third Monday in March, of that year, and on the 16th of July, in the same year, were by him levied on said slave—then in the hands of the plaintiff—and on the 14th of August, afterwards, the said sheriff, by virtue of said last mentioned executions and levies, sold and delivered said

Benjamin H. Sandeford v. James A. W. Hess.

slave to the defendant, at the price of $700. The plaintiff forbid the sale.

The Circuit Judge, upon these facts, charged the jury that, whether the sale made by Raines to the plaintiff, was with, or without, Landis' consent, was immaterial, and that the defendant had the better title.

We should have stated that the plaintiff failed to read or produce any judgments in support of the justice's executions under which he claims to have purchased; and that the judgments and executions upon which the defendant relied to maintain his title were read.

The question now is, whether the judgment of the Circuit Court can be maintained? And we think it can. Beyond all question, if the sale to the plaintiff is to be regarded merely as a sale by Raines, and not the *official act* of the constable, the plaintiff, as against the defendant, has no title, since the teste of the executions from the Circuit Court entirely overreached his purchase. *Daley* v. *Perry and Shelton*, 9 Yer., 442.

It is not necessary here for us to consider the question, whether an officer may, with the consent of the debtor, sell property levied on at private sale. (7 Bac. Ab., Title Sheriff N., 215; 1 Bos. and Pull., 360; 5 Hum., 577.) Nor as to his power, even with the consent of the debtor, to sell, after he has taken a delivery bond, and before the restoration of the property to him again on the day of sale. (3 Hum., 532; 4 Hum., 383: 2 Sneed, 93.) Nor whether the Circuit Judge should have submitted to the jury the question, whether, upon the facts of this case, this sale was not to be regarded as made by the officer, and not by

Albert G. McLellan *et al.* v. Charles D. McLean *et al.*

Raines; because, we think, the failure of the plaintiff to exhibit and read the judgments in support of the executions under which he claimed, is fatal to his title.

It is laid down, that where a purchaser, through sale under a judgment and execution, sues, as such, to recover the property purchased, he must, in general, produce the judgment, execution, &c., for they are parts of his title. 4 Philips on Ev., Cowen and Hill's Notes, part 2, 789, 790; *Carter* v. *Simpson*, 7 Johns. R., 535; *Yates* v. *St. John et al.*, 12 Wend., 74. The case in Wendell is a direct authority. The rule applies to both real and personal estate.

A purchaser of personal property at sheriff's or constable's sale, cannot maintain an action of *trover* or *replevin* against the plaintiff who subsequently causes the same property to be sold by virtue of a judgment and execution in his favor, without *proving the judgment*, as well as the execution, under which his purchase was made. 12 Wend., 74.

The judgment of the Circuit Court will be affirmed.

Albert G. McLellan *et al.* v. Charles D. McLean *et al.*

1. TRUST AND TRUSTEE. *Trust created by parol. A trust may be carved out of an absolute bequest by parol.* If a testator makes an absolute bequest of property to another, with the verbal agreement with the legatee that she will, at her death, dispose of the property equally between his and her relations, a trust is thereby created in favor of the relations, which will be enforced in a Court of Equity, if such legatee fail to execute the agreement.

2. SAME. *Same. Same. May be established by parol evidence.* Such a trust, resting upon a parol agreement, must of necessity be proven by parol testimony.

3. SAME. *Same. Same. Trust need not be noticed in the bequest.* It is not necessary, in order to establish the trust, that there should be any mention of it in the bequest. If the evidence establishes the trust, it will be enforced, although the gift of the property is absolute and unconditional.

FROM MADISON.

This cause was heard before Chancellor WILLIAMS, at the February Term, 1859, who decreed for the defendants. The complainants appealed.

McLANAHAN, STEPHENS, BROWN, and TOMLIN, for the complainants, contended that the proof clearly shows that the bequest of the property was made by the testator to his wife upon an express agreement that she would, at her death, divide the same, equally, between his and her relations. Such was the distinct understanding of the parties before and at the time the will was made; and it was executed under the belief, by the testator, that the agreement would be carried out. This being so, a trust was thereby created in favor of the relations of the testator, the complainants, who do not get an equal share of the property under and by virtue of the will of the wife.

This is a trust that can be created by parol, and, when established, will be enforced in equity. And it is not necessary that there should be any reference to it in the will. 1 Story's Eq., § 256, and cases cited; *Richardson* v. *Adams*, 10 Yer., 273; *Drakeford* v. *Wilks*,

---
Albert G. McLellan et al. v. Charles D. McLean et al.
---

3 Atk., 539; *Thynn* v. *Thynn*, 1 Vern., 296; *Wicket* v. *Ruly*, 3 Brown's Par. Cases, 16; 2 Ves. & Bea., 259; 10 Eng. Con. Ch., 241.

YERGER, SCURLOCK, and MORRILL, for the defendants.

A. W. O. TOTTEN, on the same side, cited and commented upon the following authorities:

Patton v. *McLure*, Mar. & Yer., 333; *Allison* v. *Rutledge*, 5 Yer. 193; *Blair* v. *Snodgrass*, 1 Sneed, 26; *Grant* v. *Nailor*, 4 Cranch, 235; Story's Eq. Pl., §§ 765, 766, 767, 768; 6 Ves., 61; 3 Atk., 141; 9 Ves., 518; *Chamberlain* v. *Agar*, 2 Ves. & Bea., 259; 1 Vernon, 296; 7 Simons, 644; 2 Vern., 106, *Smitheal* v. *Gray*, 1 Hum., 491; *Boyd* v. *McLean*, 1 J. C. R., 582; 2 J. C. R., 409; 2 Story's Eq. Jur., §§ 705, 706; *Richardson* v. *Adams* 10 Yer., 274; 3 Atk., 539; 14 Eng. Ch. R., 473; 1 Eng. Ch. R., 259; 9 Simons' 320; 9 Eng. Ch. R., 411; 2 Spence's Eq. Jur., 68–71; 2 Story's Eq., Jur., § 1070; *Knight* v. *Knight*, 3 Bea.; 3 Ves., 9; 11 Ves., 204.

S. W. COCHRAN, S. J., delivered the opinion of the Court.

It appears from the record in this case, that James D. McLellan and Isabella McLean intermarried in 1831. That they lived together very affectionately, and by their industry and energy, accumulated an estate, worth from seventy to eighty thousand dollars. They had no children.

In February, 1852, he died of consumption, with which he had been afflicted for a considerable time. She survived him until October, 1857, when she died.

He left a will, dated the 23d of August, 1841, to which he made a codicil, dated the 26th day of January, 1852.

The operative words of the will are as follows: "I will and bequeath to my dearly beloved wife, Isabella Caroline McLellan, all the property both real and personal, legal and equitable, that I may die seized or possessed of, or in any manner whatever entitled to; all the money, notes, accounts, choses in action, and every other species of property, that I may be entitled to, to her and her heirs forever, to dispose of as she may think proper."

By the codicil, he makes two bequests to other persons—one for $1000, and one for $200.

This bill is filed by the brothers and sisters, and the heirs of deceased brothers and sisters, of James D. McLellan, who charge that before and at the date of said will there was a mutual agreement and understanding between the testator and his wife, that at the death of the survivor, their property should be equally divided among their respective relations, giving one-half to his, and the other half to her relations. That in consequence of her promise to divide the estate at her death, he made his will, giving the whole of his estate to her in *fee simple.*

The conversations between the parties, their declarations and acts, proven, establish, very satisfactorily, the

Albert G. McLellan *et al.* v. Charles D. McLean *et al.*

fact, that such an agreement or understanding did exist between them. And the proof discloses the fact that he was very solicitous upon the subject. That when he was about to leave home, on a journey to Florida, for the benefit of his health, from which he did not expect to return alive, he exacted from her a renewal of the promise; and that upon hearing of his death she would have her will written, giving to his relations one half and to hers the other half of their property.

At her death she left a will, in which (with some inconsiderable exceptions) she gave the property to her relations and those of her deceased husband, but not equally. She gave more to the McLeans than to the McLellans.

The complainants seek an equal division of the estate between the two families, insisting that Mrs. McLellan took the estate clothed with a trust, in favor of his and her relations, equally, raised by the agreement or understanding between her and her husband.

It is insisted on the part of the defendants, that as the gift is absolute in the will, a trust cannot be raised by parol.

We are of the opinion, from authority, that such a trust can be created by parol agreement; and the agreement being in parol, must of necessity be proven by parol evidence. And that, in this case, Isabella C. McLellan took the estate in trust, to be divided, at her death, equally between her relations and those of her deceased husband.

The subject and object of the testator's bounty being subject to no uncertainty, and the proof of the agreement being satisfactory.

Albert G. McLellan *et al.* v. Charles D. McLean *et al.*

The case of *Padmore* v. *Gunning*, 7 Simons, 644, is very similar to the case under consideration. The facts, as stated in that case, are, that the testator communicated to his wife his desire and determination to give the whole of his property, real and personal, to his two natural daughters, after the death of his wife; and upon receiving that communication, she proposed that he should leave his property to her, and undertook and promised that if he would do so, she would carry into effect his desire and determination in favor of his said natural daughters. And upon the faith of such undertaking and promise, he made his will, which, after other provisions, concluded thus: "And as to the rest, residue and remainder of my estate, of every nature and kind, and all the property I have, I give, devise, and bequeath, the same to my dear wife, her heirs, administrators, and assigns, for her own separate use and enjoyment, having a perfect confidence she will act up to those views which I have communicated to her in the ultimate disposal of my property after her decease." It was held that such a state of facts would create a trust, which a Court of Equity would enforce.

Here was an absolute gift of the property, on the face of the will, and the trust was created by a parol agreement. The clause that he had perfect confidence that she would act up to his views, &c., in the ultimate disposal of his property after her decease, could not aid in discovering what those views were. The objects of his bounty, and the manner of the disposal, were left to be discovered by parol evidence; and this provision tends to give a discretion to the devisee, to act up to his views or not. The terms are not imperative;

nor do they convey the idea of any provision on her part to act up to his views.

To the same effect, in principle, are the cases of *Thynn* v. *Thynn*, 1 Vern., 296; *Drakeford* v. *Wilks*, 3 Atkins' Rep., 539; *Wicket* v. *Raby*, 3 Brown's Parliamentary Cases, 16; and *Richardson* v. *Adams & Wife*, 10 Yer., 273.

The decree of the Chancellor sets up the trust, so far the decree is right; but that part which excludes from the account the profits accruing after the death of James D. McLellan, and includes any of the estate converted or used by Isabella C. McLellan in her lifetime, is erroneous.

An account of the estate should be taken, as it existed at the death of Isabella C. McLellan, giving one-half in value to the complainants, to be divided among them according to the statute of descents and distributions; and commissioners will be appointed to value the property and make the division.

E. W. TIPTON v. JAMES SANDERS et al.

1. LAND LAW. *Grant. Occupant claims. Transfer of. Presumption.* The statutes prescribe the mode by which the transfer and ownership of the occupant claims or entries might be established before the entry-taker; and after the issuance of a grant it will be *presumed*, when the title comes collaterally in question in a Court of Law, that all the preliminary steps necessary to the making of the entry, and obtaining of the grant, were regularly pursued.

2. SAME. *Act of* 1849, *ch.* 188. *Act of* 1851, *ch.* 326, § 1. *Effect of hiatus between. Grant.* The effect of the act of 1851, ch. 326, § 1, was to resuscitate the right and prolong the time for perfecting titles to land; and, as against all persons who acquired no intervening right during the *hiatus* between the expiration of the act of 1850, and the passage of the act of 1851, the title of previous enterers, who have obtained grants, is as perfect as if no such interval had occurred.

3. SAME. *Same. Same. Illustration of the principle.* T obtained a grant on the 1st of January, 1856, founded on an entry made on the 4th of August, 1849, which purports on its face to be a consolidation of six occupant extension entries, (of which T. was assignee,) made on the 19th of October, 1840. S. obtained a grant for the same land on the 10th, of November, 1849, founded on an entry made on the 7th of July, 1847. *Held*, that under the acts of 1851 and 1853, the right of T. to perfect his title was revived and continued, and this right was perfect against all persons who had acquired no right during the intermission between the act of 1850 and 1851; that the entry and grant of S. were void *ab initio*, and were not revived by the accidental intermission in the extension law.

FROM OBION.

At the October Term, 1858, verdict and judgment were rendered for the defendants, WILLIAMS, J., presiding. The plaintiff appealed.

COCHRAN & ENLOE, for the plaintiff.

M. R. HILL, and DAVIS & SMITH, for the defendants.

McKINNEY, J., delivered the opinion of the Court.

This was an action of ejectment, brought by Tipton against Sanders. Judgment was for the defendant.

The question for our determination, is one of title. The plaintiff claims under a grant to him or 1200

E. W. Tipton *v.* James Sanders *et al.*

acres of land, lying in Obion county, issued on the 1st day of January, 1856. This grant is founded on an entry made by Tipton on the 4th day of August, 1849, which purports on its face to be a consolidation of six occupant extension entries, (of which he was assignee,) made on the 19th day of October, 1840.

The defendant sets up claim to 140 acres of the land covered by the plaintiff's title, under a grant to Parham and Woodring, issued on the 10th of November, 1849, and founded on an entry made on the 7th of July, 1847.

The Circuit Judge instructed the jury, that the plaintiff's grant was void, so far as it interfered with the grant under which the defendant claimed; on the ground, as said in the argument, of the interval between the acts of 1849–50, and 1851–2, extending the time for perfecting titles to lands previously entered, south and west of the congressional reservation line.

By the act of 1849–50, ch. 138, the time was extended "until the *first day of September*, 1851." The act of 1851–2 was passed on the 13th of November, 1851. It provides: "That the enterers of land in any of the land offices in this State, and the assignees of such entries, shall have time until the first day of March, 1854, to have their entries surveyed and granted." And by the act of 1853–4, ch. 24, sec. 1, passed on the 20th December, 1853, it is enacted, "That enterers of land in any of the land offices in this State, and the assignees of such enterers, shall have time until the first day of April, 1856, to have their entries surveyed and granted."

It will be observed, from the dates of these acts,

E. W. Tipton *v.* James Sanders *et al.*

that there was a period of time, from the 1st of September, 1851, to the 13th of November of the same year, not covered by any act for extending the time for perfecting titles to lands previously entered. And by reason of this intermission, it is assumed, that the relation of the plaintiff's grant to the occupant extension entries on which it is, in law, grounded, was cut off; and thereby, it is supposed, the defendants younger entry became valid, and the grant issued thereon an indefeasible title.

This conclusion is entirely erroneous. The title of the plaintiff, under his consolidated entry and the grant founded thereon, relates to the date of the occupant extension entries, made on the 19th of October, 1840, by force of the act of 1846, ch. 80, and other statutory enactments of similar import. And notwithstanding the consolidation entry was not surveyed until the 9th of March, 1855, nor a grant obtained until the 1st of January, 1856, the validity of the title is not impaired.

What would have been the result, if the defendants' entry had been made *during the interval* which occurred between the 1st of September, and the 13th of November, 1851, we need not stop to inquire. Be this as it may, it is very clear, that the effect of the acts of 1851-2, and 1853-4, above recited, was to resuscitate the right, and prolong the time for perfecting the plaintiff's title to a period beyond the date of his grant; and it is no less clear, that, as against all persons who acquired no intervening right, during such interval, the title of the plaintiff is as perfect as if no interval had occurred.

The idea, that the defendants' entry and grant,

though inoperative *before*, took effect instantly, on the happening of the accidental intermission in the extension law, is altogether fallacious. This could not be so, for the simple reason, that both the entry and grant, in their inception, were mere nullities. The entry was made on the 7th of July, 1847, long prior to the expiration of the time limited by the act of 1849–50, for making a survey and obtaining a grant, by the plaintiff; and directly in the face of the statute, forbidding an entry to be made of any lands to which another, at the time, had an existing occupant or pre-emption right; and declaring such entry, and the grant obtained thereon, to be void. And being thus void *ab initio*, nothing short of the sovereign power of the Legislature could impart to such entry and grant any legal effect.

Upon this point, the case of *Sampson* v. *Taylor*, 1 Sneed, 600, is not at variance with our present determination.

The objection, that the plaintiff's grant is unavailing for want of proof of the transfer to him of the occupant entries upon which the consolidated entry and grant are based, is not tenable.

The statutes prescribed the mode by which the transfer and ownership of the occupant claims or entries might be established before the entry-taker. And after the issuance of a grant, it will be presumed, when the title comes collaterally in question in a Court of Law, that all the preliminary steps necessary to the making of the entry, and obtaining the grant, were regularly pursued.

Judgment reversed.

H. B. WILLIAMS *v.* A. DONELL *et al.*

1. LAND LAW. *Grant. Presumption of.* If a person who enters land, and those claiming under him, have the exclusive, uninterrupted, and adverse possession of said land, claiming the same to the extent of the boundaries of the entry, for a period of twenty years, a grant, commensurate with the boundaries of said entry, will be presumed.

2. SAME. *Same. Same. Not necessary to show the probable issuance of a grant.* It is not indispensable, in order to lay a proper foundation for the legal presumption of a grant, to establish the probability of the fact, that, in reality, a grant ever issued. It will afford a sufficient ground for the presumption to show, that, by legal possibility, a grant might have issued. And this appearing, it may be assumed—in the absence of circumstances repelling such a conclusion—that all that might lawfully have been done to perfect the legal title, was in fact done, and in the form prescribed by law.*

3. SAME. *Same. Same. Presumption rebutted. Act of* 1819, *ch.* 1. Ever since the passage of the act of 1819, and prior to the act of Congress of 1841, the lands south and west of the Congressional Reservation Line might have been appropriated, and grants obtained therefor, by virtue of North Carolina *land warrants*. And the fact that an entry and possession under it, are prior to the act of 1841, does not repel the presumption of a grant. To destroy the foundation of the presumption, it should appear that the issuance of a grant, in the given case, was a legal impossibility.

FROM SHELBY.

This cause was heard before Judge HUMPHREYS, who instructed the jury that, upon the facts of the case,

---

* Presumptions of this kind are adopted from the general infirmity of human nature, the difficulty of preserving muniments of title, and the public policy of supporting long and uninterrupted possession. The twenty years possession does not produce the belief that there was a grant, but as a matter of public policy to quiet titles, the law presumes a grant. *Chilton* v. *Wilson's heirs,* 9 Hum., 405; 2 Tenn., 818; M. and Y., 228, *Ricard* v. *Williams,* 7 Wheaton, 109; *McDonald* v. *McNeal,* 10 John. R., 380; 1 Meig's Dig., 920.

(which are stated in the opinion of the Court,) they might presume the issuance of a grant in favor of the defendants. Verdict and judgment for the defendants. The plaintiff appealed.

KORTRECHT & ORNE, and T. P. SPURLOCK, for plaintiff.

J. T. SWAYNE, JESSE L. HARRIS, and H. D. SMALL, for defendants.

McKINNEY, J., delivered the opinion of the Court.

This was an action of ejectment, brought by Williams, to recover a tract of land lying in Shelby county. Verdict and judgment were for the defendants.

The plaintiff's title is a grant issued to him on the 1st of February, 1851, upon an entry made on the 27th of September, 1849. The defendants claim under an *entry* of 200 acres, made by George Ford and Wilson Sanderlin, of the same land; the original certificate of the survey of which, dated the 23d of November, 1833, was submitted as evidence to the jury. The plaintiff's grant includes sixty-nine acres of the land embraced by said entry under which defendants claim—to recover which this action was brought.

It is not shown that, in point of fact, a grant ever issued on the entry to Ford and Sanderlin. But it is proved, that about the year 1831—some twenty-six years before the commencement of the present action—George Ford entered into possession of said land, having purchased an improvement thereon from one Stuart, who was previously in possession; and that Ford, and those

H B. Williams *v.* A. Donell *et al.*

holding by purchase under him, have had the exclusive, uninterrupted, and adverse possession of said land, claiming the same to the extent of the boundaries of said entry, from 1831, up to the commencement of this suit, on the 19th of January, 1857.

Upon this state of facts, his Honor instructed the jury, that they might presume a grant to the defendants, commensurate with the boundaries of said entry.

This instruction is supposed to be erroneous. The argument is, that the presumption of a grant was absolutely repelled, for the reason that, until after the passage of the act of Congress of 1841, no grant could, by law, have issued for this land, on the entry made by Ford and Sanderlin, in 1833; that the legal title was in the United States up to 1841, when Tennessee was first empowered to dispose of it. This position is incorrect. There was a mode known to the law by which a grant might have been obtained for this land, long prior to the year 1841. Ever since the act of 1819, chapter 1, at least, the land might have been appropriated, and a grant obtained therefor, by virtue of a North Carolina *land warrant.* This was a familiar method of acquiring title to lands, south and west of the Congressional Reservation Line.

It is not indispensable, in order to lay a proper foundation for the legal presumption of a grant, to establish a probability of the fact, that, in reality, a grant ever issued. It will afford a sufficient ground for the presumption, to show, that, by legal possibility, a grant might have issued. And this appearing, it may be assumed—in the absence of circumstances repelling such conclusion—that all that might lawfully have been done to

H. B. Williams *v.* A. Donell *et al.*

perfect the legal title, was in fact done, and in the form prescribed by law.

But it is supposed that this principle cannot avail the defendants in the present case, because, as is alleged, the entry of Ford and Sanderlin was based upon an occupant right, and not upon a North Carolina warrant. How this matter is, does not certainly appear from the record—the entry itself not being set forth in the bill of exceptions. All that we have is the certificate of survey, which seems to have been admitted as evidence instead of the entry; and that merely states, that it was made "by virtue of the occupant law." This is by no means conclusive of the fact assumed. It does not negative the possibility of an appropriation by a different method. A location under the occupant law, would not preclude the party from afterwards appropriating the same land by "warrant."

To destroy the foundation of the presumption, it should appear that the issuance of a grant, in the given case, was a legal impossibility. The contrary of this, we have seen, is established in the present case.

No objection can now be urged, that the entry itself was not produced on the trial; that must be treated as having been waived—the objection not having been taken in proper form, and at the proper time.

Judgment affirmed.

Planters' Bank *et al. v.* A. H. Douglass *et al.*

PLANTERS' BANK *et al. v.* A. H. DOUGLASS *et al.*

1. BILLS AND NOTES. *When the acceptor of a bill may sue.* The acceptor of a bill who has paid the amount out of his own funds, may maintain an action of assumpsit against the drawer, founded on an implied promise of the drawer to the acceptor. But the mere fact of acceptance without payment, gives him no right of action.

2. SAME. *Mortgage. When foreclosed by an acceptor.* The acceptor of a bill not being able to maintain an action, directly, against the drawer without payment, he cannot do so, indirectly, by a bill in Chancery to foreclose a mortgage executed by the drawer to secure the acceptor. He has no right to a foreclosure of the mortgage until he has paid the bill.

3. SAME. *Same. Holder of the bill* If a mortgage is executed to indemnify an acceptor for money actually paid upon such acceptance, the acceptor not having the right to foreclose said mortgage until payment, the indorsee or holder of such bill cannot demand a foreclosure of the mortgage.

FROM MEMPHIS.

The bill was dismissed by Judge CARUTHERS, at the November Term, 1858. The complainants appealed.

KORTRECHT and ORNE, for the complainants.

SCOTT and DIXON, on the same side, assumed that the bank, as the holder of the bills is not compelled to sue at law, but are entitled in equity to the benefit of the collateral security, given by drawers to acceptors of the bills. There a trust is created for the better security of the debts, and a Court of Equity will see that it is not defeated. And this is so whether the bank was apprized of the security at the time she discounted the bills or not. When the fact came to the knowledge of the bank, she had a right to affirm the trust, and enforce its performance. 3 Yer., 264, and authorities cited; 2 J. C. R., 418; 4 J. C. R., 136.

YERGER & FARRINGTON, and SMALL & FOUTE, for the defendants, relied upon the following authorities to show that neither Shaw & Co. nor the bank could foreclose the mortgage executed by the defendants: Meigs' R., 256; 5 Sneed, 86; White & Tudor's L. C. in Eq., 99, 100; 12 Leigh, 387.

McKINNEY, J., delivered the opinion of the Court.

The object of the bill is to obtain satisfaction of several bills of exchange, of which the bank is holder, out of certain real property mortgaged by the defendants, for the indemnity of the complainants, G. W. Shaw & Co.

The defendants were extensively engaged in the manufacture of *flour*, in the city of Memphis; and the complainants, Shaw & Co., were commission merchants, of New Orleans.

On the 24th of June, 1857, an arrangement was made between them, by which it was agreed that Shaw & Co. should be the sole agents of defendants for the sale of flour in the New Orleans market. In consideration whereof, Shaw & Co. undertook to give the defendants "a standing credit, of not exceeding fifteen thousand dollars, in *acceptances*, having not less than sixty days to run—this credit and arrangement to extend for six months;" for which acceptances they were to receive two and a half per cent. commission.

The defendants, Douglass, Dawell & Co., were to make weekly shipments of flour, proportioned to the amount of the acceptances Shaw & Co. might be under; and for the sale of the flour the latter were to receive two and a half per cent. commission.

As an indemnity to the complainants, Shaw & Co., the defendants conveyed, in trust, certain real estate, situated in the city of Memphis. The object and intention of the mortgage is stated on the face of the instrument as follows, namely:

"If at the end of six months from this date—at which time the agreements and arrangements hereinbefore set forth are to cease—and if then, after a settlement of accounts, the said Douglass, Dawell & Co. shall be found to be indebted to the said G. W. Shaw & Co., in any amount upon the transactions between the firms aforesaid, then and in that case" the trustee is empowered to sell, &c.

It is alleged, that during the continuance of the above arrangement, bills were accepted by Shaw & Co., for the defendants, to the amount of upwards of $63,000, and beyond the proceeds of the flour shipped, to the extent of more than $14,000.

It seems, that as the bills were drawn, from time to time, they were regularly purchased by the Branch of the Planters' Bank at Memphis, from the defendants, and the proceeds paid out on their checks.

Planter's Bank *et al. v.* A. H. Douglass *et al.*

The bank is now the holder of seven of said bills, which remain wholly unpaid; and Shaw and Co. having failed, they have joined with the bank in bringing this bill, to have satisfaction of said unpaid bills out of the mortgaged property.

This is resisted by the defendants. They allege that no settlement has ever been made between Shaw & Co. and the defendants. They deny any indebtedness on their part to Shaw & Co.; and state in their answer, that the proceeds of the flour shipped by them to the complainants, Shaw & Co., exceed the cash advances on the acceptances of the latter, to the amount of more than three thousand dollars, which sum they claim to be really due to them from Shaw & Co. They also deny that Shaw & Co. are the holders of any of said bills, or that there is any balance in their favor for money paid on their acceptances.

These statements of the answer of defendants are not disproved. And, assuming the facts to be as stated, can any relief be decreed in favor of Shaw & Co., or the bank?

So far as regards Shaw & Co., we are at a loss to perceive on what principle any decree can be made in their favor, either upon the proper construction of the mortgage deed, or upon general principles of law. The mere fact of the *acceptance* of the bills, without payment, gives them no right of action against the drawers of the bills. It is the actual payment of the bill that gives the acceptor, who has paid the amount out of his own funds, the right to maintain an action of assumpsit against the drawer, founded on an implied promise of the latter to the former.

If, therefore, Shaw & Co. could not directly maintain an action against the defendants for the money, upon what principle shall they be allowed, indirectly, to accomplish the same end, by enforcing a foreclosure of the mortgage? The question needs only to be stated. It requires no answer. And if Shaw & Co. have no claim to such relief *a fortiori*, the bank, as holder of the bills, can have none.

The indemnity provided was to secure the acceptor for money actually paid upon their acceptances; and not for the security of the indorsee or holder of the bills.

It results, therefore, that the decree dismissing the bill is correct, and it is affirmed.

C. R. BELOTE et al v. JAMES WHITE.

WILL. *Construction. Trust and trustee. Chancery. Power coupled with a personal trust. Limitations, statute of. Bar of equitable estates.*
The testator bequeathed certain real and personal estate to three trustees, to be held by them in trust for the use and benefit of his daughter, B., and her children, present and future, and said trustees, or any two of them, or the survivor were vested with power to sell and convey any part or all of the property, for the use and benefit of said daughter and her children; to vest and revest the proceeds, and to manage the whole in any way they might think promotive of the interest of the beneficiaries. And, at the death of the daughter, B., the whole of said property was to be equally divided between all of her living children, and the heirs of such as may have died. The daughter, B., had two children born after the death of the testator, both of which died before their mother, and without issue. In the division of the real estate of the testator, the tract of land in controversy fell to B. and her children. A trustee was appointed by

C. R. Belote *et al. v.* James White.

decree of the Chancery Court, in place of those appointed by the will, who sold and conveyed the tract of land, in 1847. Held:

1. That the three trustees were vested, under the will, with the legal estate to the *entire* property, only during the life of the daughter, B ; and at her death, the legal title and the trusts of every kind imposed upon them by the will, ceased, and were at an end, and the entire estate, legal and equitable, freed of the trusts, vested in the children.

2. At the testator's death, the daughter, B., and her children then living, took an equitable estate in the property, as tenants in common, in equal shares; the interest of B. being for life only, with remainder to her children, theirs being in fee; and the estate was subject to and did open to let in after born children.

3. Upon the death of the children, without issue, their interest, by the terms of the will, devolved upon the other children. So, the four children owned an equitable estate in 6-7, and the mother an equitable estate for life in 1-7, the entire estate, legal and equitable, vesting, at her death, in the children.

4. The *power of sale* conferred upon the trustees was discretionary, and a thing entirely of *personal trust and confidence* in them, or any two of them, or the survivor, and could be executed by no one else; it could not be devolved upon others, either by the deed or will, or other act of the trustees, or be executed by their heirs or personal representatives, nor could a Court of Chancery have forced the trustees to execute it, or execute it itself by its clerk and master, or otherwise; nor could a trustee appointed by the Court do so. Upon the death of the trustees the power become extinct and gone, and the sale and conveyance by the new trustee, in 1847, is void.

5. The trustees having taken an estate only for the life of the daughter, B., the bar under the first section of the act of 1819, could only be to that extent.

6. The act of 1819 bars equitable as well as legal titles, and operates as an extinguishment of the same, investing the adverse claimant with a perfect title in fee simple. When, therefore, the equitable owner is *sui juris*, and can sue, but omits to do so for seven years, the entire title and fee are, by operation of the statute, placed in the possessor. And this is so, although the legal title be in a trustee, and whether he be capable of suing or not.

FROM HENDERSON.

Verdict and judgment for the defendants, at the March Term, 1858, READ, J., presiding. The plaintiffs appealed.

J. R. & S. R. HAWKINS, for the plaintiffs.

L. M. JONES, and M. &. H. BROWN, for the defendant.

WRIGHT, J., delivered the opinion of the Court.

This is an action of ejectment by the plaintiffs, to recover 500 acres of land in the county of Henderson; and judgment being against them, they have appealed in error to this Court.

The decision of the cause depends upon a construction of those parts of the will of Samuel Dickens, which relate to the devises and bequests in favor of his daughter, Elizabeth B. Belote, and her children.

They are as follows: "I give and bequeath to John D. Martin, Andrew L. Martin, and Edmund H. V. Dickens, the survivor, or survivors of them, in trust, for the use and annual support of my daughter, Elizabeth B. Belote, and her children, my stock in the Planters' Bank of Tennessee, consisting of forty shares; I also give to the said trustees, twenty shares of the residue of my stock in the Farmers' and Merchants' Bank of Memphis; the dividends of said sixty shares of Bank stock, if needed, to be applied to the support and maintenance of my said daughter Elizabeth, and her present and future children, and to their education. I also vest the said trustees with the power to sell the whole, or any part of said bank stock, if they deem it expedient, and to invest the proceeds in that way, they may deem advisable, and to the interest of my said daughter Elizabeth and children; and if not sold before the expiration of the charter of said banks, to revest the said amounts or proceeds, as they may judge best. I give and bequeath to the said trustees for the said uses and purposes, all the property, both real and personal, I may own at the time of my death in the State of Indiana."

After various devises and bequests to his other children, the testator then proceeds as follows: "All the rest of my lands and real estate, I give and bequeath to my said sons, Thomas Dickens, Robert F. Dickens, Samuel B. Dickens, Edmund H. V. Dickens, and to my daughters, Martha L. Bugg, Ann V. Martin, Sally Martin, Mary Jane Dickens, and to the said trustees, John D. Martin, Andrew L. Martin and Edmund H. V. Dickens, in trust, for the uses and purposes heretofore mentioned, which I give and bequeath to them, my said children and said trustees, and their heirs respectively, to be divided between them respectively."

He then provides for the equalization of his estate among his children, because of certain advancements theretofore made them.

The testator then, in like manner, gives the residue of his personal estate to his children, and to the said trustees of his daughter, Elizabeth B. Belote and her children, save the estate he had, in the will, given his wife; and provides that all of his children shall be made equal in his estate, the said trustees to represent and be substituted for his said daughter, Elizabeth B. Belote.

Finally: He directs that "all the property, both real and personal, herein devised to John D. Martin, Andrew L. Martin, and Edmund H. V. Dickens; they are to hold in trust for the use and benefit of my daughter, Elizabeth B. Belote and her children, present and future, and they, the said trustees, or any two of them, or the survivor, are hereby vested with full power and authority to sell and convey the whole, or any part thereof, for the use and benefit of the said Elizabeth and children, to vest and revest the proceeds, and to manage the whole in any way they may think will promote the interest and comfort of my said daughter Elizabeth. I further give the said trustees power and authority, if they think proper, and it be the wish of my said daughter Elizabeth, to allot to any one or more of her children, as they may settle off, a part of the said property, not to exceed a child's part, before the death of the said Elizabeth; and after her death, the whole of the said property to be equally divided between all her living children, and the heirs of those which may be dead; the said heirs taking their ancestor's share, or the share the ancestor would have been entitled to if alive; and where advancements have been made, the same to be accounted for by the parties to whom made."

This will was executed the 14th day of January, 1839, and proven at the August Term, 1840, of the County Court of Madison county, and John D. Martin, the executor named therein, qualified.

The testator died seized of the tract of land in dispute; and in the division of his estate among his devisees, the same was allotted to the said trustees for Mrs. Belote and her children.

The plaintiffs, Samuel D. Belote, William D. Belote, Charles R. Belote, and Reginald H. Belote, are the only children of the said Elizabeth B. Belote living at her death. She died a *feme covert*, in Weakley county, on the 18th of August, 1849, having been so from the year 1826.

The said Samuel D. Belote was born March the 9th, 1827; William D. Belote, February the 23d, 1829; Charles R. Belote, August the 27th, 1833; and Reginald H. Belote, May the 2d, 1838.

Elizabeth B. Belote had two children, to-wit: Beatrice R., born the 11th of June, 1842, and Edmund V., born the 2d of November, 1844, both of whom died in infancy, before the death of their mother.

The first question is, what estate did John D. Martin, Andrew L. Martin, and Edmund H. V. Dickens, as the trustees of Mrs. Belote and children, take? What estate did she take? And what estate did her children take?

Answer: We think it clear, the trustees took the legal estate to the entire property only during the life of Mrs. Belote; and that at her death, the legal title and the trusts, of every kind, imposed upon them, by the will, ceased and were at an end; and the entire estate, legal and equitable, freed of the trusts, become invested in the plaintiffs. This is so, by the express language and limitations in the will. The words, " and after her death the whole of the said property to be equally divided between all her living children," can have no other meaning. And upon the authority of the cases of *Smith et al. v. Thompson*, 2 Swan, 386; *Aiken et al. v. Smith*, 1 Sneed, 304; and *Ellis v. Fisher*, 3 Sneed, 231; there can, we think, be no question, that this is the proper construction of this will.

We think it equally plain, that at the testator's death, Elizabeth B. Belote and the plaintiffs, who were then her only children, took an equitable estate, as tenants in common, in this property, in equal shares of one-fifth each; her interest being for life only, with remainder, as to that, to them, and their estates in fee; that the estate was subject to open for after born children, and did open upon the births of Beatrice R., and Edmund V., in 1842 and 1844; and that upon their deaths, their shares, by the terms of the will, devolved upon the plaintiffs, so that they owned an equitable estate of six-sevenths; and she, for life, in one-seventh; and the entire estate, legal and equitable, as before stated, being invested in the plaintiffs at their mother's death. Hill on Trus., ch. 2, sec. 2, pp 65, 66; *Haywood's Heirs* v. *Moore*, 2 Hum., 584.

This much, we think, is clear. We are also inclined to the opinion, upon the proof in this record, that Edmund H. V. Dickens, with Andrew L. Martin, must be held to have accepted the trusts of this will for Mrs. Belote and children, and that the decree in the Chancery Court at Huntingdon, in 1844, under the proceeding instituted by John D. Martin, Edmund H. V. Dickens, and Ann V. Martin, the widow and executrix of Andrew L. Martin, and by Mrs. Belote, for herself and children, had the effect to invest Joseph H. Talbot with the legal title and trusts of the estate, in the same way and to the same extent as held by his predecessors, (1 Sneed, 297;) though, as we shall presently see, *not with the same powers*. But in the view we take of this case, it cannot be very material to consider the effect of this decree, since the result is the same, whether the le al estate remained with Edmund H. V. Dickens, or with him and John D. Martin, or with the heirs of Andrew L. Martin, or went by the decree, to Talbot.

Though the *trusts* in this will for Mrs. Belote and children were imperative and well defined, and such as a Court of Chancery might execute, yet the *power of sale* conferred upon the trustees was, in our opinion, *discretionary*, and a thing entirely of *personal trust* and *confidence* in Andrew L. Martin, John D. Martin, and Edmund H. V. Dickens, or any two of them, or the survivor, and could be executed by no one else.

It could not be devolved upon others, either by the deed or will, or other act of the trustees, or be executed by their heirs or personal representatives, because the will did not so provide. Nor could a Court of Chancery, as we apprehend, have forced the trustees to execute it, or execute it, itself, by its clerk and master, or otherwise. Nor could a trustee appointed by the Court do so. But upon the death or refusal to act of the trustees, the power became extinct and gone. And, in this case, if we allow that the legal title and trusts were, lawfully, by the decree, devolved upon Talbot, yet he could not sell this land, the power being incapable of transmission or delegation to him. Hill on Trustees, (edition of 1846, by Trowbat,) 472, 473, 483, 484, 485, 486, 487, 488, 489, 495; *Cole* v. *Wade*, 16 Ves., 28–46; 9 Ves., 75, Comb's case; *Alexander* v. *Alexander*, 2 Ves., 643; *Coxe* v. *Day*, 13 East., 113; *Down* v. *Worrall*, 1 Mylne & Keene, 561; *Berger* v. *Duff*, 4 Johns. Ch. Rep., 368. The case of *Cole* v. *Wade*, shows that a very clear distinction exists between a *power*, and the *estate and trusts*, the subject matter of it; and that while the power may be gone, or incapable of transmission, the trusts may still remain and be executed.

How could a Court of Chancery here substitute the master, or another trustee, for Andrew L. Martin, John D. Martin, and Edmund H. V. Dickens? It was not *imperative* that a sale should be made. The testator intended that Mrs. Belote and her children should have the benefit of the judgment of these trustees, or some two of them, or the survivor, as to the necessity and propriety of a sale. But how could Talbot's judgment be their judgment?

We think, therefore, that the sale by him, as against the plaintiffs, was unauthorized, and is void; and that Dudley L. Williams, the purchaser, acquired no title.

The deed to Williams is dated the 7th of April, 1847, and he and those holding under him have had possession ever since; and the suit was instituted the 14th of July, 1855—more than seven years after the possession—and the question is, as to the effect of the statute of limitations upon the case under the first section of the act of 1819—the deed being upon its face—a conveyance in fee-simple.

If we assume that the legal title was either in Talbot or Edmund H. V. Dickens, in 1847, when the adverse possession began, whether they were, by their acts, estopped to sue or not; or if we say the legal title was in Andrew L. Martin's heirs, and they were *sui juris*, and could have sued, still the plaintiffs cannot be barred upon the title of the trustees, because it was only an estate for the life of Mrs. Belote; and, upon the authority of *Smith et al.* v. *Thompson*, 2 Swan, and the other cases above referred to, decided by this

C. R. Belote *et al. v.* James White.

Court, the bar could, at most, only have been to that extent. 2 Swan, 386; 1 Sneed, 304; 3 Sneed, 231.

The plaintiffs then, as to the bar of the statute, must stand on their own title. This is a case for land, held by tenants in common, and the rule is different from a contest to recover personal estate. Though the plaintiffs could *join in a suit*, yet each could sue for his share separately. *Barrow's Lessee* v. *Navee*, 2 Yer., 27. And one may be bound and the others not. 2 Yer., 227; *Shute* v. *Wade*, 5 Yer., 1.

There can, we think, be no doubt that the possession of Williams, the purchaser, was wrongful and tortious, as against the plaintiffs, and also as to their mother, from the date of his deed, in April, 1847; and that, *in equity*, a cause of action and right of suit accrued to all and each of them from that time. The sale by Talbot being a breach of trust and void, they could instantly have sued in equity for a recovery of this land. The act of 1819 bars equitable as well as legal titles, and operates as an extinguishment of the same, and invests the possessor with a perfect title in fee-simple.

Whenever the equitable owner is *sui juris*, and can sue, but omits to do so for seven years, the entire title and fee are, by the statute, placed in the possessor. And this is so, though the legal title be in a trustee, and whether he be capable of suing or not.

The statute, therefore, as to six-sevenths of this land, began to run against the plaintiffs from the time the adverse possession commenced, though they were then all infants. And two of them, viz: Samuel D. Belote and William D. Belote, having failed to sue for three years after they came of age, are barred; but as to Charles R. and Reginald H. Belote, they having sued within three years after the removal of their disability—the latter, in fact, while yet an infant—are saved by the proviso in the statute. *Guion* v. *Anderson*, 8 Hum., 326.

As to the remaining one-seventh, in which Elizabeth B. Belote had an equitable life estate, none of the plaintiffs are barred, because their interest in it was a mere remainder, and they sued within seven years after her death. 8 Hum., 327, 328; *Miller* v. *Miller*, Meigs' Rep., 484.

It follows, also, that the plaintiffs, so far as not barred, have a legal status in Court, and can, at law, maintain this suit—the same having been instituted when their legal title to the possession was perfect, by the death of their mother.

Whether any of the plaintiffs, after they became *sui juris*, and with a full knowledge of their rights, and for the purpose of binding themselves, have so adopted and recognized the sale made by Talbot to Williams, by an acceptance of the purchase money paid by him for this land, or otherwise, as to estop them from suing for their unbarred interests in the same, the proof in the record does not show. How this is, will, of course, be open to evidence upon another trial. *Cherry* v. *Newsom*, 3 Yer., 369; 4 Hum., 336; 1 Sneed, 318.

The result is, the judgment of the Circuit Court is reversed, and a new trial granted.

Tribute of Respect

TO THE MEMORY OF THE

HON. WILLIAM B. REESE,

FORMERLY ONE OF THE JUDGES OF THE

Supreme Court of Tennessee.

Upon the death of the Hon. WILLIAM B. REESE, the members of the Bar held a meeting in the city of Knoxville, and adopted resolutions suitable to the occasion.

The Attorney General for the State was appointed to present the proceedings of the meeting to the Supreme Court, at its next term, and ask that they be spread upon the minutes. This request he complied with, and upon their presentation said—

May it please the Honorable Court:

Upon the death of that distinguished man, the Hon. WM. B. REESE, the members of the Bar of this city, held a public meeting, in order to testify, in a proper manner, their respect for his memory.

Tribute of Respect to the

I was selected, as their honored representative, to present their proceedings to this Court, and to request that they be entered upon the records thereof.

The character and eminent services of Judge REESE are so fully and so ably presented in the biographical sketch prefixed to the resolutions adopted, and the resolutions so appropriately express the feelings of all who knew that profound jurist and pure patriot, that nothing remains for me, in discharge of this melancholy duty, but to present the proceedings and ask that the request of those friends and neighbors of the lamented dead, be granted.

In a few appropriate remarks, by his Honor, Judge McKinney, referring to the character, ability, uprightness and public career of Judge REESE, the permission of the Court was given, to have said proceedings spread upon the minutes, which was accordingly, done.

At a meeting of the Bar of this city, held in the Court House, on Saturday the 7th instant, the following proceedings were had:

Hon. Horace Maynard announced the death of Hon. WM. B. REESE to be the melancholy occasion of the meeting. Hon. W. H. Sneed was called to the chair, and James W. Humes, Esq., appointed Secretary.

Col. Sneed, upon taking the Chair, said:

"It is most fit and proper that we—the members of the Knoxville Bar—should meet thus to pay our tribute of respect to the memory of Judge REESE, who adorned every walk of life in which he was called upon to act. His character, finished and rounded by thorough mental and moral training, and illustrated by a long course of public usefulness, may thus be delineated—he was a scholar, "and a ripe and good one," a profound jurist and upright Judge, a useful and enterprising citizen, and a christian gentleman."

On motion of Col. Samuel R. Rogers, the Chairman appointed Samuel R. Rogers, Hon. John H. Crozier, Hon. Horace Maynard, Hon. T. C. Lyon, C. W. Nelson, Esq., Gen. J. C. Ramsey, Jas. R. Cocke, Esq., Col. O. P. Temple, Gen. C. M. Alexander, Robt. H. Armstrong, Esq., and Col. John Baxter, as a committee to report a suitable preamble and resolutions.

The committee reported the following, which were unanimously adopted:

"We meet to pay a just and well merited tribute of respect and veneration for the memory of an old, learned, and highly distinguished member of this Bar, and one who has dignified and adorned the highest position on the Tennessee Bench. The Hon. W. B. REESE is no more; he died this morning at his residence, near this city. For several years his health has declined, and for the last few months it has been evident that the infirmities of age and the ravages of pulmonary consumption, would soon terminate his life. On the 4th he was still able to take his accustomed ride in his carriage, and on the glorious return of the birth day of his country's independence, his patriotic bosom still glowed with the fervor and zeal so characteristic in earlier life. But scarcely had the reverberations of the cannon, announcing another recurrence of the 4th of July, ceased— scarcely had the enthusiastic celebration of it by his countrymen been hushed to silence, when the tenacity of life which had so long sustained the flickering lamp, gave way, and its light was suddenly extinguished forever by the dampness of death.

Judge REESE was born in Jefferson county, Tenn., on the 29th of November, 1793. He was the son of James Reese, Esq., one of the most worthy of the first settlers and pioneers of Tennessee. From his father, a lawyer, and an active member of the Franklin Legislature, our deceased friend inherited much of that manly self-reliance, and laudable ambition for usefulness and distinction, which laid the foundation of his future fame, his eminent success and rapid elevation in professional and literary attainment. His mental endowments were of the highest order. He had, not only genius, but the higher attributes—intellectual vigor, independent thinking, profound research, and patient investigation. Indications of these mental traits were early in life developed, and a theatre for their culture, enlargement and exercise was fortunately at hand. He became a pupil in the classical school of the Rev. Dr. Henderson, at Cave Spring, in his native county, and afterwards a student of Blount College, under the Presidency of its first President, Rev. Sam'l Carrick. After the death of President C., in 1808, the deceased matriculated in Greeneville College, Tenn., and under the instruction of the late Dr. Coffin, he graduated there with the first honors of his Alma Mater. He afterwards, in following out his long cherished inclinations, turned his studies to the law, and was licensed as an attorney, in 1817. In 1821, he married Sarah Macklin Cocke, daughter of General Cocke, and again married in 1834, Henrietta M. Brown, daughter of Dr. Preston Brown, of Kentucky.

A sudden and brilliant professional success awaited him, and at once he assumed a prominent position at the Bar, at that time illustrious by the names of White,

Emmerson, Williams, Cocke, McKinney, McCampbell, Anderson, Lea and Jarnagin, members of it. In 1831, he was elected Chancellor, and presided over his district, composed of the counties of East Tennessee, and one-half of Middle Tennessee, until he was called upon to take the last step and the highest reward in a lawyer's success.

It has already been said that the career of Judge REESE was a successful one. His thorough acquaintance with legal science—his extensive general information, furnishing a never failing source of illustration and argument—his care in the preparation of his cases, his logical power, piercing wit, and terrible sarcasm, made him a formidable adversary to even those distinguished men who adorned the Bar of East Tennessee, when he practiced in her Courts. But Judge REESE was eminently qualified by nature and education for the duties of the Bench. An impartiality that knew no bias—an in-born love of justice that experienced no abatement—an almost instinctive perception of the truth, joined to his profound knowledge of the law—his patience and industry in research—his enlargement of mind, by a general and varied learning—his solidity of judgment—combined to make him one of the first Judges that Tennessee has yet produced. No member of the Bar—no true Tennessean, can recollect but with pride the high character of her Supreme Court throughout the Union, when he occupied a seat in that Court, with his equally distinguished brothers, Green and Turley. When he was Chancellor, his opinion was, in two cases, adopted by the Supreme Court, presided over by Mr. Justice Catron. When he was Supreme Judge, his judgment in the case of *Polk v. Faris*, 9 Yerger, drew forth a high compliment from Chancellor Kent, a happy fate, indeed, *laudari a viro laudato*.

One distinguishing peculiarity of Judge REESE as a Judge, we cannot omit to mention. Being fully convinced that the cause of general justice, and the happiness and prosperity of the people of the State depended in a great measure upon the maintenance of the rules of law, and the fixed and uniform application of its principles to cases as they arose, he would never permit himself to regard any hardship that might follow from their operation in any particular case. Hence, he contributed, in a high degree, to give the law in Tennessee a fixed and stable character.

But it is right, and certainly appropriate, that we, the acquaintances and neighbors of Judge REESE, should make brief allusion to him in some of the other relations of life. In those purely domestic, we decline to enter, further than to say that some of us knew him as a son, dutiful, obedient and affectionate—as the head of his family, kind, faithful, considerate, sympathising and indulgent. No one had a more enviable reputation for integrity, or for public and private virtue, and, as has been well said of another, no one was more distinguished for practical judgment and strong common sense—a trait more remarkable, as it was accompanied in him by the scintillations of genius, and the sprightliness of a vigorous imagination. He thought quick, yet accurately and deep. To look at a subject at all, was to penetrate it with an eagle's glance—to think was to dissect—to handle, was to unravel and analyze. His conversational powers were such as to invest any, the most trite and common topic, with a magic and interest at once novel and instructive. As a good citizen, he was liberal and enlightened, enterprising, and full of an enlarged and active public spirit. When the *project* of connecting Tennessee with the South Atlantic sea-ports, by artificial channels of communication, was first spoken of in 1828, he at once espoused that mode of internal improvement, and threw the great weight of his influence and judgment into its support—nursed the then unpopular scheme through a sickly and protracted infancy—afterwards, presided at conventions of its advocates, assembled at different periods in North Carolina and Virginia —made a most liberal contribution to its treasury, and at the time of his death was a zealous and active director of the East Tennessee and Georgia Railroad.

Judge REESE was also a devoted friend and patron of science and learning. His attainments in Polite Literature were, indeed, remarkable—so much so as to have elicited the admiration of such scholars as Legare, Everett, Grimke, King, Dickson and the like. The seclusion and retirement of his mountain home, and the absence of libraries and other educational facilities, had the effect only to throw him upon his own great intellectual resources. In this way he was self-taught—he was his own instructor. Amid the cares of his father's farm, every leisure moment was devoted to study. A great economist of time, and patient of mental labor, he achieved an amount of scholastic attainment in literature and science, that would have done credit to the tall sons of Edinburg, Cambridge and Princeton, in their palmiest days. He richly deserved the diploma of L.L.D., conferred upon him in 1845, by the East Tennessee University. In 1851, he was induced by the earnest solicitations of the Trustees of the East Tennessee University, to accept the Presidency of that institution—a position he occupied until declining health forced him to relinquish it. But even under the pressure and debility of disease and age, his fondness for literary pursuits continued ardent and unabated. A few days, only, before his death, an early friend called to see him; and though scarcely able to articulate distinctly, his conversation turned at once upon Polite Literature, Belles Lettres and Philology in general—another instance of the "ruling passion strong in death."

As a friend of science, it is due to the memory of Judge REESE to say, that when the Association for rescuing from oblivion the early and brilliant incidents in the civil, military and political history of Tennessee was organized here in Knoxville, in 1830, he earnestly and actively co-operated in the object—gave to its patrons the first whisper of encoragement, and his constant support—was elected the first President of the East Tennessee Historical and Antiquarian Society, and continued in that position to the day of his death.

In 1846, Judge REESE became a member of the Episcopal Church in Knoxville. He had manifested through a long life, the influence of the lessons of his early training by pious parents, and in his last illness was sustained by the christian's faith, and cheered by the christian's hope.

Therefore, *Resolved*, That in the death of Judge

REESE, the bar of America has lost one of its ablest members, and the community in which he lived and died, one of its most useful and valued citizens, a just Judge, a profound jurist, a sincere friend, and a good man.

Resolved, That we tender our sympathy to the friends and family relatives of the deceased; and as a mark of respect to his memory, we will attend the funeral ceremonies at his late residence.

Resolved, That the chairman designate some person to present a copy of these proceedings to the Supreme Court, at its next term, with a request that it be spread upon the records, and inserted in the next volume of the Reports.

Resolved, That these proceedings be published in the several papers of this city.

On motion of Hon. Horace Maynard, the chairman appointed the Hon. John W. Head, the Attorney General and Reporter for the State, to present the proceedings of this meeting to the Supreme Court, at its next term at Knoxville, and to request that they may be entered on the records of the Court, and inserted in the next volume of the Reports of Tennessee.

The meeting then adjourned.

W. H. SNEED, *President.*

JAS. W. HUMES, *Secretary.*

INDEX.

ABATEMENT.

Plea of. When proper, and what it must aver. Writ. Code, § 3828. A party may plead, in abatement of a summons, that it was served on him while in attendance as a witness upon the Circuit Court; but great strictness and accuracy is required in a plea of this character: and to be good, it must set out the Court which he was attending, the suit in which he was a witness and that it was then pending in the Court, the parties to the suit, and the party for whom he was summoned. *Baker* v. *Compton,* 471.

See CERTIORARI. CRIMINAL LAW. MANDAMUS. PRACTICE AND PLEADING. SUMMARY PROCEEDINGS.

ABETTOR.

See CRIMINAL LAW.

ACCEPTANCE AND ACCEPTOR.

See BILLS AND NOTES. PARTNERSHIP. TRUST AND TRUSTEE.

ACCOUNT.

1. *Assignment of. Practice.* The assignment of an account vests in the purchaser, only an equitable interest in it, and the promise of the debtor to the assignee to pay him said account is necessary to enable him to maintain an action in his own name for its recovery. Without such promise, the assignee would have to sue in the name of the assignor, for his use. *Mt. Olivet Cemetery* v. *Shubert,* 116.

2. *Same. Promise by agent.* A promise made by the treasurer of an incorporated company to pay an account transferred to a third person, is sufficient to authorize the assignee to sue the company in his own name, unless it is shown that the treasurer had no authority to bind the company. Authority will be presumed unless the contrary is shown. *Ibid.*

See PRACTICE AND PLEADING.

ADMINISTRATORS AND EXECUTORS.

1. *Devastavit. Scire facias. Debt.* When an administrator or executor has been guilty of a *devastavit*, he becomes personally responsible, and his liability may be enforced, either by an action of *debt* on the judgment obtained against him suggesting a *devastavit*; or, by *scire facias*, founded on such judgment, suggesting, in like manner, a *devastavit*. Cope & Co. v. McFarland, 543.

2. *Same. Judgment conclusive.* In either form of proceeding on a judgment against an administrator or executor, suggesting a *devastavit*, he will not be allowed to plead any plea which assumes to place his defence merely on the want of assets. The judgment is, in general, conclusive upon him. *Ibid*

3. *Settlement of executor—effect of. Infants.* Settlements made by an executor or administrator, if the legatees or distributees are infants, are not in the nature of settled or stated accounts, so as to require them to surcharge and falsify the same before they can be opened. Such settlements are only *prima facie* correct, and may be opened for a general account. They are, however, *prima facie* evidence for the executor or administrator in taking the general account. Elrod v. Lancaster, 571.

4. *Same. Same. When a decree between defendants conclusive.* A decree between defendants will be conclusive and binding upon them where an antagonism exists, so as to make them actors against each other; but if a part of the defendants are minors, and have no regular guardian, and a person is appointed guardian *ad litem* for them, who is a defendant, and whose interest in the suit is in conflict with theirs, the decree pronounced in the cause will not bar a subsequent suit by said minors against said defendant. *Ibid*.

See DECREE. SCIRE FACIAS. LAND LAW. LIEN. STATUTE OF LIMITATIONS. SURETIES. WILLS.

ADMINISTRATION.

See ADMINISTRATORS AND EXECUTORS. SURETIES.

ADMISSIONS.

See EVIDENCE.

ADVANCEMENTS.

See SALE OF REAL ESTATE. STATUTE OF LIMITATIONS.

AGENCY.

See PARTNERSHIP. PRINCIPAL AND AGENT. SUMMARY PROCEEDINGS.

INDEX.

AGREEMENT.

See CONTRACT. PRINCIPAL AND SURETY.

AIDER AND ABETTOR.

See CRIMINAL LAW.

AMENDMENTS.

See ATTACHMENT. SUMMARY PROCEEDINGS.

APPROPRIATIONS.

County Judge. Justices of the County Court. The County Judge has no power to make appropriations of county moneys. This power belongs to the Justices of the County Court. A proceeding, therefore, to compel an appropriation of money out of the county treasury, should be against the Justices, and not against the County Judge. *Connell v. The County Judge of Davidson,* 189.

ASSETS

See ADMINISTRATORS AND EXECUTORS.

ASSIGNMENT.

See BILLS AND NOTES. CHANCERY JURISDICTION. CHANCERY PRACTICE. DEED OF TRUST. LAND LAW. REGISTRATION. SALE OF REAL ESTATE. ACCOUNT.

ATTACHMENT.

1. *Verbal sale of real estate. Equitable interest. Creditor and debtor.* A creditor can be on no higher ground than his debtor, in attaching equitable interests of the latter. And if the debtor has done any act, or entered into any agreement which would preclude *him* from asserting an equity that he once had, his creditor would, likewise, be precluded from so doing. *Wood v. Thomas,* 160.

2. *Same. Case in judgment.* A. and B. entered into an agreement for the sale and purchase of real estate. The contract was in parol. A. paid B. $200, and executed his note for the remainder of the purchase money, B. verbally agreeing to make him a title to the land when the purchase money should be paid. Subsequent to this agreement, the trade between A. and B. was cancelled, and the land sold to C., who refunded to A. the $200 paid by him, and executed his notes to B., in the place of the notes previously given by A., which notes were delivered up to A. After this latter agreement a creditor of A.'s attached his interest in the land and the fund. It was held

that A. had parted with his equitable interest both in the land and fund, and it could not be attached at the instance of his creditors. *Ibid.*

3. *Parties Corporation. Stockholders.* Stockholders are distinct parties from the corporation in which they are stockholders, and legal proceedings against them cannot reach it. Hence, if an attachment is sued out in a proceeding in which the stockholders are made parties, but the corporation not, and is levied upon the effects of the corporation, no *lien* is *acquired* by virtue of the levy of said attachment. *Lillard* v. *Porter*, 177.

4. *Same. Amendment. Effect of.* If an attachment is sued out and levied upon the property of a party who is not a defendant in the suit, and the bill is subsequently amended, bringing such party before the court, the lien of said attachment takes effect at the time of the filing of the amended bill, and does not relate back and attach at the time of the levy of the attachment. And if, after the levy of said attachment, but before the filing of the amended bill, said property is attached by another, in a proper proceeding against the owner, a prior lien is, thereby, acquired. *Ibid.*

5. *Act of 1843, ch. 29, § 1. In what cases an attachment will lie.* By the act of 1843, ch. 29, § 1, in all cases where a debtor shall be absconding or concealing himself, or his property or effects, a creditor may sue out an attachment against the property debts, *choses in action*, and effects of such debtor, in the same manner that such process may be obtained against absconding or non-resident debtors under the different statutes in force in this State. *Wilson* v. *Beadle*, 510.

6. *Same. Judgment not necessary before suing out the attachment. Chancery Jurisdiction.* The act of 1843, confers upon the Chancery Court jurisdiction for the recovery of demands purely legal in attachment cases, and no previous suit or judgment, on the part of the creditor, is necessary before suing out the attachment. *Ibid.*

7. *Act of 1852, ch. 365, § 10. Fraudulent conveyances.* By the act of 1852, ch. 365, § 10, a creditor is authorized to file a bill for an attachment, without a judgment at law and an execution with a return of *nulla bona*, in all cases where a conveyance is made by a debtor, of property, either real, personal or mixed, of any description to which he has a legal or equitable title, for the purpose of hindering, delaying, or defrauding his creditors. *Ibid.*

8. *Same. Same. Embraces choses in action.* This act not only embraces conveyances of what is, strictly, termed property, but also fraudulent assignments of claims, and every species of *choses in action*. *Ibid.*

ATTORNEY.

See EVIDENCE.

BAIL.

1. *Recognizance Power of justice of the peace to take. Act of 1715, ch. 16, § 1.* By the act of 1715, ch. 16, § 1, in all criminal offences that are bailable by law, the committing magistrate is required to "admit the party to bail." The act is silent as to the form in which bail shall be taken, but it may be done by bond or recognizance. *Pugh v. The State,* 227.

2. *Scire facias. Demurrer. Judgment nisi.* The judgment *nisi* must show that the recognizance was returned into Court, but it is not necessary that it should be expressly stated in the judgment. It is sufficient, if it stated that it appeared to the Court that such a recognizance had been entered into before the committing magistrate. *Ibid.*

3. *Same. Not necessary that it should show when the Court met.* It is not necessary that a writ of *scire facias,* issued upon a judgment *nisi* against bail, should show on what day the Court at which the judgment was rendered commenced. The Courts will take judicial notice of the terms of the several Courts within the territorial limits of the State, and the days on which the terms commence. And if the day on which the forfeiture is taken is recited in the *sci. fa.*, the Court can see, without an express statement, whether it was on a day after the commencement of the term. *Ibid.*

4. *Same. Need not recite that the prisoner was adjudged guilty.* A *scire facias* need not recite that the prisoner was adjudged guilty, by the justice, of the offence charged. No formal judgment of the guilt of the accused, by the committing magistrate, is required. The adjudication that the party shall stand committed, or give bail for his appearance to answer the charge before the tribunal having cognizance of the offence, is a sufficient performance of the duty imposed, by law, on the examining magistrate. *Ibid.*

BANKS.

See CRIMINAL LAW. PAYMENT. CENTRAL BANK.

BILL OF EXCEPTIONS.

See PRACTICE AND PLEADING.

BILL OF SALE.

See SLAVES.

BILLS AND NOTES.

1. *Demand and notice. What sufficient evidence of notice. Act of* 1820, *ch.* 25, § 4. *Code* §§ 1800 *and* 1801. A Notary Public is a public officer, and when he certifies that he has done an official act, it is presumed that he has performed that duty according to law, until the contrary is shown. Hence, if he certify in or on his protest, that he notified the drawers and endorsers, it is, *prima facie,* good; and it is not necessary that he should state the time when the notice was given, the post office to which it was sent, &c. The act of 1825, carried into the Code, secs. 1800 and 1801, does not expressly require it. *Golladay, Cheatham & Co.,* v. *The Bank of the Union,* 57.

2. *Same. Effects in the hands of the drawee.* If the drawer of a bill has no effects in the hands of the drawee to meet it, or some good reason to believe it will be accepted, he is bound to the payee, or holder, without demand or notice. It is, however, presumed that the drawee has such effects, until the contrary appears; and this presumption is not changed by a waiver, or want of acceptance of the bill. *Ibid.*

3. *Same. Waiver of notice.* If the drawer of a bill, with a *knowledge* that he is discharged from its payment for want of notice, acknowledge the debt and promise to pay it, he, thereby, waives demand and notice, and is liable for the same. *Ibid.*

4. *Note executed to raise money. Surety.* If a party become surety on a note with the understanding that it shall be passed to a particular individual, and to no one else, he is not liable on said note unless passed to that person. But if he signed as surety with the general purpose to enable the principal to raise money on the note, without limiting him to the person to whom he should pass it, he would be liable, although the note was passed to another than the payee, and the holder thereof could maintain a suit in the name of the payee for his use. *Perkins* v. *Ament,* 110.

5. *Assignment. Consideration. Fraud. Notice of equity.* If a note is assigned to a party, before due, with notice, actual or constructive, that it is void, or subject to be impeached in the hands of the payee, either for fraud or want, or failure of consideration, he will hold it subject to the same equities to which it was liable in the hands of the payee. *Ryland* v. *Brown,* 270.

6. *Same. What sufficient notice of an equity against the note.* Whatever is sufficient to put a person upon inquiry, is equivalent to notice; and when a person has sufficient information to lead him to a knowledge of a fact, he will be presumed to be cognizant of that fact. *Ibid.*

7. *Same. Same. What the recital of the consideration imposes.* The recital in a note, that it was given for land, does not require a person

to examine, at his peril, the records, before taking such note, for the purpose of ascertaining whether, as between antecedent parties liens might not exist, growing out of unpaid purchase money. He would, at most, only be required to know that the maker of the note was in the peaceable possession of the land under a title sufficient in law to invest him with a fee simple estate, accompanied with the usual covenants for his indemnity. *Ibid.*

8. *Recital of consideration. Question reserved.* The recital of the consideration in negotiable paper is unusual, but its negotiability is not, thereby, affected. And if it be merely stated that the consideration of the note is the purchase of land or merchandise, is an innocent holder bound to know that the purchaser acquired a good title to the land, or that he received the goods bargained for? *Ibid.*

9. *Equity against. Suit prematurely brought.* If a note given for land is transferred to an innocent party, it would be premature, on the part of the maker of said note, to commence suit to avoid payment thereof, on the ground of failure of the consideration, before there is an attempt, or a contemplated attempt, to subject the land to a prior equity, if such exists. *Ibid.*

10. *Protest. Notary Public. Act of* 1835, *ch.* 11. As a general principle, protest of a bill or note must be made by a notary at the *place* of *payment.* And the authority of a notary public is confined to the county for which he was appointed and commissioned. He has no power to do an official act in another county. Hence, a protest of a bill or note must be made by a notary of the county in which the place of payment is fixed. *Neely* v. *Morris, Tanner & Co.*, 595.

11. *Indorsement. Evidence. Proof of joint interest in plaintiffs.* When several persons sue as endorsees of a bill, if the bill is indorsed *in blank,* there is no necessity for their proving that they were in partnership together, or that the bill was indorsed or delivered to them jointly. The indorsement in blank conveys a joint right of action to as many as agree in suing on the bill. *Ibid.*

12. *Same. Same. Same.* But when a bill is payable or indorsed *specially* to a firm, it must be proved that the firm consists of the persons who sue as plaintiffs on the record. *Ibid.*

13. *When the acceptor of a bill may sue.* The acceptor of a bill who has paid the amount out of his own funds, may maintain an action of assumpsit against the drawer, founded on an implied promise of the drawer to the acceptor. But the mere fact of acceptance without payment, gives him no right of action. *Planters' Bank* v. *Douglass.* 699.

14. *Mortgage. When foreclosed by an acceptor.* The acceptor of a bill not being able to maintain an action, directly, against the drawer

without payment, he cannot do so, indirectly, by a bill in Chancery to foreclose a mortgage executed by the drawer to secure the acceptor. He has no right to a foreclosure of the mortgage until he has paid the bill. *Ibid.*

15. *Same. Holder of the bill.* If a mortgage is executed to indemnify an acceptor for money actually paid upon such acceptance, the acceptor not having the right to foreclose said mortgage until payment, the indorsee or holder of such bill cannot demand a foreclosure of the mortgage. *Ibid.*

See CHANCERY PRACTICE. CONTRACT. DEMAND AND NOTICE.

BOND.

See BAIL. WRIT OF ERROR.

CARRIERS.

1. *Common. Delivery of goods. Notice.* Carriers by railroads, or steamboats engaged in the internal coasting and river trade, in the absence of a contract for a particular mode of delivery, must deliver freight received by them to the owner, consignee, or some authorized agent, or safely land it upon the wharf at the place of destination, or deposit it in their depot houses, and promptly notify the consignee. If delivered to a drayman, cartman, or any other person not authorized by the consignee, to receive it, it is at the risk of the carrier. *Dean v. Vaccaro & Co.*, 488.

2. *Same. Same. Same. Effect of usage or custom.* The usage or custom of a port cannot dispense with delivery, or notice of the landing, of the goods. Nor will the fact, that the consignee and others, had submitted to a delivery of goods to a drayman, before, when no loss occurred, bind him to yield his legal right to notice when it is to his interest to assert it. *Ibid.*

3. *Same Measure of damages if goods not delivered.* Upon failure to deliver goods by a carrier, as required by law, the net value of the goods at the place of delivery is the measure of damages. *Ibid*

CANTRAL BANK OF TENNESSEE.

Change of name. Act of 1854, ch. 94, § 68. The act of 1854, ch. 294, § 68, chartered the Eastern Division Mining Company, with banking powers, and the privilege of changing its name and title whenever deemed necessary. Under the power thus conferred, the name of said corporation was changed to the Central Bank of Tennessee. *Lillard v. Porter*, 177.

CERTIORARI AND SUPERSEDEAS.

1. *What the petition must show. Code, § 3180.* By § 3130 of the Code, when the certiorari extends only to a part of the judgment, or the

cause is brought up by one of several parties, a certified copy of the proceedings complained of shall be made out by the proper officer and filed in lieu of the original papers and the suit, as to parties who do not join in the application, shall not be affected. And if the whole judgment is not complained of the petition must show in what the error consists, and the amount of the same. A general statement that the judgment is for a much larger amount than the plaintiff is entitled to, is not sufficient. *O'Sullivan* v. *Larry*, 54.

2. *Petition must show merits. Abatement.* When a party has lost his right of appeal, and is driven to the extraordinary remedy furnished by the writ of certiorari, he must show merits. A trial in the wrong civil district is a matter in abatement, and cannot be taken advantage of by certiorari. It does not involve the merits of the case. *Ibid.*

3. *Justice of the peace. Civil district. Code.* §§ 4114 *and* 4118. If it were conceded that objection to a trial out of the proper district could be made available by certiorari, the petition for the writ must state such facts as will enable the Court to see that the case was tried in the wrong district, as regulated by §§ 4114 and 4118 of the Code. A statement that the trial was had without the civil district of, both, the plaintiff and defendant, is not sufficient. *Ibid.*

4. *Judgment. Interest. Costs Procedendo. Code,* §§ 312?, 8138. Prior to the adoption of the Code, the practice, upon dismissing a petition for a writ of *supersedeas,* was to discharge the *supersedeas* and award a *procedendo* to the justice to issue execution. But, by the proper construction of §§ 3124 and 8138 of the Code, judgment is to be rendered in the higher Court for the amount of the justice's judgment with interest thereon, at the rate of twelve and one-half *per cent. per annum* against the principal and sureties in the *certiorari* bond, and also for costs of suit. *Lownes, Orgill & Co.,* v. *Hunter,* 848.

See CRIMINAL LAW.

CESSION ACT.

See LAWS IN FORCE. LAND LAW.

CHANCERY.

1. *Sale of land. Rescission of contract. Registration. Attachment.* If a contract for the sale of a tract of land is entered into, and a title bond executed; and, thereafter, said contract is rescinded by the parties, either in writing or by parol, a specific performance cannot be enforced by the vendee. The creditors of the vendee stand upon no higher ground than he occupies, and cannot claim a specific performance of such contract, so as to subject the land to the payment of their debts, although the contract of rescission is not registered before the levy of their attachments upon the same. *Fleming* v. *Martin,* 43.

2. *Same. Same. Same. Fraud.* If the rescission of the contract was prompted by a motive to benefit the vendee, or injure his creditors, it would be a *fraud* upon the creditors; and would not affect them. Otherwise, if it was made to save the vendor. The registration laws do not apply to such a contract. *Ibid.*

3. *Same. Sale of equitable interest. Question reserved.* If, instead of a rescission of the contract of sale, the vendee sells his equitable interest to a third person, and the contract of sale is not registered before the land is attached, a different question would arise. It would then be a contest between a purchaser and the creditors of the vendee, and the question, as to the effect of a non-registration of the sale of such equitable interest, as against the creditors, is reserved. *Ibid.*

4. *Lien of vendor for other debts. Question reserved.* Would the vendor, if the contract is executory, have the right to retain a lien upon the land by virtue of his having the legal title, until all his debts against his vendee, both for the land and otherwise, as well as liabilities for him, are paid or secured, in preference to attaching creditors? *Ibid.*

5. *Decree. Effect of upon the rights of persons not parties.* Although a decree is not, in form, binding upon persons who are not parties, yet it is in effect, if the determination of the question presented by the record necessarily involves the determination of their rights and the validity of their title. *Goss* v. *Singleton,* 67.

See CHANCERY PRACTICE. CHANCERY JURISDICTION. CONTRACT. DECREE. ESTOPPEL. WILLS.

CHANCERY COURT.

Is a Superior Court. A Court of Chancery is a Superior Court within the sense and meaning of the term, as contradistinguished from an inferior one, and the validity of its decrees is not to be tested by the rules applicable to a Court of peculiar, special, and limited jurisdiction. *Hopper* v. *Fisher,* 253.

CHANCERY JURISDICTION.

1. *Partition.* A Chancery court has general power and authority to make partition of lands between tenants in common. This jurisdiction existed at the common law, and has since been declared and recognized by several statutory enactments. *Hopper* v. *Fisher,* 253.

2. *Same. Ejectment. Decree, when collaterally attacked.* If it appears that the Chancery Court, whose decrees are impeached in a collateral proceeding by ejectment, had jurisdiction over the subject matter of the decrees, and undertook to, and did declare the rights of the parties, there being infant defendants, who were represented by a guar-

dian *ad litem*, it will be presumed that the defendants were duly served with process, or in some way had the proper notice so as to give the Court jurisdiction of their persons; and the decrees will be held good, although it may not appear in the transcript of the record offered as evidence in the suit in ejectment, that the infant defendants were served with process, or had any notice of the proceedings, or that a guardian *ad litem* was appointed by order of the Court. *Ibid.*

3. *Innocent purchaser. When protected.* If a deed is procured from a *feme covert* by fraud and coercion, and the conveyee sells and conveys the land to another person, for a valuable consideration, who has no notice of the circumstances under which the deed was procured from such *feme covert*, he is, in contemplation of law, an innocent purchaser, and will be protected in his right. *Coleman v. Satterfield*, 259.

4. *Husband and wife. Fraud in sale of wife's land.* Although, in such a case, the wife is not entitled to relief against such third person, yet she is entitled to a decree against the party who fraudulently procured the deed from her, for the value of the land; for, in consequence of his wrong, the estate is irrecoverably lost to her. *Ibid.*

5. *When surety entitled to relief.* A surety has a right to bring his principal and the creditor into a Court of Chancery, to compel the payment of the debt for which he is bound. *Croone v. Bivens*, 839.

6. *Same. Partnership. Question reserved.* If one partner, who is bound for the firm debts, sells his interest in the firm to his co-partners, who agree to pay the debts and release him, can he be regarded in the light of a surety for them, and come into a Court of Chancery to compel payment of the debts? *Ibid.*

7. *Fraudulent conveyances may be attacked without judgment.* Code, § 4288. Under section 4288 of the Code, a creditor may, without first having obtained a judgment at law, come into Chancery to set aside fraudulent conveyances of property, or other devices resorted to for the purpose of hindering and delaying creditors, and subject the property, by sale or otherwise, to the satisfaction of his debt. *Ibid.*

8. *Mistake. Correction of.* If, by *mistake*, a writing contains less or more, or something different from the intention of the parties, and this is made to appear by clear and satisfactory proof, a Court of Equity will reform the writing, so as to make it conform to what the parties intended. *Cromwell v. Winchester*, 889.

9. *Same. Same. Case in judgment.* A lot in Memphis was conveyed, in 1848, to a trustee, for Mrs. Elizabeth Armour and "her children forever." In addition to the *intrinsic* evidence in the deed, parol evidence was introduced to show that it was the intention of the conveyor to create an estate in fee. Held, that it was a proper case for the

47

interposition of a Court of Equity, to reform the deed, so as to make it convey an estate of inheritance, and thereby carry out the intention of the parties. *Ibid.*

10. *Waiver. Act of* 1852, *ch.* 365, § 9. Prior to the passage of the act of 1852 it was the settled rule that if a party neglected to make his defence at law, whether the defence were purely legal, or, from its nature, both legal and equitable, and no obstacle in the way of such defence existed in the legal forum, he could not afterwards avail himself of it in a Court of Equity. But this rule is so far changed by the act of 1852, that. at least, in all cases not unfit for the investigation of a Court of Equity, if the defendant neglect to avail himself of the objection to the jurisdiction, by demurrer, and answers to the merits of the bill, the objection is *waived* and cannot afterwards be insisted. *Stockley* v. *Rowley, Ashburner & Co.*, 498.

11. *Garnishment. Judgment by motion. What it must show.* In a summary proceeding by motion, enough must appear upon the record to show that the Court before which the proceeding is had, has jurisdiction, and likewise all the facts necessary to authorize the judgment must be assumed therein. If these requisites do not exist, the judgment is a nullity, and a proceeding by garnishment founded upon such a void judgment, is likewise a nullity, and money received thereon by the garnishing creditor, will be ordered to be refunded, by a Court of Chancery. *Haynes* v. *Gates.* 598.

12. *Same. Effect of notice to the garnishing creditor that the fund has been assigned.* Notes were placed in the hands of an attorney for collection, and his receipt taken. These notes were assigned to another party, the receipt of the attorney handed over to him, and a guaranty of the solvency of the notes indorsed on the receipt. After the money was collected by the attorney, a garnishment was served on him at the instance of a creditor of the assignor. Before this process was taken out, both the creditor and the attorney had notice of the transfer of the notes and fund. The attorney appeared and answered to the garnishment, and judgment was rendered against him, and he paid the money over to the creditor. In the view of a Court of Equity, this is a manifest fraud upon the assignee of the notes, and the garnishing creditor must be regarded as having received the money, and as holding it for the assignee; and, in a Court of Equity, will be required to refund it. And this, perhaps, would be so, even though the creditor had obtained possession of the money in ignorance of the fact that it belonged to another. *Ibid.*

13. *Gaming securities. Act of* 1789, *ch.* 8, § 1. The act of 1789 makes all gaming contracts and all gaming securities absolutely void, at law, as well as in equity, and it provides a new remedy in the legal forum for the recovery of "money or goods" lost at gaming, and paid or delivered. This act was not designed, nor does it interfere with the previously well established jurisdiction of Courts of Equity to compel

gaming securities to be delivered up and cancelled. In transactions contravening public policy, relief may be given in equity to a *particeps criminis;* but the relief is given, always, in aid, not in subversion, of the public policy. *Rucker* v. *Wynne,* 617.

See ATTACHMENT. CHANCERY. DECREE. HUSBAND AND WIFE. SET-OFF. SPECIFIC PERFORMANCE. USURY.

CHANCERY PLEADING.

Demurrer. Presumption. It is only in cases when it clearly appears from the face of the bill that the equity of complainant is barred, that the bill will be dismissed on demurrer, and every reasonable presumption is to be made in favor of, rather than against, the bill. *Lincoln* v. *Purcell,* 143.

See INNOCENT PURCHASER.

CHANCERY PRACTICE.

1. *Bill of review. New matter.* A paper writing was mislaid. In the pleadings in the original cause, it was conceded by the parties to be a *title bond,* and the decree pronounced upon that hypothesis. The instrument was found after the decree passed. A bill of review was filed for new matter, charging that said paper writing was found, and was a deed of bargain and sale. Held, that the instrument was not a deed, and a bill of review will not lie. *Cleveland* v. *Martin,* 128.

2. *Lien. Assignment.* If the vendor of real estate retain the legal title as security for the purchase money, it has the effect of a mortgage for that purpose, and the assignment of the note given for the purchase money, carries with it the benefit of the security. *Ibid.*

3. *Same. Assignment by parol.* A debt or *chose* in action may be assigned for a valuable consideration, by parol, and whatever passes the debt will carry with it the security for its payment. No deed or writing is necessary. A sale and delivery of the note is sufficient. *Ibid.*

4. *Same. Extension of time. New note.* If the assignee of the note given for the purchase money, and the creditor and his securities extend the time of payment upon a new note, executed with an express stipulation that the lien or security should continue as before, the security for the note will remain as effective as if the time had not been extended and the new note given. *Ibid.*

5. *Re-hearing before the Supreme Court. Depositions. Evidence. Parties.* After the decree was pronounced by the Supreme Court, one of the defendants applied for a re-hearing, upon the ground that the deposition of an incompetent witness was admitted and the decree set-

tied the rights of persons who were not parties to the suit. A rehearing was refused, and the Court held:

1. That there being no exception in the Court below to the reading of the deposition, the evidence was properly heard. And, if the testimony was rejected, the result would be the same.

2. Although the beneficiaries are not parties to the record, the pleadings and proof establish the trust in their favor; the evidence *pro* and *con.* has been heard, and if the parties were turned loose to litigate anew, the depositions in this cause would be admissible in a suit by the *cestui que trust* against the defendant, and in no aspect of the case could the latter be benefitted by another contest about the property.

3. A Court of Chancery cherishes forms no further than they contribute to the main object of its existence, the attainment of substantial justice. It struggles against technical rules which merely impede this object.

4. The rule requiring all persons in interest to be made parties to suits in equity, is a rule of discretion, founded in the anxiety of those Courts to do justice among all the parties having an interest in the subject matter, or object of the suit. It is, in most cases, not a right of the parties brought before the Court, but rather a rule prescribed by Courts of Equity to themselves.

5. If persons whose interest is apparent are not made parties, they may be allowed, if they wish it, to bring forward their claim by petition, and have the benefit of the proof already taken, and will not be driven to a second contest. *Birdsong* v. *Birdsong*, 289.

See DECREE. CHANCERY. CHANCERY JURISDICTION.

CHARGE TO THE JURY.

See CIRCUIT COURT.

CHOSES IN ACTION.

See ATTACHMENT. DEED OF TRUST.

CIRCUIT COURT.

1. *Charge to the jury.* A charge upon a question of law having no relevancy to any evidence in the cause, whether erroneous or not, is not ground of reversal, unless it is shown to have done harm to the party against whom the verdict is given. *Mt. Olivet Cemetery* v. *Shubert*, 116.

2. *Charge to the jury.* The verdict of a jury will not be set aside if there is any proof to sustain it; and the jury should be left to the

free and fair exercise of their judgment, and not subjected to threats or coercion to induce them to surrender their honest convictions. Hence, it is error in the Circuit Judge for which a new trial will be granted, to say to the jury that he must keep them together until they can agree, and that it would be better for them to find a wrong verdict than not to agree at all, as any error that might be committed could be corrected by the Supreme Court. *Taylor* v. *Jones*, 565.

See OFFICERS DE FACTO. SUMMARY PROCEEDINGS.

CIVIL DISTRICTS.

See CERTIORARI.

CLIENT.

See EVIDENCE.

CODE CITED AND CONSTRUED.

When it went into effect. Act of 1847, *ch.* 89. There is no positive enactment as to the time when the Code should go into effect. The general rule is, that all statutes are in force from the date of their enactment, unless some other time is prescribed therein; but the act of 1847, ch. 89, enlarged this rule to forty days after the passage of any general law. The Code adopts the act of 1847, ch. 89, computing, however, the forty days from the adjournment of the Legislature, *sine die*. The Legislature that enacted the Code adjourned on the 22d day of March, 1858, and the Code went into operation on the first day of May, thereafter. *Chapman* v. *The State*, 86.

Section	3828,	Witness,	471
"	1800, 1801,	Protest,	57
"	3180,	Certiorari,	54
"	4114, 4118,	Certiorari,	54
"	3124, 3138,	Judgment,	848
..	4288,	Fraudulent conveyances,	889
	545,	Taxation,	461
..	5581,	Costs	555
"	4865,	Slaves,	180
..	5089,	Witness,	455
..	4701,	False pretences,	501
"	3197, 3201,	Costs,	116
"	2865, 2866,	Plea,	97
"	2886, 2887,	Plea,	898
"	2404, 2405,	Jurisdiction,	879
"	2279,	Statute of limitations,	603
..	3603,	Penalty,	124
	3591,	Jurisdiction,	312
"	3117, 3162,	Bond,	507

COMMON CARRIER.

See CARRIERS.

COMPANY.

See RAILROAD COMPANY.

CONSIDERATION.

See BILLS AND NOTES. CONTRACT. DEED. EVIDENCE. PRINCIPAL AND SURETY.

CONSTABLE.

See SUMMARY PROCEEDINGS.

CONSTITUTIONAL LAW.

1. *Sale of slaves. Act of* 1856, *ch.* 112, § 8. *Art.* 11, § 7, *of the Constitution.* The act of 1856, ch. 112, § 8, which declares, "That the title of all persons to any slave or slaves sold under proceedings in the Circuit, Chancery or County Court, under the act of 1827, and to which the heirs, distributees, or legatees were not made parties, shall be forever barred, unless suit to recover said slave or slaves shall be instituted within six months after the passage of this act," is in violation of article 11, § 7, of the Constitution, and is void. *Morgan* v. *Reed,* 276.

2. *Art.* 2, §§ 28, 29. *Taxation.* An important and fundamental distinction is made by the Constitution, between *property* and *privileges,* in regard to the power of taxation delegated to the Legislature. The rule laid down as to the former, is, that "all property shall be taxed according to its value;" and "no one species of property from which a tax may be collected, shall be taxed higher than any other species of property of equal value." But the rule as to privileges, is the discretion of the Legislature: the latter are to be taxed in such manner as may, from time to time, be directed by the Legislature. *Adams* v. *Mayor and Aldermen of Somerville,* 363.

3. *Same. Same. Corporations. Act of* 1854, *ch.* 17, § 6. *Negro traders.* Hence, the act of 1854, ch. 17, § 6, incorporating the town of Somerville, and conferring power on the mayor and aldermen, by ordinance, "to license, tax, and regulate auctioneers, grocers, merchants, retailers, brokers, coffee houses, confectioneries, retailers of liquors, hawkers, pedlers, negro traders, and tavern keepers," is constitutional. And an ordinance passed by the mayor and aldermen, by virtue of said charter, requiring "that all negro traders who shall expose negroes for sale within the corporate limits of the town of Somerville, he or they shall pay a yearly license tax of twenty dollars," is not in conflict with the Constitution, and may be enforced. *Ibid.*

4. *Code, § 545. Tax on articles manufactured of the produce of this State. Merchants.* Section 545 of the Code, which provides that "salt sugar, coffee, spun cotton, garden seed, iron, and articles manufactured in this State, may be sold without paying a tax, but these articles are not exempt in the hands of any person who sets himself up as a merchant or grocer," is not in violation of article 2, § 80, of the Constitution. This section not only refrains from taxing the articles mentioned, but saves the producer or manufacturer from any tax for the privilege of selling them. But when they become articles of merchandise and profit in the hands of a merchant by occupation, they direct that reference shall be had to them as well as foreign articles, in estimating the amount to be paid for exercising the occupation or privilege of a merchant. It is only a different mode of taxing the privilege, and not a tax upon the articles. *State* v. *Crawford, McNeill & Co.*, 460.

See LAWS IN FORCE. LAND LAW.

CONSTRUCTION OF WRITINGS.

1. *Deed. Made to separate use of wife and children.* Property was conveyed, by deed, to trustees, to be sold and divided "in equal shares between Elizabeth Frierson, Solomon H. Shaw, *Sally Simmons*, Clara Brown, and Caty Grady's children; that portion that may belong to *Sally Simmons*, and the children of Emily Shaw and Caty Grady, (the two last being dead, leaving children,) to be held by said trustees in trust, for the only proper use, benefit, and behoof of the said *Sally Simmons and her children*, and the children of Caty Grady and Emily Shaw, not to be subject to the control or debts of any other person, either their husbands or otherwise, the same being intended to be held in trust by said trustees, for the use and benefit of the said last-named children of the said Simpson Shaw, and their heirs:" *Held* that the children of Sally Simmons are not vested with an equal interest with the mother, as joint owners. That it was the intention of the donor to give the entire estate to the daughter, to her separate use, by which she would be enabled to support herself and children, as a family, and the children take no interest that can be reached by their creditors. *Moore* v. *Simmons*, 545.

2. *What requisite to constitute a deed.* A deed must take effect *in præsenti*, but this may be so without the present enjoyment or possession passing, either in fact or in right. It is sufficient if a vested right to the present or future enjoyment passes. But it must be a right to some specific thing *then* owned by the person executing the conveyance; and the conveyee designated in the instrument. An instrument possessing these requisites, and wanting nothing in form, substance, or legal ceremonies to give it effect, as a title, *in præsenti*, is a deed, and not a testamentary paper. *Swails* v. *Bushart*, 561.

See CONTRACT. LAND LAW. RAILROAD COMPANY. WILLS.

CONTRACT.

1. *Inadequacy of consideration. Fraud. Chancery.* The mere inadequacy of price, independent of other circumstances, when the parties stand on equal ground, and deal with each other without any imposition, or oppression, will not be sufficient to authorize a Court of Equity to set aside a sale. Inadequacy of consideration is only a badge of fraud. *Birdsong* v. *Birdsong,* 289.

2. *Same. Same. Same. When advantage is taken.* If, however, advantage be taken, on either side, of the ignorance or distress of the other, it affords a new and distinct ground of equity; and a very great inadequacy of price will form a presumption of oppression. *Ibid.*

3. *Same. Undue influence.* A contract will be set aside when it is obtained by undue influence over a person greatly under the power of another, if there is inadequacy of consideration, or a clear ground of inference that a confidence reposed had been abused. or advantage taken of incompetency, weakness of understanding, or clouded or enfeebled faculties. *Ibid.*

4. *Same. Same.* It is not necessary that the influence should be due to antecedent or extraneous circumstances it may have arisen in the course of the same transaction in which it was exerted. It is sufficient to show such a condition of dependency from any cause, as to raise the presumption that the party was unable to protect himself, and to justify the interference of the law to protect him. *Ibid.*

5. *Same. Same. Drunkenness.* Contracts made by persons under the influence of liquor, without being completely intoxicated, are governed by the same principles which apply to other cases where one party is in a position to expose him to the exercise of an improper influence by the other. If carried so far that the reasoning powers are destroyed, the contract is void; but when it falls short of this, the contract will not be avoided, unless undue advantage has been taken, by one party, of the condition of the other. *Ibid.*

6. *Same. Same. Same.* If a party, while excited by liquor, has been led into a hard and disadvantageous bargain, it will be set aside by a Court of Equity. And the same rule applies to persons whose minds are enfeebled by habitual intoxication, although not intoxicated when the contract is made. *Ibid.*

7. *When not set aside if made under undue influence.* A contract will not be set aside on the ground of undue influence, apart from fraud, when proper in itself and for the advantage of the party who seeks to annul it. For example, the conveyance of a man habitually intemperate, but not actually drunk, of all his property in trust for his wife and children. *Ibid.*

8. *Illegal. Effect of. Note.* A contract containing on its face an illegal stipulation cannot be enforced either at law or in equity. Therefore, no suit can be maintained in the Courts of Tennessee on a note executed in this State stipulating *on its face* for usurious interest, if no other place of payment is designated where a greater rate of interest is allowed. *Thompson v. Collins, Kellogg & Kirby* 441.

9. *Same. Plea.* If a note purports on its face to have been executed beyond the limits of the State, and the declaration avers that fact, and contains a stipulation for the payment of *ten per cent.* if not paid at maturity, it is competent for the defendant to put in issue, by a proper plea, the fact as to whether it was executed in Tennessee or not. If executed in Tennessee, it would be illegal on its face and the plaintiff would be repelled from the Court. *Ibid.*

10. *Recoupment. Damages. Act of* 1856, *ch.* 71, § 1. In a suit upon a contract, if the defendant has sustained damages by reason of the plaintiff's non-performance of his part of the agreement sued on, such defendant has the right to abate the plaintiff's recovery by the amount of such damages, and have judgment over against him for any amount or balance for which he may be found liable. *Overton v. Phelan,* 445

11. *Same. Measure of damages.* The amount of damages to which the defendant is entitled in abatement of the claim against him in such case, is the damages which he would be entitled to recover in a cross-action by him against the plaintiff for the non-performance of his part of the contract. *Ibid.*

12. *Construction. Railroad Company. Liability of. Slaves.* The defendant in error hired to the plaintiff in error, for the year 1856, two slaves. The contract of hiring contained the following stipulation; "And all risks incurred, or liability to accidents, whilst in said service, is compensated for and covered by the pay agreed upon: the said railroad company assuming no responsibility for damages from accident, or any cause whatever." This stipulation does not relieve the company from liability for any injury or loss resulting from the wilful wrong or gross negligence of said company, or its agents, but it is responsible for the same. *Memphis and Charleston R. R. Co. v. Jones,* 517.

See CHANCERY. PARTNERSHIP. RAILROAD COMPANY. SLAVES. SPECIFIC PERFORMANCE.

CORPORATIONS.

See ATTACHMENT. CONSTITUTIONAL LAW. ESTOPPEL.

COSTS.

1. *Liability of surety in the Chancery Court.* In a Court of Equity, where it is in the power of the Chancellor to award costs against

either party without regard to the result of the suit, a person becoming security for costs undertakes with reference to that discretionary power, and is subject to its exercise whether his principal succeeds or not. And a bond conditioned that the complainant "shall successfully prosecute a bill of complaint this day filed by him," &c., "or pay all costs incident on failure thereof," will bind the surety for the costs, although his principal may succeed in the suit, if taxed to him by the Court. *Allison* v. *Stephens*, 251.

2. *How taxed when the defendant is acquitted. Code, § 5581.* If the defendant, in a State prosecution, is tried for a public offence, and acquitted on the merits, his costs cannot be taxed to, and paid by the State. The State, or the county, according to the nature of the offence, pays, only, the costs accrued on behalf of the State in the cases specified in § 5585 of the Code. *Tucker & Oaks* v. *The State*, 555.

See CERTIORARI. CRIMINAL LAW. NON-SUIT. JAIL INSPECTORS.

COUNTERFEITING.

See CRIMINAL LAW.

COUNTY COURT.

See APPROPRIATIONS. JUDICIAL SALES.

COURT.

See COUNTY COURT. SUPREME COURT. CIRCUIT COURT. CHANCERY COURT.

COVENANT OF SEIZIN.

See DEED.

COVENANT OF WARRANTY.

See SALE OF REAL ESTATE.

CREDITOR AND DEBTOR.

See ATTACHMENT. DEED OF TRUST. LIEN. PARTNERSHIP. FRAUDULENT CONVEYANCES.

CRIMINAL LAW.

1. *False pretence. Act of 1842, ch. 48. Release of the penalty.* The power to release the penalty imposed by the act of 1842, for obtaining goods under false pretences, on the recommendation of the jury, where the goods do not exceed ten dollars, is vested, *alone*, in the Circuit Judge. If he decline to do so, the power cannot be exercised by the Supreme Court. *Chapman* v. *The State*, 36.

2. *Same. Same. False pretence to be taken in its legal sense.* It is not every falsehood or pretence that will constitute the offence created by the act of 1842. False pretence is to be taken in its legal, and not in its literal sense. The obtaining a quart of whiskey by falsely pretending to be sent for it by another, is not sufficient to constitute the offence. *Ibid.*

3. *Slaves. Purchase of liquor from. Aider and abettor.* The sale of liquor by a slave is a criminal offence, and a white man who tempts him to commit the offence, by purchasing liquor from him, is an aider and abettor, and as much guilty, as a principal offender, of a misdemeanor, as if the seller had been of his own color. *State v. Bonner,* 135.

4. *Act of* 1831, *ch.* 108, §§ 1 *and* 2. *Slaves. Unlawful assemblage of.* Under the act of 1831, ch. 103, §§ 1 and 2, if the number of slaves assembled is *unusual,* or if the assemblage is at a *suspicious time* and *place,* the offence is complete. It is not necessary to show that the time and place are suspicious, and the number unusual. If either one is made out the offence is complete. But in either case, it must be shown that the owner of the land on which the slaves met, had *knowledge* of, and *permitted* the assemblage, without the *express authority* of their owners. *Leetch v. The State,* 140

5. *Evidence. Onus of proof. Code,* § 2691. It devolves upon the defendant to show, by positive or circumstantial evidence, that the owners of the slaves gave permission to them to assemble. But this provision is not carried into the Code, and the question is not, now, of much importance. *Ibid.*

6. *Selling liquor to a slave. Code,* § 4865. By section 4865 of the Code, any person who sells liquor to a slave except in the *master's presence,* or upon his written order, is guilty of a misdemeanor. The law contemplates a *visible* presence of the master; such a presence as necessarily, implies a knowledge of, and assent to the act of selling the liquor to the slave. If the master watch at a short distance, with a view to detect the party in the violation of the law, he is not present within the meaning of this provision of the law. *Brown v. The State,* 180.

7. *Same. Presentment. Incapacity to obtain license.* It is not necessary to aver in the presentment or indictment, that the defendant is a licensed grocery keeper, to authorize the Court to pronounce judgment of incapacity to obtain a license in future. It is sufficient to warrant such judgment if the fact appears in evidence on the trial, or is otherwise satisfactorily established, before rendition of the judgment. *Ibid.*

8. *Same. Code,* §§ 4865 *and* 2678. The offences defined in secs. 4865 2678 of the Code, however similar, are not the same, and the convic-

tion, whether upon the one section or the other, must be followed by the prescribed punishment. *Ibid.*

9. *Homicide. Self-defence.* To excuse homicide on the ground of self-defence, the danger to life, or of great bodily harm, must be either real, or honestly believed to be so, at the time of the killing, and such belief of danger must be founded on reasonable grounds. There must not only, be sufficient cause to authorize the fear of death or great bodily harm, but such fear must be really entertained, and the killing done under an honest and well founded belief that it is absolutely necessary in self-defence. *Rippy* v. *The State,* 217.

10. *Same. Same. Antecedent menaces.* The danger must be present and imminent. There must be some words or overt act at the time clearly indicative of a *present* purpose to do the injury. Previous threats, or even hostile acts, how violent soever they may be, will not, of themselves, excuse a homicide. *Ibid.*

11. *Same. Same. Same. Evidence.* The character of the deceased for violence, as well as his animosity to the defendant as indicated by his words and actions, then and before, are proper matters for the consideration of the jury in ascertaining whether the defendant had reasonable cause to fear, and did fear, that his life would be taken, or great bodily harm done him. *Ibid.*

12. *Costs. Taxed to the prosecutor. Certiorari and supersedeas. Justices of the peace* The power given to magistrates to tax the prosecutor, in criminal cases, with the costs, when the prosecution is frivolous or malicious, is discretionary; but it is a legal and not an arbitrary discretion, and is subject to revision by the Circuit Court by virtue of the constitutional writ of *certiorari. State* v. *Green,* 356.

13 *Same. Same. In what cases the prosecutor should be taxed with the costs.* To authorize a taxation of the costs in a criminal proceeding to the prosecutor, the proof should be clear and conclusive that the prosecution was frivolous or malicious, and known to the prosecutor to be without foundation. It may, and often does happen, that sufficient apparent cause exists, when, upon investigation, it turns out to be otherwise. *Ibid*

14. *Same. Same. Judgment. Certainty of.* If a warrant is taken out upon the oath of the prosecutor, for a criminal offence, and upon the trial judgment is rendered by the justice, on the warrant, discharging the defendant and taxing the prosecutor with the costs, without stating in the judgment the name of the prosecutor, it is not void, and should not be quashed for uncertainty. To hold that such a judgment was void for uncertainty, would be too technical for justices' proceedings. *Ibid.*

15. *Same. Same. Evidence. Question reserved.* If the evidence is

not taken down by the committing magistrate, would his judgment taxing the prosecutor with the costs be subject to the revisory power of the Circuit Court, or does it apply alone, to cases where the proof is reduced to writing by the justice, as required by law? *Ibid.*

16. *Gaming. Witness examined before the Grand Jury. Act of 1824, ch. 5. Code, § 5089.* By the act of 1824, ch. 5, incorporated in the Code, § 5089, any person who is summoned and examined as a witness before the grand jury as provided in said act, is not liable or bound to answer to any criminal proceedings for any offence about which he may have been so examined as a witness; but this statute was intended to relieve such persons, only, in cases, although guilty with others, where they had informed against them for the identical offence, and not in all cases of like offences. *Owens v. The State,* 455.

17. *Same. Same Plea in abatement.* If a party wish to avail himself of the benefit of the protection of the act of 1824, ch. 5, by a plea in abatement, he must aver, specifically, in his plea, that he was examined before the jury as to the particular offence charged against him in the indictment. An averment that he was summoned and went before the grand jury to testify as to unlawful gaming, &c., is not sufficient. *Ibid.*

18. *Juror. Power of the Court when juror refuses to be sworn.* The Court has the power, in a criminal case, before the jurors are sworn, to discharge one of the number upon his persistent refusal to take the oath; but after the juror has been actually discharged for this cause, the Court has no power to recall him and force him upon the prisoner without his consent. *Isaac v. The State,* 458.

19. *False pretence. Code, § 4701.* The Code, § 4701, provides that "every person who by any false pretence, or by any false token, or counterfeit letter, with intent to defraud another, obtains from any person any personal property *on* the signature of any person to any written instrument, the false making of which is forgery, shall, on conviction," &c. The word *on*, in the third line, after "property," is, by misprint, or clerical error, substituted for *or*, and it should read, "or the signature of any person to any written instrument," &c. *Roberts v. The State,* 501.

20. *Same. Passing counterfeit coin.* The offence of passing counterfeit coin is a distinct, substantive felony, of higher grade from that of obtaining goods by false pretences, created by the act of 1842; and if the false pretence be the passing of counterfeit coin, the indictment cannot be sustained. *Ibid.*

21. *Same. Same.* To constitute the offence of passing counterfeit coin, the spurious coin passed must be a representation of genuine coin on both sides. If it be a piece of spurious metal, about the size of current coin, representing it on one side, but merely an advertise-

ment on the other, and not purporting to be coin, the passing of it (the other requisites existing) is a false pretence, under the statute. *Ibid.*

22. *Passing a counterfeit bank note. Rule as to resemblance.* If a party is indicted for passing a counterfeit resemblance or imitation of a genuine bank note, to authorize a conviction, the imitation or resemblance must be such as to be capable of imposing on persons of *ordinary observation. Dement v. The State,* 505.

23. *Discharge of jurors.* Pending the selection of the jury, and before the jurors had been charged with the trial of the prisoner, two of them were discharged by the Court, with the consent of the Attorney General and the prisoner. In this there was no error. *Nolen v. The State,* 520.

24. *Statement made by one juror to his fellow jurors. New trial.* A new trial will not be granted in a criminal case upon the unsupported affidavit of the prisoner, to the effect that after the jury retired from the bar, one of the number made a statement as of his own knowledge, that the prisoner was a violent, dangerous man. And the jurors are not bound to appear in Court and convict themselves of a violation of duty. *Ibid.*

25. *Evidence. Parol, to establish the existence of Free Banks.* Act of 1851-2, *ch.* 118. Upon an indictment for fraudulently keeping in possession the counterfeit resemblance or imitation of the note of a Free Bank, created by the act of 1851-2, ch. 118, parol evidence is not admissible to establish the existence of said bank. The memorandum required by said act, or a copy thereof, duly certified, either by the Register or Secretary of State, must be produced. *Trice v. The State,* 591.

26. *Fraudulently keeping in possession the counterfeit note of a Free Bank. When note described of a different denomination from any issued by the bank.* By the 3d section of the act of 1851-2, ch. 118, the banks organized under its provisions are empowered to issue and circulate notes of the different denominations authorized to be issued by the incorporated banks of the State. And, therefore, the fact that the counterfeit note, for having possession of which a party is indicted, is of a denomination different from any issued by the bank, will not defeat the prosecution. It is sufficient that the bank had lawful authority to issue notes of the denomination of that described in the indictment. *Ibid.*

See BAIL. COSTS.

CUSTOM.

See CARRIERS.

DAMAGES.

Measure of. Obligation for railroad bonds. If an obligation is executed for a sum of money, to be paid in the bonds of a railroad company, and said obligation is not complied with, the measure of damages in an action thereon, or when offered as a set-off, is the nominal value of the bonds, and not the value at which they might be rated in the market. *Memphis and Little Rock R. R. Co.* v. *Walker,* 467.

See CARRIERS. CONTRACT. RAILROAD COMPANY. SLAVES. TRESPASS.

DE BENE ESSE.

See DEPOSITIONS.

DEBT.

See ADMINISTRATORS AND EXECUTORS.

DECREE.

When a decree between defendants conclusive. A decree between defendants will be conclusive and binding upon them where an antagonism exists, so as to make them actors against each other; but if a part of the defendants are minors, and have no regular guardian, and a person is appointed guardian *ad litem* for them, who is a defendant, and whose interest in the suit is in conflict with theirs, the decree pronounced in the cause will not bar a subsequent suit by said minors against said defendant. *Elrod* v. *Lancaster,* 571.

See ADMINISTRATORS AND EXECUTORS. CHANCERY. CHANCERY JURISDICTION. CHANCERY PRACTICE.

DEED.

1. *Consideration. Covenant of seizin.* The defendant executed a deed to the plaintiff in 1851 for a lot of ground in the city of Memphis, for the consideration of four thousand dollars. The deed contained, simply, a covenant of general warranty in the usual form. About eighteen months after the execution of said deed, the defendant executed to the plaintiff another deed for the same lot without any new consideration. This deed was made to bear the same date and to recite the same consideration of the first deed, and in no respect differed from it, except that it contained a covenant of seizin, and that the lot was free from all incumbrances. *Held,* that, if in the absence of fraud the defendant voluntarily and understandingly executed the second deed with the intent and for the purpose of carrying out the original agreement between the parties at the time of making the contract, and to supply the omission in the first deed: or, if the original contract were *silent* as to the covenants incorporated in the second deed, and

the vendor, at the instance of the vendee, and with knowledge that the first deed was defective, in respect to the proper and necessary covenants—fairly and voluntarily executed the latter conveyance as a farther and better assurance of title to the purchaser intending that the former deed should be abandoned and the latter substituted in its stead, the second deed would be valid and binding without any new or additional consideration. *Park* v. *Cheek*, 451.

2. *Same. Estoppel.* In such a case the vendee would be estopped to question his liability on the covenants of the second deed, on the score of want of consideration. *Ibid.*

See CONSTRUCTION OF WRITINGS DEED OF TRUST. EVIDENCE. STATUTE OF LIMITATIONS.

DEED OF TRUST.

1. *Not void if creditors are required to present their claims within a specified time.* A deed of trust was executed on the 12th of May, 1857, providing for the payment of the "home creditors," by name, of the bargainors, and then directed that the remainder of the fund in the hands of the trustee be divided *pro rata* among their New York and Philadelphia creditors, to whom they owed $21,000 ; but said creditors were not otherwise referred to than by this general description. The benefit of this provision was confined to such of those creditors as would present their claims to the trustee on or before the 25th day of December, 1858, and they were to be notified by him. Held, that this was a just and prudent provision, and did not render the deed void. *Mayer & Co.* v. *Pulliam*, 846.

2. *Assignment of choses in action. Probate. Registration.* An assignment of *choses in action* is not embraced by the registry acts, and such assignment is as good without as with registration. If made to a third person, as trustee, for the benefit of creditors, it is good against subsequent attaching creditors without probate and registration. *Ibid.*

See LAND LAW.

DEMAND AND NOTICE.

Bank notes. When for any purpose, demand of payment of bank notes is necessary, the demand must be made at the place where the notes are, *upon their face*, made payable. *Ware* v. *Street & Co.*, 609.

See BILLS AND NOTES. PAYMENT.

DEMURRER.

See BAIL. CHANCERY PLEADING. PRACTICE AND PLEADING.

DEPOSITIONS.

1. *Effect of release after deposition taken. Witness.* If the deposition of a witness is taken, who is incompetent at the time his testimony is given, the subsequent release of the interest, on the trial, will not operate to remove the objection existing at the time the deposition is taken. The witness must be competent at the *time* his testimony is given. *Ford* v. *Grieshaber*, 485.

2. *Taken before issue, or by collusion.* If a deposition is taken in a cause, to which an infant is a party, before the same is at issue, and it does not appear to have been taken *de bene esse*, and there is reason to believe that there was collusion between the complainant and the *next friend* of the infant, the deposition will be rejected. *Gaugh and wife* v. *Henderson*, 628.

See CHANCERY PRACTICE. EVIDENCE.

DESCENT AND DISTRIBUTION.

See LAND LAW. STATUTE OF LIMITATIONS.

DEVASTAVIT.

See ADMINISTRATORS AND EXECUTORS

DEVISE.

See TRUST AND TRUSTEE.

DISABILITY.

See EVIDENCE. STATUTE OF LIMITATIONS.

DISCLAIMER.

See TRUST AND TRUSTEE.

DISTRIBUTION.

See SLAVES.

DRUNKENNESS.

See CONTRACT.

EJECTMENT.

See CHANCERY JURISDICTION. LAND LAW.

ENTRY AND ENTRY-TAKER.

See LAND LAW.

EQUITABLE INTEREST AND ESTATE.

See ATTACHMENT. STATUTE OF LIMITATIONS. WILLS.

ESCHEATS.

What necessary to establish an escheat. To entitle the State to recover lands alleged to have escheated, it must appear that the owners were *foreigners*, that they died without *issue*, and left no relations within the United States entitled, by law, to succeed to said land. If there is an omission to prove these facts, a verdict in favor of the State will be set aside, and a new trial granted. *Catham* v. *The State*, 553.

ESTOPPEL.

1. *By answer in Chancery. Corporation.* If a party, by his answer in Chancery, admits the existence of a corporation by a particular name, he cannot be heard to deny, in said suit, that admission. *Lillard* v. *Porter*, 177.

2. *Feme covert. Sale of slaves. Coverture* confers no privilege or license to commit either fraud or falsehood under sanction of an oath; nor protection from the consequences. And if a married woman makes a solemn disclaimer on oath, in a deposition or otherwise, of title to slaves which are legally hers, she is estopped from thereafter claiming them. *Cooley* v. *Steele*, 605.

See DEED. LIEN. STATUTE OF LIMITATIONS. WARRANTY.

EVICTION.

See SALE OF REAL ESTATE.

EVIDENCE.

1. *Payment. Receipt not conclusive.* A receipt of payment or delivery is only *prima facie* evidence of the fact, and not conclusive, and, therefore, the fact that it recites may be contradicted by oral testimony. *Mt. Olivet Cemetery* v. *Shubert*, 116.

2. *Depositions. Competency. Objection to must be specific.* If a deposition contains matter that is relevant and competent, and that which is incompetent, an objection, to be available, must be specifically made to such parts as are incompetent. A general objection to the reading of the deposition will not do. *Ibid.*

3. *Partner not a competent witness.* One of the co-partners of a firm, in a contest between third persons and the firm, is not a competent witness to prove the existence of the partnership, or that the debt sued for was created for or on account of the firm. *Philips* v. *Henry and Shackleford*, 188.

4. *Privileged communication. Attorney and client.* Communications between a client and his attorney are under the seal of confidence, and cannot be disclosed in proof. It is not necessary to the application of this rule of evidence that a suit should be pending or anticipated, nor that there should be a regular retainer, or the payment of a fee. But the communication must be in a professional character, in relation to some act passed, or right or interest in existence. *McMannus* v. *The State,* 218.

5. *Same. Same. Does not apply to abstract legal questions.* This rule of evidence relative to privileged communications, does not apply to cases where abstract legal opinions are sought and obtained on general questions of law, either civil or criminal. In such cases, no facts are or need be disclosed, implicating the client, and so there is nothing, of a confidential character, to conceal. *Ibid.*

6. *Hearsay. Admissions of guardian.* The statements of a guardian relative to a contract for the hire of a slave, made by him as guardian, in a suit to which he is not a party, are not admissible. First, because it is mere hearsay evidence. If admissible the guardian must be called on as a witness Second, the evidence is inadmissible on the principle that the admissions by a guardian, though the plaintiff, or a party on record is not evidence against the infant. *Dement* v. *Scott,* 867.

7. *Settlement. Receipt.* The fact that the defendant had paid, in part, for articles or work and taken a receipt therefor, or taken receipts from the plaintiff and another person, before the same were found to be defective, does not change the rule as to damages, or lessen the plaintiff's liability, or preclude the defendant from showing that the plnintiff is the person really liable to him. *Overton* v. *Phelan,* 445.

8. *Statement of slave. When admissible.* The principle admitting as evidence the representations of a slave made to a physician, or other person, is confined to statements made as to the nature, symptoms, effects, and duration of the malady under which he is laboring. A representation to a person, by the slave, without any question being asked, to the effect that she had become diseased after the plaintiff purchased her, and in consequence of ill-treatment, is not admissible. *Nored* v. *Adams,* 449.

9. *Onus probandi. Recitals of a deed. Consideration.* The burden of proof, when a party attacks the consideration of a deed, and attempts to prove that it was paid by another than the person recited in the deed, is upon the party attacking the same; and he must disprove, by clear and satisfactory evidence, the truth of the fact recited. *Gaugh & Wife* v. *Henderson,* 628.

10. *Disability. Infancy. Presumption from lapse of time.* So long as a party is under a disability, or within the saving of the statute of limitations, lapse of time furnishes no presumption against her, and does not operate prejudicially to her rights. *Ibid.*

See BILLS AND NOTES. CHANCERY PRACTICE. CRIMINAL LAW. DEPOSITIONS. PARTNERSHIP. SALE OF PERSONALTY. FORCIBLE ENTRY AND DETAINER. SLAVES. SUMMARY PROCEEDINGS. TRUST AND TRUSTEE. WARRANTY. WILLS.

EXECUTION.

1. *Levy of. What property to be levied on first.* It is the duty of the officer into whose hands an execution is placed, first to levy on the personal property of the defendant or defendants, before making a levy on land. If there be several defendants, all primarily liable, the officer may proceed against the goods and chattels of either one to levy the whole debt, leaving the question of contribution to be settled among the defendants. And if some of the defendants have personal property liable to the satisfaction of the debt, and others have not, it is the duty of the officer to proceed against the former, or either of them, until property sufficient is found to discharge the debt. *Hassell* v. *Southern Bank of Ky.*, 881.

2. *Return of. Summary proceeding. Case in judgment.* The officer cannot screen himself from liability for an insufficient return, by returning that one of several defendants had no property subject to execution. To protect him, his return must show that the money could not have been made out of either defendant. Thus, a return on an execution against several defendants, "no personal property to be found in my county, of E. W. Tipton," (one of the defendants,) "on which I can levy for said debt and cost," is an insufficient return, and the officer is liable therefor, upon motion. *Ibid.*

3. *When it may be collaterally attacked.* An execution cannot be attacked, collaterally, except by showing a total want of jurisdiction to render the judgment upon which the execution issued, so as to make it void. It cannot be done for mere errors that may exist in the proceedings and judgment, which do not render the judgment void. *Wells* v. *Griffin & Co.*, 568.

See ADMINISTRATORS AND EXECUTORS. SALE OF PERSONALTY. SLAVES. STAY OF EXECUTION.

FACTOR.

1. *Lien upon goods consigned. Possession.* Where the consignor remains owner of the goods consigned, no special property can exist in the factor, or any lien general or special, unless he have possession, either actual or constructive, of the goods. If the goods are in *transitu*, or if the factor has only a right of possession, the lien does not attach. *Woodruff* v. *the Nashville and Chattanooga Railroad Company*, 87.

2. *Same. Power of the owner.* If the factor has no property in the goods, and no lien upon them, the owner has a perfect right to dispose of them as he may please, and the factor cannot control him in this right. *Ibid.*

3. *Question reserved.* Can a factor, who has neither the actual nor constructive possession of the goods, and no property in them, maintain an action against a mere wrong-doer, acting in opposition to the rights of both him and the owner? *Ibid.*

4. *Same.* If a factor has made acceptances, or incurred liability upon the faith of the consignment of goods to him, but has no property in them, nor possession, either actual or constructive, do such acceptances or liability give him a lien upon or property in the goods consigned? *Ibid.*

5. *Lien ceases when liability discharged.* If such lien exists, it ceases upon payment of the bills drawn, or liability incurred. And if the factor is under no liability for the consignor, or owner, at the time of the institution of his suit, it cannot be maintained. *Ibid.*

FALSE PRETENCES.

See CRIMINAL LAW.

FEME COVERT.

See ESTOPPEL. SPECIFIC PERFORMANCE.

FORCIBLE ENTRY AND DETAINER.

1. *Three years possession.* The uninterrupted possession of the premises in controversy, by the defendant, continuously, for the space of three years immediately preceding the commencement of the action, is, if the estate of the defendant has not determined within that time, a bar to any proceeding by writ of forcible entry and detainer. *Philips v. Sampson,* 429.

2. *When title may be enquired into.* As a general rule, the title cannot be enquired into, in this form of action; yet it is admissible to look to the title to define the boundaries; or, in view of the question of damages, or rents to be recovered in an action brought by a mere intruder against the rightful owner of the land; or, where the claimant by fraud induces another to take a lease, or to enter under him upon a false representation as to his title. In such cases, and, perhaps, others, the title may be looked to, in the determination of the question, whether the case made out constitutes, in law, a wrongful entry or detainer. *Ibid.*

3. *Evidence. Case in judgment.* Both claimants derive title from the same source—one dating back to 1795, and the other to 1838. The

premises were rented by the agent of the older claimant, to a tenant, for the years 1847 and 1848. At the end of 1848 he rented it to the defendant, who held under that title until this suit was instituted. The other claimant procured an instrument of writing purporting to have been executed on the 18th of November, 1848, from the person in possession that year, recognizing his tenancy under him, and agreeing to deliver the possession to him on the first of January, 1849. *Held*, that the instrument of writing thus executed, the party being a competent witness, is inadmissible as evidence of the character of his holding; and the three years continuous possession of the tenants under the elder claimant, is a bar to the action of the plaintiff. *Ibid.*

FRAUD.

See BILLS AND NOTES. CHANCERY. CHANCERY JURISDICTION. CONTRACT. ESTOPPEL. PARTNERSHIP. POWER. RAILROAD COMPANY. SALE OF REAL ESTATE SLAVES. SPECIFIC PERFORMANCE. TRUST AND TRUSTEE. WILLS

FRAUDS, STATUTE OF.

Statute of. A promise by a company, or its agent, to pay an account due from said company, which has been assigned to a third person, is not within the statute of frauds, and need not be in writing. *Mt. Olivet Cemetery v. Shubert*, 116.

See SALE OF REAL ESTATE.

FRAUDULENT CONVEYANCES.

Debtor and creditor. What liable to creditors. A conveyance of an interest not liable to creditors, though fraudulent, is not within the provisions of the statute of frauds. Neither can the creditor coerce the debtor to labor for his benefit. If, therefore, a debtor, by an agreement with his son, permit him to have the use of his horse and the services of two other sons, who are minors, to raise a crop, and furnish the family with provisions for that year out of the crop—reimbursing himself for the supplies thus furnished, and also to retain reasonable wages, and whatever beyond this remained of the proceeds of the crop was to go to the payment of the father's debts—such agreement is not a fraud upon the creditors of the father, and the crop raised is not liable to execution. *Leslie v. Joyner*, 514.

See ATTACHMENT. CHANCERY JURISDICTION. SALE OF REAL ESTATE.

FRAUDULENT SALES.

1. *Liability of purchaser from vendee with notice of the fraud.* If goods are procured by fraud under color of a contract of purchase

and the same are received by a third person with notice of the fraud in obtaining them; or under circumstances sufficient to put him on inquiry; or such third person fails to put himself on the footing of a *bona fide* purchaser for a valuable consideration; then, by the mere act of receiving the goods and appropriating them to his own use, he is guilty of a conversion, for which the original owner of the goods may maintain an action of *trover*. *Gage, Dater & Massey* v. *Epperson*, 669.

2. *Same.* Such third person is thus liable, although he may have received the goods *before* the owner took any steps, or made known his determination to reclaim them. Being affected with notice of the fraud, he is chargeable with all the legal consequences of the same. He cannot excuse himself upon the ground that the owner might acquiesce in the fraud, and abandon his legal right to treat the sale as a nullity and reclaim the goods. *Ibid.*

GAMING.

See CHANCERY JURISDICTION. CRIMINAL LAW.

GARNISHMENT.

See CHANCERY JURISDICTION.

GIFT.

See TRUST AND TRUSTEE.

GRANT.

See LAND LAW.

GUARDIAN AND WARD.

When an infant may bind himself, or guardian, or parent, for necessaries. If an infant is under the care of a parent, or guardian, who has the means and is willing to furnish him what is actually necessary, he can make no contract for any article whatever, that will bind himself, his parent, or guardian, without the consent of his legal protector and adviser. But an infant is liable for necessaries suitable to his rank and condition, when he has no other means of obtaining them except by the pledge of his own personal estate. *Elrod* v. *Myers*, 38.

See EVIDENCE. SALE OF REAL ESTATE.

HEARSAY.

See EVIDENCE.

HEIRS.

See LAND LAW.

HIATUS.

See LAND LAW.

HIRE.

See SLAVES.

HOMICIDE.

See CRIMINAL LAW.

HUSBAND AND WIFE.

1. *Husband's right to the real estate of the wife.* By the common law the husband, by marriage, gains an estate of freehold in the lands of his wife, which he may convey by his own deed to another, and the wife can take no step, either at law or in equity, to regain the possession of the land, so long as the *coverture* lasts. But her ultimate fee simple interest is not affected by her disability, and on its termination she will be remitted to her right of action to recover the possession. *Coleman* v. *Satterfield*, 259.

2. *Same. When wife may sue. Cloud upon her title. Chancery jurisdiction.* Although the husband, by his own act may, by the principles of the common law, defeat the wife's enjoyment of the possession and profits of her land, yet he has no power over her title or interest in fee; of this she can, alone, be divested by her own *voluntary* act, in the form prescribed by law. And the attempt to deprive her of it by fraud, force, or undue influence, either on the part of her husband or a stranger, furnishes her in a suit by next friend, a clear ground for redress in equity, by having said deed declared null, and the cloud removed from her title, although she may not be entitled to the present possession of the land. *Ibid.*

3. *Same. Same. Rights of the wife under the act of* 1849–50. The act of 1849–50 materially changes the common law. It not only protects the husband's interest in the lands of his wife from seizure and sale by his creditors *during* her life, but it likewise disables the husband to sell or dispose of such interest, without her joining in the conveyance. And if a conveyance has been procured from her by fraud, or other improper means, whether by her husband or a stranger, she may maintain a bill by next friend, to have it set aside and to have the possession restored to her—making the husband a defendant. *Ibid.*

See CHANCERY JURISDICTION. STATUTE OF LIMITATIONS. TRUST AND TRUSTEE. WARRANTY.

IMPROVEMENTS.

See SALE OF REAL ESTATE.

INDEX. 761

INDORSERS.

See BILLS AND NOTES.

INFANTS.

See ADMINISTRATORS AND EXECUTORS. EVIDENCE. SALE OF REAL ESTATE. GUARDIAN AND WARD. STATUTE OF LIMITATIONS.

INFLUENCE.

See CONTRACT.

INNOCENT PURCHASER.

Notice. Chancery pleading. Registration. Case in judgment. If a party have either actual or constructive notice of title, he cannot avail himself of the plea of an innocent purchaser, for value, without notice. A bill of sale, evidencing the title of the complainants, was registered in the county where the bargainor and bargainees resided. The bargainees, subsequently, removed to another county with the slaves, where they were sold by the trustee to the defendant. *Held*, that the defendant was bound to trace the residence of the parties and the history of the title of the slaves, by a search of the Register's books; that the registration of the bill of sale was constructive notice to him, and if he failed to make such search, he was guilty of gross negligence, and could not rely upon the plea of being an innocent purchaser. *Parker v. Hall*, 641.

See CHANCERY JURISDICTION. TRUST AND TRUSTEE.

INSOLVENCY.

See SET-OFF.

INTEREST.

See CERTIORARI.

JAILS AND JAILERS.

1. *How jails are built, and are public prisons.* Jails are usually built by the County Courts, out of the funds in the County Treasury, but the Legislature may authorize them to be constructed by the towns and cities; and, unless restricted by law, they, *all*, become the public prisons of the State, to be used for the safe custody of offenders. And it does not lie in the power of any county, town, or city, to exclude the State, or its officers, from the custody and control of them. *Felts v. The Mayor and Aldermen of Memphis.* 650.

2. *Sheriffs entitled to the custody of the jails.* At the common law the custody of jails of right belonged and was annexed, as an in-

cident, to the office of sheriff. He was amenable for escapes, and subject to amercements if he had not the bodies of prisoners in Court; and, therefore, had the appointment of jailers and the custody of the jails. These common law rights of the sheriff have not been abridged by the Legislature; and they have the right to the custody and control of the public prisons of their respective counties. *Ibid.*

3. *Same. When the sheriff may be restored to the custody of the jail, by mandamus.* If a jail, built by authority of law, is placed in the possession and under the control of another, than the sheriff, by the County Court, or the Mayor and Aldermen of a town or city, and the sheriff of the county virtually refused all legal authority and control over it, he may be restored to his rights by a writ of *mandamus.* *Ibid.*

4. *Jail in Memphis.* The acts creating the Court in, and amending the charter of the city of Memphis, clearly imply that there should be a jail within the jurisdiction of said Court, as well for the safe-keeping of offenders against the State laws, as the city ordinances. Hence, the jail built by the corporate authorities is a prison of the State, under the care and control of the sheriff of the county. *Ibid.*

JAIL INSPECTORS.

Powers of. Costs. Physician's bills. The power conferred upon jail inspectors, to "make rules and regulations for the preservation of the health and decorum of the prisoners," is confined to general sanitary and police regulations. It does not authorize them to charge the county with physician's bills for medical attention to the prisoners. Such bills do not form an item of costs provided for by law in prosecutions, either, for felonies or misdemeanors. *Connell v. The County Judge of Davidson,* 189.

JOINT ESTATE.

See STATUTE OF LIMITATIONS.

JOINT INTEREST.

See BILLS AND NOTES.

JUDGMENT.

See ADMINISTRATORS AND EXECUTORS. ATTACHMENT. BAIL. CERTIORARI. CHANCERY JURISDICTION. CRIMINAL LAW. LIEN. OFFICERS DE FACTO. PARTNERSHIP. SALE OF PERSONALTY. SCIRE FACIAS. STAY OF EXECUTION. SURETIES.

JUDICIAL SALES.

1. *County Court. Jurisdiction in setting aside sales after confirmation.* The jurisdiction of the County Court, under the law authorizing the

sale, by that tribunal, of the property of decedents, for partition, &c., is limited, alone, to the making and completion of the sale. After such sale has been completed, by the confirmation of the report, if any matters of equity exists, or should arise, entitling the purchaser to be relieved against the payment of the purchase money, resort must be had to a Court of Equity. *Bond* v. *Clay*, 379.

2. *Same. Same. Code, §§ 4204, 4205, does not enlarge the jurisdiction.* Sections 4204 and 4205 of the Code are merely declaratory of the law as it previously existed in regard to the jurisdiction of the County Court in sales of property for partition. &c. No new and enlarged jurisdiction is conferred upon that Court by the Code. *Ibid.*

See SURETIES.

JURISDICTION.

Rule for, as to Superior and Inferior Courts. The rule for jurisdiction is, that nothing shall be intended to be out of the jurisdiction of a Superior Court but that which specially appears to be so; and, on the contrary, nothing shall be intended to be within the jurisdiction of an Inferior Court but that which is so expressly alleged. *Hopper* v. *Fisher*, 258.

See SALE OF REAL ESTATE. JUDICIAL SALES. SUMMARY PROCEEDINGS.

JURORS.

See CRIMINAL LAW.

JUSTICES OF THE PEACE.

See BAIL. CERTIORARI. CRIMINAL LAW. STAY OF EXECUTION. SUMMARY PROCEEDINGS.

LAND LAW.

1. *Entry and entry taker. Act of* 1777, *ch.* 1, § 18. By the Act of 1777, ch. 1, § 18 if any entry taker is desirous of making any entry of lands in his own name, such entry shall be made in its proper place before a justice of the peace of the county not being a surveyor or assistant, which entry the justice shall return to the County Court at its next sitting &c.; and every entry made by, or for such entry taker, in any other manner, is illegal and void, and any other person may enter, survey, and obtain a grant for the same land. *Egnew* v. *Cochrane*, 820.

2. *Same. Same. Not repealed.* The 18th section of the act of 1777 has not expired or become obsolete by non-user, nor changed by practice and usage; neither has it been repealed by the act of 1706,

or by the 6th section of the act of 1801, ch. 8, or by the act of 1806, ch. 1, or by the act of 1819—said section of the act of 1777 is in full force. *Ibid.*

3. *Same. Same. Applicable to lands south and west of the Congressional Reservation Line.* The 18th section of the act of 1777 is applicable to, and embraces that portion of the State south and west of the Congressional Reservation Line. *Ibid.*

4. *Same. Common law.* Upon common law principles, the entry taker cannot make an entry in his own name, before himself, because it is against public policy. *Ibid.*

5. *Same. Question reserved.* Is a grant obtained by the entry taker, upon an entry before himself to be regarded as void and open to attack in a Court of Law, or only voidable at the suit of the party aggrieved, in a Court of Equity? *Ibid.*

6. *Same. Same.* What would be the effect of a purchase from the grantee thus obtaining a grant upon his own entry, and can a person holding a younger entry and grant call in question the prior grant of the same land to the entry taker? *Ibid.*

7. *Occupant claim. Act of 1843, ch. 8, § 4. Administrators and executors.* The act of 1843, ch. 8, § 4, provides that in all cases where an occupant claimant south and west of the Congressional Reservation Line, " may have heretofore died, or may hereafter die, without having perfected his title to his occupant claim it shall be the duty of the administrator or executor, by the use of the first money which shall come to his hands, to perfect the title to the occupant claim of his testator or intestate, in the name and for the use of the heirs at law, of such decedent claimant " This act is retrospective, and applies to all cases occurring before its passage, when the administration has not been settled up, and the administrator or executor discharged of the trust. *Gray* v. *Davis*, 860.

8. *Same. Same. Same. Application of the principle. Trust and trustee.* The testator died in 1834. He was the owner, at his death, of an occupant claim south and west of the Congressional Reservation Line, the title to which had not been perfected. His widow was duly qualified as his executrix. She received money and assets of the estate, but had made no settlement of her administration at the time of the filing of the bill in this case. In 1846 the widow caused said lands to be entered, and she procured a grant therefor, in her own name; and afterwards, by her will, devised the land to two of her children. Held, that not having closed her administration, and been discharged of the trust prior to the passage of the act of 1843, she was bound to carry out its provisions, and must be held to have taken the legal title as trustee for the heirs, and her devisees can stand in no better condition. *Ibid.*

9. *Words of inheritance.* "*Heirs*" *necessary to create a fee.* At common-law, the word "*heirs*" is indispensable to convey an estate of inheritance. Without the use of that term in deeds an estate for life only, is created. But this rule has been changed in Tennessee, by statutory enactment   *Cromwell* v. *Winchester,* 889.

10. *Grant. Hiatus between the expiration of the act of* 1850, *and the passage of the act of* 1851. *Abandonment of an entry.* If land was entered previous to the expiration of the act of 1850, but no grant issued until after that time, and a third person, during the *hiatus* between the 30th of August, 1851, the time the act of 1850 ceased, and the passage of the act of the 13th of November, 1851, entered the same land; but, upon discovering the conflict with the older entry, which being left in the entry taker's office, was recorded by the deputy without his knowledge, such subsequent enterer could not hold the land in opposition to the older entry   *Bullock* v. *Tipton,* 408.

11. *Entry. Assignment of.* If, upon a promise made prior to the discovery of said conflict, the second enterer of the land assigns his entry to a third person, without consideration, and with a full knowledge of the prior claim, and the abandonment of the second entry, the assignee can have no higher equity than his assignor, and could not, by virtue of such second entry, defeat the title of the older enterer. *Ibid.*

12. *Legal title. Valuable consideration. Prior equity   Question reserved.* If a party procures from the State the legal title to a tract of land, and has paid a valuable consideration therefor, will a Court of Equity take it from him at the instance of one who, with a full knowledge of his previous rights, seeks to come in under an *hiatus* in the extension law upon an entry made upon a mere nominal consideration? *Ibid.*

13. *Ejectment. Construction. Trust deed. Notice of sale.* H sold a tract of land to R and J, and executed a bond for title on payment of the purchase money, for which notes were executed. Afterwards H made an assignment of these notes and his title to the land to A, for the benefit of creditors, reciting in the deed his previous sale to R and J, and his obligation to make them a title upon payment of the purchase money. The deed provided that if the notes were not paid within a reasonable time, the trustee, A, should dispose of them to the highest bidder, at public auction, the sale to be made at the court-house, after giving notice thereof for the space of twenty days by public advertisement at three or more public places. The trustee sold the notes of R and J, to M, at public auction, and executed to him a deed in fee to the land. Afterwards R and J paid the purchase money to M, who, thereupon, conveyed said land, in fee, to them. In the conveyance from the trustee to M, and from him to R and J, the covenant to convey, on payment of the purchase money, executed by H to R and J, is specially recited. *Held;*

1. That, by the proper construction of the deed from H to A, the lands previously sold by A to R and J were not intended to be sold by the trustee, but the object was merely to enable the trustee, on collecting the notes from R and J to transfer to them the title, in pursuance of the bond before mentioned; or, if they failed to pay in a reasonable time, and a sale of the notes at public auction should become necessary, that the trustee might be in a condition to transfer the title to the purchaser, as a security to him for the payment of said notes. And, by the conveyances thus made, R and J acquired a valid title to the land.

2. That a stranger to the title thus derived from H, and a trespasser upon the premises, cannot be heard to set up, as an objection to the validity of the title of R and J, that it does not appear that the twenty days' notice of the sale of their notes was given by the trustee, even if the title could be successfully assailed on this ground, by a party in interest. *Matthewson v. Spencer*, 424.

14. *Cession Act. Constitution, art.* 1, § 81. The validity of North Carolina land claims is recognized by the Constitution of Tennessee, art. 1, § 81. It is, in substance, declared that the sovereignty and right of soil of Tennessee are subject to the conditions and provisions of the "Cession Act," and shall not "extend to affect the claim or claims of individuals to any part of the soil which is recognized by the aforesaid Cession Act" *Fogg v. Williams* 474.

15. *Same. North Carolina land claims. State a trustee for the claimants.* The relation between the State of Tennessee and the owners of North Carolina land warrants, or other claims, is that of *trustee* and *cestui que trust*. The State, as trustee, cannot divest the claimants of their right, either directly or indirectly And this trust is so incorporated with the claims and the land appropriated by them, as to affect all subsequent enterers of the same land. *Ibid.*

16. *Same. Same.* Independent of the exercise of any power or authority in Tennessee, the owners of land appropriated under North Carolina land warrants, may be regarded as invested with an estate in fee-simple, merely by force of the Cession Act and the acts of Congress and of the General Assembly of Tennessee, passed in pursuance thereof. *Ibid.*

17. *Same. Same. Power of the Legislature to annex conditions. Act of 1850, ch.* 188. The Legislature, therefore, does not possess the power to annex subsequent conditions, by which the failure of claimants under North Carolina land warrants, to apply for a grant within a limited time, shall work a forfeiture of their estates. *Ibid.*

18. *Power of the Legislature to annex conditions to the procuring of grants. Question reserved.* Has the Legislature the power to annex subsequent conditions and limitations in regard to the time within

which the enterers of land, deriving their right from the exclusive sovereignty and right of soil in Tennessee, shall perfect their titles? *Ibid.*

19. *Act of* 1851, *ch.* 826. *Occupant claim. Time to perfect title.* By the act of 1851, ch. 826, it is unlawful for any person to enter land on which another resides, or which is cultivated, or has been previously entered by him, until such person gives at least thirty days' notice in writing to the person residing on or cultivating said land, or to the previous enterer or his assignee, of his intention to enter the same. Any entry made, or grant obtained contrary to the provisions of said act, are void. And time is given until the first of March, 1854, to have surveys made and grants issued. *Scott* v. *Price & Bell,* 532.

20. *Same. Same.* The language of the act of 1851 is general, and embraces all land which had been previously entered under authority of law, no matter when, and without any distinction as to the origin or nature of the right of entry. It applies to an occupant enterer, and protects him as fully as it does the general enterer. *Ibid.*

21. *Descent. An occupant right descends to heirs.* Upon the relinquishment of the public lands, by Congress, to the State, the occupant laws previously enacted, conferred upon those who complied with their provisions, an inheritable interest in the lands. And upon the death of any person having an occupant right, or of his assignee, such right is cast by descent upon his heirs. *Ibid.*

22 *Act of* 1851, *ch.* 826. *Assignee protected.* The right of the assignee of an original occupant claim is protected by the act of 1851, without an actual residence on the land by such assignee, or his heirs. *Ibid.*

23. *Grant. Occupant claims. Transfer of. Presumption.* The statutes prescribe the mode by which the transfer and ownership of the occupant claims or entries might be established before the entry-taker; and after the issuance of a grant it will be *presumed,* when the title comes collaterally in question in a Court of Law, that all the preliminary steps necessary to the making of the entry, and obtaining of the grant, were regularly pursued. *Tipton* v. *Sanders,* 690.

24. *Act of* 1849, *ch.* 188. *Act of* 1851, *ch.* 826, § 1. *Effect of hiatus between. Grant.* The effect of the act of 1851, ch. 326, § 1, was to resuscitate the right and prolong the time for perfecting titles to land; and, as against all persons who acquired no intervening right during the *hiatus* between the expiration of the act of 1850, and the passage of the act of 1851, the title of previous enterers, who have obtained grants, is as perfect as if no such interval had occurred. *Ibid.*

25. *Same. Same. Illustration of the principle.* T. obtained a grant on the 1st of January, 1856, founded on an entry made on the 4th

of August, 1849, which purports on its face to be a consolidation of six occupant extension entries, (of which T. was assignee,) made on the 19th of October, 1840. S. obtained a grant for the same land on the 10th, of November, 1849, founded on an entry made on the 7th of July, 1847. *Held*, that under the acts of 1851 and 1853, the right of T. to perfect his title was revived and continued, and this right was perfect against all persons who had acquired no right during the intermission between the act of 1850 and 1851; that the entry and grant of S. were void *ab initio*, and were not revived by the accidental intermission in the extension law. *Ibid.*

26 *Grant. Presumption of.* If a person who enters land, and those claiming under him, have the exclusive, uninterrupted, and adverse possession of said land, claiming the same to the extent of the boundaries of the entry, for a period of twenty years, a grant, commensurate with the boundaries of said entry, will be presumed. *Williams* v. *Donell*, 695.

27. *Same. Same. Not necessary to show the probable issuance of a grant.* It is not indispensable, in order to lay a proper foundation for the legal presumption of a grant, to establish the probability of the fact, that, in reality, a grant ever issued. It will afford a sufficient ground for the presumption to show, that, by legal possibility, a grant might have issued. And this appearing, it may be assumed—in the absence of circumstances repelling such a conclusion—that all that might lawfully have been done to perfect the legal title, was in fact done, and in the form prescribed by law. *Ibid.*

28. *Same. Same. Presumption rebutted. Act of* 1819, *ch.* 1. Ever since the passage of the act of 1819, and prior to the act of Congress of 1841, the lands south and west of the Congressional Reservation Line might have been appropriated, and grants obtained therefor, by virtue of North Carolina *land warrants*. And the fact that an entry and possession under it, are prior to the act of 1841, does not repel the presumption of a grant. To destroy the foundation of the presumption, it should appear that the issuance of a grant, in the given case, was a legal impossibility. *Ibid.*

See STATUTE OF LIMITATIONS.

LAPSE OF TIME.

See EVIDENCE.

LAWS IN FORCE.

What portions of the law of North Carolina in force. Cession act. Constitution of 1796 *and* 1834. By the Cession act, the laws in force and use in the State of North Carolina at the time of its passage, were to be and continue in force within the ceded territory until repealed or altered by the Legislature thereof. And by the Constitution of 1796, it was declared that all the laws then in force and use in said territory, not inconsistent with it, should continue to be in force and use in this State until they should expire, be altered, or repealed by the Legislature. The Constitution of 1884 has a clause to the same effect. *Egnew* v. *Cochrane*, 820.

LEVY.

See EXECUTION. ATTACHMENT.

LICENSE.

See CRIMINAL LAW.

LIEN.

1. *Equality among partners.* Partners in lands have an equity against each other, for the purpose of producing equality among themselves; and this equity fastens itself, and is a lien, upon their respective interests in the partnership lands, of which neither can be deprived by the other, or a creditor of his, or purchaser from him with notice. *Williams* v. *Love*, 80.

2. *Same. Death of the partner having the lien.* It is immaterial whether the amount of the inequality is ascertained at the death of the partner in whose favor this inequality exists. If the indebtedness arise from transactions occurring in the lifetime of such partner, the lien may be enforced by his personal representative. *Ibid.*

3. *For indebtedness to person holding the legal title to land.* If two persons are the joint owners of lands, but the legal title is in one of them, and the other, who has a mere equity in the land, is indebted to the one who has the legal title, the latter cannot be forced to part with the legal title, until the discharge of his indebtedness to him, and until he is freed from liability for him. *Ibid.*

4. *Same. Rights of purchasers and creditors.* A purchaser of an equitable title must always abide by the case of the person from whom he buys. And if the person thus having an equitable interest in land, sell or mortgage the same, or his interest is attached by a creditor, the purchaser, mortgagee, or creditor, takes it incumbered with the equity existing against him. *Ibid.*

5. *Same. Rights of the personal representative.* If the party thus holding the legal title, and an equitable lien on the land for satisfaction of indebtedness to him, dies before the enforcement of such equitable lien, the same right exists in favor of his personal representative, heirs and devisees. *Ibid.*

6. *Same. When mortgagee becomes indebted to the person holding the legal title.* If a person who has an equity in land, mortgages the

same to a third person, and the mortgagee becomes indebted to the person holding the legal title to the land, and then assigns his claim upon the mortgagor, together with his lien. the land, by reason of the indebtedness of the mortgagee, becomes subjected to an additional equity against him, and his assignee occupies no higher ground, and must yield to the superior equity of the person holding the legal title. *Ibid.*

7. *General and special.* Liens are of two kinds, general and particular, or special. A particular lien is the right to retain a thing for some charge or claim growing out of or connected with that identical thing. A general lien is the right to retain a thing not only for charges and claims specifically arising out of or connected with the identical thing, but also for a general balance of accounts between the parties in respect to other dealings of a like nature. *Woodruff v. The Nashville and Chattanooga R. R. Co.*, 87.

8. *By contract, not in the nature of a mortgage or vendor's lien.* An express lien, created by contract and reserved on the face of the conveyance, is not, in all respects, equivalent to a mortgage, because the legal estate passes by the conveyance, and vests in the purchaser. Neither is it, in all respects, in the nature of the vendor's lien. The latter, when the legal estate has been conveyed, exists only by implication of law, and is the mere creature of a Court of Equity. A lien created by contract, and reserved on the face of the conveyance, is regarded as a *specific lien*, forming an original substantive charge upon the estate thus conveyed, and as affecting all persons who may, subsequently, come into possession of the estate with notice, either actual or constructive, of its existence. *Lincoln v. Purcell*, 143.

9. *Same. Statute of limitations.* This being the nature and effect of the lien, the presumption of law is that the purchaser of the land upon which the lien is reserved, holds under and consistent with the lien until the contrary is shown by him. And the statute of limitations will not run until he disclaims the lien, and assumes to hold adversely to it, with the knowledge of the party having said lien. *Ibid.*

10. *Same. Same. Adverse possession.* Act of 1819, ch. 28, § 2. The debt of a mortgagee, or lien of a vendor, or other lien for the payment of money, is not barred, under the act of 1819. ch. 28 § 2, by the mere lapse of seven years before filing a bill to enforce them. To create the bar, under that section, the possession must be, in legal contemplation, adverse. *Ibid.*

11. *Same. Same. Does not run until the money is due.* A cause of action must exist for the full period of seven years before suit brought in order to create the bar, and a note payable in stonework to be done at any time called for, cannot be sued on without a previous request to do the work, and the statute of limitations will not begin to run until such request is made. *Ibid.*

12. *Release by trustee.* If a party hold as a naked trustee, a lien, for another, a release by him, of such lien to a person having a knowledge of the character of his claim, is a nullity. *Ibid.*

13. *Same. Liability of the trustee. Estoppel.* If a naked trustee execute a release, under seal, of a lien for the payment of money, in which he acknowledges the reception of the money, he will be treated as holding the money in trust, and rendered liable for the same. And his acknowledgment would be an estoppel upon him, both at law and in equity, to deny the fact of having received the money. *Ibid.*

14. *On slaves. Reserved by parol contract.* As respects personal property, no lien exists by implication of law, and in no other mode can a valid lien be created in favor of the seller of a personal chattel, when the legal title and possession have been parted with, than by express contract, which, at least, as against creditors and subsequent purchasers without notice, must be in writing, and duly proved and registered. *Woods* v. *Burrough,* 202.

15. *Judgment. Priority of, when several have been rendered.* If several judgments are rendered against a party at different terms of the Court, and he, thereafter, acquires the legal title to real estate, the *liens* of the several judgments attach, together, upon the property, at the same instant; and all stand upon the same footing, as respects the proceeds of the sale of the same. *Relfe & Co.* v. *McComb,* 558.

See ATTACHMENT. CHANCERY. CHANCERY PLEADING. SALE OF REAL ESTATE. SPECIFIC PERFORMANCE. FACTOR.

LIFE ESTATE.

See STATUTE OF LIMITATIONS. WILLS.

LIMITATIONS.

See STATUTE OF LIMITATIONS.

LIMITATION OVER.

See WILLS.

MANDAMUS.

1. *When the proper remedy.* In general, where a man is refused to be admitted, or wrongfully turned out of any office, or franchise that concerns the public, or the administration of justice, he may be admitted or restored by a writ of *mandamus. Felts* v. *The Mayor and Aldermen of Memphis,* 650.

2. *When prosecuted by a public officer the suit enures to the benefit of each successor. Sheriff. Abatement.* When a suit for a writ of *mandamus* is prosecuted by a sheriff, or other public officer, in his official capacity, for the public benefit, the law regards the name of the office, and not the adjunct name of the individual, and in it are implied all the successors that shall ever be to it—each successor, for the time of his term, being the real plaintiff to support the action, whether described by name or not. And, if one dies, or his term of office expires before the determination of the suit, it will not abate, but shall be continued by his successor. *Ibid.*

See JAILS.

MENACES.

See CRIMINAL LAW.

MERCHANTS.

See CONSTITUTIONAL LAW.

MISTAKE.

See CHANCERY JURISDICTION. RAILROAD COMPANY. WILLS.

MORTGAGE.

When foreclosed by an acceptor. The acceptor of a bill not being able to maintain an action, directly, against the drawer, without payment, he cannot do so, indirectly, by a bill in Chancery to foreclose a mortgage executed by the drawer to secure the acceptor. He has no right to a foreclosure of the mortgage until he has paid the bill. *Planters' Bank* v. *Douglass*, 699.

See BILLS AND NOTES. LIEN.

MOTION.

See SUMMARY PROCEEDINGS. WRIT OF ERROR.

NECESSARIES.

See GUARDIAN AND WARD.

NEGOTIABLE PAPERS.

See BILLS AND NOTES. PARTNERSHIP.

NEGRO TRADERS.

See CONSTITUTIONAL LAW.

NON-SUIT.

Costs. Taxation of. Act of 1794, ch. 1, § 74. Code, §§ 3197 and 3201. The plaintiff took a non-suit, which was set aside and he taxed with the costs of the Term. No exception was taken to the action of the Court. After verdict for the plaintiff, the defendant moved the Court to tax the plaintiff with all costs that accrued before the non-suit, which the Court refused. The Circuit Court did not err. The case is not embraced by the act of 1794, ch. 1, § 74, nor by §§ 3197 and 3201 of the Code. *Mt. Olivet Cemetery v. Shubert*, 116.

NOTARY PUBLIC.

See BILLS AND NOTES.

NOTES.

See BILLS AND NOTES. CHANCERY PRACTICE. CONTRACT.

NOTICE.

See DEMAND AND NOTICE. BILLS AND NOTES. CHANCERY JURISDICTION. CARRIERS. LAND LAW. RAILROAD COMPANY. FRAUDULENT SALES. INNOCENT PURCHASER. STATUTE OF LIMITATIONS. SUMMARY PROCEEDINGS.

OCCUPANCY.

See LAND LAW.

OFFICERS DE FACTO.

1. *Acts of, when binding.* The acts of officers *de facto* are valid when they concern the public, or the rights of third persons who have an interest in the act done. But a different rule prevails where the act is for the benefit of the officer, because he is not permitted to take advantage of his own wrong. *Venable & Co. v. Curd & White*, 582.

2. *Same. Circuit Court. Judgment. Times of holding the Court. Illustration of the rule.* By an act of the Legislature the times of the sitting of the Circuit Court for Henry county were changed. This change was not known to the officers of the Court, the act having been passed but a short time before a term of said Court was to be held. The Court was held by the presiding Judge at the time before fixed by law, but at a different time from that required by the law *then* in force. A judgment was rendered by the Court thus sitting, the justice of which was not controverted. Held, that the judgment is valid; that the judgments and decrees of a judge regularly in office are valid, if he hold his Court under color of law, although the law may be repealed, or invalid. *Ibid.*

See PATROLS.

ONUS PROBANDI.

See EVIDENCE.

OYER.

See PRACTICE AND PLEADING.

PARTIES.

See ATTACHMENT. CHANCERY PRACTICE. SALE OF REAL ESTATE.

PARTITION.

See CHANCERY JURISDICTION.

PARTNERS.

See EVIDENCE. PARTNERSHIP. LIEN.

PARTNERSHIP.

1. *Power of partners to bind the firm.* Each partner is the authorized agent of the firm, and may bind it in all matters within the scope of the partnership business, but not beyond this, except by authority, express or implied, from the other members of the firm. *Scott, Baker & Co.* v. *Bandy,* 197.

2. *Same. Acceptance for accommodation.* It is not within the scope of the business of a mercantile firm to draw, accept or endorse the paper of neighbors for accommodation. Hence, one partner cannot bind the other members of the firm, by note, endorsement, or acceptance, in any transaction unconnected with the partnership business, and known to be so by the party taking it; nor for the party's own debt. *Ibid.*

3. *Same. Same. Evidence. Subsequent ratification.* An act of one partner, beyond the scope of his authority, may be rendered obligatory on the firm by antecedent or subsequent sanction by the other members of the firm. Proof of such sanction may be presumptive. That one member was in the habit of extending accommodations to others, in the name of the firm, with approbation, or without dissent, would be sufficient evidence of authority, and the firm would be bound. *Ibid.*

4. *Evidence. Competency of a partner as a witness.* A partner is not a competent witness to prove the existence of the partnership; but when proven, he is competent to prove the justice of the demand against the firm. This principle does not render a partner competent to prove that an obligation created by him in the name of the firm, and not within the scope of the partnership business, was authorized, or adopted, by the other members, so as to render the firm liable. *Ibid.*

5. *Sale, by one partner, of his interest in the firm. Lien.* Where a partner sells his interest in the partnership concern, either to his co-partners or strangers, he has no lien on the partnership property for the payment of partnership debts for which he is liable. He cannot pursue specifically, or have an account of the effects of the late firm of which he was a partner, to the end that they may be subject to the satisfaction of claims existing against the firm. *Croone v. Bivens*, 889.

6. *Same. Same. Contracts to pay the debts of the firm.* The fact that when such partner retired, his co-partners stipulated to pay the debts of the concern, and indemnify him, can make no difference, he having trusted to the personal covenants of his assignees; unless he retains an interest in, or lien upon the effects transferred, or stipulates that they shall be applied in payment of the partnership debts. *Ibid.*

7. *Agency of each partner.* Each partner is the agent of the partnership, and, therefore, the act of each in transactions properly relating to the partnership business, is regarded as the act of all, and binds all. But it is only in the capacity of an authorized agent of his co-partners that he has power to bind them. Hence, in order to bind the firm, the act must, ordinarily, be done in the name of the firm, otherwise, it will only bind the individual partner as his own private act. *Venable & Co. v. Levick, Brother & Co.*, 861.

8. *Same. Sale of goods to one partner presumed to be for the firm.* A sale of goods to one partner within the scope and course of the partnership business, is in judgment of law, a sale to the partnership, and the seller of the goods will not be affected by any fraudulent intention of the purchasing partner in buying them, or by his subsequent misapplication of them, if the seller be clear of the imputation of collusion. *Ibid.*

9. *Same. Same. Negotiable securities.* The same principle applies to negotiable securities drawn, indorsed, accepted, or negotiated by one partner within the scope and course of dealing of the partnership in the absence of fraud on the part of the person receiving such securities. *Ibid.*

10. *Same. Same. Same. When the firm not bound. Fraud. Constructive knowledge.* But if goods be sold to one partner on his private account, and for his individual benefit, or, if partnership security be taken from him for a debt which the creditor knew at the time was the private or individual debt of the particular partner, without the previous knowledge or consent of the other partners, it would be a fraudulent transaction as to them, and clearly void. So, if from the subject matter of the contract, or the course of dealing, or the circumstances of the transaction, the creditor was chargeable with constructive knowledge of the fraudulent purpose, or intended misapplication on the part of the particular partner, the partnership cannot be made liable. *Ibid.*

11. *When a fraud for a person to take a partnership engagement without the authority of the firm.* If the public have the usual means of knowledge given them in regard to the existence and business of a partnership, and no acts have been done or suffered by the partners to mislead or deceive, every one is presumed to know the nature and extent of the partnership with whose members he deals; and where a person takes a partnership engagement without the knowledge or authority of the firm, for a matter that has no reference to the business of the firm, and is not within the scope of its authority, or its regular course of dealing, he is, in judgment of law, guilty of a fraud, and cannot enforce such engagement. *Ibid.*

12. *Contract with one partner. When illegal. Usury.* If one partner borrows money for the benefit of the firm, and executes the firm note for the amount borrowed, but at the same time enters into a *verbal contract* with the lender to pay usurious interest for the use of the money, such independent parol agreement will not bar the right of recovery on said note. This contract, though illegal and void, is, in legal contemplation, separate and distinct from the contract evidenced by the note, and does not fall within the principle in the case of *Hutchins* v. *Turner.* *Bowers* v. *Douglass,* 876.

13. *Death of a partner. Remedy of creditors. Act of* 1789, *ch.* 57, § 5. By the act of 1789, ch. 57, § 5, modifying the common law doctrine, all "obligations or assumptions of co-partners" are declared to be joint and several, and to survive against the personal representative of a deceased partner, as well as against the surviving partner. The effect of which is to give the joint creditors the same remedies *at law* against the estate of the deceased partner which they were entitled to in equity. *Saunders* v. *Wilder,* 577.

14. *Same. Same. Judgment.* Creditors may, therefore, obtain judgment against the survivor and the representative of the deceased partner, jointly; or, at their election, against either, separately; and proceed to enforce satisfaction against either. Of this, neither the representative of the deceased partner, nor the survivor can complain, but they have their remedy over against each other. *Ibid.*

See CHANCERY JURISDICTION.

PATROLS.

1. *Pleading. What a general replication to a plea justifying an act upon the ground of being a patrol puts in issue.* All matters which confess and avoid, whether alleged by the plaintiff or defendant, must be specially pleaded. Therefore, if a person justify a battery upon a slave upon the ground that he was a patrol, and acting in discharge of his duty, the plaintiff must, if he wishes to rely upon excessive punishment, plead it specially: it is not admissible under a general replication to the plea of the defendant. *Tomlinson* v. *Darnall,* 588.

2. *Public officers. What prima facie evidence of appointment.* Proof that a person has notoriously acted as a public officer, is *prima facie* evidence of his official character, without producing his commission or appointment *Ibid.*

3. *Same. Pleading. Slave. What replication of excess admits.* If a party justify a trespass upon a slave upon the ground that he was a patrol, and the plaintiff replies that the punishment was excessive, the replication admits the justification as alleged, and precludes the plaintiff from offering any evidence to disprove it. *Ibid.*

PAYMENT.

1. *Presumption of, after the lapse of sixteen years.* If a bond or note under seal, be suffered to lie dormant for the space of sixteen years, without demand being made, or payment of interest, or other explanatory circumstances to show that it is still in force, payment will be presumed upon the mere fact of lapse of time. *Thompson v. Thompson,* 405.

2. *Same. Effect of.* This presumption of payment, like other legal or artificial presumptions, derives from the law a certain technical force and effect, which courts and juries cannot disregard. Until rebutted, or displaced by evidence, it has all the force and effect of plenary proof of the fact of payment, and the jury are bound so to regard it. *Ibid.*

3. *Less than sixteen years.* The fact of payment may be inferred by the jury from the circumstances of the particular case, in a shorter period than sixteen years, but the presumption of law does not attach until the full expiration of that time. *Ibid.*

4. *In bank notes. Effect, if genuine, though worthless.* A payment of indebtedness in *genuine* bank notes, supposed by both parties to be good, though in fact worthless, is binding, and the loss must, in the absence of fraud, fall upon the party receiving them. It is otherwise if the bank notes are not genuine—not what they purport to be. *Ware v. Street & Co.,* 609.

5. *Same. Demand and notice, and tender of worthless bank notes.* A payment in bank notes is not upon the same footing as a payment in promissory notes, or bills, so as to avoid the payment by presentation and refusal to pay. If a payment is made in *genuine* bank notes, circulating and received as money, such payment cannot, in the absence of fraud, be avoided by demand, refusal, and notice or tender to the payor. *Ibid.*

See EVIDENCE.

PERSONALTY.

See SALE OF PERSONALTY.

PETITION.

See CERTIORARI AND SUPERSEDEAS. SALE OF REAL ESTATE.

PLEA.

See ABATEMENT. ADMINISTRATORS AND EXECUTORS. CONTRACT. CRIMINAL LAW. PRACTICE AND PLEADING.

PLEADING.

See PATROLS. PRACTICE AND PLEADING.

POSSESSION.

See LIEN. FORCIBLE ENTRY AND DETAINER. SLAVES. STATUTE OF LIMITATIONS. TRESPASS. FACTOR.

POWER.

1. *Fraud in its exercise. Question reserved.* If fraud intervenes in the exercise of a power of appointment, does it vitiate the entire acts of the trustee, or only such appointments as are fraudulent? *Cruse v. McKee*, 1.

2. *Referred to in the instrument executing it. Question reserved.* The rule, according to the weight of authority, seems to be, that although it is not necessary to the due execution of a power, that it should be recited or expressly referred to, yet, there must be something to show that the party intended to execute it. But since the act of 1827, an executor has no power to sell slaves under the will, unless the power is conferred therein; and it is difficult to see, if this power is conferred, why an absolute bill of sale, without reference to the power, is not a good execution of it. But the question is reserved. *Gee v. Graves and wife*, 239.

See WILLS

PRACTICE AND PLEADING.

1. *Suit prematurely instituted. Abatement. Demurrer.* The fact that a suit has been prematurely brought is, properly, matter for what is termed a plea in abatement to the action of the writ, unless the objection is apparent upon the face of the record; and then it is ground of demurrer, or may be taken advantage of on the trial. But, if not so apparent, it must be pleaded in abatement. And if this be not done, the defendant loses the benefit of the defence. *Carter & Pulliam v. Turner* 52.

2. *Writ of error. Plea not filed. Act of 1852, ch. 152, §§ 4, 5. Code, §§ 2865, 2866, 2872, 2878.* Since the passage of the act of 1852, ch. 152, §§ 4 and 5, the provisions of which are incorporated into the Code, sections 2865, 2866, 2872 and 2878, the want of a plea in a record brought up by writ of error, is regarded as a matter of form for which the judgment of the Court below will not be reversed. *Cornelius & Davis v. Merritt*, 97.

INDEX. 779

3. *Account. Record. Bill of exceptions.* An account, unless made so by a bill of exceptions, is no part of the record in a cause, and cannot be noticed upon a writ of error, so as to raise the question whether there is a variance between the parties to the suit, and the account sued on. *Ibid.*

4. *Authority of general agent. Principal bound by contracts of agent.* If a general agent make a contract within the scope of his agency, the principal is bound by such contract, though in violation of instructions, unless the party with whom the contract is made knew that the agent was violating his instructions. *Mt. Olivet Cemetery v. Shubert,* 116.

5. *Profert. Demurrer. Oyer.* The plaintiff is bound to make profert of, and to produce in Court, the notes declared on, having them in possession. But the omission to file them with the declaration, is not a matter that can be reached by demurrer, profert being made in proper form. If the plaintiff fails to file the notes, the defendant may ask to have his demand of oyer entered, and have the judgment of the Court whether he is bound to answer until the notes are filed. *Anderson v. Allison, Anderson & Co.,* 122.

6. *Same. Same. Motion to take the demurrer from the file.* If the defendant demurs because the notes are not filed, it being an improper defence, the plaintiff may move the Court to order the demurrer to be taken off the file, and to enter up judgment by default, for want of a defence to the action. *Ibid.*

7. *Pleas sworn to. Code, §§ 2886, 2887.* By the provisions of the Code, the plaintiff, in his pleading, may require the answer of the defendant to be given under oath, and the answer of the defendant thus put in, has the same force as an answer in Chancery requiring two witnesses, or one with corroborating circumstances, to overturn it. And this applies to every description of plea, or defence, to any civil action at law. *Baker v. Ammon,* 898.

See PATROLS. RAILROAD COMPANY. ROADS. WRIT OF ERROR. ACCOUNT.

PRESENTMENT.

See CRIMINAL LAW.

PRESUMPTION.

See CHANCERY PLEADING. EVIDENCE. LAND LAW. PAYMENT. TRUST AND TRUSTEE.

PRINCIPAL AND SURETY.

1. *Agreement to become principal. Consideration.* If an obligation is incurred by two, to raise money to discharge the debt of one, the

other, who is in no way bound for the original debt, cannot, by agreement, become the principal, and the one whose debt is paid become the surety, so as to make him first liable on the obligation thus assumed, unless there is a legal consideration to sustain the promise made to become the principal. *Bates* v. *Whitson*, 155.

2. *Same. Same. Case in judgment.* A bill of exchange was drawn by two partners. Money was retained by one partner to discharge the bill of exchange, but he appropriated $700 of the fund to his individual debts, and the bill, to that extent, remained unpaid. After the death of this partner, one of his administrators, together with the other partner, executed a note in bank, in payment of the $700. This note was indorsed by the indorsers on the bill of exchange. The partner who was joint maker of the note paid it after judgment, at the request of the administrator, who promised to refund the amount paid. The estate of the deceased partner proved to be insolvent, and his administrator, who had jointly executed the note, refused to refund the money out of his individual means. The partner who paid the debt moved for judgment, as surety, against him. *Held,* that it does not appear that it was understood by the parties that the administrator was to be individually liable for the debt, and become the principal in the note; and, if it did so appear, there is no consideration to support the promise, and it cannot be enforced. *Ibid.*

See SURETIES.

PRIVILEGED COMMUNICATIONS.

See EVIDENCE.

PROBATE.

See DEED OF TRUST.

PROCEDENDO.

See CERTIORARI.

PROCESS.

See SUMMARY PROCEEDINGS.

PROFERT.

See PRACTICE AND PLEADING.

PROMISE.

See ACCOUNT.

PROSECUTOR.

See CRIMINAL LAW.

INDEX. 781

PROTEST.

See BILLS AND NOTES.

PURCHASER.

See LIEN.

QUESTION RESERVED.

See BILLS AND NOTES. CHANCERY. CHANCERY JURISDICTION. CRIMINAL LAW. LAND LAW. POWER. RECOGNIZANCE. SALE OF REAL ESTATE. FACTOR.

RAILROAD COMPANY.

1. *Conditional subscription of stock. Notice.* If a party, who has subscribed stock to a railroad company, can renounce and abandon his subscription, it can be done, only, by notice to the agent, or to the company, in proper time. *Cunningham v. Edgefield and Kentucky Railroad Company*, 23.

2. *Same. Fraud vitiates subscription, if notice is given in a reasonable time.* If a subscription is fraudulently obtained from a person, and he is injured thereby, the contract of subscription would be void, although the name of the subscriber was accepted and entered upon the stock-book of the company, unless, by his failure to notify them in a reasonable time after the fraud was discovered, the company would be injured by its release. *Ibid.*

3. *Same. Effect of parol condition.* A parol condition to the subscription of stock to a railroad company will not, if violated, invalidate the subscription, because it forms no part of the written contract of the parties. *Ibid.*

4. *Same. Effect of an innocent mistake. Contract.* If a party is induced to take stock in a railroad company by false representations which are not fraudulent, and which form no part of the contract of subscription, he is not entitled to be relieved from the payment of the amount of his subscription. But if he acts upon such representations to his injury, he is entitled to relief, although they may have been innocently made. *Ibid.*

5. *Liability to tenant for trespass.* If a railroad company, in violation of a contract with the landlord, enter upon land held by a tenant, and commit a trespass upon the tenant's possession, by destroying his vegetables &c., said company is liable, in an action on the case, to the tenant for the damages sustained by him. Otherwise, if there is no contract with the company, by which the tenant is protected in his possession of the premises. *Louisville and Nashville Railroad Company v. Faulkner*, 65.

6. *Statutory remedy exclusive.* The statutory remedy given to land proprietors, for land taken for the construction of railways, is, in general, exclusive of all other remedies, and not merely cumulative. *Colcough* v. *The N. & N. W. R. R. Co.,* 171.

7. *Same. Damages.* The remedy prescribed in the charter of the Northwestern Railroad Company, embraces not only just compensation for the land taken, but likewise all such incidental loss, or damage, as must necessarily or reasonably result from the appropriation of the land and construction of the road in the manner authorized by the charter. *Ibid.*

8. *Same. Same. Confined to the land taken.* This statutory remedy is confined to the land taken, and the damages incident thereto. It does not extend to, and embrace damage or injuries to adjoining land, not authorized by the charter to be taken; nor to damages resulting from carelessness, negligence, or wilful trespasses in the execution of the work. *Ibid.*

9. *Same. Remedy not limited to the owner of the fee.* This statutory remedy is not limited to the owner of the fee. A life interest, or a term of years may be carved out of the fee; and in such case the tenant for life, or lessee, as well as the remainderman, or lessor, is within the spirit and meaning of the charter, and they are entitled to recover compensation for the damage or injury by them respectively sustained. *Ibid.*

10. *Practice. Proceeding may be joint or several.* The persons vested with the several interests which constitute the entire estate, may join in a proceeding under the statute to obtain compensation; or, as they have several interests, may proceed separately. In either mode of proceeding, the compensation for the entire damage must be apportioned according to the injury to their respective interests. *Ibid.*

11. *Construction of charter. Lands taken. Act of 1858.* The eighth section of the charter of the Mississippi Central and Tennessee Railroad Company, which does not materially differ from most of the other railroad charters, provides that where the company and owner of the soil required for the road fail to agree upon the terms of purchase and sale, the Court shall appoint commissioners to value the land taken, &c. It is not necessary, under this charter, that the parties should make an effort to agree, and fail, before the Court has jurisdiction to appoint commissioners to assess the value of the land. *Bigelow* v. *The Mississippi Central and Tennessee Railroad Co.,* 624.

See CONTRACT. DAMAGES.

RATIFICATION.

See PARTNERSHIP.

RECEIPT.

See EVIDENCE.

RESCISSION OF CONTRACT.

See SLAVES. SPECIFIC PERFORMANCE.

RECORD.

See PRACTICE AND PLEADING.

REGISTER.

See REGISTRATION.

REGISTRATION.

1. *Law of the owners domicil prevails, in alienation of personal property.* The transfer of personal property is controlled by the laws of the owner's domicil, or the place of transfer, no matter where the property may be situated; but in ascertaining and giving preferences and priorities, the government where the property is situated will not extend this comity so far as to prejudice its own citizens, but will protect their interest. *Allen v. Bain,* 100.

2. *Assignments. Pennsylvania. Registry act of.* By the law of Pennsylvania, "all assignments, so as aforesaid to be made and executed, which shall not be recorded in the office for recording deeds in the county in which such assignor resides, within thirty days after the execution thereof shall be considered null and void, as against any of the creditors of the assignor." *Ibid.*

3. *Same. Same. What it embraces. Different in Tennessee.* This act is held to embrace assignments of legacies in payment of debts due from the assignor. But by the construction given to the registry acts of Tennessee, they do not embrace legacies. *Ibid.*

4. *Same. Attachment. Priority. Case in judgment.* B., to whom a legacy was coming in Tennessee, transferred it in Pennsylvania the place of his domicil, in payment of a debt. The assignment was not registered in Pennsylvania, but was registered in Tennessee. A., a creditor of B., attached said legacy for the satisfaction of his debt. The attachment was levied after the registration of the assignment in Tennessee. Held, that the assignment not having been registered in Pennsylvania, it is void against the creditors of B., and the attaching creditor. A., has priority of satisfaction. *Ibid.*

5. *Vacancy in the office of register. Deputy register. Act of* 1851-2. By the act of 1851-2, each county register is authorized to appoint one deputy; and all deeds previously registered by *deputies* are declared to be valid. The act also provides that when the register shall die, the deputy may continue to act until the appointment of a suc-

cessor; and all instruments registered by a deputy during a vacancy in the office, by death, are declared as effectual as if made by the principal register. Although a vacancy occasioned by the *removal* of the register is not embraced by the words of the act, it is within the spirit of the law, and conveyances registered by a deputy during such a vacancy are as effectual as if the vacancy had been occasioned by death. *Maley* v. *Tipton*, 408.

6. *Same. Register de facto.* The acts of an officer *de facto* are valid as respects third persons who have an interest in them, and as concerns the public, in order to prevent a failure of justice. Hence, if the office of register becomes vacant by the removal of the incumbent, and his deputy continues to act, the acts of such deputy, being an officer *de facto*, are valid and effectual without the aid of any statutory enactment. *Ibid*

See CHANCERY. DEED OF TRUST. INNOCENT PURCHASER.

REHEARING.

See CHANCERY PRACTICE.

RELEASE.

See DEPOSITIONS. LIEN. SURETIES.

RECOGNIZANCE.

Lien of. When taken by a magistrate. Question reserved. A recognizance entered into in a Court of Record, forms a direct and specific lien upon all the lands owned by the party at the time of its acknowledgment, or afterwards acquired by him. And from the force and effect of a magistrate's recognizance, upon its being returned into a Court of Record, the legal consequence, as respects the lien, must necessarily be the same; but whether the lien in the latter case shall be held to attach only upon the return of the recognizance into Court, is reserved. *Pugh* v. *The State*, 227.

See BAIL. SURETIES.

RECOUPMENT.

See CONTRACT.

REMAINDER AND REVERSION.

See WILLS.

INDEX.

RENTS.

See SALE OF REAL ESTATE.

REPLEVIN.

See SALE OF PERSONALTY

REPLICATION.

See PATROLS. PRACTICE AND PLEADING.

RETURN.

See SUMMARY PROCEEDINGS.

REVIVOR.

See SUMMARY PROCEEDINGS.

REVOCATION.

See WILLS.

ROADS.

1. *Practice. Contest to be decided by the Court, and not submitted to a jury.* In contests about roads, the jurisdiction, in the first instance, is given, exclusively, to the County Court; and, upon appeal to the Circuit Court, to the Judge. It is the duty of the Circuit Judge to hear and determine the controversy, and not shift the labor and responsibility from himself to a jury. *McWhirter v. Cockrell,* 9.

2. *When to be established. Rights of the community and of individuals.* Whenever the necessity for a road is imperative, it is the duty of the Court to establish it, although injurious to individuals, upon making compensation for the injury, as provided by law. This is to be done with as little injury to private property as practicable, and only when the advantage to the public is sufficiently great to outweigh the private injury. The Court should look, carefully, to the interest of all citizens, and never exercise the right of eminent domain, unless it is clearly and imperatively demanded for the public good. *Ibid.*

SALE OF PERSONALTY.

1. *Judgment. Execution. Trover. Replevin. Evidence.* A purchaser of personal property at a sheriff's, or constable's sale, cannot maintain an action of *trover* or *replevin* against a party who subsequently causes the same property to be sold by virtue of a judgment and exe-

cution in his favor, without producing in evidence the judgment, as well as the execution under which his purchase was made. *Sandeford v. Hess,* 680.

2. *When made after the teste of an execution issued from the Circuit Court.* The owner of personal property cannot sell and make a good title to the same after the teste of an execution issued from the Circuit Court. *Ibid.*

3. *Private sale of property after levy of an execution. Question reserved.* Can an officer sell property levied on, at private sale, with the consent of the debtor, especially after he has taken a delivery bond, and before the restoration of the property to him? *Ibid.*

4. *Same. Same.* If property is levied on by an officer, and is sold at private sale by him and the debtor, (the debtor conveying the title,) is it to be regarded, in a contest with a third person as to the validity of the title, as a sale made by the officer? *Ibid.*

See PARTNERSHIP. FRAUDULENT SALES.

SALE OF REAL ESTATE.

1. *Vendor and vendee. When vendee bound to accept title.* In the absence of fraud, the purchaser of real estate is bound to accept a title which is perfect at the time it is to be made, although it may have been defective at the time of the sale. *Gss v. Singleton* 67.

2. *Same. Same.* The purchaser of real estate is compelled to accept the title if it has become "*indefeasible*" by operation of the first section of the act of 1819. *Ibid.*

3. *Jurisdiction. Covenant of warranty. Fraud.* If there be no fraud in the sale of real estate, the purchaser, on failure of title, must rely, alone, on his covenants of warranty. And if there be no covenants of warranty, he has no remedy, either in law or equity, for his money. *Stipe v. Stipe,* 169.

4. *Same. Eviction. Breach of warranty.* The purchaser of real estate has no remedy on his covenants of warranty, either in a Court of Law or Equity, until there is a breach of the warranty; and there is no breach until eviction. But if there be a breach of the covenant, the remedy at law is plain and adequate, and a Court of Equity has no jurisdiction. *Ibid.*

5. *Eviction. Question reserved.* Is the payment of a judgment which is an incumbrance upon the land, by a purchaser with covenants of warranty, an eviction *pro tanto? Ibid.*

6. *Rent. When it passes by the sale.* The sale of land passes the right to the rents that subsequently become due as incident to the reversion,

but not the rents then in arrear. Rent is not due, where the contract for renting is by the year, until the end of the year, and the rent is not in *arrear* until due. Rent, therefore, not due at the time of the sale, passes with the reversion, unless there is a stipulation to the contrary, in the contract. *Gibbs* v. *Ross*, 437.

7. *Frauds, statute of. By whom agreement to be signed.* To make a contract for the sale of real estate valid, it must be in writing and signed by all the owners, by themselves, or by some person lawfully authorized to sign their names. *Frazer* v. *Ford*, 464.

8. *Same. Same. Must be binding upon all.* The language in the statute of frauds, "the party to be charged therewith," means the persons who sell the land. The filing of a bill by all the owners, in the absence of a memorandum or writing as required, with an express ratification of the contract and a tender of title, will not remedy the defect and compel the purchaser to take the land. To make the contract obligatory it must be mutual. *Ibid.*

9. *Guardian. Parties. Form of the petition.* In a proceeding for a sale of the real estate of minors, it is immaterial whether the petition is filed in the name of the guardian, for the minors, naming them, or in the names of the minors, by their guardian. If all the other steps taken are regular, the fact that the petition is filed in the name of the guardian, for his wards, will not vitiate the sale. *Elrod* v. *Lancaster*, 571.

10. *Same. When guardian may purchase.* In sales of the real estate of infants, made by a Court of competent jurisdiction, the guardian of the infants may purchase, if he act fairly, with the utmost good faith, and the transaction is free from any imputation of design on his part to gain a benefit to himself, to the prejudice of the interests of his wards. Yet his conduct will be watched with jealousy. *Ibid.*

11. *Fraud. Infancy. Improvements. Rents.* A lot was purchased in the city of Memphis with a fund raised by contribution. The title was made, by direction of the contributors, to A, an infant of tender years. The creditors of A's father obtained judgments against him—levied upon said lot, and had it sold under a writ of *venditioni exponas;* and H, one of the creditors, purchased the same. The sheriff executed a deed to H. H sold and conveyed the lot, and there were several intermediate conveyances, before the defendant, Greenlaw, acquired the title. Subsequent to the sale, and purchase of H, a bill was filed in the Chancery Court against A, the minor, and others, to set aside the deed made to her, upon the ground that the father had paid the purchase money, and the conveyance was executed to the infant daughter to protect the lot from his creditors. This suit was conducted, collusively, by the complainant and *next friend* of the infant, and a decree was pronounced divesting her of her title. *Held,* that said sale, by virtue of the *venditioni exponas*, and the proceedings in

the Chancery Court—together with the conveyances made by H and those claiming under him—were void; and A is entitled to the lot, with the accruing rents—she accounting for such improvements as may have enhanced the value of the property. *Gaugh & Wife* v. *Henderson*, 628.

12. *Venditioni exponas. When lost.* A sale of land under an order of condemnation and a writ of *venditioni exponas*, is not void if the writ cannot be found, provided it appears by the testimony of the clerk, the memorandum on his execution docket, and the recitals in the sheriff's deed, that the writ did issue and the sale was made by virtue of the same. *Ibid.*

13. *Fraudulent conveyances. Question reserved.* If land is purchased and paid for by a father, but the deed made to his infant daughter, (the legal title never having vested in him,) for the purpose of protecting the property from the creditors of the father, can said land be seized and sold by execution at law at the instance of the creditors; or, must it be done by a decree of a Court of Equity? *Ibid.*

14. *Voluntary conveyance. Advancement. Question reserved.* If a father, not being indebted at the time, purchase a tract of land and have the title made to an infant daughter, it being done *bona fide*, will it not be regarded as an advancement, or a voluntary settlement upon the child; and can subsequent creditors of the father impeach the conveyance merely upon the ground that it is voluntary? *Ibid.*

15. *Lien. Assignment.* If the vendor of real estate retain the legal title as security for the purchase money, it has the effect of a mortgage for that purpose, and the assignment of the note given for the purchase money carries with it the benefit of the security. *Cleveland* v. *Martin*, 128.

See ATTACHMENT. CHANCERY. CHANCERY PRACTICE. SPECIFIC PERFORMANCE. TRUST AND TRUSTEE.

SAVING OF THE STATUTE.

See STATUTE OF LIMITATIONS.

SCIRE FACIAS.

Administrator and executor. Judgment. What the scire facias must aver. A *scire facias* against an administrator or executor, to render him personally liable on a judgment rendered against him in his representative character, must allege a *devastavit*; and, also, the fact of a judgment obtained against him in his character of executor or administrator, for a *scire facias* will not lie on a judgment against him individually, or against his testator, or intestate *Cope & Co.* v. *McFarland*, 543.

See ADMINISTRATORS AND EXECUTORS. BAIL.

INDEX.

SECURITIES.

See SURETIES.

SELF-DEFENCE.

See CRIMINAL LAW.

SET-OFF.

1. *When allowed.* A debt or demand, to be set-off, must be an existing debt or demand at the commencement of the plaintiff's suit. Otherwise, it cannot be allowed. *Brazelton v. Brooks,* 194.

2. *Same. Insolvency of the party. Chancery jurisdiction.* If a party, who is insolvent, recovers a judgment against one to whom he is indebted, but who was not a creditor, so as to entitle him to his set-off at law, the latter may come into a Court of Chancery and be allowed to set-off his demand against the judgment thus recovered against him. *Ibid.*

3. *Chancery jurisdiction. Waiver of a defence.* If a bill is filed seeking to set-off a demand against a judgment recovered against the complainant, and the defendant answers, virtually submitting to the set-off, it is error for the Court to refuse the relief. The answer is a waiver of any objection to the jurisdiction of the Court. *Ibid.*

4. *Obligation to be discharged in bonds.* An obligation for money to be paid in the bonds of a railroad company, by a given day, may, if not complied with, be the subject of set-off in a suit against the original holder of said obligation, or his assignee, for money due said company. And this is so, whether the obligation fixes the value at which the bonds are to be received or not, the law having established a rule by which the value may be ascertained and rendered certain. *Memphis and Little Rock R. R. Co. v. Walker,* 467.

SETTLEMENT.

See ADMINISTRATORS AND EXECUTORS. EVIDENCE. WILLS.

SHERIFF.

See MANDAMUS. JAILS. SUMMARY PROCEEDINGS.

SLAVES.

1. *Sale of under a will. Bill of sale or other writing not necessary, if possession delivered.* If a sale of slaves is made under a power created by a will, and is absolute, and possession delivered by the executor no bill of sale, or other written evidence is necessary to transfer

the title to the purchaser. The verbal sale accompanied by delivery of possession, is as operative to pass the title, as a bill of sale. *Woods* v. *Burrough*, 202.

2. *Hire. Compensation for keeping, when allowed.* A party who purchases slaves from an executor who sells without authority, is a wrongdoer, and is not entitled to compensation for the support and raising of the slaves, and for physicians' bills, taxes, &c., beyond the hire. And this relief is afforded him incidentally, by allowing him to *recoup* against the claim for hire. *Gee* v. *Graves and wife*, 289.

3. *Warranty. Fraud. Tender. Rescission of contract.* If, upon the sale of a slave, a warranty is made, and the vendor is attempted to be made liable upon the ground of fraud or deceit, for defects covered by said warranty, to authorize a recovery it must be shown that the vendee returned, or tendered the slave to the vendor in a reasonable time, or was prevented from doing so by the death of the slave. *Conner* v. *Crunk*, 246.

4. *Same. Same. Same. Rule confined to cases of warranty.* This rule is confined to cases where there is a contract of warranty which covers the defects upon which the suit is based. But if redress is sought against a party, upon the ground of fraud, who has made no warranty, or for a fraud not covered by the warranty, the principle does not apply, and a tender of the slave is not necessary to entitle the vendee to recover for the fraud and deceit. *Ibid.*

5. *Contract of hire. Liability of the hirer.* To work at digging a race, which, in some cases, might require the blasting of rock and standing in water, is not properly embraced by a contract to work on or at the mill. The race, though necessary to the mill, is distinct from it, and might demand exposure to extra hazardous employment. *Dement* v. *Scott*, 367.

6. *Same. Same. Voluntary exposure by the slave.* The hirer having power to control the slave, is bound to restrain him from wilful exposure, by the obligations which the law impose on him. And he is responsible for the consequences of any exposure of which he has knowledge and does not prevent, although it may be voluntary by the slave, and against his orders. *Ibid.*

7. *Same. Same. Same. Previous disease of the slave. Rescission of contract of hiring.* If a hired slave is diseased at the time of the contract, and this fact is not communicated to the hirer, either from fraud or ignorance of its existence, the hirer has the right, upon coming to a knowledge of the fact, to abandon the contract, and return the slave; but he is not justified in requiring the slave to perform a kind or amount of labor for which he has not the physical capacity, and which, of necessity, must destroy his life more speedily. *Ibid.*

8. *Warranty. Fraud. Evidence.* Where the contract for the sale of a slave is in writing, and contains no warranty, or a refusal to warrant, parol evidence is inadmissible to superadd a warranty. But if the contract is induced by an oral warranty which the seller knows to be false, and is made for the purpose of throwing the other party off his guard, and fraudulently obtaining his consent to the bargain, evidence of such verbal warranty is admissible to show that the assent of the party to the contract was obtained by falsehood and fraud, and therefore has no legal existence. The same principle applies in the case of false and fraudulent representations made under like circumstances. *Smith v. Cozart*, 526.

9. *Same. Same. Effect of stipulation that the slave is sold as unsound.* A stipulation in the bill of sale that the slave is sold as unsound property, is, in itself, an exclusion of all warranty; but such a stipulation will be of no avail where the seller has been guilty of a wilful and intentional false representation or concealment, or has resorted to any contrivance to deceive and mislead the purchaser. *Ibid.*

10. *Same. Same. Measure of damages.* If there is a breach of the warranty of the soundness of a slave, or a fraudulent representation or concealment of her unsound condition — the slave not having been returned or offered to be returned — the proper measure of damages is the difference in value between the slave, if in the condition in which she was *represented* to be at the time of the sale, and her then *actual* condition, and not the value of the slave or the price paid for her. *Ibid.*

11. *Pass to the distributees. Sale of, by execution. Act of* 1827. Slaves pass to distributees in like manner as lands go to the heirs, and cannot be seized and sold upon an execution at law against the personal representative. The representative, or creditors, must, to subject them to the payment of debts, proceed under the act of 1827. *Saunders v. Wilder*, 577.

See CONSTITUTIONAL LAW. CONTRACT. CRIMINAL LAW. ESTOPPEL. EVIDENCE. LIEN. PATROLS. STATUTE OF LIMITATIONS.

SPECIFIC PERFORMANCE.

1. *Feme covert. Contract by.* A covenant to convey real estate, executed by a *feme covert*, who is not invested with power to sell and convey the same as a *feme sole*, is void, and will not be specifically executed by a Court of Chancery. *Pilcher & Cataulis v. Smith & Wife*, 208.

2. *Feme covert. Fraud.* The legal disability of coverture carries with it no license or privilege to practice fraud or deception on other innocent persons, nor will the disability be permitted to protect a person

in doing so. Thus, if a married woman covenant to convey land, and, by reason of her coverture, the covenant is void, it would be a fraud for her to avoid the contract without restoring the purchase money, and it will not be permitted. *Ibid.*

3. *Same. Rescission of contract. Refunding of the purchase money.* A married woman cannot avoid a sale of real estate made by her, without refunding the consideration money paid by the purchaser. *Ibid.*

4. *Same. Chancery jurisdiction. Specific performance. Rescission of contract. Lien.* A purchaser of real estate from a *feme covert* whose covenant is void, has a right to come into a Court of Equity to obtain, either a specific execution, or rescission of the contract. And if the *feme covert* resist a specific execution, and the contract is rescinded, as an incident to the rescission, the Court will order the re-payment of the purchase money, and declare a lien upon the land to secure its payment. *Ibid.*

5. *Not enforced if title defective.* A specific performance of a contract for the sale of land will not be enforced, unless the vendor can make the vendee a good and indefeasible title. *Starnes & Wife* v. *Allison,* 221.

STATUTE OF LIMITATIONS.

1. *When one capable of suing. Slaves.* If one of several parties who have a joint right to slaves is free from disability, and in a condition to be capable of suing, the statute of limitations will run against, and bar the right of all of said parties in case there is an adverse holding of the slaves for a period of three years. *Morgan* v. *Reed,* 276.

2. *Same. Severance of the joint right.* A sale by one or more of the joint owners of slaves who are *sui juris,* of their interest in them operates as a severance of the joint interest, and leaves the parties under disability at liberty to sue separately for their slaves, as if there had never existed a unity of title or of interest between them and the other joint owners. And, consequently, the statute of limitations will not bar the right of those under disability, until after three years from the removal of the same, as to all. *Ibid*

3. *Same. Same. Estoppel.* If two of the distributees of an estate, who are *sui juris,* administer, and in that capacity, petition and procure an order for the sale of the slaves of their intestate, in which they have a joint interest, but which proceeding is void against the other distributees, who are then minors, by reason of the latter not being made parties, such adult distributees are placed under an *estoppel,* and, thereby, disabled from suing: and the fact that they were co-distributees, and *sui juris,* (the joint interest of the parties having

been severed by the sale,) will not bar the right of the infants to sue and recover, at any time within three years after the youngest arrives at age. *Ibid.*

4. *What will arrest it. Descent cast.* If a parent place a son in possession of land under a verbal gift, and the possession is held by the son adversely to the father and all other persons, the death of the father will not arrest the running of the statute. By the *descent cast* the heirs are placed exactly in the shoes of their ancestor. And the statute having attached and commenced running against him in his lifetime, it continues to run without intermission against his heirs. Its operation can, in such case, be arrested, only, by a suit at law, or in equity, effectually prosecuted. *Haynes* v. *Jones,* 872.

5. *Same. Same. Saving of the statute.* The ancestor being free from disability when the adverse possession is taken and the running of the statute commenced, there is no saving or exception in the statute in favor of his heirs; and they, though infants or *femes covert,* are bound to sue just as much as their ancestor would have been had he lived, before the expiration of seven years from the adverse possession. *Ibid.*

6. *Possessory right. Act of* 1819. *Advancement.* If a child is placed in the possession of land by the parent, under a parol gift as an advancement, and such child holds said land adversely to the parent and the other heirs for a period of seven years, he will be protected under the second section of the act of 1819, to the extent of his enclosure, for which he must account at the estimated value put upon the land at the time of the advancement. *Ibid.*

7. *When it will bar a life estate.* If a person own a life estate in a slave, which he can sell and transfer, or which can be sold by execution, and such person, for a valuable consideration, sells and transfers said slave to another, who takes possession thereof and holds and claims the slave, adversely, for a period of three years, the statute of limitations will perfect his title and protect the possession, so far as the life estate is concerned, against the person from whom the slave was purchased, his creditors, and all other persons, except the owner of the remainder. *Bradford* v. *Caldwell,* 496.

8. *Bar of two years, as to administrators and executors. Act of* 1789. *Code,* §§ 2279, 2280. The delay necessary to remove the limitation of two years, provided by the act of 1789, (Code, § 2279,) must be a delay at the request of the administrator or executor, for a *definite time,* or to an *event which may occur,* and thereby render the period *certain.* A payment of part of the claim, and a promise to credit a note due the estate for so much of the balance as may be just, will not take the case out of the statute. *Birdsong* v. *Birdsong,* 608.

9. *Trust and trustee. When the statute runs against the title of a trustee. Infants.* The principle that when the trustee is barred all the beneficiaries are barred, whether under disability or not, applies, only, when the trustee can sue, but fails to do so. If the trustee estops himself from suing by a sale of the property—thus uniting with the purchaser in a breach of trust—the wrong is to the beneficiaries, not to him. He cannot sue, and the beneficiaries, if under disability, are not affected by the statute. *Parker* v *Hall*, 641.

10. *Same. Same. Time given persons. under disability, to sue.* In such case, if the beneficiaries are all under disability at the time the adverse possession commences by the sale of the trustee, they are allowed the time, within which to sue, given in the statute, after the disability is removed as to all of them. If any one is capable of suing at the time of the sale, the bar will be perfected within the time allowed by the statute, from that date. *Ibid.*

11. *Land law. Tenants in common. Deed by one co-tenant. Adverse possession.* If real estate is held in common, and one tenant assumes to convey the entire land, or any specific part of it, by metes and bounds, his deed will be a *color of title*, and possession under it for seven years, will be adverse to the title of the co-tenants, and bar their right to recover the land conveyed. *Weisinger* v. *Murphy*, 674.

12. *Same. Same. Notice. Ouster.* Such deed and possession of the land is an actual ouster and disseizin of the co-tenant, which he is bound to notice. In order to create this adverse relation, no formal or other notice, from the vendee in possession, is necessary. *Ibid.*

13. *Husband and wife. Joint estate of. Tenancy by the curtesy.* By marriage, the husband derives an estate of freehold in the real estate of the wife. He is jointly *seized* with his wife, and during the existence of the *coverture* he is not tenant by the curtesy; and cannot be, unless he survive her. If there be a disseizin during the coverture, it is a disseizen of the entire joint estate, and the husband and wife must, jointly, bring suit to recover the possession. If they neglect to sue for seven years, during which period there is an adverse possession of the land, their joint right of action will be barred. *Ibid.*

14. *Same. Same. Same. Extinguishment of husband's interest.* If the joint right of husband and wife is barred by the statute of limitations, the husband's interest is extinguished. And if he survive his wife, he has no right to, or interest in her real estate as tenant by the curtesy. *Ibid.*

15. *Same. Same. Wife surviving. Must sue within three years.* If the wife survive her husband, she has, by the *proviso* of the statute, only three years next after their coverture shall cease, within which to sue; and if she neglects to sue within that time her right is barred. *Ibid.*

16. *Same. Same. Husband surviving. Heirs of wife must sue within three years.* If the husband survive the wife, his interest in the estate having been extinguished, her heirs, though under the disabilities of infancy, coverture, &c., must sue within three years next after her death, or their right of action will be barred. Cumulative disabilities are not allowed to suspend or arrest the statute after it has commenced running. *Ibid.*

17. *Same. Same. If severed by the deed of the husband, when the bar of the statute is formed.* The case is different where there is no joint right of suit in husband and wife, as when the husband makes a conveyance of the lands of the wife, she not joining therein. In such case the husband, by his deed, has estopped himself from suing, and the wife cannot sue alone, nor can she or her heirs sue the husband's vendee until after the death of the husband. The estate becomes one of remainder in the wife or her heirs, with the right to sue therefor at any time within seven years next after the husband's death. *Ibid.*

18. *Equitable titles.* The act of 1819 bars equitable as well as legal titles, and operates as an extinguishment of the same, investing the adverse claimant with an perfect. title in fee simple. *Belote* v. *White,* 708.

See TRUST AND TRUSTEE. LIEN. WILLS

STATUTES CITED AND CONSTRUED.

1777, ch. 885,	Penalty,	124
1858, ch. 89,	Motion,	29
1789,	Statute of limitations,	603
1827,	Slaves,	577
1851–2,	Register,	408
1852, ch. 152, §§ 4, 5,		97
1794, ch. 1, § 74,	Costs,	116
1851, ch. 826,	Occupancy,	582
1850–1,	Hiatus,	408
1843, ch. 8, § 4,	Land law,	360
1717, ch. 1, § 18,	Entry-taker,	320
1851–2, ch. 113,	Banks,	591
1824, ch. 5,	Witness,	455
1831, ch. 103, §§ 1, 2,	Slaves,	140
1843, ch. 29, § 1,	Attachment,	511
1852, ch. 365, § 10,	Attachment,	511
1715, ch. 16, § 1,	Bail,	227
1820, ch. 25, § 4,	Protest,	57
1852, ch. 365, § 9,	Jurisdiction,	493
1789, ch. 8, § 1,	Gaming,	617
1856, ch. 112, § 8	Constitution,	276
1854, ch. 17, § 6,	Taxation,	368
1856, ch. 7, § 1,	Set-off	445
1842, ch. 48,	False pretences,	36

STAY OF EXECUTION.

1. *Justices' docket. Act of 1835.* The fact that the name of the stayor is not written in the most appropriate place on the justice's docket, or that the docket is not made out with all the formality prescribed by the act of 1835, will not vitiate the security, or discharge the stayor from his liability. *Lownes, Orgill & Co. v. Hunter,* 848.

2. *Irregularities in the judgment.* If the judgment upon which a party undertakes to stay execution remains in force, the stayor cannot go behind it in search of irregularities upon which to be discharged from his liability. If the party prejudiced by the supposed irregularity submits to it, it does not lie in the mouth of the surety for the stay of execution to complain. *Ibid.*

STOCKHOLDERS.

See ATTACHMENT.

SUBSTITUTION.

See SURETIES.

SUIT.

See PRACTICE AND PLEADING.

SUMMARY PROCEEDINGS.

1 *Motion against sheriff and securities. Revivor by motion. Act of 1858, ch.* 89. Prior to the act of 1858, the remedy by motion did not extend to the personal representative of a deceased officer, or of his security, and could not be maintained against either By that act, if the officer, or either of his securities, shall die during the pendency of a suit by motion, against them, it may be revived against the personal representative of such officer, or security, in the same way that suits are revived against personal representatives in other cases. *Burroughs v. Goodall,* 29.

2. *Same. Same. Act of 1858 does not have a retrospective operation.* If the Legislature could have given the act of 1858 a retrospective operation, it is manifest that it was not done; and is, therefore, to be construed as applicable, only, to cases arising after its passage. *Ibid.*

3. *Same. Same. Death of the principal abates the motion as to the securities.* It is only through their principal, and jointly with him, that the securities can be reached by motion. And the abatement of the motion as to the principal, of necessity, works an abatement as to the securities. Even under the act of 1858, no step can be taken against the securities until the motion is revived against the personal representative of the principal. *Ibid.*

4. *Sheriff. Amendment of return.* The motion, and not the notice that it will be made, is the commencement of the suit; and the sheriff may be permitted to amend his return upon a summons at any time before the motion is made, even after service of the notice, that it will be made. *Hill* v. *Hinton*, 124.

5. *Same. Evidence. Return of summons.* In a summary proceeding against the sheriff for the non-return of a summons, the enquiry is confined to the face of the return. Extrinsic evidence is not admissible. *Ibid.*

6. *Same. Process. Non-return of. Act of* 1777, *ch.* 8, § 5. *Code* § 3608. By the 3608 § of the Code, taken with some modifications from the act of 1777, a penalty of $125 is recoverable by motion of the party aggrieved against any sheriff or other officer who fails to execute and make return of any process issued from any Court of Record, and delivered to him twenty days before the return day. This means that he shall, not only hand in the writ, but return that he has executed it, or state a sufficient reason why he has not done so. *Ibid.*

7. *Same. What sufficient return.* The return "not to be found in my county," would be more perfect and proper, but great strictness is not required when a motion is made for a penalty. Hence, the return "not found," although informal, is sufficient. *Ibid.*

8. *Jurisdiction. Circuit Court. Justices of the peace. Acts of* 1801, 1823, *and* 1835. *Code,* § 3591. By the provisions of the acts of 1801, 1823, and 1835, and the 3591 section of the Code, the Circuit Court and justices of the peace have concurrent jurisdiction of motions against officers for failing to pay over money collected by them, and for the non-return of executions within thirty days. But justices of the peace are confined to cases where the amount is within their jurisdiction. The Circuit Court is not limited as to amount. *Drewry* v. *Vaden,* 312.

9. *Motion. Constable. Notice.* In a summary proceeding, by motion, against a constable, the notice is sufficient if it describes the note placed in the constable's hands for collection—the date and amount—the date and amount of the judgment rendered upon it, and the execution issued to him in the case—that the execution had not been returned into the office from which it issued within thirty days thereafter, nor the money due thereon paid over according to law; and that, therefore, judgment is demanded against the officer and his securities for the amount of the judgment of the justice of the peace, with legal interest from the rendition thereof, and twelve and one-half *per cent.* interest on the same from the time it was demanded, by way of damages. *Lashley* v. *Wilkinson,* 482.

10. *Same. Same. Same.* The validity of a notice, for the non-return of an execution, is not affected by the fact that it demands, as a legal

conclusion, more or less by way of interest, or damages, than the plaintiff is entitled to. The law fixes the officer's liability upon the case stated, and it is the duty of the court to give judgment for the proper amount. *Ibid.*

11. *Same. Same. Same. Variance.* If the notice is, in other respects, good, a *variance* between the date of the execution produced on the trial and the one described in the notice will not be fatal. *Ibid.*

12. *Constable. Sureties of, when liable.* When a constable executes his receipt for a claim, placed in his hands for collection, he assumes the double relation of *private agent* and *officer*. When his term of office expires, all his authority, as an officer, ceases. His agency continues until revoked by the principal. His sureties are liable, *alone,* for his official misconduct. They are not liable for his negligence as a *private agent. Crittenden* v. *Terrill,* 588.

13. *Same. Liability as agent.* When a constable thus becomes the agent of a party, he is personally liable to him for any negligence in failing to sue on the claim, or to take out execution, or to do any other unofficial act. But for these his sureties are not liable. *Ibid.*

14. *Same. Case in judgment.* A note was placed in the hands of a constable for collection. He executed his receipt therefor, and obtained judgment on the note. After the expiration of his term of office, he took out an execution on the judgment, and placed it in the hands of his successor in office, who collected the money and paid it over to him. He failed to pay it over to the plaintiff, who proceeded, by motion, against him and his sureties. Held, that after the expiration of his term of office, the constable could do no official act that would bind his sureties, and they were not liable. That the plaintiff's remedy, if any, was against him as his agent. *Ibid.*

SUPERSEDEAS.

See CERTIORARI AND SUPERSEDEDAS.

SUPREME COURT.

See CHANCERY PRACTICE.

SURETIES.

1. *Recognizance. How far surety liable.* Pending the suit in the Circuit Court, the former securities were released, and the following recognizance entered into by the new surety: "Joab Parks comes into open court and acknowledges himself the defendant's security in the sum of $1000, in the room and stead of M. D. Cardwell and John A. Rogers, their former securities, conditioned that they defend their suit successfully, or in case of failure to pay all costs." *Held,* 1: That an

undertaking, by recognizance, for costs, is as binding as if by bond, and is good, although the party to whom bound is not named, if the parties to the suit are named. and the party agrees to be the defendant's security for costs. 2: That the act prescribing the sum for which bond is to be taken in cases of contested wills, is directory, and the bond may be for a larger sum; and the fact that the former sureties were only bound in the sum of $500, does not change the undertaking of the new security. *Parks* v. *Allen*, 528.

2. *Entitled to substitution before payment of the debt.* Sureties are entitled to the benefit of all securities which the creditor obtains against the principal debtor; and this is so, whether the debt has been paid by the surety, or not, if the principal has become insolvent. *Henry* v. *Compton*, 549.

3. *Same. Case in judgment.* A slave was sold under a decree of court, which decree retained a lien on the slave for the payment of the purchase money. The purchaser gave bond and security for the price. He became insolvent, and the slave was levied on by his creditors. The surety of the purchaser, not having paid the debt, filed a bill to enjoin the sale of the slave by the creditors, and to be *substituted* to the *lien* retained by the decree. It is held that the surety is entitled to the relief asked for. *Ibid.*

4. *Bound by the litigation of his principal.* A surety in a replevin bond is bound by the result of the litigation with his principal. And, if the Court had jurisdiction of the subject matter and of the parties, he is bound by the orders and judgment. *Wells* v. *Griffin & Co.*, 568.

5. *Judgment. Form of.* A judgment "that the plaintiff recover of the defendant and of William S. Wells, the security on the replevin bond, the said sum of $1427.28, the damages so by the jury aforesaid assessed, and the costs of the suit, and that execution issue, to be levied of the proper goods and chattels, rights and credits of the said intestate, in the hands of the said administrator to be administered," is, in legal effect, a judgment against Wells in his own right and against the administrator in his representative character. *Ibid.*

6. *Release of, by erasure of name of one. Covenant.* If two or more persons become the surety of a third person, to a bond, and the obligees and principal obligor erase the name of, and release one of the sureties, without the knowledge or consent of the co-securities, or their subsequent ratification of the same, they are not bound on said bond. *Mitchell* v. *Burton* 618.

7. *Same. Same. Signed by others after erasure.* But if the obligation after such erasure, is presented to other persons, who sign the same as sureties, they are bound by their undertaking, although they may be ignorant of the circumstances of the erasure and of the fact that the other sureties on the bond are released thereby. The erasure was

visible, and they should have ascertained all the facts in reference thereto, before signing the obligation, and not having done so, are bound by their act. *Ibid.*

8. *Administrators and executors. Judicial sales. When sureties liable on administration bond.* The bond given by an administrator only binds the sureties for the faithful performance of his duties in his capacity as administrator, and not for the performance of any duty imposed by an appointment of the Court. And if, upon the petition of an administrator and the distributees of his intestate, a slave is ordered to be sold, and the adminstrator appointed commissioner to make the sale, his sureties in the administration bond, are not liable for the proceeds of such sale, in the event he sells the slave and fails to pay over the proceeds to the distributees. *Reeves* v. *Steele*, 647.

See BILLS AND NOTES. CHANCERY JURISDICTION. COSTS. SUMMARY PROCEEDINGS.

TAXATION.

See CONSTITUTIONAL LAW. NON-SUIT.

TENANTS IN COMMON.

See STATUTE OF LIMITATIONS.

TENANT BY THE CURTESY.

See STATUTE OF LIMITATIONS.

TENDER.

See PAYMENT. SLAVES.

TITLE.

See FORCIBLE ENTRY AND DETAINER. HUSBAND AND WIFE. SPECIFIC PERFORMANCE.

TRESPASS.

1. *Exclusive possession sufficient to support this action.* An actual and exclusive possession by a party, even though it be by wrong, is sufficient to support an action of trespass against a mere stranger or wrong-doer, who has neither title to the possession in himself, nor authority from the legal owner. *Criner* v. *Pike*, 898.

2. *How possession lost.* The fact that the property in suit, a mare, was in her usual *range* in the woods, or had gone to the defendant's in the neighborhood, if this be so, where he killed her, did not destroy the plaintiff's possession, so as to prevent him from sustaining the action. *Ibid.*

3. *Measure of damages.* Ordinarily, in such cases, the party in possession is either the owner of the property, or answerable over to the owner; and in either case he is entitled not only to damages for the taking, but also for the value of the same. *Ibid.*

4. *Same. Mitigation.* The defendant may prove, in mitigation of damages, that the goods did not belong to the plaintiff, and that they have gone to the use of the true owner, either by being restored to him in *specie*, or taken upon legal process in payment of his debts. *Ibid.*

See RAILROAD COMPANY.

TROVER.

See SALE OF PERSONALTY.

TRUST AND TRUSTEE.

1. *Husband and wife. Sale of real estate settled upon the wife. Privy examination of the wife.* If real estate is conveyed by the husband to a trustee, for the sole and separate use of the wife, with power to the trustee, at her request in writing, to sell and convey the same, and re-invest the proceeds as she may direct, a simple request in writing is sufficient. A formal power to the trustee, accompanied with the *privy examination* of the wife, is not required. *Cardwell* v. *Cheatham,* 14.

2. *Same. Same. Breach of Trust. Fraud.* It is the duty of both the trustee and purchaser, in the event the property is sold, to see that the fund is paid over to the trustee, and re-invested for the benefit of the wife, as directed by the terms of the trust. And if, in violation of the provisions of the deed, the purchaser contract with the husband, pay him the purchase money, and, upon the written authority of the wife, the trustee conveys title to him, such sale and conveyance is a breach of trust—a fraud upon the power, and will, upon the application of the wife, be set aside. *Ibid.*

3. *Same. Same. Innocent purchaser.* If the purchase is made *bona fide*, without notice of the breach of a trust reposed in the trustee, the purchaser is not bound to see that the purchase money is re-invested in other property for the use of the wife. *Ibid.*

4. *Same. Same. Same. How this defence to be made.* If a party rely upon the defence that he is an innocent purchaser without notice, he must set it out, specifically, by plea or answer; and establish the facts relied on by proof. *Ibid.*

5. *Gift. Acceptance. Benefit. Presumption of.* In general, any gift by deed, will, or otherwise, is supposed *prima facie*, unless the contrary appears, to be beneficial to the donee. Consequently, the law

presumes, until there is proof to the contrary, that every estate i accepted by the person to whom it is expressed to be given. *Goss v. Singleton*, 67.

6. *Same. Not perfect until acceptance.* The gift is not perfect until ratified by the assent of the donee; and a disclaimer of the trust operates as evidence that such assent was never given. *Ibid.*

7. *Same. Acceptance discretionary.* The law does not force the donee to accept the gift of an estate, whether made in trust, or otherwise. and therefore it is competent for the person appointed trustee to refuse both the estate and the office attached to it, provided he has done no act to deprive himself of that right. *Ibid.*

8. *Same. Disclaimer. How made.* There is some conflict of authority as to whether a parol disclaimer is sufficient. But it is well settled that the renunciation may be by deed, by matter of record, or any written instrument, or by an answer in Chancery. *Ibid.*

9. *Same. Same. Relates back to the gift.* A disclaimer, or refusal to accept the trust will relate back, and be held to have been made at the time of the gift, if no act has been done to preclude the party. *Ibid.*

10. *Same. Same. Effect of. Devise in trust.* The legal effect of a proper refusal or disclaimer of the trust is, that all parties are placed precisely in the same situation relatively to the trust property, as if the disclaiming party had not been named in the trust instrument, whether it be a deed or will. Hence, if all the trustees disclaim a devise in trust, the legal estate will vest in the heir of the devisor. *Ibid.*

11. *Trust does not necessarily pass with the property.* A trust is the mere creature of equity, and does not necessarily inhere in the property so as to be inseparable therefrom, but may remain in the trustee or elsewhere wholly unaffected by an unauthorized sale of the property, the subject of the trust. *Ibid.*

12. *Effect of the appointment of a trustee.* If, by reason of the disclaimer of the trustees, the property descends to the heir-at-law, who is also the *cestui que trust*, the legal estate is cast upon the *cestui que trust*, who applies to a court of competent jurisdiction, and has a trustee appointed, in whom the legal estate is vested, coupled with the trusts, the legal estate is by necessary implication divested out of the *cestui que trust. Ibid.*

13. *Same. Statute of limitations. Effect of.* If, from the time the legal title to real estate, the subject of the trust, is thus vested in the trustee, there is an adverse holding of the same for a period of seven

years, the party's title becomes indefeasible by the act of 1819, as against the trustee, and equally so as against the *cestui que trust*. *Ibid.*

14. *Conveyance in trust for the wife and children.* If a person who is addicted to the excessive use of ardent spirits, and is a spendthrift, makes a conveyance of all his property in trust for the benefit of his wife and children, such conveyance will not be set aside by a Court of Chancery, although procured by the influence of another, and under such circumstances as would have authorized a Court of Equity to have annulled it if the conveyance had been made to a stranger. *Birdsong* v. *Birdsong*, 289.

15. *Same. When conveyance absolute.* If such conveyance is absolute, a Court of Equity will execute the trust for the benefit of the wife and children. *Ibid.*

16. *Trust created by parol. A trust may be carved out of an absolute bequest by parol.* If a testator makes an absolute bequest of property to another, with the verbal agreement with the legatee that she will, at her death, dispose of the property equally between his and her relations, a trust is thereby created in favor of the relations, which will be enforced in a Court of Equity, if such legatee fail to execute the agreement. *McLelland* v. *McLean*, 684.

17. *Same. Same. May be established by parol evidence.* Such a trust, resting upon a parol agreement, must of necessity be proven by parol testimony. *Ibid.*

18. *Same. Same. Trust need not be noticed in the bequest.* It is not necessary, in order to establish the trust, that there should be any mention of it in the bequest. If the evidence establishes the trust, it will be enforced, although the gift of the property is absolute and unconditional. *Ibid.*

See LAND LAW. LIEN. STATUTE OF LIMITATIONS. WILLS.

USURY.

When it may be recovered back in equity. The rule in equity is to apply the excess of interest to the satisfaction of the principal, and when that is paid in this way, all that is paid afterwards may be recovered by the borrower as so much money had and received by the lender to his use. And this may be done although the party has been sued at law, and failed to make the defence. *Threadgill* v. *Timberlake*, 895.

See PARTNERSHIP.

VACANCY.

See REGISTRATION.

VARIANCE.

See SUMMARY PROCEEDINGS.

VENDITIONI EXPONAS.

See SALE OF REAL ESTATE.

VENDOR AND VENDEE.

See SALE OF REAL ESTATE.

VOLUNTARY CONVEYANCES.

See SALE OF REAL ESTATE.

WAIVER.

See BILLS AND NOTES.

WARRANTY.

1. *When it embraces visible defects. Evidence.* A general warranty of soundness, whether in writing or by parol, does not extend to an unsoundness or defect which is plain and obvious to the purchaser, or of which he had cognizance. But to exclude a defect or disease from the operation of the warranty, it must be of such a character or description as to disclose to the vendee, not only the *existence*, but the *extent* of the defect or disease, and if this is not so, it is covered by the warranty. And parol evidence to show that the defect was obvious, or that the seller disclosed the unsoundness at the time of the sale, is admissible, notwithstanding the warranty may be in writing. *Fisher v. Pollard*, 815.

2. *Husband and wife. Liability of the wife on joint warranty with the husband. Estoppel.* If land is conveyed to the wife, with authority to her by joint deed with her husband to dispose of the same, and she join her husband in a deed for the land, with covenants of warranty, such warranty can only affect her by way of *estoppel*, if she attempts to assert any title in opposition to the one thus warranted. She would not be liable on her covenants in the joint deed. And it would not prohibit others from acting as trustees for her, and thereby secure her a benefit. *Fletcher v. Coleman*, 884.

3. *Same. Same. Case in judgment.* A tract of land was conveyed to the wife, with authority to her to dispose of the same by joint deed with her husband. She joined her husband in a conveyance of the land to a third person, with covenants of warranty. After the execution of this deed the original vendor filed a bill, and procured a decree for the sale of the land, to pay the purchase money. The trustee of the *feme covert* bid off the land for her, and gave bond and security

for the purchase money. Subsequent to the sale, and before any title was vested in the *feme covert*, the parties and the sureties entered into an agreement by which the sureties paid the trustee $1000, and were substituted as the purchasers. Held, that the warrantee of the wife could not be substituted to the title, the wife having acquired none, and not being liable on her warranty; nor could he be indemnified out of the $1000 paid by the sureties. *Ibid*

4. *When implied.* When goods are ordered and supplied, or manufactured for a particular purpose, there is an *implied warranty* that they are reasonably fit and proper for that purpose. And this rule especially applies in a contest between the manufacturer and purchaser of the articles. *Overton v. Phelan*, 445.

See SALE OF REAL ESTATE. SLAVES.

WIFE.

See HUSBAND AND WIFE. STATUTE OF LIMITATIONS. TRUST AND TRUSTEE.

WILLS.

1. *Construction of. Power of appointment.* The will of. David Baggerly contained the following clauses: "To my beloved wife Rebecca, I give and bequeath all the lands owned by me, lying on the south side of the Yadkin river, in Iredell county, during her lifetime; and also, all my household goods and effects of every description, and also my negro women, Fanny and Rina, and a negro boy named James." * * * "It is further my will and desire, that my negroes, Fanny, Rina, and James, be disposed of by my wife Rebecca, with their increase, *to the whole or any one or more of my children she may think proper, at her decease.*" Upon these clauses it is held:

1. That the wife took an estate for life, with power to dispose of the property to one or more of the *children*, as she chose; but, in the event she failed to exercise the power, or made an invalid appointment, it would go, equally, to the children and grandchildren of the testator.

2. That the power of appointment to children does not embrace grandchildren, and the exercise of it in their favor is void.

3. That the appointments of the wife, so far as they are in conformity with the power, are not void, because others, invalid, are included in her will. Those in accordance with the power will be sustained, and those not, rejected.

4. That the property not disposed of in conformity with the power will be equally divided among the children and grandchildren, *per*

stirpes, under the will of the testator, without regard to the property held under the valid appointments of the wife. It is not, as in a case of intestacy, a case for collation of advancements. *Cruse* v. *McKee*, 1.

2. *Same. Same. A power must be executed in good faith.* A person clothed with a power of appointment, must exercise it in good faith for the end and purposes designed; and, in all cases, when a discretion is given in the selection of the objects amongst a class, good faith must be observed, and if discriminations are made to secure advantage to the trustee, or a stranger, his act will be held vicious and corrupt, and the appointment declared void. *Ibid.*

3. *Revocation of. Mistake. Fraud.* If the maker of a will burns a paper, which she thinks is her will, but by *mistake* or the *fraud* of others, burns a different paper, with the intention of revoking said will by its destruction, and honestly believed that she had done it, and continued in that belief, without any subsequent recognition, or even knowledge of its existence, it would amount to a revocation of the will. *Smiley* v. *Gambill*, 164.

4. *Same. Evidence.* Revocation is a question of intention, and the acts, conduct, and declarations of the maker of the will are admissible for the purpose of ascertaining whether it was revoked. Revocation may be established as other facts, by positive or circumstantial evidence. *Ibid.*

5. *Same. Revocation a question of law.* While it is the province of the jury to determine the facts, what amounts to a revocation is a question of law. *Ibid.*

6. *Construction. Life estate.* If land and slaves, together with a sufficiency of all kind of stock for an ample support, household and kitchen furniture, are bequeathed by a testator to his wife for life, with a remainder in the land to his son—the residue of the property to be sold at her death or marriage, and the money to be equally divided between his children named in the will—the widow takes an estate for life in the property bequeathed, with the right to *enjoy and use this* property in *specie*, and the same cannot be sold by the executors. *Forsey & Wife* v. *Luton*, 188.

7. *Tenant for life. Rights of.* The rents and use of the land, the hire and labor of the slaves, crops, young animals—the offspring of those originally given—new furniture &c., and the entire fruits of the life estate, belong, absolutely, to the tenant for life, and make no part of the estate of the testator. *Ibid.*

8. *Same. Liability of. Remaindermen. Rights of.* If the tenant for life wastes, or converts any part of the estate for life to unauthorized uses, her estate will be liable for the amount so wasted or converted. But if the property were consumed in the use intended to be

INDEX. 807

made of it, or perished by time, or death of animals, or wear and tear of furniture and farming tools, the rights of the remaindermen are defeated, and they are entitled to nothing, except what remains of the original stock. *Ibid.*

9. *Same. Executor. Liability of.* If an executor participate, with the tenant for life, in a breach of trust, in the sale of any part of the estate for life, he is jointly liable with her for the value of the property sold. If she received the proceeds of the sale, her estate is, primarily, liable to the remaindermen. *Ibid.*

10. *Construction. Persons taking as a class.* The fifth clause of the will is as follows: "I give all the balance of my land to my brother Hiram during his natural life; and, at his death, my will is, that all my lands be sold—except what I have given above to my two nephews—and the proceeds of said lands to be equally divided between all my brothers' and sisters' children." Held, that the fund vests in the described class, as a class, as it exists at the time fixed for distribution of the same; and, under this clause, it goes to the children of the brothers and sisters of the testator, as a class, living at the termination of the life estate. *Beasley* v. *Jenkins,* 199.

11. *Construction of. Settlement. Power of appointment.* The will contains the following clauses: "I give, devise, and bequeath unto my daughter, Mary C. Rudder, all my estate or property of every description," * * * "of which I may die seized or possessed," * * * "to have and to hold all of said estate or property unto her, the said Mary C. Rudder, her heirs and assigns forever. But if the said Mary C. should marry, said estate or property is to be her own sole and separate estate, and the same, and every part and parcel thereof, as well as its increase and profits, shall remain free from the contracts and obligations of any person with whom she may intermarry, during her *coverture,* as though she had remained *sole.*" * * "In the event of the death of my said daughter without lawful issue living at the time of her death, it is my will that all the estate and property devised and bequeathed unto her, shall go as she may, by any instrument in the nature of a last will under hand and seal, witnessed by three or more witnesses, direct; and the power to dispose of the same and its increase in the event of her death, without issue, either before or after the age of twenty one years, and either while single or covert, is hereby given her, to be exercised and executed in the manner just prescribed, and in no other manner; but in the event she leaves issue, she may provide for that issue in whatever manner she deems best, and in that event my intent is not to limit her power over her estate at her death, in any manner whatever." Held:

1. That the property bequeathed to the said Mary C. Rudder, and its increase and profits are restricted to her separate use, and guarded against the contracts and obligations of her husband.

2. She may, *at her death*, whether she be a minor or of age, single or covert, if she have no issue then living, dispose of her property, at discretion, by an instrument under seal in the nature of a will, with three or more witnesses. This power is to be exercised in the manner prescribed, and in no other. The daughter cannot dispose of the property by deed, gift, or sale.

3. In the event she leave issue, she may provide for that issue as she thinks best, not confining her to an equal distribution of the property among them. Her power is to be unlimited, but it must be exercised at the time and in the manner pointed out by the testator.

4. If the daughter marry, and she and her husband sell the real estate, a specific performance of the contract cannot be enforced, because they cannot convey a good title to the purchaser. *Starnes and Wife* v. *Allison*, 221.

12. *Construction. Power of executor to sell property bequeathed.* The testator directed that his property, both real and personal, should be kept together and managed by his executor for the benefit of his wife, *during* her widowhood, and the maintenance and education of his children ; but in case his wife married she was to have the use and enjoyment of certain of the property during her natural life, and at her death, the same to be sold and equally divided between his the testator's, children. The widow remained single, and, at her death, the executor sold and conveyed one of the slaves mentioned in the will. It is held, that the testator did not intend that his executor should sell any of his estate unless his wife married again, and the sale of the slave by him, was unauthorized and void, and communicated no title to the purchaser. *Gee* v. *Graves and Wife*, 239.

13. *Construction. Limitation over.* When, by a will, an absolute gift of the property is made in the first instance, followed by a limitation over on the death of the devisee or legatee, the absolute gift is not taken away by the gift over, unless the gift over may itself take effect. *Alston* v. *Davis*, 266.

14. *Same. Same. Illustration of the principle.* The testator divided his estate among his children, of whom Rebecca Davis was one, and provided that her share should be vested in the hands of a trustee or trustees, for her use and benefit during her natural life, not subject to the control or obligations of her husband, and at her death, to be equally divided among her bodily heirs. By the proper construction of the will, in the event there are no "bodily heirs" (which in this connection means children) of the said Rebecca Davis, the gift becomes absolute. The testator did not, in that event, die intestate as to the remainder, so that the same would go to his heirs at law, under the statutes of distribution. *Ibid.*

15. *Holographic. What meant by "valuable papers." Act of* 1784, *ch.* 10, § 5. Before the passage of the act of 1784, no devise of land was good unless it was signed and witnessed by two subscribing witnesses. This act made an exception in favor of holographic wills. The first requirement of the act is, that the will shall be found among the "*valuable papers or effects*" of the deceased, or shall have been lodged in the hands of some person for safe keeping. "Valuable papers," as used in this act, consist of such as are regarded by the testator as worthy of preservation, and. therefore, in his estimation, of some value. They are not confined to deeds for land, bills of sale for slaves, obligations for money, or certificates of stock. Any others which are kept and considered worthy to be taken care of by the owner of them, are *valuable* in the sense of the act of 1784. *Marr* v. *Marr*, 808.

16. *Same. What "found" implies.* To be "*found* among his valuable papers," implies that it must have been placed there by the writer, or with his knowledge and assent, not surreptitiously by some other person; and so deposited with the intention at the time, that it should be his will. *Ibid.*

17. *Same. Not every paper thus deposited and found is a will.* All the requirements of the act of 1784 may be complied with, and the paper invalid as a testament. The paper thus found must be a *will*. And if a *will* it may be attacked, as other testamentary papers, for want of competency of the testator, for fraud and undue influence, or that it was never legally assented to by the maker, as a complete and finished act; not signed—with an attesting clause, but not witnessed, &c. *Ibid.*

18. *Same. How revoked. Declarations of the testator.* When the requisites of the act of 1784 have been complied with, it amounts to a publication of the will, and gives it the same dignity as if it had been regularly executed and witnessed, and requires something more than verbal declarations to revoke it. There must be some act done. clearly indicating an intention of revoking the will—such as cancellation, destruction, removal from the place of deposit, or reclamation from the hands of the person with whom it may have been lodged. *Ibid.*

19. *Same. Evidence. Declarations of the testator.* The declarations of the testator are admissible as evidence for the purpose of showing whether the requirements of the law exist, so as to establish the paper propounded, as a will; but when these are established by proof, such declarations cannot have the effect to defeat the testamentary character of the paper, or to work a revocation of it, as a will. *Ibid.*

20. *Construction. Estate tail. Rule as to realty and personalty.* As a general rule, whenever the words of a will, if applied to real property, would create an estate tail, they will, when applied to personalty, vest the absolute property in the first taker. *Clark* v. *Clark*, 886.

21. *Same. Same.* The testator, by his will, bequeathed to his daughter, who was a *feme sole*, certain slaves and sums of money, with directions to his executor to invest the money in young negroes for her benefit. The bequest is subject to the following provision, namely: "The said negroes with their increase shall be *entailed* on my said daughter Martha J., and her children, and not be taken for the debts of her husband." It is held, that the above rule has no application to this clause. That by the use of the word *entailed* it was not the intention of the testator to create an *entail* in the technical sense of that term. And the daughter took the negroes and money to her sole and separate use for life, free from the marital right of any future husband, with remainder to her children. *Ibid.*

22. *Construction. Life estate. Remainder.* The testator bequeathed certain property to his wife, during her widowhood, and then provided: "And at her death or marriage the said land and negroes, with their increase, to be equally divided among my children and surviving heirs of the body of those who may have deceased before that period, except the children of my daughter Nancy." * * * "It is my will and desire that my wife keep possession of the property of such of my children as may be under age, without paying hire, as a compensation for maintaining and educating said children; and as they arrive of lawful age, or marry. my executors are authorized and required to allot to such child or children an equal part," &c. "And at the death or marriage of my wife, I desire that my whole estate be equally divided among the following children: I mean and wish it clearly understood before I name them, viz: It is my express meaning and wish that all my children share alike in my general estate, and all those who have not received any part thereof, are to be made equal with my children beforementioned, viz:" * * "to them and their lawful issue, or the survivors of them, as before stated, forever. And if any of my children should die before they come of age, or marry. (or, in that case, leave no child,) it is my will and desire that their part or parts be equally divided among the survivors of them, or their lawful issue, except the children of my daughter Nancy, to whom I have given all I intend." The widow survived the marriage of her daughter Jemima, but died first. A negro girl, Leah, was allotted to Jemima, upon her marriage or arrival at age. This suit is by the children of the daughter, Jemima, to recover said slave Leah and her increase, she having been sold by the husband. It is held:

1. That the widow took an estate for life or widowhood in the land and slaves given her, and, at her death or marriage, the same with its increase, was to be equally divided among such of the testator's children as may *then* be living, and the surviving issue of such of his children as may have died before that period, except the children of his daughter Nancy.

2. That if a child died before the period of division, viz., the death or marriage of the widow, leaving children who remained alive until

the period of division, then they took the share of the deceased child; but if such child left no children living at the time of the division, the share of the child went to the surviving children, and the surviving issue of such as may have died before that period.

8. That no remainder was created in favor of any of the grandchildren of the testator whose parents were living when the particular estate of his widow ceased; and the daughter, Jemima, took an absolute estate in the woman Leah and her increase, and the title to them passed by the marriage to her husband, who might sell or otherwise dispose of them. *Seay* v. *Young*, 417.

28. *Construction of. Power. Implied gift over, in default of appointment. When persons take per capita.* In the second clause of his will, the testator bequeathed seven slaves to his wife, during her life, or widowhood, and at her death, or marriage, to be disposed of as he should afterwards direct in his will, unless she died his widow, in which event he gave her the privilege of giving said slaves to whom she pleased, among his children or grandchildren. In the fourth clause he makes his four sons his residuary legatees. In the fifth clause he directs that, in case of the marriage of his wife, said slaves shall be equally divided among his children, if living; and if any of them be dead, leaving issue, that issue to receive the share of its parent. His wife died without having again married, and without disposing of said slaves under the power given her. Upon the construction of this will it is held:—

1. That the testator did not intend to die *intestate* as to these slaves. That the legal presumption is, that he did not so intend, and that presumption is not overturned by anything contained in the will.

2. From the context, it is apparent that said slaves were not intended to, nor do they pass to the four sons under the residuary clause. Nor do they go to his children under the fifth clause of the will.

3. Under the second clause of the will there is a gift, by implication, of the slaves to the children and grandchildren of the testator, subject to the power of appointment by the widow, at her death, among them. And the power not having been exercised by the widow, the shares go, under said clause, to the children and grandchildren.

4. When the donee of a power has a life interest in the subject of the power which is to be exercised by will, or at the death of the donee, or at or before that time, the objects will be considered to be those who answer the particular description at the time the power is to be exercised. And, therefore, the children and grandchildren of the testator, living at the death of his widow, are entitled to the slaves.

5. The grandchildren of parents living at the death of the widow are not embraced. Grandchildren are mentioned merely as substi-

tutes for children, and to take only in the event of the parents being dead. And the slaves go to the children living, and the grandchildren whose parents are dead, living at the time of the death of the widow.

6. The children and grandchildren, living at the death of the widow, take the slaves *per capita*, and not *per stirpes*. *Rogers* v. *Rogers*, 661.

24. *Construction. Trust and trustee. Chancery. Power coupled with a personal trust. Limitations, statute of. Bar of equitable estates.* The testator bequeathed certain real and personal estate to three trustees, to be held by them in trust for the use and benefit of his daughter, B., and her children, present and future, and said trustees, or any two of them, or the survivor were vested with power to sell and convey any part or all of the property, for the use and benefit of said daughter and her children; to vest and revest the proceeds, and to manage the whole in any way they might think promotive of the interest of the beneficiaries. And, at the death of the daughter, B., the whole of said property was to be equally divided between all of her living children, and the heirs of such as may have died. The daughter, B., had two children born after the death of the testator, both of which died before their mother, and without issue. In the division of the real estate of the testator, the tract of land in controversy fell to B. and her children. A trustee was appointed by decree of the Chancery Court, in place of those appointed by the will, who sold and conveyed the tract of land, in 1847. Held:

1. That the three trustees were vested, under the will, with the legal estate to the *entire* property, only during the life of the daughter, B; and at her death, the legal title and the trusts of every kind imposed upon them by the will, ceased, and were at an end, and the entire estate, legal and equitable, freed of the trusts, vested in the children.

2. At the testator's death the daughter, B., and her children then living, took an equitable estate in the property, as tenants in common, in equal shares; the interest of B. being for life only, with remainder to her children, theirs being in fee; and the estate was subject to and did open to let in after born children.

3. Upon the death of the children, without issue, their interest, by the terms of the will, devolved upon the other children. So, the four children owned an equitable estate in 6-7, and the mother an equitable estate for life in 1-7, the entire estate, legal and equitable, vesting, at her death, in the children.

4. The *power of sale* conferred upon the trustees was discretionary, and a thing entirely of *personal trust and confidence* in them, or any two of them, or the survivor, and could be executed by no one else; it could not be devolved upon others, either by the deed or will, or other act of the trustees, or be executed by their heirs or personal

representatives, nor could a Court of Chancery have forced the trustees to execute it, or execute it itself by its clerk and master, or otherwise; nor could a trustee appointed by the Court do so. Upon the death of the trustees the power become extinct and gone, and the sale and conveyance by the new trustee, in 1847, is void.

5. The trustees having taken an estate only for the life of the daughter, B., the bar under the first section of the act of 1819, could only be to that extent.

6. The act of 1819 bars equitable as well as legal titles, and operates as an extinguishment of the same, investing the adverse claimant with a perfect title in fee simple. When, therefore, the equitable owner is *sui juris*, and can sue, but omits to do so for seven years, the entire title and fee are, by operation of the statute, placed in the possessor. And this is so, although the legal title be in a trustee, and whether he be capable of suing or not. *Belote* v. *White*, 703.

WITNESS.

See CRIMINAL LAW. DEPOSITIONS. EVIDENCE. PARTNERSHIP.

WRIT.

See ABATEMENT.

WRIT OF ERROR.

1. *Bond. Code, § 3177.* The bond to be given upon suing out a *writ of error*, whether the application be to the clerk of the court, or a judge thereof, or to the court itself, and whether a *supersedeas* issue or not, must, by § 3177 of the Code, be the same as in an appeal in the nature of a writ of error. *Patrick* v. *Nelson & Co.*, 507.

2. *Same. Upon an appeal in the nature of a writ of error. Code, § 3162.* By the Code, § 3162, in actions founded upon liquidated accounts signed by the party to be charged therewith, bonds, bills single, &c., upon an appeal in the nature of a writ of error, the bond shall be taken, and the securities bound for the payment of the whole debt, damages and costs, and for the satisfaction of the judgment of the superior court, where the cause may be finally tried and determined. The bond must be the *same* if a case is brought up by a *writ of error*. *Ibid.*

3. *Same. Motion to dismiss for want of. What may be looked to.* Upon a motion to dismiss for want of a sufficient bond, the court cannot look to, or decide whether there be error in the record or not. It is sufficient to authorize the dismissal of the writ if it appear that the proper bond has not been executed by the party. *Ibid.*

HARVARD LAW LIBRARY

HARVARD LAW LIBRA

See PRACTICE AND PLEADING.